D1567507

Game Programming Gems 3

Game Programming Gems 3

Edited by Dante Treglia

CHARLES RIVER MEDIA, INC.

Hingham, Massachusetts

Publisher: Jenifer Niles
Production: Publisher's Design and Production Services, Inc.
Cover Design: The Printed Image
Cover Image © Naughty Dog, Inc. 2002.

CHARLES RIVER MEDIA, INC.
20 Downer Avenue, Suite 3
Hingham, Massachusetts 02043
781-740-0400
781-740-8816 (FAX)
info@charlesriver.com
www.charlesriver.com

This book is printed on acid-free paper.

Dante Treglia. *Game Programming Gems 3*.
ISBN: 1-58450-233-9

Library of Congress Cataloging-in-Publication Data

   Game programming GEMS 3 / edited by Dante Treglia.
      p. cm.
   ISBN 1-58450-233-9
   1. Computer games—Programming.   2. Computer graphics.   I. Treglia, Dante.
   QA76.76.C672 G363 2002
   794.8'15265—dc21

                          2002006817

Printed in the United States of America
02 7 6 5 4 3 2 First Edition

Contents

Foreword xi

Preface xv

Acknowledgments xix

About the Cover Image xxi

Contributor Bios xxiii

SECTION 1   GENERAL PROGRAMMING 1

Introduction 3
Kim Pallister

1.1   Scheduling Game Events 5
Michael Harvey and Carl Marshall

1.2   An Object-Composition Game Framework 15
Scott Patterson

1.3   Finding Redeeming Value in C-Style Macros 26
Steve Rabin

1.4   Platform-Independent, Function-Binding Code Generator 38
Allen Pouratian

1.5   Handle-Based Smart Pointers 44
Brian Hawkins

1.6   Custom STL Allocators 49
Pete Isensee

1.7   Save Me Now! 59
Martin Brownlow

1.8   Autolists Design Pattern 64
Ben Board

1.9   **Floating-Point Exception Handling** 69
          Søren Hannibal

1.10   **Programming a Game Design-Compliant Engine Using UML** 73
          Thomas Demachy

1.11   **Using Lex and Yacc To Parse Custom Data Files** 83
          Paul Kelly

1.12   **Developing Games for a World Market** 92
          Aaron Nicholls

1.13   **Real-Time Input and UI in 3D Games** 109
          Greg Seegert

1.14   **Natural Selection: The Evolution of Pie Menus** 117
          Don Hopkins

1.15   **Lightweight, Policy-Based Logging** 129
          Brian Hawkins

1.16   **Journaling Services** 136
          Eric Robert

1.17   **Real-Time Hierarchical Profiling** 146
          Greg Hjelstrom and Byon Garrabrant

SECTION 2   MATHEMATICS 153

          Introduction 155
          John Byrd

2.1   **Fast Base-2 Functions for Logarithms and
          Random Number Generation** 157
          James McNeill

2.2   **Using Vector Fractions for Exact Geometry** 160
          Thomas Young

2.3   **More Approximations to Trigonometric Functions** 170
          Robin Green

2.4   **Quaternion Compression** 187
          Mark Zarb-Adami

2.5   **Constrained Inverse Kinematics** 192
          Jason Weber

2.6 **Cellular Automata for Physical Modeling** 200
Tom Forsyth

2.7 **Coping with Friction in Dynamic Simulations** 215
Miguel Gomez

SECTION 3   ARTIFICIAL INTELLIGENCE 227

Introduction 229
Steven Woodcock

3.1 **Optimized Machine Learning with GoCap** 231
Thor Alexander

3.2 **Area Navigation: Expanding the Path-Finding Paradigm** 240
Ben Board and Mike Ducker

3.3 **Function Pointer-Based, Embedded Finite-State Machines** 256
Charles Farris

3.4 **Terrain Analysis in an RTS—The Hidden Giant** 268
Daniel Higgins

3.5 **An Extensible Trigger System for AI Agents,
Objects, and Quests** 285
Steve Rabin

3.6 **Tactical Path-Finding with A*** 294
William van der Sterren

3.7 **A Fast Approach to Navigation Meshes** 307
Stephen White and Christopher Christensen

3.8 **Choosing a Relationship Between Path-Finding and Collision** 321
Thomas Young

SECTION 4   GRAPHICS 333

Introduction 335
Jeff Lander

4.1 **T-Junction Elimination and Retriangulation** 338
Eric Lengyel

4.2 **Fast Heightfield Normal Calculation** 344
Jason Shankel

4.3   **Fast Patch Normals** **349**
Martin Brownlow

4.4   **Fast and Simple Occlusion Culling** **353**
Wagner T. Corrêa, James T. Klosowski, and Cláudio T. Silva

4.5   **Triangle Strip Creation, Optimizations, and Rendering** **359**
Carl S. Marshall

4.6   **Computing Optimized Shadow Volumes for Complex Data Sets** . . . **367**
Alex Vlachos and Drew Card

4.7   **Subdivision Surfaces for Character Animation** **372**
William Leeson

4.8   **Improved Deformation of Bones** **384**
Jason Weber

4.9   **A Framework for Realistic Character Locomotion** **394**
Thomas Young

4.10 **A Programmable Vertex Shader Compiler** **404**
Adam Lake

4.11 **Billboard Beams** **413**
Brian Hawkins

4.12 **3D Tricks for Isometric Engines** **417**
Greg Snook

4.13 **Curvature Simulation Using Normal Maps** **424**
Oscar Blasco

4.14 **Methods for Dynamic, Photorealistic Terrain Lighting** **433**
Naty Hoffman and Kenny Mitchell

4.15 **Cube Map Lighting Techniques** **444**
Kenneth L. Hurley

4.16 **Procedural Texturing** **452**
Mike Milliger

4.17 **Unique Textures** **459**
Tom Forsyth

4.18 **Textures as Lookup Tables for Per-Pixel Lighting Computations** . . . **467**
Alex Vlachos, John Isidoro, and Chris Oat

4.19 **Rendering with Handcrafted Shading Models** **477**
Jan Kautz

SECTION 5   NETWORK AND MULTIPLAYER **485**

Introduction **487**
Andrew Kirmse

5.1   Minimizing Latency in Real-Time Strategy Games **488**
Jim Greer and Zachary Booth Simpson

5.2   Real-Time Strategy Network Protocol **496**
Jan Svarovsky

**5.3   A Flexible Simulation Architecture for
Massively Multiplayer Games** **506**
Thor Alexander

5.4   Scaling Multiplayer Servers **520**
Justin Randall

5.5   Template-Based Object Serialization **534**
Jason Beardsley

5.6   Secure Sockets **546**
Pete Isensee

5.7   A Network Monitoring and Simulation Tool **557**
Andrew Kirmse

5.8   Creating Multiplayer Games with DirectPlay 8.1 . . . . **561**
Gabriel Rohweder

5.9   Wireless Gaming Using the Java Micro Edition **573**
David Fox

SECTION 6   AUDIO **583**

Introduction **585**
Scott Patterson

6.1   Audio Compression with Ogg Vorbis **587**
Jack Moffitt

6.2   Creating a Compelling 3D Audio Environment **595**
Garin Hiebert

6.3   Obstruction Using Axis-Aligned Bounding Boxes **600**
Carlo Vogelsang

6.4   **Using the Biquad Resonant Filter** 606
           Phil Burk

6.5   **Linear Predictive Coding for Voice Compression and Effects** 613
           Eddie Edwards

6.6   **The Stochastic Synthesis of Complex Sounds** 622
           Phil Burk

6.7   **Real-Time Modular Audio Processing for Games** 630
           Frank Luchs

           Appendix: About the CD-ROM 639

Foreword

Mark DeLoura

madsax@satori.org

Hello, and welcome to *Game Programming Gems 3!* Thanks for picking up this latest volume of game-programming wisdom. For the life of this series, we have been firm believers that involving more people and perspectives will make the information more valuable to you. In that vein, I'm proud to introduce the book editor for *Gems 3*, Dante Treglia. Dante is the lead software engineer for developer support at Nintendo, and he's done an incredible job researching and organizing the material you'll find in this book. Dante has recruited a strong team of section editors and advisors to assist him—for more info on them, and for more info on the wisdom contained within this volume, please see Dante's Preface.

A Vision for the Future

The purpose of the *Gems* series is to encourage game developers to share their knowledge. Open standards and open source are the stable foundations that allow game technologists to share and evolve their work. But as the industry grows, so do the stakes, and so does the likelihood of someone asserting their patent or hiding their interface from you. At the time this volume was being published, the reign of Game-Cube, XBox, and PlayStation 2 had just begun. Can you envision the complexity of the next generation of game consoles? How challenging will it be to develop for them if you don't have intimate knowledge of how they work and how you can take advantage of their similarities and differences? It becomes increasingly important for us to share information and push for open-source libraries as our real-time systems become more complex.

It's great news that our industry is doing so well. We're all fond of pointing to our revenue numbers and comparing them to Hollywood's. But where are we heading? What does the future have in store for us? There are two particular trends that point us toward the future of our industry. One is the evolutionary growth of the major consoles into networked entertainment devices, as opposed to simple stand-alone game machines. A second trend is that of the aging gaming populace, for whom games have always been a part of their lives; and as this group ages, their tastes mature as well. This group of folks demands more mature themes. They might still enjoy a simple fighter, shooter, or platform game; but complex story lines, such as that found in *Deus Ex*, and playgrounds like *The Sims* and *Grand Theft Auto 3* are rising to the top of the charts.

Music and movies both began as entertainment that had to be sought out by going to concerts or the theatre. As the technology became available to make this entertainment available on-demand, it crept into our homes through radio and television, accompanied by advertising. We all take for granted this ready availability of free music and movies today, and games will also make their way into our homes in this way.

The technology to make this possible hasn't been available until just recently. All three of the current game consoles are planning out their network strategies. The accessibility of broadband is a limiting factor in the success of this vision. It's not going to be a huge success story overnight, and perhaps not even during this round of consoles. But the technology will make it possible; and as broadband becomes more ubiquitous, games will find their way into homes along with music and movies, and (of course) along with lots of advertising.

The Direction of Game Technology

But where is games technology heading right now? Game engines and game platforms follow or outpace Moore's Law, and this remarkable rise in complexity is placing strains on our industry. It impacts product cycles, lengthening development time and cost substantially. Many reactions to this can be seen: Some publishers 'rev' their titles each year, shipping regardless of whether the game is good or not ("It'll be better next year!"); middleware is used in more and more game projects to reduce time-to-market; development teams are growing, and software engineering is making its way to the game industry; publishers are buying out developers in order to get exclusive titles for their money outlay; and the disparity in quality between top-tier games and second-tier games is dramatic. As a whole, taking a risk is getting harder to do. And as a result, games are either unique and tasty, or derivative and half-baked.

What impact is this going to have on the way that we create games? In the short term, all of these trends will certainly continue. But online broadband gaming to the home will significantly change what we create and how we create it. As broadband takes off, you might find your technology locked to a particular platform and ISP. Standards will need to evolve quickly at this time in order to ensure that your success isn't overly dependent on your platform manufacturer. The broadband space should be as open as the Internet is today, and platform manufacturers will need to be aware of how important it is to foster their development communities and encourage them to create great games through keeping the platform open.

When you're creating games for the true mass market, you'll want to focus even more on the story and less on the technology. Also, incorporating the players into your games is a fabulous way to extend the value of your game. Releasing your tools to the public so that player-created content can prosper will encourage the loyalty of your players and encourage the next generation of game developers. Everyone wants to create, explore, and share the worlds they imagine. We in the game industry are lucky enough to be able to create our visions—supplying that same gift to your player community ultimately enriches all of our lives.

What Should You Do?

It is of paramount importance to continue sharing with other professional developers and budding game developers. We are blessed with a number of high-quality industry conferences, Internet forums, and mailing lists. Think about it—if knowledge is power, then anyone who restricts your access to the information you need to create a high-quality game is really restricting your power and ability to create your vision. Demand open source from your game-platform providers. You should be in control.

As it is natural for there to be some industry consolidation over time, continue to be vocal about having choices. It's important that we as an industry create experiences that appeal to everyone, not just a narrow band of folks whom we think of as 'gamers.' You need to be able create the vision that is in your head. If the government, your publisher, your platform provider, or your advertisers restrict what you create, is it really your art anymore? Or is it just a marketing piece, or an agenda-driven experience?

Stay active in the game-development community, and get involved in industry outreach efforts. Our industry is only going to get bigger. Be prepared and be proactive, and we'll all continue to be able to create what we see in our dreams.

In Closing

It's a true pleasure for me to see how our *Gems* family has grown. You'll find that a few of the authors from the original *Game Programming Gems* (2000) have returned in this volume. You'll also find that a few of those authors have gone on to create their own books of wisdom! If you enjoy the type of material you've found in this series, I encourage you to check out their works, since they are what made this series possible.

But don't forget to share your *own* wisdom with everyone, as well.

Preface

Dante Treglia,
Nintendo of America, Inc.

treglia@yahoo.com

Welcome to *Game Programming Gems 3!* This is the third volume of a series geared toward providing advanced game programmers with valuable, insightful, and practical information on a variety of programming techniques. By publishing the experience of expert game programmers, we encourage the game development community to work together and achieve the ultimate goal of making better games. We hope that you will learn time-saving techniques and be inspired to create new and exciting features with them.

If you are a beginner, this book offers a true cross-section of the challenges facing today's game programmers. We have provided many references to help you find all the resources you need to further your understanding of the topics presented. If you are an advanced game programmer, the true value of this book is in the incredible amount of time it will save you. The authors spent many months organizing their thoughts, code, and illustrations to present a concrete understanding of their problem space, so you don't have to be an expert in their area in order to gain wisdom from them. This leaves you with more time to add cutting-edge features to your own games.

The momentum initiated by the first two *Gems* books was evident by the 215 submissions we received from game programmers who were eager to share their experiences with the community. The quantity and quality of the submissions was pleasantly surprising, so choosing which proposals to include was an arduous task. To help with this process, we recruited experts for each of the sections to ensure that the gems were valuable to you, the professional game programmer. The section editors for *Gems 3* are:

- General Programming—Kim Pallister, Intel Corporation
- Mathematics—John Byrd, Electronic Arts
- Artificial Intelligence—Steven Woodcock, Wyrd Wyrks
- Graphics—Jeff Lander, Darwin 3D, LLC.
- Network and Multiplayer—Andrew Kirmse, LucasArts Entertainment Company
- Audio—Scott Patterson, Next Generation Entertainment

Our goal was to select gems that are long-lasting, practical, unique, and last but definitely not least, fun and interesting. We concentrated on issues that would benefit game programmers for many years. Many of the gems presented here are tightly packed nuggets of information that you can immediately utilize. Other gems are more complex and involved, and offer the details and insight necessary to incorporate the ideas into real games.

The Sections

Networked, multiplayer PC games have many success stories—*Everquest, Asheron's Call, Ultima Online, Counter-Strike,* and *Unreal Tournament,* to name a few. Even as this book goes to press, the three major console manufacturers (Sony, Nintendo, and Microsoft) are all poised to launch their network strategies to the masses, following the trail blazed by Sega with the network-ready Dreamcast. At the same time, a market for wireless gaming is emerging as cell-phone technologies and distribution increase. The need for a network-related section in the *Game Programming Gems* series was evident, so we have premiered the Network and Multiplayer section in this volume. Topics range from template-based object serialization to network monitoring and emulation tools, as well as wireless gaming.

The other day, I was watching TV with a friend, when a commercial featuring a talking dog came on. After the pitch, my friend turned to me and exclaimed, "Hey! That was pretty good animation!" Just then, I realized that in my lack of sleep, for a brief moment, I was actually listening to the dog as if it were just another talking entity. I was temporarily immersed in the realism of the animation and graphics. I look forward to the day that I catch myself being truly immersed in a game like that. Each generation of graphics processors brings us closer to that reality. Vertex shaders and pixel shaders are some examples of technologies that will make this realism possible. The Graphics section of this book includes many gems that will help you create more-realistic characters and immersive environments. Topics include high-level, programmable vertex shaders to help you extract the power of modern graphics chips, normal distribution functions (NDFs) to create interesting surface effects, and textures as look-up functions to easily achieve advanced graphics algorithms on a per-pixel basis.

Networking and graphics are two very specific areas of game programming; however, in order to utilize them, a game framework must be established. Enter the General Programming section—this section presents a wide variety of topics, from game design management tips to very effective debugging techniques. There is something for every game programmer in this section.

At the heart of every algorithm lies mathematics. The Mathematics section includes a nice collection of the more math-intensive contributions. You will find generally useful topics, such as fast base-2 logarithms and trigonometric functions, as well as more-specific techniques, like constrained inverse kinematics and friction simulation. And the best part is, these authors have done the necessary background mathematics for you.

At the heart of every game lies artificial intelligence (AI). The Artificial Intelligence section covers a gamut of topics—from improved refinements on path-finding to tips on choosing a relationship between path-finding and collision models. The techniques presented are easily used to create more-intellectually stimulating games.

Visual and intellectual interactivity is only half the battle. The ear has an amazing influence on our perceptions. Have you ever heard a real gun being fired? It's much more realistic in person than in the movies. The burst of a blast cap is enough to propel your body into an adrenaline rush. Why? Our ears are fine-tuned instruments that alert us to danger, its direction, and its proximity. So, as audio programmers, I encourage you to strive for that adrenaline-pumping audio in your games. The audio section covers topics to help you achieve this goal, from creating 3D audio to creating convincing audio using stochastic techniques.

Conclusion

I am very excited to bring you this third volume of *Game Programming Gems*. I hope that you benefit from the ideas presented in this book and in turn share your ideas with the rest of the development community through similar efforts. We work in an exciting and dynamic multibillion-dollar industry; let's help each other keep it that way (when we're not busy playing games).

We all remember the odd corners of every experience. I'd like to leave you with a little gem I discovered along the way:

```
main(k){float i,j,r,x,y=-16;while(puts(""),y++<15)for(x
=0;x++<84;putchar(" .:-;!/>)|&IH%*#"[k&15]))for(i=k=r=0;
j=r*r-i*i-2+x/25,i=2*r*i+y/10,j*j+i*i<11&&k++<111;r=j);}
```

—Ken Perlin, http://mrl.nyu.edu/~perlin/

Acknowledgments

First, and foremost, I want to thank the 67 contributors that made this book possible. Their willingness to share their ideas and hard-earned experience with you is the spirit that drove not only this volume, but the entire book series. Many of the authors are second- and third-time offenders. Thank you all. I want to especially thank the section editors for dedicating their already very busy schedules to ensure the validity of the content within rigid time constraints.

I would like to extend a very special thanks to Mark DeLoura, who selected me as the editor of this book and offered the needed help and inspiration to see it through (including flying out to Seattle to help me edit gems for the final two weekends!). Jenifer Niles, the publisher, is wonderful to work with. Her guidance and responsiveness are truly appreciated. I would like to especially thank Jessica Leppaluoto, who helped me organize, prepare, and edit the book. I could not have done this without her support.

The third group of people I would like to thank are my coworkers at Nintendo, who have supported and encouraged me. Thanks for putting up with my sleep-deprived, caffeine-buzzed state. I especially appreciate the friendship, leadership, and input from Howard Cheng, Ramin Ravanpey, Eugene Kwon, Tian Lim, Carl Mueller, and the rest of the gang at Nintendo.

Last, but definitely not least, I want to thank my wonderful family for all their love and support. Hi Mom!

About the Cover Image

Bob Rafei, Naughty Dog

The cover image is from *Jak and Daxter: The Precursor Legacy*, a character action game developed by Naughty Dog, Inc., produced by Sony Computer Entertainment, and released in December 2001 for the Playstation 2. The in-game geometry was built and assembled in Maya, with multiple levels of detail. The water utilizes a combination of animated geometry, animated textures, and environment map reflection. Jak and Daxter are captured celebrating in a frame from a victory dance, triggered by picking up one of the seven power cells (substituted here with gems), hidden in

Sentinel Beach. Jak's and Daxter's game models use IK structure, vertex morph tools (for facial expressions), and movable *uv*-mapped pupils to give them a full range of expressions as well as groovy dance steps, as in the dance illustrated above. A particle system was used to create a wide array of visual enhancements—from kicked up dust particles to fireballs, butterflies, and the streaked glow effect displayed above.

Contributor Bios

Thor Alexander

thor@hardcodedgames.com

Thor Alexander has spent the last 10 years working to bring believable, autonomous characters to the game industry. Recently, he founded Hard Coded Games (Austin, TX) to bring state-of-the-art AI and machine learning to online games. Previously, he held senior AI programming and design positions at Electronic Arts, Microsoft, and Xatrix Entertainment, as well as being a founding member of Asgard Interactive and CEO of Harbinger Technologies, Inc. He is the inventor of the hyperSim autonomous character system as well as GoCap (Game Observation Capture), a machine learning process used to train AI characters by watching how real people play games.

Jason Beardsley

jbeardsley@ncaustin.com

Jason has been writing network and server code for online multiplayer games since 1996. He has computer science degrees from Massachusetts Institute of Technology (MIT) and Binghamton University. Currently, Jason is employed at NCsoft/Austin, working on a next-generation, online title.

Oscar Blasco

oscar@asidesoft.com

Oscar started to code his own little programs when he was a child. He has always been completely self-taught, continually learning and improving his skills. He worked at Crytek Studios on character programming and as a research programmer. Now he is focused on finishing his studies and working on the new Titan2 engine at Aside Software.

Ben Board

ben_board@yahoo.com

Ben's programming career was founded on his Dad's early adoption of the ZX81, BBC Model B, and Amstrad 8086 PC. After cutting his milk teeth on BASIC, Ben was studying C by 12 and never looked back, at least until his study at Cambridge University introduced him to OOP. After a dismal brush with the real working world

Ben found his true purpose in life, joining Bullfrog Productions' excellent Theme Team in 1997, where he wrote the AI for Theme Park World (among other things). In late 2000 he took the plunge and helped to establish start-up Dogfish Entertainment in the role of lead programmer on their inaugural title, but fate intervened and sadly the company closed in early 2002. But every knock is a boost: he is now extremely proud to be helping Godalming's finest, *Big Blue Box*, to finish the sublime *Project Ego*: a game which even he would admit is better than 3D Monster Maze.

Martin Brownlow

mbrownlow@shiny.com

Martin started programming at age 10 on his friend's ZX81. After completing his education, Martin began his career at Virtuality, Ltd. (U.K.) writing VR arcade games. After three years, he moved to the U.S. to work for Shiny Entertainment. He has worked on several games for Shiny, including *MDK* and *Sacrifice*, and is currently knee deep in the *Matrix* video game.

Phil Burk

philburk@softsynth.com

Phil Burk is a computer programmer and designer who specializes in interactive and experimental music systems. He started by creating home-brew analog synthesizers and computers, with a focus on guitar processing. In 1981, he began collaborating with Larry Polansky and David Rosenboom at the Mills College Center for Contemporary Music. Together, they developed HMSL (Hierarchical Music Specification Language), which has been used by composers worldwide to explore the boundaries of live computer music. HMSL is a Forth-based object-oriented composition language that supports MIDI and DSP-based synthesis. Phil then worked at the 3DO company developing the first DSP-based sound synthesis system for a video game console. At CagEnt, a 3DO spin-off, he developed a custom RISC-style digital signal processor (DSP) designed specifically for unit generator-based synthesis and sound effects. He is currently developing JSyn, a synthesis API for Java that allows composers to embed interactive computer music pieces into a Web page. Phil has also worked on many projects as consultant, including designing the audio module for a digital television ASIC, and developing MIDI tools and telephony-related applications in Java.

John Byrd

jbyrd@well.com

John Byrd is currently a senior project manager for *Freekstyle* at Electronic Arts. Before that, he was a director of developer technology at Sega, where he created the Sega Dreamcast (Katana) SDK and supported hundreds of game development projects. He has also served as a senior engineer at 3DO. John is the founder of Bosslevel, an online game-industry forum. John has a degree in computer science from Harvard, and he can play a banjo passably well.

Drew Card

dcard@ati.com

Drew Card is currently a software engineer in the 3D Application Research Group at ATI, where he is focusing on the application of shader-based rendering techniques. He has worked on SDK applications as well as having contributed to the ATI demo engine. Drew is a graduate of the University of South Carolina.

Christopher Christensen

cchristensen@naughtydog.com

Christopher first started programming in 1982 on an Apple II+ machine. In 1994, despite having recently gotten a master's degree in computer engineering, he took a job programming PC role-playing games at Interplay Productions. He has been in the game industry ever since and currently is a programmer at Naughty Dog in Santa Monica, California.

Wagner Corrêa

wtcorrea@research.att.com

Wagner Corrêa is a Ph.D. student in the Department of Computer Science at Princeton University. He has been working with computer graphics for about 10 years, and his master's thesis was on object-oriented game engines. Wagner has published several research papers, including two recent SIGGRAPH papers. He is a member of the Princeton Graphics and Geometry Group, and is currently working on developing a walkthrough system for real-world environments.

Mark DeLoura

madsax@satori.org

Mark is the creator of the *Game Programming Gems* series of books. He currently can be found at Sony Computer Entertainment America, where he is manager of developer relations, working diligently to lead developers to the SIMD promised land. Mark has also spent time hacking code as lead software engineer at Nintendo of America and hacking articles as editor-in-chief of *Game Developer* magazine. He is still a fervent believer in virtual reality; and at his core, he's a tree-hugging peacenik who believes that ultimately, technology will bring the whole planet together in peace and love. Either that or it will overthrow humanity and reduce the planet to flaming embers. While we're waiting for either eventuality, Mark will continue to be found online, kicking your butts in multiplayer, first-person shooters.

Thomas Demachy

thomas@abunth.com

When Thomas was a kid, his mother found program listings under his pillow. After several years in scientific and high-performance computing, he left the sunny French Riviera to work as a programmer for Titus Interactive Studio near Paris, France, where he recently took part in *Robocop* for PlayStation 2. Apart from video games, his main interests usually deal with the sea, such as sailing or island hopping around the world.

Mike Ducker

mike@ducker.org.uk

Mike started programming at the stunningly late age of 16, working his way through Turbo Pascal until discovering C++ during his AI degree at Essex University. After graduating, and at a loss for choosing a career, a lucky job application landed him his first game programming position at Anco Software in late 1997. After three years of GUI, graphics, and AI programming, Mike returned to academia at Sussex University undertaking a master's in artificial life. He has since returned to the game industry as an AI programmer, briefly working with Ben Board at Dogfish Entertainment prior to its collapse, before securing a position at Lionhead Studios, working alongside Richard Evans on an, as of yet, unannounced title.

Eddie Edwards

eddie@tinyted.net

Eddie was educated in mathematics at Christ's College, Cambridge. He briefly worked in software engineering before taking the plunge into video games in 1994 with a *Wolfenstein 3D* conversion. Since then, he has worked at a variety of studios on a variety of games, including (most recently) Naughty Dog's *Jak and Daxter*. He is currently setting up a studio in the U.K.

Charles Farris

charlesf@vr1.com

Charles Farris is a senior software engineer at VR1 Entertainment (Boulder, CO). Since getting into the game industry in 1998, Farris has been AI lead on *Hired Guns* and *Nightcaster*, and is currently working on the AI for *Nightcaster II*. He holds bachelor's degrees in ocean engineering and applied mathematics from the Florida Institute of Technology, and has a master's degree in applied mathematics from the Colorado School of Mines.

Tom Forsyth

tomf@muckyfoot.com

Focused on 3D graphics since seeing *Elite* on his ZX Spectrum, Tom has always tried to make hardware beg for mercy. He has written triangle-drawing routines on the Spectrum, Sinclair QL, Atari ST, Sega 32X, Saturn, Dreamcast, and PC—and he's sick of them. He's very grateful that we now have hardware to draw the things for him. After two excellent years writing 3D graphics card drivers at 3Dlabs, Tom moved to Mucky Foot Productions, Ltd.—a games company in Guildford, U.K.—and is currently obsessed with displacement maps and the BRDF of Wesley Snipes' skin.

David Fox

dfox@citycom.com

David works for Next Game, creating Web and wireless multiplayer games. He is the author of several best-selling books about Internet technologies, and his writing frequently appears in publications such as *Gamelan* and those to be found at Salon.com and Developer.com. David has presented topics in Java gaming at Sun Microsystems' JavaOne conference for the past three years, and he has been a winner of the Motorola-Nextel Developer's Challenge for the past two years.

Byon Garrabrant

byon@byon.com

Byon Garrabrant has been programming games professionally since 1988, starting with PC conversions of coin-op arcade machines. He created *Castles, Castles II,* and *Conquest of the New World* for Interplay before joining Westwood Studios in 1997 to colead programming on *Command & Conquer: Renegade.*

Miguel Gomez

kikomu@seanet.com

Miguel Gomez is a software engineer at the SAAM institute, a developer of modeling and analysis software for medical research. His previous experience includes graphics and physics programming for *PGA Tour '96* (Electronic Arts), *Hyperblade* (Activision), *Baseball 3D* (Microsoft), and *Destruction Derby 64* (Psygnosis). He holds a bachelor's degree in physics and a master's degree in applied mathematics, both from the University of Washington.

Robin Green

robin_green@playstation.sony.com

Robin has worked in the game industry for seven years, starting at Electronic Arts (U.K.), moving into R&D at Bullfrog Productions, and ending up in the R&D department at Sony Computer Entertainment America. He has contributed technology and support for, among others, *Dungeon Keeper 2* and *Sim Theme Park,* as well as a tutorial on steering behaviors at SIGGRAPH 2000. He is also a fully paid-up member of the C++ Language Police (Const Correctness Division).

Jim Greer

jamesfgreer@mindspring.com

Jim Greer started in the game industry in 1991 at Origin Systems, where he worked on *Ultima VII* and *Ultima VIII*. Later, in 1995, he cofounded a game studio in Austin, Texas, which developed *Netstorm: Islands at Wa*r for Activision. *Netstorm* was an online, real-time strategy game that had the distinction of being voted the "#1 Game of All-time that Nobody Bought," according to C-Net's game reviewers. Since then, he has worked on Web games for shockwave.com and ea.com. On the side, he's been helping out on *Shadow Garden*, an interactive art project (see http://www.mine-control.com for more info). He's also an avid tournament poker player.

Søren Hannibal

sorenhan@yahoo.com

At age 11, Søren started programming on a Commodore 64, and he spent most nights of the following eight years programming demos and being active in the demo scene. In 1993, his hobby became his career path when he moved away from Denmark to pursue his first job in the industry. Since then, he has been the lead programmer on titles by Core Design, Ltd. and Scavenger, Inc., and has received his bachelor's degree. Søren is currently having fun writing character technology for his second title at Shiny Entertainment, a game based on the *Matrix* movie license.

Michael Harvey

michael.harvey@intel.com

Mike is a senior software engineer in the graphics and 3D technologies group within Intel Labs. He is currently working on simulation technologies for a next-generation, 3D Web-based engine.

Brian Hawkins

winterdark@sprynet.com

Brian Hawkins graduated with a bachelor's degree in mathematics and computer science from Carnegie Mellon University, and immersed himself in computer graphics research at Justsystem Pittsburgh Research Center. After two years, his desire to hold a finished product in hand led him across the United States to join Activision in Los Angeles, where he worked as the game core and user interface lead on *Star Trek: Armada*. In addition, he contributed to *Civilization: Call To Power* and *Call To Power 2*. Brian is now a lead programmer at Seven Studios on *Defender*, the remake of the classic title. His interests range across the board, so feel free to email him on any topic.

Garin Hiebert

ghiebert@creativelabs.com

Garin Hiebert is a programmer at Creative Labs, Inc., where he works on a variety of projects. He has contributed to the audio code of several games and has been an active contributor to OpenAL. He continues to work on the Macintosh OpenAL codebase, cross-platform testing code, and an OpenAL programmer's guide.

Dan Higgins

dan@stainlesssteelstudios.com

Dan is a proud member of *Empire Earth*'s AI team, which consists of the talented Bob Scott and the amazing Chad Dawson. His background is in writing high-performance search engines for the History Channel, A&E (Arts & Entertainment) Channel, and the Biography Channel. At a previous job, Dan did some COM integration architecture programming, but will only recall the details of it after a few stiff drinks and a lot of tears. In *Empire Earth*, Dan was responsible for the path-finding, terrain analysis, computer-player military, and animal AI. He is a computer science graduate of Frostburg State University in Maryland, and has a borderline maniacal passion for C++, games, STL, and optimization.

Greg Hjelstrom

greg@westwood.com

Greg Hjelstrom has worked for Westwood Studios since 1995 on titles such as *Command & Conquer Tiberian Sun*. His most recent project was colead programming *Command & Conquer: Renegade*.

Naty Hoffman

naty@westwood.com

Naty Hoffman is a senior graphics programmer at Westwood Studios, where he has spent five years making pretty space explosions for *Earth and Beyond*, a massively multiplayer space game. Prior to that, he worked on microprocessor architecture at Intel, where he was the architect for the Pentium Processor with MMX and at least partly to blame for the MMX, SSE, and SSE2 instruction set extensions. He has spoken at GDC and has been published in *Game Developer* magazine.

Don Hopkins

xardox@mindspring.com

Don Hopkins is a programmer and user interface designer who has been researching and developing interactive graphical systems on various platforms. Don has worked as a migrant research programmer and user interface flower child for the University of Maryland Parallel Processing Lab, Heterogeneous Systems Lab, and Human Computer Interaction Lab, as well as The Turing Institute, Carnegie Mellon University Computer Science Department, Kaleida Labs, and Interval Research Corporation. He's also worked as a commercial software developer, implemented *The Sims'* character animation system and user interface, ported *SimCity* to Unix, created interactive TV- and Web-programming toolkits in ScriptX for Kaleida Labs, and developed and used real-time visual data-flow programming languages with David Levitt for Levity and Interval Research. Levitt and Hopkins have started a company called ConnectedMedia, where they're currently developing a consumer product called ConnectedTV: a personalized entertainment guide with TV remote control for the Palm and other devices.

Kenneth Hurley

khurley@nvidia.com

Kenneth started his career in the game industry in 1985 with a company called Dynamix. He has also worked for Activision, Electronic Arts, and Intel, and is now currently in Developer Relations at NVIDIA Corporation. His current job includes research and development, and instructing developers on how to use new technology from NVIDIA. His credits in the game industry include *Sword of Kadash* (Atari ST), *Rampage* (PC, Amiga, Apple II), *Copy II ST*, *Chuck Yeager's Air Combat Simulator* (PC), *The Immortal* (PC), and *Wing Commander III* (PlayStation). While at NVIDIA, he contributed the following packages/demos: NVASM (Geforce3 vertex/pixel shader assembler), NVTune (NVIDIA's performance-analysis tool set), DX7 refract demo, Minnaert lighting demo, particle physics demo and the brushed metal effect, cloud cover demo, and the photorealistic face demo. He has a bachelor's degree in computer science from University of Maryland University College.

Pete Isensee

peteis@xbox.com

Pete has been programming games professionally for almost a decade. He's shipped titles ranging from CD-ROM action/adventure stories to casual online games, working on platforms ranging from PC to Mac to Xbox. He's currently an engineer with the Xbox Advanced Technology Group. He has a degree in computer engineering, and was a C++ template geek long before templates were cool.

John Isidoro

jisidoro@csa.bu.edu

John Isidoro is part of the 3D Application Research Group at ATI, and is simultaneously working toward a Ph.D. in computer science at Boston University. At ATI, he codeveloped the Radeon 8500 technology demos and screen savers, as well as many other applications. His research interests are real-time graphics, shader programming, image-based rendering, multiview reconstruction, nonrigid region tracking, and using graphics hardware in new and innovative ways. He was published at the ICCV '98, CVPR '00, and in *Game Programming Gems 2*, and *ShaderX* (Wordware Publishing, Inc.).

Jan Kautz

kautz@mpi-sb.mpg.de

Jan is working on his Ph.D. at the Max-Planck-Institut für Informatik in Saarbrücken, Germany. His main research area is interactive realistic lighting and shading using graphics hardware.

Paul Kelly

paul_kelly2000@yahoo.com

Paul Kelly holds a master's degree in computer science from the University of Central Florida. He has earned credits on *NCAA Football '99*, *Die Hard Trilogy 2: Viva Las Vegas*, and *Duke Nukem: Land of the Babes*. His programming-related interests include 3D graphics and artificial intelligence. When not programming, Paul enjoys playing soccer.

Andrew Kirmse

ark@alum.mit.edu

Andrew was the co-inventor and director of *Meridian 59* (1996), and the graphics programmer on *Star Wars: Starfighter* (2001). He has degrees in physics, mathematics, and computer science from Massachusetts Institute of Technology (MIT). Andrew now works at LucasArts Entertainment Company.

James Klosowski

jklosow@us.ibm.com

James Klosowski is a research staff member at the IBM Thomas J. Watson Research Center. His main research interests are in computer graphics, visualization, and applied computational geometry. James received a B.S. in computer science and mathematics from Fairfield University in 1992, and an M.S. and Ph.D. in applied mathematics from the State University of New York at Stony Brook in 1994 and 1998, respectively. His research interests in computer graphics include interactive visualization of large datasets, collision detection, volume rendering, and adaptive network graphics. Recently, his research has focused on visibility culling, simplification of complex geometric models, and parallel rendering of distributed data.

Adam Lake

adam.t.lake@intel.com

Adam Lake is a senior software engineer in the Intel Architecture Labs (Hillsboro, OR). Previous to working at Intel Labs, he obtained an M.S. in computer science at the University of North Carolina (UNC) at Chapel Hill, studying computer graphics and virtual reality. He has over 10 years worth of experience developing projects in C/C++ using Microsoft Visual Studio and GNU C/C++. Previous to studying at UNC-Chapel Hill, he worked at Los Alamos National Laboratory in the Applied Theoretical Physics and Computational Science Methods (XCM) group and earned a B.S. in computer science with a minor in math at the University of Evansville. There, he worked on a computer-aided design application for physicists, called "Justine." More information on Adam is available at http://www.cs.unc.edu/~lake/vitae.html. In his spare time, he is a mountain biker, road cyclist, hiker, camper, avid reader, snowboarder, and Sunday driver.

Jeff Lander

jeffl@darwin3D.com

Jeff Lander is the founder of Darwin 3D, a company geared toward a higher adaptation of real-time 3D graphics. Jeff has worked as a programmer for over 10 years in the video game, television, and film arenas, where he has developed many real-time graphic applications. Darwin 3D's many game and entertainment clients include Activision, MGM Animation, QuantumWorks Corporation, and Rhythm and Hues Studios. Jeff has also written extensively for *Game Developer* magazine and has spoken at many industry trade shows and conferences.

William Leeson

wleeson@indigo.ie

Since 1996, William has been tormenting the academic world with papers on global illumination and parallel rendering. He received his Ph.D. from Trinity College Dublin in 2001, and during the following year, he did research into character animation.

Eric Lengyel

lengyel@terathon.com

Eric Lengyel is a cofounder and director of technology at Terathon Entertainment in Sacramento, California. He is also the author of *Mathematics for 3D Game Programming & Computer Graphics* (Charles River Media, Inc., 2002). Eric holds a master's degree in mathematics from Virginia Tech.

Frank Luchs

frank@visiomedia.com

In 1983, Frank Luchs wrote his first music program for the Atari computer and started his dual music/programming career. His projects have ranged from producing and composing scores for movie and TV, to sound design and programming of custom applications and multimedia software. He has produced and composed hundreds of songs, jingles, and movie scores (e.g., Germany's most-known crime serial, *Tatort)*. He is the founder of Visiomedia Software Corporation, a company specializing in virtual instruments. At Visiomedia, he designed the Sphinx Modular Media System, which is the base for the software synthesizers Saccara, Chephren, and Cheops. A lighter version of Sphinx has been adapted as open source for this book. Frank currently works in the movie business in Munich, Germany. When he's not programming, he enjoys making a lot of noise with his synthesizer gear and composing electronic symphonies.

Carl S. Marshall

Carl.S.Marshall@intel.com

Carl S. Marshall is a senior software engineer in the Graphics & 3D Technologies Group, Intel Labs. He has an M.S. in computer science from Clemson University, where he conducted research in the area of virtual reality. He has previously written for *Game Programming Gems 2* (2001), and has worked on the NPR and other aspects of the Shockwave3D graphics engine. Currently, Carl is pursuing research interests in intelligent path-finding and real-time photorealistic and nonphotorealistic 3D graphics algorithms.

James McNeill

james_mcneill@ameritech.net

James McNeill, a consulting programmer specializing in 3D graphics, is currently living in Chicago, Illinois. He has worked with Sinister Games, an Ubisoft company in North Carolina, and at Westwood Studios, where he did graphics programming for the PC game *Blade Runner*. Gamers can hear James' voice in a couple of Westwood titles: He voiced the House Atreides infantry in *Dune 2000* and many of the vehicles in *Command & Conquer 2*.

Mike Milliger

mikem@2015.com

Mike has spent the last two years surviving the Normandy beach in *Medal of Honor: Allied Assault*, as well as blue-haired maelstroms, artists with knives, and animators with monkeys—not to mention a drooling problem. Currently, he is the lead programmer at 2015, working on their next first-person shooter. Shoot him an email and tell him to sit down.

Kenny Mitchell

kmitchell@westwood.com

Kenny Mitchell started coding "graphics" on BBC model A & ZX81 and led unpublished/hobby campaigns in the Speccy/C64 and ST/Amiga wars. He has a BSc(Hons) in artificial intelligence and computer science, a MSc in object oriented software engineering, and a PhD on 3D Data Environments. Kenny was the graphics/technology lead and crash bug fixer on: HEDZ PC, Pirates PS2 & XBox with R&D on engines with voxels, NURBS, subdivision surfaces, displacement mapping, BSP/portals and terrain. Recently published articles cover full scene anti-aliasing and terrain rendering. He is Director of 3D Computer Graphics Software Engineering at Westwood Studios.

Jack Moffitt

jack@xiph.org

Jack Moffitt founded the Icecast project in late 1998 and has played pivotal roles in several early Internet radio start-ups, including Green Witch Internet Radio and iCast, a CMGi company, and is widely regarded as one of the leading industry experts in streaming media. His experience in the areas of software development, databases, load management and scaling, streaming media, system administration, architecture, and security is extensive. Jack is also the executive director of the Xiph.org foundation. The Xiph.org foundation is a nonprofit technology and research organization focused on interoperable and patent-free multimedia technologies and standards, such as the Icecast streaming media server and the Ogg Vorbis codec project.

Aaron Nicholls

aaron_feedback@hotmail.com

Aaron Nicholls is a development lead at Microsoft Corporation in Redmond, Washington. From a young age, his passion for graphics programming, AI, and physics simulation, combined with a love for great games, sparked his interest in game development. In recent years, he has also applied his foreign-language skills to software internationalization. Aaron was previously published in *Game Programming Gems 2* (2001), and he welcomes your correspondence and feedback.

Chris Oat

coat@ati.com

Chris Oat is a software engineer in the 3D Application Research Group at ATI, where he explores novel rendering techniques for real-time 3D graphics applications. His current focus is on pixel- and vertex-shader development for PC gaming. Chris is a graduate of Boston University.

Kim Pallister

kim.pallister@intel.com

Kim Pallister is a technical marketing manager and processor evangelist with the Intel Software and Solutions Group. He is currently focused on real-time 3D graphics technologies and game development.

Scott Patterson

scottp@tonebyte.com

Scott Patterson was a contributing author in *Game Programming Gems 2* (2001), and now serves as editor for Section 6: Audio for this edition of *Game Programming Gems 3,* as well being as a contributing editor. Over the past 12 years, he has done game programming of audio, graphics, and logic systems, as well as tool programming for audio and graphics development, and some content creation. In the past, he has worked for Naughty Dog, Midway, and Microprose. Currently, he is designing and developing game systems as R&D team leader for Next Generation Entertainment. His work on *Game Programming Gems 3* has been made possible with the patience, love, and support of his wife, Alison; his son, Nick; and his daughter, Grace. Luckily, they all enjoy 'computer geeking,' too.

Allen Pouratian

allenp@csua.berkeley.edu

Were it not for the words, power, and love of Jesus Christ, Allen Pouratian would still be arrogant, selfish, lustful, and unemployed. Instead, he has a future as a disciple of

Jesus, and quite possibly as a software engineer. When he is not reading the Bible, he enjoys reading http://evolutionlie.faithweb.com.

Steve Rabin

steve@aiwisdom.com

Steve Rabin is a 10-year game industry veteran working at Nintendo of America. He's written AI for three published games and was a contributor to both *Game Programming Gems* (2000) and *Game Programming Gems 2* (2001). He served as the AI section editor for *Game Programming Gems 2* and is the founder and chief editor of *AI Game Programming Wisdom* (Charles River Media, Inc., 2002). Steve has spoken on AI at the Game Developers Conference and holds a degree in computer engineering from the University of Washington, where he specialized in robotics.

Justin Randall

jrandall@soe.sony.com

Justin Randall is a programmer currently employed by Sony Online Entertainment (Austin, TX). He is working to complete *Star Wars Galaxies*, a massively multiplayer role-playing game in the *Star Wars* universe. His work has shipped with several titles, including real-time strategy and first-person action games.

Eric Robert

eric.robert@videotron.ca

Eric is a software engineer for the Ubi Soft Entertainment's core technology group located in Montréal, Canada. He is currently involved in the development of a next-generation, multiplatform engine. Sometimes he enjoys testing his coworker's skills by introducing hidden 'features' in the source code that behave (amazingly) just like bugs. At home, he likes a quiet evening with his wife—or even better, with his compiler. In his spare time, Eric tries to keep his fingers safe when he works on his table saw.

Gabriel Rohweder

grohwed@hotmail.com

Gabriel wrote his first game in Apple BASIC at the age of 13. Several years later, he found himself graduating with a computer science degree from Ball State University. After a short stint working as a database programmer and as a network engineer, he knew that it was time to fulfill his childhood dream of working in the game industry. He now works for Microsoft as a software design engineer on the DirectPlay team.

Greg Seegert

gseegert@alum.wpi.edu

Greg Seegert is a programmer at Stainless Steel Studios, where he worked extensively on the hit RTS game, *Empire Earth*. When not programming, Greg is thinking about programming, reading about programming, or dreaming about programming. He has been programming since he was 10, and although he hasn't matured much socially since then, Greg plans to continue to program. In the process, he hopes to get really good at it.

Jason Shankel

JShankel@maxis.com

Jason Shankel has been a professional game programmer since 1992. Currently, he is a senior software engineer at Electronic Arts/Maxis, but someday he hopes to become a real boy.

Cláudio Silva

csilva@research.att.com

Cláudio Silva is a senior member of the technical staff at AT&T Labs-Research. His current research focuses on architectures and algorithms for building scalable displays, rendering techniques for large datasets, 3D scanning, and algorithms for graphics hardware. Cláudio received his Ph.D. in computer science from the State University of New York at Stony Brook. While a student, he worked at Sandia National Labs, where he developed large-scale scientific visualization algorithms and tools for handling massive datasets. Cláudio has published over 40 papers in international conferences and journals, and presented courses at various conferences, including ACM SIGGRAPH, Eurographics, and IEEE Visualization.

Zack Booth Simpson

zsimpson@sprynet.com

Zack Booth Simpson joined Origin/Electronic Arts in 1991 as a programmer on *Ultima* and left in 1995 as the director of technology. (He later returned as a research fellow.) In 1995, he cofounded Titanic Entertainment, which created *NetStorm: Islands at War*. In 1997, Zack abandoned the game industry and now creates interactive installation artwork, travels the world, and teaches math. His home page is at http://www.totempole.net.

Greg Snook

gregsn@microsoft.com

Greg has worked in the game industry for over eight years, contributing to titles by Viacom New Media, Kinesoft, TerraGlyph, and Past Tree. Greg can currently be found at Bungie Studios within Microsoft, working on XBox titles so secret it would take at least three drinks for him to tell you about them. Greg also likes to lament over the epic gladiator title he poured his soul into, which was eventually published as a screenshot on the back cover of *Game Programming Gems 2* (2001).

William van der Sterren

william@cgf-ai.com

William van der Sterren develops tactical AI for computer games and simulations. He is a developer/consultant and founder of CGF-AI. William has spoken at the Game Developers Conference, and contributed to *AI Programming Wisdom* (Charles River Media, Inc., 2002), and the *Game Programming Gems* series. Having worked as a research scientist in the fields of embedded systems and defense simulations, William is currently working as the AI lead programmer on a next-generation console title.

Jan Svarovsky

jan@svarovsky.com

Jan has been programming for almost 20 years. He graduated from Cambridge University (England) in 1995, joined Bullfrog, and worked in R&D, writing AI technology, experimental 3D engines, network code, and two of the first-ever 3D-accelerator PC conversions. He worked on two Bullfrog technology-led projects as sole or lead engine programmer before joining Mucky Foot Productions, Ltd. and becoming lead programmer on *StarTopia*, a game released in June 2001. His homepage can be accessed at http://www.svarovsky.com/jan.

Dante Treglia

treglia@yahoo.com

Dante remembers spending his formative years blearily plotting individual pixels with his Atari 400 BASIC cartridge. Years later, he discovered that you could create fancy graphics in Mathematica without pecking out dots on the screen—and as a result, he found himself with a bachelor's degree in mathematics from the University of Georgia. However, once faced with the real world, he quickly realized that he had missed his true calling and decided to revisit programming at Clemson University. At Clemson, he spent most of his time hacking OpenGL while wearing five-pound head-mounted displays connected to multimillion-dollar VR hardware. After receiving his master's degree, Dante re-entered the real world and luckily landed a job at Nintendo of America. He is currently lead software engineer in developer support, where he continues to work on fun virtual-reality experiments—on much more affordable mediums.

Alex Vlachos

Alex@Vlachos.com

Alex Vlachos is a senior software engineer in the ATI 3D Application Research Group, where he has worked since 1998, focusing on 3D-engine development. Alex is the lead programmer for ATI's graphics demos and screen savers, and he continues to write 3D engines that showcase next-generation hardware features. In addition, he's also developed N-Patches (a curved surface representation, which is part of Microsoft's DirectX8), also known as PN Triangles or TRUFORM. Prior to working at ATI, he worked at Spacetec IMC as a software engineer for the SpaceOrb 360, a 6°-of-freedom game controller. He was published in *Game Programming Gems* (2000) and *Game Programming Gems 2* (2001), the ACM Symposium on Interactive 3D Graphics, and *ShaderX* (Wordware Publishing, Inc.). Alex is a graduate of Boston University. His Web page can be found at http://alex.vlachos.com.

Carlo Vogelsang

cvogelsang@creativelabs.com

Carlo Vogelsang has worked on games as early as 1998. Has been credited with music/sound programming and additional programming with the following game development companies: Epic MegaGames, Inc., Digital Extremes, Triumph Studios, Orange Games and Secret Level. Carlo currently works at Creative Labs.

Jason Weber

jason.p.weber@intel.com

Jason Weber began by building a 3D night-vision terrain-simulation package for the Army Research Lab, complete with animated trees and grass. He now works in Intel's graphics and 3D-technologies group, developing the animation and skeletal deformation technologies used in Macromedia's Shockwave3D. Jason has presented papers at SIGGRAPH and the Game Developers Conference. His Web site can be found at http://www.imonk.com/baboon.

Stephen White

swhite@naughtydog.com

Stephen White is the programming director at Naughty Dog and has over 15 years of professional video game-programming experience on a wide variety of platforms. Some of Stephen's more notable products are: *Jak and Daxter: The Precursor Legacy*,

Crash Bandicoot: Warped, Crash Bandicoot: Cortex Strikes Back, Brilliance, and *Deluxe Paint ST*. He is very passionate about creating video games, and has been involved in practically all aspects of video game development. Stephen is a devoted husband to Linda (wife of 10 years) and a devoted father to Logan (son of 10 months).

Steven Woodcock

ferretman@gameai.com

Steven Woodcock's background in game AI comes from over 18 years of ballistic missile defense work building massive real-time war games and simulators. He did a stint in the consumer arena with arcade and console games, then returned to the defense world to help develop the AI for the national missile defense system. He maintains a Web page dedicated to game AI at www.gameai.com, and is the author of a number of papers and publications on the subject. He now pursues game AI through a variety of contract work, helps moderate the Game AI roundtables at the Game Developers Conference, and has had the honor of serving as contributor to and technical editor for several books and magazines in the field. Steve lives in gorgeous Colorado Springs at the foot of Pikes Peak with his lovely wyfe Colleen, an indeterminate number of pet ferrets, and one neurotic red basenji. Hobbies include shooting, writing, playing games, and working on old GMC trucks (go figure).

Thomas Young

thomas.young@bigfoot.com

Thomas cut his teeth many years ago coding hardware tricks for the Amiga. After obtaining a degree in AI from Sussex University, he joined Gremlin Interactive (Sheffield, U.K.) as an AI programmer. Two themes of his work in AI over the years have been the problem of giving characters an understanding of the obstructions in their environment and the problem of getting characters to move realistically. In 2000, he left Gremlin (now Infogrames, Sheffield House) to work as an independent contractor, and has set up a company to provide sophisticated path-finding systems under a middleware license (http://www.pathengine.com).

Mark Zarb-Adami

mark@muckyfoot.com

Mark Adami has coded games since he was 10 years old, when he got an Atari 800 for Christmas with a BASIC cartridge, but no games. Eight years later, he studied computer science at Cambridge University before working at Bullfrog and now Mucky Foot. Titles he has worked on include *Syndicate Wars* and *Urban Chaos*.

GENERAL
PROGRAMMING

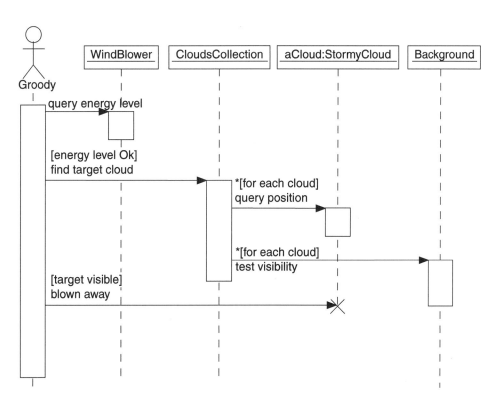

Introduction

Kim Pallister, Intel Corporation

Kim.Pallister@Intel.com

While attending a conference a few years ago, I attended a lecture by Ken Perlin at which I was treated to an amusing anecdote. He was relating a story about a time that he and several other graphics pioneers had been arguing the merits of their favorite high-level languages.

> *"C++ is the best high-level language!" argued one.*
>
> *"Java is the best high-level language!" said another.*
>
> *"The best high-level language," said yet another, "is a graduate student."*

Ken, of course, got a good laugh out of most of the audience—with the exception of a couple of the more-academic types, whose guffawing carried on for quite some time afterward.

A funny joke, for sure; but if you give the statement some thought, it has an element of truth to it. Programming has always been about devising a way to tackle a problem (sometimes, if we're lucky, a particularly ingenious way) and instructing the computer to solve the problem in that way. Whether the problem is a small one with the solution implemented in assembly or a large one tackled in C++—or a very large one implemented in English using a 'graduate student compiler'—the art being practiced is the same.

Keeping this in mind, we were faced with the dilemma of deciding what level of problem/solution to focus on for the gems of this section of *Game Programming Gems 3*.

Would it be best to focus on low-level gems—things nestled quietly in craftily written functions, such as ways to use only N instructions for a given function or ways to coerce the processor to do it for you? Would it have been better to focus on high-level problems? Or should we concentrate on the key teachings of industry veterans (as these are exactly where the gems come from) in areas like engine design or tool development?

In facing these challenges, we applied the time-honored practice of abstraction. What qualifies a 'gem,' regardless of level, scope, or problem domain, is its key insight into tackling a problem. That insight either lets the reader tackle the problem successfully for the first time or gives those with experience a new trick to add to their arsenal for the next time they are faced with the same challenge.

Consider the oft-quoted line below:

> *We have seen that computer programming is an art, because it applies*
> *accumulated knowledge to the world, because it requires skill and*
> *ingenuity, and especially because it produces objects of beauty.*

> —Donald E. Knuth, *The Art of Computer Programming, 1974*

There's an element of abstraction that applies to Knuth's view as well. Anybody who's done any level of programming, from highly optimized assembly to large systems, has, at some point, come up with an approach or a solution to a problem that is not only correct, but which is also beautiful. These revelations invoke the same awe-inspired phrases as Archimedes', when he fell in his tub and exclaimed "Eureka!"—or, in our contemporary translations: "Dude, that rocks!" and "Who's da man?!". Alas, such is progress.

The gems in this section cover a broad range of subjects. We cover high-level topics like framework design and saving games. We look at programming topics varying from customizing STL allocators, to a number of C-style macros, to floating-point exception handling. We look at using design aids and tools like UML, and Lex and Yacc to make the development of complex games easier. We even have a couple of gems that cover areas like localization, user interface design and implementation. Finally, keeping in mind what are often overlooked-till-way-too-late areas, we cover some ways of better debugging and profiling games.

It's a wide range of topics, but they all share that key element of offering the author's insight—and this qualifies them as gems. Now go ahead and dive in!

1.1

Scheduling Game Events

Michael Harvey and Carl S. Marshall,
Intel Labs

michael.harvey@intel.com,
carl.s.marshall@intel.com

M anaging events in a game—animation updates, object collisions, and so forth—can be a daunting task if there is no clear understanding of how the events are organized and executed. This gem will explain how a scheduler can provide both organization and flexibility to your game framework.

ON THE CD

We will begin by describing what a scheduler is and why it is useful, and end with advanced topics on scheduler development. A simple scheduler is provided as source code on the CD-ROM.

With the growing sophistication of computer games, real-time events and simulations are virtually a standard in today's game architectures. What is needed is a way to manage and execute multiple events per frame, or many times within a frame's timestep. A scheduler can manage game events in a very flexible fashion, as well as facilitate a modular approach for extensibility.

A few examples of game technologies that can effectively utilize a scheduler are physics simulations, character animation, collision detection, game AI, and rendering. A key aspect in all of these technologies is *time*. Many of these simulation technologies can become enormously complex, with hundreds of independent objects and processes being updated at various time intervals. For instance, a physics simulation will break down time into small, discrete intervals for each object in order to update the object's motion [Bourg01]. By providing a finer resolution of time, the simulation will have a much higher degree of accuracy. In this case, many objects and time intervals are managed by the same scheduling code, so efficiency is a vital concern in preventing scheduling bottlenecks.

Another important aspect of the scheduler is its ability to add and remove objects on the fly. This allows for new entities to come into a game and participate in the simulations along with the rest of the game's entities without missing a beat, and then be removed from scheduling when they are no longer needed.

Scheduler Concepts

The basic components of the scheduler are a task manager, an event manager, and a clock (see Figure 1.1.1). With these components, the scheduler can generate time- or frame-based events and execute event handlers. Throughout this gem, we will refer to event handlers as *tasks*.

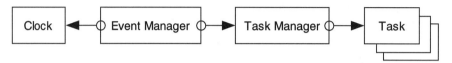

FIGURE 1.1.1   *Basic scheduler architecture.*

Task Manager

The *task manager* handles the registration and organization of tasks. Each task has a standardized interface that contains a callback function for the manger to execute. The task manager maintains a list of tasks, along with scheduling information about each one—such as start time, execution frequency, duration, priority, and other required properties. It might also contain a user-data pointer or performance statistics.

Event Manager

The *event manager* is the heart of the scheduler. Each task in the task manager defines one or more *events* that it handles. An event is a moment in time when a task is to be executed. For example, in Figure 1.1.2, Task1 defines events at times 10 and 15. The event manager generates events as needed to trigger the execution of tasks.

Real-Time Versus Virtual Time

A real-time scheduler is fairly simple in concept—the event manager sits in a loop, watches a real-time clock, and as soon as a target time is reached, it fires an event. In a real-time system, latency is critical. If a task takes too long, then it might interfere

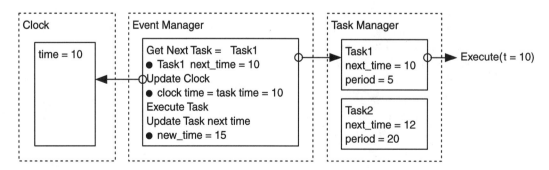

FIGURE 1.1.2   *Event processing.*

with the start of the next task. Since each task occurs exactly at its scheduled time, the time between tasks is essentially wasted from the scheduler's frame of reference.

From the task's point of view, time is only a number. Times can be compared, and elapsed time can be computed, based on this comparison number. The scheduler can simulate a given time or the passage of time by manipulating this number, independent of real-time—hours can pass in the blink of an eye, or time can be halted. This is the basis of *virtual time*.

Virtual time is extremely useful because it allows the scheduler to execute tasks when it is most convenient to do so, instead of when real-time dictates. It allows a sequence of events to be run quickly forward, stopped, recorded, and replayed. It also makes it possible to debug a 'real-time' application by stepping one interval at a time.

A virtual time scheduler divides time into frames. Tasks are executed in batches between frames, running in 'virtual time,' and then are synchronized with real-time when each frame is rendered. If the frame rate is high enough, the illusion of real-time is achieved. However, a few dozen milliseconds between frames is a lot of time for the computer, especially if it is managed efficiently. By batching all tasks together into a single block, the remaining time can be used for something else (see Scalability). Latency issues can be almost eliminated.

We'll refer to virtual time as *simulation time* in this gem, since all objects within the simulation use it as a reference. If simulation time is stopped, then simulation pauses as well. When it resumes, objects in the simulation do not detect any break in continuity. Simulation time starts at zero at the beginning of the simulation.

Tasks are executed sequentially while simulation time is updated between tasks. As an example, assume each frame has a length of 20 ms (see Figure 1.1.3). If we have events that occur at 51 ms and 54 ms, then they will be processed during Frame 2. The event manager does not know how long Frame 2 is until it has ended; so at the beginning of Frame 3, it looks at real-time and sees 60 ms. It can now process the tasks scheduled for Frame 2. Task1 is the first, at 51 ms; but the simulation clock is still at the beginning of Frame 2. The clock is advanced to 51 ms and Task1 is exe-

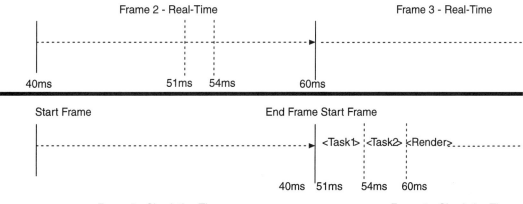

FIGURE 1.1.3   *The difference between real-time and simulation time in Frame 2.*

cuted. Once Task1 is done, the clock is advanced to the next event at 54 ms and Task2 is executed. No more events are scheduled for this frame, so the clock is set to the end of the frame (60 ms) and the frame is rendered. (If you are using an offscreen buffer, the frame was probably already rendered, and this is merely copying the image to the display.) Any unused time can be used for additional processing (see Scalability on how to use those extra processing cycles).

In this model, task execution and frame rendering always lag slightly behind real-time. But this is not perceptible to the viewer, and it allows us to work with a variable frame rate. If the frame rate slows down, the scheduler can compensate so that the simulation appears to run at a constant rate. If the frame rate is fixed, the scheduler can predict the start and end times, and perform event processing in advance. However, if the machine becomes significantly overloaded, the scheduler cannot compensate, and the game will become slower.

Event Types

Frame events are the simplest types of events and occur once per N frames, or every frame ($N = 1$). They can also occur before or after the render event. *Time events*, on the other hand, occur in simulation time and are not specifically synchronized with frames. For example, a time event can occur every 10 ms, regardless of the rendering frame rate. It is also possible to combine time events and frame events. For example, an event could be scheduled to occur 10 ms after the start of every frame, or it could execute five times per frame, evenly distributed in simulation time.

Clock

The *clock* component of the scheduler keeps track of real-time, the current simulation time, and the frame count. The accuracy of the clock will determine the accuracy of the simulation—a 1-ns resolution clock will be much more accurate than a 1-ms resolution clock. For most purposes, 1-ms resolution is adequate. If greater resolution is required, one could use the 1-ms hardware clock and subdivide the real-time ticks as needed to increase the resolution. A floating-point clock could be used as well, although careful attention would have to be paid to dealing with rounding errors.

Sequencing

The event manager handles the sequencing and generation of events. Since tasks are triggered by events, proper ordering occurs naturally. For example, let's define two tasks:

    Task1:   Run every 5 ms from 5 to 15, normal priority.
    Task2:   Run every 4 ms from 11 to 19, high priority (see Table 1.1.1).In some
              cases, tasks might be set to execute at the same time. In the example,
              both Task1 and Task2 execute at time 15. Since Task2 has higher
              priority than Task1, it is executed first. If priorities are equal, or no

Table 1.1.1 Task Execution Order

Time	Task
5 ms	Task1
10 ms	Task1
11 ms	Task2
15 ms	Task2
15 ms	Task1
19 ms	Task2

priority system is implemented, they are handled round-robin. Priority is also useful for ordering frame-based tasks.

Task Manager Details

ON THE CD

With hundreds of potential tasks, the task manager must manage things intelligently. A brute-force search for the next task is clearly not very efficient. While many methods are possible, the example programs on the CD-ROM make use of an ordered list. The tasks are stored in a list according to their next execution time—the head of the list is always the next task to be executed. The event manager only needs to look at the first task to determine when the next event should occur. When an event occurs, the foremost task is 'popped' off the list and executed, its next time is updated, and it is re-inserted into the list according to its updated execution time.

Besides avoiding lengthy searches, this approach also has the advantage that frequent tasks stay close to the front of the list (almost like a cache). Infrequent tasks stay out of the way and 'bubble up' automatically at the proper time.

It is often the case that a registered task must be modified on the fly, which might involve adjusting its priority, period, duration, or even deleting it before it is finished. In order to update a task, there must be some external means to locate it. A unique registration ID can be assigned to locate the task in the list.

A Simple Scheduler

ON THE CD

Now that we have discussed the various concepts and components of a scheduler, we will demonstrate how a simple scheduler can be built and utilized. Code for the examples provided can be found on the CD-ROM. The provided sample scheduler (Scheduler, Clock, and ITask) can also be used as a library. Two sample clients are provided (sample.exe and win.exe).

Design

The scheduler's design hinges on two components—the scheduler engine itself and the ITask plug-in interface (see Figure 1.1.4).

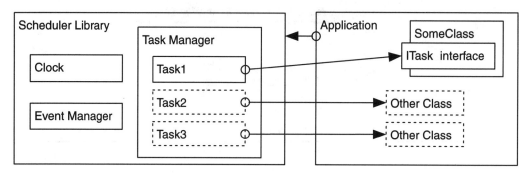

FIGURE 1.1.4   *Relationship between scheduler components and client application.*

In order for the scheduler to run, someone needs to call it. In a non-GUI program, this is as simple as coding a loop and executing:

```
while (running)
    scheduler.ExecuteFrame();
```

There are two ways to integrate a scheduler into a message-pump GUI, such as Windows. The first is by modifying the message loop to process messages and then execute the scheduler. This is the most obvious approach, but it suffers from scheduler 'freezes' while a window is being resized.

The second approach is to create a Windows timer, and use that to call the scheduler. Since timers are not interrupted by window dragging, the scheduler runs continuously in the background. A sample application (Win) has been provided on the CD-ROM that shows how to use a scheduler in a Windows application. Let's look at this application more closely.

ON THE CD

The core Windows code is quite simple. The scheduler is run off a WM_TIMER message and has two types of scheduled events. One updates the position of each ball every 15 ms, while the render event writes all the balls to an offscreen buffer. Windows can then paint the screen from this offscreen buffer on an as-needed basis. The simulation and rendering occur without any special Windows programming. This example demonstrates the use of multiple simulation tasks and adding/removing tasks on the fly.

Often, games have frame rates that vary, depending on system capacity and load, yet the velocity of moving objects remains constant. While both sample applications have a fixed frame rate, the provided scheduler does support this constant velocity technique. The key is in the Clock.Update() method that samples the actual real-time and advances the simulation by the elapsed time. If an object moves N units in 60 ms, it does not matter whether the system renders two 30-ms frames or three 20-ms frames—the object moves the same distance in the same real-time, so the velocity is constant. If you wish to have the velocity of simulated objects increase or decrease with the frame rate, change the `Clock.Update()` method so that it advances in fixed intervals, instead of reading the real-time clock.

So, how does the scheduler manage time, anyway? We need to register some events and see how it works.

Scheduling

The first step in scheduling a task is to specify it as a time event, a frame event, or a render event. This code will schedule a frame event that starts on Frame 200, runs every third frame, and ends before Frame 210 (start 200 + duration 10):

```
scheduler.Schedule(TASK_FRAME, 200, 3, 10,
pSomeHandler, pUserPointer, &id);
```

This task would run on Frames 200, 203, 206, and 209. After executing the final iteration, the task expires and is deleted by the task manager. Tasks with duration 0 are perpetual and never expire. In certain cases, you might want to remove a task before it is complete, or you might want to manually end a perpetual task. To do this, you `Terminate()` it using the task ID.

How does the frame get updated? Each time the scheduler `ExecuteFrame()` method is called, it first calls `Clock.BeginFrame()`, which starts a new frame by updating the frame count and computing new frame start and end times. After updating the frame count, it executes all time events, advances the simulation time to the end of the frame, executes all frame events, and then finally executes the render task. (In the sample scheduler, the render task is a special frame task that does not have a start, period, or duration—It always executes once per frame.)

The entire simulation can be stopped or restarted using the `Run()` and `Stop()` methods. When the scheduler is stopped and then restarted, it computes the elapsed time and subtracts it from the total simulation time. While stopped, the scheduler still performs renders and frame events, but time events are suspended.

Advanced Concepts

There are a number of ways in which the scheduler can be improved or better utilized. Scalability, simulation and multithreading are a few of these methods.

Scalability

A common problem in game development is scalability. The game should take advantage of all the available processing power to provide a richer experience, but it still needs to function well on less-powerful systems. Computationally expensive features need to be throttled down or turned off completely. The game should also 'play well' in a multitasking environment—a game that utilizes most of the CPU might prevent the OS from responding to user input in a timely manner. In addition, if the OS launches any housekeeping tasks in the background, it could slow the game down. Ideally, the game should adjust dynamically to the conditions of the system.

Collecting the performance data is half the battle. Since the scheduler can become a bottleneck by handling all processes, it is a perfect place to put performance monitors.

As described earlier, the clock takes a snapshot of the current time and compares it to the last frame to determine elapsed time. The scheduler can also determine the elapsed time of each task by comparing the start time to the end time. This information can either be communicated to the task, or it can be used to determine whether or not to run the task and/or how often.

One way to provide scalability is to require time budgets—the more power, the more time allowed. A task might have a 'time budget' per frame. The scheduler tracks the accumulated budget and the accumulated running time, and only executes the task if the current budget exceeds the actual time. For example, a task might have a time budget of 2 ms per frame, but it runs in 3 ms on a slow CPU. The scheduler will skip every third frame in order to keep the task within its budget (see Table 1.1.2).

Table 1.1.2 Time Budget Per Task

Frame #	Budget	Actual
Frame 1	2	3
Frame 2	4	6
Frame 3	6	—
Frame 4	8	9

Some tasks might have a time budget 'threshold'—if they exceed their budget, instead of running part of the time, they do not run at all. The scheduler can also determine the time needed to perform the entire simulation by summing all of the tasks. The difference between processing time and frame length is idle time. Ideally, the game should use all the available time to improve gameplay, but should not use *more* than what is available, or the frame rate will slow down. The scheduler can add tasks to fill idle time or remove tasks to reduce the load. (There must, of course, be some way to specify which tasks can safely be added or removed.) By supplying overall system usage statistics to tasks, the tasks can then scale themselves to use more or less time based on the data received. It is probably best to have a 5% to 10% idle target to allow for minor fluctuations in actual processing time without slowing things down.

Other options that provide scalability include increasing or decreasing of time budgets, scheduling of idle tasks (which only run during idle time), garbage collection or other housework, graphics enhancements, or improvement of the AI. When doing this type of management, it is important to avoid oscillation between extremes. This can be done by limiting adjustments to small incremental changes rather than large jumps, or by statistical analysis of the effect of previous adjustments in order to improve prediction.

Simulation

The scheduler can be used to drive a simulation system. Most simulation engines break time down into discrete steps for purposes of animation and collision detection. The scheduler described in this gem is perfect for this type of simulation system.

In a simple example of a lunar lander, the lander has a vertical velocity and a forward velocity. Each timestep adds gravity. If we use AI to control the vertical thruster of the lander, then at each timestep, the AI samples velocity and adjusts thrust to compensate, allowing for a controlled descent. The timesteps need to be small enough to give the AI time to react—otherwise the lander will hit the ground before it can respond effectively. For collision detection, again, you want small timesteps so that the lander will intersect the surface rather than passing completely through it.

Multithreading

It is possible for the scheduler to manage the execution of subthreads [Carter01, Dawson01]. There are many reasons why you might wish to do this. For example, some tasks might work better as a continuous process rather than a series of discrete events [Otaegui01]. Such tasks can be written as a thread, and the scheduler can control how much time the thread is allowed for processing. This approach allows true preemptive multitasking while actually enforcing a time budget.

Multiprocessing systems are slowly becoming more common, and it is likely that multiprocessing will become a standard feature in the near future. Games that are able to take advantage of multiple processors will be able to outperform games written for a single CPU. An easy way for a game to utilize multiple CPUs is to make it multithreaded and let the OS do the work of distributing the threads on available processors.

A multi-CPU scheduler could activate several threads at once so that they could run concurrently. It could also spawn event handlers into specific threads so that multiple events can be handled concurrently.

Conclusion

There are a variety of reasons to use a scheduler—portability, flexibility, and support of simulations. A quality scheduler needs to be flexible and efficient. This gem has covered some of the basic scheduler concepts, has provided a sample scheduler, and has shown how to integrate it into conventional and GUI-based applications. Help organize your events by using a scheduler in your next game.

References

[Bourg01] Bourg, David M., *Physics for Game Developers,* O'Reilly, 2001.
[Carter01] Carter, Simon, "Managing AI with Micro-Threads," *Game Programming Gems 2,* Charles River Media, Inc., 2001.

[Dawson01] Dawson, Bruce "Micro-Threads for Game Object AI," *Game Programming Gems 2*, Charles River Media, Inc., 2001.

[Llopis01] Llopis, Noel, "Programming with Abstract Interfaces," *Game Programming Gems 2*, Charles River Media, Inc., 2001.

[Mirtich00] Mirtich, Brian, "Timewarp Rigid Body Simulation," Computer Graphics Proceedings, SIGGRAPH 2000: pp. 193–200.

[Otaegui01] Otaegui, Javier, "Linear Programming Model for Windows-Based Games," *Game Programming Gems 2*, Charles River Media, Inc., 2001.

1.2

An Object-Composition Game Framework

Scott Patterson, Next Generation Entertainment

scottp@tonebyte.com
scott@gameframework.com

This gem will present a design for a game framework based on object composition and explain its advantages and design philosophy. We will present reasons why this kind of framework can be useful for implementing the work required for games.

This game framework can serve as a reference for your own game systems. You can create new systems with the capabilities that you need and create new tasks that perform the actions that you need.

When we talk about a programming framework, we are referring to a system of objects that work together to provide certain services. An application framework is a collection of classes that provide the services necessary for creating applications. Our goal in this gem is to find out what kind of framework we can build to help create game applications.

There are good reasons to use a framework to build an application. Getting something running quickly is a primary reason. Time is money, after all. Frameworks typically contain built-in features, consistent behavior and structure, and well-known rules for object access, object ownership, and object lifetimes.

ON THE CD

In this gem, we first summarize game development stages to get an overview of the work that is required. We then discuss the game framework design issues. Finally, we present an overview of the game framework implementation provided on the CD-ROM.

Game Development Stages

The need for a game framework will vary as development progresses. Table 1.2.1 shows a listing of typical game development stages and identifies the typical goals at each stage.

Table 1.2.1 Typical Goals During Game Development

Stage	Goal
Concept	Design of functionality and aesthetics. Creation of character, story, and mission concepts.
Prototype	Demonstration of key gameplay elements through proof-of-concept demos. Demonstration of technology.
Playable	Demonstration of at least one mission or level being played from start to finish.
Production	Completion of designs and implementation for all missions and levels.
Wrapping	Integration of various game modes and screens. Includes story segments, training, mission/level selection, win/lose, status/scores, save/load, pause/restart, options/configuration.
Testing	Solving design and implementation problems. Solving compatibility issues. Integration of alternate drivers.
Release	Shipping the game on its first platform. Party!
Conversion	Alternate language versions. Alternate platforms.

During the early stages (concept, prototype, playable), the choice of framework might be focused on getting the program running quickly. At this time, it is quite possible that the framework does not seem as important as creating the demonstration of concepts. However, if the framework is not also designed to be useful for the other stages of game development, then you might find yourself losing time to refactoring.

During the production stage, tools such as viewers and editors become essential. Viewers are necessary for developers to see how their content looks "in the game." Editors are required for developers to make adjustments to any aspect of the game. While these kinds of tools can be separate from the game application, it is often required for viewer and editor capabilities to be incorporated into the game. To do this, there must be code for the "consumer" aspect as well as for the "developer" aspect. The goal is to build a framework that leverages the shared components of these features, yet allows them to be developed independently.

During the wrapping stage, we must integrate the various game modes and screens into one seamless product. This integration sometimes suffers from scheduling delays or restructuring of the original design. Having a framework to help manage these game modes and screens, and even the transitions between them, will help this process go more smoothly.

During the testing stage, we might need the ability to start the game in various modes or at certain points within the game. We want our framework to provide this kind of flexibility to make it easy to define these various modes and entry points. We might also want to include the ability to switch between drivers while inside the game. If our framework binds a particular type of video technology to our application, switching video drivers would not be possible. Whether we provide driver-switching or not, we can add logging capabilities to our framework to aid the process of compatibility testing.

After we reach the release stage, the game team might go on to do conversions of the game, or it might be shipped off to other developers to do the conversions. Either way, if our framework is hard to port to another platform, it will cause delays. We would rather have the conversion team spend their time putting in new features and enhancements for each platform, rather than spend their time struggling to get it working.

Game Framework Design

Now that we have an idea of the kind of work required to make games, we can look at the design issues in creating a framework. We will cover platform dependence, game dependence, object composition, inheritance, frame-based code, function-based code, operation order, object lifetimes, and task integration.

Platform-Independent Versus Platform-Dependent

Games are usually filled with many concepts that transcend operating systems and platform technologies. These concepts determine the player's enjoyment through "gameplay" and "depth." Conversely, games are also commonly written to take advantage of specific hardware features that help identify the presentation quality. This presentation quality is often responsible for extending a game's feeling of "immersion."

Frameworks need not be bound to operating systems and technologies. We can define platform-independent system interfaces for our framework rather than platform-dependent system interfaces. Even though these interfaces are platform-independent, we can use a factory system to create the concrete implementations for specific platforms.

The more we can separate the game's conceptual work from platform specifics, the easier it will be to replace only the platform-specific code for conversions. So, part of our goal in creating a game framework is making it easy to keep game concepts independent of the operating system and platform technology details whenever possible or practical.

Game-Independent Versus Game-Dependent

If we want to use a framework for many games, it makes sense to have the framework be game independent. However, if we are going to use a framework for a single game on several platforms, it might be acceptable to have portions of the framework be game dependent.

For example, if our game controls a specific type of character that has many dynamic visual details that depend on the character's state, we might want the rendering code to access game-specific states and decide how the object should be rendered. This kind of situation can reduce the number of system interface calls, which simplifies and speeds up the code.

Object Composition Versus Inheritance

One way to make an application framework intuitive is to use the template method design pattern, and create objects that are a subclass of an application class. When we do this, we treat application initialization and destruction as algorithms that subclasses can redefine. This kind of design pattern is called "class behavioral" because it uses inheritance to distribute behavior between classes.

Another way to define the steps of application initialization and destruction (without inheritance) is to define these steps as a list of tasks to process. A task system class can coordinate task execution, and a resource system can reference and manage the task lists and task objects. Now we are "object behavioral" because we are using object composition and our resource system as our mediator for these objects.

Using a task system like this means that we can now build a framework based on object composition rather than inheritance. Our task system controls task objects through their interfaces, and our tasks perform work by calling object interfaces. This also means that our framework will not have the typical inverted control structure that is a result of the template method. Instead, our task objects control the software. Perhaps this is an object framework rather than a class framework, but it is a framework nonetheless.

The *Design Patterns* book [GoF94] discusses many advantages of object composition. It also highlights two principles of object-oriented design:

* Program to an interface, not an implementation.
* Favor object composition over class inheritance.

Frame-Based Versus Function-Based Operation

There are many types of software that are not concerned with frame timing, where functions may take seconds, minutes, or even longer to complete. This function-based operation can be much easier to program than frame-based operation.

Most games must be visually and aurally responsive, with many animations and details being calculated every frame. Each time a visual image and/or audio buffer is rendered, we have created a frame. Games may be rendered at speeds up to 50 or 60 frames per second. This kind of frame-based operation requires game software to execute in short spurts of time. If a lengthy operation (over 1/60th of a second) is to be performed, it must be broken into shorter pieces or be performed as a background task.

For our framework, frame-based operation will require a frame system class that can tell our task system class when to call frame-synchronized tasks. Our task system will also be able to process tasks that are not frame-synchronized, which we will call "asynchronous tasks."

Since the frame system controls when to call frame-synchronized tasks, we can also offer the ability to manually step through frames and choose particular frame rates. This can be useful for checking animation playback details as well as for other debugging and testing purposes.

Dynamic Versus Static Operation Order

There are many types of software operations that need to be done in a specific order. For these operations, we must call functions in a particular order or submit tasks in a specific order to our task system. This is an example of static operation order.

Games are normally filled with various screens and transitions that are not typically connected in a specific order. Instead, the player's actions determine what happens next. This is an example of dynamic operation order.

For our framework, we can provide dynamic operation order by enabling task objects to access the task system interface and submit new tasks.

Dynamic Versus Static Object Lifetimes (and Ownership Issues)

In hierarchical systems, we might find that base objects own certain objects that are used by inherited objects, while inherited objects can create objects that the base objects know nothing about. Often the lifetimes of such objects are built into the hierarchy, and inherited objects cannot dynamically create and delete them. The lifetimes of these objects are static in this sense.

In an object-composition framework, it could be confusing to know when a particular object owns another object. To resolve this, we can assign object ownership to our resource system. This way, any task can connect with system resources as needed and not be given management responsibilities. We give our resource system the power of object ownership and our tasks the power of object access, which limits the confusion over ownership issues.

We can make the lifetimes of these objects dynamic by having tasks issue commands to our resource system. We can direct the resource system to load and dump objects in collections. For example, a load collection command can be issued before tasks that need the loaded objects are started. A dump collection command can be issued after those tasks are finished. Alternatively, we can have objects around for the entire lifetime of the application.

Horizontal Versus Vertical Integration of Tasks

In hierarchical systems, it might seem like we are always "under" other objects that control us and that our relationship with those objects is "fixed." Tasks feel vertically arranged, and changes to higher parts of the system can have far-reaching effects on the operation of lower parts of the system.

In object-composition framework, it might seem like our programming environment is "flat" and our relationships with certain objects is more "dynamic." Tasks feel horizontally arranged, and changes to certain tasks in the system will have little or no effect on other tasks in the system.

Game Framework Implementation

Now we present an overview of the implementation of our framework that meets these challenges. The framework is composed of systems and tasks. A special kind of task called the "frame player" provides high-level control of audio-visual rendering and logic.

Systems

The Systems_t class contains pointers to the *pure interfaces* [Stroustrup97] of the systems that our game will use. We choose to provide access to these systems through pure interfaces so that dynamic system switching is possible and platform-dependent system code is separated from the platform-independent code that accesses the systems. The interfaces available in the Systems_t class are summarized in Table 1.2.2.

Table 1.2.2 The Interfaces Available in the Systems_t Class

System	Summary
LogSys_t	Handles all message logging from the game. Optional output types include text boxes or files.
ErrorSys_t	Handles error information and states.
TimeSys_t	Reports timing information.
FactorySys_t	Creates objects using Factory IDs.
ResourceSys_t	Manages object instances using Instance IDs.
TaskSys_t	Manages task execution and control.
WindowSys_t	Provides window system management and control.
FrameSys_t	Provides frame synchronization services and control.
InputSys_t	Provides input device management and control.
VisualSys_t	Provides visual system management and control.
AudioSys_t	Provides audio system management and control.
NetworkSys_t	Provides network system management and control.

Each system has an Init(Systems_t *pSystems) and a Shutdown() method. Passing the Systems_t pointer to the objects allows them to access any of the system interfaces. Including the Systems_t class does not create compiler dependencies on the systems code because the systems are accessed through pointers that only require forward references. This is important, as Systems_t pointers are used in many of the framework's classes. Reducing physical dependencies is an important goal of good *physical design* [Lakos96].

Because each of these systems is defined as a pure interface that hides all implementation details, we can dynamically switch system implementations as long as those implementations do not have static link dependencies. The break-up of dependent implementations into dynamically loadable components is an example of the packages pattern [Noble01].

ON THE CD

The source code on the CD-ROM demonstrates how to dynamically switch visual systems. This is done using dynamic link libraries, each of which provides different implementations of the VisualSys_t interface. Here is an example of how to control the switch of visual systems:

```
FactorySys_t *pFS = m_pSystems->GetFactorySys();
pFS->DeleteVisualSys( m_pSystems->GetVisualSys() );
pFS->SetVisualSysDriverID( m_nVisualSysDriverID );
m_pSystems->SetVisualSys( pFS->CreateVisualSys() );
```

Tasks

The TaskSys_t class provides an interface to the task system. Using the Post_TaskCommand function, we can post a task as either a frame-synchronized task or an asynchronous task. The only difference is when the tasks are called. Frame-synchronized tasks are called when the frame system reports that it is time to run the next frame. Asynchronous tasks are called in each loop of the task system.

Post_TaskCommand allows us to add and remove tasks at any time. Here is an example of how to post task commands to stop the current asynchronous task and start a frame-synchronized task:

```
// get the task system
TaskSys_t *pTaskSys = m_pSystems->GetTaskSys();
// get the resource system
ResourceSys_t *pResSys = m_pSystems->GetResourceSys();
// remove the current asynchronous task
pTaskSys->Post_TaskCommand( ASYNC_REMOVE, this );
// get the new task to start
Task_t *pTask = pResSys->GetTask( INSTANCE_ID_TASK_INTRO );
// push back the new frame-synchronized task
pTaskSys->Post_TaskCommand( FRAMESYNC_PUSH_BACK, pTask );
```

Here we see that we can access any task using its instance ID by calling the resource system's GetTask function. Tasks are passed to the Systems_t pointer when they are connected to the system via the task's Connect(Systems_t *pSystems) function.

Layers

Throughout the game development process, there is typically a great amount of work associated to visual rendering design. Rendering can be managed in a high-level manner using a layer system. The importance of a layer system comes into play when the game screen is rendered in a layered fashion. For example, during a 3D game, we might have the world rendered as one layer and perhaps game objects as another layer, and then a "heads-up display" as a third layer. We want the ability to push new layers onto the scene and have them appropriately affect visuals, audio, and input-handling logic.

To control layers of visual screens, audio data, and input-handling logic, we introduce a special kind of task called the FramePlayer_t. This task is intended to be frame-synchronized and manages audio-visual-layer (AVLayer_t) objects and logic-layer (LogicLayer_t) objects.

Audio-visual-layer objects are called each frame as follows:

```
// Update AV Layers
for( each audio-visual layer (forward-order)  )
{
    AVLayer_t *pAVL = contents of iterator;
    pAVL->Update();
}

// Begin Render Visual
if( m_pSystems->GetVisualSys()->BeginRender() )
{
for( each audio-visual layer (forward-order) )
    {
        AVLayer_t *pAVL = contents of iterator;
        pAVL->RenderVisual();
    }
    m_pSystems->GetVisualSys()->EndRender();
}
// End Render Visual

// Begin Render Audio
if( m_pSystems->GetAudioSys()->BeginRender() )
{
    for( each audio-visual layer (forward-order) )
    {
        AVLayer_t *pAVL = contents of iterator;
        pAVL->RenderAudio();
    }
    m_pSystems->GetAudioSys()->EndRender();
}
// End Render Audio
```

We can see that each audio-visual layer is updated first with an Update() call. This is when the audio-visual objects are updated, depending on their state of animation. Following this update call, we render the visuals and audio.

Logic-layer objects are called each frame as follows:

```
// Update Logic Layers
for( each logic layer (reverse-order) )
{
    LogicLayer_t *pLL = contents of iterator;
    pLL->Update();
    if( pLL->IsExclusive() ) break;
}
```

We can see that each logic layer is simply updated with an Update() call. While audio-visual-layer updates are meant to handle animation, logic-layer updates are used to handle game logic and player input.

Since the logic layers are processed in reverse, and since they stop processing if they're marked exclusive, the last logic layer in the m_LogicLayerPtrList can "override" previous logic layers. So, pushing back a logic layer can exclusively change the way player input is handled, such as is required for game menus, viewers, and editors. In contrast, if we push forward a new audio-visual layer, we only add a new set of items to display and hear.

Just as the task system has task commands, the FramePlayer_t class has layer commands. Here is an example of how to post layer commands:

```
AVLayer_t *pAVL;
LogicLayer_t *pLL;
// get the resource system
ResourceSys_t *pResSys = m_pSystems->GetResourceSys();
// get the task to modify
Task_t *pTask = pResSys->GetTask(INSTANCE_ID_TASK_INTRO);
// we know it is a frame player
FramePlayer_t *pFP = (FramePlayer_t *)pTask;
// push back an audio-visual layer
pAVL = pResSys->GetAVLayer(INSTANCE_ID_AVLAYER_INTRO);
pFP->Post_AVLayerCommand(PUSH_BACK, pAVL);
// push back a logic layer
pLL = pResSys->GetLogicLayer(INSTANCE_ID_LOGICLAYER_INTRO);
pFP->Post_LogicLayerCommand(PUSH_BACK, pLL);
```

Here we see that we can get any audio-visual layer using its instance ID by calling the resource system's GetAVLayer function. Similarly, we can get any logic layer using its instance ID by calling the resource system's GetLogicLayer function. Layers are passed to the Systems_t pointer when they are connected to the system via the layer's Connect(Systems_t *pSystems) function.

With this layer system, we can now change audio-visual layering dynamically. All of the various game modes and screens mentioned in the wrapping stage can be implemented using layer and task commands. For example, we can push back an audio-visual layer for a "heads-up display" when needed. Similarly, we can push back audio-visual and logic layers for floating menus. When creating new modes and screens, we have the option of editing the layering of our frame-player task using the layer commands, or we can switch between frame-player tasks using the task commands mentioned earlier.

Finally, a sophisticated use of layer and task manipulation is in transitions. Items on one game screen (the first audio-visual layer) can be gradually covered by items of another game screen (the second audio-visual layer). When the transition is complete and only the second layer is visible, the first layer can be removed from audio-visual processing.

Source Code

ON THE CD

The CD-ROM includes source code to the game framework implementation and some additional documentation. The code with this book is meant to highlight game framework concepts and not game technology concepts. Code updates will be available at http://www.gamefgramework.com. Figure 1.2.1 illustrates the modes, tasks, and layers that are implemented in the source.

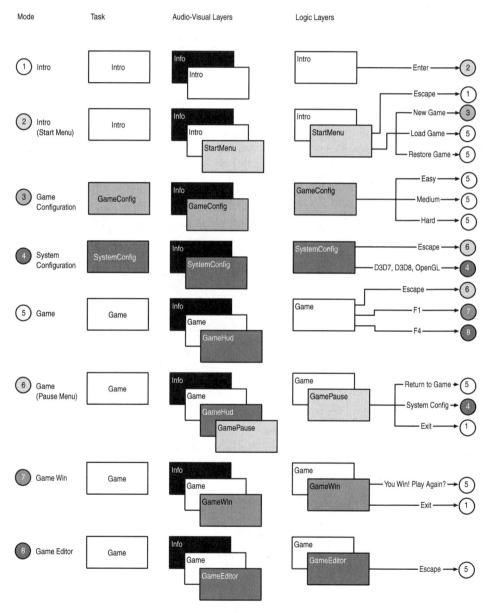

FIGURE 1.2.1   *Using the game framework: An example of how game modes can be implemented using tasks, audio-visual layers, and logic layers.*

References

[Boer00] Boer, James, "Object-Oriented Programming and Design Techniques," *Game Programming Gems*, Charles River Media, Inc., 2000: pp. 8–19.

[Boer00] Boer, James, "Using the STL in Game Programming," *Game Programming Gems*, Charles River Media, Inc., 2000: pp. 41–55.

[GoF94] Gamma, E., et al., *Design Patterns: Elements of Reusable Object-Oriented Software*, Addison Wesley Longman, Inc., 1994.

[Lakos96] Lakos, John, *Large-Scale C++ Software Design*, Addison Wesley Longman, Inc., 1996.

[Llopis01] Llopis, Noel, "Programming with Abstract Interfaces," *Game Programming Gems 2*, Charles River Media, Inc., 2001: pp. 20–27.

[Meyers96] Meyers, Scott, *More Effective C++*, Addison Wesley Longman, Inc., 1996.

[Meyers98] Meyers, Scott, *Effective C++*, Second Edition, Addison Wesley Longman, Inc., 1998.

[Meyers01] Meyers, Scott, *Effective STL*, Addison Wesley Longman, Inc., 2001.

[Noble01] Noble, James, *Small Memory Software: Patterns for Systems with Limited Memory*, Addison Wesley Longman, Inc., 2001.

[Stroustrup97] Stroustrup, Bjarne, *The C++ Programming Language*, Third Edition, Addison Wesley Longman, Inc., 1997.

[Vlissides98] Vlissides, John, *Pattern Hatching: Design Patterns Applied*, Addison Wesley Longman, Inc., 1998.

1.3

Finding Redeeming Value in C-Style Macros

Steve Rabin, Nintendo of America, Inc.
steve@aiwisdom.com

The lowly C-style macro (#define) is a powerful construct that is severely misunderstood. Many people and books characterize it as evil and outdated, replaced by the inline functionality in C++. Unfortunately, that's a simplistic view that doesn't take into account the unique functionality that the macro possesses. Shamefully, many C++ books fail to explain the basic properties of macros or even acknowledge their existence. However, solid explanations can still be found in classic C books such as [Kernighan88].

In a nutshell, the macro is a directive to the compiler's preprocessor to do some creative text replacement. Thus, no type-checking or other safety checks take place, and this is where many programmers get into trouble. As a simple rule, macros shouldn't be used to create function-like behavior or constants. For a discussion of the pitfalls of macros, please refer to [Dalton01], [Hyman99], and [McConnell93].

However, this gem isn't about the problems with macros; it's about proving that macros are useful and desirable in many surprising ways. Macros allow you to perform fancy text replacement before actual compilation, and that's exactly what the following tricks exploit. Note that the source code that appears in each example can also be found on the CD-ROM.

ON THE CD

Disclaimer

With macros, it's easy to be carried away into a world of bad programming practices. However, that's not the intention of this gem. While individuals have their own boundaries as to what is acceptable, it is generally understood that making new *dialects* of C/C++ by using macros is undesirable. Anyone coming onto a project should be able to read your code with a minimal amount of effort. So, as you read these tricks, understand that each one must be carefully weighed for its benefit versus the possibility of obfuscation. Confined use of these examples is probably the most reasonable way to benefit from this gem.

Macro Trick #1: Turning Enums into Strings

There are two special operators that let you do some tricky text manipulation inside of a macro. The first operator is #, and it will instruct the macro to put quotes around the argument that follows it. For example:

```
#define CaseEnum(a)    case(a): LogMsgToFile(#a, id, time)

switch( msg_passed_in )
{
    CaseEnum( MSG_YouWereHit );
        ReactToHit();
        break;

    CaseEnum( MSG_GameReset );
        ResetLogic();
        break;
}
```

After the compiler's preprocessing step, the previous code becomes:

```
switch( msg_passed_in )
{
    case( MSG_YouWereHit ):
        LogMsgToFile( "MSG_YouWereHit", id, time );
        ReactToHit();
        break;

    case( MSG_GameReset ):
        LogMsgToFile( "MSG_GameReset", id, time );
        ResetLogic();
        break;
}
```

With this macro scheme, you can easily dump enum names in a reliable and meaningful way, as actual strings, to a log file or the screen. Without this trick, you would need to have a lookup table of all enums-to-strings. Unfortunately, lookup tables are often poorly maintained and, thus, not reliable. The other solution is to use strings in the first place, instead of enums, but it's doubtful you would want to perform routine string compares inside your game. Therefore, the macro trick is a sound solution that is both fast and reliable.

Another variant is to read in the enumeration from a header file and interpret the single list into both an enumeration and an array of string names. The following shows how this can be done:

```
// data.h

DATA(MSG_YouWereHit)
DATA(MSG_GameReset)
DATA(MSG_HealthRestored)
```

```
// data.cpp

#define DATA(x) x,

enum GameMessages
{
    #include "data.h"
};

#undef DATA
#define DATA(x) #x, // make enums into strings

static const char* GameMessageNames[] =
{
    #include "data.h"
};

#undef DATA
```

Macro Trick #2: Compile-Time Constants from Binary Representations

The other special macro operator is ##. This operator lets you paste two arguments together. For example:

```
#define cat(a,b)   a ## b

value = cat( 1, 2 );
```

The preprocessor will turn the previous line into:

```
value = 12;
```

While this simple example is useless (shown just to illustrate the concept), the ## operator can be exploited in very interesting ways. The following trick allows you to create compile-time constants using binary representations. What is especially interesting is that this runs completely in the preprocessor with no runtime code generated. (Special thanks to Jeff Grills who provided this implementation.)

Here's the usage:

```
const int nibble = BINARY1(0101);       // 0x5
const int byte   = BINARY2(1010,0101);  // 0xa5

// 0xa5a5a5a5
const int dword = BINARY8(1010,0101,1010,0101,1010,0101,1010,0101);
```

Macro source:

```
#define HEX_DIGIT_0000 0
#define HEX_DIGIT_0001 1
```

```
#define HEX_DIGIT_0010 2
#define HEX_DIGIT_0011 3
#define HEX_DIGIT_0100 4
#define HEX_DIGIT_0101 5
#define HEX_DIGIT_0110 6
#define HEX_DIGIT_0111 7
#define HEX_DIGIT_1000 8
#define HEX_DIGIT_1001 9
#define HEX_DIGIT_1010 a
#define HEX_DIGIT_1011 b
#define HEX_DIGIT_1100 c
#define HEX_DIGIT_1101 d
#define HEX_DIGIT_1110 e
#define HEX_DIGIT_1111 f

#define HEX_DIGIT(a)        HEX_DIGIT_ ## a

#define BINARY1H(a)         (0x ## a)
#define BINARY1I(a)         BINARY1H(a)
#define BINARY1(a)          BINARY1I(HEX_DIGIT(a))

#define BINARY2H(a,b)       (0x ## a ## b)
#define BINARY2I(a,b)       BINARY2H(a,b)
#define BINARY2(a,b)        BINARY2I(HEX_DIGIT(a), HEX_DIGIT(b))

#define BINARY8H(a,b,c,d,e,f,g,h) (0x##a##b##c##d##e##f##g##h)
#define BINARY8I(a,b,c,d,e,f,g,h) BINARY8H(a,b,c,d,e,f,g,h)
#define BINARY8(a,b,c,d,e,f,g,h)  BINARY8I(HEX_DIGIT(a), \
    HEX_DIGIT(b), HEX_DIGIT(c), HEX_DIGIT(d), HEX_DIGIT(e), \
    HEX_DIGIT(f), HEX_DIGIT(g), HEX_DIGIT(h))
```

Macro Trick #3: Adding a Descriptive Comment to Standard Assert

The standard Windows assert (found in assert.h) is already a macro. It's extremely helpful, even indispensable to good software engineering—but it can be improved. The biggest improvement is to add a descriptive string so that a meaningful message is displayed when an assert is triggered.

With the following macro, you can easily expand the standard assert to include a descriptive string:

```
#define assertmsg(a,b) assert( a && b )
```

Example use:

```
assertmsg( time > 0, "Trigger::Set - The arg time must be > 0" );
```

When time is less than or equal to zero, the assert will be raised and the embedded message is displayed as part of the failed assertion. You can read more about this trick, as well as other assert tricks, in [Rabin00].

Macro Trick #4: Compile-Time Assert

Occasionally, you'll have a situation where you want a build to immediately fail if a particular condition isn't satisfied at compile time. Depending on the size of your project, this can save a lot of time and trouble. The following macro allows you to verify a statement at compile time, which in effect is a compile-time assert.

```
#define cassert(expn) typedef char __C_ASSERT__[(expn)?1:-1]
```

For example, if you're working on cross-platform code, you might want to check at compile time that enumerations are the same size as an unsigned integer. Given an enumeration such as MyEnum, you can check this by writing:

```
cassert( sizeof(MyEnum) == sizeof(unsigned int) );
```

If a false statement is passed into cassert, it will fail at compile time because it attempts to define an array with a negative size. Defining a negative-size array is a blatant compile error that will immediately stop the build.

Macro Trick #5: Determining the Number of Elements in an Array

Sometimes it's useful to know the number of elements in an array. However, there is no obvious way to query this, since it is not stored explicitly—only defined at initialization time.

The trick to computing the number of elements in an array is to divide the overall size of an array by the size of a given element. For example, if the total size of an array is 120 bytes and each element takes up 12 bytes, there must be 10 elements in the array. The size of each element, in bytes, is known at compile time, and the following macro neatly returns the number of elements.

```
#define NumElm(array) (sizeof(array) / sizeof((array)[0]))
```

Macro Trick #6: Making __LINE__ into a String

Several very useful macros exist by default. These include:

```
__LINE__ //an integer of the line number where it appears
__FILE__ //a string containing the file name where it appears
__DATE__ //a string containing the date when it was compiled
__TIME__ //a string containing the time when it was compiled
```

The main use for these macros is to record information that is useful in debugging. For example, when an assert macro is placed in your code, it takes advantage of the __FILE__ and __LINE__ macros. Should the assert be triggered, these values are displayed; thus, you know the exact filename and line number where the problem occurred.

Since these values are normally used for printing out debugging information as strings, here are several macros to turn the __FILE__ string and the __LINE__ integer into a single string containing both:

```
#define _QUOTE(x) # x
#define QUOTE(x) _QUOTE(x)
#define __FILELINE__ __FILE__ "(" QUOTE(__LINE__) ")"
```

This trick doesn't work with Microsoft Visual C++, since it replaces __LINE__ differently than other compilers. Instead of replacing the macro __LINE__ with a simple integer, it is replaced by (__LINE__Var+offset), where __LINE__Var is an internal variable that represents the line number where the function starts, and offset is an actual integer representing the offset from the start of the function. Therefore, with Microsoft Visual C++, the macro trick might produce a result like:

```
"C:\project\main.cpp((__LINE__Var+5))"
```

However, this macro trick produces the desired result with both Metrowerks CodeWarrior and SN Systems ProDG (a gcc-based compiler).

Macro Trick #7: Protecting Against Infinite Loops

The possibility of an infinite loop often looms over particular parts of your code, especially parts that depend on outside data or scripts. A practical safeguard is to create a counter that increments every time through the loop and, if it should get too high, asserts. That is exactly what this next trick will do, except that it will be done in a transparent manner that can be optionally compiled out for release builds.

This trick creates a macro called "while_limit," which behaves similar to the while keyword; however, it takes a second argument that defines the number of iterations at which it will raise an assert. For example, consider the following code:

```
while_limit( node != 0, 1000 ) {
    //some work
    node = node->next;
}
```

The previous example will assert if the loop spins more than 1,000 times. By raising an assert instead of hanging, testers can more easily diagnose bugs. As an added bonus, if the tester chooses to ignore the assert, the while_limit will exit the infinite loop and continue normal program execution.

Here's the macro source:

```
static bool while_assert( bool a )
{
    assert( a && "while_limit: exceeded iteration limit" );
    return( a );
}
```

```
#define UNIQUE_VAR(x) safety_limit ## x
#define _while_limit(a,b,c) \
    assert(b>0 && "while_limit: limit is zero or negative");\
    int UNIQUE_VAR(c) = b; \
    while(a && while_assert(--UNIQUE_VAR(c)>=0))
#define while_limit(a,b) _while_limit(a,b,__COUNTER__)
```

Note that a new default macro, __COUNTER__, is used in the previous code. The macro __COUNTER__ expands to an integer, starting with zero, and increments by one every time it is used. This allows us to create a unique variable each time we use while_limit. This unique variable is used to keep track of loop iterations. The first time a while_limit occurs, the variable's name will be safety_limit0. (The second time, the variable's name will be safety_limit1.) This unique-naming trick is necessary so that multiple while_limit macros could be used without their loop-iteration variable names clashing (causing compile errors due to multiple definitions).

The macro __COUNTER__ is not a standard ANSI C macro and is not implemented in all compilers. However, it is implemented in Microsoft Visual C++ and Metrowerks CodeWarrior. For SN Systems ProDG and other gcc compilers, an alternative trick exists by using the __LINE__ macro to help create the unique variable name. The following code will work with both SN Systems ProDG and Metrowerks CodeWarrior. (Both variations of while_limit work with Metrowerks CodeWarrior.)

Alternate while_limit macro:

```
static bool while_assert( bool a )
{
    assert( a && "while_limit: exceeded iteration limit" );
    return( a );
}

#define _UNIQUE_VAR(x) safety_limit ## x
#define UNIQUE_VAR(x) _UNIQUE_VAR(x)
#define while_limit(a,b) \
    assert(b>0 && "while_limit: limit is zero or negative"); \
    int UNIQUE_VAR(__LINE__) = b; \
    while(a && while_assert(--UNIQUE_VAR(__LINE__)>=0))
```

Macro Trick #8: Small, Specialized Languages

Macros can be quite powerful, and this trick probably demonstrates this best. Using the text-replacement property of macros, you can create your own small, specialized language that compiles directly into C/C++. Before you jump to conclusions, remember that we're still striving for readable, maintainable, and debuggable code.

In the article "Implementing a State Machine Language" (*AI Game Programming Wisdom* [Rabin02]), there is an example of a macro language that standardizes the construction of state machines and enforces some good programming practices. Consequently, it makes the state machine easier to build and easier to read. Here is an example of a state machine using the macro language:

```
BeginStateMachine

    State( STATE_Wander )
        OnEnter
            // C++ code for state entry
        OnUpdate
            // C++ code executed every tick
        OnExit
            // C++ code for state clean-up

    State( STATE_Attack )
        OnEnter
            // C++ code for state entry

EndStateMachine
```

While the previous code looks like a completely new scripting language, it compiles into C/C++ using only six macro keywords. The benefit is that native C/C++
code can be freely inserted, and it is trivial to debug, since the full power of the debugger is still available. Once you understand the behavior of the state machine, the
macro language actually hides the unnecessary details and lets you code the internals
in a simple and natural way.

The six macro keywords are as follows (OnEvent is a helper—it's not used
directly):

```
#define BeginStateMachine    if(state < 0){if(0){
#define EndStateMachine      return(true);}}else{assert(0); \
                             return(false);}return(false);
#define State(a)             return(true);}} \
                             else if(a == state){if(0){
#define OnEvent(a)           return(true);}else if(a == event){
#define OnEnter              OnEvent(EVENT_Enter)
#define OnUpdate             OnEvent(EVENT_Update)
#define OnExit               OnEvent(EVENT_Exit)
```

If you want to explore this macro-scripting language further, please see [Rabin02]
for an in-depth explanation.

Macro Trick #9: Simplifying Class Interfaces

One of the goals of C++ is to separate the declaration of a class from its definition.
This is very useful; it allows you to see the interface that a given class exposes—its *declaration*, usually placed in a header file—without having to understand its actual
implementation of that functionality (the *class definition*, usually placed in a .CPP
file).

Unfortunately, the way C++ implements the separation of class declaration and
definition ends up causing a fair amount of extra work. Namely, the signature (function name and parameters) of every non-inline function must be stated twice, once in
the class declaration and once in the definition.

```
// class declaration in Elmo.h
class Elmo
{
    void TickleMe(int x, int y = 0);
};

// class definition in Elmo.cpp
void Elmo::TickleMe(int x, int y)
{
    // actual implementation of Elmo::TickleMe() goes here
}
```

Because the signature of `Elmo::TickleMe()` exists in two places, every time we wish to change the parameters of the method—or change the function's name, or change it to be *const*, perhaps—we need to change it in two places.

Usually, this isn't a big deal. In most cases, a method will belong only to one class, and it's not problematic to change it in only two places. However, there are some cases where this aspect of the C++ language can cause you a lot of work. And in some situations it can become very easy to incur subtle bugs when you change a function's signature—bugs that your compiler won't be able to warn you about.

For example, imagine we have a base class named `BaseClass`. There are three classes derived from `BaseClass`—`D1`, `D2`, and `D3`. `BaseClass` declares a virtual function `Foo()`. `BaseClass::Foo()` comes with a default implementation in `BaseClass`; it's not a pure virtual function. Further, let's assume that the derived class `D3` overrides `Foo()`, so that `D3::Foo()` does something different than `BaseClass::Foo()`.

Now, let's say we add a parameter to `BaseClass::Foo()`, and we forget to update `D3::Foo()` at the same time. Sadly, our compiler will now lose the connection between `BaseClass::Foo()` and `D3::Foo()`—it will assume that they are two entirely different functions, and that `D3::Foo()` is an entirely separate function from `Base-Class::Foo()`. When we try to call `Foo()` as a virtual function on objects of class `BaseClass`, `D3::Foo()` will not get called on objects of type `D3`, as we originally intended.

Ideally, we want a method's signature to exist in only one place. It would be nice to be able to declare `BaseClass::Foo()` and provide implementations in both `Base-Class` and `D3` without also having to provide an additional declaration of `D3::Foo()`.

There's also an argument in support of productivity: With inheritance in C++, we often end up making many shallow class hierarchies with a single parent and many children. These generally tend to be much more useful than deep, everything-includ-ing-the-kitchen-sink hierarchies, which attempt to artificially conglomerate many unrelated pieces of functionality into a single, massively extended family.

With shallow hierarchies, we begin with a base class that exists primarily to declare an interface—that is, it declares some number of virtual functions, most of which will be pure virtuals. Quite often, we end up with a large number of classes in such a family, with a single base class and perhaps a dozen other classes derived from that base class. The problem is that we need to redeclare all of the methods we want to override in all of the derived classes we implement. If we have a base class with 10 functions, and we derive 10 classes from that base class, that's 100 extra function declarations, all of which essentially exist only to say, "I, too, implement the functionality declared in the base class." All of this extra text can make header files difficult to maintain and hard to read.

Let's imagine we have a class called `Creature`, and we intend to derive various different classes of creatures from this base class. `Creature` defines three pure virtual functions, as shown:

```
class Creature
{
    public:
        virtual std::string GetName() const = 0;
        virtual int GetHitPoints() const = 0;
        virtual float GetMaxVelocity() const = 0;
};
```

Furthermore, assume we derive several different classes of creature (`SnowCrab`, `NordicYeti`, and `SnowshoeBandit`) from this base `Creature` class. Each of our three methods—`GetName()`, `GetHitPoints()`, and `GetMaxVelocity()`—now exists in seven places: once in the declaration of `Creature`, and once each in the declaration and definition of `SnowCrab`, `NordicYeti`, and `SnowshoeBandit`.

So now let's assume we make a minor change and modify `GetHitPoints()` to return a float instead of an int. We now have to go and modify `GetHitPoints()` in *seven different files*—Creature.h, SnowCrab.h, SnowCrab.cpp, NordicYeti.h, NordicYeti.cpp, SnowshoeBandit.h, and SnowshoeBandit.cpp.

One good way to handle this is to wrap the methods into what can be called an *interface macro*. This is a macro that simply declares all of the `Creature` methods, like so:

```
#define INTERFACE_Creature(terminal)                       \
    public:                                                \
        virtual std::string GetName() const ##terminal \
        virtual int GetHitPoints() const ##terminal     \
        virtual float GetMaxVelocity() const ##terminal

#define BASE_Creature        INTERFACE_Creature(=0;)
#define DERIVED_Creature      INTERFACE_Creature(;)
```

The beauty of this is that we can now vastly simplify the class declarations of `Creature` and all of the classes derived from it:

```
// Creature.h
class Creature
{
    BASE_Creature;
};

// Skeleton.h
```

```
class SnowCrab
   : public Creature
{
    DERIVED_Creature;
};

// NordicYeti.h
class NordicYeti
   : public Creature
{
    DERIVED_Creature;
};

// etc.
```

Now, whenever we want to change one of the methods in `Creature`, we no longer have to touch SnowCrab.h, NordicYeti.h, or SnowshoeBandit.h—all we need to change is the interface macro (`INTERFACE_Creature` in Creature.h). We still need to modify the implementations in the various .cpp files; but given that the function is changing, we'd need to do that anyway.

Furthermore, our class declarations have become much more readable. When we look at the class declaration of `NordicYeti` in NordicYeti.h, we see `DERIVED_Creature` plus some number of other methods specific to a `NordicYeti` and not shared with other creatures. This immediately tells us what functionality belongs specifically to `NordicYeti`, and that if we want to see the declaration of the creature-level functionality, we should look for it in Creature.h, since that's where it properly belongs.

It's important to note that this interface macro is entirely different from the concept of an 'interface' in a language such as Java or C#. In these sorts of languages, you can treat an interface as an object—you can pass it around as a reference and call any of its methods. An interface macro, however, is just a way of encapsulating a set of related function declarations to hide some of the unnecessary duplication that the structure of the C++ language forces you to maintain.

Very special thanks to Paul Tozour for supplying this macro trick.

Conclusion

Hopefully, these examples have given you some renewed hope in macros and have expanded your personal toolbox of solutions. Just remember to carefully weigh the cost versus the benefit; always strive to make your code easier to understand and more robust. Used judiciously, these macros should make your programming tasks just a little easier and the results a little less prone to error.

References

[Dalton01] Dalton, Peter, "Inline Functions Versus Macros," *Game Programming Gems 2,* Charles River Media, Inc., 2001.

[Hyman99] Hyman, Michael, and Phani Vaddadi, *Mike and Phani's Essential C++ Techniques,* APress, 1999.

[Kernighan88] Kernighan, Brian, and Dennis Ritchie, *The C Programming Language,* Prentice Hall, 1988.

[McConnell93] McConnell, Steve, *Code Complete: A Practical Handbook of Software Construction,* Microsoft Press, 1993.

[Rabin00] Rabin, Steve, "Squeezing More Out of Assert," *Game Programming Gems,* Charles River Media, Inc., 2000.

[Rabin02] Rabin, Steve, "Implementing a State Machine Language," *AI Game Programming Wisdom,* Charles River Media, Inc., 2002.

1.4

Platform-Independent, Function-Binding Code Generator

Allen Pouratian, Sony Computer Entertainment RTime

allenp@csua.berkeley.edu

An automatic function binding tool scans your C code for function prototypes, assigns unique integers to each function, writes out code that hashes the prototype text names to the integers, and then writes out code for a 'switch' to bind these integers to the code that calls the functions.

Once the code generated by the binding tool is compiled into your program, such an interface forms the core of a scripting engine or a network RPC executor without the usual tedious and error-prone maintenance programming.

This gem is an extension of [Bilas00], from the original *Game Programming Gems* (2000).

Youth and Wisdom

Back when we were young punks hacking on our first machines, we lacked the wisdom to tweak our software without a rebuild. Later, we wised up a tad and started using command line arguments. Later still, we used option files. Those of you who are in-crowd material wrote a tool to make your option files [Rabin00].

Now that we're older punks, we'll design a tool to write the code that handles the internals of calling any function in our programs by text name. For example, it sure would be nice to avoid hard-coding the loading of a level, and script it instead. Also, if the design guy orders a new class of enemy bots for your shoot-em-up, wouldn't it be great if the code needed to send the new function calls to the other client machines wrote itself automatically?

Cygwin

Before the fine souls at Red Hat published their Cygwin [Cygwin01] package, such a coding stunt was not cheap. The Cygwin libraries allow most POSIX code to build and run in Windows 9x/NT/2000/XP environments. Thus, the ancient and venerable compiler-generation tools Lex and Yacc, along with grammars and specifications found for free on the Internet [Degener95], mean that everything necessary for parsing C structures, typedefs, and function prototypes is mostly already complete on all GNU-supported platforms—complete, that is, on platforms where sufficient clue has been scraped together to complete the porting task. Since GNU support strengthens by the week, genuine versions of Lex and Yacc are there for downloading.

Ghost of Gems Past

The prequel to this gem, ([Bilas00]), thoroughly discussed the issues surrounding various function-binding mechanisms. Gradually, we were led through the simple yet impractical and painful first and second design attempts. Through the lessons grew the design for an automated and elegant Windows-, x86-, Visual C++ 6.0-specific solution. Specifically, functions tagged for compile-time DLL export were parsed from compiler-generated export files into a table at runtime. This table then allowed the look-up of function text names for associated IDs and their subsequent execution.

The Gist

As we peruse the Lex specification for C [Degener95], we notice `#define` and `#include` are missing. The C preprocessor handles these and forwards the results to the compiler. Fortunately, the writers of gcc have broken out the preprocessor into a separate utility, called "cpp."

Here is what we will do. First, take a C module whose functionality you want exported, and run it through cpp. Then, for 'Phase 1' of this tool, take the product generated by cpp and extract function prototypes with the tool you will write with Lex and Yacc. Next, in 'Phase 2' of this tool, take these extracted function prototypes, assign integer IDs to each of them, and generate C code for a table that associates the IDs with the prototypes. In 'Phase 3,' we must write out yet more C code for a function that resolves function names into IDs, preferably with a 'move-to-front,' chaining hash table. Finally, our tool generates a `switch` statement on said ID, which serves up the hard-coded function call with properly cast arguments. Thus, tool-generated C code leaves the platform specifics of calling functions to the compiler. Just compile and link in the tool-generated C code, and you're ready to go.

Once we have Lex'd and Yacc'd together our function prototype-reading tool, we need it to shove out some fast C code to bind function text names to IDs. Surprisingly, using a clever 'move-to-front' hash-table chaining mechanism [Zobel01] beats all trees, including self-adjusting splay trees [Sleator85] by at least threefold! Following the Paredo principle, which states that 20% of the data is needed 80% of the time, the most commonly accessed elements are kept at the chain's top.

After compiling and linking our tool-generated C code into our games, we are ready to reap the rewards! We can call our script-execution function on any script file, or we can write a new function for our server, and execute it on the server from any client with no coding effort for translation and invocation.

Keep in mind that if all you desire is a way to call your C, C++, or Objective-C functions from scripts written in Perl, Python, or Tcl/TK, then visit www.swig.org. Support for binding yet more languages to C/C++/objective-C code is in the works.

The Details

The task of writing tokenizers for compilers surfaces so often that Mike Lesk and Eric Schmidt (Bell Labs) decided to write a tool to simplify the task. Review Chapter 1 of the respective O'Reilly book [Levine95] if you need convincing that Lex will cut your workload drastically.

We use regular expressions [Borsodi01] to express the tokens, and slam out C code to handle each respective expression. Lex handles the dirty work of writing C code to extract the token and calls your C code when it's found. The following Lex code identifies some famous scientists and mathematicians of history:

```
%{
/* Put any C code here. It need not be a comment. */
%}

%% [\t ]+ /* ignore white space */ ;

Newton | newton    { printf("Issac Newton\n") ; }
Pascal | pascal    { printf("Blaise Pascal\n") ; }
Pasteur | pasteur  { printf("Louis Pasteur\n") ; }

[a-zA-Z]+ {printf("%s: don't recognize \n", yytext); }

\&.|\n { ECHO; /* normal default anyway */ }

%%

main()
{
    yylex();
}

/* Again, any C code of yours can go here */
```

Between the opening %{ and %}, we insert any C code we want at the top of the generated C code for this Lexer. Then, we nest the tokens we seek to extract between the two %% groupings, followed by bracketed C code that we want executed when the desired Lexeme is found. After the trailing %%, we again insert any C code we need.

Fear not, for you can also call functions and declare/assign variables from the C code that follows each regular expression. Just make sure you link the Lex library into your applications. If you use the Unix make utility, this is most commonly done by adding –ll to the line that summons the linker.

Yacc in Two

The engineers of the 1970's Bell Labs were an industrious bunch, so Yacc was written to ease the task of writing parsers. Just as English grammar specifies the syntax of English sentences, we write a grammar for C so Yacc can distinguish a line of C from a line of Ada. Here is a simple Yacc grammar that will parse the simplest of English sentences:

```
%{
/* Put any C code here. It need not be a comment. */
#include <stdio.h>
%}

%token NOUN VERB PRONOUN

%%
sentence: subject VERB {printf("Baby talk!\n"); }
    ;

subject: NOUN | PRONOUN ;

%%

#define ERROR_RETURN( intReturnValue, expression,
stringExplanation ) \
    if( expression ) \
    { \
        printf("Function Failure: %s in %s at line
        %d\n", stringExplanation, \
        __FILE__, __LINE__ ) ; \
        return intReturnValue ; \
    } \

extern FILE *yyin;

main(int argc, char* argv[])
{
    FILE *fp ;

    ERROR_RETURN( 1, argc != 2 , "main-->wrong number of arguments")
;

    fp = fopen(argv[1], "r" ) ;
    ERROR_RETURN( 2, !fp , "main-->Invalid input
file") ;

    yyin = fp ;

    while(!feof(yyin))
    {
        yyparse();
    }

    fclose( fp ) ;
```

```
    }

    yyerror(s)
    char *s;
    {
        fprintf(stderr, "%s\n", s);
    }
```

Like cousin Lex, Yacc allows direct insertion of any C code between %{ and %} into the generated C file. This time, in addition to a C-style comment, we have arranged for the loading of stdio.h. The words that follow %token designate tokens that the grammar will recognize. Should you choose to use Lex with Yacc, these macro definitions will be common between your Lex and Yacc specifications.

Between %% groupings, we describe what are called *productions* of the grammar, where the grammar's syntax is described to Yacc unambiguously. Typically, a programmer will include C code they want executed after a desired production. Following the trailing %%, we again include all C code we want to include with the C code generated by Yacc. There is no need to link in a Yacc library the way we must with Lex.

Scripting

Once your level-loading functions are exported, a script provides welcomed flexibility during development. Imagine changing a triggered sound with the change of a named WAV file, or any attribute of anything, without a rebuild. Visualize your producer doing this instead, so that you can take time to hunt down another memory leak. If, a week before shipping, someone deems that a game level is too dark—feel your schedule pressure lessen as they adjust one variable at the top of your level-loading script.

AI Directives

In a Gamasutra article, Charles Guy discussed modeling AI (Artificial Intelligence) biologically with procedural directives [Guy99]. Again, the exported functionality allows tweaking by the nontechnical personnel working on the project. AI needs AI (Artificial Intervention—Yours!) to function acceptably, and scripts defining such behavior will speed the process and lessen headaches in the long run.

Networking

Once you have function binding integrated into your RPC system, you need not worry about extending functionality when you expand your API. Say we're planning a four-person, peer-to-peer network game, where in order for Player A to fire a missile, `fire_missile()` must be called on computers A, B, C, and D. If the foundation for the calling mechanism on Machine A is laid once in a generic way using ANSI C variable-length argument lists (which refer to the aforementioned tool-generated, function prototype table of IDs and encoded argument lists), no extra coding effort will be needed to translate and execute each new function at the other end of the network pipe.

Conclusion

Exporting and binding functions with tool-generated C code can save us lots of work in manually binding functions for scripting and RPC engines. Converting tasks that traditionally required programmer modification over to the hands of designers and artists helps speed the iterative design cycle significantly.

References

[Bilas00] Bilas, Scott, "A Generic Function-Binding Interface," *Game Programming Gems,* Charles River Media, Inc., 2000.

[Borsodi01] Borsodi, Jan, "Regular Expressions Explained," available online at http://www.zez.org/article/articleprint/11/, 2000.

[Cygwin01] http://www.cygwin.com.

[Degener95] Degener, Jutta, "ANSI C Grammar, Lex Specification," available online at http://www.lysator.liu.se/c/ANSI-C-grammar-l.html, 1995.

[Degener95] Degener, Jutta, "ANSI C Yacc Grammar," available online at http://www.lysator.liu.se/c/ANSI-C-grammar-y.html, 1995.

[Guy99] Guy, Charles, "A Modular Framework for Artificial Intelligence Based on Stimulus Response Directives," available online at http://www.gamasutra.com/features/19991110/guy_01.htm.

[Levine95] Levine, Mason, Brown, *Lex & Yacc,* O'Reilly & Associates, 1995.

[Rabin00] Rabin, Steve, "The Magic of Data-Driven Design," *Game Programming Gems,* Charles River Media, Inc., 2000.

[Sleator85] Sleator, Tarjan, "Self-adjusting Binary Search Trees," *JACM,* Vol. 32, No. 3, July 1985: pp 652–686.

[Zobel01] Zobel, Heinz, Williams, "In-Memory Hash Tables for Accumulating Text Vocabularies," available online at http://goanna.cs.rmit.edu.au/~hugh/zhw-ipl.html.

1.5

Handle-Based Smart Pointers

Brian Hawkins, Seven Studios

winterdark@sprynet.com

At any time, an object in a game can die and leave any pointers to that object dangling with dangerous consequences. Handles are a common method for preventing these invalid pointers from being used, but handles incur a substantial overhead if used for every action to be performed on an object. To reduce this overhead, there is often a conversion provided from a handle to a pointer, but this can lead to accidental storage of the raw pointer without any method of tracking its use. A better solution is to wrap the handle inside a smart pointer. This provides familiar syntax as well as greater safety and debugging options.

A smart pointer is a C++ class that uses syntax similar to a regular pointer, but it provides added functionality that is not normally available to a regular pointer. One of the most common jobs performed by a smart pointer is ownership management of the object data. There are many smart pointer implementations available with different ownership strategies for each (deep copy, copy on write, reference counting, and destructive copy), and it is important to consider which type is necessary for the task at hand. Andrei Alexandrescu provides a good overview of many smart-pointer features in *Modern C++ Design* [Alexandrescu01].

Let's consider when to use handle-based smart pointers. First, the object should have a distinct owner that controls when it is destroyed—for example, if the scene manager is the only one allowed to destroy a game object. If there is no distinct owner to determine when the object is destroyed, reference counting might be a better option. Second, the object's destruction time should be unknown. A game object that is killed by the player is an example of an unpredictable destruction time. If the time an object is deleted is certain, it is usually not necessary to incur the overhead of handles. Finally, handle-based smart pointers are only necessary when several objects need to store pointers to the same object, such as four players that each require a reference to the same vehicle object. Otherwise, there is most likely a better solution with smaller overhead.

Usage

Now that you know when and why to use handle-based smart pointers, we can move on to the details of implementing them safely and efficiently. But first, a description of how handle-based smart pointers are used will help in understanding what the implementation is designed to accomplish.

The first step is to create the object instance and assign the resulting dumb pointer (the term "dumb pointer" is often used to refer to a built-in pointer type) to a smart pointer. There is no reason to keep the dumb pointer around, so this operation can be performed in one line:

```
t_HandlePointer<class> l_handle(new class);
```

The designated owner of the object instance can then assign this handle to anyone that requires a reference to that instance:

```
t_HandlePointer<class> l_handleCopy = l_handle;
```

When the object's lifetime is over, the instance's owner destroys the object. Because the owner stores a smart pointer, a function is required rather than the delete operator (operator delete):

```
g_Destroy(l_handle);
```

Using a handle pointer is as close to using a dumb pointer as possible. For example, the handle pointer can be dereferenced using operator-> or operator*. The handle pointer can also be checked to determine its validity using the same conditional that would be used to check for a null dumb pointer:

```
if(l_handle) {
    l_handle->m_Member();
    (*l_handle).m_Member();
}
```

This check should always be done if there is a possibility that the object has been destroyed, thus invalidating the handle pointer.

Handle

The handle is at the heart of a handle-based smart pointer and therefore must be implemented efficiently. The primary operations that are performed on the handle are conversion to a pointer and tests for validity. A very efficient way to convert from handle to pointer is to store the pointer in an array and include the array index as part of the handle. The conversion then takes two simple operations to complete: First, obtain the index from the handle; and then, look up the pointer in the array using the index.

The preceding conversion is only valid if the handle is still valid. There must therefore be a method of determining that the contents at the index match the handle used for the conversion. To accomplish this, a unique identifier can be assigned to each handle and stored with the associated pointer in the array. When the handle is invalidated, both the pointer and unique identifier are removed from the array. Future attempts to use the handle can be detected as invalid because the unique identifier is no longer at that location in the array. Figure 1.5.1 shows a possible layout using this method.

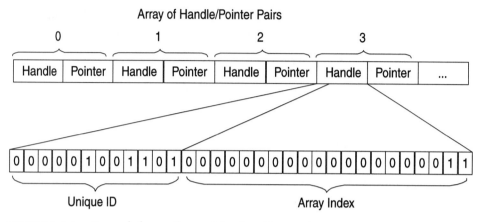

FIGURE 1.5.1   *Example layout for resolving handles to pointers.*

While there are several methods for generating a unique identifier, a simple method usually suffices for handles. Simply start with one as the first unique identifier, and increment by two every time a new unique identifier is requested. The added advantage of this method lies in the fact that zero is never a unique identifier because the one bit is always set. Notice that no mention is made about checking for a duplicate unique identifier. As long as the bit count of the unique identifier is reasonably large compared to the number of objects in existence at any one time, the chances that the same identifier will occur at the same location in the array is small enough to ignore. Preventing the unique identifier from wrapping around will eliminate this minute possibility, although it will also limit the total number of objects.

Smart Pointer

ON THE CD

The smart pointer wraps the handle to provide familiar syntax when using the handle. Since there are several good books and articles on all the details of making smart pointers, we will concentrate on the issues that are specific to handle-based smart pointers. These issues can be broken down into construction, destruction, dereferencing, and validation. The sample implementation provided on the CD-ROM provides a fully working example.

Construction and Destruction

Constructing a smart pointer from a dumb pointer requires the creation of a handle. The constructor passes the dumb pointer to a handle manager in order to create this handle. The handle and the dumb pointer, which will be used for validation and dereferencing, are then stored in the smart pointer.

The handle manager is typically a Singleton class [GoF95]—a class with one global instance. This is necessary to provide a central location for handle/pointer pairs for later handle lookups. The manager also ensures there is only one handle per pointer, but this comes with a performance penalty. This check can be avoided if a dumb pointer is assigned to a single handle-based smart pointer immediately on object creation, and all subsequent use is through the smart pointer or copies of the smart pointer.

Normally, an object is destroyed using the `delete` keyword; but that is not possible with smart pointers. One option is to add a member function to the smart pointer that will call `delete` on the dumb pointer. This can lead to confusing code, however, when the same variable has `operator->` and `operator.` applied to it. A better alternative is to use a friend function that deletes the dumb pointer when given a smart pointer as an argument. Once the object is deleted, the handle manager must be informed that the handle is now invalid.

Validation

If there is the possibility that the object was destroyed, the smart pointer must be checked for validity before it is dereferenced. There are two important conditionals that are used when checking a handle-based smart pointer: equality and inequality. Internally, both tests must query the handle manager to determine if the handle is still valid.

The inequality test is a simple matter of overriding `operator!`, but the equality test requires a little bit more work to prevent strange behavior on the part of the smart pointer. A simple class must be created that disables `operator delete` by declaring, but not defining the operator, and then returning a pointer to a global instance of the class from a conversion operator if the handle is valid. Otherwise, the conversion function can return a null pointer. More information on why this is the preferred method can be found in *Modern C++ Design* [Alexandrescu01].

Dereferencing

The most useful feature of a smart pointer comes from the dereferencing operators `operator->` and `operator*`. These operators are the reason for keeping a copy of the dumb pointer in each smart pointer; this way, we can quickly return the pointer or a reference to the object. These operators should be extremely simple and efficient because they will be the most-frequently used handle-based smart pointer features. Debugging versions of these functions can also perform validation of the handle as an added protection against the mistake of the caller not testing the smart pointer before dereferencing it.

Conclusion

Handle-based smart pointers can be an efficient and powerful technique when used with the right types of objects. The combination of handles and smart pointers simplifies object management and retains syntax familiar to all programmers.

We've covered the specific issues relating to smart pointers using handles, but there is a lot more information available on smart pointers. *Modern C++ Design* [Alexandrescu01] and *More Effective C++* [Meyers96] both contain a wealth of useful information on smart-pointer implementation and uses.

References

[Alexandrescu01] Alexandrescu, Andrei, *Modern C++ Design*, Addison Wesley, 2001.
[GoF95] Gamma, Erich, et al., *Design Patterns*, Addison Wesley, 1995.
[Meyers96] Meyers, Scott, *More Effective C++*, Addison Wesley, 1996.

1.6

Custom STL Allocators

Pete Isensee, Microsoft Corporation

pkisensee@msn.com

Many games use custom memory allocation strategies, providing their own `mal-loc` and `free` functions or overriding the global `operator new` and `delete`. The C++ STL (Standard Template Library) provides a powerful extension that allows you to use your own allocation and deallocation methods with all standard C++ container objects, including strings. This gem shows how to create custom allocators and integrate them into game code.

An Example

As an example, suppose your game creates a list, manipulates it in some way, then throws the list away—all within a single function:

```
std::list<int> MyList;
for( int i = 0; i < 100; ++i ) // build the list
    MyList.push_back( i );
MyList.reverse(); // manipulate the list
```

If this function is called once per game loop, the penalty you would pay for allocating and freeing list nodes could easily convince you not to use STL lists. Suppose you could customize the list so that all memory allocations came from the *stack* rather than the heap. Deallocations would be free, because stack memory is automatically reclaimed when the stack object goes out of scope. Here's how the stack-based list code might look using a custom allocator:

```
// Create custom allocator object
const size_t nStackSize = 100 * 12;
unsigned char Stack[ nStackSize ];
StackAlloc<int> sa( Stack, nStackSize );

// Tell the list about the custom allocator
std::list<int, StackAlloc<int> > MyList( sa );

// This code is the same
for( int i = 0; i < 100; ++i ) // build the list
    MyList.push_back( i );
MyList.reverse(); // manipulate the list
```

StackAlloc is a custom STL allocator. The StackAlloc type is specified as a template parameter in the list declaration, and the StackAlloc object is passed to the list constructor. In this example, the stack is specified as just large enough to allocate 100 nodes. In most STL implementations, a list node consists of the object and two pointers. The full implementation of StackAlloc is available on the CD-ROM.

ON THE CD

Performance-wise, this particular optimization produces code that runs *two to three orders of magnitude* faster than the first version, depending on the compiler and platform. Clearly, custom allocators offer huge performance benefits, and the beauty of allocators is that you can write your own implementations that use whatever allocation techniques make sense for your game.

Allocator Basics

STL containers include vector, deque, list, map, set, multimap, and multiset. The basic_string object also meets the qualifications for a container. All STL containers allocate memory to store objects in the container. These containers allow you to provide custom allocators that define how memory will be managed. For example, list is defined as the following:

```
template <typename T, class Allocator = allocator<T> >
class list { ... };
```

The Allocator parameter is a default template parameter. In normal usage, it's not specified, and the default allocator, allocator<T>, is used. The default allocator will be covered in more detail later.

```
std::list<int> IntList; // uses default allocator<int>
```

Allocator Requirements

Any allocator object must meet the minimum requirements set forth by the C++ Standard in Section 20.1.5 of [Cpp98]. These requirements are not difficult to follow and involve writing mostly boilerplate code. However, it's beneficial to understand all portions of the allocator class.

Typedefs

All allocator objects must include the typedef names shown here. These typedefs are almost always defined as listed in this section. However, the C++ Standard allows implementations to provide alternative definitions. For instance, the pointer typedef might refer to *far* pointers, or some other pointer type particular to the platform. In practice, the freedom to define alternate types is limited, especially since C++ has no way of defining a reference type other than good old T&. The moral of the story: Don't alter these typedefs without fully understanding the ramifications.

```
typedef size_t    size_type;
typedef ptrdiff_t difference_type;
```

```
typedef T*          pointer;
typedef const T*    const_pointer;
typedef T&          reference;
typedef const T&    const_reference;
typedef T           value_type;
```

Construction and Copying

Allocators are regular C++ objects, so there must be a way to construct them, copy them, and destroy them. Here are the declarations for the constructors and destructor:

```
allocator() throw();
allocator( const allocator& ) throw();
template <typename U>
    allocator( const allocator<U>& ) throw();
~allocator() throw();
```

Notice the unusual template member constructor, which allows an allocator to be constructed given an allocator of another type. Some compilers do not support template members yet, so this constructor may not exist in your implementation. Note also that the C++ Standard explicitly requires that neither the constructors nor destructor throw an exception.

Utility Functions

Allocator objects must provide a small set of utility functions. The most interesting utility function is max_size, which returns the maximum number of objects that could be conceivably allocated via allocate.

```
pointer address( reference r ) const
{
    return &r;
}

const_pointer address( const_reference c ) const
{
    return &c;
}

size_type max_size() const
{
    return numeric_limits<size_t>::max() / sizeof(T);
}
```

Allocation

The allocate function is one of the two critical functions in the allocator object, and is the focus of custom allocation strategies. The C++ Standard says that allocate must return a pointer to raw memory of sufficient size to hold n objects of size T, where n is always greater than zero. The function does *not* construct the objects.

The second parameter is an allocation "hint," commonly a pointer to another memory block used to improve locality of reference. The hint parameter is generally not used.

```
pointer allocate( size_type n, const void* pHint );
```

Here's just one example of how this function could be written to conform to the Standard:

```
pointer allocate( size_type n, const void* )
{
    assert( n > 0 );
    return pointer( malloc( n * sizeof(T) ) );
}
```

Deallocation

The `deallocate` function is the second critical function of the allocator object. The C++ Standard states that this function must free storage for *n* objects of size *T*, where the raw memory of those objects begins at a non-null storage location *p*. The `pointer` p must have been previously returned by `allocate` from an equivalent allocator object, and the function must not throw an exception.

```
void deallocate( pointer p, size_type n );
```

Here's an example of how this function could be written to conform to the Standard:

```
void deallocate( pointer p, size_type )
{
    assert( p != NULL );
    free( p );
}
```

In-Place Construction and Destruction

Notice that unlike `new` and `delete`, `allocate` and `deallocate` don't construct or destroy objects—they only deal with raw memory. For performance reasons, allocators specifically separate out these operations. For instance, `vector::reserve()` allocates raw memory, but only constructs `vector::size()` objects. Only if and when `vector::resize()` is called would uninitialized objects actually be constructed.

The allocator `construct` function allows existing memory to be used for constructing an object in place. You cannot call a constructor directly in C++, but the *placement new* operator provides the functionality needed. Placement new doesn't actually allocate memory—it calls an object's constructor using existing memory.

```
void construct( pointer p, const_reference c )
{
    // placement new operator
```

```
        new( reinterpret_cast<void*>(p) ) T(c);
    }
```

The `destroy` function allows an object to be explicitly destroyed without releasing the memory. You *can* call a destructor directly in C++, which is exactly what `destroy` does.

```
    void destroy( pointer p )
    {
        // call destructor directly
        (p)->~T();
    }
```

The C++ Standard defines these functions very precisely. They must always behave as shown here. The real purpose of these functions is to hide the notational complexity from containers.

Rebind

Suppose you've defined your own allocator object for a list of integers.

```
    list<int, MyAlloc<int> > IntList;
```

You might be inclined to believe that `MyAlloc<int>::allocate` would be called whenever a new item was added to the list. You would be mistaken. Most containers (`vector` being an exception) don't actually allocate the objects they store. They allocate *nodes*. Each node contains an object plus one or more pointers. That means that allocators must have some way of converting from type *T* to type *node*, whatever type *node* may be. The solution is called `rebind`.

```
    template <typename U>
    struct rebind
    {
        typedef allocator<U> other;
    };
```

Rebind simply allows `allocator<T>` to allocate objects of another type, U. For example, given allocator a of type *T,* you can allocate an object of type *U* with the expression:

```
    T::rebind<U>::other(a).allocate( 1, NULL );
```

Don't worry if you don't understand the gory template details. The important thing to remember is that the allocator you define for a given type has a way to allocate objects of different types (and sizes). The other important thing to know about `rebind` is that it requires a compiler with support for *member templates* in order to work properly. STL implementations that work with nonconforming compilers must provide their own mechanism for allocating nodes. For instance, older versions of the

Dinkumware STL library [Dinkum] provide the function _Charalloc to support nonconforming versions of Microsoft Visual C++.

Comparing

The C++ Standard says two things about comparing allocators. First, it states that allocators are considered equivalent if and only if storage allocated by one can be deallocated via the other. Then, it says that STL implementations are *permitted* to assume that allocators "be interchangeable and *always* compare equal to each other." If these statements sound contradictory, that's because they are. What the Standard is saying is that allocator comparison is implementation-dependent. Some STL implementations allow allocator comparison. Other implementations always compare allocators as equivalent.

```
template <typename T1, typename T2>
bool operator==( const allocator<T1>&,
                 const allocator<T2>& ) throw();
template <typename T1, typename T2>
bool operator!=( const allocator<T1>&,
                 const allocator<T2>& ) throw();
```

In many cases, it's perfectly fine to assume that allocators are interchangeable. The classic case is when the allocator has no data members. In other cases, you might really want to compare allocators (for more detail on this issue, see Allocator State Data, below).

The Default Allocator Object

The C++ Standard requires that all STL implementations include a default allocator object called "allocator<T>." This is the allocator that's used if a custom allocator is not specified. In other words, this is the allocator that your code is probably using at the moment, so it makes sense to know what it is doing.

The default allocator object is defined in the C++ Standard in Section 20.4.1 [Cpp98]. You can find the default allocator for your version of the STL in the <memory> header file (or one of the headers included by <memory>).

The standard says the default allocator must call operator new to allocate storage. If not enough memory is available, it throws the bad_alloc exception. A typical implementation of the default allocate function looks like this:

```
pointer allocate( size_type n, const void* )
{
    assert( n > 0 );
    return pointer( operator new( n * sizeof(T) ) );
}
```

The Standard says the default deallocate function must call operator delete(p). A typical implementation of the default deallocate is:

```
void deallocate( pointer p, size_type )
{
    assert( p != NULL );
    operator delete( p );
}
```

As you might expect, the default allocator object simply wraps `new` and `delete`. Implementations are free to provide additional optimizations in the default allocator if they wish. You can examine your version of the STL to see how the default allocator is implemented.

Writing Your Own Allocator

As mentioned above, every allocator object must meet the minimum requirements set forth by the C++ Standard. To be useful, it also has to function within any compiler-specific limitations. The best way for *you* to meet these requirements (and limitations) is by copying the default allocator from `<memory>` and then customizing the `allocate` and `deallocate` functions, and potentially the constructors, destructors, and comparison operators as well.

ON THE CD

Here's the partial implementation of the `StackAlloc` allocator shown at the introduction of the gem. Full source code is included on the CD-ROM. The `allocate` function simply returns a pointer to the next unused portion of stack memory, then updates the number of bytes that have been allocated. If it runs out of stack space, it throws `bad_alloc()`. The `deallocate` function doesn't need to do anything, because stack space is automatically reclaimed. All of these functions are inlined template functions, so `deallocate` is a no-op in a release build.

```
template <typename T>
class StackAlloc
{
public:

    // boilerplate typedefs here . . .

    // critical ctor
    StackAlloc( unsigned char* pStack,
      size_t nMaxBytes ) throw()
    :
        mpStack( pStack ),
        mBytesAllocated( 0 ),
        mMaxBytes( nMaxBytes )
    {
    }

    // other ctors, dtor . . .

    // utility functions . . .

    // construct, destroy, rebind . . .
```

```
pointer allocate( size_type n, const void* )
{
    void* pRaw = mpStack + mBytesAllocated;
    mBytesAllocated += ( n * sizeof(T) );

    if( mBytesAllocated+1 > mMaxBytes )
        throw std::bad_alloc();

    return pointer(pRaw);
}

void deallocate( pointer p, size_type )
{
    assert( p != NULL );
}

// member data . . .
};
```

Potential Uses

When should you write your own allocator? If after profiling your game, you've determined that the default allocator is a bottleneck, consider providing a custom allocator. If your entire game uses a custom solution and you don't want operator new being called at all, but you do want to use STL containers, consider writing a custom allocator.

There are far too many allocation strategies to possibly list them all, but Table 1.6.1 lists a selected number of strategies to consider when creating a custom allocator.

Table 1.6.1 Allocation Strategies

Type	Description
Fixed-Size Pools	All allocations are the same size; reduces memory overhead per allocation.
Shared Memory	Allocations use shared memory. See [Stroustrup97] for an example.
Multiple Heaps	Allocations come from different heaps, depending on the allocation size or type.
Single Threaded	Allocations and deallocations are not thread-safe; useful within single-threaded code.
Garbage Collected	Deallocations don't free memory; garbage collector function is called to free memory.
Stack Based	All memory resides on the stack. Useful for containers with short lifetimes.
Static Memory	Allocations come from program data space (static memory).
Never Delete	Deallocations never free memory; memory is reclaimed when application exits.
One-Time Delete	Deallocations never free memory; memory is reclaimed by custom function.
Aligned	Memory is aligned to meet certain requirements. Examples include page-aligned memory or SSE instruction-aligned memory.
Debugging	Allocation logging, pinpointing leaks, checking for memory overwrites, peak allocation size, and so forth.

Allocator State Data

As mentioned above, STL implementations might allow any allocator to be equivalent to any other. That implies that unless your particular implementation supports comparable allocators, it's dangerous for allocators to hold per-object data/state of any kind. If you're writing an allocator that must work across multiple implementations, the only safe path is writing allocators with no per-object data. The nice thing about this restriction is that allocators in such implementations generally have no space overhead. The drawback is that it might be more difficult to accomplish your task with a custom allocator.

One of the easiest ways to see if your STL implementation supports allocators with per-object data is to examine the implementation of `list::splice`. In the nominal case, the splice function splices one list to another by shifting pointers, which is very fast. Now, consider the case where the allocators for the lists are truly different—using different heaps, for example. Splice *cannot* simply change pointers, because the resulting list would contain some nodes allocated on one heap and some on another. The resulting list wouldn't "know" how to delete some of its nodes!

In the list `splice` function, if there are two code paths based on the comparison of allocators, it's likely you have an implementation that supports allocators with per-object data. If not, it's likely your implementation assumes that allocators are all equivalent.

Recommendations

Below is a list of recommendations for writing a custom allocator.

* Copy the default allocator from `<memory>` and replace `allocate` and `deallocate`. If your allocator has state data, update the constructors and destructor. Don't forget to include the global comparison functions.
* Be aware that using `allocator<T>` does not necessarily mean that only blocks of `sizeof(T)` will be allocated. The `rebind` function allows other types—and therefore other sizes—to be allocated.
* Typedefs are your friends, especially when dealing with template code. Use typedefs for allocators and containers that use custom allocators. If you need to make a change, only the typedef will need to be altered.
* Be wary of creating allocators that hold per-object data or that contain "state." Your STL implementation might not support such allocators. Examine the list `splice` function to determine if your implementation supports allocators with per-object data.
* Due to current compiler technology, not all allocator implementations conform to the C++ Standard. When in doubt, examine the default allocator in `<memory>` to determine how your implementation works around compiler limitations.
* Don't add custom allocators until you need to. The great thing about the allocator architecture is that allocators can be replaced with very few code changes.

Implementation Details

ON THE CD

The code included on the CD-ROM is designed to work with Microsoft Visual Studio Version 6 and Visual Studio .NET. It was tested with STL implementation Versions 3.08 and 3.10 from Dinkumware. These versions *do* support allocators with per-object data and allow nontrivial comparison functions.

Example allocators are provided for a number of strategies, including multiple heaps, stack-based allocators, and static allocators. There's also an allocator that simply wraps `malloc` and `free`.

Conclusion

Writing a custom allocator is a matter of copying some boilerplate code and customizing a handful of key member functions. Allocators have some curious features, and a working knowledge of these features is critical to understanding how allocators work. It's also important to note that different STL implementations might not support allocators with per-object data and might provide custom member functions to avoid compiler issues. Regardless of the complexities, custom allocators can significantly improve performance and are definitely worth understanding.

References

[Alexandrescu01] Alexandrescu, Andrei, *Modern C++ Design*, Addison Wesley, 2001.

[Austern98] Austern, Matt, "What are Allocators Good For?," *C/C++ Users Journal*, available online at http://www.cuj.com/experts/1812/austern.htm, May 1998.

[Austern99] Austern, Matt, *Generic Programming and the STL*, Addison Wesley, 1999.

[Cpp98] ISO/IEC 14882, *ANSI C++ Standard*, August 1998.

[Dinkum] Plauger, P. J., et. al., "Dinkumware Standard Template Library," available online at http://www.dinkumware.com.

[Josuttis99] Josuttis, Nicolai, *The C++ Standard Library: A Tutorial and Reference*, Addison Wesley, 1999.

[Meyers01] Meyers, Scott, *Effective STL*, Addison Wesley, 2001.

[Plauger01] Plauger, P. J., et. al., *The C++ Standard Template Library*, Prentice Hall, 2001.

[Stroustrup97] Stroustrup, Bjarne, *The C++ Programming Language*, Third Edition, Addison Wesley, 1997.

1.7

Save Me Now!

Martin Brownlow, Shiny Entertainment
mbrownlow@shiny.com

Many recent games have been released with one vital feature missing, and this one feature has probably generated more user complaints than any other element of a game. What could possible cause so much commotion? It is none other than the ability to save the game at any point. Saving your game on demand is generally taken for granted by the game-playing public; and if this functionality is missing, the public will complain loudly and often.

However, some categories of games can get away without it. Several game types would actually almost be ruined if you could save at any point. Could you imagine *Bubble Bobble* if you could save the game whenever you wanted? Unfortunately, most modern PC games do not realistically have the luxury of excluding a save game feature.

It is possible to argue that the ability to save at any point can significantly decrease the difficulty of a game, hence adversely affecting or severely curtailing the longevity of a game. This is reason enough for not implementing it. Most games instead support saving only at specific points where certain things can be taken for granted, simplifying the implementation. Unfortunately, this approach usually has a detrimental effect on the whole gameplay experience. Players feel cheated and often think that the feature was omitted to artificially inflate the playing time by making them replay the same 20 minutes over and over again. A better approach would be to allow saving the game at any point, but revoking that ability during crucial gameplay areas, such as the ubiquitous boss encounter.

Why Is It So Difficult?

Saving a game at an arbitrary position is one of those annoying tasks—to the layperson it seems remarkably simple, but when you get right down to the nuts and bolts, you discover that hard work is involved.

During the course of a game, even with clever object reuse, memory gets fragmented and object lists get jumbled. So, at any given time, it is nearly impossible to say where in memory a new object will be generated. A solution to this is to replace all pointers in the game with handles, which are then de-referenced through a lookup table. However, if you are not using handles, another solution is to change all pointers to handles as they are written to disk, and then de-reference the handles back into pointers after loading. Note that this will require several passes through the 'save data' prior to saving and after loading.

Another large hurdle is deciding exactly what to save for each object. Once this decision is made, it is necessary to write functions that read and write the data for each object type. Since most games have many types of objects, this can become an onerous task. Also, whenever any data structures change, all saved games are invalidated and new code must be written. This is often why the task of writing the save code is postponed until the end of the project. In the worst cases, the code is either not properly tested or it is omitted altogether as pressure mounts to finish the game within the time constraints.

What we need is a little automation. Ideally, we should only have to specify what data elements and types to save for each object class, pass a list of object instances to save, and let the save-game manager handle the rest. In this gem, we will be discussing a SAVEMGR class framework that manages game saves with this automation. The class files are available on the CD-ROM.

ON THE CD

The SAVEMGR **Class**

The SAVEMGR class is designed to make writing a save-game function quick and easy. After implementation, the process of saving a game becomes trivial. Simply specify all objects that should be saved with calls to AddSaveObject(), and then call Save() to save the game. Loading a game is simpler still—just call Load() and the game is loaded.

SAVEMGR builds a list of all the objects that are to be saved with each call to AddSaveObject(). When the Save() function is invoked, SAVEMGR goes through this list and calls the Save()member function for each object. When a pointer to an object needs to be saved, SAVEMGR searches through this list to find the referenced object. The position in the list (beginning from one; zero is reserved for NULL pointers) becomes the object's ID, which is then saved in place of the pointer. Note that if the object being referenced by the pointer is not in the list, then the game cannot be properly saved.

When reading a file, SAVEMGR first reads the number of objects in the file. Then, for each object, it reads its class ID and calls the SAVEMGR::MakeObject() function to instantiate an empty object of the correct type. Next, SAVEMGR calls the object's Load() function, which reads the object's data. When all objects have been loaded in this manner, SAVEMGR makes a final call to each object's PostLoad() function, which de-references object pointers from object IDs back into usable pointers.

The SAVEOBJ **Class**

Every savable class should be derived from the SAVEOBJ class and must implement the pure virtual functions GetSaveID() and GetSaveData(). Optionally, a class can override the Save(), Load(), and PostLoad() virtual functions, but it must be careful to call the base class version of the functions before returning.

How does it know what data to save for each object? That is where the GetSaveData() function comes in. For each class, a static array should be defined that specifies the data elements to write into the save file. This array defines the offset, type, and length of each piece of data. The GetSaveData() function should return a pointer to the correct array for the class. To retain simplicity, the SAVEMGR class defines several macros for common types, including pointers, allocated data, and contiguous data blocks. Also, for class hierarchies, there is a macro allowing the class to refer to its parent's save data description.

The GetSaveID() member function must return a unique ID for each type of class. This ID is then used by the user-defined SAVEMGR::MakeObject()factory function to create a class of the correct type during loading.

Data Types and Extensions

The SAVEMGR class natively supports the saving of several different data types through macros that create the save table. These macros automatically fill out the SAVERECORD structure by calculating the offset and length of the given data. The default types supported are contiguous generic data, pointers, allocated memory, and the save table of the base class. These are listed in the save table through the macros SAVEDATA, SAVEPTR, SAVEALLOC, and SAVEBASE, respectively.

The SAVEDATA macro has two parameters; the first is the type of the class, and the second is the member variable name. For example, the mat member variable in the PLAYER class would be declared with the macro SAVEDATA(PLAYER,mat). Similarly, the SAVEPTR macro takes the type of the class and the member variable name.

The SAVEALLOC macro takes three parameters—the type of the class, the member variable for the memory pointer, and a member variable containing the length of the allocation.

Finally, the SAVEBASE macro takes a single parameter—a pointer to the save data table for the base class. For instance, for a class PLAYER derived from the class OBJECT, the save table could contain an entry SAVEBASE(OBJECT::obj_savetable). If the OBJECT class was derived from another class, say MASTEROBJ, then the OBJECT save table could contain an entry SAVEBASE(MASTEROBJ::mobj_savetable). Then, the PLAYER class would automatically save the data elements for its base OBJECT class and also its base MASTEROBJECT class.

These macros work by finding the offset of the given data element and its size, then writing this into the save table. The SAVEALLOC function is slightly different, however. This macro saves not only the offset of the pointer to the allocated data, but also the offset of a variable containing the size of the data that has been allocated. It is often necessary to save data types that are specific to the current game state. For instance, we might need to save a pointer to a resource that has been changed from the default. To do this, extra macros need to be defined, and the code to handle these macros must be placed in the SAVEMGR member functions WriteData(), ReadData(), and CorrectData(). For our example, the code in WriteData() must translate the

resource pointer into some recoverable form (like the resource ID), and ReadData()
must translate it back.

Overriding the Default Functions

In some cases, it is desirable not to save certain data to the file, since it is derivable
from other elements in the object. This is where the overridable Save(), Load(), and
PostLoad() functions come in.

When an object is saved, the save manager calls SAVEOBJECT::Save(). This in
turn calls SAVEMGR::SaveData(), which actually writes the data out. If there is work to
be done before saving (for instance, deriving Euler angles from a matrix) then we
must override the Save() function. Note that the base Save() function must be called
to perform the actual write.

Similarly, the Load() function can be overridden. However, there will be no data
in the class until you have called the base class's Load() function. Finally, the PostLoad()
function can be overridden and called for each object after all the objects have been
loaded. Its primary purpose is to restore all the pointers in the object, but it should
also be used to restore any data not saved in raw form (for instance, converting Euler
angles to a matrix).

A Simple Example

The following code demonstrates saving a simple class.

```
class PLAYER : public SAVEOBJ
{
public:
    /* constructors/members omitted */
    int         GetSaveID();
    SAVERECORD *GetSaveData();

protected:
    /* This is the table returned by GetSaveData() */
    static SAVERECORD player_savedata[];

    /* This is the data for the PLAYER class */
    MATRIX      mat;
    NTT         *targetNTT;
};

/* The data saved for class PLAYER */
SAVERECORD PLAYER::player_savedata[] =
{
    SAVEDATA(PLAYER,mat),
    SAVEPTR(PLAYER,targetNTT),
    SAVEDONE()
};

SAVERECORD *PLAYER::GetSaveData()
{   /* return the data table for PLAYER */
```

```
        return player_savedata;
    }

    int PLAYER::GetSaveID()
    {   /* return a unique ID for this class */
        return PLAY_ID;
    }

    /****************************************
        This is the class factory function.
        It takes a classID and makes an
        object of the correct type
    ****************************************/
    SAVEOBJ *SAVEMGR::MakeObject( int classID )
    {
        switch( classID )
        {
        case PLAY_ID:
            return new PLAYER();
        }
        return NULL;
    }
```

The PLAYER class is derived from the SAVEOBJECT base class and defines the inherited pure virtual functions GetSaveID() and GetSaveData(). GetSaveID() returns the value PLAY_ID, which is then used later in the class factory function, SAVEMGR::MakeObject(), to create a class of the correct type. The GetSaveData() function returns a pointer to the save table for the PLAYER class, which defines the data that will be saved and loaded. The save table defines just two member variables that need saving—the mat variable and the targetNTT pointer.

Conclusion

ON THE CD

Saving and loading games is arduous and requires careful data conversion and management. With care and a little automation, however, this task can be transformed into a simple task of maintaining one table of data for each type of class. The code provided on the CD-ROM is a skeleton for a save/load manager. Many enhancements are possible. For example, the output stream could be passed through a compressor layer or a cryptographic layer. You might want to add a header to the file to enable quicker parsing, or include a miniscreenshot to display in the file manger. It is even possible to extend the SAVERECORD entry to enable backward compatibility.

Autolists Design Pattern

Ben Board, Dogfish Entertainment, Ltd.

ben_board@yahoo.com

A C++ game programmer frequently finds it necessary to gain selective access to the set of all objects of a type *T* (e.g., CAIPedestrian), where *T* is a leaf type of the hierarchy derived from a base type *B* (e.g., CAIObject). Since there is often a list in the game containing pointers to all objects derived from *B*, identifying the relatively few entries of type *T* requires a wasteful search.

A sensible alternative is to create a separate list containing just those objects of type *T*, enabling immediate access to those objects in isolation. However, this method has some problems:

- We must decide where the list itself should be stored.
- We must ensure objects are added to the list on creation and removed on deletion.
- Rogue additions or deletions must be guarded against.

Creating each list requires several lines of code in a number of places, and it is easy to introduce bugs, particularly by using copy and paste, or forgetting a step in the process. An ideal solution would be if the programmer could somehow mark the class as "to be listed," and, with no further programmer effort, the class itself would create the list, store it intelligently, and guarantee that it contained just the existing instances of itself. This gem provides just such a solution with a design pattern called *autolists* that achieves all these features, removes much of the potential for bugs, and only requires half a line of code for each class to be listed.

Implementation

Consider a class, CListMe. We would like each instance of CListMe to be added to a special new list on construction and removed on destruction, and we would like to be able access this list simply, but in a suitably object-oriented manner.

Autolists achieve this by way of a single C++ template class, TAutolists<T>. TAutolists<T> has these crucial features:

- It has a static, private member variable of type list-of-pointers-to-*T*s.
- On construction, it casts its this pointer to type T* and adds itself to that list.

- On destruction, it finds its entry in the list and removes it.
- TAutolists exposes a read-only interface, allowing useful query functions without allowing the list to be altered directly.

To mark a CListMe as "to be listed," simply derive it publicly from TAutolists <CListMe>:

```
class CListMe : public TAutolists<CListMe>
{
    ...
    // no further references to TAutolists required
};
```

Since the constructor for CListMe must call the parent constructor (that of TAutolists<CListMe>), the class's this pointer (cast to a CListMe pointer) is added to the list. When the object is destroyed, the reverse process happens, and the pointer is removed from the list, which is hidden in the parent class' private scope. In both cases, the derived class has nothing further to do to make this happen.

Access to the resulting list is via the TAutolists interface—no direct access is allowed to the list object itself. The following is a typical example of autolist usage:

```
CListMe* pLM = TAutolists<CListMe>::GetAutolistFirst()

while (pLM)
{
    // use pLM here

    // finally:
    pLM = TAutolists<CListMe>::GetAutolistNext();
}
```

GetAutolistFirst() and GetAutolistNext() both return a T*, which will point to either a valid existing T object or NULL if the end of the list has been reached. There is almost no danger that a returned non-NULL T* pointer refers to a nonexistent object, given the restrictions on removals from the list. There is nothing for the programmer to forget to do!

Note the explicit scope qualifications of GetAutolistFirst() and GetAutolist-Next() by use of the prefix TAutolists<CListMe>::. This is not strictly necessary in the case where only one function of that name is visible (more on this shortly).

It is difficult to use this implementation incorrectly—there are two interface functions, which do not take any arguments. We could use an iterator system, but by exposing an extra type, requiring the declaration of another variable in the autolist loops, adding parameters to the list lookups, and essentially replicating a tiny subset of the regular list functionality without all the other useful stuff you can do with iterators—it would be taking a step backward from the no-brainer, no-bugs purity of this pattern.

Comments on the Implementation

Now, let us discuss some of the details of this implementation.

Cost

The cost of autolisting a class is trivial: one static list object containing one list element per object listed (as it would be with any list), one static iterator per list, and the virtual function table entry for the TAutolists virtual destructor.

Nested Iterations

In the implementation presented, nested iterations of the list are not allowed. If GetAutolistFirst() for a list is called while another iteration is in progress further up the call stack, the iterator would become corrupted. This is addressed by asserting that the iterator is NULL on starting a new iteration, but if nested accesses are likely to be useful, it is simple to replace the single static iterator in the TAutolists class with an array (or list) of iterators to manage an iterator 'stack' within GetAutolistFirst/Next().

Autolists Without Constructors

A second point to make is that some games avoid using constructors and destructors in favor of Initialize and Shutdown methods that are explicitly called shortly after construction and before deletion in order to gain more control over these important phases of an object's life. In this case, it might be necessary to dilute the automation of the pattern by moving the addition to and deletion from the list to separate functions, say InitializeAutolists() and ShutdownAutolists(), and require that the autolisted type call these explicitly—a step that must be remembered by the programmer, but at a very small cost when considering the benefit.

Downward Casting

One might raise an eyebrow at the cast down the inheritance tree that takes place in the TAutolist constructor. We recognize this issue, but can see no practical cause for concern, since there is little theoretical doubt about the type safety of the cast. The compilers used do not complain, and problems have yet to be seen while adding to, removing from, or querying a list. It might ease the programmer's conscience if a dynamic cast is performed rather than a static one by enabling run-time type identification (RTTI). However, no such problems should occur.

Other Storage Methods

The name of this pattern implies that lists are the only (or the preferred) method of storing the instances of a certain class. This is not necessarily the case. A sister class to TAutolists might be TAutomaps, for example, which stores each new object in an STL map. Indeed, one might create a suite of classes covering a range of aggregate methods to suit the expected populations of classes and to optimize their accesses. We have chosen the (STL) list example merely for simplicity.

Use of Multiple Inheritance

It is also worth discussing the potentially controversial use of multiple inheritance (MI) implied by this pattern. In order to mark a class with one existing parent as "to be listed," it must add `TAutolists`, a second parent. This is only a cause of limited concern; the problems associated with MI are dealt with in the natural use of the pattern.

The principal problem raised by the use of MI is name clashing—a type in a hierarchy ends up inheriting two or more functions with the same name from its parents. This problem might be mitigated by carefully naming the public interface by including the word "Autolist" in the `Get*()` functions. The chances of finding that name elsewhere in a hierarchy are slim. Of course, a name can always clash with itself: Consider the perfectly sensible and useful situation in which class `CBase` is a parent to class `CDerived`, and both are autolist clients:

```
class CBase : public TAutolists<CBase>
{
    ...
}

class CDerived : public CBase, public
    TAutolists<CDerived>
{
    ...
}
```

Within member functions of `Cbase`, it is possible to access other members of your own type by referring to the autolist interface without the usual explicit scope qualification:

```
void CBase::ExamineOtherCBases()
{
    CBase *pBase = GetAutolistFirst();
    // not strictly necessary to write
    // TAutolists<CBase>::GetFirst(), because this
    // way is unambiguous
}
```

However, this is not the case within `CDerived`, which inherits two functions called `GetAutolistFirst()` (one from its own `TAutolists` inheritance, and one via the inheritance from `CBase`). In this instance, it is necessary to fully resolve the scope:

```
void CDerived::ExamineOtherDerived ()
{
    CDerived *pDerived = GetAutolistFirst();
    // syntax error – ambiguous call
```

```
CDerived *pDerived =
    TAutoLists<CDerived>::GetAutolistFirst();
// no error, and arguably clearer syntax
}
```

In our project, we have imposed the rule that all uses of autolists, whether or not the scope is ambiguous, should explicitly state the scope in question, partly for readability and partly to maintain good habits.

Conclusion

Autolists are a design pattern intended to ease the common game-programming task of tracking all instances of a particular class type, without the programmer manually maintaining a list per type (a bug-prone operation requiring several steps).

This is achieved by a single template class, TAutolists, which, when used as a parent class for a class T, creates a new list of pointers-to-T, hides its implementation behind a simple interface, and causes each new instance of T to be added to the list on creation and removed from the list on deletion—all in half a line's worth of additional code. Autolists list your objects so you don't have to. The TAutolists<> class definition can be found on the CD-ROM.

ON THE CD

1.9

Floating-Point Exception Handling

Søren Hannibal, Shiny Entertainment

sorenhan@yahoo.com

Most programming packages for creating Windows applications create applications in which floating-point exceptions are often handled automatically, causing the processor to keep quiet about any floating-point errors that might occur. This gem will show you how to make your program crash when one of these errors occurs, by only adding three lines of code. It will also give you a few hints on how to locate the bugs.

Why Provoke Crashes?

Why should these errors be exposed in the first place? There are at least three good reasons:

- **Cross-Platform Compatibility:** Since other processors and other operating systems might be much less forgiving, any code that could potentially cause floating-point exceptions might crash on some platforms and run on others.
- **Performance:** Depending on the design of the processor, an instruction causing an exception might be slower than a well-executed instruction. Furthermore, since many operations work differently with illegal or infinite floating-point values, the code might run much slower or even lock up. For example, the following loop will lock up if x is an infinite number, as half infinite is still infinite:

```
int counter=0;
while(x>1.0f)
{
    x=x/2.0f;
    counter++;
}
```

- **To Avoid Sloppiness:** Although most floating-point errors are very innocent, they can easily hide bigger problems that typically surface at 2:00 a.m. the night before a major deadline.

It is important not to think of this gem as introducing bugs into programmers' code; our goal is only to expose the bugs that are already there. Therefore, it is in the best interest of every programmer to use the method in this gem to find and fix any code that causes floating-point exceptions.

Does Your Program Handle Floating-Point Exceptions?

Some compilers (e.g., Microsoft Visual Studio 6) disable floating-point exceptions by default; and therefore, you should always perform a test when switching programming environments. Here is a short piece of test code that, when put into a program, should generate a division-by-zero error. You should be careful to put the test somewhere in the core of your program and not in the very beginning, as some library calls, such as in the DirectX8 IDirect3DDevice8::Reset(), might disable the floating-point exceptions every time it is called.

```
volatile float x=1.0f;
volatile float y=0.0f;
for(int i=0;i<10;i++)
{
    x=x/y;
}
```

The code uses volatile to prevent the compiler from optimizing the division by zero out. When put into a project, it should be easy to see if your program ignores floating-point exceptions or crashes it.

Exception Types

The biggest consideration when enabling the floating-point exceptions is which types of exceptions to use. The Windows system routines allow access to six different types:

- _EM_INVALID—Invalid Exception. This should always be enabled.
- _EM_ZERODIVIDE—Division by Zero Exception. This should also be enabled.
- _EM_OVERFLOW—Overflow Exception. This should probably be enabled, except if the application is written to work with infinite numbers.
- _EM_INEXACT—Exception for an Inexact Result. This exception should definitely not be enabled, as most floating-point operations are slightly imprecise and would set the flag.
- _EM_UNDERFLOW—Underflow Exception. This occurs when an operation gives a smaller result than the floating-point register can contain, and it is rounded to zero. This exception should not be enabled, since, for example, the dot-product of two perpendicular vectors, with slight imprecision, would result in very small numbers.
- _EM_DENORMAL—Denormal Exception. Denormals are slightly specialized cases of floating-point numbers and are the smallest floating-point numbers available in

the IEEE754 standard. A very small number would become denormal before becoming zero. Denormals can therefore be unavoidable; and as a general rule, this exception should not be enabled. However, denormals are expensive compared to normal floating-point values, and by testing your code with this flag on, you might discover areas that can be modified to avoid denormals.

The Code

The code for enabling the floating-point exceptions is really simple. It reads the old control register values, modifies them, and writes them down again. The code is:

```
#include <float.h>
void enableFPExceptions()
{
    int i = _controlfp (0,0);
    i &= ~(EM_ZERODIVIDE|EM_OVERFLOW|EM_INVALID);
    _controlfp (i,MCW_EM);
}
```

The tricky part is where to place it within the program. As mentioned above, some libraries overwrite the floating-point exception flags. Therefore, after incorporating this function into your code, it is very important that you test it. Again, the test code should be at the core of the program, not just immediately after enabling the exceptions. Note that changing the floating-point exception flags can be expensive, so it should not be done for every frame. If you know which library functions overwrite the control register, it would perhaps be a good idea to reset the flag before the library call and set it again afterward.

Exception Handling in Released Projects

You should also consider whether to enable floating-point exceptions in your released programs or not. There are arguments for and against this, and the answer depends on the type of program. For a game, it might make sense to disable all exceptions; a bug probably will not have any long-term effects when the program is closed down. On the other hand, there is an argument for enabling them in programs such as level editors, since a level might get corrupted in memory and then saved to disk.

Debugging Floating-Point Exceptions

Ok, so you enabled the exceptions and your program crashes. But the code next to the crash looks fine. What is wrong, then?

Unfortunately, the crash does not occur right away. Because today's processors have multistage pipelines, the floating-point error occurs at the earliest stage during the next floating-point instruction, which might not even be in the same function. Therefore, it is very useful to switch to disassembly mode and look at the actual floating-point registers instead of looking at source-level debugging output. Remember this when you are trying to locate bugs that make no sense (at first).

Conclusion

There are three reasons to check for the floating-point exceptions—cross-platform compatibility, performance, and avoidance of sloppiness. The code to check for floating-point exceptions is simple, but care has to be taken to put it in at the right place and to test it carefully. Debugging can be confusing because of the delayed multistage pipeline, but looking at disassembly instead of source-level output makes it easier.

There is no reason not to check for floating-point errors, and doing so offers the potential for more stability and higher performance. By using the information presented in this gem, you will be on your way to writing better code in minutes.

1.10

Programming a Game Design-Compliant Engine Using UML

Thomas Demachy,
Titus Interactive Studio
tdemachy@titus.fr

L et's admit it—as programmers, we are sometimes compelled to turn down great game-design ideas because the game engine cannot cope with them. On the other hand, we might be disappointed when the game designer frowns at a brand new weather-control system, just because the game takes place underground.

We have all faced these situations, usually due to the fact that game design and engine programming are parallel tasks. Even if there are frequent interactions between designers and programmers, both have their own ideas of what the game should be.

This gem will explore collaborative work between the game-design team and the programming team, using a common graphic language—Universal Modeling Language (UML). By working together on the same model, designers and programmers will focus on the game, and only the game, and thus reduce both delays and development costs.

The Object Is in the Game

Object-oriented programming (OOP) was modeled after the real world. Consider an object—it is unique and identifiable, and therefore can be described with properties, such as its shape or color. In addition, any object interacts with the world and thus has a specific behavior.

These two observations are the foundations for object-oriented methods. These methods have been successfully applied to the software industry for more than 20 years, and many language implementations are available—Smalltalk, Java, and Visual BASIC, to name a few.

For several reasons, OOP just recently came to our industry with the growing use of C++ as a game programming language. For instance, [GPG01] presents many contributions concerning the benefits of using C++. However, there is more to C++ than a 'plus' added to C. It is a completely different paradigm, with a strong motto: "Think Object!".

Software and Game Design Share History

Recently, one of the most difficult challenges faced in game design is how to break away from linear or multilinear storytelling. Too often, situations are described with each and every interaction specifically defined. It becomes impossible for the player to freely choose their own unique path.

In a lecture entitled "The Future of Game Design" [Smith01], Harvey Smith (Ion Storm) promotes object-oriented game design in order to gain 'global consistency' (among other benefits). He demonstrates that by using object classes that inherit properties from one another, a more credible game universe can be achieved. Sound familiar? It probably does.

A Solution for Collaborative Work

Since game design is becoming more object-oriented, now is the time to work together and use a common language. The Universal Modeling Language was first introduced in the mid-90s and enables this collaborative opportunity. UML is a graphic-modeling toolbox, mainly used for software design; but it was intended from the start to be applied to any kind of design. This gem is not intended to be a UML tutorial. There are plenty of resources available in books or on the Web, several of which are listed in the References section.

All the World's a Stage

When considering design tools, it's important to take the dynamic aspect of game's design into account. If the world were really a stage, then a modeling language would have its own actors. This is the case for UML. From the game scenario, you can identify characters and actions. For UML, an actor is an entity with a role, such as the player, a nonplaying character, a vehicle, ... even a weather-control system. It introduces actors, use cases, sequences, and collaborative diagrams.

Introducing *Groody*

Both the game designer and the programmer use the game scenario as the starting point. Imagine you are working on a 2D platform game called *Groody*. The fairly basic scenario would go something like: *Groody features a hero running through a scrolling background. He can jump from one white cloud to another, but must blow stormy clouds away by using his wind blower. If a stormy cloud hits Groody, he might catch a cold.*

Defining Which Case to Use

The first step is to identify the actions and actors. For *Groody*, we identify three actors that can initiate an action—the game player, Groody, and the stormy cloud. Note that the game player and its virtual avatar are two different actors—you don't run in front of your screen like the hero does in the level. We then need to define the 'main actions' of the scenario. For UML, these actions are formalized as use cases. Use cases are very important because they define how the system will be built. In Figure 1.10.1, actors are drawn as stick figures, and use cases are drawn as ovals. The lines between the objects symbolize communication. The supported actions can be stereotyped as "uses" or "extends," linking several cases together. In this diagram, the *Run Through Level* case uses the *Jump* over white clouds case. Each use case must also be described in plain language, including normal control flow, alternative operation, special cases, and so on.

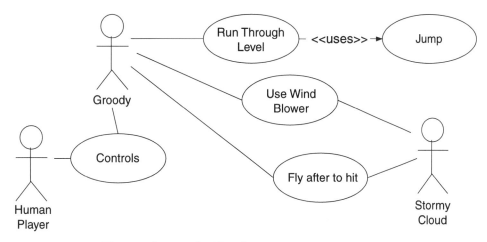

FIGURE 1.10.1   *Use case diagram for Groody.*

Unwrapping the Action

Use cases are wonderful for creating a quick draft of the design concepts, but they can be far too abstract and can be misinterpreted as more-detailed concepts. In an actor use-case relationship, each time that an instance of an actor is created, it will execute an instance of the use case, also called the "scenario." This scenario is unwrapped along a timeline and represented in the sequence diagram (see Figure 1.10.2).

A sequence diagram features the dynamic interactions between objects. If we focus on the **Use Wind Blower** use case, a typical scenario would be:

- Groody checks to see if he has energy cells left for the wind blower.
- For each cloud in the level, check if there is a clear line of sight (LOS).
- The first cloud with a clear LOS is hit and blown into thin air.

Several sequences are defined for each use case. It is the sum of all these scenarios that describes a use case.

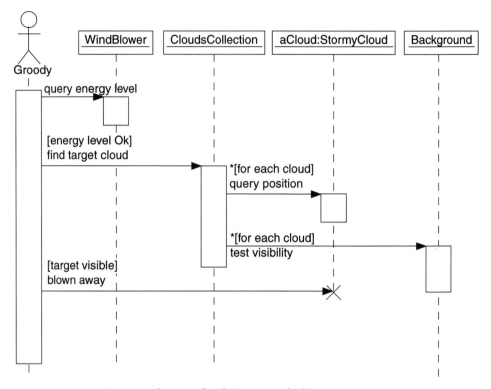

FIGURE 1.10.2   *Sequence diagram for the Use Wind Blower use case (time goes downward).*

From Sequence to Collaboration

Sequence and collaboration diagrams are two sides of the same mirror—they convey exactly the same information. The only difference is that the sequence is time-based, whereas the collaboration is object-based (see Figure 1.10.3). The magic of UML resides in this simple translation, which is the link between the dynamic and the static parts of the model.

Classes Move ... Like Stones Do

The game of *Go* is paradoxical in a way. Opponents attack one another and gain territories, essentially by laying down stones that will never be physically moved. The dynamic is born from the static. We have, until now, focused on the dynamic nature of objects and their relationships. In the game engine, however, the dynamic—the behavior—is based on the object properties.

Next, we will focus on the static representation for the game world and on the most popular diagram for UML, the class diagram.

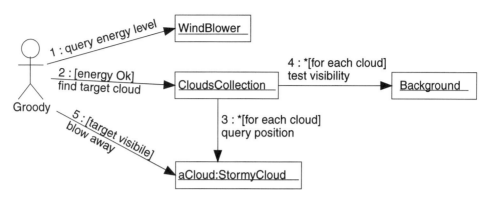

FIGURE 1.10.3   *Collaboration diagram for the Use Wind Blower use case.*

Two Ways To Talk About Classes

Leaning toward ever-more realistic simulations, modern games have to manage several thousands of objects, each interacting with a subset of the domain. Class generalization (or inheritance) is one of the most powerful object-oriented mechanisms. By classifying objects and creating hierarchies, it drastically downsizes the system's complexity.

Usually, inheritance cannot be identified from the dynamic analysis, since it mainly links object properties. During the class design, the secret to efficient collaboration between the programmer and the game designer is 'vocabulary' (see Figure 1.10.4). Both domains share the same object-oriented paradigm, but where the

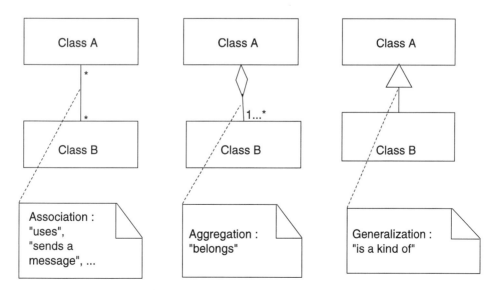

FIGURE 1.10.4   *A word for each association.*

programmer uses the terms "association," "aggregation," or "generalization," the game designer will refer to "uses," "possesses," or simply "is a kind of." The words are different, but the graphical representations for these concepts are the same.

Creating an Object Hierarchy

The collaboration diagram usually makes a good starting point. The messages become class operations to be transferred in the class initiating the message. Communicating classes are in an association relationship, except when the link is asymmetrical. In this case, we have an aggregation. There is aggregation when you can say that one object is part of another, and when the destruction of the owner will force the destruction of the owned.

From the collaboration diagram (Figure 1.10.3), we define the messages as the operation from the calling class. Figure 1.10.5 shows a representation of a class diagram after one use-case analysis.

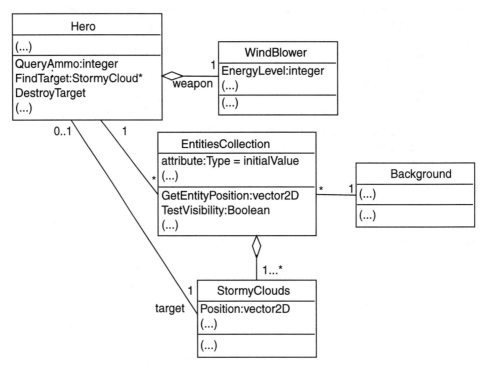

FIGURE 1.10.5   *Class diagram (incomplete), after one use case analysis.*

Collaborate and Iterate

UML has more advantages than just simplifying communication between game designers and programmers. The main idea behind UML is the iterative modeling process. It means that it is not necessary (and not even desirable) to develop the whole game design in UML before beginning the engine implementation. The process is incremental, back and forth between game designer and programmer. The use of case tools, such as those listed in the References, below, will smooth the entire process. In fact, several of these tools have code-generation and reverse-engineering features. Thus, a programmer can code the game engine and go back to the design when needed.

Because of its graphical nature, a UML model can be modified at very low cost. For instance, when introducing a new enemy, say a snake, you might want to create an abstract enemy class and specialize the cloud class from this new one. This modification implies a minor modification to the class diagram (see Figure 1.10.6). We must introduce the enemy abstract class, create the snake subclass, and then inherit the stormy cloud from the enemy class with the generalization link.

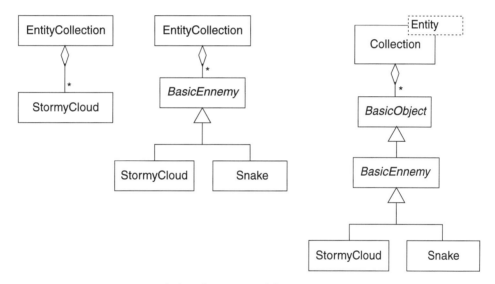

FIGURE 1.10.6 *Incremental class diagram modifications.*

While implementing source, it implies inheritance modifications, just as with other design techniques. However, if you use a UML case tool, the code modifications will be automatically rebuilt.

Modifications are not restricted to class hierarchy and can be done at any level. In the sequence diagram (Figure 1.20.2), the Groody actor is responsible for polling the level to find StormyCloud targets. For implementation reasons or to increase the reusability of the code, it might be preferable to introduce a combat resolver, establishing the interface between the shooter and the target (see Figure 1.10.7). The new scenario would be:

1. Groody informs the combat resolver that he is shooting.
2. The combat resolver determines if there is enough energy left in the wind blower.
3. The combat resolver finds a stormy cloud in Groody's line of sight.
4. When a cloud is targeted, the combat resolver informs it that it is being blown into thin air.

This new scenario results in a new sequence diagram (Figure 1.10.7), which in turn produces a new collaboration diagram. The new class, CombatResolver, is simply inserted into the class diagram. Implementation constraints do have consequences on the game design, however. Using a case tool, the whole process might take a few minutes.

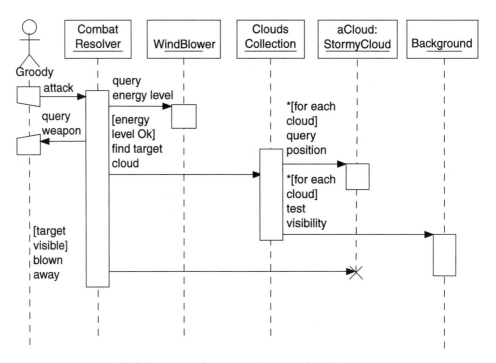

FIGURE 1.10.7   *Modified version of sequence diagram from Figure 1.10.2.*

Implementation Issues

Throughout this gem, we have not written one line of code. This demonstrates the capacity of UML to be completely language-independent. However, implementation can be done from the class diagram at any time. If you are using a UML tool, it can usually build the source code from the design automatically.

Hard Coding vs. Scripting

Since UML can be translated into many languages, you can choose what will be hard-coded and what will be described with a script. Usually, this decision is made very early in the development process. Using a UML design, functions and classes can be included in the hard-coded areas or in the scripts.

If you choose an object-oriented script language, such as embedded Python [Python02], you can also use UML to code these game scripts. In fact, there is another UML diagram perfectly adapted for behaviors and AI—the state diagram, as shown in Figure 1.10.8. The state diagram has been widely covered for AI state machines [Dybsand00]. It unrolls all the different states that an object can encounter, along with the conditional transitions.

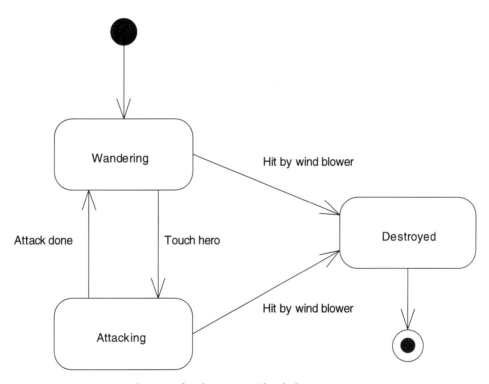

FIGURE 1.10.8 *State diagram for the StormyCloud class.*

Applying UML to Your Project

Several books, like [Muller97], describe the rules for widely used languages when translating the class diagram into plain code. However, the best option is to use a case tool that supports the whole iterative process, can generate the code in a chosen language, and can even reverse-engineer your code. This way, you have all the latitude necessary to keep both the UML model and the code consistent.

Currently, the most popular UML tools are Together ControlCenter [Together02] and Rational Rose [Rational02]. The latter has been reviewed in *Game Developer Magazine* [Sari01], a sign that it is making its way into the game-development community. There is also an open-source case modeler, ArgoUML [Argo02]; but since it is Java based, it does not implement complete code generation yet.

Conclusion

This gem proposed techniques for using UML for game programming. It demonstrated that using a modeling language can help game designers create object-oriented designs and emphasize the collaborative work between the programmer and the designer. The most recent version of UML (1.3) has many more features to offer that can be adapted for your team collaboration.

Using a case tool gives you the ability to work incrementally with object-oriented methods, while keeping complete control over the code and increasing maintainability, documentation, and reusability of the game engine.

References

[Argo02] ArgoUML Project, available online at http://www.argouml.org.

[Dybsand00] Dybsand, Eric, "A Finite-State Machine Class," *Game Programming Gems,* Charles River Media, Inc., 2000: pp. 237–248.

[GPG01] DeLoura, Mark, *Game Programming Gems 2*, Charles River Media, Inc., 2001.

[Muller97] Muller, Pierre-Alain, *Instant UML*, Wrox Press, Inc., 1997.

[Python02] Python 2.2 Script Language, available online at http://www.python.org.

[Rational02] Rational Software Corporation, http://www.rational.com.

[Sari01] Sari, Jonathan, "Product Review: Rational Rose," *Game Developer Magazine,* July 2001: pp. 10–11.

[Smith01] Smith, Harvey, "The Future of Game Design: Moving Beyond *Deus Ex* and Other Dated Paradigms," available online at http://www.igda.org/Endeavors/Articles/hsmith_intro.htm.

[Together02] TogetherSoft Corporation, http://www.togethersoft.com.

1.11

Using Lex and Yacc To Parse Custom Data Files

Paul Kelly

paul_kelly2000@yahoo.com

Most game engine subsystems have reached quite a state of complexity—they require a great deal of data to configure the behavior of that subsystem. It is beneficial to have that data specified outside of code and loaded at game initialization. Data should be in a format that is easy to modify, which can be done with a custom data file. Briefly, the format of the custom data file will contain the data and descriptions of the data. The separation of data from the code by using a custom data file has several benefits:

- Creating a custom data file for the subsystem helps organize the data so that it is easy to modify with a text editor [Boer01].
- Artists and game designers can change behaviors of the subsystem to balance gameplay.
- Data is managed outside of source code. If data is stored within code, then it is usually the programmer's responsibility to make data tweaks, which would be a tremendous bottleneck to a project.

The custom data file is input to a tool. The tool takes the text description of the data as input and transforms the textual data into a binary form. The binary file can then be loaded directly into memory at game initialization. This data transformation by the tool will require a parser. However, writing custom parsers for all game subsystems would require a great deal of work. Why reinvent the wheel?! Lex and Yacc, an application toolset that allows programmers to create a 'programming language' for a game subsystem, can do most of the work for you. Lex and Yacc can extract data from a text file and pass the data along to a tool for further processing. This gem presents methods for using Lex and Yacc within a tool for processing custom data files that can be compiled into binary data for a game subsystem.

The different sections of this gem break down the process of how to build a lexer and parser for a custom data file, as well as how to build a simple data file format. The first two sections provide a brief description of the basic functionality of Lex and Yacc. The third section covers how both work together to parse custom data files. Refer to [Levine92] for a more complete reference for Lex and Yacc.

The last two sections cover methods of using Lex and Yacc to generate game data. The first method will discuss generating game data from a custom data file for a game subsystem. The second method will cover creating loadable game data from intermediate export data files. Finally, an example will be given. The examples in this gem were tested using the non-GNU Flex and GNU Bison (instead of Lex and Yacc). See *Availability of Flex and Bison,* at the end of this gem, for instructions on how to obtain these applications.

Lex

Lex generates a source code file that specifies a lexical analyzer (also know as a lexer or a scanner). In general, a lexer takes an input text file and combines the characters of the text into individual pieces called tokens, which are assigned a meaning by the lexer. The tokens can then be passed to the parser [Aho86]. In our case, the parser would be created by Yacc.

There are three sections to every Lex file: a C code section and the lexer specification, which is followed by another C code section. The first is used for inserting include files and the declaration of constants, macros, global variables, function prototypes, and other data types that are used by the lexer and the last (C code) section. The second section defines the lexer. A lexer is defined by regular expressions that will be used to tokenize the input. The last section is where code, such as utility functions for processing input, will be located.

Yacc

Yacc is a parser generator. Yacc generates a source code file that specifies a parser (and an optional header file to be used by the Lex-generated code that contains token defines). In general, a parser takes the tokens produced by the lexer and combines them into phrases that have a particular meaning. Actions can be associated with the phrases. In our case of using custom data files, these actions are used to determine how the text file should be interpreted into binary data.

A Yacc specification has a similar setup as a Lex specification. The first section contains C code and is usually used for inserting include files and the declaration of constants, macros, global variables, function prototypes, and other data types that are used by the parser and the second C code section. The second section contains the parser definition. The parser definition consists of production rules and the associated action when a production rule is matched. The last section contains another C code section that contains code used within the parser specification. Functions for error reporting and other input processing functions are located in this section.

Advantages and Disadvantages

So, what is the advantage of using Lex to write lexers and Yacc to write parsers? [Levine92] points out that even a small lexer written in C that handles a simple command language is three times as long as the equivalent Lex program. This could mean that the C version could take three times as long to debug. When using Lex, there is only a need to debug the regular expression or other code that determines string matches for tokenizing the text. The same argument can be made for using Yacc.

Nevertheless, there are disadvantages to using a lexer created by Lex and parser created by Yacc. The disadvantages are the same for both. The generated code is often much larger than it would be if you wrote it yourself. This is due to the necessary code that handles all the functionality of Lex and Yacc—wasted space if that functionality is not used. Also, the execution time of code generated by Lex and Yacc tends to be slower. This because optimizations that could be performed in the coding of a lexer or a parser cannot be performed within a Lex lexer and a Yacc parser with as much relative ease.

Interaction of Yacc with Lex

We have a general understanding of how Lex and Yacc work independently. How do they work together to construct a parser for a tool? As shown in Figure 1.11.1, source files generated by Lex and Yacc are compiled and linked into a tool that uses them. The tool will assign the Yacc global variable, yyin, to be a pointer to the custom data file. Next, the tool will call yyparse() to start the parsing of the input text file. (See Listing 1.11.4 for an example main() for a tool.) The source code that Yacc generates has calls to the lexer functions created by Lex to grab the tokens of the input (the custom

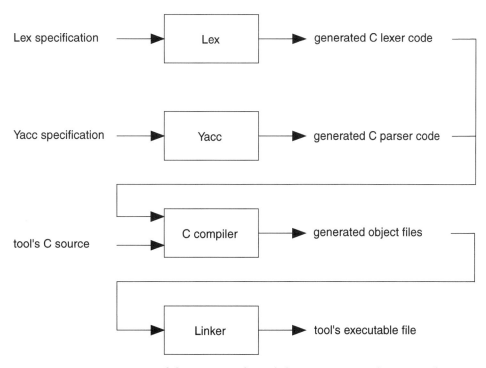

FIGURE 1.11.1   *Overview of the creation of a tool that uses a Lex and Yacc specification.*

data file). Data is passed from Lex to Yacc by using the Yacc %union and another Yacc global variable, yylval. Data is passed to the tool from Lex and Yacc through global variables. The values of the global variables are assigned within the actions of the parser specification (see Figure 1.11.2). The introduction to Lex and Yacc given above is a very basic one. For more information about Lex and Yacc, see [Levine92].

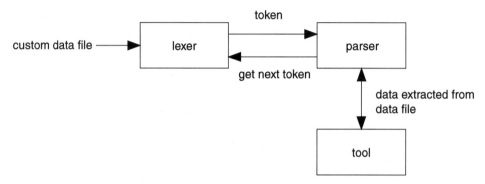

FIGURE 1.11.2   *Interaction of lexer, parser, and a tool that uses them.*

Custom Data File for a Game Subsystem

A custom data file can be used to specify data for a game subsystem. The structure of the custom data file can be difficult to define. However, most game data has some kind of structure that can be exploited to form a data file format that is both sensible in design and intuitive to the user. It is best to start simple and build on working custom data file formats. For example, take a game that has a weapon system. A weapon can have static and dynamic data. Static weapon data would include things like maximum ammo in a clip, ammo type, and firing rate, to name a few. The static data can be configured using a custom data file. Listing 1.11.1 (on the CD-ROM) is an example of a custom data file for a weapon system, the Lex specification for the custom data file, and the Yacc specification for the custom data file.

ON THE CD

Listing 1.11.1 Weapon data custom data file.

```
START_AMMO
        AMMO  9MM
                DAMAGE     5
        END
        AMMO  50CAL
                DAMAGE     15
        END
END

START_WEAPON
```

```
WEAPON MP5
    AMMO_CLIP    30   /* num bullets in clip  */
    AMMO_TYPE    9MM /* in millimeters        */
    FIRE_RATE    60   /* in rounds per second */
END

WEAPON DESERT_EAGLE
    AMMO_CLIP    10
    AMMO_TYPE    50CAL
    FIRE_RATE    150
END
END
```

The custom data file must have enough structure so that a Yacc specification can be made to uniquely identify all the elements of the file. This is mostly achieved in the above example by delimiting sections with start and end symbols. Listing 1.11.1 can be used as a template for most simple data-file formats. More-complicated formats will use a similar structure, but will probably embed more nested substructures (areas surrounded by a start symbol and an end symbol).

A similar custom data file, Lex specification, and Yacc specification can be used for power-up data, AI attributes, inventory data, player attributes, vehicle properties, and any other data for which a custom data file can be created. These systems would have a similar data file to the weapon system's data file.

A custom data file can be created for menu or HUD system data, where data within those items might be dynamic, but the items themselves usually don't change. A whole specification can be created for menus within a data file that can be used to build all the screens of the game. For those of you familiar with Windows programming, the resulting file would be similar to a Windows resource file. The specification would tell the location of elements of the menu screen and the possible range of values.

Combining Data Exporters with Lex and Yacc

ON THE CD

Lex and Yacc can also be used to parse text data exported from tools like 3DMax. It is sometimes easier to spot errors in model, terrain, and animation data exports if it is exported first to a text file for visual inspection. A parser can be written to convert the text data to a binary file that can be loaded at game initialization. The parser could also do error checking on the data if that is desired. An example of this kind of parser can be found on the CD-ROM. The Packer program takes a text description of a .md3 Quake III model file and converts it to its binary representation. Unpacker is also included on the CD-ROM. It converts a .md3 in binary form to its text form.

A Complete Example

ON THE CD

We will now present an example (on the CD-ROM) using the custom data file format of the weapon system presented in Listing 1.11.1. We'll start by looking at the Lex specification in Listing 1.11.2 (on the CD-ROM). The lexer code (generated by Lex) is called from the parser (generated by Yacc) whenever a new token is needed. As you can see, the lexer simply returns the next token it encounters. If the input text is "START_WEAPON," the token constant TKN_START_WEAPON is returned to the Yacc function that called for the token. The Yacc functions retrieve tokens until a parse match is obtained. In addition to the type of token, values used in the parser actions can be returned to the Yacc function via yylval.

Listing 1.11.2 Lex specification for weapon data custom data file.

```
%{
/* C code section for Lex specification */
/*** INCLUDES ***/
#include "weapon_y.h"   /* include token macros
                           generated by yacc */

#include <stdlib.h>
#include <string.h>

/*** PROTOTYPES ***/
void RemoveComment (void);
%}

/*** LEXER SPECIFICATION ***/
%%
START_WEAPON    {     return TKN_START_WEAPON; }
START_AMMO      {     return TKN_START_AMMO; }
END             {     return TKN_END; }
WEAPON          {     return TKN_WEAPON; }
AMMO            {     return TKN_AMMO; }
AMMO_CLIP       {     return TKN_AMMO_CLIP; }
AMMO_TYPE       {     return TKN_AMMO_TYPE; }
FIRE_RATE       {     return TKN_FIRE_RATE; }
DAMAGE          {     return TKN_DAMAGE; }

[0-9]+          {     yylval.integer = atoi (yytext);
                      return TKN_INTEGER; }

"/*"            {     RemoveComment (); }

[a-zA-Z0-9]*[a-zA-Z][_a-zA-Z0-9]*
{   strcpy (yylval.string, yytext);
    return TKN_IDENTIFIER; }

%%
/* C code section for Lex specification */

/* function to remove a comment from the input data file. */
void RemoveComment (void)
{
    int   c1 = 0, c2 = input();

    for (;;)
    {
```

```
            if (c2 == EOF)
            {
                break;
            }
            if (c1 == '*' && c2 == '/')
            {
                break;
            }
            c1 = c2;
            c2 = input();
        }
    }
```

Next, we'll inspect the Yacc specification in Listing 1.11.3. The Yacc specification is a Backus-Navr Form (BNF) grammar [Aho86] with embedded actions. This Yacc specification starts with the values that can be returned from the lexer, designated with the %union{} group. Next are the token types the lexer can return. These constants will be placed in a header file. (A command-line argument to Yacc is necessary to generate the header file and that header filename will need to be included in the Lex specification file.) The second section of the Yacc specification is the parser definition. When a parser match occurs, any action associated with the match is executed. For instance, when "WEAPON MP5" is parsed, the action strcpy(weapon_tbl[weapon_cnt], $2->string); is executed, and then the parse continues until the whole input file is processed (assuming no errors have occurred). This action specifies copying the production rule's second token's string value (returned by Lex) into the weapon table. The $2 denotes the token and the field specifies what data is expected to be returned from Lex. These are unioned fields so be careful! In this case, $2->string will be the string "MPS."

Listing 1.11.3 Yacc specification for weapon data custom data file.

```
%{
/*** INCLUDES ***/
#include "weapon.h"
#include <string.h>
#include <stdio.h>

/*** GLOBAL VARIABLES ***/
extern char *yytext;
%}

/*** TOKENS ***/
// return types for tokens
%union
{
    int     integer;    // for INTEGER token
    char    string[80]; // for IDENTIFIER token
}

// used by the lexer as return values so that the
```

```
// parser knows which tokens have been found
%token TKN_START_WEAPON TKN_START_AMMO TKN_END
%token TKN_WEAPON TKN_AMMO
%token TKN_AMMO_CLIP TKN_AMMO_TYPE TKN_FIRE_RATE
%token TKN_DAMAGE

// tokens that can return a value from Lex to Yacc via // yylval
%token <integer> TKN_INTEGER
%token <string> TKN_IDENTIFIER
%%


/*** YACC SPECIFICATION ***/
// weapon_data is the start symbol
weapon_data:        /* lamda rule - empty rule */
                    | weapon_data weapon_section
                    | weapon_data ammo_section

weapon_section:   TKN_START_WEAPON weapon TKN_END
weapon:
    /* lamda rule - empty rule */
    |   weapon TKN_WEAPON TKN_IDENTIFIER
            { strcpy (weapon_tbl[weapon_cnt], $3); }
        weapon_attribute TKN_END
            { weapon_cnt++; }
weapon_attribute:
    /* lamda rule - empty rule */
    | weapon_attribute ammo_clip
    | weapon_attribute ammo_type
    | weapon_attribute fire_rate

ammo_clip:
    TKN_AMMO_CLIP TKN_INTEGER
        {weapon [weapon_cnt].ammo_clip = $2;}
ammo_type:
    TKN_AMMO_TYPE TKN_IDENTIFIER
        {strcpy (weapon [weapon_cnt].ammo_type, $2);}
fire_rate:
    TKN_FIRE_RATE TKN_INTEGER
        {weapon [weapon_cnt].fire_rate = $2;}

ammo_section:      TKN_START_AMMO ammo TKN_END
ammo:
    /* lamda rule - empty rule */
    |   ammo TKN_AMMO TKN_IDENTIFIER
            { strcpy (ammo_tbl[ammo_cnt], $3);}
        ammo_attribute TKN_END
            { ammo_cnt++;}
ammo_attribute:
    /* lamda rule - empty rule */
    | ammo_attribute TKN_DAMAGE TKN_INTEGER
        {ammo [ammo_cnt].damage = $3;}
%%
int yyerror (const char *msg)
{
    printf ("%s at '%s'\n", msg, yytext);
    return 0;
```

```
        }
```

Listing 1.11.4 shows the general shell of a main() function from a tool that would use the lexer and parser generated by Lex and Yacc.

Listing 1.11.4 The tool source code.

```c
#include "y.tab.h"

WEAPON_DATA weapon;

int main (void)
{
    FILE *in;

    in = fopen ("weapon.data", "r");
    yyin = in;
    yyparse();

    /* process data in weapon and write out as binary
       data */

    return 0;
}
```

Conclusion

This gem shows how Lex and Yacc can be used to create parsers for custom data files. With Lex and Yacc, you are given access to tools that can generate a very powerful parser. Take the time to get to know and become familiar with these tools; your time spent will be repaid tenfold in future time savings.

Availability of Flex and Bison

Flex, a version of Lex that can be found on the GNU Website, and Bison, GNU's version of Yacc, are available for free at the GNU Website [GNU02]. See [Flex02] and [Bison02] for FTP download information.

References

[Aho86] Aho, Alfred, et al., *Compilers: Principles, Techniques, and Tools,* Addison Wesley, 1986.
[Bison02] Free Software Foundation, March 2002. Bison Flex is available for download at ftp://ftp.gnu.org/gnu/bison/.
[Boer01] Boer, James, "A Flexible Text Parsing System," *Game Programming Gems 2,* Charles River Media, Inc., 2001.
[Flex02] Free Software Foundation, March 2002. Flex is available for download at ftp://ftp.gnu.org/gnu/non-gnu/flex/.
[GNU02] Free Software Foundation, "GNU's Not Unix!—the GNU Project and the Free Software Foundation (FSF)," available online at http://www.gnu.org/, March 2002.
[Levine92] Levine, John, et al., *Lex & Yacc,* O'Reilly & Associates, Inc., 1992.

1.12

Developing Games for a World Market

Aaron Nicholls, Microsoft Corporation

aaron_feedback@hotmail.com

Until recently, developing games for multiple language markets was often done as an afterthought. Once the product was ready (or nearly so) for release in its core language market, the coding work to support other languages would begin, with test and localization soon following. The resulting products were often delayed and very limited in terms of language support. However, in recent years, many companies have released games in multiple language markets simultaneously, and titles such as *Starcraft* and *Diablo 2* have enjoyed phenomenal sales worldwide.

In order to capitalize upon the full market for a game, it is important to understand the technical obstacles and processes related to globalization. In addition, integration of globalization techniques into the entire developmental process is essential. In this gem, we will present the main issues related to the design, development, and testing of world-ready games, as well as some solutions to the inherent problems.

Market Potential

Traditionally, many games companies have had a tendency to focus on their local market, ignoring the global potential of a quality title. Many titles have received universal praise and strong sales in the U.S., but no attempts were made to introduce the titles to new markets. In other cases, a title is released worldwide, but the game is entirely in English—only the manual is translated. Fans of a specific genre and avid gamers in the know might be willing to put forth the effort to tackle a game that is not in their native tongue. However, as a wider audience embraces PCs and game consoles, it is important to appeal not only to the hardcore gamer, but to casual gamers as well.

In the past few years, there have been several game releases that have identified the size of the international game market. For example, in 2000 and 2001, South Korea proved to be a very promising market. Both *Starcraft* and *Diablo 2* were big hits, each selling more than 3 million copies worldwide. Of that total, approximately one third of the sales were in South Korea alone, with over a million copies of each game sold there. The games became cultural phenomena of a sort, with the game characters featured in toys and on potato chip bags.

Such success stories have not only been the case with American games selling outside of the U.S. As of January 2002, the best-selling, massively multiplayer, online role-playing game was not *Ultima Online, Asheron's Call,* or *Everquest,* but the Korean game *Lineage* with over 4 million copies sold—and it hadn't even launched in the U.S. and Europe yet! With such examples of success, it is easy to understand the importance of designing a game from the ground up to appeal to a world market of gamers.

First Things First—Display and Input

When dealing with international game development, one of the first challenges is in displaying the desired language(s). In addition, you might choose to provide input options and customizations particular to each language version of your game.

Fonts

First of all, you need fonts that contain all of the characters that must be displayed. While bitmap fonts are still used in some games, many have moved to TrueType and OpenType fonts for ANSI and Unicode character display, respectively. Unicode fonts can contain characters for multiple languages, but they can result in much larger file sizes, also.

Fortunately, the latest versions of Windows and MacOS support input and display of a wide variety of languages, including the necessary fonts. However, games typically use their own fonts (with the possible exception of install/uninstall), and it is important to consider a game's target markets when obtaining or developing fonts. In addition, keep in mind that while English text may look perfectly clear in an 8-point font, applying the same size to a traditional Chinese font might produce illegible text. Your game should be designed with enough flexibility to take such issues into account.

Line Breaks and Sorting

If your game supports multiline text input or display, one of the problems that can arise is that of breaking multiple lines of text. The rules for line-breaking are relatively simple for English and other European languages, but things are not as simple for many other languages. For example, in Chinese and Japanese, spaces typically are not used to distinguish individual words in a sentence. Instead, sentences consist of characters with no spacing, although similar (but double-byte) punctuation is still used. As such, it may be necessary to use more-advanced guidelines for determining where to break lines and wrap words. When dealing with multi-byte text, you can adopt the following rule: Lines may be broken before, after, or between double-byte characters. However, when a line break is needed within single-byte characters, you should break at the last space or double-byte character.

In addition to line/word breaking, sorting rules also vary from language to language, and sorting by character code is usually insufficient. Fortunately, these rules are usually defined in the operating system and are typically exposed to you as the developer through system APIs.

Input Method Editors (IMEs)

Once you have your characters displaying properly, you need to deal with input as well. While some games allow input only in English, this can be very limiting when dealing with saving games, chatting with other players, or jotting down in-game notes (for those games with such features). Many users do not speak English as a first language, and limiting input to English can distract gamers and reduce immersion into a game. Although supporting input of European characters requires few changes from an English-based product, other languages, such as Korean, Chinese, and Japanese, might require more work to support.

The first problem with implementing support for input of these languages is that each of them has thousands of characters—far too many to fit on a keyboard. When developing computer-based games, it might be possible to implement or use existing input method editors (IMEs). An IME is a program that converts keyboard scan codes (and, more recently, pen- or mouse-driven input) into character codes.

For example, for a user to input the word *"sushi"* in Japanese, they will first activate the IME (usually with a user-defined keystroke or a dedicated key on a Japanese keyboard). The IME then activates, and it intercepts the English letters "s-u-s-h-i" or a Japanese phonetic equivalent as they are typed by the user. The IME then gives the user a choice of candidate words corresponding to the phonetic spelling input by the author. Once the user selects the desired word (or string), the actual character codes representing the desired Japanese input are sent to the target application. If you choose to support IME input in your game, you should familiarize yourself with the IME message codes and architecture for your platform (see References for Web links to IME information).

Input Options Without IMEs

Unfortunately, IME support is not always an option. Due to UI design or development constraints, it may be impractical to implement or use an existing IME. This is usually the case when the target platform is a game console. However, with basic knowledge of the target language(s) for a game, it might still be possible to provide the user with some level of input support.

For example, in a Japanese game, it is possible to allow users to input player names in Japanese by providing an onscreen virtual keyboard containing only the katakana or hiragana (collectively referred to as Kana) characters. These are two sets of phonetic characters, either of which can be used to represent any word in the Japanese language. Although either alphabet is sufficient to represent any Japanese word phonetically, each has its own use, somewhat like upper- and lowercase letters in English. A hiragana or katakana keyboard to allow input in Japanese can be implemented in approximately the same amount of screen space required for an English upper/lowercase keyboard. An example of such an interface can be seen in Figure 1.12.1, taken from Microsoft's Japanese Xbox user interface. However, it is of course necessary to weigh the benefits of such a solution with the impact of such a feature on testing and development.

A

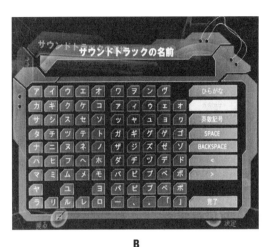
B

C

FIGURE 1.12.1 *On-screen keyboard for input of (A) Japanese hiragana characters, (B) Japanese katakana characters, and (C) English characters, from Microsoft Xbox. Screen shots reprinted by permission from Microsoft Corporation.*

Units and Display Formatting

When developing a game, it is important that the interface not interfere with immersion into the game itself. One way in which you can provide the user with a familiar interface is to default to the date, time, and number formats that the user is likely to prefer. It can be disorienting to go through savegame files as DD/MM/YY when you expect dates to be displayed in YY/MM/DD format. Similar problems can occur when dealing with numeric and time formats (is it 1,234.56 or 1.234,56?), as well as units for speed, weight, or distance.

While it might be appropriate in many cases to choose the most common default format for the target market, keep in mind that some operating systems (especially Windows and MacOS) allow users to specify these preferences in great detail. In addition, some console makers hard-code these formats differently, depending on the target market for the console. If your game retrieves these settings from the system, you can provide the user with their preferred display formats automatically.

Character Sets

When implementing support for various languages into a game, there are several different character encoding schemes that can be used. While there seems to be a gradual move toward Unicode on some platforms, there are advantages and disadvantages to each character encoding scheme. Typically, the scheme you choose will depend on your platform, target languages, and any dependencies you might have on legacy or other code that is not world-ready.

Single-Byte Character Sets (SBCS)

In addition to character display, another issue that has to be dealt with is character encoding. When dealing with traditional ASCII text, one byte is required to store one character. This is called a "single-byte character set" (SBCS) and is often used to encode data from English and other European languages.

However, even within SBCS, there are multiple systems for encoding. The ASCII standard uses 7 bits to store characters, with the 8th bit (originally) used for parity checking. This allows 128 characters (0–127) to be stored, which is sufficient for English text, punctuation, and a few control characters. Unfortunately, this is not sufficient for many other European languages, which need to represent accented characters, additional letters, and symbols that are not typically used in the English language.

In order to represent these additional languages, several extensions to the ASCII standard were proposed. Since the parity bit is no longer needed, the full 8-bit range is utilized, with characters 0–127 typically kept identical to ASCII specifications and characters 128–255 used to store additional characters, punctuation, and symbols. In Windows, for example, these are represented by a form of the ANSI character set known as ISO-8859. However, in order to represent various languages, multiple code pages (or encodings of characters to numerical values) have been developed. Typically, SBCS code pages differ only in the definition of the upper-range characters 128–255. However, since single-byte character sets can only represent 256 symbols, it is still not possible to represent even the full range of European languages, much less languages such as Chinese, Japanese, or Korean (often referred to collectively as CJK).

Double and Multi-byte Character Sets (DBCS/MBCS)

To represent a wider range of characters, larger character sets were developed. As the name implies, a double-byte character set (DBCS) uses two bytes per character, and a multibyte character set (MBCS) contains characters of varying length. One example of this is the Japanese Shift-JIS encoding scheme, which uses characters of one or two bytes.

In the Shift-JIS system, single-byte characters fall from 0x00 to 0x7F for ASCII characters and 0xA0 to 0xDF for Japanese single-byte kana. Double-byte characters consist of lead bytes and trail bytes, and lead bytes fall in the range excluded by the single-byte characters, namely 0x81 to 0x9F and 0xE0 to 0xFC. Such systems can encode tens of thousands of characters through this extended encoding; but they are trickier to develop for because character-counting, word-wrapping, and cursor-movement algorithms have to compensate for varying character sizes. In addition, since the lead-byte ranges vary for different MBCS encodings, your code might need to provide different cases for different Asian languages. Although the term DBCS is often used for encodings such as Shift-JIS, MBCS is a more appropriate definition and is the notation used in the C/C++ standards.

Programming for Various Byte-Size Character Sets

When working with SBCS data, while code pages might be a concern, characters and bytes are always one-to-one, requiring few code changes. Memory allocation, cursor movement, searching, editing, and word breaking remain relatively trivial. However, when coding for DBCS or MBCS data, it is necessary to take into account the fact that a character does not necessarily correspond to a byte, and vice-versa.

To begin with, when allocating memory for DBCS/MBCS strings, confusing bytes with characters can lead to disastrous results. For example, if a player's name is allocated as a 16-byte string, and the input algorithm counts user input by characters instead of bytes, a buffer overflow can occur, leading to instability and/or security problems. In addition, the interface needs to handle cursor movement, editing, and searches in terms of characters, rather than bytes.

In particular, searches are another area that can be problematic. For example, when parsing a file path, it is essential to distinguish between a forward or backslash and the same character code used as a nonlead byte of a double- or multibyte character. Failure to do so can lead to file-loading problems, savegame corruption, and other serious bugs that are only reproducible when specific characters in certain languages are used.

Since such problems are so difficult to identify (and often discovered by isolated customers after release), it is necessary that your test team understands and tests for these types of issues in order to prevent them from reaching the finished product. First of all, care must be taken in development to ensure that all string search and parsing algorithms are DBCS/MBCS-aware. In addition, identifying a core set of such 'danger characters' and including them in all string-algorithm testing can be effective in detecting problems before the production stage.

MBCS-Specific Problems

In MBCS systems, editing can be even more complicated. For example, merely hitting the backspace key while editing can trigger a full string parse, required to determine the number of bytes to delete. First of all, we don't immediately know if the byte immediately before the cursor represents a single byte or part of a multibyte character. We can determine that by stepping backward one character at a time until we reach either the beginning of the string or a character sequence that is definitively a single- or multibyte character. From that point, we can determine the number of bytes in the character to be deleted.

In the worst case, it might require parsing back to the beginning of the string. As such, it might actually be more efficient to parse the string from the beginning, especially when dealing with short strings. However, there is an alternative. Many systems contain MBCS-aware APIs for solving such problems. In Windows, for instance, the CharPrev, CharNext, and IsDBCSLeadByte APIs make this process easier by encapsulating this functionality into a simple system call.

Unicode

Fortunately, there is a way to support a variety of languages with a single codebase and without having to deal with code pages and characters of varying lengths. The Unicode standard defines approximately 40,000 characters in a constant two-byte format, supporting characters, symbols, and codes necessary to display the majority of major languages in a single code page. Although the standard also specifies extensions for supporting millions of characters and a plethora of languages (even Klingon!), the double-byte Unicode standard is typically sufficient for most games, and its flexibility and universal nature has made it the encoding system of choice for many serious, world-ready games. For more information on Unicode, please see [Unicode02] or the latest published version of the standard. At the time of this writing, the latest version is *Unicode Standard 3.0.*

Interface and Design Considerations

In addition to the character input, encoding, and display issues that were described above, there are several other areas of the game interface and design that must be taken into account when developing a game for multiple markets. These include device input and video output, as well as UI design and game content.

Video Output

When developing for game consoles, it is important to keep video standards in mind. While televisions in the United States, Canada, Mexico, and Japan use the NTSC standard at 30 (60 interlaced) frames per second, most other countries use PAL/ SECAM, which runs at 25 (50 interlaced) frames per second. As such, be aware that pre-rendered video for your game might need to be provided in both formats. In addition, it is a good idea to ensure that your game does not synchronize rendering or animation to a particular standard.

Keyboard Input

A common problem encountered when producing a PC game for a world market is that of keyboard input. While joysticks and gamepads are for the most part standardized, keyboards can vary from region to region. Some games anticipate a predefined set of expected scan codes (representing the physical position of a key on the keyboard) or virtual key codes or vkeys (typically representing the actual character on the key). If your game is to have appeal in multiple language markets, it is important to ensure that it works equally well with various keyboard layouts.

The problem arises when gamers use different keyboard layouts to play the game. In the best case, they find that certain keys just aren't available for mapping. In the worst case, keys are misnamed or don't work in the game, a very frustrating experience. For example, the scan code for the right square bracket "]" on a U.S. English keyboard maps to "+" on the German keyboard and "$" on the French. In addition, the upper range of vkeys contains several values that vary from language to language, specifically 0xba-0xbf, 0xc0, 0xdb-0xde, and 0xe2. For more details on scan codes, virtual keys, and ASCII character codes, please refer to Table 1.12.1. Fortunately, using a more-advanced input API, such as Windows DirectInput, can insulate your game from some of these implementation details; it provides a layer of abstraction and includes APIs for mapping codes to keys.

Table 1.12.1 Virtual Keys, Glyphs, and ASCII Codes for Scan Codes

Scan code	English			German			French		
	Vkey	Glyph	ASCII	Vkey	Glyph	ASCII	Vkey	Glyph	ASCII
0x0c	0xbd	-	0x2d	0xdb	ß	0xdf	0xdb	)	0x29
0x0d[1]	0xbb	=	0x3d	0xdd	`	0xb4	0xbb	=	0x3d
0x1a[2]	0xdb	[	0x5b	0xba	ü	0xfc	0xdd	^	0x5e
0x1b	0xdd	]	0x5d	0xbb	+	0x2b	0xba	$	0x24

(Continues)

Table 1.12.1 Virtual Keys, Glyphs, and ASCII Codes for Scan Codes (*Continued*)

	English			**German**			**French**		
0x27	0xba	;	0x3b	0xc0	ö	0xf6	0x4d	m	0x6d
0x28	0xde	'	0x27	0xde	ä	0xe4	0xc0	ù	0xf9
0x29[1]	0xc0	`	0x60	0xdc	^	0x5e	0xde	?	0xb2
0x2b	0xdc	\	0x5c	0xbf	#	0x23	0xdc	*	0x2a
0x32	0x4d	m	0x6d	0x4d	m	0x6d	0xbc	,	0x2c
0x33	0xbc	,	0x2c	0xbc	,	0x2c	0xbe	;	0x3b
0x34	0xbe	.	0x2e	0xbe	.	0x2e	0xbf	:	0x3a
0x35	0xbf	/	0x2f	0xbd	-	0x2d	0xdf	!	0x21
0x56[3]	0xe2	\	0x5c	0xe2	<	0x3c	0xe2	<	0x3c

1 Not available on German keyboard
2 Not available on French keyboard
3 Not available on U.S. keyboard

Language-Neutral UI Design

Regardless of the character encoding and input method systems used in a game, one of the universal problems encountered is with UI design and text layout. This is particularly problematic in the localization process, when resources from various languages are brought into the game. Even if your game's engine and UI is designed to handle a wide range of character types, it is practically guaranteed that you will encounter resizing and/or overlapping issues when you first localize your game.

When developing a user interface, it is good practice to leave additional space in both the UI and the necessary data storage to take into account languages that might use longer strings or different fonts. For example, strings translated from English to German can grow considerably in size. If a UI is built with the English product in mind, with graphical buttons or UI components just large enough for the English strings, it might be impossible to produce the same interface for German without either modification or excessive abbreviation.

One often-quoted guideline is that when using English as your source language, you should leave enough room in the UI for strings to grow 30% to 50%. In addition, shorter strings might require even more room for growth, especially when a German product is to be produced from an English product. This way, your UI will be less likely to require changes when you begin localizing to languages that might require longer strings.

In addition, it might be necessary to accommodate a taller font in order for detailed Chinese or Japanese characters to be legible, especially on a console where the target display device is typically a low-resolution television without sharp pixel rendering. If the UI does not provide sufficient leeway for such a change, users might be faced with an interface that is unfriendly or difficult to read. Another problem that can occur is overlapping; strings of text overlap improperly due to size and formatting differences between languages. Although overlapping and truncated strings might be found through manual testing of the in-game UI, it is also possible to automate this process and programmatically detect potential string problems before they reach the product.

Culture-Neutral Game Design

In addition to making sure that the interface is designed for its target language, it is important to ensure that your game does not make any invalid assumptions regarding cultural associations or expectations. For example, if your game expects the character to drive on the left-hand side of the road, American gamers might be surprised to see traffic coming at them in the right-hand lane unless you make a point of telling them otherwise. In addition, if you have a 'call' button in the UI with an image representing its function, it might be best to use an icon that is relatively universal, rather than a picture of an old-fashioned rotary dial or a traditional British phone booth.

Cultural and Political Sensitivity Issues

One final issue is that of cultural and political sensitivity. While many games might be set in a fantasy or science-fiction setting, your game will need to sell in the real world, and it probably won't do that by violating cultural norms or governmental standards. For example, if you choose to develop a game that has strong adult themes, Nazism, or violent material, you might need to consider toning it down or providing a filter for potentially offensive content, depending on your target market.

In addition, keep in mind the political environments of the markets where you anticipate selling your game. For example, if your game shows a map that contains disputed regions (such as Kashmir, the western Sahara, or the Falkland Islands), take care not to offend gamers or officials in your target market. This might mean modifying the detail of the map or shipping different maps for different markets. In addition, when dealing with disputed territories, such as Taiwan, it might be best to avoid referring to them with the term "country." Flags are another touchy issue, as they might change frequently and exist for regions that are not recognized countries. Lastly, you should take care not to offend if your game refers to existing governments, places, or people. When making a game for a world market, it is important to consider the political ramifications of your content. Otherwise, you might risk alienating gamers in your target market or even having your game banned.

Localization

Once you've developed your game to display, input, and handle data in your target language, you still have a problem—your game isn't actually in the target language yet. Localization is the process of translating content and adapting interface/internal configurations to prepare a software product for another language market. Ideally, it should not involve any changes to the code. Proper care should be taken during the design and development process in order to ensure that the localization process goes smoothly.

Hard-Coded Strings

Quite possibly, the biggest impediment to the localization process is that of hard-coded strings and resources. When developing software, it is standard practice to store all strings in a resource file outside of the source code. This allows for easy access to and modification of in-game text. If such strings are actually embedded in the code rather than the resources, it can be difficult to find or modify them, although this might not be a problem if the strings don't need to be changed during the life of the product.

This problem escalates when localizing a product, as having text in the wrong language is unacceptable. In Windows, for example, many system paths are localized in many of the products, but not all. As such, any reference to system paths (and memory allocation for such strings) should query the system rather than hard-coding them. In order to prevent localization problems due to hard-coded strings, it is important to establish and follow proper coding standards.

Over-Localization

As important as localization is for a successful product, it is important to prevent what is called "over-localization." This is where the localization process goes to far, localizing resources that should not be modified. For example, names of in-game objects should not be localized because they are not exposed to the user, and changing their names might break code that depends upon them. In order to prevent over-localization, all resources and strings should be marked with flags that indicate whether or not they should be localized. In addition, when localizing dialogue and media, you might wish to document your content before it is sent to localization to ensure that the gamer receives the same experience regardless of the language. For example, if a character speaks broken English in the U.S. version, then the script and voice for that character in the localized French version should similarly portray the character as less than fluent in French.

Localizing Media

Localization becomes more complicated when applied to nontextual resources. For example, if your game contains graphical resources with embedded text, it is unreasonable to expect localizers to possess the proper software and skills to edit the image and localize it. Instead, all text embedded in graphics should be stored in a separate layer and coordinated with external string tables for ease of localization. This also makes it easier to modify the text in the core language product. In addition, the graphic should be large enough to allow string wrapping or font changes necessary in the localization process.

In addition, when producing audio or video, remember that the localized version may run longer, especially if the original version contains quickly spoken text. As such, it is best to ensure that in-game audio/video clips are long enough to accommodate various-length localized versions, and that gameplay is not affected by these differences. In addition, if you are targeting multiple language markets, please keep in mind that it can be much more expensive to localize full-motion video (FMV) than video sequences using the game's engine. The balance of FMV versus in-game sequences is something that must be determined early on in the project. One alternative that may help you avoid some of these problems is to localize only subtitles for video sequences. This significantly reduces problems with media synchronization; but you need to balance those advantages with the potential impact on the user experience and immersion that it might have on your game.

Another concern in localization is ensuring that the game has the same feel in multiple target languages. For example, if you choose to localize audio or video in your game, it is a good idea to ensure that the character and tone of the original is taken into account. If a character is to sound paranoid and edgy, it is important that the message gets across in all languages. In addition, if your game has a character that is a New York mobster, for a Japanese version, you might choose a voice actor that can speak with a stereotypical, modern Osaka Yakuza accent if that is appropriate to your genre. Lastly, keep in mind that if you use a celebrity in your game, he or she might not be as well recognized in much of your international market.

String and Audio/Video Concatenation

One final concern is that of concatenation of strings and media. Due to variations in grammar and overall sentence structure, concatenating multiple strings to make a single sentence can be very problematic. As such, if your game must use string concatenation, it is important to involve localization at an early stage to ensure later localizability. Concatenation is an even greater problem when dealing with audio and video, and extra care should be taken with a product that will be localized.

Design and Planning Considerations

Once you understand the core issues involved in developing games for a world market, it is important to integrate this knowledge into the design and development process. There are several ways to plan multiple language releases of the same game. To begin with, some teams choose to focus on the core language product initially, with consideration for localized versions later in the project. This method has several problems.

To begin with, the localized versions might be considerably delayed, missing the halo of excitement that can follow a successful release. In addition, this approach tends to increase the work for localization and testing, and might significantly hamper functionality in other languages. However, this could be the only choice if a game is released for a certain market, but strong interest is shown in other language markets.

Modifying a Game After the Fact

If you are trying to add multiple language support for a game that is already shipped or that is late in the development process, your choices are limited. First of all, trying to convert the entire game to Unicode late in the project is expensive, time-consuming, and error prone. As such, it is usually not even an option. However, it is possible to provide a moderate level of support for various languages at a reasonable development and test cost.

To begin with, it is possible to reduce support for various languages while still providing desired functionality. For example, you might choose to support only European languages in the game UI itself, but implement wider support in the install engine and file system. As an alternative, it might be acceptable to allow input only in English, but modify the game engine to support storage and display of a wider range of languages. Finally, you can modify the game to support MBCS (such as Shift-JIS), but this can incur a large development hit and bug risk. In addition, cross-language functionality might be limited, such as chat. The determining factors should be a balance of the cost/time involved and the user experience you wish to provide.

Doing it Right the First Time

Although the above options are valid and have been used many times, successful globalization should be designed from scratch. To begin with, it is much cheaper to develop a product the right way from the onset, as opposed to tacking on desired features after the fact. In addition, if all versions of the game run off the same code base, development is less complicated and support issues are reduced because only a single platform must be supported and maintained.

In the long run, it is also cheaper and faster to incorporate globalization and localization into the core design process. While this integration may incur a small delay the first time around, it can greatly improve the speed with which multiple language versions of your game can ship. In addition, you'll be able to ship these versions simultaneously, and if you choose to release multiple languages in a single media, you can reduce manufacturing and support costs further.

Testing

So far, the focus of this gem has been primarily on design and implementation. However, it is important that the same standards of internationalization be applied to testing as to development. Testing of different localized versions of a product need not be redundant. If your game is single-code base and world-ready, a full test pass needs be performed on only one language version. Testing on other language versions of the game can focus on localization and functionality specific to those versions, although sanity testing should be performed across the product. The following are several areas of testing that might require specific attention when dealing with an international game.

I Can't Read It—How Do I Test It?

One of the first obstacles to testing a localized game is the language barrier. If you're like most companies, you picked your test team because of their technical skills and testing ability in a number of languages seemed a low priority. However, a good test team can test for the majority of functionality bugs without having to learn another language.

To begin with, your testers should know your game inside and out. If they have been testing the original-language version long enough, they should be able to walk through the UI with their eyes shut. As long as everything functions as planned, testers should be in familiar territory. One exception might be warning and error messages. If they are localized in the test builds, it might be necessary to provide testers with a list of common error/warning messages and phrases ("not found," "not enough space available," etc.) and their localized counterparts.

In addition, if you have someone on staff that speaks the language and can be on call, they can help to quickly identify problems when they occur. With some experience, testers should become familiar with common messages and known problems in the localized product, so only new or infrequent issues will require attention. However, in-game verification and other testing might require someone fluent in your target language. Many technical recruiting, staffing, and contracting companies have experience finding and providing testers with native language experience. You could find it worthwhile to contract one or more testers who are fluent in your target language once localized builds are available. In addition, there are several international companies to which you can outsource localized testing.

Danger Characters

Once your team is ready to tackle the testing of a world-ready product, you need to identify your highest-risk areas and integrate this knowledge into your test process. One place to start is with so-called "danger characters." These are characters that, due to their usage or their position in a codepage, tend to cause a disproportionate number of problems in applications. In particular, danger-character testing is important when dealing with originally SBCS code that has been modified to be MBCS/DBCS compliant. When dealing with such code, it is not unusual to find search or parsing algorithms that treat strings as being strictly single-byte.

Most operating systems reserve certain characters in their file paths, such as the forward/back slashes and the pipe character. A common problem occurs when the filename/path-parsing algorithm is single-byte, generating errors for filenames that are perfectly valid. For example, if a user enters a Chinese filename with a double-byte character whose code happens to be 0x5C (the ASCII code for the backspace character) in the second byte, a single-byte algorithm will likely detect this as a backslash and improperly parse the file path.

In addition, off-by-one errors are not uncommon when dealing with MBCS codepages. These occur when comparisons leave out or include one too many characters, such as a greater-than instead of a greater-than-or-equals. For example, in Shift-JIS, the character value 0xDF represents the highest of the single-byte kana codes, while 0xE0 marks the beginning of the second DBCS range for leading bytes. In such a case, it may be useful to test your boundary values (0xDF and 0xE0 in this case) to ensure that your code does not contain off-by-one bugs.

In order to produce a list of danger characters, you should evaluate your target language/codepage and identify the following characters:

- Any values that the filename/path parser might search for or consider invalid, such as the pipe, backslash, brackets, file delete marker, and so forth.
- The beginning and ending values for each character range if you are using an MBCS character set.
- The lowest and highest possible character values, and also one character beyond those in each direction (these should be noted as invalid characters).

You should first test these values to ensure that valid and invalid values are treated properly. In addition, for any SBCS values, you should find an MBCS character that includes those values as trailing bytes to ensure that your filename/path parsing will not fail on these values. To be most effective, you should create a universal test string that includes one each of the invalid characters and enter it everywhere possible. If you cannot read the target language, you can have a native speaker write down what the string looks like and how to enter it. In addition, if your game is Unicode and allows multiple-language input, a good test string should include text (preferably danger characters) from multiple languages as well.

Buffer Allocation

Another common programming bug that can occur when developing world-ready games is in buffer allocation. This type of error is common when a distinction is not made between characters and bytes. For example, if a string is allocated to be 16 bytes, it will only hold eight characters if they are double-byte. Testers should know the buffer limits for different strings (they should be detailed in the game specification, including whether the limits are in characters or in bytes), and perform boundary testing on them with both single- and double-, or multibyte characters if possible.

Hardware Configuration

Another issue that can arise in testing localized games is that of hardware configuration and input. To begin with, internationally, a wide variety of keyboards are used, and certain market areas (such as Korea and Japan) might have their own, language-specific keys on their keyboards. In addition, there can be other variations in hardware worldwide, such as localized drivers on the PC and different default hardware configuration/controllers on consoles. When testing for these markets, it is important to consider the most-popular configurations (which may affect your supported hardware configurations) and test with these devices to ensure compatibility with your target market.

System Configuration

World-ready system configurations comprise their own kettle of fish. With regards to testing, the two things you should look out for are system incompatibilities and user settings. While system incompatibilities are typically spotted early in the development cycle due to their severity, user settings are often overlooked. These include, but are not limited to, time, date, and unit formats. PCs and some consoles allow a certain degree of customization in this area, and you should test to ensure that your game respects the users' preferences.

Input Testing

One more area that should be given special testing in a world-ready product is that of editing and input. Two functions in particular that should be tested (if available in your game) are cursor movement and text editing. Cursor-movement testing typically covers selection and movement of the cursor through text, while editing includes such functionality as delete, backspace, copy, cut, and paste. To test for problems in these areas, you can create a string composed of a mixture of different double-byte (and single-byte if available) characters, and make sure that cursor movement, selection, and editing are character-based. In no case should you ever be able to move the cursor to the middle of a character or cut off the leading or trailing byte of a multibyte character.

UI and Localization Testing

When performing localization and UI testing, a sanity check can be performed by a non-native speaker who will look for truncation, resizing, and other obvious visual problems. However, many other problems require the eye of a native speaker, notably context, string order, and translation testing. Context and string order testing refers to verifying the UI content (mostly text) and ensuring that strings are in the right places, and that all text is comprehensible and translated properly for the appropriate context. String order problems can occur when a string has to be broken into two or more parts to accommodate a variable component. Since sentence structures and order are different in various languages, care must be taken in both localization and testing to verify that all resources are properly presented and in context.

Translation testing focuses on the validity of the translation itself and can be somewhat vague due to the difficulties of communicating the same message in multiple languages. If your company performs in- house localization, you might be able to involve the localization team in the testing process, since they are familiar with both the content and the target language. In addition, proper checks in the localization process can identify mistakes in the original text prior to translation, thus correcting problems before they reach the test team.

Conclusion

As you can see, there are several factors to take into consideration in order to develop a world-ready game. In this gem, we have tried to list the major issues that concern this process, along with ways of anticipating and resolving them as they relate to game development. Although it can be a complex process, integrating globalization and localization into your design process allows you to capitalize on a larger market and produce a better design as well as a better gaming experience.

References

[Aliprand00] Aliprand, Joan, *The Unicode Standard, Version 3.0*, Addison Wesley Publishing Co., 2000.

[Dmoz02] Open Directory Project, "Open Directory - Help Central," available online at http://www.dmoz.org/Computers/Software/Globalization/. The Open Directory Project's software globalization page has links to almost any related topic. March 2002.

[DrIntl02] Dr. International, *Developing International Software*, Microsoft Press, 2002.

[Kano95] Kano, Nadine, *Developing International Software*, Microsoft Press, 1995. The entire book is accessible online at http://www.microsoft.com/globaldev/dis_v1/disv1.asp.

[Lunde98] Lunde, Ken, and Gigi Estabrook, *CJKV Information Processing*, O'Reilly, 1998.

[MicrosoftGlobalDev02] Microsoft Corporation, "Microsoft: Global Software Development!," available online at http://www.microsoft.com/globaldev. Microsoft's global software development page includes step-by-step globalization guidelines, solutions to common problems, and links to other resources. March 2002.

[MicrosoftIME02] Microsoft Corporation, "Microsoft Global Input Method Editors (IMEs) Further Enhance East Asian Text Input," available online at http://www.microsoft.com/Windows/ie/downloads/recommended/ime/, Microsoft IME download page for pre-Windows 2000 systems, March 2002.

[Shmitt00] Shmitt, David, *International Programming for Microsoft Windows*, Microsoft Press, 2000.

[Unicode02] Unicode Consortium. The Unicode home page, available online at http://www.unicode.org, contains general information, standards documentation, code charts, and conference proceedings. March 2002.

1.13

Real-Time Input and UI
in 3D Games

Greg Seegert, Stainless Steel Studios

gseegert@alum.wpi.edu

Developing a safe, fast, and responsive user interface and input system for your game remains an often-overlooked programming task, but it is one of the most vital components in a successful title. In this gem, we will explore various implementation details, tricks, and optimizations that will assist you in creating the best UI and input system possible. We will also examine the important role that a user interface and input system fulfill in eliminating perceived network latency. This gem assumes a basic familiarity with DirectX, and the code samples and accompanying code are implemented with DirectX8, although the concepts could be applied to any 3D API.

Implementing the User Interface

When creating a 3D game, it is helpful to utilize the power of the available 3D hardware to render 2D elements as well. To draw our UI elements, we will simply render flat polygons to the screen after setting up our world, view, and projection matrices. The following code sample illustrates setting up Direct3D to render polygons two-dimensionally:

```
// an LPDIRECT3DDEVICE8 variable named "d3dDevice"
// has been previously instantiated.

D3DXMATRIX tempMatrix;

// make an identity matrix
D3DXMatrixIdentity(&tempMatrix);

// set dx8's world and view matrices
d3dDevice->SetTransform(D3DTS_WORLD, &tempMatrix);
d3dDevice->SetTransform(D3DTS_VIEW,  &tempMatrix);

// set the projection matrix using
// the width and height of the viewport
tempMatrix._11 =  2.0f / width;
tempMatrix._41 = -1.0f;
tempMatrix._22 = -2.0f / height;
```

```
tempMatrix._42 = 1.0f;

d3dDevice->SetTransform(D3DTS_PROJECTION,&tempMatrix);
```

After we have set up our world, view, and projection matrices, we must simply render two triangles to the screen. The two triangles will form our polygon, which we can color or texture to use as a background, button, or any other 2D component of a user interface. First, after the corresponding UI object is instantiated, create a vertex buffer consisting of the vertices used to specify the two triangles. Set the position of each vertex to be the location you want in *screen pixel coordinates*. Then, for each frame call, DrawPrimitive() to render the vertex buffer as a triangle list [MSDN101]. The method of using screen coordinates simplifies the encapsulation of any 2D user interface elements you choose to develop. It is also important to point out that DirectX8 offers a method for rendering a sprite in screen coordinates that may be useful [MSDN201]. An excellent resource to accomplish this goal using OpenGL is the gem "Using 3D Hardware for 2D Sprite Effects" [McCuskey00].

User interfaces have grown increasingly complex over the years. The end user expects a high level of functionality, and it is the programmer's job to supply these features. Table 1.13.1 lists common controls that should be implemented in any robust UI.

Table 1.13.1 Suggested UI Elements For Implementation

• Backgrounds	• Edit Box	• Sliders
• Button	• List Box	• Static Text
• Check Box	• Radio Button	• Tool Tips
• Combo Box	• Scroll Bar	• Pages or Forms

Specifying User Interface Elements

Once the code is written and the various UI elements are tested, it is time to put them into the game. There are many ways to accomplish this goal. Each and every screen and element could be hard-coded into the game. However, this method requires programmer intervention to change even the simplest aspect of how the UI is displayed. Ideally, we would like to be able to specify the UI in an external file, allowing designers to create and modify the interface as they see fit with virtually no programmer intervention.

XML: It's Not Just for Microsoft Anymore

XML is an acronym for eXtensible Markup Language. Anyone vaguely familiar with the syntax of HTML will most likely be comfortable with XML. In fact, HTML is itself an 'older cousin' of XML. XML's true power is its extensibility—it essentially allows the creation of a unique markup language. The backbone of XML is the DTD (Document Type Definition). The DTD specifies the constructs and syntax used in the particular instance of XML. The DTD can then be used to ensure that a corresponding XML file adheres to the correct syntax. The XML standard is well defined, and there are numerous resources available to assist in writing and parsing XML [W3C102]. Because of the object-oriented and data-driven nature of XML, it is an ideal candidate for specifying not only a user interface but also virtually all data-driven elements of the game engine.

The following code segment is a sample taken from an imaginary XML file used to specify a user interface screen. As you can see, the XML file logically outlines the user interface elements in a manner that is easy to parse as well as to read and edit.

```
<!-- This will create a UI screen with a background,
    a title, list box, and an ok button. These are
    all user-defined tags -->
<UISCREEN NAME="screen0" BACKGROUND="screen0_bg.tga">
    <UITEXT NAME="text0" LEFT="10%" RIGHT="90%"
            TOP="10%" BOTTOM="25%">
        <UITEXTITEM>This is the title.</UITEXTITEM>
    </UITEXT>
    <UILISTBOX NAME="list0" LEFT="30%" RIGHT="70%"
            TOP="40%" BOTTOM="70%">
        <UITEXTITEM>This is item 1.</UITEXTITEM>
        <UITEXTITEM>This is item 2.</UITEXTITEM>
        <UITEXTITEM>%1001%</UITEXTITEM>
    </UILISTBOX>
    <UIBUTTON NAME="button0" LEFT="40%" RIGHT="60%"
            TOP="80%" BOTTOM="90%">
        <UITEXTITEM>OK</UITEXTITEM>
        <UIEVENT ONCLICK="PushScreen"
                PARAMETER1="screen1"/>
    </UIBUTTON>
</UISCREEN>
```

ON THE CD

The DTD for the above segment contains the allowable tags, their parameters, and the tags that can be nested under them. One DTD can be used to verify any number of XML data files. The sample shown here and corresponding DTD can be found on the CD-ROM.

In this example, the occurrences of <UITEXTITEM> specify text, with %value% indicating a string table entry. Positions for each UI entity are specified in percentages. Using percentages helps to ensure the UI is displayed as expected in a variety of screen resolutions. The <UIEVENT> tags specify what events are valid for a specific UI entity and what actions to take when those events are fired. For example, when button "button0" is clicked, the UI code will execute the PushScreen action with screen1 as a parameter. Implementing the actions to fire could be accomplished through the use of function pointers or through a C++ class that is derived from an abstract base class requiring a string name. The action could then be mapped to the appropriately named object, and code would be executed with the specified parameters.

To parse an XML file, you can write or reuse a custom parsing routine. Alternatively, there are a number of free SDKs available that support XML parsing on a variety of platforms [W3C202]. For Windows developers, Microsoft offers the Microsoft XML Core Services (MSXML) 4.0 SDK, which includes full-featured XML parsing accessible through C and C++ interfaces [MSDN301].

Localization Considerations

As games continually increase in both size and scope, so do their target audiences. In order to maximize market penetration, it is imperative to design a game to be easily localizable to any other language. The user interface is on the forefront of this effort, as translated text will eventually be displayed on the screen. The following guidelines should always be considered throughout the development of the user interface and the game engine itself.

- Never hard-code any text that might eventually be translated; use a string table instead.
- Use MBCS or Unicode strings.
- Be wary of string concatenation.
- Process WM_CHAR messages for all text displayed to the user.
- Design UI controls to accommodate potentially large strings.
- Use fonts that support multibyte languages.

The most obvious tenet is to never hard-code any text. Instead, use a string table for all text (excluding debug text, of course). It is also important to use MBCS (multibyte character strings) or Unicode (wide character) strings throughout the game. If you do not, certain languages will appear to have garbled text. The Standard Template Library (STL) offers a wide character version of the string class, appropriately named wstring. Use caution when concatenating strings. Sentences are formed differently in other languages, so it is important to store sentence format in the string table as well. Also, never use DirectInput to process keyboard inputs that will be directly displayed to the user as text. Instead, use WM_CHAR messages. When processing WM_CHAR messages, Windows will perform the translation based on local information. An equally important task is to design UI controls to accommodate large strings or to expand to fit the displayed string. A short English phrase could easily become twice as long when translated to another language. Lastly, the font used must be carefully chosen and able to display multibyte languages. Some system fonts support multibyte languages, making them good selections. If you absolutely must use a custom font, however, a clever solution is to specify the font to use in the string table itself. Then, the localization team could choose the appropriate font for the language they are translating to if necessary.

The Input System

The user's game experience incorporates more than simply the textures used for backgrounds and buttons. Your primary goals should include ensuring that all user input is responsive and performs as the user expects it to. We will now explore several useful tricks to achieve this for the keyboard, mouse, and joystick.

The Keyboard

`DirectInput` allows two methods of retrieving data from various input systems: immediate and buffered. Immediate data returns a snapshot of the current state of the device, while buffered data consists of a sequence of events that have occurred since the last buffered data call. When used for the keyboard, immediate mode returns an array of 256 bytes representing the state of the keyboard keys. If the high bit is set for a particular key index, the key is down. Immediate mode appeals to many Windows programmers due to its simplicity, its similarity to the Win32 `GetKeyboardState()` call, and the desire to know exactly what the state of the keyboard is at any given moment. Although this approach is effective, it seems to perform best when the game is only processing a small amount of keyboard commands, such as left, right, up, down, and shoot. What about a flight simulator, RTS game, or another game with potentially hundreds of hotkey combinations? It could be rather inefficient to loop through every hotkey that might or might not have been pressed, checking against the array returned by `GetDeviceState()` at every update. Handling events when a key is released will also require maintaining a copy of the keyboard state as of the previous update. Additionally, this approach does not handle the case where a user manages to press and release one or more keys between updates to the input system.

How To Never Miss an Input

Fortunately, `DirectInput`'s buffered data mode offers a viable alternative. Rather than calling `GetDeviceState()`, we will call `GetDeviceData()`. This will return a list of keyboard events that have occurred since the last call to `GetDeviceData()`. Each keyboard event specifies whether the key was pressed or released, which key it was, and provides a high-resolution time of when the event occurred. No matter how frequently or infrequently the input system is refreshed, we will know exactly what events occurred and in what order.

The next step is to package up the input event, and put it on a queue of inputs to be processed by the game engine. We will maintain three queues: "just pressed," "pressed," and "just released." Storing our inputs in these three queues allows us to fire actions depending on the state of the key. For example, holding down the forward-arrow key could accelerate a car in a racing game, while tapping the "A" key could shift gears. The other items to consider are the 'modifier' keys. These keys, which include CTRL, SHIFT, and ALT, are no different than any other key as far as `DirectInput` is concerned. This is the desired behavior, as we might wish to fire events when those particular keys are pressed. However, we will also use these keys as modifiers. For example, CTRL-A will be considered a unique key separate from CTRL and A. For this reason, the input system will maintain a current modifier state consisting of bit flags that will be updated as the appropriate modifiers are pressed and released. Therefore, each packaged input event will consist of the key for that event as well as the current modifier state. Packing the combination of key and modifier state into a single 16-bit value will allow us to identify a unique key combination for sorting and comparison purposes.

On each occasion that the input system is refreshed, we will add any input events to the appropriate queue. When we are ready to process these inputs, the game engine will iterate through the queues. Each hotkey that we will be checking for can be stored as a map of input events to hotkey pointers. This way, look-up is considerably fast for locating the corresponding hotkey (if it exists) and executing the game engine code.

We now know exactly what keys the user pressed, no matter how often the input system is refreshed. Furthermore, this method for processing input can serve as an important optimization, since we are quickly processing a much smaller list of what the user actually did, rather than checking against every possible key combination. Refer to the CD-ROM for further implementation details.

ON THE CD

The Mouse and Joystick

The mouse and joystick can benefit from buffered input in precisely the same manner as the keyboard. Instead of key presses, we will package and process mouse and button clicks. However, buffered input should not necessarily be used to interpret the axis movement of either the mouse or joystick. During pauses in the execution of the game engine, the mouse cursor or joystick controls might appear to jump around the screen as the buffered axis inputs are processed. The simple solution is to use buffered *and* immediate input. The buffered input is used to process buttons and clicks, while the immediate data modifies the axes.

A Smooth and Responsive Cursor

One fairly common implementation of the mouse in games is to run the mouse in its own thread. This remains a good approach, as the mouse can be updated and rendered independently of other processing being performed by the game engine. However, the mouse thread might be capped to yield away time, allowing more processor cycles for physics, AI, and graphics. Although this makes perfect sense, capping processing of the mouse thread can exhibit undesirable behavior on certain machine configurations. If the game is running at over 60 fps (frames per second), a mouse pointer updating only 10 times per second will appear jerky and unresponsive. In this case, the solution is to separate the updating of the mouse axes from the processing of the buttons. Then, the position of the mouse can be updated and the mouse pointer rendered every single frame, achieving the smoothest possible movement.

The Role of the UI in the Fight Against Lag

As the popularity of network games increases, so does users' expectations of as fast and enjoyable online experiences as possible. At times, the user's expectations can be rather unrealistic. A user running a complex network game on a 28.8k-baud modem will expect gameplay as smooth as those users connected directly on a LAN. There is only a certain degree of optimization and tuning that can be applied to the network code—given the unpredictability of network connections; if the user is not transmitting data fast enough, there is not much more that can be done to accomplish this feat.

The best way to attack this problem is to simply hide the network latency from the user. Some of the most successful online games, like *Quake* and *Half-Life*, use a method known as client-side prediction. Essentially, the simulation is run on the client's machine as fast as possible, with the client predicting the position and actions of other entities in the game. When network updates are received from the server, the client is corrected if it is not synchronized with the server.

A similar methodology can be applied to all aspects of the user interface and input. Any and all feedback of the game, including updating UI buttons or selecting units, should be performed *instantly* on the client. For example, if the user presses the trigger button, the gun should fire immediately as the network message is sent to the server. If the user sends a chat message, it should be displayed on the screen instantaneously. If the user clicks a button to build another unit, the onscreen counter should increment without delay. What happens, however, if the command is not allowed, rejected by the server, or the network packet is lost?

There are a number of potential solutions to this problem. It is possible to occasionally compare the UI with the state of the game world, making corrections when necessary. To help prevent these errors in the first place, the same server-side validation of commands and actions can be performed on the client, although this could duplicate code and increase processing demands. Lastly, a method of guaranteed message delivery could be implemented for the game. This will allow the client to update the user interface, knowing that eventually the server will receive the command. However, the drawback to this approach should be fairly obvious. In a high network loss situation, the client could potentially be forced to resend a message many times. Combined with lag, this method could aggravate, rather than relieve the problem.

Conclusion

ON THE CD

Hopefully, you have found the ideas and tips presented in this gem useful. Though we have only scratched the surface, keeping these points in mind will help you build a fast, safe, and robust user interface and input system for your game. The CD-ROM contains a complete keyboard input system that is easily adaptable for any game. The input system implements the fast, buffered-input method mentioned previously. Additionally, the input system is localization friendly and can read hotkey assignments from an external file, allowing completely customizable hotkeys. Also available on the CD-ROM is a simple C++ XML parser, as well as the XML samples used here.

References

[McCuskey00] McCuskey, Mason, "Using 3D Hardware for 2D Sprite Effects," *Game Programming Gems,* Charles River Media, Inc., 2000.

[MSDN101] msdn.microsoft.com, "IDirect3DDevice8::DrawPrimitive," available online at http://www.msdn.microsoft.com/library/en-us/dx8_c/directx_cpp/ Graphics/Reference/CPP/D3D/Interfaces/IDirect3DDevice8/DrawPrimitive.as p, 2002.

[MSDN201] msdn.microsoft.com, "ID3DXSprite::Draw," available online at http:// www.msdn.microsoft.com/library/en-us/dx8_c/directx_cpp/Graphics/Refer- ence/CPP/D3DX/Interfaces/ID3DXSprite/Draw.asp, 2002.

[MSDN301] msdn.microsoft.com, "MSXML 4.0 RTM," available online at http://www.msdn.microsoft.com/downloads/sample.asp?url=/MSDN- FILES/027/001/766/m sdncompositedoc.xml, 2001.

[W3C102] World Wide Web Consortium, "Extensible Markup Language," available online at http://www.w3c.org/XML/, 2002.

[W3C202] World Wide Web Consortium, "Extensible Markup Language (Soft- ware)," available online at http://www.w3c.org/XML, 2002.

1.14

Natural Selection: The Evolution of Pie Menus

Don Hopkins

don@DonHopkins.com

Pie menus are a naturally efficient user-interface technique—directional selection of pie slice-shaped targets. The cursor starts out in the inactive center region of a pie, and all target slices are large, nearby, and in different directions. Pie menus are quite easy for new users. You simply follow the pop-up directions to use them. They are also extremely efficient for experienced users. Once you know the directions, you can quickly and reliably 'mouse ahead' without looking. Fitts' Law [Fitts54] explains the pie menu advantage—their fast selection speed and low error rate is due to their large target size and the small distance between each item.

The evolution of user interface design is driven not only by theory, but also by practice. We'll examine the successes and failures of a few real-world examples, not only to avoid re-inventing the square wheel, but also to encourage further creativity. The examples presented here are intended to inspire you to think outside the box and design new kinds of fun, efficient, and reliable user interfaces.

The Feng GUI of Pie Menus

User interface design is not just a process of raw artistic creation nor a legalistic application of interface guidelines and theories. It's the exploration and discovery of naturally efficient ways of solving problems, given competing sets of constraints. The outcome is always different, because the trade-offs and constraints always vary, but many of the underlying principles are universal.

'Feng GUI' seeks to understand the dynamic flow of mental and physical energy. It orchestrates the flow of attention and gesture throughout the interface as a whole. Fitts' Law is useful for scientifically analyzing performance speed and error rate, but it doesn't capture the human side of the equation. Feng GUI tries to prevent unfortunate accidents (like the 2000 Florida presidential election 'Butterfly Ballot') before they happen.

When designing a pie menu, think of Martha Stewart arranging a bunch of flowers into a beautiful bouquet. You must work with what you're given, try to play off the visual and semantic symmetries and relationships, and arrive at a pleasing pattern that's both enjoyable and easy to remember.

To construct a memorable pie menu tree of submenus, you should emulate Alexander Calder's creating a hanging mobile sculpture. The task not only requires a sound understanding of scientific engineering principles, but also aesthetic judgment calls and acrobatic balancing acts.

Doug Engelbart, who invented the mouse and pioneered interactive user interfaces, strongly believes that the human-tool co-evolution should be based on rigorous exploratory use in a wide variety of real-world applications. So don't just talk about pie menus—use them, evaluate their performance, and improve upon them!

Researching and Evaluating Pie Menus

The essential idea of directional menu selection has been around for a long time in various forms and with different names. Many examples of implementations exist, and a detailed history can be found at [PieMenu02].

Many studies have also been done on their effectiveness compared to other UI approaches. Gordon Kurtenbach and Bill Buxton (University of Toronto) have demonstrated many interesting results with their empirical research and controlled experiments with marking menus and various input devices. At Alias|Wavefront, they have successfully applied them to Maya, a high-end 3D animation environment, so users can design their own marking menus to customize their environment. In their research, they studied the learning curve from novice to expert user. They found that there are three stages of behavior along the learning curve:

1. Novice users click up the menu, wait for it to display, look for the desired label, move the mouse, and click to select the highlighted item.
2. Intermediate users remember the direction, click up the menu, move in a desired direction, wait for the menu to pop up and highlight the desired item, and release the button to confirm the selection.
3. Expert users simply press down the button, move in a desired direction, and release the button without hesitating.

Because the physical motions of novice, intermediate, and expert users are the same, pie menus transparently train you to become an expert. Each time you make a selection, you're rehearsing the expert mouse-ahead gesture. The intermediate stage is like an escalator along the learning curve. It helps novice users become experts by exercising their skills and increasing their confidence to mouse-ahead. Your muscles quickly and unconsciously learn to mouse-ahead without looking.

Jaron Lanier (VPL Research) put it well: "The mind may forget, but the body remembers." Pie menus exploit your body's ability to remember muscle motion and direction, even when your mind has forgotten the names of the corresponding items.

The nature of the input device used has a significant effect on the selection speed and error rate. Mice have been found to be faster and more accurate than trackballs, and pens are faster and more accurate than mice.

The maximum usable breadth (number of items) and depth (submenu nesting level) is limited by the maximum error rate the application can tolerate. Nuclear power-plant interfaces should stick to single level-two and four-item pie menus, which are extremely reliable. A game like *SimCity* or an editor like Maya can get away with using deeper menus with more items because it's easier to recover from selecting the wrong item.

Experienced users perceive single-level pie menus with two, four, and six items to be error-free, and eight items to be very reliable. Kurtenbach and Buxton measured the error rate at less than 10% with four items four levels deep as well as with eight items two levels deep.

Increasing the number of items in a pie menu has an obvious detrimental effect on the selection speed and error rate, but the relationship is not simply linear. Even numbers of items are easier to use and remember because more of the items are on-axis and symmetrical. On-axis items are easier to select than off-axis items, so it's good to put commonly used items to the North, South, East, and West, and less-common items along the diagonals.

This even/odd effect is most pronounced when comparing 7 versus 8 items, and 11 versus 12 items. Eight and 12 items are especially easy to use, because the directions are mentally more familiar and physically more on-axis. As the number of items increases, the negative effect of adding another item decreases. So, it's often helpful to add an extra item to 11-, 7-, and even 3-item menus, just to make them nice and even.

When designing nested pie menus, the depth versus breadth trade-off seems to be about even. So, it's best to let the semantics of the items determine how they should be arranged: shallow menus with many items, or deep menus with few items.

It's worth noting that some menus still work better as linear menus. Most linear menus and submenus aren't arranged to take advantage of the pie menu directions, and pie menus with too many items are huge and unwieldy. To solve those problems, modifiable pie menus have been developed that the user could customize, and scrolling and paging pie menus can handle any numbers of items.

Plugging in Pie Menus

Component technologies, like ActiveX and Dynamic HTML behaviors, make it possible to implement general-purpose, easily reusable plug-in user-interface components. Pie menus can provide configuration languages, property sheets, and special-purpose editors, which enable designers and users to create and customize their own menus without programming.

ActiveX (also known as COM and OLE) is a component technology developed by Microsoft. We developed an open-source ActiveX pie menu component that can be plugged into any OLE control container, including those used by Internet Explorer, Visual BASIC, Visual C++, and many other tools and applications. They're easily created and customized through scripting languages like Visual BASIC or JavaScript, and they have property sheets to configure their many options, for editing, and to preview the pie menus (see Figure 1.14.1).

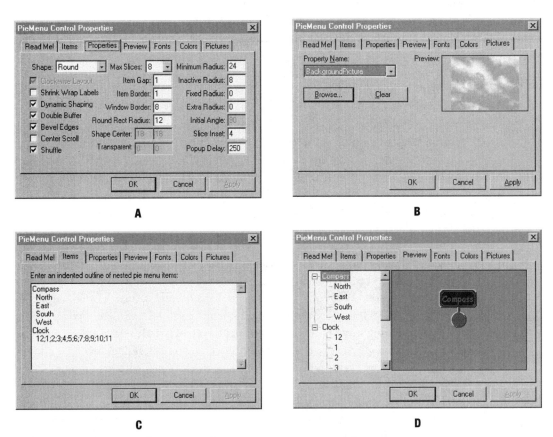

FIGURE 1.14.1 (A-D)   *Editing control properties using an example program.*

ActiveX pie menus support many properties and methods to control their appearance and behavior. You can customize pie menus by writing scripts that manipulate their properties, call methods, and handle callback events signaled during tracking. However, their graphical abilities are quite limited when compared to Dynamic HTML (see Figure 1.14.2).

The open-source JavaScript pie menus for Internet Explorer solve this problem nicely [JavaScript02]. They're tightly integrated with the Web browser and can take advantage of all of its features. They're easily and completely configured in XML as well as being extremely flexible, because you define their appearance with Dynamic

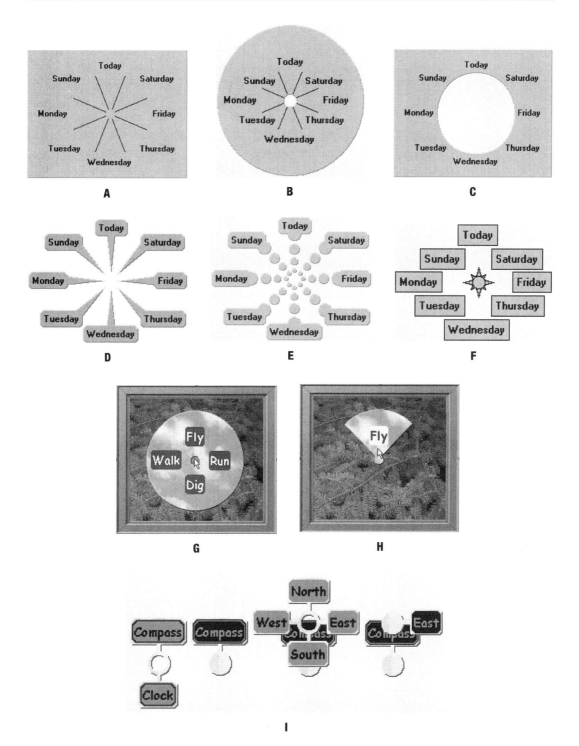

FIGURE 1.14.2 (A–I)   *Pie menus implemented using Dynamic HTML.*

HTML. These menus a easy for Web page designers to use for static pages and for Web server programmers to use for dynamic online services because they're implemented as modular 'Dynamic HTML Behavior Components.'

JavaScript pie menus are specified in XML, so it's possible for people to manually write them with a text editor. It is also possible for programs to dynamically generate them from a database. The JavaScript pie-menu component code is cleanly distinct from the Web page and XML pie-menu specification. You can customize their behavior by writing event handlers on the Web page in JavaScript, VBScript, or other languages. They can provide rich, dynamic graphical feedback, because scripts can reach into the pie menus and Web pages, and actually modify the Dynamic HTML on the fly.

Using XML to specify pie menus has many advantages. The format is independent of the implementation, so the same pie menus can be used across many different platforms. Web servers and browsers can automatically transform application-specific XML formats into pie menus by using standard XML-processing tools, like XSTL and distributed XML databases. For example, an XSLT style sheet can dynamically generate a Web page with 'Punkemon' pie menus, based on an XML database of trading-card attributes and links to animations [Punkemon02] (see Figure 1.14.3).

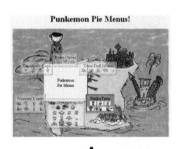  

A   B   C

FIGURE 1.14.3 (A-C)   *The 'Punkemon' example.*

ON THE CD

The XML pie menu schema enables editors to automatically validate, construct, and edit pie menus. The pie menu schema is on the CD-ROM as well as [PieSchema02]. An example editor can be seen in Figure 1.14.4, which is available online [PieEditor02].

Fasteroids [Fasteroids01] is both a real-time video game and an empirical user interface experiment; it enables you to compare linear menus and pie menus. The JavaScript pie menus also support the old-fashioned linear menu style, and they can be instrumented to record the selection time for experimental purposes. *Fasteroids* alternates between pie menus and linear menus (as shown in Figure 1.14.5), and prompts you to select a certain item to blow up the asteroids. It records and displays

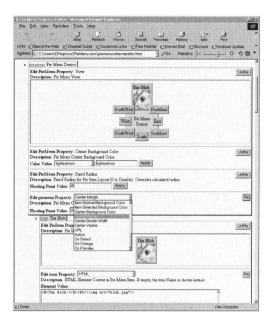

A   B

FIGURE 1.14.4 (A-B) *Pie menu schema and editor.*

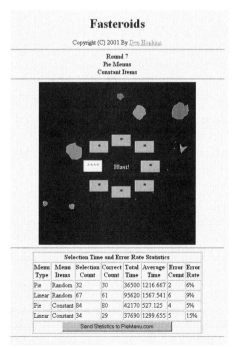

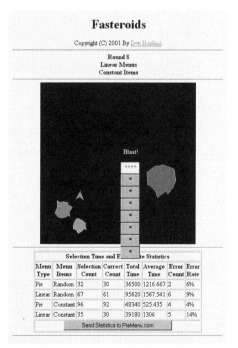

A   B

FIGURE 1.14.5 (A-B) *The Fasteroids game and experiment.*

the average selection time and error rate, so you can compare pie menus and linear menus for yourself.

Future Directions

Pie menus work well with touchscreens on handheld devices like the Palm Pilot and the Pocket PC. 'Finger Pies' are easy enough to use with your finger, so no pen is required. A product we have developed called ConnectedTV makes your handheld into a customizable entertainment guide and remote control that's designed to be held in one hand and operated with the thumb and finger. ConnectedTV lets you use finger pies to make your own personalized television schedule, filter, and program-search guide; you can flip back and forth through show descriptions and movie reviews, and send infrared remote-control commands to change the TV channel and operate other equipment.

Fast, inexpensive motion detectors that are sensitive enough to detect the direction of gravity will soon be built into consumer electronic equipment like cell phones, handheld computers, remote controls, and games. Motion detectors will enable convenient one-handed scrolling, dialing, panning maps, tilting pie menus, continuous gesture recognition, and many other exciting interaction techniques.

Going to Town with *SimCity*

In 1991, we first ported *SimCity* to Unix. It featured pie menus (see Figure 1.14.6) for quickly selecting *SimCity* editing tools, which was a useful shortcut for the original *SimCity* command palette.

Static pie menus whose items don't change can be carefully designed for ease of use and nicely illustrated for aesthetic appeal. We translated the *SimCity* tool palette into a convenient set of static pie menus. Icons in the pie menus are arranged in the same pattern as the palette, so they're easy to learn and quick to use.

Pop-up pie menus let you quickly switch tools without moving back and forth between the map and the tool palette. You soon learn to mouse-ahead through the pie menus and submenus just by flicking in the appropriate directions. Thanks to Moore's Law, you can now run *SimCity* so fast, it's a strategy twitch game, running at decades per second. Thanks to Fitts' Law, pie menus help you keep up with accelerated *SimCity* time by mousing-ahead without looking, and without wasting centuries dragging though linear menus.

The icons of the *SimCity* tool palette and pie menus are different sizes and shapes than the original, square *SimCity* tool icons. Their sizes and shapes are related to the prices and functions of the tools. Small icons stand for inexpensive tools, like parks or bulldozers. Large icons stand for expensive tools, like power plants or airports. Long icons suggest linear tools, like roads or railroads. And square icons are for square buildings, like residential zones or fire stations. The purpose behind this oddball icon design is to make remembering and differentiating between them easier (see Figure 1.14.6).

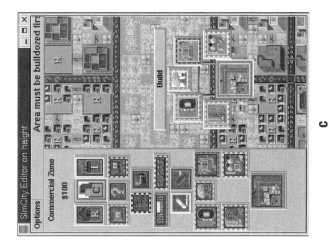

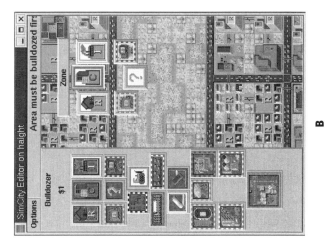

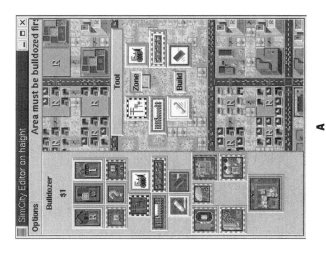

FIGURE 1.14.6 (A–C)   *SimCity's pie menus.*

Living at Home with *The Sims*

The pie menus in *The Sims* use a combination of desaturation, darkening, and alpha blending to feather the edges of the menu (see Figure 1.14.7 and Color Plate 1). This was done because we didn't want the pie menus to obscure too much of the scene behind them. You can see through the pie menu as the animation continues on in real-time behind it. The head of the currently selected person is drawn in the center of the pie menu and follows the cursor by looking at the currently selected item.

It was necessary to somehow separate the head from the rest of the scene. Otherwise, it looked like a giant head was floating in a room of the house, which was somewhat disconcerting and violated the 'Principle of Least Astonishment.' Simply drawing a solid menu background would obscure too much of the scene behind the menu. Using a partially transparent menu background still did not visually separate the head from the background scene enough. It looked muddy and cluttered, instead of crisp and bright.

Instead of simply alpha-blending the menu background, we actually lowered the contrast, which darkens the image and desaturates the background. The effect was to cast a colorless shadow with soft, feathered edges over the animated background, against which you can easily see the head and menu item labels.

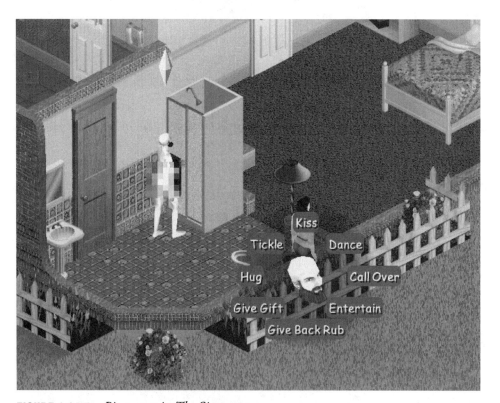

FIGURE 1.14.7 *Pie menus in The Sims.*

Instead of drawing a circular edge around the pie menu, the gray shadow gradually tapers off, suggesting that the active pie menu target area is not confined to a small circle. The labels are drawn around the pie menu center with high-contrast drop shadows, so they're easy to read.

The animated head in the center needed to look sharp and bright against the pie menu background. So, the shadow effect looks at the Z buffer to clip around the head in the menu center, keeping it crisp and bright. That gives it visual 'pop,' which clearly separates the user interface from the world, without drawing dividing lines or unnecessary visual clutter.

Conclusion

Pie menus benefit from the natural consequences of Fitts' Law. They're neither the only nor the best user interface technique to take advantage of this effect. However, they're a great improvement over today's standard linear menus and a stepping stone to developing even better user-interface techniques.

The proven advantages that pie menus have over linear menus are their higher speed and lower error rate. They also have the potential to be carefully designed and conveniently automated in many different ways, which increases their usefulness for many applications.

Computer games and handheld consumer electronic devices are reshaping the way user interfaces are designed because of their new and unusual demands. Real-time games require quick, responsive, engaging user interfaces. Handheld computers and phones must be useful for a wide range of people in real-world conditions, so they demand high reliability and ease-of-use.

Designing a good user interface requires balancing many competing demands and guidelines. It's extremely important not to squander the user's time or attention—consider it your most rare and precious resource. Don't get tripped up on metaphors—take a step back and look at what's really going on. Think in terms of the user's goals, mental models, and physical actions.

Be prepared to throw away your first design. Use your own system on an everyday basis. Continuously iterate the design, based on feedback from empirical testing and the users themselves. Every application and user has different requirements that demand different trade-offs at different times.

Designing good pie menus takes thought and effort, like writing Haiku. Limit the number of items in each menu, and group them together into memorable, balanced submenus. Arrange the items in natural directions to exploit their semantic relationships and physical associations. Don't exclusively use pie menus when other techniques are more appropriate, like sliders, scrolling lists, keyboards, or handwriting recognition. It's a good idea to provide multiple ways of accomplishing the same task when it makes the application easier to use.

Feng GUI seeks to integrate the lessons of real life, empirical research, and theoretical principles, and apply them to the enlightened design of efficient, reliable user interfaces. The "Butterfly Ballot" debacle demonstrated how badly designed user interfaces can have enormously consequential effects on the real world. By striving to design user interfaces with good Feng GUI, you can improve people's lives and affect the world in many positive ways.

References

[Fasteroids01] Hopkins, Don, *Fasteroids,* available online at http://www.PieMenu .com/fasteroids.html, March 2002.

[Fineman01] Fineman, Howard, "Unsettled Scores," *Newsweek*, September 17, 2001.

[Fitts54] Fitts, P. M., "The Information Capacity of the Human Motor System in Controlling the Amplitude of Movement," *Journal of Experimental Psychology*, 1954: Vol. 47, pp. 381–391.

[JavaScript02] Hopkins, Don, "Open Source JavaScript Pie Menus," available online at http://www.PieMenu.com/JavaScriptPieMenus.html, March 2002.

[PieEditor02] Hopkins, Don, "Pie Menu Schema Editor," available online at http://www.PieMenu.com/piemenuschemaeditor.html, March 2002.

[PieMenu02] Hopkins, Don, "Pie Menu Central," available online at http://www .piemenus.com/, March 2002.

[PieSchema02] Hopkins, Don, "Pie Menu XML Schema," available online at http://www.PieMenu.com/piemenuxmlschema-1.0.xsd, March 2002.

[Punkemon02] Hopkins, Don, "Punkemon Pie Menus," available online at http:// www.PieMenu.com/punkemon.xml, March 2002.

1.15

Lightweight, Policy-Based Logging

Brian Hawkins, Seven Studios

winterdark@sprynet.com

odern debuggers are powerful and very useful, but there are still places they cannot reach. This is where a simple, lightweight logging system is of great value. Logging can be used when a debugger is not available, which is often the case for game designers and testers. Logging also allows the examination of the current game state and similar information, while the game continues running under normal operation.

To accomplish this end, an efficient logging system that is configurable at both compile time and runtime is introduced in this gem. The entire system can be placed into a library, thus maintaining compile time flexibility through the use of policies [Alexandrescu01], and includes the ability to remove the logging calls from the final game. Runtime configuration allows the modification of logging data without the need to recompile. This also allows developers to share the same code, but only log the information they want to see. Thus, code can be entered into a source control system without the need to remove logging calls that might be useful later. We will also concentrate on performance throughout the gem.

Policies

Policies define a class interface that is compile-time bound as a template parameter. Policies are similar to the 'traits', used by the Standard Template Library (STL) and the Strategy Design Pattern [GoF95]. The end user of a policy-based class can then create a class that conforms to the specified interface. This class is passed as a template parameter to configure an instance of a policy-based class without the need to change the original class code. This makes policies useful in creating robust libraries, a concept that will be used throughout the design of the logging system. More information on policies and policy design can be found in *Modern C++ Design* [Alexandrescu01].

Debug Flag

Debugging flags are used to provide runtime configuration. These flags act as a boolean type for determining whether to perform various debugging operations.

129

When designing a flag, there are several decisions that need to be made. These decisions can be grouped into three main choices—initialization, assignment, and storage type— that can be turned into policies, allowing the final decision to be made by the flag user. We can then provide implementations of these choices that are useful for logging.

Initialization

The most important decision is the method of initialization. The policy interface for initialization is:

```
class t_InitializationPolicy
{
    typedef /*type*/ t_Type;
    static bool m_Convert(t_Type i_value);
};
```

The first part of the interface defines the argument type used for initialization. This is the type that will be passed to the flag's constructor. The debug flag has access to this type because it is defined as t_Type. The second part of the interface is a function that takes an argument of t_Type and converts it to a boolean value. This function must be declared as static, so that it can be accessed without the need to instantiate an instance of the class. With these two pieces, the constructor for the debug flag can be implemented to take an argument, convert it to boolean, and then store the boolean value.

Assignment

The interface for the assignment policy is identical to the initialization interface. The two interfaces are separate in order to allow different types for initialization and assignment. Thus, the primary difference is only that the assignment policy is used to implement operator=, while the initialization policy is used to implement the constructor.

Boolean Storage Type

The final decision is the boolean storage type. The primary use of this policy is to make the flag either a constant or a mutable boolean flag. By defining the type of the flag as constant, assignment is disabled. By defining the type as a normal boolean, assignment is made possible. It is also possible to provide more-complex types, as long as they support assignment from boolean and conversion to boolean. The policy interface for this is:

```
class t_BooleanPolicy
{
    typedef /*type*/ t_Boolean;
};
```

Configuration File

The debugging flags greatly benefit from the ability to be initialized using a configuration file, since debugging information can then be enabled without recompiling. For this purpose, a Singleton class [GoF95] is created that provides initialization from a single configuration file.

Initialization

The first step is to initialize the configuration Singleton class by parsing the configuration file. A sorted string array, using `std::vector` or a similar array class, is created based on the contents of the configuration file. Once an array of available strings is sorted, we can use a binary search, such as `std::binary_search` [Meyers01], to find a particular string. Because most debugging flags are initialized at the start of an application, there is not as much of a concern for performance. Even so, the binary search should be efficient.

Use PIMPL

The public interface for the configuration file is simple and should not change, whereas the private implementation has several options that might change for various reasons. The PIMPL, or Private Implementation, design pattern [Sutter00] is ideal for separating the public interface from the private implementation. The public class contains a pointer to a private implementation class, and the public class passes all function calls along to the private implementation. The private implementation can then be created in a separate header or in the source file. If private changes are required later, there will be no effect on users of the public interface. This paradigm also discourages the user of the public interface from relying on private implementation details.

Configurable Flags

The functionality of the debugging flags and the configuration class can be combined into a single configuration flag. The best approach for this is to provide an initialization policy for the debug flag that uses a Singleton configuration class. The definition of `t_Type`, above, would become a string, and the conversion function would call the configuration Singleton class to convert the string to a boolean.

Logging

The log class brings all the components together with several policy interfaces to form the workhorse of the logging system.

Flag Policy

Enabling and disabling of a log instance is based on the flag policy provided. The flag policy interface is:

```
class t_FlagPolicy
{
        typedef /*type*/ t_InitializationType;
        typedef /*type*/ t_AssignmentType;
        t_FlagPolicy(t_InitializationType i_value);
        t_FlagPolicy& operator=(t_AssignmentType i_value);
        operator bool() const;
};
```

The first two parts of the interface are type definitions for the constructor and operator=. The flag policy must also support a constructor that takes the initialization type and an assignment operator that takes the assignment type. Note that this policy differs from the others described previously because an instance of the flag is created within the log class, causing the need for a constructor. Finally, the flag policy must support conversion to a boolean value. The debugging flag described earlier fits the required interface.

Operator<<

There are two primary methods for logging messages: variable-length argument lists or operator<<. While variable-length argument lists are a traditional method for logging operations, this method introduces potential problems:

- Lack of argument checking.
- Lack of type safety.
- Lack of extensibility.
- No support for user class types.

In the best case, these problems could lead to garbage information in the logging system. In the worst case, logging could end up corrupting or crashing the game. For example, if a string is specified in the output format, but is not included in the argument list, an invalid memory address is likely to be referenced. On many platforms, certain memory addresses throw an exception even when the data is only being read, causing the game to crash if the invalid memory address happens to land within one of these ranges.

The operator<< solves all of the problems previously listed, but it introduces a new one. Variable argument list syntax would invoke only one function call, whereas operator<< could invoke an unspecified number of functions calls. A buffer is needed to store the result of each subsequent call until the entire log is collected and ready for dispatch.

Given the tradeoffs, operator<< is the still the best approach, so we deal with the buffer issue by defining a buffer policy.

Defining a Buffer Policy

A buffer implementation, which determines how the log string is stored until being dispatched, is specified by the buffer policy:

```
class t_BufferPolicy
{
        typedef /*type*/ t_Type;
        static const string m_ToString(const t_Type &i_buffer);
        static void m_Clear(t_Type &o_buffer);
};
```

The first part of the interface is the buffer class type, an instance of which will be created with each log class. Note that the buffer type must support all instances of operator<< that are to be logged. This allows the log class to pass on all operator<< calls to the buffer policy with a template member function:

```
template <typename t_Type>
    t_LogImplementation& operator<<(t_Type i_value)
{ m_buffer << i_value; return(*this); }
```

Although a new class could be implemented, in most cases, the STL's std::stringstream is the best choice. The standard string stream also supports the other two buffer policy functions.

The m_ToString function converts the contents of the buffer to a standard string. The standard string will then be passed to the dispatch policy (described later). The m_Clear function is used to clear the buffer once it has been dispatched.

Performance

The most important performance issue to address is log instances that have been disabled. Enabled logs are not as much of a concern because they are already bottlenecked by the performance of I/O. For disabled logs, a boolean test and a branch should be all that is performed. This prevents the use of a single function for the purposes of logging, which would require the evaluation of all function arguments. Since overloaded operators are really just functions with convenient calling syntax, they are not useful, either.

Instead, it is necessary to fall back to a trusted C paradigm—logical AND, &&. By placing the boolean test before && and the logging function after, the entire logging call is short-circuited when the boolean test is false. There are two steps to accomplishing this result. First, for simplicity, define a macro:

```
#define LOG(type) (type) && (type)
```

Note that a macro must be used to ensure the logical AND behavior is preserved. A template function would result in a function call that would defeat the purpose of using logical AND. Second, define an inline implementation of operator bool for the log class that only calls the dispatch function when the internal flag is true:

```
operator bool() { return(m_flag && m_Dispatch()); }
```

This will expand to result in only one test and one branch for disabled flags. You might be wondering about the dispatch call, which appears to be called twice due to the two boolean conversions in the LOG macro. It is called twice for each log, but the first call performs no dispatch because the buffer is empty.

Dispatch Policy

Once the buffer is full and operator bool is called on the log class, the string is extracted, then the buffer cleared. The string is then passed to the dispatch function defined by the dispatch policy:

```
class t_DispatchPolicy
{
    static void m_Dispatch(const string &i_string);
};
```

This function can be defined to do any number of things, including writing to the console, writing to a file, displaying the message onscreen, or all of the above.

Usage

The first step in using the logging class is to create an instance of the class. Because templates are used, it is often helpful to define a shorthand type for various sets of template arguments. For example:

```
typedef t_FlagImplementation<
    t_FlagConfigurationPolicy,
    t_FlagBooleanMutatorPolicy,
    t_FlagMutablePolicy> t_ConfigurationFlag;
typedef t_LogImplementation<
    t_ConfigurationFlag,
    t_StandardOutDispatchPolicy,
    t_StringStreamBufferPolicy> t_Log;
```

From this, instances can be created that are initialized from the configuration file:

```
t_Log LOG_MEMORY("MEMORY");
t_Log LOG_SCRIPT("SCRIPT");
```

Logging information is very similar to using the standard I/O streaming library. The following is an example of a log:

```
LOG(LOG_MEMORY) << "Memory used is " << l_memoryUsage
        << "\n";
```

There is also the option to change the state of the logging instance later, for example:

```
LOG_SCRIPT = false;
```

Conclusion

ON THE CD

With the information presented in this gem, a logging library can be created that is both flexible and efficient. Extensions can be made without the need to change the library code through the use of policies. Several basic policies are provided here and on the CD-ROM, but there is still a wealth of new policies that can be written for specific implementations. We encourage you to explore them.

References

[Alexandrescu01] Alexandrescu, Andrei, *Modern C++ Design*, Addison-Wesley, 2001.
[GoF95] Gamma, Erich, et al. Richard Helm, Ralph Richard, Johnson, Ralph, and John Vlissides, John, *Design Patterns*, Addison -Wesley, 1995.
[Meyers01] Meyers, Scott, *Effective STL*, Addison -Wesley, 2001.
[Sutter00] Sutter, Herb, *Exceptional C++*, Addison -Wesley, 2000.

1.16

Journaling Services

Eric Robert,
Ubi Soft Entertainment, Inc.
eric.robert@videotron.ca

Debugging interactive applications is not a trivial task. Lots of things can go wrong without leading to a crash or without getting caught by proofing code. Also, timing issues, which are often involved, just make matters worse.

It is not uncommon to have some sort of state machine with unexpected behavior under specific conditions. The faulty logic that triggered this condition could be very far from the experienced problem in terms of both time and code. Many intermediate states could get executed before reaching the point where the error is finally noticed. This occludes the real problem from the programmer and significantly increases debugging time. Without any kind of execution history, the problem must be reproduced over and over until the iterative process narrows down and gives a clear picture of what is really happening.

Programmers typically try to trace the code using their debugger. If this is not possible, they will start adding some debugging code to generate primitive tracing information where it might be needed. This is a long and arduous task. On the other hand, breaking into the code only reveals the current state of the application. What went wrong could be light-years away and might not be retraced. Since debuggers typically provide many effective ways to stop execution and to monitor memory, they are of limited help when it comes to interactive applications. What is needed is some way to trace the program's flow without breaking it.

Therefore, a solution could be to provide real-time information about what is going on under the hood in a flexible and efficient way. This is what this gem will focus on.

Managing the Information

An important consideration about real-time debugging is the amount of information presented to the user. It must be understood that having too much information is just as bad as not having enough. A monstrous amount of information will slow down the system and overwhelm the user. Needless to say, too little information is also quite useless.

The ideal balance must be reached by presenting the right debugging information at the right time. Therefore, the user should be actively involved in the selection of the source of that information. Being able to focus reporting precisely on a specific system or subsystem can be a very precious tool. This way, journaling services can be used to mimic the debugging process and provide support for a divide-and-conquer approach known to help find and correct bugs.

Thus, the system should consist of a logical state (on/off) associated with each system or subsystem to support the activation or deactivation of reporting functions. It should be built so that it can provide easier control over groups of states. For example, the journaling of a complete system could be disabled without having to specify each and every associated subsystem:

```
Journaling::setDisable("/Core/Loading/...");
```

Another consideration is the location where reports will be written. The user might want data to be presented directly on-screen, sent directly to a file, or maybe even across the network if the monitored application is remote. This kind of flexibility is most welcome in console projects, since debugging is often somehow limited.

By providing an extensible framework from which alternative output locations can be developed and integrated, the system's usability will increase substantially.

The System Hierarchy

Our journaling services are built around three classes: the Switch, the SwitchBox and the Journal. Many concrete services can then be built using these basic components.

The Switch is the primary interface that users interact with. It contains a logical state and the associated output location wrapped in a Journal. Each Switch is owned

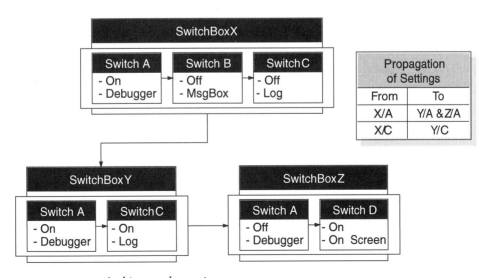

FIGURE 1.16.1 *Architectural overview.*

by a `SwitchBox`, which is part of the `SwitchBox` tree. By naming each element with strings, the user can refer to them using the path notation.

```
mySwitch = Journaling::getSwitch("/Core/Loading/Trace");
```

In the hierarchy, each `SwitchBox` is an internal node, and each `Switch` is a leaf. So, in this example, both "Core" and "Loading" are `SwitchBoxes` and "Trace" is a `Switch`.

The goal here is to have a `Switch` associated with a particular reporting facility for a particular system or subsystem. Thus, a complete area of the program could control its reporting facilities with a simple query on the current state of its `Switch`.

```
if(mySwitch->getState()) {
    mySwitch->getJournal() << "Some Trace";
}
```

Before presenting some code, it is worth mentioning that while designing this system, we considered the journaling services to be basic services. Thus, we didn't use any kind of dynamic memory allocation (since the memory manager could eventually use those services, creating a dependency loop). We also decided that the whole system should be available before the program entrance (`main`), since the service might be useful for tracking construction of global objects. Because the initialization order of global objects cannot be controlled in a portable manner, we aimed for objects that will be initialized on demand.

First, users must declare their own `SwitchBox` and `Switch` singleton objects in order to use them in services. The initialization procedure for both classes is done using the same method. The singleton instance is constructed on its first access using a static factory method that will insert the object into its owner's singly linked list. Note that macros are available for these tasks, but the generated code for a `Switch` is presented here.

```
// Header file
class SwitchSample : public Switch
{
    typedef Root OwnerType;

    static Switch * ourInstance;
    static Switch * staticFactory();

public:

    SwitchSample();

    static Switch * getInstance() {
        if(ourInstance) {
            return ourInstance;
        }

        return staticFactory();
    }
```

```
    };


    // Source file
    SwitchSample::SwitchSample() :
        Switch(OwnerType::getInstance(),
            "My name",
            "My description") {}

    Switch * SwitchSample::staticFactory() {
        static SwitchSample instance;
        ourInstance = &instance;
        return ourInstance;
    }

    Switch * SwitchSample::ourInstance =
        SwitchSample::getInstance();
```

Using the helper macros usually make more sense.

```
    DECLARE_SWITCH(SwitchSample, Root);
    IMPLEMENT_SWITCH(SwitchSample,
            "My name",
            "My description");
```

The singly linked list is implemented without memory allocation by considering each inserted item as a node of the list. Thus, both classes supply a link to the next list item (called the brother), allowing insertion.

```
    void SwitchBox::addSwitch(Switch * item) {
        if(mySwitches) {
            item->myBrothers = mySwitches;
        }

        mySwitches = item;
    }
```

This kind of structure will enable the implementation of a hierarchical propagation of settings. This could be useful to enable (or disable) a Switch for a system and all its subsystems at once. Since everything is related somehow to the Root node, it also provides a way to list and manage everything in the system.

It also gives the opportunity to provide a number of operations on the whole SwitchBox tree at once. A class named Journaling implements many of these operations.

```
    // Disable everything at once.
    Journaling::disableAll();

    // Print the whole tree.
    std::cout << Journaling::getRoot();
```

Due to the way instances are defined, the initialization of some branches in the SwitchBox tree will be forced if they are used before main. It is only after this process that the whole tree is really available for operations. Hence, even if the system works for global objects, it is somewhat limited.

Each Switch supplies two singly linked lists that use forward iterators. One is for Switch and the second one is for SwitchBox children. They support both increment operators and the indirection operator that returns a reference to the associated list item. Thus, in the previous example, if a Switch named "Trace" is added to the existing SwitchBox named "Core", changing the state of the "Core/Trace" could propagate at the lower level and update the "Core/Loading/Trace" accordingly.

```
void Switch::setState(bool state, bool recursive) {
    myState = state;

    if(recursive) {
        myOwner->propagateState(this);
    }
}

void SwitchBox::propagateState(Switch * source) {
    SwitchBox::Iterator i = getChildrenBegin();

    while(i != getChildrenEnd()) {
        SwitchBox * node = &(*i++);
        node->setState(source);
    }
}

void SwitchBox::setState(Switch * source) {
    Switch::Iterator i = getSwitchesBegin();

    while(i != getSwitchesEnd()) {
        Switch * leaf = &(*i++);

        if(!strcmp(leaf->myName, source->myName)) {
            leaf->myState = source->myState;
        }
    }

    propagateState(source);
}
```

Other mechanisms could also be built around the hierarchical system already in place. These might include some sort of extended name-matching using wildcards or regular expressions. However, the basic functionality presented here should be enough to efficiently use the system and control the flow of information.

The supplied code sample also implements the Journal propagation and some searching facilities in the SwitchBox tree using path notation. A more elaborate implementation could provide (at least) a console command so that the user could modify the system's Switch states in real-time. Maybe a stand-alone user interface would be useful for remote debugging on systems that do not support a keyboard.

The Journal Interface

An output location is associated with a Switch instance using the Journal abstraction. It simply provides a way to output formatted text to different devices. Since instances of Journal will be shared, this resource is reference counted.

One way to implement this is by using the standard libraries with the std::iostream. Since the design is extensible, we can build our own streams fairly easily. As an example, a debug stream (specific to Win32) is presented here.

For those not familiar with the std::iostream design, it can be divided into two layers. The first implements all formatting concepts with manipulators and operators. The other provides the underlying buffering mechanism. This separation will enable us to build our own buffering system and support alternate output locations while benefiting from standard formatting operations. Our debugger stream is built around a simple deviation from the std::streambuf. Since we only need an output stream, the input part of the buffering is disabled (by default).

The first step is to build a std::streambuf. A fixed-size buffer is provided for buffering, and only two virtual methods need to be implemented. The first one transfers the data within the buffer to the debugger with a Win32 call. Note that one character is reserved for the null termination. The second function deals with overflow situations.

```cpp
class DebuggerStreamBuf : public std::streambuf
{
    char myBuf[512];

public:

    DebuggerStreamBuf() {
        setp(myBuf, myBuf + sizeof(myBuf) - 1);
    }

protected:

    virtual int sync() {
        size_t len = pptr() - pbase();

        if(len > 0) {
            myBuf[len] = 0;
            OutputDebugString(myBuf);
            setp(myBuf, myBuf + sizeof(myBuf) - 1);
        }

        return 0;
    }

    virtual int_type overflow(int_type c) {
        sync();

        if(c != traits_type::eof()) {
            myBuf[0] = c;
```

```
            pbump(1);
            return c;
        }

        return traits_type::not_eof(c);
    }
};
```

The journal provides two additional virtual functions used to delimit the beginning and the end of a reporting event. For the debugger journal, only the end is used, which provides synchronization with the debugger. So, to implement this journal, the std::ostream subsystem must simply be initialized with the above std::streambuf.

```
class DebuggerJournal : public Journal
{
    DebuggerStreamBuf myStreamBuf;

public:

    DebuggerJournal() {
        init(&myStreamBuf);
    }

    virtual char endReport() {
        *this << std::endl << std::flush;
        return 0;
    }
};
```

More-elaborate journals can be built using this method. In the supplied code sample, we added a journal that uses a Win32 message box. This way, we can retrieve the user's answer and act accordingly.

Other implementations can be used to extend the system and add more types of journals. For example, it would be useful to have multiple output locations for a unique reporting event. However, since the Switch class only contains a single Journal reference, a new type of Journal that can handle this case needs to be designed. A quick way to resolve this problem is to forward the formatted data string to all other instances of Journal that could be kept in a std::vector.

```
virtual int sync() {
    size_t len = pptr() - pbase();
    if(len > 0) {
        myBuf[len] = 0;
        for(int i = 0; i < myJournals.size(); ++i) {
            *(myJournals[i]) << myBuf;
        }

        setp(myBuf, myBuf + sizeof(myBuf) - 1);
    }
```

```
        return 0;
    }
```

Building Journaling Services

Some typical journaling services are presented here that use the system presented in the previous section to control the flow of information.

Information Reports

The first service only reports data to the associated journal. It provides the very basic functionality needed to use the system.

```
#define REPORT(Leaf, Expression)                        \
    do {                                                \
        Switch * leaf = Leaf::getInstance();            \
                                                        \
        if(leaf->getState()) {                          \
            Journal& journal = *leaf->getJournal();     \
                                                        \
            journal.beginReport();                      \
            journal << Expression;                      \
            journal.endReport();                        \
        }  \
    } while(0)
```

Note that all services are designed as macros to enable conditional compilation and remove some or all reporting facilities on specific builds.

Tracing Information

Another useful idea is the stack trace. Knowing what portion of the program is currently executing (without stopping it) can be valuable. This is especially true when debugging optimized releases or if associated debugging information is not available.

The method presented here simply keeps track of the whole call stack at all times. Each method must contain some code that will update the stack as the program runs. If one of the methods is missing this piece of code, it will simply not be shown. The journaling will report (when enabled) the Enter and Leave events. Nevertheless, because the stack must be valid even when not reporting, the housekeeping code will always get executed.

```
void foo() {
    TRACE(TraceSwitch); // Add the stack trace here.
    ...
}
```

This implementation simply pushes the current function name and the associated Switch on the stack. Since many compilers now support a predefined macro describing the current function name, it will be used here. To differentiate between functions having the same name, we chose to use the function's signature. Note that a pointer to the parent is kept to enable us to walk back up the stack to its top.

```
class StackTracer
{
    StackTracer * myParent;
    Switch * myLeaf;

    const char * myName;

public:

    StackTracer(Switch * leaf, const char * name) :
        myLeaf(leaf), myName(name) {
        myParent = ourParent;

        reportEvent("Enter -- ");
        ourParent = this;
    }

    ~StackTracer() {
        reportEvent("Leave -- ");
        ourParent = myParent;
    }

protected:

    void reportEvent(const char * prefix) {
        ...
    }

    static StackTracer * ourParent;
};
```

The helper macro can then be easily defined with the compiler-specific definition of the function's signature. Note that we are using a predefined compiler macro that was not available in any version prior to Microsoft Visual Studio .NET. Thus, some compilers might not support this feature. Some other compilers, like Metrowerks CodeWarrior, support this with the GCC extension __PRETTY_FUNCTION__, which does the same thing.

```
#define TRACE(Leaf)  \
    StackTracer      \
    stackTop(Leaf::getInstance(), __FUNCSIG__)
```

At any moment, this 'virtual' call stack can be used to report the current position of the program. For example, the next service reports the call stack when an unexpected condition occurs. This way, the user has more-valuable information than just the traditional filename and line number.

Interactive Reports

Finally, to give an overview of interactive reports, the common assertion macro will be presented. Normally, if the assertion fails, a message box is displayed to prompt the user to choose between aborting the application, debugging it, or simply ignoring the error. The assertion's logic should not be associated with the Journal, since it could be used with any other interactive services. Therefore, the behavior of this report differs with the above trace service in handling the endReport event. It should only communicate the user's answer so that it can be dealt with appropriately. All supported values are enumerated in the Journal interface.

```
#define ASSERT(Leaf, Condition)                     \
    do {                                            \
        Switch * leaf = Leaf::getInstance();        \
                                                    \
        if(leaf->getState() && !(Condition)) {      \
            char result =                           \
                displayAssert(leaf->getJournal(),   \
                    #Condition,                     \
                    __FILE__,                       \
                    __LINE__);                      \
                                                    \
            if(result == Journal::ABORT) {          \
                System::Terminate();                \
            }                                       \
            if(result == Journal::BREAK) {          \
                System::Break();                    \
            }                                       \
        }                                           \
    } while(0)
```

Note that this opens the door to something interesting. By using another Journal, it is possible to run the application unattended. Assertions will still get caught and reported, but no message box will wait on the user.

Conclusion

To summarize, we presented a simple and extensible system built to control the flow of real-time information, along with some basic tools to report it. However, it should be clear that the quality of that information and its adequate separation into usable topics are definitively up to the programmer. Remember that time invested in producing information reports will pay off when it's time to debug.

References

[Reeves01] Reeves, Jack, "The (B)Leading Edge: Using IOStreams, Part I," The C/C++ User's Journal Experts Forum, available online at http://www.cuj.com/experts/1901/reeves.htm, January 2001.

[Stroustrup00] Stroustrup, Bjarne, *The C++ Programming Language Special Edition,* Addison Wesley, 2000.

1.17

Real-Time Hierarchical Profiling

Greg Hjelstrom and Byon Garrabrant, Westwood Studios

greg@westwood.com
byon@byon.com

When developing most games, a primary goal is to get maximum performance out of your code. Knowing where to spend your optimization effort is key to attaining this goal. We've all heard variations on the old adage: "A program spends 90% of its time in 10% of the code." Profiling is an invaluable tool for finding that 10% of the code that needs to be optimized.

Two types of profiling strategies are often employed—sampling and explicit timing. A sampling profiler works by frequently sampling the position of the instruction pointer while the program runs. This generates a huge amount of raw data that is then processed to generate profiling data. Sampling profilers can often tell you exactly in which line of code most of the time is being spent. Many commercial profilers work this way because modifications to the application code are unnecessary. Unfortunately, it isn't always practical to use sampling in real-time, due to the amount of overhead involved in gathering and processing the sampled data.

The other profiling method that is commonly used is to explicitly time blocks of code. These measurements can then be displayed in real-time and can aid in finding transient performance problems. This is important because bottlenecks in games are often dependent on many factors. It is useful to see how the profiling data changes as the user plays the game and triggers various events. Also, these profiling samples will typically be logically organized. For example, one might log how much time the code spends processing AI, rendering, and physics. Then, at any point in time, you can see which subsystem in the code is taking the most time. The only drawback to this type of profiling is that it only gives a general idea of where the code-processing time is being spent. For example, once you know the AI is running extremely slow, you typically have to use a sampling profiler or temporarily add more timing measurements to find out why the AI is running slowly.

Ideally, we would like to have the best of both worlds—real-time profiling with as much detail as a sampling profiler. This gem will describe a system that, while not attaining the resolution of a sampling profiler, can efficiently support thousands of profiling samples that are logically and hierarchically organized. A 'profile tree' is constantly updated and can be browsed in real-time, and we can find out where the CPU is spending its time.

The Profile Tree

The profile tree is an *N-ary* tree made of profile nodes. An N-ary tree is a tree where each node of the tree can have any number of child nodes. The topology of this tree is determined by the placement of profiling macros in the application's code. Since each node in the tree typically has only a few children, searching and data presentation is efficient.

Each profile node corresponds to a single explicit timing sample of a block of code. Each node tracks the total amount of time spent within that block of code and the total number of times that code has been executed. Samples, which are taken within the scope of another sample, correspond to a child node of that sample. Whenever a new profiling call is made, a new child node is added to or reused in the current node.

For a real-world example, we can examine how this profiling system was used in *Command & Conquer Renegade. Renegade* had a total of over 1,000 profile nodes(see Color Plate 1). However, the profiler was efficient because there were only an average of 2 children for any given node, and the worst-case node only had 15 children. As we will show later, the cost of this algorithm is proportional to the number of children in a node.

Usage

To use this profiling system, PROFILE macros must be placed at key points in the code. As will be described later, placing a PROFILE macro in the code will cause a profile node to be generated. This node will be responsible for timing the scope of the corresponding code. A good strategy is to place a PROFILE macro at the top of each subsystem in the application, and refine it as needed.

```
void My_Function(void)
{
    PROFILE("My_Function")
    ...
}
```

It can be helpful to break large routines into several independent profile samples. This is easily accomplished by adding additional scoping brackets to the function, each with their own PROFILE macro. Here is an example:

```
void BigFunction(void)
{
    {
        PROFILE("BigFunction Part 1")
        ...
```

FIGURE 1.17.1   *This is a screenshot the real-time hierarchical profiler running inside of Command & Conquer Renegade. Only one node of the tree is shown, but the user can navigate the tree in real-time.*

```
    }
    {
        PROFILE("BigFunction Part 2")
        ...
    }
}
```

It can also be useful to 'flatten' the profile structure of a member function in a class hierarchy. The following example shows how you can combine time spent in a particular layer of an overridden function, even when it is called through many different derived classes. In this example, time spent in BasePhysics::Timestep() is not included in CarPhysics::Timestep(), and all time spent in BasePhysics::Timestep() will be combined into a single profile sample, even when called from other derived classes (assuming they use this profiling strategy).

```
void CarPhysics::Timestep(void)
```

```
{
    {
    PROFILE("CarPhysics::Timestep");
    ...
    }
    BasePhyics::Timestep();
}
```

Browsing the Profiling Data

This profiling system generates a lot of data, so the user must have a way to navigate it easily. An iterator is provided that can be used to navigate through the tree and display statistics for the children of the current node. Using this system, a user can chase down a bottleneck in real-time by walking up and down the profile tree, and focus on areas of code that are taking a lot of time. For example, a representative profile sample for the main loop of *Renegade* is listed in Table 1.17.1.

Table 1.17.1 Profile Data for Main Loop

Name	%Parent	%Total	Ms/Frame	Ms/Call	Calls/Frame
0-Audio	2.01	2.00	0.35	0.35	1
1-Render	51.64	51.40	8.95	8.99	1
2-Network	1.70	1.69	0.30	0.30	1
3-Think	43.19	42.99	7.49	7.49	1
4-Pathfind	0.04	0.04	0.01	0.01	1
Unlogged	1.42	1.42			

In this case, the time is mostly split between Render and Think. Navigating the tree is achieved by assigning a numerical index to each child of the current node. The user is allowed to enter either the parent of the current node or any of its children. Assume the user wanted to investigate the Render child. They would get a new display, as shown in Table 1.17.2.

Table 1.17.2 Profile Data for Render

Name	%Parent	%Total	Ms/Frame	Ms/Call	Calls/Frame
0-Switch_Thread	16.39	8.58	1.47	1.47	1
1-Post_Render	0.28	0.14	0.02	0.02	1
2-End_Render	8.04	4.21	0.72	0.72	1
3-DialogMgr	0.09	0.01	0.01	0.01	1
4-Render_Game	49.55	25.95	4.44	4.44	1
5-Begin_Render	1.70	0.89	0.15	0.15	1
6-Shadow_Gen	22.83	11.96	2.05	2.05	1
Unlogged	1.12	0.09			

Since `Render_Game` takes a large portion of this node's time, the user could then descend the tree to get a breakdown of that node. This process can continue as long as there are children of the node you are interested in.

All of the statistics in the profiling system represent running totals and averages. It can be useful to use the reset feature to throw out historical data. For example, when the frame rate drops, we often reset the profiler to get a more accurate measurement of what the code is doing at that time. When the profile system is reset, the tree is not actually destroyed; only the timing data contained in the nodes are zeroed out.

Implementation

The implementation relies on an accurate way to sample time. We used the 64-bit cycle counter feature of Pentium CPUs. This counter is incremented every time the CPU executes an instruction. By saving the state of the counter at the start of a profiling sample and subtracting that value from the state of the counter at the end of a profiling sample, you can very accurately compute the amount of time elapsed. We then divide the number of instructions by the CPU clock speed to determine the amount of time spent. Our profile nodes accumulate the amount of time in a floating-point variable.

CProfileSample

This is a small C++ class whose only task is to call the `Start_Profile()` method of `CProfileManager` in its constructor and the `Stop_Profile()` method in its destructor. This automates the task of starting and stopping a profile sample during the scope of this object. To further simplify the usage, the `PROFILE` macro is used to automatically create a `CProfileSample` object and to easily remove profiling code from release builds.

```
class   CProfileSample {
public:
    CProfileSample(const char * name)
    {
        CProfileManager::Start_Profile(name);
    }
    ~CProfileSample(void)
    {
        CProfileManager::Stop_Profile();
    }
};

#define PROFILE(name) CProfileSample __profile(name)
```

CProfileManager

The profile manager is the external interface to the profiling system. It maintains the `CurrentNode` pointer into the profile tree that corresponds to the scope of the currently executing code. It also contains methods for accessing the profile tree for display purposes.

The `Start_Profile()` method is used to start a profile sample. It detects recursion by comparing the name of the requested profile with the name of the current node. When the subnode that matches the given name is found, it becomes the current node. The overhead incurred in this search will be proportional to the number of immediate children linked to the current node. Typically, this is a small number, rarely as large as 10. In addition, since we use static strings for all of our profile sample names, pointer compares are used rather than slower string compares when looking for a particular profile sample.

In the case that a child with the given name does not exist, a new node will be created and linked to the tree. Note that node creation will only occur on the first pass through a particular code path. In any case, the node's `Call()` method is then called to begin timing.

```
void CProfileManager::Start_Profile(const char * name)
{
    if (name != CurrentNode->Get_Name()) {
        CurrentNode=CurrentNode->Get_Sub_Node(name);
    }
    CurrentNode->Call();
}
```

The `Stop_Profile()` method is used to end a profile sample. The first task is to call the `Return()` method on the current node to complete and record the timing. Since the profile manager has maintained the current node being sampled, no searching overhead is incurred in this operation. Assuming we are not in a recursive function, the parent node becomes the current node.

```
void CProfileManager::Stop_Profile( void )
{
    // go to parent unless recursed
    if (CurrentNode->Return()) {
        CurrentNode = CurrentNode->Get_Parent();
    }
}
```

The remaining methods in the profile manager are either accessors or perform simple administrative functions. For example, the application calls the `Increment_Frame_Counter()` method once per frame in order to support calculation of the number of calls per frame for any profile sample. The `Get_Iterator()` and `Release_Iterator()` methods provide and destroy an iterator that is used to access the profile tree.

CProfileNode

The `CProfileNode` is a C++ class that is private to the profiling system; it stores the total time spent in a block of code and the number of calls of that block of code. When the CPU is in the scope of a node, the node also stores the starting time.

To start a profiling sample, the profile manager calls the Call()method on the node. This method simply increments the call counter and, if we are not recursing, records the starting time.

```
void CProfileNode::Call( void )
{
    TotalCalls++;
    if (RecursionCounter++ == 0) {
        Profile_Get_Ticks(&StartTime);
    }
}
```

At the end of a profiling sample, the Return() method is called. After checking if we are not recursing, the elapsed time is computed and added to the TotalTime variable. This function also returns whether or not the code is recursing, so the profile manager knows if the node is completed, in which case it would return to the parent node.

```
bool CProfileNode::Return( void )
{
    if (--RecursionCounter== 0 && TotalCalls != 0 ) {
        __int64 time;
        Profile_Get_Ticks(&time);
        time-=StartTime;
        TotalTime += (float)time / Tick_Rate();
    }
    return ( RecursionCounter == 0 );
}
```

CProfileIterator

This object provides an easy way to browse the profile tree. It contains methods for navigating the tree and displaying the contents of a particular node. Typically, a node along with its immediate children are displayed to the user. For each child, several statistics are available: total time spent, total number of calls, calls per frame, and time per frame.

Conclusion

ON THE CD

With the ability to hierarchically profile code in real-time and sample thousands of blocks of code efficiently, we've found this to be a useful tool for code optimization. It is our hope that readers will find this system useful in improving their own code. You will find an implementation of these classes on the CD-ROM.

References

[GPG00] Rabin, Steve, *Game Programming Gems*, Charles River Media, Inc., 2000.

MATHEMATICS

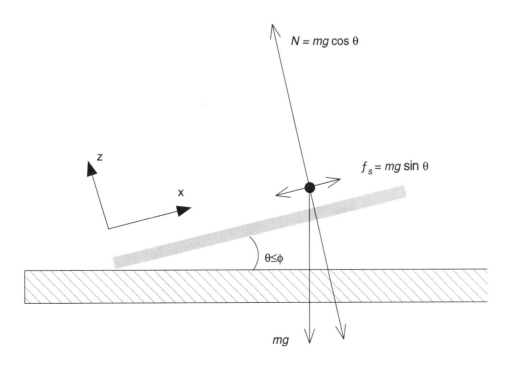

INTRODUCTION

John Byrd

jbyrd@well.com

Why should we care about deeper math in game programming? After all, optimization is all about unrolling tight loops and getting vertex data transformed in a cache-coherent way. Besides, hardware nowadays practically does all your 3D math and rendering for you! The reason we should care is simple: Programs do not work exactly right when we ignore the math.

Old-school, 3D-game machines like the 3DO, Sega Saturn, and the Sony PlayStation use affine textures. The resultant headaches from playing first-person shooters did not go away until perspective-correct textures burst on the game scene in 1996 with the Nintendo64. Something along the rendering pipeline needs to solve second-order partial differential equations in *uv* space in order to render a perspective-correct texture. The math is 'icky' and complicated, but you must do it.

Say you are resampling a digital audio signal from 44.100 kHz to 11.025 kHz in real-time. So, you throw away three out of four samples and send the result to the DAC. However, for some reason the audio doesn't sound right; there are weird overtones that weren't in the original sample. Perhaps you should have used a low-pass filter before resampling to avoid Nyquist artifacting. The math is unpleasant and complicated, but you must do it.

Representing object orientations in Euler form is easy to understand; it's the way we learned to do it in college. However, in a real game, we need to interpolate from one orientation to another, and doing this in Euler space often causes our object to thrash wildly as a mysterious force called "gimbal lock" takes over. However, we can interpolate cleanly between orientations if we work in quaternion space—The math is unpleasant and complicated, but you must do it.

Game mathematics gems are at their very best when they are relevant and applicable to the common hardware features of the day. In days of yore when a single-precision multiply took many microseconds to complete, one transcendental function implementation was just as costly as any other. There's no way you would consider doing such an exotic thing in a game loop without a table lookup. Nowadays, on most hardware, you can pretty much assume that you can pipeline at least four multiplies and maybe an add. In this section, you will find some plucky transcendental function implementations from Green that take advantage of these hardware features. Does your path-finding algorithm keep failing due to insufficient precision? Take a look at Young's algorithm, which is optimized for 128-bit architectures. Having trouble keeping all your quaternions in memory? With Adami's method, you can squash a quaternion into 32 -bits without introducing a lot of artifacting.

Game programmers rely on math the way that producers rely on game programmers. If your eyes tend to glaze over at double integrals and you slept through Taylor polynomials in undergraduate math, you can still do your job as a game programmer, but you had better choose your algorithms with care, because they're going to be doing the work on your behalf.

2.1

Fast Base-2 Functions for Logarithms and Random Number Generation

James McNeill

james_mcneill@ameritech.net

In this gem, three utility functions are presented for computing values associated with the base-2 logarithms of integers. They are simple, efficient, and correct for any 32-bit input value, in contrast to their floating-point alternatives.

The Integral Base-2 Logarithm

The need to compute integral base-2 logarithms arises occasionally during the game-development process. The integral logarithm is the real logarithm, rounded up or down to the nearest integer as required. This logarithm is useful when rounding texture image dimensions up to the nearest power of two, padding data to the nearest power of two before using the Fast Fourier Transform, or determining the number of levels a quadtree needs in order to subdivide a grid.

Although the logarithm can be calculated using an expression such as `int(floor(log(n)/log(2)))` or `int(ceil(log(n)/log(2)))`, the floating-point division can underflow and give incorrect results. A simple test program of the above expressions using 32-bit floating-point arithmetic on an Intel processor showed the problem occurring as low as $n = 65536$. There are also some environments that are devoid of floating-point functionality, but a mechanism for computing the integral logarithm is still desired.

To avoid these issues, we use the two integer-only routines described in this gem. They provide correct results over the entire 32-bit input range and are also more efficient than the corresponding floating-point methods. The expression `log2le(n)`, which stands for "$\log_2$ less-than-or-equal-to n", finds the largest non-negative integer x such that $2^x \leq n$. The expression `log2ge(n)`, which stands for "$\log_2$ greater-than-or-equal-to n," finds the smallest non-negative integer x such that $2^x \geq n$. The code for both of these functions can be found on the CD-ROM.

Bit Masks and Random Number Generation

The third utility function provided in this gem, `bitmask(n)`, computes a mask in which all bits used by numbers from one up to, and including, *n* are set to one.

One use for `bitmask()` is in generating uniformly-distributed random integers that fall within a specified range. As an example, suppose a random number generator `rand()` generates uniformly-distributed random integers in the range 0 to 32767, but we need a sequence of random numbers in the range [0, 2]. A common approach is to use the modulus operator to map the source range to the target range:

```
int randomNum = rand() % 3;
```

As described in [Booth97], there are a couple of problems with this method. The modulus operator is typically fairly slow, and the results are slightly biased away from a uniform distribution. Because the target range [0, 2] does not evenly partition the source range of [0, 32767], values of `randomNum` are not evenly distributed. Zero and 1 each have 10,923 values of `rand()` that map to them, while 2 has only 10,922 values that map to it. This is admittedly a small difference, but the disparity can be larger. For instance, if we used this technique to generate numbers in the range [0, 32766], zero would be twice as likely as any other number.

One way to get evenly distributed results is to generate random numbers and throw them away until we get one within our desired range:

```
do { randomNum = rand() } while ( randomNum > 2 );
```

Now, with our example, this would take a very long time, since values of `rand()` are far more likely to be out of the desired range than in it. However, the above procedure can be modified to be quite fast. First, use the modulus operator with an integral divisor in the range of `rand()` to get to an intermediate range of random numbers as close as possible to the target range. Then, reject any values from the intermediate range that fall outside the target range:

```
do { randomNum = rand() % 4 } while ( randomNum > 2 );
```

Since most random number generators have a range that is a power of two, we can use bit masking instead of the modulus operator to speed things up:

```
do { randomNum = rand() & 3 } while ( randomNum > 2 );
```

This is where our function `bitmask()` comes in. It computes the necessary bit mask for use in the previous algorithm, so we can write a general function for getting random numbers over an arbitrary range:

```
unsigned random( unsigned range )
{
    if ( range < 2 )
        return 0;
```

```
        unsigned mask = bitmask(range-1);
        unsigned n;
        do { n = rand() & mask; } while (n >= range);
        return n;
}
```

Assuming the values of rand() are evenly distributed, the expected number of loop iterations is less than two and approaches one as the intermediate range's size approaches that of the target range. This is substantially faster and more reliable than the alternatives.

How the Functions Work

The functions are specialized for 32-bit integers. This limits the number of distinct return values to 32 or 33, depending on the function. The function log2le() returns a value ranging from 0 to 31, log2ge() returns a value ranging from 0 to 32, and bitmask() returns a bit mask ranging from 0 to 0xFFFFFFFF.

One possible algorithm would be to simply store the 32 or 33 return values in an array and do a binary search through it to find the correct result. The functions here follow this approach, but do so without the stored array, since the array entries are easily computed as needed. Only a few registers are used as a result. Finally, the loops have been unrolled for speed.

ON THE CD

The implementations of each function can be found on the CD-ROM.

References

[Booth97] Booth, Rick, *Inner Loops: A Sourcebook For Fast 32-Bit Software Development*, Addison-Wesley Developers Press, 1997: pp. 223–224.

2.2

Using Vector Fractions for Exact Geometry

Thomas Young, PathEngine

thomas@pathengine.com

It tends to happen near the end of the project. A particularly ingenious tester figures out that there is a certain corner on a certain level where path-finding fails, leaving enemies stuck. Someone else notices that jumping into another corner lets you wander off the edge of the world. After days of nerve-racking debugging, you figure out the source of the problem—error due to approximation.

In game programming, fewer problems are more subtle or insidious than round-off errors. Perhaps you try to add code to the system to catch these errors. You check for tolerances and write a lot of special-case code. Unfortunately, this merely converts the precision problem into a set of other nasty problems. What error tolerances are acceptable? How can we guarantee that the code will work? Lastly, who will ever be able to figure out our code when the sequel comes out?

This gem considers examples in constructive solid geometry and in path-finding where approximation at points of intersections can cause the algorithms to fail. Techniques are offered for representing these intersection points without approximation. This enables us to eliminate errors without adding complexity to our algorithms.

The Problem

When a polygon is rendered to screen pixels, the user won't notice if the least significant bit of the green value is incorrect. Even if screen coordinates are off by a pixel or two, it's probably okay as long as there are no visual artifacts, such as cracks between polygons.

On the other hand, there are some key algorithms in game programming that are sensitive to even small round-off errors in mathematical calculations. In particular, a problem arises when an algorithm needs to reuse the results of calculations with implicit round-off errors. With a complex algorithm, we often depend on constraints holding true for our data structures as the algorithm proceeds. Perhaps we depend on this to have the algorithm terminate.

When we try to represent fractional values as floating-point or fixed-point numbers, we often introduce round-off errors that can affect the results of our algorithms.

We can't represent 1/3 exactly using a fixed-point or floating-point number of finite precision. Examples of this kind of problem arise in constructive solid geometry (CSG) and points-of-visibility path-finding.

Constructive Solid Geometry

Consider the problem of Boolean operations between meshes in two dimensions. In order to process the mesh efficiently, we will want to specify certain validation conditions for that mesh. For example, we can require all faces to be convex. We then depend on this validation condition for the algorithm to work.

As part of the Boolean process, we might detect an overlap between two faces and resolve this by introducing extra vertices where edges intersect (see Figure 2.2.1).

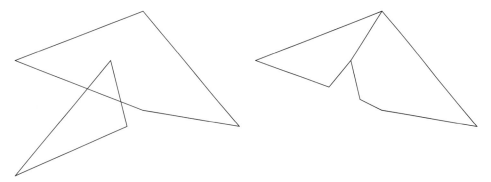

FIGURE 2.2.1   *Boolean subtraction in two dimensions.*

Approximation at these intersections can lead to nonconvex geometry (see Figure 2.2.2).

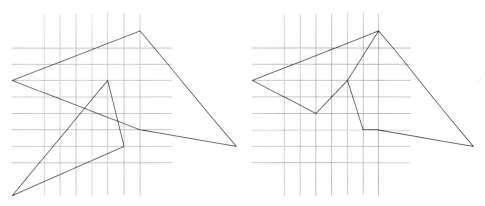

FIGURE 2.2.2   *Approximation results in a nonconvex face.*

The same problem exists in three-dimensional constructive solid geometry for edges created at the intersection of faces and for vertices created at the intersection of an edge with a face.

Path-finding

[Young01] demonstrates how silhouette regions can be used to optimize points-of-visibility path-finding. Each point of visibility corresponds to a corner in the environment. A point is considered for connection if it appears as a silhouette from the perspective of the source point.

Figure 2.2.3 shows how approximation at an intersection can cause path-finding to fail. The boundary of a silhouette region intersects with another line, which might be an expanded external edge, another region boundary, or a portal. Approximation at the intersection means that our source point is incorrectly determined to be outside of the silhouette region, so a connection to the associated point of visibility is not generated. The line from the source point to the target point just clips the edge of the obstacle and is, therefore, blocked by collision. The result is that the path-finder fails to generate a path to the target area.

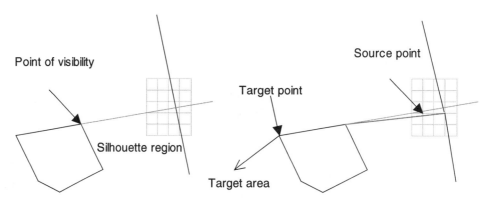

FIGURE 2.2.3   *Path-finding fails because the source point is incorrectly determined to be outside a silhouette region.*

One solution to this problem is to treat the lines bounding our silhouette regions as infinite lines. To test if the source point is in a given region, we test inside of each bounding line. However, it is a lot quicker to keep track of which region a point is in by detecting which edges are traversed as a point is moved. If our path-finder has to deal with overlapping geometry, then this traversal also serves to delineate between different levels of geometry.

In order to perform our traversal, we need to be able to determine which side of our traversal an intersection is on. In Figure 2.2.4, the traversal ends inside the silhouette region because the intersection is to the right of the line of traversal.

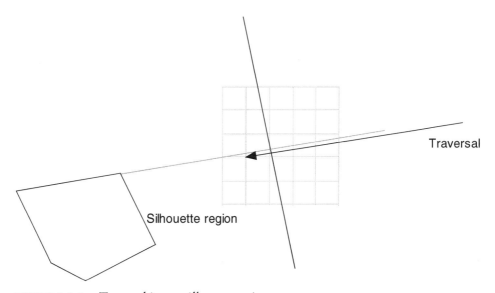

FIGURE 2.2.4   *Traversal into a silhouette region.*

Why Not Just Use Floats?

Floating-point representation only gives us greater precision near zero. At the edges of the number range, we actually get less precision than with an integer representation because of the bits required to store the exponent. Floating-point representation implies a grid that looks something like Figure 2.2.5, but with many more graduations. Thus, the problem still occurs, since results are still approximated to a grid.

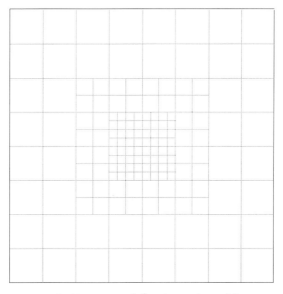

FIGURE 2.2.5   *A floating-point grid.*

Even adding arbitrary precision doesn't solve the problem. For example, we cannot represent 1/3 exactly no matter how many decimal places we use. Some errors will occur with a similar frequency no matter how small our grid is. Unless error probability becomes infinitely small, reducing the frequency of that error just serves to make life harder for our testers.

A Solution: Vector Fractions

We can solve this problem by representing the points of intersection without approximation. We propose vector fractions as one way of achieving this.

Intersection of 2D Lines

Consider two infinite lines in two dimensions, represented with start points and axes $S_1 A_1$ and $S_2 A_2$. As long as the lines are not parallel, they will intersect, allowing us to represent the intersection I as a fractional distance along the axis of one of the lines (see Figure 2.2.6 and Equation 2.2.1).

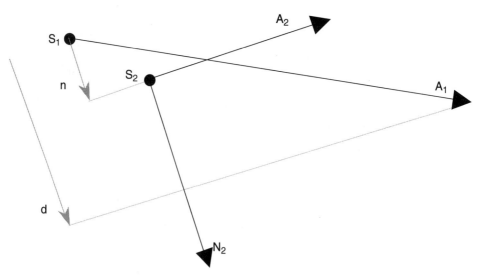

FIGURE 2.2.6   *Representing the point of intersection as a vector fraction.*

$$I = S_1 + \frac{nA_1}{d}$$

(2.2.1)

The numerator and denominator elements n and d are determined by taking dot products with N_2, a vector normal to the axis of the second line (Equation 2.2.2 and Equation 2.2.3). These values will be proportional to the lengths of the arrows shown in Figure 2.2.6.

$$n = \left(S_2 - S_1\right) \cdot N_2 \tag{2.2.2}$$

$$d = A_1 \cdot N_2 \tag{2.2.3}$$

Intersection of a 3D Line with a Plane

The method extends easily to the intersection of a three-dimensional line with a plane. In this case, we can take dot products with the plane normal to obtain a fractional distance along the three-dimensional line for the intersection.

Working with Vector Fractions

We can apply the same kinds of techniques for working with vector fractions that we use with normal fractions. Most importantly, when we work with vector fractions, cross-multiplication enables us to perform certain operations without explicit division. By eliminating division, we can perform the required geometric operations without approximation. Operations involving addition, subtraction, and multiplication of integer values will yield integer values.

Testing Side of Line for an Intersection

To determine if a point **P** is on the right of an infinite line defined by start **S** and axis **A,** we can test for the inequality in Equation 2.2.4. This equation assumes that the direction of increasing x is to the right of the direction of increasing y:

$$\left(P_x - S_x\right)A_y < \left(P_y - S_y\right)A_x \tag{2.2.4}$$

To apply this to a point represented as a vector fraction, we simply substitute a fractional representation for **P** (Equation 2.2.5) and then multiply everything by d_p to avoid division, giving us the inequality in Equation 2.2.6. This gives us one way to implement the traversal we require through path-finding regions.

$$P = B + \frac{C}{d_p} \tag{2.2.5}$$

$$\left(B_x d_p + C_x - S_x d_p\right)A_y < \left(B_y d_p + C_y - S_y d_p\right)A_x \tag{2.2.6}$$

Generalizing to Other Operations

It is easy to extend this approach to more-general operations on vector fractions. To perform comparisons between **P** and a second point **Q** (also represented as a vector fraction, as shown in Equation 2.2.7), we transform the points to a common denominator by multiplying both points by $d_p d_q$. Addition of **P** and **Q** yields a vector fraction result, as shown in Equation 2.2.8.

$$Q = D + \frac{E}{d_q} \tag{2.2.7}$$

$$P + Q = B + D + \frac{d_q C + d_p E}{d_q d_q} \tag{2.2.8}$$

Another Way To Traverse—Using Order of Intersection

Another way to solve our traversal problem is by comparing the distances for two intersections along a common axis. Figure 2.2.7 depicts the traversal problem. We need to determine the side of our traversal line ($\mathbf{S}_3\,\mathbf{A}_3$) for an intersection of region boundaries ($\mathbf{S}_1\,\mathbf{A}_1$ and $\mathbf{S}_2\,\mathbf{A}_2$). If we know that the traversal line crosses the boundary line $\mathbf{S}_1\,\mathbf{A}_1$ from right to left, then we can compare fractional distances for intersections along the axis $\mathbf{A}_1$. The inequality in Equation 2.2.9 is true when the boundary vertex is to the right of traversal.

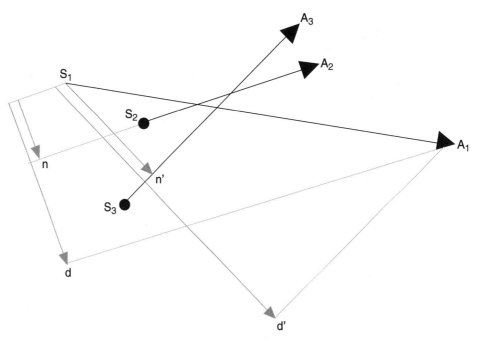

FIGURE 2.2.7   *Determining order of intersection.*

$$nd' > n'd \tag{2.2.9}$$

Number Ranges

By using integer coordinates and eliminating division, we can perform geometric operations without approximation and without requiring any extra precision. However, we have to think carefully about number ranges to avoid the possibility of overflow. The ranges that must be supported will depend on the coordinate range allowed for our geometry, together with the exact operations performed on this geometry.

Deriving Ranges

Let us assume that the coordinates of all points in our geometry are in the range $[0, r]$. Let us also assume that axis vectors are always formed by subtracting a start point from an end point.

The range of vectors formed by subtraction of points will be from $[-r, r]$. Both the numerator and denominator in Equation 2.2.1 were determined by dot products of these vectors and therefore will have a range $[-2r^2, 2r^2]$ for the two-dimensional case. For the three-dimensional case, the range is $[-3r^2, 3r^2]$ for dot products of three-dimensional vectors. Extending the two-dimensional analysis to Equation 2.2.6 gives us a range $[-6r^4, 6r^4]$ for each side of the inequality. For Equation 2.2.9, we get $[-8r^4, 8r^4]$.

Fitting the Ranges into Integer Data Types

Say we allow 128 bits to represent $-8r^4$ to $8r^4$. This gives us Equation 2.2.10 for r. Solving and rounding to integer coordinates yields a value for r.

$$8r^4 = 2^{127} - 1 \tag{2.2.10}$$

$$r = 2^{31} - 1 \tag{2.2.11}$$

Points and vectors can be stored in 32 bits, the results of dot products in 64 bits, and products of dot products in 128 bits. For different constraints or if different computations are required, a different set of ranges and, therefore, a different set of data types might need to be chosen.

Managing Range Constraints

Defining different data types for different stages of computation can help with managing the different ranges. For example, points and vectors could be implemented as different types, as well as dot products and multiplied dot products. With this method, we can use the compiler to check that the correct types are used for a computation.

It is a good idea to include range checking in the debug build. The impact on performance can be limited by only checking ranges when data types are constructed from other data types that do not have a defined range. We would then make sure to avoid this kind of construction as often as possible.

At compile time, it might not be possible to know what ranges will be required for complex operations. In this case, or simply as an alternative to working out ranges in advance, it is possible to use an integer class that dynamically allocates storage as required to represent arbitrarily sized integers. There are a number of packages available that can do this. See, for example, [GMP02] and [Haible02].

Implementation Details

Working with Big Integers

For platforms with a register size of 64 bits, working with big integers need not be a problem. For these platforms, multiplication of two 64-bit values will be performed in the silicon and yield a 128-bit result across two registers. Addition, subtraction, and comparison of 128-bit register pairs is also not a problem.

For platforms with a 32-bit register size, multiplication of 64-bit integers is a little more expensive; but if done correctly in assembly, it might not be too costly. Be careful with the standard 64-bit extensions provided by your compiler, as the code generated by these can be slower than you would expect. If multiplication of 64-bit integers is too costly, then an alternative is to reduce the ranges so that only 32-bit multiplication is required.

Which Kind of Traversal Should We Use?

We have a choice between Equation 2.2.6 and Equation 2.2.9 for implementing our traversal. Let's consider these equations in terms of the operations required for implementing them.

For Equation 2.2.6, we can precalculate $\mathbf{B}d_p$ and store the result together with our fractional representation. Now, testing the inequality only requires four multiplies. However, our intermediate results are obtained by multiplication of a dot product and a point coordinate. So given r as derived in Equation 2.2.11, two of these multiplies must be performed with 128-bit sources. Ideally, we need to avoid multiplying numbers this large because of the resulting performance hit.

One solution is to reduce the range permitted so that the two final multiplications for Equation 2.2.6 can be performed with 64-bit sources. This is the fastest option. Alternatively, we can use Equation 2.2.9 with six multiplies that all can be performed with a 64-bit source.

Optimizations

The ranges derived above are theoretical limits that will rarely be reached in practice. If you are a gambler, you can use fewer bits than are theoretically required for intermediate values, and perhaps overflow will never occur. Another alternative is to check for overflow and use a separate code path when the overflow occurs. Branch prediction on the target processor can help improve code performance in this situation. The vast majority of the time there will be no overflow, so we need to set up our code so that the branch is predicted correctly for this case.

Vector fractions based on a dynamic integer class can result in some very large numbers and a very slow program. In this case, it might be worthwhile to reduce the size of the numbers involved. We can do this by finding the greatest common denominator of the numerator and denominator of the fraction. Then, we divide both numerator and denominator by this value.

A simpler optimization is to detect when an intersection falls exactly on the coordinate grid and proceed as if it were a normal point. This is only worthwhile if the savings offset the cost of the test.

Conclusion

The mathematical basis for vector fractions is not complicated, but they provide an elegant solution for dealing with points at intersections without introducing the error of approximation. The elimination of artifacts from approximation removes a major headache when implementing geometric algorithms.

It's important to avoid overflow when using vector fractions. The compiler can help us with this if we use different types for different stages of computation. If we know what geometric queries we need, we can abstract the notion of a vector fraction as either a class or as a set of functions.

The cost of the change can be as little as a few extra multiplies and some extra bits to manipulate. Adding these extra calculations means that you'll no longer need special-case checks for the results of an approximation.

References

[GMP02] GMP, "GMP," available oneline at http://www.swox.com/gmp/, January 2002.

[Haible02] Haible, Bruno, "CLN - Class Library for Numbers," available online at http://www.ginac.de/CLN/, January 2002.

[Young01] Young, Thomas, "Optimizing Points-of-Visibility Pathfinding," *Game Programming Gems 2*, Charles River Media, Inc., 2001.

2.3

More Approximations to Trigonometric Functions

Robin Green,
Sony Computer Entertainment America

robin_green@playstation.sony.com

The art and science of writing mathematical libraries has been consistent over the past 10 years. Many computer science reference books that were written in the 1970s and 1980s are still in common use, and, as mathematics is the universal denominator, these books are usually considered as the last word on the subject. In the meantime, hardware has evolved, instruction pipelines have grown in length, memory accesses are slower than ever, multiplies and square-root units are cheaper than ever before, and more specialized hardware is using single-precision floats. It is time to go back to basics and review implementations of the mathematical functions that we rely on every day. With a bit of training and insight, we can optimize them for our specific game-related purposes, sometimes even outperforming general-purpose hardware implementations.

Measuring Error

Before we look at implementing functions, we need a standard set of tools for measuring how good our implementation is. The obvious way to measure error is to subtract our approximation from a high-accuracy version of the same function (usually implemented as a slow and cumbersome, infinite series calculation). This is called the *absolute error* metric:

$$error_{abs} = \left| f_{actual} - f_{approx} \right| \tag{2.3.1}$$

This is a good measure of accuracy, but it tells us nothing about the *importance* of any error. An error of 3 is acceptable if the function should return 38,000, but an error of 3 would be catastrophic if the function should return 0.008. We will also need to graph the *relative error:*

$$error_{rel} = 1 - \frac{f_{approx}}{f_{actual}} \quad \text{when } f_{actual} \neq 0 \tag{2.3.2}$$

When reading relative error graphs, an error of zero means there is no error; the approximation is exact. With functions like `sin()` and `cos()`, where the range is [−1.0, 1.0], the relative error is not that interesting. But functions like `tan()` have a wider range, and relative error will be an important metric of success.

Sine and Cosine

For most of the examples, implementations of the sine and cosine functions shall be considered, but many of the polynomial techniques, with a little tweaking, are applicable to other functions, such as exponent, logarithm, and arctangent.

Resonant Filter

When someone asks you what is the fastest way to calculate the sine and cosine of an angle, tell them you can do it in two instructions. The method, called a *resonant filter*, relies on having previous results of an angle calculation and assumes that you are taking regular steps through the series (see Figure 2.3.1).

```
int   N = 64;
float PI = 3.14159265;
float a = 2.0f*sin(PI*N);
float c = 1.0f;
float s = 0.0f;

for(i=0; i<N; ++i) {
    output_sine   = s;
    output_cosine = c;
    c = c − s*a;
    s = s + c*a;
    ...
}
```

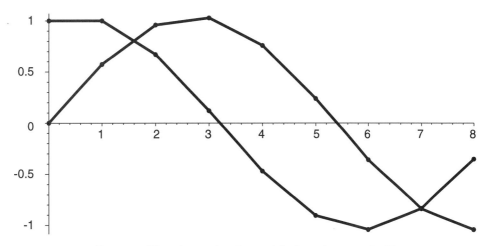

FIGURE 2.3.1   *Resonant filter sine and cosine—eight iterations over* $3\pi/2$.

Note that the value of c, used to calculate s, is the newly updated version from the previous line. This formula is also readily converted into a fixed-point version, where the multiplication by a can be modeled as a shift (e.g., a multiply by 1/8 converts to a shift right by three places).

If you plan to use this technique to fill look-up tables for later use, you must pay close attention to a (the step size) and to the initial values of c and s. The technique relies on the previous value feeding back into the system, so the initial values of s and c affect the final amplitude of the waves (e.g., starting with $s = 0.5$ and $c = 0.5$ gives a peak value of 0.7). As fast as this technique is for generating sine wave-like signals, you cannot rely on samples at fractions of a cycle returning accurate values. For example, say we were looking to take seven steps around a quarter of a circle:

```
N = 7;
a = 0.5*sin(PI*N);
...
```

The values for iterations seven and eight (counting from zero) are listed in Table 2.3.1.

Table 2.3.1 Testing the Accuracy of the Resonant Filter

Iteration	Sine	Cosine
7	1.004717676	0.158172209
8	0.9917460469	-0.0597931103
...	...	...
27	1.000000000	-0.000000002

The end points of this function miss the correct values of 1.0 and 0.0 by quite large amounts (see Table 2.3.1 and Figure 2.3.2). If, however, we extend the table to generate the whole cycle using 27 samples, we find that the final values for s and c are correct to nine decimal places. Adding more iterations will reduce this error, but won't make it disappear. Clearly, this approximation is useful for generating long sequences of sine-like waves, especially over entire cycles; but it is not well suited to accurate, small-angle work.

Goertzels Algorithm

A more accurate approach to the same problem is *Goertzels algorithm*, which uses and updates the two previous values (i.e., it's a *second order* filter). With it, we can calculate a series of sine and cosine values in the series $x_n = \sin(a + n*b)$ for integer values of n:

```
float cb = 2 * cos(b);
float s2 = sin(a + b);
float s1 = sin(a + 2*b);
float c2 = cos(a + b);
float c1 = cos(a + 2*b);
```

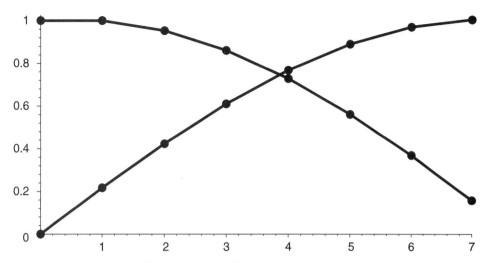

FIGURE 2.3.2   *Resonant filter quarter-circle test, seven iterations over π/2.*

```
float s,c;

for(i=0; i<N; ++i) {
    s = cb * s1 - s2;
    c = cb * c1 - c2;
    s2 = s1;
    c2 = c1;
    s1 = s;
    c1 = c;
    output_sine   = s;
    output_cosine = c;
    ...
}
```

The technique is only slightly more expensive to run than the previous method, but it has greater setup costs. However, if the setup can be done at compile time, the algorithm is still very efficient (see Figure 2.3.3).

There are some pitfalls associated with this algorithm, as it is a second-order filter. Because the values of *s* and *c* are constructed from the two previous samples, the algorithm actually outputs a result three iterations later than you might expect. To compensate for this, we need to initialize the sequence carefully, subtracting three steps from the initial value of *a:*

```
// step = N steps over 2*PI radians
float b = 2.0f*PI/N;
// minus three steps from origin
float a = 0.0f - 3.0f * b;
...
```

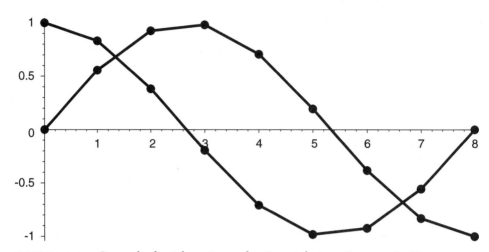

FIGURE 2.3.3   *Goertzels algorithm: sine and cosine, eight iterations over* $3\pi/2$.

Adding in these alterations and putting Goertzels to the quarter-circle test, we find that it passes the test well, producing more-accurate results than the resonant filter for fractions of complete cycles (see Figure 2.3.4).

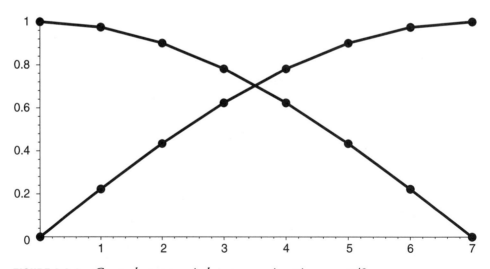

FIGURE 2.3.4   *Goertzels quarter-circle test, seven iterations over* $\pi/2$.

Table-Based Solutions

As clock speeds rise and memory-access latencies become longer and longer, sine and cosine tables fall out of favor and are no longer the fastest method in all situations. New architectures that provide vector units with closely coupled, fast RAM can still give single-cycle access time for small tables, so the technique must not be discounted and will be with us for some time to come.

The idea is to precalculate a table of samples from a function at regular intervals and use the input value to the function to hash into the table, look up the two closest values and linearly interpolate between them (see Figure 2.3.5). In effect, we are trading off storage space against speed.

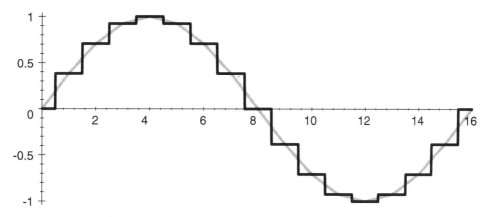

FIGURE 2.3.5   *Table-based sine(16 samples) with and without linear interpolation.*

In order to speed linear interpolation (*lerp*) between samples, we can precalculate the difference between adjacent samples, saving a subtract per look-up, especially on SIMD machines where a look-up usually loads a four-vector of floats at a time.

$$\sin(x) \approx \text{table}[i] + \Delta * \left(\text{table}[i+1] - \text{table}[i]\right)$$

$$\approx \text{table}[i] + \Delta * \text{gradient}[i] \qquad (2.3.3)$$

Precalculating these differences turns the lerp operation into a single multiply-add.

Using a table poses the question: How many samples do we need to get N digits of accuracy? The table-based sine with 16 samples is shown in Figure 2.3.5, and the absolute error graph is shown in Figure 2.3.6.

The largest error (or *maximal error*) occurs where the curvature of the function is highest—in fact, when two samples straddle the top of the curve. The size of the maximal error where the step size is $\Delta x = x_{n+1} - x_n$ can be shown to be:

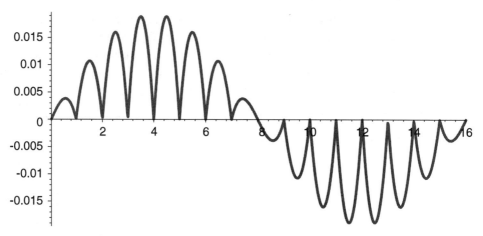

FIGURE 2.3.6   *Absolute error of 16 sample, linearly interpolated sine table.*

$$E = 1 - \cos\left(\frac{\Delta x}{2}\right) \tag{2.3.4}$$

So, for a table of 16 samples covering one whole cycle, the maximum relative error will be $1 - \cos(\pi/16) = 0.0192147$, giving us just under two decimal places of accuracy in the worst case. Turning the problem around, given a known accuracy, how many entries will we need in the table? We just reverse the inequality. For example, to approximate $\sin(x)$ to 1% error we only need 23 entries:

$$E = 1\%$$

$$1 - \cos(\pi\ /\ N) < 1\%$$

$$\cos(\pi\ /\ N) > 0.99$$

$$N > \pi/\arccos(0.99)$$

$$\approx 22.19 \tag{2.3.5}$$

Using a process called *range reduction*, we can reconstruct the whole cycle from just 45° of samples, meaning that we only need a table of 23/8 = 3 entries. Equation 2.3.4 will give you the hard upper bound on the error, an error that almost never occurs. For a slightly lower bound, you can use a small-angle approximation to the arccos(), as π/N should hopefully be a very small angle, giving you a bound of:

$$N = \frac{\pi}{\sqrt{2E}} \tag{2.3.6}$$

Applying Equation 2.3.6 to various error factors gives us a feel for situations where tables would be well used and where more-accurate methods must be used. See Table 2.3.2 for some example values.

Table 2.3.2 Size of Table Needed To Approximate Sin(X) to a Given Level of Accuracy

	E	360° Range	45° Range
1% accurate	0.01	23	3
0.1% accurate	0.001	71	9
0.01% accurate	0.0001	223	28
1.0°	0.01745	17	3
0.1°	0.001745	54	7
8-bit int.	2^{-7}	26	4
16-bit int.	2^{-15}	403	51
24-bit float	10^{-5}	703	88
32-bit float	10^{-7}	7025	880
64-bit float	10^{-17}	~infinite	8.7e+8

Range Reduction and Reconstruction

The sine and cosine functions have an infinite domain. Every input value has a corresponding output value in the range [0, 1] and the pattern repeats every 2π units. To properly implement the sine function, we need to take any input angle and find out where inside the [0, 2π] range it maps to. This process, for sine and cosine at least, is called *additive range reduction*, and is shown in Figure 2.3.7.

To do this, we need to find out how many times we need to subtract 2π from the current value to reduce it to the target range. We divide the input value by 2π, truncate the result toward zero (i.e., convert it to an integer), and subtract that many copies of 2π from it.

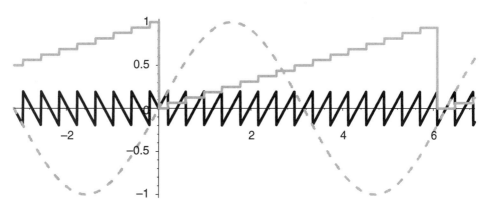

FIGURE 2.3.7 *Additive range reduction where C=2π/16.*

```
const float C = 2*PI;
const float invC = 1/C;

int k = (int)(x*invC);
y = x - (float)k * C;
...
```

In this example, the value of k only tells us how many full cycles we need to subtract, but if we were to range-reduce using fractions of a cycle then the lower digits of k would tell us which 'quadrant' the remainder belongs to. Why is this useful? Because of these well known relationships:

$$\sin(A + B) = \sin(A)\cos(B) + \cos(A)\sin(B)$$

$$\cos(A + B) = \cos(A)\cos(B) + \sin(A)\sin(B) \qquad (2.3.7)$$

If we range-reduce to $y \in [0..\pi/2]$, that means we have four segments to our cycle, and k mod 4 will tell us which segment to use. If we multiply Equation 2.3.7 through, we find that $\sin(B)$ and $\cos(B)$ collapse into the constants zero and one, and we get four special cases:

$$\sin\left(y + 0 * \pi / 2\right) = \sin(y)$$

$$\sin\left(y + 1 * \pi / 2\right) = \cos(y)$$

$$\sin\left(y + 2 * \pi / 2\right) = -\cos(y)$$

$$\sin\left(y + 3 * \pi / 2\right) = -\sin(y) \qquad (2.3.8)$$

leading to code like:

```
float table_sin(float x) {
    const float CONVERT = (2.0f * TABLE_SIZE) / PI;
    const float PI_OVER_TWO = PI/2.0f;
    const float TWO_OVER_PI = 2.0f/PI;

    int k = int(x * TWO_OVER_PI);
    float y = x - float(k)*PI_OVER_TWO;
    float index = y * CONVERT;
    switch(k&3) {
        case 0:  return sin_table(index);
        case 1:  return sin_table(TABLE_SIZE-index);
        case 2:  return -sin_table(TABLE_SIZE-index);
        default: return -sin_table(index);
    }
    return(0);
}
```

Why stop at just four quadrants? To add more quadrants, we need to *reconstruct* the final result by evaluating Equation 2.3.7 more carefully, using either in-lined constants or a table of values:

```
...
s = sin_table(y);
c = cos_table(y);
switch(k&15) {
    case 0:    return s;
    case 1:    return s * 0.923880f + c * 0.382685f;
    case 2:    return s * 0.707105f + c * 0.707105f;
    case 3:    return s * 0.382685f + c * 0.923880f;
    case 4:    return c;
    case 5:    return s * -0.382685f + c * 0.923880f;
    ...
}
```

Note how we have had to approximate both the sine *and* cosine in order to produce just the sine as a result. For very little extra effort, we can easily reconstruct the cosine at the same time, and the function that returns them both for an input angle, traditionally present in FORTRAN mathematical libraries, is usually called `sincos()`.

You will find that most libraries use the *range reduction*, *approximation*, and *reconstruction* phases in the design of their mathematical functions, and that this programming pattern turns up over and over again. In the next section, we will generate an optimized polynomial that replaces the table look-up and lerp.

Polynomial Approximations

A person's first introduction to approximating functions usually comes from learning about the *Taylor Series* in high school. Using a series of differentials, we can show that the transcendental functions break down into an infinite series of expressions—for example:

$$\sin(x) = x - \frac{x^3}{3!} + \frac{x^5}{5!} - \frac{x^7}{7!} + \frac{x^9}{9!} - \dots \tag{2.3.9}$$

If we had an infinite amount of time and infinite storage, then this would be the last word on the subject. As we have a very finite amount of time and even less storage, let's start by truncating the series at the ninth power and multiply through to five significant digits:

$$\sin(x) \approx x - \frac{1}{6}x^3 + \frac{1}{120}x^5 - \frac{1}{5040}x^7 + \frac{1}{362880}x^9$$

$$= x - 0.16667x + 0.0083333x^5 - 0.00019841x^7 + 0.0000027557x^9 \tag{2.3.10}$$

This is one of the classic infinite series—it exhibits alternating signs and drastically reducing factors (1/x! plummets toward zero), two signals that this series is going to converge toward the correct value fairly fast. The problems lie in the approximation error. If you graph the absolute error of this function (shown in Figure 2.3.8), you find that it is very accurate for small angles around the origin of the Taylor expansion, but the error increases almost exponentially away from x = 0. Truncating the

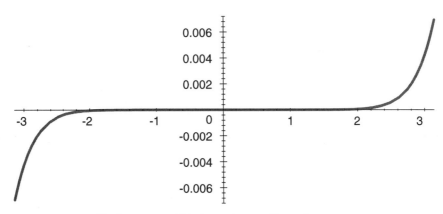

FIGURE 2.3.8   *Absolute error of Taylor series over $[-\pi, \pi]$.*

series later will decrease the error; however, it is more costly, opens you up to more danger of numerical error, and each additional term is another load/multiply-accumulate in your program. We need good accuracy across the *whole* range, and we need it using as few terms as possible.

How about reducing the input range? If you reduce the range of the sine function that we're trying to approximate, then, yes, we reduce the error because there's less to go wrong! Along with reducing the range, we could also Taylor-expand around the center of the range we want to approximate. This will halve the overall error, but at the cost of doubling the number of constants we need—now we need to calculate every power from zero to nine, not just every second one. We can do better than to use a Taylor series as a technique for generating fast polynomial approximations.

Minimax Polynomials

The Taylor expansion has a poor *maximal error*. If only we could find a way to take some of this error and spread it out across the whole range. In fact, thanks to a theory by Chebychev, it can be shown that every approximation has one special polynomial that has an equal amount of error everywhere—where we have 'minimized the maximal error,' and it's called the *minimax polynomial.* Its characteristics are:

- For a power N approximation, the error curve will change sign $N + 1$ times.
- The error curve will approach the maximal error $N + 2$ times.

The method used to find these polynomial approximations is called the *Remez Exchange Algorithm,* and it works by generating a set of linear equations. For example:

$$\sin(x) - a + bx_n + cx_n^2 = 0 \quad \text{for a set of values } x_n \in \left[a..b\right] \qquad (2.3.11)$$

These are solved to find the required coefficients *a, b,* and *c*; the maximal error is found and fed back into x_n. This highly technical optimization problem is sensitive to floating-point accuracy and is difficult to program, so we call on the professionals to do it for us. Numerical math packages, like Mathematica and Maple, have the necessary environments with the huge number representations and numerical tools needed to give accurate answers.

The arguments needed to calculate a minimax polynomial are:

- the function to be approximated,
- the range over which the approximation is to be done,
- the required order of our approximation, and
- a weighting function to bias the approximation into minimizing absolute (weight 1.0) or the relative error.

Let's find a seventh-order polynomial approximation to sin(x) over the range [0, π/4], optimized to minimize relative error. We start by looking at the Taylor expansion of sin(x) about $x = 0$, just to get a feel for what the polynomial should look like. The result shows us that the series has a leading coefficient of 1.0 and uses only the odd powers:

$$\sin(x) \approx x - 0.166666667x^3 + 0.00833333333x^5 - 0.000198412698x^7 \qquad (2.3.12)$$

A raw call to minimax will, by default, use all coefficients of all available powers to minimize the error, leading to some very small, odd-looking coefficients and many more terms than necessary. We will transform the problem into one of finding the polynomial in the expression:

$$\sin(x) \approx x + x^3 P(x^2) \qquad (2.3.13)$$

First, we form the minimax inequality, expressing our desire to minimize the *relative error* of our polynomial P:

$$\left| \frac{\sin(x) - x - x^3 P(x^2)}{\sin(x)} \right| \le error \qquad (2.3.14)$$

Divide through by x^3:

$$\left| \frac{\dfrac{\sin(x)}{x^3} - \dfrac{1}{x^2} - P(x^2)}{\dfrac{\sin(x)}{x^3}} \right| \le error \qquad (2.3.15)$$

We want the result in terms of every second power, so we substitute $y = x^2$:

$$\left| \frac{\dfrac{\sin\left(\sqrt{y}\right)}{y^{3/2}} - \dfrac{1}{y} - P(y)}{\dfrac{\sin\left(\sqrt{y}\right)}{y^{3/2}}} \right| \le error \qquad (2.3.16)$$

So, we have reduced our problem to finding a minimax polynomial approximation to:

$$P(y) = \frac{\sin\left(\sqrt{y}\right)}{y^{3/2}} - \frac{1}{y} \qquad (2.3.17)$$

with the weight function:

$$W(y) = \frac{y^{3/2}}{\sin\left(\sqrt{y}\right)} \qquad (2.3.18)$$

In order to evaluate the function correctly in the arbitrary, precision environment of Mathematica or Maple, it is (ironically) necessary to expand the first expression into a Taylor series of sufficient order to exceed our desired accuracy in order to prevent the specially written, arbitrary accuracy sine function from being evaluated:

$$P(y) = -\frac{1}{6} + \frac{y}{120} - \frac{y^2}{5040} + \frac{y^3}{362880} - \frac{y^4}{39916800} + \frac{y^5}{6227020800} - \dots \qquad (2.3.19)$$

Our last task is to transform the range we wish to try and approximate. As we have substituted $y = x^2$, so our range $[0, \pi/4]$ is transformed to $[0, \pi^2/16]$. Running these through the minimax function, looking for a second-order result gives us:

$$P(y) = -0.166666546 + 0.00833216076y - 0.000195152832y^2 \qquad (2.3.20)$$

Resubstituting this result back into Equation 2.3.12 gives us the final result:

$$\sin(x) \approx x - 0.166666546x^3 + 0.00833216076x^5 - 0.000195152832x^7 \qquad (2.3.21)$$

In order to reconstruct these coefficients as single precision floats, we need only record the first nine significant digits (see proof below), giving us Figure 2.3.9, the absolute and relative error curves over our range with a maximum absolute error of 2.59e-9 at $x = 0.785$.

Here is a loose proof. In single precision, numbers in the range $[10^3, 2^{10}] = [1000, 1024]$ have 10 bits to the right of the decimal and 14 bits to the right. There are therefore $(2^{10} - 10^3)2^{14} = 393,216$ representable values. If we use a decimal notation with eight digits, we can represent $(2^{10} - 10^3)10^8 = 240,000$ values. We therefore need nine decimal digits to be able to reconstruct the correct binary number. Similar constructions along the number line show a need for between six and nine digits. For more, see [Goldberg91].

Optimizing for Floating-Point

The same technique we used to remove a coefficient can be used to force numbers to machine-representable values. Remember that numbers like 1/10 are not precisely representable using a finite number of binary digits. We can adapt the technique above to force coefficients to be our choice of machine-representable floats. Remem-

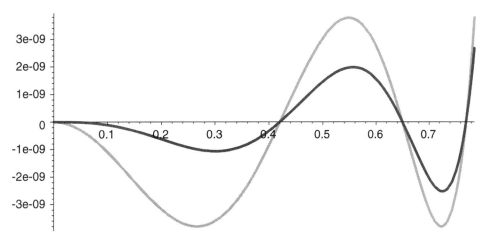

FIGURE 2.3.9   *Absolute and relative error of approximation over* $[0, \pi/4]$.

bering that all floating-point values are rational numbers, we can take the second coefficient and force it to fit in a single precision floating-point number:

$$k = -\frac{2796201}{2^{24}} = -0.16666656732559204101562500000 \tag{2.3.22}$$

Now that we have our constant value, let's optimize our polynomial to incorporate it. Start by defining the form of polynomial we want to end up with:

$$\sin(x) = x + kx^3 + x^5 P(x^2) \tag{2.3.23}$$

Now we form the minimax inequality:

$$\left| \frac{\sin(x) - x - kx^3 - k^5 P(x^2)}{\sin(x)} \right| \le error \tag{2.3.24}$$

which, after dividing by k^5, substituting $y = x^2$, and solving for $P(y)$, shows us that we have to calculate the minimax of:

$$P(y) = \frac{\sin\left(\sqrt{y}\right)}{y^{5/2}} - \frac{1}{y^2} + \frac{k}{y} \tag{2.3.25}$$

with weight function

$$W(y) = \frac{y^{5/2}}{\sin\left(\sqrt{y}\right)} \tag{2.3.26}$$

Solving this and resubstituting gives us a seventh-degree optimized polynomial over the range $[0, \pi/4]$ with a maximal error of 3.39e-8 at $x = 0.557$, but with better single precision floating-point accuracy:

$$\sin{(x)} \approx x - \frac{2796201}{2^{24}}x^3 + 0.00833220803x^5 - 0.000195168955x^7 \quad (2.3.27)$$

The absolute and relative error of float-optimized approximation over $[0, \pi/4]$ are shown in Figure 2.3.10.

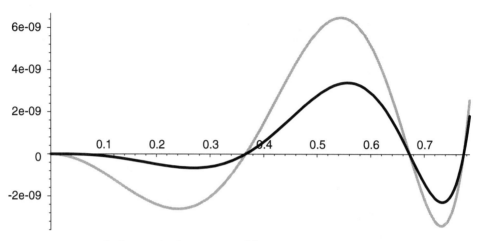

FIGURE 2.3.10   *Absolute and relative error of float-optimized approximation over* $[0, \pi/4]$.

A Note on Convergence

How do we choose the degree of polynomial that we need to approximate a function to a given accuracy? We can easily calculate how many bits of accuracy an approximation provides. First, we calculate the maximum error within the range (this will be a small value, typically something like 5e-4) and take the base-2 logarithm of this value using $\ln(error)/\ln(2)$, giving us a negative number that tells us how many bits we will need after the decimal point to be able to represent this value. Generating a table of this value for several important functions shows us some interesting results (see Table 2.2.3).

Table 2.3.3 Number of Significant Bits of Accuracy Versus Degree of Minimax Polynomial Approximating the Range [0, 1]

	2	3	4	5	6	7	8
e^x	6.8	10.8	15.1	19.8	24.6	29.6	34.7
$\sin(x)$	7.8	12.7	16.1	21.6	25.5	31.3	35.7
$\ln(1+x)$	8.2	11.1	14.0	16.8	19.6	22.3	25.0
$\arctan(x)$	8.7	9.8	13.2	15.5	17.2	21.2	22.3
$\tan(x)$	4.8	6.9	8.9	10.9	12.9	14.9	16.9
$\arcsin(x)$	3.4	4.0	4.4	4.7	4.9	5.1	5.3
$\sqrt{x}$	3.9	4.4	4.8	5.2	5.4	5.6	5.8

Firstly, it shows how well we can use polynomials to approximate $\exp(x)$ and $\sin(x)$, as each additional power gives us pretty much four bits of accuracy. For a 24-bit single precision floating-point value, we will only need a sixth- or seventh-power approximation. The table also shows how badly $\sqrt{x}$ is approximated by polynomials; each additional power only adds half a bit of accuracy—this is why there are no quick and easy approximations to the square root; we must use range reduction with Newton's algorithm and good initial guesses to calculate it. Another surprise is $\tan(x)$. After all, it's only $\sin(x)/\cos(x)$ isn't it? Rational functions like this are not well approximated by ordinary polynomials and require a different toolkit of techniques.

Conclusion

The task of writing low-accuracy mathematical functions using high-accuracy techniques has not been covered in any depth in the literature. But with the widespread use of programmable DSPs, vector units, high-speed yet limited hardware, and more-esoteric shading models, the need to write your own mathematical functions is increasingly important.

Introductions to polynomial approximation always start by saying how accurate they can be, and this obsession with accuracy continues through to extracting the very last bit of accuracy out of every floating-point number. Why this obsession with accuracy? Because if you can build high-accuracy polynomials with less coefficients, you can also build tiny, low-accuracy approximations using the same techniques. The levels of accuracy you can obtain with just two constants as well as the hugely reduced range can be amazing. Hopefully, this gem has given you the confidence to grab a math package and generate some of your own high-speed functions.

References

[Cody80] Cody & Waite, *Software Manual for the Elementary Functions*, Prentice Hall, 1980.

[Crenshaw00] Crenshaw, Jack W., *Math Toolkit for Real-Time Programming*, CMP Books, 2000.

[DSP] The Music DSP Source Code. Archive available online at http://www.smart-electronix.com .

[Goldberg91] Goldberg, Steve, "What Every Computer Scientist Should Know About Floating Point Arithmetic," *ACM Computing Surveys,* Vol. 23, No. 1, March 1991.

[Hart68] Hart, J. F., *Computer Approximations*, John Wiley & Sons, 1968.

[Moshier89] Moshier, Stephen L., *Methods and Programs for Mathematical Functions*, Prentice Hall, 1989.

[Muller97] Muller, J. M., *Elementary Functions: Algorithms and Implementations*, Birkhaüser, 1997.

[Ng92] Ng, K. C., "Argument Reduction for Huge Arguments: Good to the Last Bit," SunPro Report, July 1992.

[Story00] Story, S. and Tang, P. T. P., "New Algorithms for Improved Transcendental Functions on IA-64," Intel Report, 2000.

[Tang89] Tang, Ping Tak Peter, "Table Driven Implementation of the Exponential Function in IEEE Floating Point Arithmetic," *ACM Transactions on Mathematical Software,* Vol. 15, No. 2, June 1989.

[Tang90] Tang, Ping Tak Peter, "Table Driven Implementation of the Logarithm Function in IEEE Floating Point Arithmetic," *ACM Transactions on Mathematical Software,* Vol. 16, No. 2, December 1990.

[Tang91] Tang, Ping Tak Peter, "Table Lookup Algorithms for Elementary Functions and Their Error Analysis," Proceedings of 10th Symposium on Computer Arithmetic, 1991.

[Upstill90] Upstill, S., *The Renderman Companion*, Addison Wesley, 1990.

2.4

Quaternion Compression

Mark Zarb-Adami,
Muckyfoot Productions

mark@muckyfoot.com

Many of today's computer games use large amounts of animation data, and a large portion of the memory used for each animation frame is consumed by the rotation of the bones. Typically, the rotation data is stored as quaternions. In this gem, we propose and compare methods for compressing a four-float quaternion into a 32-bit quantity.

Quaternions

A quaternion $Q(x, y, z, w)$ can be used to represent a rotation matrix. If we consider all rotation matrices to represent a rotation of angle θ about axis $A(X, Y, Z)$, then the quaternion for the rotation would be:

$$Q = (sX, sY, sZ, c)$$

where:

$$s = \sin(\theta)$$

$$c = \cos(\theta)$$

It is important to note that quaternion $Q(x, y, z, w)$ and quaternion $Q'(-x, -y, -z, -w)$ represent the same rotation. This is because a rotation of θ about axis A is equivalent to a rotation of $-\theta$ about axis $-A$. Also, note that all the quaternions we consider in this gem are normalized. This means that for every quaternion $Q(x, y, z, w)$:

$$x^2 + y^2 + z^2 + w^2 = 1$$

Smallest Three Method

We can compress a quaternion by quantizing each element of the quaternion down to a byte. This is very fast, but it is also inaccurate. Because the quaternion is normalized, we can improve the accuracy of quantization by eliminating one of the elements. Given three of the elements, we can calculate the fourth one. Now, we have to decide which element to exclude. If we remove the biggest element, we will have smaller numbers to store! In fact, none of the three smallest elements of a quaternion can have an absolute value larger than $1 / \sqrt{2}$. To understand why this is the case, consider the following. The *second* largest element of a normalized quaternion will be *largest* when two elements of the quaternion have the same value and the other two are zero, as in *Q(v, v, 0, 0)*. If we normalize this quaternion, then *v* must equal $1/\sqrt{2}$.

We don't have to store the sign of the largest element, since we can make sure it is always positive. If it isn't positive already, simply negate the quaternion as described previously.

Polar Methods

Since we can store a direction vector *(x, y, z)* using just two angles, *yaw* and *pitch*, we can also store a quaternion as *(yaw, pitch, w)*. Note that storing *(x, y, z)* with *yaw* and *pitch* removes information about its length, but we can restore the correct length with *w*, since the quaternion is normalized. If we ensure that *w* is always positive, then we don't have to store its sign. Once again, if *w* is negative, we simply negate the quaternion.

The trouble with storing a direction vector as *yaw* and *pitch* is that the encoded vectors are not evenly dispersed over a sphere. They are instead concentrated at the poles. When the pitch of the vector is $\pi/2$, and the vector points straight up at the pole, we do not want to store a *yaw*. However, when the pitch of the vector is zero and the vector lies along the equator, we want to store many *yaw* values. Say we wanted to use *n* bits to encode a direction vector. One solution would be to spread points evenly across the surface of the sphere, store *(x, y, z)* or *(yaw, pitch)* for each point in a lookup table, then store an *n*-bit index into that table. While this is okay for small values of *n*, the size of the lookup table quickly becomes uncomfortably large!

However, there is an effective method for encoding a direction vector without the use of a lookup table. First of all, we store the signs of *x*, *y*, and *z* separately so that we can assume that *x*, *y*, and *z* are all positive. This reduces the problem to an eighth of the sphere. The next step is to number points inside this eighth of a sphere as in Figure 2.4.1.

Notice that the square numbers appear on the left-hand side of the diagram. This allows us to find the row and column of an encoded number, *e*, like this:

```
row = floor(sqrt(e));
column = e - row*row;
```

Now, if we let *pitch* be the row of *e*, and if we let *yaw* be the column of *e*, we can efficiently store and retrieve these values. Notice how we will not waste any *yaw* values at the pole, and that we have plenty of possible *yaw* values at the equator.

Implementation

Now, let's discuss the implementation for the methods we have discussed.

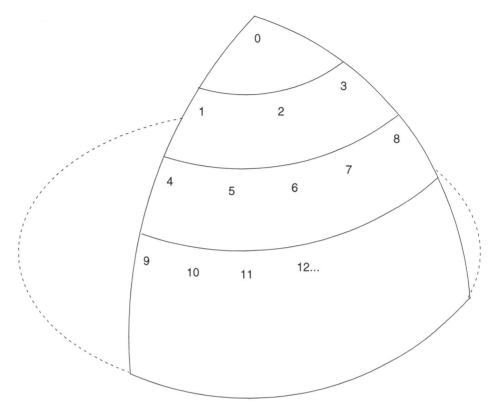

FIGURE 2.4.1 *Numbering over an eighth of a sphere.*

Smallest Three

The *smallest three* method neatly stores a quaternion into 32 bits. We need two bits to store the index of the implied (largest) element, leaving 10 bits for each of the three smallest elements. Since we know each of the stored elements lie in the range $[-1/\sqrt{2}, 1/\sqrt{2}$. we can interpolate those values to $[0, 1023]$ so that the values are represented as integers.

Polar

After experimenting with various bit allocations, we found the best compression when we allocated 11 bits to w. We need an additional 3 bits to store the sign of x, y, and z, leaving 18 bits to store *yaw* and *pitch*. If we are encoding *yaw* and *pitch* as a single number, then we can store 2^{18} values in 512 rows. Alternatively, we can allocate 9 bits for *yaw* and 9 bits for *pitch*. We know they are both in the range $[0, \pi/2]$, so we interpolate these values to $[0, 511]$ and store them as integers.

Converting from *yaw* and *pitch* to a vector requires sine and cosine calculations for both *yaw* and *pitch*, so we recommend using a fast polynomial approximation

[Edwards00] to calculate these values. Moreover, because *yaw* and *pitch* are always within $[0, \pi/2]$, we can tailor (no pun intended) the approximations to this particular range. We can expand a Taylor series about $\pi/4$ (instead of about 0) and use values between $[0, \pi/4]$ as sample points for a Lagrange series. A Taylor series to order five, or a Lagrange series to order four or five is sufficient. The order-four Lagrange series is slightly faster, but you lose a bit of accuracy. Also, the order-five Lagrange series gives a more accurate approximation than the order-five Taylor series.

The animation data for our game *Blade II* is stored hierarchically, hence the vast majority of the quaternions have only a small angle of rotation, θ. Since w is $cos(\theta/2)$, w is usually close to 1 for this data. Note that this would be true to a lesser extent even if the quaternions had random angles of rotation, simply because of the nature of the *cosine* function. So, to get more resolution for values near to 1, we store $\sqrt{1-w}$ instead of w and recover w at decompression time.

Performance

To quantify the performance of each compression method, we used the quaternions from our *Blade II* as data. We compressed and decompressed each quaternion Q to get another quaternion, Q'. We converted Q and Q' to matrices, and transformed a set of points with the resulting matrices. Then, for each point, we calculated the distance between the point transformed with Q and the point transformed with Q'. We represent these distances as error for that compression method. We also measured the decompression speed of each method. Figure 2.4.2 shows the relative performance of each compression method on our hierarchical data. The approximation method used for the polar methods was an order-five Lagrange polynomial.

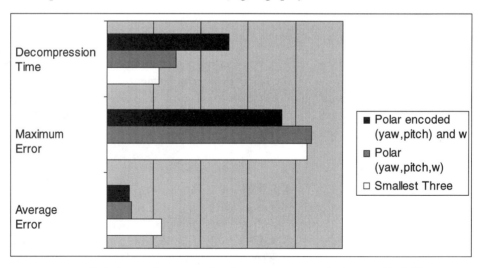

FIGURE 2.4.2   *Relative performance of each compression method using Blade II quaternion data.*

Conclusion

The real test of the compression of each algorithm comes from observing the characters in your game. The worst-case scenario for *Blade II* is when errors accumulate down the skeleton, especially if the character is holding a long lever (like a shotgun) in his hand! There is a visible improvement when using the *polar* methods compared to the *smallest three* method.

Acknowledgments

I want to thank Jan Svarovsky and Mike Diskett for their help in developing the ideas in this gem.

References

[Edwards00] Edwards, Eddie, "Polynomial Approximations to Trigonometric Functions," *Game Programming Gems*, Charles River Media, Inc., 2000.
[Svarovsky00] Svarovsky, Jan, "Quaternions for Game Programming," *Game Programming Gems*, Charles River Media, Inc., 2000.

2.5

Constrained Inverse Kinematics

Jason Weber, Intel Corporation

jason.p.weber@intel.com

Much of the animation currently used in interactive applications relies on stored fragments of motion-captured or hand-authored data. Although these motions can be beautifully polished, the repeated use of a limited set of actions can become readily apparent. One key to holding the attention of a user is to continually provide new and unique environments.

To provide unique animations at runtime, we first need an abstract means to control and deform a mesh, such as with an embedded skeleton. Then, we need to generate motion for that skeleton from events or items in the proximity of the mesh. Forward kinematics allows us to simply adjust bone angles like a jointed, wooden artist's model. However, we also need the reverse calculation to find suitable angles that will arrange terminal segments, like hands and feet, where we want them. Inverse kinematics (IK) provides a fast and robust method to position an arbitrary chain of bones so that an end bone attempts to align with a movable 'effector.' By providing solutions in real-time, we allow characters to react spontaneously and uniquely to an unpredictable environment.

We describe a well-known method called "cyclic coordinate descent" and demonstrate how to constrain the angular solutions based on the physical limits of the joints. We specifically target the constraint format provided with 3ds max.

Bones Hierarchy

The skeletal structure is basically a hierarchy of transforms, like a scene graph. At each transform, we define a bone length, which is really a displacement along that transform's local *x*-axis. By default, the origin of all child bones is positioned at the point on the end of the parent bone. We allow for an additional arbitrary displacement, but in most cases it is zero, because bones usually connect end-to-end.

For clarity, we will not refer to a "model space" in which the overall character is placed. We will refer to the space that the root bone moves in as the "world space," even though in a real scenario, it will probably be just a node in some greater scene graph. At each transform in the bone hierarchy, that transform, relative to its parent, will be called a "local" transform.

At this stage, we represent all rotations using quaternions because of their smooth interpolative qualities [Bobick98]. A quaternion is a four-dimensional extension to complex numbers. So, just as a complex number can be used for two-dimensional rotational computations, $w + x\mathbf{i} + y\mathbf{j} + z\mathbf{k}$ ($\mathbf{i}^2 = \mathbf{j}^2 = \mathbf{k}^2 = -1$, $\mathbf{ij} = \mathbf{k} = -\mathbf{ji}$) can effectively represent three-dimensional rotations. Conversions to and from quaternions, as well as operations using quaternions, can include nontrivial mathematics, but small libraries and clear examples are readily available [Flipcode98]. We use right-handed unit quaternions of the form (w, x, y, z) where $(1, 0, 0, 0)$ represents an identity of no rotation. The values are similar to the angle/axis format, where a rotation of $(2\cos^{-1} w)$ radians occurs about a nonunit vector (x, y, z).

A reference pose for the skeleton describes the state of the hierarchy so that it aligns with a given undeformed source mesh. (BiPed™, in 3ds max, calls this the "figure mode.") The motion of the bones away from reference is used to deform the mesh to any arbitrary position. The deformation techniques are a different topic [Weber02], so all we have to know about here is that the IK algorithms or interpolated motion data supply a bone-indexed set of world-aligned transforms at each frame. After the parent-relative quaternion values have been determined for a frame, the bone graph is traversed, and the world transforms are generated through simple quaternion-quaternion concatenation and quaternion-matrix conversion.

Cyclic Coordinate Descent

The IK system attempts to rotate a chain of participating bones so that the tip of the end bone is located at a movable control point, called an *effector*. There are many complex and expensive ways to generate inverse kinematic solutions, but fortunately there is a reasonably simple algorithm that is quite fast and surprisingly robust, called "cyclic coordinate descent" (CCD), which is nicely outlined in [Lander98]. We use quaternions for all the rotational operations.

Each iteration starts with the deepest child bone in the chain. The bone is rotated about its base so that it points directly at the effector. Next, the parent of that bone is rotated about its base so that an imaginary line from the base of that parent to the tip of the newly rotated child points toward the effector. This is repeated for every bone in the chain so that each bone's imaginary line from its base to that same end bone's endpoint rotates toward the effector. Multiple iterations through the chain can further refine the solution to produce a smoother distribution of angles. Even if the effector cannot be reached, the solver can make a solid attempt without becoming shaky or unstable.

This method can create a tendency to make the lowest child disproportionally dynamic, such as using full wrist deflection just to pick up a ball. It is possible to bias the solution by having some bones only rotate a fraction of the desired change for each iteration, but this might increase the number of iterations needed to reach a static solution. To pick up a ball, it is probably easier just to apply the IK effector to the wrist instead of the fingertips, and then use a generic pick-up motion for the hand.

Figure 2.5.1 shows the steps in a descent. The X symbol is the location of the effector. The dotted line represents the current base-to-tip angle. Each currently addressed bone is rotated to align the dotted line with the desired dashed line.

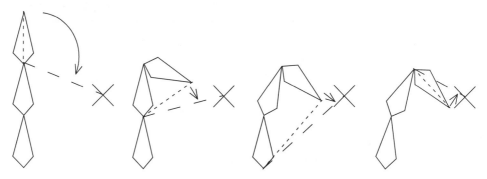

FIGURE 2.5.1   *Steps in cyclic coordinate descent. The X symbol is the location of the effector.*

If a bone participates in multiple 'effected' end bones, the participating bone can first compute an angular change to satisfy each of the solutions, then use given weighting factors to work out a blended solution.

The number of iterations required to reach an acceptable solution depends on where each new frame starts the solution. In a conventional approach, you would reset the limb to some default state at the beginning of each frame. The solver would run through 10 or so iterations to a fresh solution. However, a small change in an effector position can cause a sudden change in the solution. For example, if you are moving an effector for the hand vertically behind the back, the solver might suddenly decide that it is better to reach over the shoulder than under it. An alternative approach is to continue from the solution of the previous frame. Then, we can cut back to as little as one iteration per frame. By using this incremental method, the solver also is much less likely to flip between marginally superior, but substantially different solutions.

An important factor in generating realistic motion is limiting the angular velocity. To do this, we take the world-based quaternion of the previous frame and compare the new quaternion solution. We convert the delta to angle-axis form and limit the angle to a specified maximum. About 3 radians per second seems to be a good default limit, with smaller values increasing the sluggishness. Limiting angular acceleration turns out to have minimal value, since it appears that most biological structures can achieve full velocity during the timestep of one frame.

See [Welman93] for detailed explanation of CCD and other methods of inverse kinematics.

Rotational Constraints

The resulting IK solution will not work well with physical creatures unless we account for realistic angular limits. The basis of how constraints are defined and applied is dictated by the form in which the authoring packages export them. Therefore, we will define two conventions we need to follow.

Euler Angles

Although our rotations are computed using quaternions, the limiting angles are usually supplied from the artist using Euler angles, an alternative angular representation using three angles applied in succession. For example, Euler angles could represent the orientation of an airplane by heading, pitch, and bank where pitch is applied after rotating by the heading, and bank is applied after rotating for the pitch. Gimbal lock can occur if one of the angles is near 90°, since two of the rotation axes can align and become redundant. In that case, the third degree of freedom is lost.

Converting from an Euler representation to a quaternion or matrix is as simple as applying the three rotational transforms in succession. However, converting back to an Euler representation is weakly defined and can have multiple solutions. A conversion example is in a referenced article, [Flipcode98].

World-Aligned Constraints

Programmers would probably expect the angular limits of a particular bone to be defined relative to the position of its parent. While this is partially true, 3ds max uses world-aligned axes to define the angles about which these limits are to be applied. This means that if the world-relative reference transform of a parent bone is not aligned with the world axes, then an isolated constraint of a child about one of the parent's local axes is not possible. Because of this, the 3ds max manuals recommend that the constrained bones in the reference pose (their 'figure mode') should be *coincidentally* aligned with the world. Unfortunately, we cannot simply transform these limits about world-aligned axes to the local axes of the bone. To faithfully reproduce the artist's intentions, we have to follow these conventions exactly, making conversions back and forth as necessary.

'Kine' Each Bone, and Apply the Constraints

ON THE CD

This pseudo-code will describe the entire process of applying IK to one specific bone. This process is applied to the entire hierarchy in a child-first order. For reference, see GPGCharacter::KineBone() in the file GPGCharacter.cpp on the CD-ROM. The variable *world_relative* is true (you may note how much simpler the code would be if it were false).

Each bone contains a list of the effector solutions to which it participates. For each bone that has an effector, there are usually several bones that participate in the solution to draw that one bone toward the effector. Note that we called this participating association to an effector an "effection." Having an effection doesn't necessarily mean that the specific bone is trying to reach the effector, but rather it may be helping a descendent bone meet the effector. For example, the upper arm can help the hand reach for a ball.

The float *scalar* is used to divide influence from multiple effectors. Currently in our code, it is evenly divided, so if a bone has an effection to two effectors, each will only have half the effect they would have had by themselves. The following block is applied once for each bone's effection.

```
Vector3 effected = current end of effected bone in world space
    displaced in local X by the bone length
Vector3 effector = current position of relevant control point in
    world space
Vector3 current = effected, reverse-transformed to local space
Vector3 desired = effector, reverse-transformed to local space

if the difference between current and desired is small, skip to next
    bone

normalize current and desired

compute a quaternion delta that would rotate current to desired

sum all the scaled deltas from the multiple effections and store in
    change

if velocity-limiting is on, limit change to the max per-frame angle
    allowed; this should be adjusted to the magnitude of the timestep

rotate the bone by the quaternion delta

Quaternion global_rot = parent's world rotation * this bone's local
    rotation (this is the bone's current world transform)

Quaternion parent_delta = parent's reference rotation * inverse of
    parent's current world rotation (this is how much the parent has
    deviated from reference with respect to the world)

Quaternion global_delta = parent_delta * global_rot * inverse of
    parent reference world rotation (this is the bone rotation in world-
    aligned axes adjusted for parent rotation)

convert Quaternion global_delta to Euler euler
```

The next block does the actual limiting of angles. It is applied to *euler* in each of the three axes. "Active" means it is allowed to move. "Limited" means that the angle is constrained. To avoid gimbal lock, we ignore new x and z angles when the y angle is near $\pm 90°$ (by about 5% of a radian). We retain old values of x and z until the y angle returns to a safe value.

Note the usage of a variable called *bias*. When a potential solution goes far outside the constraints, this can prevent it from flipping around and constraining to the opposite limit. A *bias* of zero means the bone is currently being limited by the minimum angle, one indicates it is being limited by the maximum angle, and two indicates no preference. When thinking about the constraints, it can be helpful to think of a pie slice in a circle where the two radials are the minimum and maximum angles. Usually, when the result ends up outside this region, you want to snap to the closest boundary (minimum or maximum). However, if the computed solution is outside the pie slice, but is nearly equidistant from both limits, it is possible that the clamping routine will flip back and forth between the minimum and maximum. So, we insert a bias indicating that in order to flip around the outside of the pie, the alternate limit must be substantially closer. In our code, we add 10° to the alternate distance before the magnitude comparison.

```
if active and not limited, skip this axis (any angle is fine)

if not active, set the angle to the reference value; skip to next
  axis

X,Z axes only: if Y angle is near 90 degrees, set angle to last
  frame's value, and skip to next axis (gimbal lock avoidance)

if current angle is within limits, reset bias to 2 (no preference),
  and skip to next axis

mindiff = minimum − angle
maxdiff = angle - maximum

adjust mindiff and maxdiff to be in range of 0 to 2*PI

if there is a bias preference, adjust angles to make flipping between
  solutions less desirable by adding the 10 degrees to the opposite
  min/max diff variable

if maxdiff<mindiff, set angle to max and bias to 1
if maxdiff>mindiff, set angle to min and bias to 0

store modified euler in case there is a gimbal lock next frame

convert euler to Quaternion global_delta

Quaternion constrained = inverse of parent reference world rotation
  * global_delta * parent reference world rotation

set bone rotation to constrained

recompute cached current world transform for this bone and all
  descendents
```

Figure 2.5.2 shows a character reaching back to an effector about 2/3 meters behind his head. Without the constraints, the solver would have immediately positioned the arm in a straight line from the shoulder toward the point. With constraints, the arm is restricted to its physical limits. Also see Color Plate 2 for an example of this technique on a scorpion tank mesh.

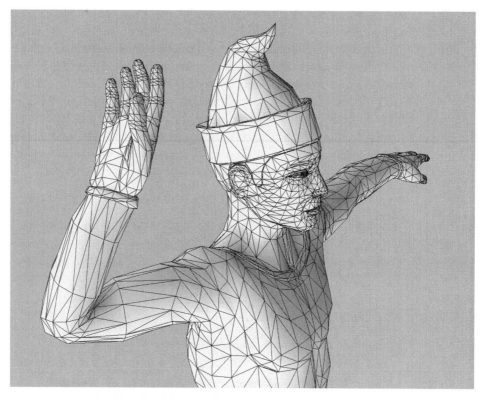

FIGURE 2.5.2 *Reaching back for an effector.*

Conclusion

Using inverse kinematics in skeletal motions can generate a level of spontaneity that is difficult to produce with pre-authored or captured motion data. By generating the motion in real-time, the characters can react uniquely to an ever-changing situation.

In our example, we use hard stops to limit the angles. By adding a springiness near the limits, we should be able to reduce the mechanical-looking motions that can sometimes occur.

References

[Bobick98] Bobick, Nick, "Rotating Objects Using Quaternions," *Game Developer Magazine,* February 1998: pp. 34–42. Also available online at http://www.gdmag.com/.

[Flipcode98] Unattributed, "The Matrix and Quaternions FAQ," available online at http://www.flipcode.com/documents/matrfaq.html, December 1998.

[Lander98] Lander, Jeff, "Making Kine More Flexible," *Game Developer Magazine,* November 1998: pp. 15–22.

[Weber02] Weber, Jason, "Improved Bones Deformation," *Game Programming Gems 3,* Charles River Media, Inc., 2002.

[Welman93] Welman, Chris, "Inverse Kinematics and Geometric Constraints for Articulated Figure Manipulation," Masters Thesis, Simon Fraser University, September 1993.

The author will make an effort to maintain a long-term archive and link site for some related resources at http://www.imonk.com/baboon/bones.

Cellular Automata for Physical Modeling

Tom Forsyth,
Mucky Foot Productions, Ltd.
tomf@muckyfoot.com

Many current game environments are mostly static. The sorts of things that move in games are restricted to either small, discrete objects, such as vehicles and people, or sometimes some larger, mechanical, or prescripted objects. In some cases, the water level in a container can move in scripted ways, but it is only a single horizontal plane that moves up or down, and there is no way for the player to directly interact with it.

In the current state of the art of games, the following effects tend to be either faked or not simulated at all:

- Fire that spreads, ignites flammable objects, and causes damage to them.
- Water that can be held in containers, flow through pipes, be pumped around realistically, walked through, weigh objects down, overflow containers, or spread over floors and down slopes.
- Oil that combines the fluid properties of water with the burning properties of flammable materials, such as wood.
- Explosions that have realistic damage radii, doing more damage indoors than outdoors, and traveling around corners in realistic ways.
- Heat that causes air to rise, causes convection currents, can be pumped around by ventilation fans, and possibly even carry scents and smells.
- Smoke and dust that spread with air currents, are generated by fires or smoke grenades, obscure vision, and choke people.
- Walls and environments that can be damaged, destroyed, set on fire, moved, or give limited protection from explosions and attacks.

Some of these features have appeared in games, but usually in heavily scripted and constrained ways; frequently they play little part in the actual gameplay and look artificial—which, of course, is exactly what they are. Using cellular automata (CA) to simulate these ideas can lead to far more dynamic and realistic behavior, and allow new types of gameplay and new tactics within games. At the very least, they allow more realism, better graphical rendering, and therefore increase player immersion.

CA Basics

Cellular automata (CA), and their close relatives, finite element analysis (FEA) and computational fluid dynamics (CFD) [CFD], are already used in plenty of applications for modeling air and water flow, heat distribution, building stresses and strains, and many other aspects of the real world. However, the main emphasis of the academic and commercial modelers is on accuracy. As game programmers, our only real concern is whether something looks good enough and runs quickly enough; and in almost every case, the simulation can be enormously simplified while still looking perfectly correct to most people.

The basics of a CA are simple. The world is divided into a grid of fixed-size cells. Each cell has various numbers associated with it to represent its state. Usual values held in cells are the air pressure, temperature, amount of water, which direction the water or air is flowing in, and so on.

Each game turn, every cell is processed, and it compares itself with its neighboring cells. Differences between them result in changes to the state of the cell and/or its neighbors according to various laws. In this gem, these laws will be based very loosely on real physical laws. One of the best-known CA is called "Conway's Game of Life" [Conway]. This is an extremely simple CA. It has a single bit of state—whether the cell is full or not—and some extremely simple rules for changing state according to the state of neighboring cells. Nevertheless, even this simple model can give rise to some extremely complex behavior.

The CAs used in games will have rules based on various physical models to determine the amount of heat, air, water, or smoke that is transferred between neighboring cells. If we run the rules quickly enough on a sufficient number of cells, water will flow downhill and find level ground, gently heated air will form convection currents, and strongly heated air will burn objects and, in turn, be heated by the burning objects.

In a three-dimensional array of cubic cells, there are three possible definitions of 'neighbor' cells:

- The six cells that share a face with the central cell.
- Those 6, plus another 12 that share an edge with the central cell.
- Those 18, plus another 8 that share a corner with the central cell.

Surprisingly, the rules that are used for physics simulations give almost the same results, whichever of the three definitions we use. Of course, the first version is far simpler, and there is only one type of neighbor cell, rather than three. For this reason, it is far easier to only consider as neighbors the six cells that share a face with the central cell.

First, choose the physical size of a CA cell. For human-size games, we decided to use cubes that are half a meter across. Any bigger, and a CA cell of air will not fit inside a narrow passageway. Smaller cubes give higher resolution and allow for smaller pipes, narrower gaps, and so on—but the extra space and processing is expensive. Different scales of games will naturally require a different size of CA cell; however, because most games are set on a human scale, for convenience, this gem will assume a scale of half-meter cube cells in its examples.

Another important consideration in a human-size game is how to model thin walls. Most internal house walls and doors are only a few centimeters thick. They will stop water flow, slow fire down, and stop smoke and air spreading, so they must be modeled in some way. Modeling them conventionally by using many small cells, and marking those occupied by the wall as solid, would require using cells of no more than about 10 cm across, which requires 125 times as many cells—an extremely expensive option.

Two possible solutions present themselves. One method, used by the first of the *X-Com* series of games in their impressive and innovative use of CAs [XCom], is to model the faces between the cells as entities, as well as modeling the cells themselves. So walls, floors, and ceilings always lie between two cells, along cell faces. This works quite well, but it does mean that there are now two distinct classes of objects—things that fill a whole cube (e.g., rock, dirt, furniture, or tall grass) and things that sit between two cells (e.g., walls, floorboards, short grass, or doors). This creates annoying special cases in the code used to model substances and their interactions, and causes code replication between the two types (spaghetti code). However, if this model fits, then it is a viable one, and it is fairly intuitive—the internal representation of objects matches their rendered shape fairly closely.

The other solution is one that retains its generality without resorting to many tiny cells. Rather than aligning cubic cells on a fixed grid, we allow the edges between cells to move about a bit according to the contents. This allows a thin wall to be chopped into half-meter squares, and each square lives in a cell. Because the walls are only a few centimeters thick, we expand the neighboring cells to take up the extra space. Even though the cells are no longer aligned on a grid, the CA code itself does not know or care what shape the objects it represents are. As far as the CA physics are concerned, everything is still half a meter thick. Most of the work in making things look otherwise is in the rendering, rather than in the CA routines. It is the job of the rendering to ensure that water goes all the way to the wall's mesh and not just to the edge of the CA cube, which would leave a large gap. The only things that need to spread adaptively like this are volumetric effects, such as smoke, fire, and water. When drawing a cell with one of these effects, the renderer needs to check each neighboring cell to see if its polygonal shape is smaller than the usual half-meter cube. If it is, it expands the size of the volumetric effect to fill the space.

In this scheme, a one-meter-wide corridor with thin wooden walls is represented by a plane of 'wood' cells, a plane of 'air' cells, and then a plane of 'wood' cells. Since the centers of the cells are each half a meter away from each other, the total apparent width from wall to wall is still one meter. Of course, the graphical representation of the world still shows that the 'cubes' of wood are not cubes at all, but flat planes a few centimeters thick; and this is the representation that will be used for any collision detection. But the distinction makes very little difference to the things that are modeled with the CA. Because these entities are fairly amorphous, the difference between what is rendered (a one-meter gap) and what is actually being modeled (a half-meter gap) is very hard for the player to see. Again, accuracy is sacrificed for speed wherever the game can get away with it.

The next factor to consider is a gameplay decision—the difference between using passive scenery and active scenery.

Passive Scenery

In this system, as far as the CA is concerned, the scenery is inert—it is not affected by the actions of the CA in any way. This is the simpler of the two representations, but it still allows discrete objects, such as the ubiquitous oil drum and crate, to float away on rivers of water or to explode or burn when heated by fire.

Because the CA only knows about cells, not polygons, the scenery must be converted into a cell representation—usually as a preprocessing step. These cells are simply marked as inert volumes that confine the actions of the CAs. Of course, the scenery is usually a collection of arbitrary polygons and is not aligned to cell boundaries. But the things being modeled with CAs are so amorphous that this difference does not matter in practice. As long as each solid polygonal wall is converted into a continuous wall of CA cells, water will not flow through and break the illusion.

Even in this system, special cases should be made for doors that can be opened and other animate or moving objects. When doors are opened, they should remove (sliding doors) or move (swinging doors) the solid cells that represent them so that water and/or fire can move through them.

Active Scenery

The far more versatile and adventurous option is to have the scenery modeled by the CA as well. This opens up the 'totally destructible world' concept that many designers are looking to as the next big thing in games, though this concept is not truly new in computer games [XCom].

In this system, rather than simply being cells of inert material, scenery is modeled by its actual properties, such as temperature, flammability, and so on. As the cells modeled with CA change their state according to the physical rules of the CA, the graphics engine changes how it renders the associated polygonal objects (e.g., sooty, damaged, etc.)

In the latter case, the graphics engine can either be of the 'Geo-Mod' type [RedFaction], or the object itself can simply have been specially marked as destructible and have an alternative, 'broken' graphical representation.

The Octree

Those considering implementing these CA methods will have quickly noticed that storing half-meter cells for even a modest-size level consumes a huge amount of memory, and the processing and memory bandwidth requirements become severe. The approach to doing this efficiently is to not store or process cells that are not participating in any interesting activities—notably inert walls and/or air at (standard) ambient temperature and pressure (STP).

An octree is ideally suited to storing this arrangement, specifically a dynamically allocated octree. In any implementation of the octree, remember that the most common operation in a CA is "find the cell next to me," so it makes sense to optimize for this type of operation when implementing the octree. If this request is made and there is no neighboring cell in the octree, it is assumed that the neighboring cell is air at STP. The physical simulations are carried out accordingly; and if they result in the 'missing' cell becoming significantly different from STP, a cell with the new properties is created and inserted in the octree. When an air cell returns to within a certain tolerance of STP, it is deleted from the octree and is no longer processed.

The octree holding CA cells can also be useful as a general-purpose octree. Many games use octrees to optimize collision detection and visibility culling, and there is no reason the octree cannot fulfill both roles and hold objects not directly related to the CA. A fairly easy adaptation to the search algorithms allows the octree to become a 'loose octree' [Ulrich00], which has several other advantages over a conventional octree. This does not change its behavior when dealing with the CA aspect of its behavior, since all CA cells are aligned to regular intervals and have a fixed size.

Practical Physics

The main thing to remember when writing CA physics routines is to keep things simple. It is surprisingly easy to write very simple routines that take major physical shortcuts, yet look perfectly natural to the player. As long as the basics of conservation of mass and energy are retained—which is frequently optional—most of the other code deals with keeping the simulations stable.

The major problem we encountered during implementation was finding good, simple models of various physical features. Most of the standard references deal with the application of Navier-Stokes equations for various materials and implementing them with as little error as possible. This enormously complicates the code, and most of the academic and commercial literature is concerned with these error reductions. For games, what is required is simplicity, not accuracy. Most of the time, finding implementations involved getting only the general feel of the behavior from the literature.

Core Processing Model

Most of the properties simulated by the CA work in similar ways. To illustrate these common methods, here is a very simple fluid simulation that just tries to achieve even distribution of pressure throughout the available space. Even this simplified model is very useful for air and fluid modeling.

```
for ( neigh = each neighbor cell )
{
    if ( neigh->Material->IsInert() ) continue;
    float DPress = cell->Pressure - neigh->Pressure;
    float Flow = cell->Material->Flow * DPress;
    Flow = clamp ( Flow,
        cell->Pressure / 6.0f,
        -neigh->Pressure / 6.0f );
    cell->NewPressure -= Flow;
    neigh->NewPressure += Flow;
}
```

The clamp() operation is performed to prevent NewPressure from going negative. The division by six is because there are six neighbor cells. In practice, even more damping might be needed to retain stability and prevent small oscillations, such as waves on the surface of water, from becoming unrealistic oscillations.

Conventionally, once all the cells have been processed in this way, the NewPressure values are copied to the Pressure values. This double-buffering is necessary, rather than simply writing directly to Pressure at the end of the routine. Otherwise, pressure will be transmitted extremely fast (sometimes instantly) in the direction that the cells are updated, and much slower in the reverse directions. This produces obvious asymmetry in heat distribution, water flow, and other processes.

The double visit to each cell can hurt performance considerably, especially as the second visit is simply a copy, and will be limited by memory bandwidth on most modern CPUs. A better method is to store the last turn that a cell was processed. When subsequently processing that cell, the turn number is checked; and if it is earlier than the current turn, the copy is done. Although slightly odd-looking, this is in fact much quicker than scanning the whole array of cells twice. The code becomes:

```
if ( cell->Turn != CurrentTurn )
{
    cell->Turn = CurrentTurn;
    cell->Pressure = cell->NewPressure;
}
for ( neigh = each neighbor cell )
{
    if ( neigh->Material->IsInert() ) continue;
    if ( neigh->Turn != CurrentTurn )
    {
        neigh->Turn = CurrentTurn;
        neigh->Pressure = neigh->NewPressure;
    }
    // same physics code as before
}
```

Air

This simple model works well for uniform redistribution of air pressure. At first glance, this is not something that is frequently modeled in games. But in fact, it is one of the most common effects—explosions and their effects on things. An explosive is simply a lump of material that produces a huge amount of air in a very short time. They can be modeled through the following steps. First, find the nearest CA cell to the center of an exploding grenade. Second, add a large number to the cell's pressure. Third, let the CA propagate the pressure through the world. Damage is done to the surroundings by either high absolute pressures or high pressure differences—in reality, both do different kinds of damage to different objects; but that is usually unnecessary complication for the purposes of a game.

The advantages of this method of modeling over conventional ones is that line-of-sight is handled automatically. Explosions in confined spaces are far more deadly at a certain range than explosions in open spaces because there is less space for the pressure to dissipate. In addition, it shows that pure line-of-sight is not protection enough from explosions—they do go around corners and obstructions to a certain degree.

Because the simulation of the flow of air is qualitatively correct to the human eye, debris and small objects can be carried along with the explosion; you don't have to worry about the illusion being shattered by debris going the wrong way or through solid walls.

Water

Water is only slightly more complex than air. The obvious distinction is that air expands to fill the available space with cells changing pressure to do so, while water stays at the bottom of its container and is incompressible.

In fact, the easiest way to simulate the transmission of pressure through water is to make it slightly compressible. This means pressure can be stored as a slight excess mass of water in the cell, above what the cell's volume should be able to hold. In practice, the amount of compression needed is tiny—allowing just 1% more water per cell per cube height is easily enough. In a static body of water whose cells can normally contain 1.00 liter of water each, the cells at the top will contain 1.00 liter, the ones under them will contain 1.01 liters, the cells under those will contain 1.02 liters, and so on to the bottom. This tiny amount of compression will be completely unnoticeable to the player, but it has enough dynamic range to allow all the usual properties of liquids. For example, the levels of water in two containers joined by a submerged pipe will be the same, even if water is poured into one of them; it will flow through the pipe to the other container.

```
if ( neighbor cell is above this one )
{
    if ( ( cell->Mass < material->MaxMass ) ||
```

```
            ( neigh->Mass < material->MaxMass ) )
      {
          Flow = cell->Mass - material->MaxMass;
      }else{
          Flow = cell->Mass - neigh->Mass
                  - material->MaxCompress;
          Flow *= 0.5f;
      }
  }
  else if ( neighbor cell is below this one )
  {
      if ( ( cell->Mass < material->MaxMass ) ||
           ( neigh->Mass < material->MaxMass ) )
      {
          Flow = material->MaxMass - neigh->Mass;
      }else{
          Flow = cell->Mass - neigh->Mass
       + material->MaxCompress;
          Flow *= 0.5f;
      }
  }
  else    // neighbor is on same level
  {
      Flow = ( cell->Mass - neigh->Mass ) * 0.5f;
  }
```

This Flow value is then scaled and clamped according to some measure of the maximum speed that the fluid can flow, allowing some fluids to appear more viscous than others, and to prevent any resulting masses from going negative.

The two cases of code for the water model deal with different situations. The first case is where one of the two cells is not full of water—such as on the surface of a body of water or if the water is splashing or falling (e.g., in a waterfall). Here, the behavior is simple—water flows downward to fill the lower cell of the two to the value Max-Mass—the mass of water that can be contained by a single cell's volume. In the previous example, the mass is one liter of water.

The second case is where both cells are full of water, or perhaps a bit over-full, such as in the middle of the body of water. Here, the flow acts to try to make sure that the upper cell has exactly MaxCompress more water than the lower cell. MaxCompress is the amount of 'extra' water that can be fitted in because of compression. In the previous example, it would be the mass of 0.01 liters of water.

Flow

So far the air and water models have ignored a fairly important property of any liquid or gas—its speed of flow. We have simply taken the difference in pressures between two cells and used that to move mass around. This is fine for relatively static environments that we wish to bring to a stable state, such as uniform air pressure or water finding its level. Many games will only use these simple properties for all the gameplay and realism they need.

However, what happens in real life is that water and air have momentum (which equals flow times mass), and the difference in pressure only influences the flow between cells; it does not rigidly set it. Storing momentum or flow is important when modeling waves, flowing rivers, and air currents. Although rivers can flow in models without momentum, they have a very visible slope of at least 10°, which looks very bizarre.

To model momentum or speed of flow during each processing step, the difference in masses determines the pressure gradient, as before. However, instead of changing the masses of the cells directly, the pressure gradient only alters the flow between the cells. The flow then changes the masses in the cells. The code is slightly more complex because flow is a three-dimensional vector and not a scalar like mass.

There are two possible ways to think about flow. The first is to think of a flow vector as being the flow through the center of the cell. This is possibly the most intuitive model—the flow and the mass of the cell are both measured at its center. However, in this case, the flow is affected by the pressure differential between the two neighboring cells, which in turn determines how mass flows from one neighboring cell to the other. Note the slightly odd result that, for a particular cell, the flow stored in it is not affected by the mass in the cell itself, but only by its neighbors. Nor does it change the mass of the cell, but only the mass of its neighbors' cells. This is a slightly surprising result; and in some cases, this can lead to odd behavior.

It is more useful to think of each component of the flow vector as being the flow between two adjacent nodes—from the 'current' node to the node in the positive relevant direction. Thus, the flow vector $\mathbf{F}$ stored at cell (x, y, z) is interpreted as meaning that $\mathbf{F}_x$ is the flow from cell (x, y, z) to cell $(x + 1, y, z)$; $\mathbf{F}_y$ is the flow from cell (x, y, z) to cell $(x, y + 1, z)$; and, similarly, for $\mathbf{F}_z$. The 'meaning' of the vector $\mathbf{F}$ is now not as intuitive, but the physical model does seem more sensible. In practice, this is the most common model; but either model can be used for simulation with appropriate adjustment of the various constants.

The most important step in this model is to carefully control oscillations. Not only does this model allow waves, but it also tends to encourage them to build up, and sufficient damping must be applied to the flow by introducing a simple friction coefficient. Otherwise, waves can build up higher and higher instead of dying down, and the liquid or gas starts to do very odd things indeed.

It is worth mentioning that, although one of the most common applications of flow is in rivers, in most 'human-size' games, large bodies of water, such as lakes and rivers, are frequently far too large to participate in gameplay. Their behavior will stay fairly constant whatever the player does; and if they do change, they will do so in highly constrained ways. They do not usually require the flexibility of a CA and are often far better modeled and rendered in more-conventional ways. We can use pre-animated meshes, collision models, and scripted events. However, there are many other genres that operate on larger scales and will want to properly simulate rivers with a CA.

Heat

Transmitting heat through the environment, whether from burning objects or from other sources, happens through three separate mechanisms: conduction, convection, and radiation.

Conduction

Conduction is the simplest mechanism to simulate. Neighboring cells pass heat energy between each other so that eventually they reach the same temperature. This is complicated because different materials are heated by different amounts by the same energy—called the specific heat capacity (SHC), which is usually measured in J/kg°C. If a hot cell made of water (high SHC and hard to heat up) is next to a colder cell made of the same mass of iron (low SHC), equilibrium will be reached at somewhere very close to the original temperature of the water, not at the average of the two temperatures. This is because when a given amount of energy is transferred from the water to the iron, the water's temperature drops far less than the iron's temperature rises.

Note that the above example is true for the same *mass* of each substance. However, iron has a far greater density than water; and therefore, for the same *volume*, they have very similar heat capacities.

```
// Find current heat capacities.
float HCCell = cell->material->SHC * cell->Mass;
float HCNeigh = neigh->material->SHC * neigh->Mass;
float EnergyFlow = neigh->Temp - cell->Temp;
// Convert from heat to energy
if ( EnergyFlow > 0.0f )
    EnergyFlow *= HCNeigh;
else
    EnergyFlow *= HCCell;
// A constant according to cell update speed.
// Usually found by trial and error.
EnergyFlow *= ConstantEnergyFlowFactor;
neigh->Temp -= EnergyFlow / HCNeigh;
cell->Temp += EnergyFlow / HCCell;
// Detect and kill oscillations.
if (((EnergyFlow>0.0f)&&(neigh->Temp<cell->Temp))||
    ((EnergyFlow<=0.0f)&&(neigh->Temp>cell->Temp)))
{
    float TotalEnergy = HCCell * cell->Temp +
                    HCNeigh * neigh->Temp;
    float AverageTemp = TotalEnergy /
                    ( HCCell + HCNeigh );
    cell->Temp = AverageTemp;
                    neigh->Temp = AverageTemp;
}
```

The code at the end is necessary if two materials with very different SHCs are side by side. In this case, the temperatures of the two can oscillate violently and can grow out of control. The physically correct solution is to integrate the transfer of heat over time. However, this approach simply finds the weighted average temperature, which is the temperature that the system would reach eventually. It is less accurate, but looks perfectly natural and is quite a bit quicker to execute. Importantly, it obeys the law of conservation of energy, so any artifacts are purely temporary. The longer-term state is the same as a more realistic simulation.

Convection

Convection is the phenomenon of heat rising. Hot areas of fluid, such as air or water, are less dense than cold areas, and thus try to rise. This can be simulated by incorporating temperature into the model of water or air. If a flow model is being used, the flow will be influenced by the relative temperatures of cells as well as their relative pressures. Otherwise, convection does not work very well, though its effects can be faked as described in the section on fire.

Radiation

Hot things glow. They emit light at various wavelengths, which travels in straight lines, hits other surfaces, and in turn heats them up. This effect is very important physically, but unfortunately it is also extremely expensive to model. Each source of heat must effectively shoot many rays out from itself and heat up whatever they hit.

Radiative heat modeling is very similar to the radiosity modeling that is used when creating lightmaps for many current games. Both are extremely expensive to model in runtime, even crudely, though there are some cunning methods that use a heavy amount of approximation to improve the speed of radiative heat modeling. Even with these algorithms, modeling even a fraction of the radiative heat seems like a prohibitive amount of work for a game. These algorithms are also extremely complex and do not involve the standard cell-to-cell interactions that model all the other physical properties mentioned. For both these reasons, we won't discuss them here.

Fire

The physics of burning materials is frequently extremely complex. There are multiple parts that burn at different rates and heats, and there are also different phases of material involved in the process.

To perform the calculations in real-time, the material models used during the process need to be trimmed down to their minimum; and for each material, an appropriate model must be chosen that emphasizes the main characteristic.

Of the many models considered, the one that finally seems to give the best results for the least amount of effort is a quadratic approximation of an exponential graph. This graph shows how much heat energy is released per unit of time when a substance burns at a certain temperature. There is a maximum amount of energy that can be released, no matter how hot the fire gets. But even at relatively cool temperatures, a lot of heat is released. This explains why open fires tend to start small, rapidly grow to a certain size, and then not grow any bigger, yet burn for a long time, despite ample availability of fuel. They are simply not generating enough heat energy to compensate for the heat lost to the environment (which is directly proportional to the temperature).

```
float Temp = cell->Temp - material->Flashpoint;
// Damage the cell.
CellDamage = Temp * material->BurnRate;
float Burn;
// Convert to actual burning value.
if ( Temp > material->MaxBurn * 2 )
    Burn = material->MaxBurn;
else
    Burn = ( 1.0f - ( 0.25f * Temp / material->MaxBurn ) ) * Temp;
ASSERT ( Burn <= material->MaxBurn );
ASSERT ( Burn >= 0.0f );
// And heat the cell up from the burning.
cell->Temp += Burn * material->BurnTemp;
```

Note that the damage done to a cell is proportional to its actual temperature, not how much heat is generated by burning. This allows materials that burn at low temperatures to nevertheless be far more severely damaged if exposed to high temperatures. By varying the factors MaxBurn and BurnTemp, burning anything can be simulated—paper, wood, oil, gunpowder, or high explosives.

Of course, one of the major aspects of fire is that it is hot, and thus it relies heavily on the modeling of heat flow by the three methods discussed previously. In real-life fires, convection and radiation are incredibly important to their behavior. Convection makes fires spread vertically far easier than spreading horizontally, such as across floors, and leads to distinctive 'walls of fire' in burning buildings. Radiation concentrates fire in corners of rooms, causing fire to spread up the corners of the room first.

Sadly, radiative heat, as mentioned above, is extremely hard to model, and convection, although slightly more straightforward, requires large numbers of air cells around the source of the fire to be modeled and updated, which is expensive. It would be far better to find some hacks that simulate some of these features without incurring the considerable expense involved.

A hack for convection effects is simply to make conduction of heat far easier in an upward direction. In real life, a section of burning wall heats the air beside it, which rises and heats the section of wall higher up. This makes it far easier for the flames to spread upward. Using this hack, conduction of heat is made artificially asymmetrical. In the model presented above, a single factor—ConstantEnergyFlowFactor—was used for heat conduction for all six neighbors of a cell. Instead of this, a higher figure is used when conducting heat upward and a lower figure when conducting heat downward.

A hack for radiation is more difficult, but it is possible that some precomputation could be done using the same techniques as radiosity to decide which parts of a room would be more susceptible to fire because of the feedback effects of radiative heat. One possibility is computing the hemispherical occlusion term [Hemispherical01] and using that to boost the heat generated by fire—generally around edges and corners.

A factor that might not be immediately obvious is that these hacks are far more controllable than any realistic solution. Convection in real life is a notoriously chaotic system, and small changes in conditions can cause it to adopt very different patterns of flow. This can make designing gameplay around the effect very tricky indeed. What game and level designers usually require is a high degree of control and pre-dictability to carefully create exciting set-pieces for the player to experience. The hacks presented above are far more predictable and linear in their behavior, which is usually a far more desirable quality in a game than absolute realism.

Dynamic Update Rates

The natures of some of the physical properties being simulated here require high update rates to maintain realism. The flow of any property from one cell to another can only proceed at a maximum speed of one cell per update cycle. Fire might spread quickly—at meters per second or faster. Water spilling from a container might move even faster—at tens of meters per second. Explosions require extremely high update rates—real-life explosion shock waves spread at the speed of sound, roughly 340 m/s.

Simulating all of the above implies that update rates of 680 cycles per second could be required. This is an awesome speed, and it seems unlikely that any current platform can sustain these sorts of update rates for a decent-size game world.

As with the optimization of not storing or processing cells at STP, it is possible to use the octree to reduce the update rates for cells that do not require fast updates to maintain realism.

When a cell is processed, it decides how fast it needs to be updated to maintain a good simulation, based on its current state. Cells involved in explosions require high update rates; cells holding flowing water, burning objects, or high heat need medium update rates; cells with fairly static water require lower update rates; and cells that hold scenery at ambient temperature require no processing at all until disturbed.

This speed of processing is then stored in the cell and is also passed up the octree hierarchy, each level being marked so that it is processed at the highest update rate of any of its children. This then allows the update routine to start at the top node of the octree and recurse down the tree. At each level, it decides if the current node would require processing of the all the child nodes.

One point to note is that this system only works if the update rates are quantized to powers of two. For example, if a child node needs to be updated every third turn, but the parent node is marked as being updated every second turn, every sixth turn the child node needs updating, but the parent does not. Because of the traversal algorithm's early-out path, the child does not get updated this time, and in the end only gets updated every sixth turn. Quantizing update rates to powers of two solves this problem and also allows some slight extra storage efficiency.

An obvious consequence of this variable update rate is that the physics routines need to be able to handle variable update rates as well. So far, all the code has assumed that it will be run at a set speed, and that the physical constants will be adjusted to give good results for that speed. With variable update rates, the physically correct behavior is to integrate the various equations over the given period. However, one of the purposes of the variable update rate is to choose an update rate that ensures the cells have a fairly constant behavior over the update interval.

This assumption makes integration simple. We just multiply the given behavior flow or rate by the time period since the last update. This slight extra complication is more than offset by the savings in processing time and memory bandwidth because of the huge reduction in the number of cells updated per second.

In many cases where the mathematics are simple, it might be more efficient to actually perform the integration. The extra accuracy of the simulation will then allow the use of an even lower update rate, further improving speed overall.

An unexpected artifact of using a variable update rate can occur when neighboring cells have very different update rates. Since one cell is being updated much more frequently than its neighbor, it can change rapidly before the other cell has time to react. The solution is to limit the maximum difference in update rates of adjacent cells. Every time a cell is processed, as well as exchanging temperature, heat, and similar information with neighboring cells, it also ensures that those cells are being updated at least a quarter as fast as itself. We found this factor purely by experimentation. Using a factor of two causes too many cells to have their update rates raised pointlessly by nearby events, when in fact nothing exciting is happening to them. Using a factor of eight or more allows more possible artifacts, but does not reduce the processing load appreciably. As with the many arbitrary factors that are found by pure experimentation, others should experiment to find what works best.

Conclusion

The use of CA methods allows the simulation of a wide range of real-world effects and situations rarely seen in games today. They allow the player to interact with them fully, flexibly, and logically, without the limitations of prescripting. This opens the way for more inventive puzzles, more lateral thinking by the player, more freedom to experiment, more realistic rendering, and overall better immersion in the game world as a real place, rather than as a collection of polygonal entities.

References

[CFD] There are innumerable references to the field of computational fluid dynamics. Unfortunately, most assume graduate physics knowledge or an extremely firm grasp of 3D calculus. One of the more comprehensible of these can be found at http://www.efunda.com/formulae/fluids/overview.cfm.

[Conway] http://www.dmoz.org/Computers/Artificial_Life/Cellular_Automata/ Conway's_Game_of_Life/.

[Hemispherical01] "Advanced Shading and Lighting," presentation at Meltown 2001: pp. 22–35. Available online at *http://www.microsoft.com/mscorp/corpevents/ meltdown2001/ppt/DXGLighting.ppt.*

[LorensenCline87] Lorensen, W. E. and Cline, H. E., "Marching Cubes: A High Resolution 3D Surface Reconstruction Algorithm," *Computer Graphics Proceedings* (SIGGRAPH 1987), Vol. 21, No. 4: pp. 163–169.

[RedFaction] *Red Faction,* developed by Volition, Inc. Published by THQ, Inc., 2000.

[Ulrich00] Ulrich, Thatcher, "Loose Octrees," *Game Programming Gems,* Charles River Media, Inc., 2000.

[XCom] *X-Com: UFO Defense* (U.S.) or *X-Com: Enemy Unknown* (U.K.), Microprose, 1994, http://www.codogames.com/UFOUnknownDefense.htm.

2.7

Coping with Friction in Dynamic Simulations

Miguel Gomez

You're at a playground, holding a block of wood. You stand at the base of a slide and shove the block of wood up the ramp. The block slides to the middle of the ramp, reverses direction, and slides back down to the bottom of the ramp.

You place the block at the fulcrum of a balanced seesaw and grab one of the ends. As you slowly tilt the seesaw, the block remains stationary at first, but then begins to slide down the seesaw. As you increase the tilt, the block slides faster, and eventually ends up at your feet again.

Can your physics model for friction handle all these cases correctly? For extra credit, can it do all this work without resorting to strange magic numbers and tolerance checking?

Modeling dry frictional forces is an important aspect of simulating mechanical systems. However, standard numerical integration schemes can fail, since friction is discontinuous with respect to velocity. This gem uses some simple one-dimensional examples to provide an intuitive understanding of the Coulomb model of friction and to illustrate numerical problems that arise when simulating frictional systems. A three-dimensional formulation is given, and a simple numerical method for computing the trajectory of an irrotational object, sliding and sticking under friction over a surface of constant incline, is presented. Important issues in extending this method to curved surfaces and polygonal surfaces are also discussed.

Coulomb Friction

There are two types of dry friction: *dynamic* (or *kinetic*) *friction*, which acts opposite to *existing relative motion* between two objects at their region of contact, and *static friction* (also known as *stiction*), which equalizes forces *tangent* to the surface that would otherwise initiate relative motion at a *stationary* region of contact. The following examples illustrate the essential differences between static and dynamic friction.

A System with Dynamic Friction

For our first example, suppose a block is placed on a flat surface. At time $t = 0$, it is given an initial velocity $v_0 > 0$ in the x^+ (positive x) direction, as in Figure 2.7.1. (Note that in general, velocity is a vector. Since we are working in one dimension, scalar values suffice.) Experiments show that this block will decelerate at a *constant* rate until it comes to rest at some time t_s, after which it remains stationary. Furthermore, the rate of deceleration is independent of the block's mass, m, and is proportional to the gravitational acceleration, g. If instead we had given the block an initial speed $v_0 < 0$ in the x^- direction, friction would have again decelerated the block until it had stopped. We can conclude that friction always acts opposite the velocity, v, of the block and that friction exerts no force on the block when $v = 0$. This implies that a correct formulation of dynamic friction for this one-dimensional system is:

$$f_d = \begin{cases} -\operatorname{sgn}(v)\mu_d N & \text{when } v \neq 0 \\ 0 & \text{when } v = 0, \end{cases} \tag{2.7.1}$$

where μ_d is the *coefficient of dynamic friction* and N is the *magnitude* of the *normal force;* that is, the force exerted on the object by the surface in the normal direction (z^+ in this example). Equation 2.7.1 constitutes a one-dimensional formulation of dynamic *Coulomb friction* [Stewart00]. Even though our block exists in the x and z

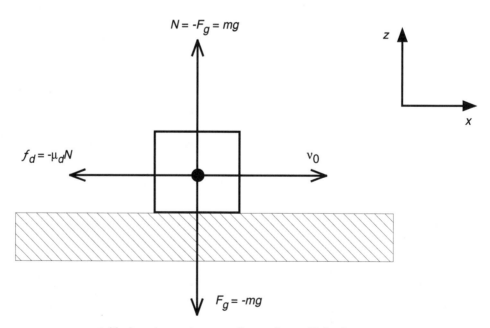

FIGURE 2.7.1 *A block set in motion on a flat surface will decelerate at a constant rate until it comes to rest. This rate of deceleration is proportional to gravitational acceleration by the coefficient of dynamic friction* μ_d.

axes, friction is represented as a scalar value, so it's okay in this simple example to think of friction as a one-dimensional force.

In this example we assume the block has no motion along the z direction; therefore, the net force in this direction is zero, and N must be exactly *equal and opposite* the gravitational force *mg*. By Newton's second law we know that $x(t)$, the x position of the block as a function of time t, satisfies the system of differential equations:

$$\frac{dx(t)}{dt} = v(t) \tag{2.7.2a}$$

$$\frac{d^2x(t)}{dt^2} = \frac{dv(t)}{dt} = -\,\text{sgn}\big(v(t)\big)\mu_d g \tag{2.7.2b}$$

Suppose again that $v_0 > 0$. Since v will not change sign before the block stops, the sgn(v) term can be omitted, and Equation 2.7.2b can be integrated directly to yield an explicit formula for $v(t)$:

$$\int_{v_0}^{v(t)} dv = -\int_0^t \mu_d g \, dt \Rightarrow v(t) = v_0 - \mu_d g t. \tag{2.7.3}$$

If the initial x-position of the block is $x_0 = 0$, integrating Equation 3 gives

$$\int_0^{x(t)} dx = \int_0^t v_0 - \mu_d g t \, dt \Rightarrow x(t) = v_0 t - \tfrac{1}{2}\mu_d g t^2. \tag{2.7.4}$$

The exact time and position at which the block comes to rest are:

$$t_s = \frac{v_0}{\mu_d g} \tag{2.7.5a}$$

and

$$x_s = x(t_s) = \frac{1}{2}\frac{v_0^2}{\mu_d g} \tag{2.7.5b}$$

respectively. For all times $t \geq t_s$, the block has stopped; in other words, the solution is simply:

$$x(t) \equiv x_s, \text{ and } v(t) \equiv 0. \tag{2.7.6a, b}$$

The position, velocity, and acceleration of the block over time are plotted in Figure 2.7.2. Notice that the acceleration of the block has a jump discontinuity (an instantaneous change in value) at t_s. *This discontinuity must be taken into account when we develop a numerical method for computing the trajectory of the block.*

Coefficients of friction depend on both the *types* of surfaces and on the *condition* of the surfaces in contact. See [Beer62] for a table of static friction coefficients for some common surfaces.

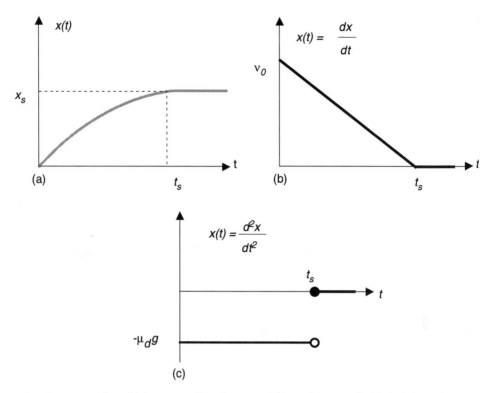

FIGURE 2.7.2   *Plots of (a) position, (b) velocity, and (c) acceleration of a block sliding along a flat surface subject to friction. Acceleration goes to 0 instantaneously when v = 0 at time t$_s$.*

A System with Static Friction

Suppose now that our block is placed on a platform at an incline $\theta > 0$; and for simplicity, let the x-axis be aligned with the platform and the z-axis point in the normal direction. Assume that the block is initially stationary, as in Figure 2.7.3. For most, if not all dry surfaces, there exists some angle $\phi_s > 0$ below which the block remains stationary and above which the block begins to slide. Static friction can therefore be thought of as a *constraint* force that must satisfy:

$$f_s \le \mu_s N, \qquad\qquad\qquad\qquad (2.7.7)$$

where is the *coefficient of static friction*.

First, suppose that the incline of the platform is at an angle $\theta < \phi_s$ so that the block is stationary. This implies that the frictional force is *equal and opposite* the x component of the gravitational force. When $\theta = \phi_s$, static friction is at its *maximum* possible value (the authors of [Pfeiffer92] refer to this state as "friction saturation") so that

$$f_s = \mu_s N. \qquad\qquad\qquad\qquad (2.7.8)$$

This implies the relationship

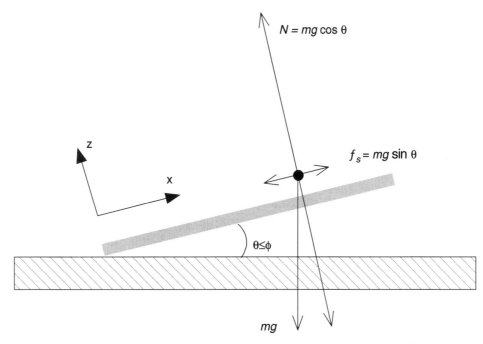

FIGURE 2.7.3   *Static friction keeps the block from sliding down a ramp.*

$$\frac{f}{N} = \frac{mg \sin \phi_s}{mg \cos \phi_s} \Rightarrow \mu_s = \tan \phi_s. \tag{2.7.9}$$

If the platform is then raised to an angle $\theta > \phi_s$, the force required to prevent motion exceeds the maximum possible static friction, and the block begins to slide.

Transitions Between Dynamic and Static Friction

Now, suppose that the block is launched at velocity $v_0 > 0$ up the ramp. By the above reasoning, if the ramp is at an incline $\theta \leq \phi_s$, the block will slide up the ramp, decelerating at a constant rate until it stops and then remains stationary. On the other hand, if $\theta > \phi_s$, static friction will not be sufficient to equalize gravity, so the block will slide up to an apex and then slide back down.

Notice also that if $\mu_d < \tan \phi < \mu_s$, then the block will be unstable when it is stationary. Even the slightest impulse will start the block sliding.

Numerical Methods

We want to implement these concepts in a practical simulation. Given an object moving along a surface, we must find some method of determining its position at each frame so it can be displayed.

It might seem that the explicit formula for $x(t)$ derived above could be used to calculate the exact position at the times we want to display the particle. Unfortunately, this approach only works for flat surfaces. For a general curved surface, an explicit formula cannot be found, so we are forced to find a time-stepping scheme that gives the position at subsequent times.

We'll start by implementing friction naïvely and see why discontinuity of acceleration is a real problem when implementing game code. Then, we'll change our friction model slightly to try to work around the acceleration problem. Last, we'll propose an altogether better mathematical model that takes care of these problems for us.

First Approach: Euler's Method

Consider the first example: a block sliding on a flat surface. Given the position $x(t)$ and velocity $v(t)$ at time t, we might try to calculate the position and velocity of the block at a later time, $t + h$, in the following way:

$$x\big(t + h\big) = x\big(t\big) + h v\big(t\big)$$ (2.7.10a)

$$v\big(t + h\big) = v\big(t\big) - h \, \mathrm{sgn}\big(v\big(t\big)\big)\mu_d g$$ (2.7.10b)

This intuitive approach is called Euler's method [Gerald97]. Due to its simplicity and speed, this is the integration method of choice for many game programmers.

Let $x_0 = 0$, $v_0 = 1$, $m = 1$, $\mu_d = 1$, $g = 9.81$, and $h = 0.02$. The exact solution indicates the block will come to rest after $t_s = 0.10194$ seconds at a position $x_s = 0.05097$ meters. Table 2.7.1 gives the numerical output of Euler's method for this initial value problem.

Table 2.7.1 Positions and Velocities Resulting from Euler's Method for a Block Sliding on a Flat Surface

t	$x(t)$	$v(t)$
0.00	0.00000	1.0000
0.02	0.02000	0.8038
0.04	0.03608	0.6076
0.06	0.04823	0.4114
0.08	0.05646	0.2152
0.10	0.06076	0.0190
0.12	0.06114	−0.1772
0.14	0.05760	0.0190
0.16	0.05798	−0.1772
0.18	0.05443	0.0190

Note: The numerical values *never converge* due to the discontinuity of acceleration at $v = 0$.

Numerical calculations nearly stop the block after about 0.1 seconds at 0.061 meters. Since Euler's method is only first-order accurate, some error should be expected. What is alarming, however, is that not only does v never converge to zero, but it oscillates about zero asymmetrically so that x actually *decreases* at a constant rate for times $t > t_s$. An animation would show the block turning around and moving back toward the origin!

It might seem practical to solve this problem by simply setting v to zero when its magnitude falls below some threshold $v_c > 0$. Unfortunately, tuning these types of 'magic numbers' so that a particular system looks intuitively correct is an art. Finding velocity thresholds that work for simulations involving several objects of different masses and friction coefficients requires a lot of time and testing. In essence, it's necessary to test each object affected by friction against every surface type on which it might possibly rest. We've simply traded one problem for another, less-tractable one. As we shall see later, velocity thresholds cause more serious problems when evaluating transitions between dynamic and static friction.

Second Approach: Reformulating Friction

In retrospect, it now seems obvious that Euler's method would fail for this problem. When v is 'small,' our integration method will cause v to overshoot zero and change sign. On the following step, acceleration is in the opposite direction, which causes v to change sign again. Since v oscillates asymmetrically about zero, the position gets a net translation every two steps.

Instead of fixing the numerical method, we might be tempted to modify our formulation so that friction is continuous at $v = 0$. One option is to replace the Coulomb formula with *viscous damping*:

$$f = -v\mu_d N. \tag{2.7.11}$$

Unfortunately, this formula will cause the block to decelerate too quickly at high speeds and not quickly enough at low speeds. Animations using this formula simply look unnatural.

Another possibility is to *regularize* friction (see [Abadie00] or [Stewart00]) so that

$$f = \begin{cases} -\dfrac{v}{v_c}\mu_d N & , \text{ when } |v| \le v_c \\ -\operatorname{sgn}(v)\mu_d N & , \text{ when } |v| > v_c , \end{cases} \tag{2.7.12}$$

for some velocity threshold $v_c > 0$. This formulation resolves the counterintuitive behavior observed at high speeds but has the same problems as viscous damping at low speeds. Furthermore, v_c is just another magic number that must be tuned to the particular system. More importantly, these alternate formulations cause problems when transitioning (either way) between dynamic and static friction.

Third Approach: Dealing with Nonsmoothness

It is possible to find a numerical method that works well, provided we understand what is going wrong. The trajectory $x(t)$ of our sample problem has two smooth domains (a function $x(t)$ is *smooth* if its first derivative is continuous and exists everywhere):

$$x\left(t\right) = \begin{cases} v_0 t - \frac{1}{2}\,\mathrm{sgn}\!\left(v\right)\mu_d g t^2 & , \text{ when } t < t_s \\ \quad\quad x_s & , \text{ when } t \geq t_s \end{cases} \tag{2.7.13}$$

The function $x(t)$ and its derivative $v(t)$ are both continuous at t_s, but acceleration $a(t)$, the first derivative of $v(t)$, is not. Euler's method, along with higher-order methods, assumes that the function $x(t)$ has a Taylor series on the interval over which we are integrating [Gerald97]. This system, however, *does not satisfy this property in a neighborhood of* t_s where v goes to zero and the discontinuity occurs. Therefore, any method that assumes a valid Taylor series for $x(t)$ will not converge to the correct solution.

Suppose that our current time is $t < t_s$ and that we want to calculate the position at some later time $t + h < t_s$. Over this interval, $x(t)$ *does* have a valid Taylor series, so we can expand $x(t + h)$ in h about t to get

$$x\left(t + h\right) = x\left(t\right) + h\frac{dx\left(t\right)}{dt} + \frac{1}{2}h^2 \frac{d^2 x\left(t\right)}{dt^2} = x\left(t\right) + hv\left(t\right) - \frac{1}{2}h^2\,\mathrm{sgn}\!\left(v\right)\mu_d g . \tag{2.7.14}$$

The Taylor series for $v(t + h)$ is

$$v\left(t + h\right) = v\left(t\right) + h\frac{dv\left(t\right)}{dt} = v\left(t\right) - h\,\mathrm{sgn}\!\left(v\right)\mu_d g . \tag{2.7.15}$$

Together, these two equations form a Taylor method [Gerald97]. Provided we integrate over time intervals $[t, t + h]$ that satisfy $t + h < t_s$, this method is *exact* for our block on a flat surface at any incline.

During any interval, we know that v will go to zero if the quantity

$$h_s = \frac{v}{\mathrm{sgn}\!\left(v\right)\mu_d g} \tag{2.7.16}$$

satisfies

$$0 \leq h_s \leq h . \tag{2.7.17}$$

If h_s satisfies this inequality at any particular step, we must set $v = 0$, and consider $x(t + h_s)$ the position of rest. In general, if the block has acceleration $a(t)$, our method has the form

$$x\left(t + h\right) = x\left(t\right) + hv\left(t\right) + \frac{1}{2}h^2 a\left(t\right) \tag{2.7.18a}$$

$$v(t + h) = v\left(t\right) + ha\left(t\right) \tag{2.7.18b}$$

At every step, we check to see if h_s satisfies

$$0 \le h_s = -\frac{v(t)}{a(t)} \le h. \tag{2.7.19}$$

When applied to our test system, this approach gives much better results. In fact, Table 2.7.2 shows that t_s and x_s are *exact*, but more importantly, $v(t) \equiv 0$ for $t \ge t_s$.

Table 2.7.2. Positions and Velocities Calculated with a Taylor Method

t	$x(t)$	$v(t)$
0.00000	0.00000	1.0000
0.02000	0.01804	0.8038
0.04000	0.03215	0.6076
0.06000	0.04234	0.4114
0.08000	0.04861	0.2152
0.10000	0.05095	0.0190
0.10194	**0.05097**	**0.0000**
0.12194	0.05097	0.0000

Note: Positions and velocities calculated with a Taylor method are exact for our test system. Calculating an intermediate time step h_s ensures that velocity goes to zero and stays there.

Transitioning Between Static and Dynamic Friction

The previous approach handles only dynamic friction. On slopes, we must evaluate whether or not a transition between static and dynamic friction will occur. When $v \ne 0$, friction is dynamic by definition, so we only need to consider these transitions when $v = 0$.

Recall the example of Figure 2.7.3. For inclines $\theta > \phi$, the block will decelerate to an apex, then slide back down. But for $\theta \le \phi_s$, it will stop at its apex and remain stationary. If the block is stationary and the forces on the block are changing over time, then we must periodically check to see if static friction can equalize tangential forces so that the block remains stationary. In other words, if the net tangential force does not satisfy the inequality

$$-\mu_s N \le F_t \le \mu_s N ; \tag{2.7.20}$$

then the block begins to slide.

There is an important subtlety, however, that must not be overlooked. When the block transitions from static to dynamic friction, its velocity is zero; so the direction of dynamic friction cannot be determined. Since the impending motion *will* be in the direction of F_t, dynamic friction must therefore act opposite to F_t.

It is now easy to see why velocity thresholds cause problems when transitioning from static to dynamic friction. Upon the first application of dynamic friction, velocity goes from zero to some value $v(t + h)$. If $|v(t + h)| < v_c$, our minimum allowable velocity, then v is set back to zero. However, since $a(t) \neq 0$, $x(t + h)$ will advance somewhat. If velocity consistently fails to rise above v_c, then the block will slowly creep down the slope at a constant speed. For any configuration of θ, a, and v_c, there exists some minimum time step $h_{\min}$ below which creep will occur.

A Three-Dimensional Formulation

We can now formulate dynamic friction in three dimensions:

$$\mathbf{f}_d = \begin{cases} -\mu_d N \hat{\mathbf{v}} & \text{when } \mathbf{v} \neq 0 \\ \\ -\mu_d N \hat{\mathbf{F}}_t & \text{when } \mathbf{v} = 0, \end{cases} \tag{2.7.21}$$

where $\hat{\mathbf{F}}_t$ is the direction of the tangential component of the net force on the object. This formulation is consistent for transitions from static to dynamic friction. Friction $\mathbf{f}_d$ is now a vector. We assume that velocity has no normal component so that the unit vector $\hat{\mathbf{v}}$ is tangent to the contact surface. The normal force is the vector $\mathbf{N} = N\mathbf{n}$, where $\mathbf{n}$ is the unit normal direction.

When $\mathbf{v} = 0$, static friction tries to counter tangential forces, and its magnitude must satisfy

$$f_s = \| \mathbf{f}_s \| \leq \mu_s N . \tag{2.7.22}$$

The interpolated Taylor method derived above will still work, provided we can accurately predict whether or not $\mathbf{v}$ goes to zero during the integration interval.

Due to the nonlinearity of the three-dimensional problem, we cannot solve for h_s exactly, so we must find some way of estimating its value. The time rate of change of the square of the magnitude of velocity is

$$\frac{d}{dt} \left\| \mathbf{v}(t) \right\|^2 = \frac{d}{dt} (\mathbf{v} \cdot \mathbf{v}) = 2\mathbf{v} \cdot \frac{d\mathbf{v}}{dt} = 2\mathbf{a} \cdot \mathbf{v} . \tag{2.7.23}$$

If we assume that the acceleration $\mathbf{a}$ and the *direction* of velocity is constant over the interval $[t, t + h]$, then only the magnitude of velocity changes over time. We can integrate Equation 2.7.23 to find h_s:

$$\int_t^{t+h} 2\mathbf{a} \cdot \mathbf{v} \, dt = 2\mathbf{a} \cdot \int_t^{t+h} \mathbf{v} \, dt = 2\mathbf{a} \cdot \left(\mathbf{x}(t + h) - \mathbf{x}(t) \right) = 2\mathbf{a} \cdot \Delta\mathbf{x} . \tag{2.7.24}$$

Since we are assuming the direction of $\mathbf{v}$ is constant and its magnitude decreases at a constant rate, we get

$$2\mathbf{a} \cdot \Delta\mathbf{x} = 2\mathbf{a} \cdot \tfrac{1}{2} \mathbf{v} h_s = \mathbf{a} \cdot \mathbf{v} h_s . \tag{2.7.25}$$

If this rate of change is negative, then we get

$$h_s = -\frac{\mathbf{v} \cdot \mathbf{v}}{\mathbf{a} \cdot \mathbf{v}} . \tag{2.7.26}$$

This reduces to the one-dimensional formula when **v** and **a** are in the same direction.

Geometric Issues

Smoothness

One common way to represent a two-dimensional surface is as a polygonal mesh. Another common representation is the heightfield, in which elevations of a surface are stored over a regularly spaced grid. Unfortunately, both of these representations can lead to convergence problems if *discontinuities in slope* are not properly dealt with.

Consider the example illustrated in Figure 2.7.4. When the block hits the slope, gravity will *instantaneously* change from acting solely along the normal direction to having a component opposite friction, and the net acceleration will experience a jump discontinuity. If this is not dealt with properly, it can lead to the same convergence problems described here.

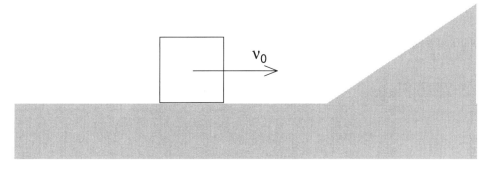

FIGURE 2.7.4 *A block sliding along a flat surface will experience a discontinuity in its acceleration when the slope suddenly changes.*

One possible remedy is to interpolate the position and velocity to the point at which the change in slope occurs. For a heightfield, this might be practical; but it could be inefficient for arbitrary polygonal meshes. This approach might also cause problems for an implementation that treats impacts (which involve instantaneous changes in *velocity*) generally.

Another possibility is to smooth the surface so that its directional derivative (see [Davis91]) is continuous. For a heightfield, this would require quadratic spline interpolation (see [Watt00]) along the x and y directions. For arbitrary polygonal meshes, a subdivision scheme might be required.

The best approach must be decided by the application developer, but the effects of discontinuities in acceleration on the convergence of the method should be kept in mind.

Curvature

Though we now have a good model for representing frictional forces operating on flat surfaces, extending this model onto curved surfaces is nontrivial. If you want to try to extend it, note the following: When the surface curves upward, integration will push the object into the slope and give v a component normal to the surface. This can be dealt with by simply resetting the position of the object and removing the normal component of velocity following the integration step.

When a surface curves downward, however, it must be decided whether or not the object should leave the surface. Although not very robust, using a velocity threshold on the normal component of velocity seems to be the most common approach. When using this approach, these thresholds must be adjusted to get the desired behavior.

Conclusion

We have used some simple one-dimensional examples to illustrate the Coulomb model of friction. We have also explored reasons why certain numerical methods are insufficient, and we have developed a simple but effective numerical method for computing the three-dimensional trajectory of an object sliding over a surface of constant incline. Now, go build yourself a playground!

References

[Abadie00] Abadie, Michel, "Dynamic Simulation of Rigid Bodies: Modeling of Frictional Contact," *Impacts in Mechanical Systems: Analysis and Modeling*, Springer-Verlag, 2000.

[Beer62] Beer, F. P. and Johnston, E. R., Jr., *Mechanics for Engineers: Statics and Dynamics*, McGraw-Hill, 1962.

[Davis91] Davis, H. F. and Snider, A. D, *Introduction to Vector Analysis*, 6th Edition, Wm. C. Brown Publishers, 1991.

[Gerald97] Gerald, C. F. and Wheatley, P. O., *Applied Numerical Analysis*, 6th Edition, Addison Wesley, 1997.

[Pfeiffer92] Pfeiffer, F. and Hajek, M., "Stick-Slip Motion of Turbine Blade-Dampers," *Philosophical Transactions: Physical Sciences and Engineering*, Nonlinear Dynamics of Engineering Systems, 1992: Vol. 338, No. 1651, pp. 503–517.

[Stewart00] Stewart, D., "Rigid-Body Dynamics with Friction and Impact," *SIAM Review*, 2000: Vol. 42, No. 1, pp.3–39.

[Watt00] Watt, A., *3D Computer Graphics*, 3rd Edition. Addison Wesley, 2000.

ARTIFICIAL INTELLIGENCE

Introduction

Steven Woodcock, Wyrd Wyrks

ferretman@gameai.com

Boy, do we have a treat waiting for you.

The gems presented here in the AI section of *Game Programming Gems 3* represent a great follow-up to the AI gems in previous books in the *Game Programming Gems* series. They cover the gamut of interesting AI topics, from architecting your game to allow for intricate expansions while avoiding hard-coded scripting, to ever-so-useful refinements on how to do path-finding for the characters who live in your game world. Each gem is a remarkable outpouring of the author's knowledge of the craft, with most of the gems being derived from the author's recent experiences in game AI development.

It is frankly amazing to this developer how the field of game AI has grown and become an integral part of the game-development cycle over the past few years. Recent polls have shown an enormous surge in the amount of time, development, and just plain CPU cycles devoted to the creation of good game AI. Quality game AI is no longer a "please don't impact the frame rate" issue—it's now a vital part of a game's development and viewed to be every bit as important as the graphics or sound. Whether this is simply because companies have the money to do AI *right,* or whether it's because they're looking for ways to distinguish themselves in an ever-more competitive market of 'me too' titles—it's a good sign of things to come. We'd like to think that these books and the AI gems presented in them have helped. With luck, so will the gems that follow.

Eight authors contributed to our section this time around, with gems that cover a remarkable breadth of AI applications. Table 3.0.1 shows how they overlap and build on each other, with several covering different aspects of the same problem in ways that can reinforce one another. For example, "Rectangle Navigation" (Board and Ducker) proposes a method for breaking the game world into areas and navigating through them with a variation of flocking; while "A Fast Approach to Navigation Meshes" (White) covers a similar technique that instead focuses on an implementation of A* and portals to connect the areas of the world together. Both approaches have their advantages and drawbacks, but together they describe powerful possibilities that are vital when dealing with games that contain huge maps and hundreds of characters.

Table 3.0.1 AI Gem Organization and Application

Gem	Architecture	Path Finding	Tactical Decisions	Terrain Analysis
Optimized Machine Learning with GoCap	x		x	
Area Navigation: Expanding the Path-Finding Paradigm		x		
Function Pointer-Based, Embedded Finite-State Machines	x			x
Terrain Analysis in an RTS—The Hidden Giant		x	x	x
An Extensible Trigger System for AI Agents, Objects, and Quests	x			
Tactical Path-Finding Using A*		x	x	x
A Fast Approach to Navigation Meshes		x		x
Choosing a Relationship Between Path-Finding and Collision	x	x		

One thing stands out in our collection of contributed gems: The game industry is rapidly shifting its attention away from experimentation with the so-called "academic" or "advanced" AI techniques, and is gravitating back toward working with tried-and-true principles. There are no neural networks or genetic algorithms presented this time around; these are valuable tools, but simply are not what most developers are using today. Whether it's terrain analysis or path-finding enhancements, the gems presented here build on techniques that are well known to any game developer—scripting, state machines, and A* path-finding. They might not be obvious at first glance; but after digesting each gem, the reader will almost certainly wonder, "Why didn't I think of that?"

This isn't because game developers are ignoring the techniques of the academic and the military worlds—far from it. The sessions at the Game Developers Conference and various discussion forums across the Web are a testament to the fact that game developers are always interested in learning new techniques no matter what their origins are. The difference is that they have very limited hardware, very limited budgets, very limited development cycles, and very limited resources. They simply *must* succeed, whether it means cheating or not. The techniques they use must therefore offer a clear and obvious benefit, or they simply will not get used—there isn't time. The academic and military worlds often don't have these restrictions, or have goals that are just plain different.

It is the hope of this developer and editor that the academic, military, and game programming worlds will continue to learn and adapt techniques from each other. It is in this spirit of mutual learning that the reader should go forth and carefully read the gems that follow, in the hopes that this book might light a path toward this goal.

3.1

Optimized Machine Learning with GoCap

Thor Alexander, Hard Coded Games

thor@hardcodedgames.com

Machine learning is an emerging technology that will make a big impact on the way games are made in the future. From a production standpoint, machine learning will bypass need for the thousands of lines of brittle, special-case AI logic that is used in many of today's games. Training a computer-controlled character by observing a human, expert player will bring great advances in the level of intelligence that can be displayed. Game designers will be able to role-play the personalities of a wide array of characters, which can be stored in libraries and then later imported into their games like traditional content assets.

This gem presents an optimized version of *GoCap*, a method we developed to train AI characters by observation [Alexander02]. Think of it as 'motion-capture for AI.' Some figures contained in this gem are shown using UML (Unified Modeling Language) notation. For an in-depth discussion of UML, see [Booch98].

GoCap Architectural Overview

To employ GoCap, we need to engineer our system to record the inputs to the system as a human plays the game, and then map them to the action that the player chooses to execute, and under the current simulation conditions. To make this useful, we will have to build the game in such a way that a human trainer can play all of the game actors, including the enemies. To do this, we must first define a few classes to support training.

ActionState

An `ActionState` is an atomic element of a finite-state graph. It stores the legal transitions that it can make to other action states in a `transitionList`. The `ActionState` also maintains an `ActionRuleSet` that enumerates all of the rules under which the state should be used. Each `ActionRule` has its own `Evaluate()` method that computes and returns some game-related value that defines the rule (see Figure 3.1.1).

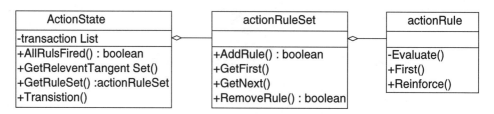

FIGURE 3.1.1   *Class diagrams for* ActionState *with* actionRuleSet *and* actionRule.

Actor Class

An actor is a simulation object that is capable of interacting with the game environment. Each actor has a control state that defines if the actor is currently under player control, AI control, or is in the training state. The control state can be swapped on the fly to transition the actor between one of these states. The actor's PerformAction() method will delegate processing to the current control state, which will determine the desired ActionState to transition to.

ControlState

A ControlState defines from where the associated actor can accept commands. When in a training state, the player controls the actor, as in the user-controlled state; except now, the computer can observe and learn from the actor's actions.

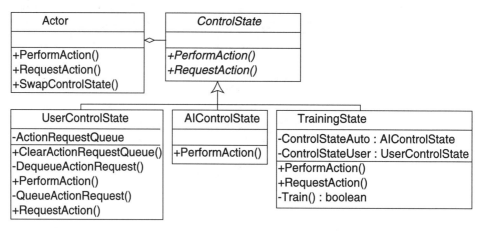

FIGURE 3.1.2   ControlState *class hierarchy.*

UserControlState

For use in client/server environments, the UserControlState maintains a queue of pending action requests that have been received from the player. This control state's PerformAction() method will pull requests from this queue when it is called. The queue can be replaced with an immediate request-handling method if the training environment runs locally, without need of a server.

AIControlState

The `AIControlState` is responsible for determining the appropriate action to perform when an actor in this state calls its `PerformAction()` method. The example presented in here implements a rule-based AI decision system encoded with hash maps.

TrainingControlState

The `TrainingControlState` adds a private `Train()` method that it will use to learn under which conditions to transition to a given `ActionState`.

Training a Car To Drive

To illustrate how GoCap works, we present the example of driving a toy car around some obstacles and the car's learning when to turn to avoid the obstacles. This example will also illustrate the process of mapping action states to the rules that detail when to use them.

Defining Action States

Our toy car has five basic action states that define the operations that it can perform and limit the transitions between them. Table 3.1.1 enumerates the states, and Figure 3.1.3 depicts the transitions between them, shown as arrows.

Table 3.1.1 Action States for Driving a Car

Action State	Description
Stop	Stop the car from moving (default state).
MoveFwd	Move the car forward in the direction it is facing.
TurnRight	Steer the car to the right.
TurnLeft	Steer the car to the left.
MoveBwd	Back the car up.

Once we have defined the states, we will need the transitions between them so that we can build the classes to implement them. Figure 3.1.4 shows the class diagram for these action states. Each state can be encapsulated in its own instance of an `ActionState`. Note that this implementation yields a state graph containing the legal transitions between states, but it does not embed any knowledge of when to make those transitions.

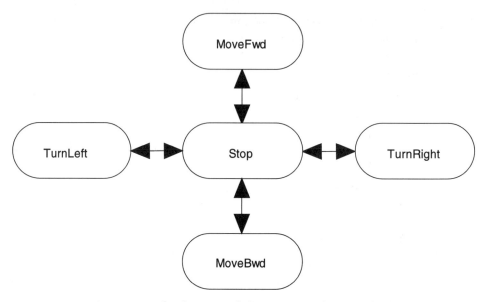

FIGURE 3.1.3   *Action states for driving and the transitions between them.*

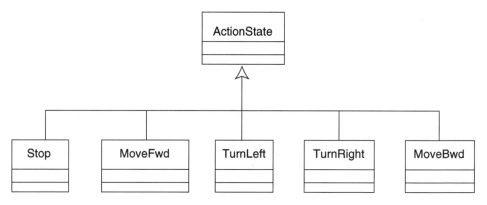

FIGURE 3.1.4   *Class diagram for movement action states.*

Defining Rules

Now we need to determine the rules that will detail when our car can transition to these action states. Each `ActionState` is associated with an `ActionRuleSet` that contains the rules under which we can use the state (see Figure 3.1.1). Each `ActionRule` has its own `Evaluate()` method that computes and returns some game-related value. For our car, we will define six sensors that will detect proximity to possible collisions. Each of these sensors will be implemented with an `Evaluate()` method. These methods will cast a ray from the car's origin, out in the sensor direction. If the sensor collides with an obstacle, then the method will compute distance to the obstacle and return the proximity as 1/distance, ensuring that the distance is always greater than or equal to 1. This yields a floating-point proximity value from 0.0 to 1.0. Table 3.1.2 details the sensors we will use. Figure 3.1.5 illustrates how these probes will be attached to our car.

Table 3.1.2 Sensors for detecting collisions.

Sensor	Description
FWD	Probe forward directly in front of the car.
FWD-L	Probe forward to the left of the car.
FWD-R	Probe forward to the right of the car.
LEFT	Probe left of the car.
RIGHT	Probe right of the car.
BWD	Probe directly behind the car.

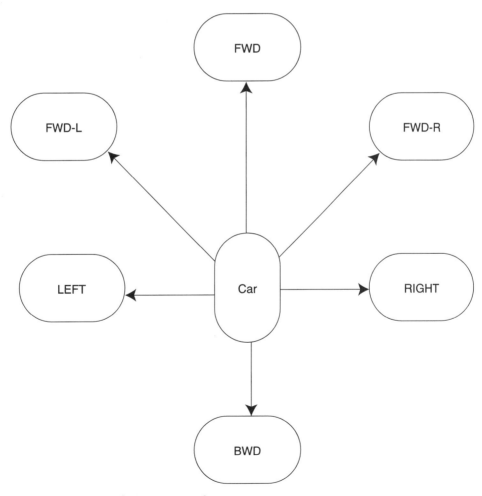

FIGURE 3.1.5   *Attaching sensors probes to a car.*

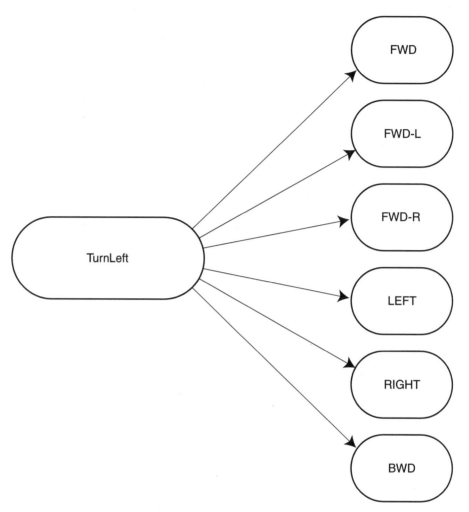

FIGURE 3.1.6   *Rules for the TurnLeft behavior.*

With our Evaluate() methods encapsulated in each rule, we can now build the ActionRuleSet for each ActionState. Figure 3.1.6 depicts the TurnLeft action state with its associated six sensor rules. Figure 3.1.7 shows the class diagram for the Turn-Left state and rules.

Learning the Rules

Now, we are ready to train our car's rules. We do this by swapping the car's actor to the training control state with a human player in the driver's seat, as described here. Pseudo code is provided to illustrate the process.

```
Actor.SwapControlState( TrainingControlState )
```

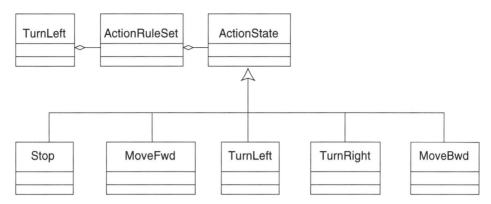

FIGURE 3.1.7 *Class diagram for* TurnLeft ActionState *rules.*

When the player steers to avoid obstacles, the training actor is informed of the action requests. The TrainingControlState will allow the user control state to perform the requested steering action as normal, but it will grab the resulting Action-State and pass it to the Train() method.

```
TrainingControlState:PerformAction( Actor )
{
    ActionState = UserControlState.PerformAction()
    TrainingControlState.Train( ActionState )
    ...
}
```

Cluster Maps for Floating-Point Valued Rules

To allow us to dynamically train the rules, each rule has a ClusterMap associated with it. A cluster map is a one-dimensional, spatial-partitioning data structure. This structure can be partitioned into a number of cells that provide coverage appropriate to the domain of the associated rule. To cover our Evaluate() method's domain of 0.0 to 1.0, we will use a 10-cell cluster map. If we required greater precision to cover the rule domain, we could increase the number of cells. A 10-cell cluster map can be implemented as a hash map that is indexed by an integer key value between zero and nine. Figure 3.1.8 shows the related classes.

The ClusterMap class provides a CalculateIndex() method that can perform an index calculation on the floating-point value returned by the Evaluate() method to transform it into an integer representation. This gives us the hash map key that corresponds to the evaluation value. We can feed this key to the Lookup() method on the ClusterMap class to get the individual Cluster object that represents the cell. The cluster map serves to round off or quantize the floating-point input value so it fits into the nearest cell.

```
TrainingControlState:Train( ActionState )
{
```

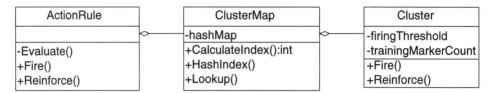

FIGURE 3.1.8   *Class diagram for* `ClusterMap`.

```
For Rule in ActionState.GetRuleSet()
    ClusterMap = Rule.GetClusterMap()
    Value = Rule.Evaluate( Actor )
    Index = ClusterMap.CalculateIndex( Value )
        Key = ClusterMap.HashIndex( Index )
    Cluster = ClusterMap.Lookup( Key )
    Cluster.Reinforce()
End For
}
```

The `Reinforce()` method is where the actual training occurs. Each `Cluster` maintains a `trainingMarkerCount` that is incremented during training. This marker indicates that the player activated this action rule with this evaluation value. As the player feeds more input into the training system, we will get more values that fall into this cluster. Every time we get a hit in the cluster, we increment the marker count until it reaches some preset firing threshold. We add this threshold to account for noise or error in the input data. In practice, you might need to set this threshold significantly high if your training data is prone to noise or error.

```
Cluster:Reinforce()
{
    trainingMarkerCount ++
    If trainingMarkerCount > firingThreshold then
        trainingMarkerCount = firingThreshold
    End If
}
```

Early in our training, the cluster maps will only contain a few training markers. As training goes on, more data flows into the system, and more rules are learned. Eventually, we will tend to reach a point of equilibrium where we have learned all of the rules that match the input action choices. We can detect this equilibrium by comparing the player's input against the action that the `AIControlState` would pick itself. When they match on a continuing basis, we can signal the player to stop training.

Swapping Control to the AI

Now that we have a fully trained rule set, we can detach our human trainer and swap to AI control. When the actor performs its next action, it calls on its decision process and newly trained rules to determine its course of action.

```
Actor.SwapControlState( AIControlState )
ActionState = Actor.PerformAction()
If ActionState Is Not None Then
    CurrentState = Actor.GetCurrentActionState()
    CurrentState.Transition( ActionState )
End If
```

The cluster's `Fire()` method can now test the evaluation values against the training markers in the cluster map. If a rule evaluates to a value that falls into a cluster that has enough markers to reach the threshold, then that rule fires. If all of the rules in the rule set fire, then the associated `ActionState` is returned for activation.

```
AIControlState:PerformAction( Actor )
{
    fired = 0
    ActionState = Actor.GetCurrentActionState()
    For Action in ActionState.GetTransitions()
        For Rule in Action.GetRuleSet()
            ClusterMap = Rule.GetClusterMap()
            Value = Rule.Evaluate( Actor)
            Index = ClusterMap.CalculateIndex(Value)
            Key = ClusterMap.HashIndex( Index )
            Cluster = ClusterMap.Lookup( Key )
            If Cluster.Fire() Then
                fired++
            End If
        End For Rule
        If fired = Action.GetRuleSet().Count() Then
            Return Action
        End If
    End For Action
    Return None
}
```

Conclusion

This gem outlined an implementation of GoCap using hash maps for the dynamic learning of rule clusters. This enhancement provides a significant performance increase over the previous version, which used sparse arrays. The nested structure of the AI decision loop makes it a good candidate for further optimization with SIMD techniques, but that is a story for another day.

References

[Alexander02] Alexander, Thor, "GoCap: Game Observation Capture," *AI Game Programming Wisdom*, Charles River Media, Inc., 2002.
[Booch98] Booch, Grady, *The Unified Modeling Language User Guide*, Addison Wesley, 1998.

3.2

Area Navigation: Expanding the Path-Finding Paradigm

Ben Board and Mike Ducker,

Dogfish Entertainment

ben_board@yahoo.com, mike@ducker.org.uk

Path-finding constitutes one of the primary areas of game AI and is a major concern in almost all modern computer games. The simple act of producing a route from A to B could introduce a significant CPU hit, depending on the complexity of the world and the manner in which the task is broken down. The traditional approach to solving the path-finding problem involves placing nodes across the game world and connecting them by edges, where the direct route linking any two points is free from obstruction.

The placement of these nodes can be achieved in many ways: by the level designer as part of the design process, by a procedural method as part of an export process, or by the nature of the game world in which the environment might be split into some set of formalized shapes, such as a tile map.

Once the world is deconstructed into nodes and connections, path-finding is normally carried out by some form of heuristic search to discover the list of connections that would provide a route from a character's start point to their goal. Arguably, the most popular form of heuristic search in computer games today is A*, an explanation of which can be found in [Stout00] or on various gaming Web sites throughout the Net. This algorithm simply expands the best node in the current list until the goal node is reached or no valid nodes remain to be expanded (i.e., the attempted path-finding has failed).

This gem presents a paradigm shift in the way a given world is deconstructed for path-finding. Rather than using nodes as the fundamental components of path-finding, it is suggested that regions of the environment be segregated into areas, each represented by one node in the search space, and that these areas be connected to one another if navigation between them is possible. Upon implementation of this paradigm in our game, we will have profited from significant improvements in the following areas:

- Speed and storage efficiency due to a huge decrease in nodes used in the search algorithm.
- Realistic movement—by moving from area to area, individuals are not restricted by unnecessarily precise waypoints.

Out with the Old

Traditionally, path-finding has used the waypoint as its fundamental component for the traversal of a simulated environment. By deconstructing the world into a series of connected nodes (connections exist between a pair of nodes if those nodes can be navigated without obstruction), the world can be viewed as a graph of vertices and edges, thus allowing state-space searches and graph theory to be directly applied. An introduction to graph theory can be found in [Sedgewick89].

This abstraction from a complex environment, possibly containing detailed 3D models obstructing much of the landscape, allows simple, yet powerful algorithms to connect two geographically dispersed points by the shortest possible route.

While the node is a sensible choice for performing state-space searches, given its similarity to the vertex in graph theory, it lends itself rather easily to certain common scenarios where its straightforward use can lead to inefficiency. Imagine the simplest form of environment—a 2D tile map. Figure 3.2.1 shows a simple tile map contain-

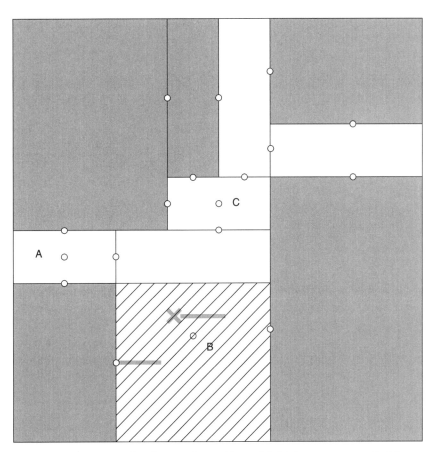

FIGURE 3.2.1 *A simple tile map for a 2D world. Light areas are walkable, dark areas are unwalkable.*

ing two types of terrain: walkable (light) terrain and unwalkable (dark) terrain. The simplest procedural method of producing nodes for this map is to place a single node at the center of each tile, and then connect each one to its horizontal and vertical walkable neighbors, as shown in Figure 3.2.2.

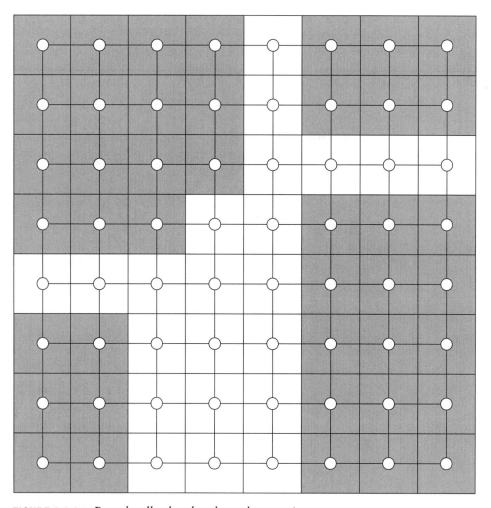

FIGURE 3.2.2   *Procedurally placed nodes and connections.*

Of course, using this procedure generates seemingly redundant nodes on the unwalkable tiles. They are only truly redundant if their type (the particular aspect that determines their navigability) is guaranteed not to change, and there are no characters in the game world that are able to use them.

Such a complete system of nodes ensures that an obstacle-free path can be found from any walkable tile to any other walkable tile (if such a path exists), but at the significant cost of time and storage per node (for every tile). A preferred solution would require fewer nodes, carefully chosen to encode the same accessibility information in less space.

Any algorithm for node application must function under the following constraints to ensure that the path it generates is free of static obstacles:

- Each node must represent a group of tiles that share the property that any pair of tiles in that group can be navigated between (without obstruction).
- Each potentially navigable tile on the map must be represented by exactly one node.

The method above recognizes those constraints only by applying a high degree of redundancy. If we could address that redundancy by identifying the minimal set of nodes necessary to encode walkable versus unwalkable regions, we could still enjoy the benefits of the graph-search approach, but in optimal space and time.

The following section explains the paradigm shift in which each node represents a nonuniform area of tiles.

In with the New

When approaching the problem of path-finding, the form of the environment should be considered so that the path-finding algorithm can be optimally written for the game in question. There are two underlying considerations for deconstructing the world:

- *The number of nodes it is deconstructed into*: The fewer the better; the fewer nodes there are, the quicker the heuristic search.
- *The usefulness of the resulting nodes for path traversal:* It is preferable that the nodes allow characters to walk the path within the maximal limits set by the walkable environment.

The use of areas rather than points is beneficial in both cases.

The world is broken into areas, each being of uniform navigability and internally traversable in a straight line without having to avoid static obstacles. If one can navigate between two areas, then the areas are connected by a 'portal' that is in the shape of the contact region between the two areas. In the tile-world example, the tiles can be split into areas as shown in Figure 3.2.3. Note that our tile-world example is rectangular, but the new approach is extendable to convex polygonal regions for the general case.

As seen in Figure 3.2.3, no points are arbitrarily used in path-finding. This mirrors the common-sense approach used by the majority of people when solving the same problem in real life. When attempting to plan a path from one position to another, you would normally only use two points: the start point and the end point. All other sections of the path are generalized areas, split up by the way you perceive the world. When walking from your bedroom to your bathroom in the morning (or early afternoon), you might consider stairs, landings, corridors, or even other rooms

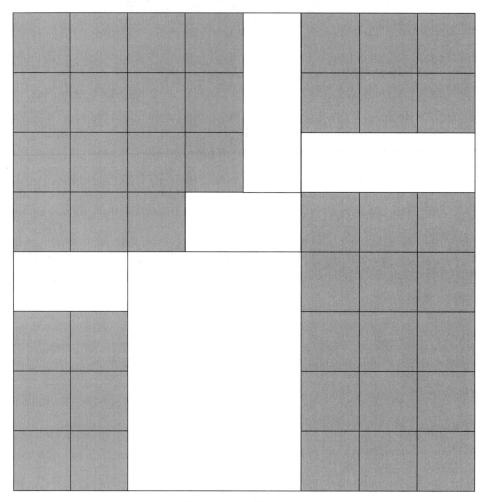

FIGURE 3.2.3   *Breaking the world into walkable areas connected by portals.*

while planning your path. You don't, however, consider particular points within these areas, unless there is some specific reason to (once at the top of the stairs, there are no more decisions to be made until you reach the bottom!). There is normally no motivation to walk to any specific spot within a corridor before you leave it; you just walk from area to area via their shared portals until you reach your destination. Any path with start and end points contained within a single area is always a straight line, barring any dynamic obstacles (such as the cat).

It should be noted that the use of areas does not overly affect the basic heuristic search algorithm. The only change that must be made is the calculation of distance from area to area. The simplest solution to this metric would be to use the distance between central points of the areas. However, Figure 3.2.4 shows that this metric will give higher values than the distances actually traveled, given a realistic path-traversal

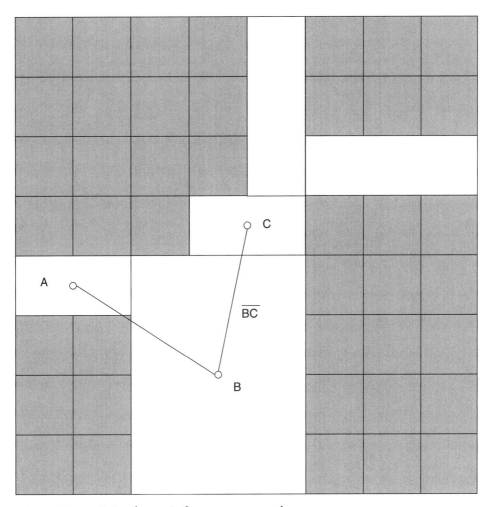

FIGURE 3.2.4 *A simple metric for movement cost between areas.*

algorithm. A better solution would be to use the distance from the central point of the portal used to enter an area to the central point of the portal used to exit that area. For instance, if your path took you from area A to B to C during your path-finding process, the distance cost of traveling from B to C would be the distance from the portal connecting A to B to the portal connecting B to C, shown here in Figure 3.2.5.

To summarize the path-generation algorithm:

- The world is split into an optimal set of areas, where each area is uniformly navigable, and any two points within the area can be traversed in a straight line without impediment.
- Each of these areas is represented by a node in a graph, and two nodes are connected by an edge if their associated areas have a common navigable interface (a portal).

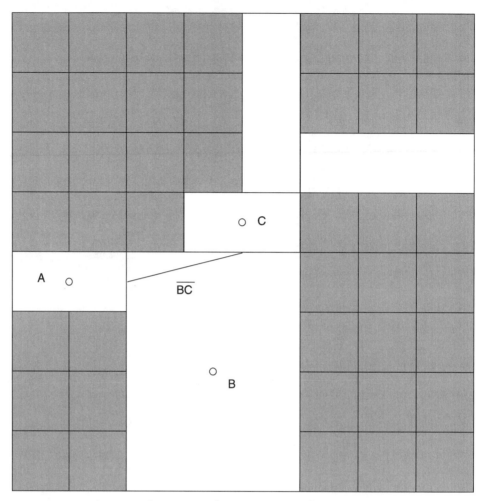

FIGURE 3.2.5 *A more realistic metric for movement cost between areas.*

- Basic paths are generated by determining the containing areas for the start and end points of the journey, finding the associated nodes, and then searching the graph to find the best route between the two points.
- Once this area-wise route is found, a specific path is created by moving between the portals linking successive pairs of areas. This is path traversal, which shall be discussed shortly.

Now that the basic concepts have been introduced, the next section will continue with the tile-world example and explain a method of producing optimal areas from the environment.

Divide and Conquer

Constructing areas from raw terrain data is a very game-specific problem. It is possible you will have to extract the processed areas from polygons flagged for terrain type, or even from open spaces in a fully 3D game. This section will focus on the simplest case as an example and show a method of rectangularizing a tile world to produce results as seen in Figure 3.2.3.

While there are many possible ways of producing a set of rectangles from a given tile set (each having its own merits and flaws), for the purposes of producing rectangles for path-finding, the following aspects are important to consider:

- *The rectangles produced should be as large as possible.* The larger the rectangles, the quicker the path-finding process will occur, since fewer rectangles are necessary.
- *The rectangles should be as square as possible.* For the purposes of path-finding, the rectangles will produce better paths if the ratio of width to height is close to one. This helps avoid the problem outlined in Figure 3.2.4 and leads toward more-realistic looking paths.
- *The rectangularization algorithm should be fast.* In games where the type of landscape can be changed dynamically and rectangularization must be performed in real-time, the algorithm for rectangularization should be as fast as possible.

The following pseudo-code rectangularizes the world with reasonable speed, producing more-evenly sided rectangles with an adjustable level of performance between optimized rectangles for path traversal and optimized speed. Where offline processing is possible, speed optimization is not a key issue and can be ignored in favor of better optimized rectangularization. The algorithm is presented as pseudo-code here due to the length of the full code, which can be found on the CD-ROM.

ON THE CD

The rectangularization function is defined as:

```
RectangularizeWorld( MapCellTypes cellType, int
    initialTestSize)
```

where the parameter cellType defines the type of environment the function will rectangularize (walkable, unwalkable, or some other defined type), and the parameter initialTestSize defines the size of the largest square tested, and is used to trade optimal rectangularization for optimal speed.

The first step in the function is to count the number of cells of the required type. This is used to abort out of the function if that cell type is lacking in the current environment. Only cells that are not already contained within an area are considered.

```
int CellCount = number of free cells of type cellType
if CellCount = 0 then exit
```

The next step is to ensure that the size of the square used for the comparisons is smaller than the square root of the number of cells of the required type. If the test size defines an area larger than the number of cells that the required type can occupy, then there is no way that the square will find an area consisting entirely of those cells.

```
if initialTestSize > sqrt(CellCount)
    then initialTestSize = sqrt(CellCount)
```

The main loop of the rectangularization process begins by testing the world with a square of the maximum defined size and decreasing that square with each iteration until it is zero.

```
for testSize = initialTestSize, testSize > 0, testSize = testSize - 1
```

The square is passed across the map from bottom left to top right:

```
For startX = 0 to mapWidth — testSize
    For startY = 0 to mapHeight - testSize
```

The square defines an area of the world that is tested for uniform cells (of the required type) such that no cell under the square is contained by another area.

```
For testX = startX to startX + testSize
    For testY = startY to startY + testSize
    If cell[testX][testY] is not free or not of the required type,
        fail
```

If the square fails, then move it to the next testing position and test again. If the square contains only free cells of the required type, then attempt to expand the square North, East, South, and West by one cell width, one direction at a time. New cells added to the area by each expansion are permanently added to the rectangle (if they are of the required type and contained by any other area). The algorithm continues to expand in all four directions until it fails to give a valid set of cells.

```
Fail = 0
While fail < 4
    For North, South, East, and West
    Expand the area by one cell width
        If the new rectangle is valid
            Fail = 0
        Else
            Fail = Fail + 1
        Contract the rectangle along this direction
```

At this point, we have an area defined by this expanded rectangle that should be added to the list of areas.

```
For x = rectStartX to rectEndX
    For y = rectStartY to rectEndY
    Cell[x][y] set to unavailable

Add new area to area list
```

```
CellCount = CellCount - new area size
If CellCount = 0 then exit
```

By altering the maximum size of the initial comparison square, it is possible to trade speed optimization for optimal rectangularization. If the initial side length is set to one, then the minimal number of rectangle comparisons will be made, hence optimizing the speed of the procedure. If it is set to a maximum value, the width of the map for instance, then far more rectangle comparisons will be made; however, the set of areas produced will adhere to the first two aspects of optimal rectangularization. It's a tradeoff that the developer must choose for their particular need.

Path Traversal

Once a path has been produced, the next step is for a character to follow that path to the destination. There are two aspects to basic path traversal: attraction toward some goal and repulsion from static obstacles along the way. The attraction is either toward the next portal on the path or toward the goal point if the character has entered the goal area. The repulsion comes from proximity to nonwalkable areas. (There are no static obstacles within each area, by definition.)

To move a character toward its next area in a realistic manner, two simple modes of attraction are used in conjunction (as seen in Figures 3.2.6 and 3.2.7):

1. Attraction to the central point of the portal.
2. Attraction along the normal of the portal. (The portal's normal is defined by a vector perpendicular to the portal's vector.)

These modes can be applied to varying degrees depending on the position of the character relative to the portal. If the character does not lie on a point along the portal normal, then attraction along the normal of the portal will not result in a convincing movement to the new area. So, some amount of attraction to the center of the portal might be necessary. Figure 3.2.8 shows the portion of area B where attraction by the normal alone will result in the transition from area B to area C.

An example attraction algorithm is to use the normal vector shown in Figure 3.2.7 while in the shaded area and a mixture of the two vectors outside that area (increasing the proportion of the central-point vector with distance along the line of the portal).

Repulsion works similarly to the normal attraction, except that the direction of the normal is reversed such that the vector is heading into the character's current area rather than out of it. In the specific case of the simple tile world described so far, it would be necessary to store a list of walls as well as portals, so that the walls could be used to repulse the characters from nonwalkable cells. In the more general case, every cell type would have its own area list, and all areas would have portals to all their neighbors. Neighbors leading to areas that a specific character could not use would repulse that character by using a different area type in the traversal algorithm.

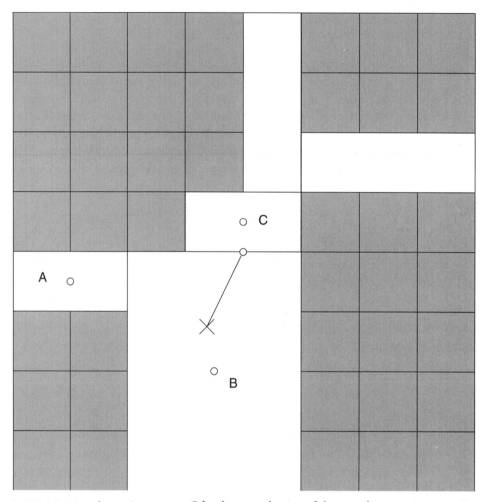

FIGURE 3.2.6 *Attraction to area C by the central point of the portal connecting areas B and C.*

Figure 3.2.9 shows the map broken into walkable and unwalkable areas, with points defining the center of each portal.

For each unwalkable area connected to the character's current area, a repulsion vector is applied along the normal to the portal. This repulsion is only applied if the character is within the confines of the portal, as shown by the shaded area of Figure 3.2.10.

Finally, once the path traversal is in place, dynamic object avoidance can be achieved by using basic flocking techniques and adding repulsion vectors from other characters in the world to the path-traversal vectors. For more information on flocking see [Reynolds87] or [Woodcock00].

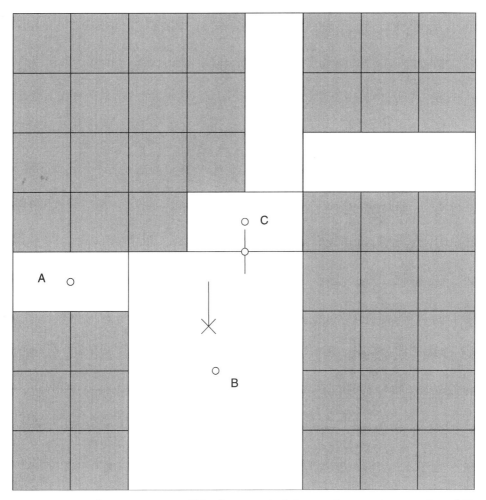

FIGURE 3.2.7   *Attraction to area C by the normal of the portal connecting areas B and C.*

Dynamic Landscapes

Deconstructing the world into areas is a CPU-intensive process that must be carried out at appropriate points during runtime, if at all. It is preferable to carry out the production of areas during some batch process as the level is loaded. However, if the environment is dynamic due to player interaction or scripted changes, then the deconstruction process might have to be called during runtime. In these cases, speed is a primary consideration, and the process of deconstruction must be approached in such a way as to avoid frame lag without reducing the quality of the areas produced. This is achievable as follows:

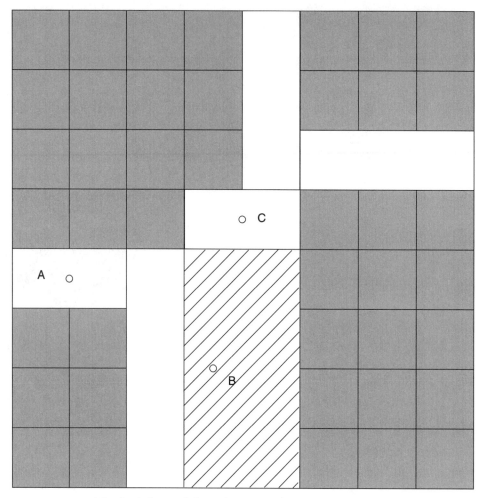

FIGURE 3.2.8   *The shaded area defines the portion of area B where attraction by the normal of the portal connecting areas B and C (shown in Figure 3.2.7) will suffice to traverse a character from area B to area C.*

- Initially, use the fastest deconstruction algorithm. With the rectangularization algorithm detailed above, choose an `initialTestSize` value of 1. This might produce an inferior set of rectangles for path traversal than a higher value would, but the speed of the process is maximized.
- During runtime, minimize redundant rectangularization (i.e., do not rectangularize areas that are unaffected by the environment change).
- Re-rectangularize the environment for optimal path traversal at an appropriate time. Reconstruct the entire world when a slight lag would not be noticed, such as when the player switches to an in-game menu.

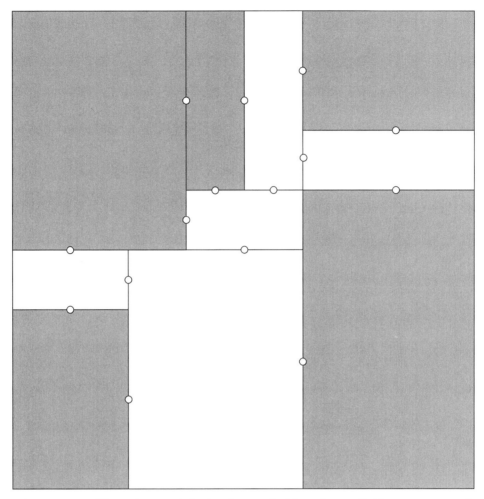

FIGURE 3.2.9 *The entire map is broken into walkable and unwalkable areas connected by portals with their centers marked by points.*

Remember, altering the set of areas not only requires deconstructing the world, but it also requires recalculating the characters that are positioned in those areas.

Advancing the Paradigm

While this gem has focused on 2D tile worlds as a simple example, the area navigation approach is applicable to every type of game world (including 3D). All that is required is a method of deconstructing the world into efficient areas that obey the rules described above as well as redefining the connecting portal region.

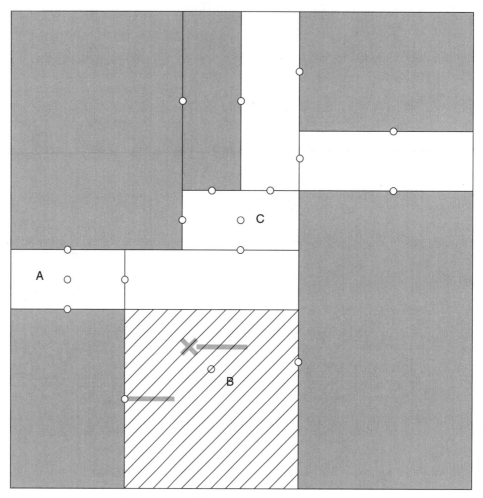

FIGURE 3.2.10 *Repulsion is applied to characters within the area defined by the normal of the portal, which is shown by the shaded section of area B.*

Conclusion

This gem presents a highly efficient algorithm for creating and following paths in a variably navigable environment—one that we are using successfully in our current title. By identifying optimal areas within the environment that are trivially navigable, representing them with a single node, then linking these nodes wherever the associated areas have a navigable interface, we are able to quickly produce paths covering long distances. Redundancy is minimized, resulting in high speed and storage efficiency. To support this process, a method of determining these optimal areas has been suggested. Also, in order to use the resulting area-wise path and apply it to a navigating character, a path-traversal method has been described. The results are inexpensive and the paths realistic.

References

[Reynold87] Reynolds, Craig, "Flocks, Herds and Schools: A Distributed Behavioural Model," Computer Graphics Proceedings (SIGGRAPH 1987): pp. 25–34.

[Sedgewick89] Sedgewick, Robert, *Algorithms,* Second Edition, Addison Wesley, 1989.

[Stout00] Stout, Bryan, "The Basics of A* for Path Planning," *Game Programming Gems,* Charles River Media, Inc., 2000.

[Woodcock00] Woodcock, Steve, "Flocking: A Simple Technique for Simulation Group Behavior," *Game Programming Gems*, Charles River Media, Inc., 2000.

3.3

Function Pointer-Based, Embedded Finite-State Machines

Charles Farris, VR1 Entertainment, Inc.

charlesf@vr1.com

The goal of this gem is to create an FSM (Finite State Machine) implementation using function pointers, inheritance, and function overloading. This implementation has three design requirements: object-oriented implementation, minimal coding, and fast execution.

The first requirement, object-oriented implementation, is very important in modern games development. Many developers are moving toward object-oriented languages, such as C++ and Java, because these languages support features like abstract object manipulation and inheritance. To be used effectively in an object-oriented programming (OOP) environment, an FSM implementation needs to be object-oriented in design.

The second requirement, minimal coding, arises from a fundamental rule in software engineering: "Keep It Simple, Stupid." Accordingly, this implementation makes the addition of FSM functionality as simple as inheriting a class and adding some member variables and functions.

Finally, this implementation uses function pointers to avoid computationally expensive if-then-else comparisons at runtime [Calder94].

What Is a Finite-State Machine?

The most general definition of an FSM describes it as a model of an event-driven system. A system's behavior is represented within an FSM as a set of states, a set of input events, and a state-transition function. A simple lightbulb example is demonstrated in Table 3.3.1 and Figure 3.3.1.

For a more in-depth description of FSMs and their application to game programming, both Eric Dysband's "A Finite-State Machine Class" [Dysband00] and Andre LaMothe's *Tricks of the Windows Game Programming Gurus* [LaMothe99] are excellent sources of information.

Table 3.3.1 Lightbulb State Transition Function

Current State	Input Event	State Transition
On	Switch On	
On	Switch Off	Off
Off	Switch On	On
Off	Switch Off	

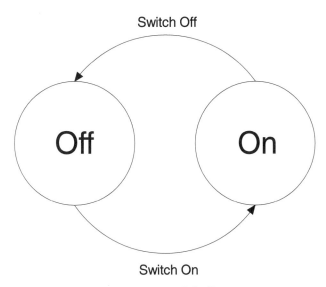

FIGURE 3.3.1 *Lightbulb FSM.*

Why Use FSMs?

In game programming, FSMs are generally used to control a game object's behavior at runtime by selectively executing portions of the object's code based on the current state. While FSMs can be used to control virtually any game object, they are extremely popular for AI programming for the following reasons:

- FSMs are useful for reducing complex behaviors into smaller, simpler behaviors.
- FSMs are useful for synchronizing an AI's behavior with external events, such as animations, sounds, or timers. FSMs allow developers to integrate animations with AI behavior without placing too many restrictions on the animator's artistic vision.
- FSMs are much easier to debug and tune than other AI techniques, such as neural networks or genetic algorithms [Woodcock00, Woodcock01]. FSMs generate

deterministic behavior during execution because state transitions are predefined for a given state and input event.

FSM Implementation

First, we need to make some assumptions regarding our game objects. Each object should be represented by a C++ class, have a function called `Update()` that is called every tick, and have a set of state functions (which are called in the `Update()` function). Given these assumptions, an FSM implementation requires a variable to track the current state and some code for handling the state transitions. Most importantly, it needs some code for mapping the current state to the appropriate state functions in the game object.

FSM Integration

FSM implementations can be integrated into game objects in one of two ways. The first and simplest method is to include an instance of the FSM within the game object. The second method is to embed the FSM within the game object via inheritance. Both methods have advantages and disadvantages, but this gem will use the second method for two main reasons. First, inherited FSMs allow greater flexibility because the FSM's state-transition logic can use the game object's data directly. Second, embedded FSMs have slightly better performance, since there is less redirection required when accessing the FSM.

The main disadvantage with inherited FSMs lies in the dependency between the FSM and the game object classes, which can pose a challenge later on in development, since changes to the inherited FSM class might require extensive modifications to the derived classes.

The Switch Implementation

The most common form of FSM implementation is the `switch` implementation. In this implementation, the current state is stored as an integer, and a `switch` statement is used to map the current state to the state function calls [LaMothe99]. The primary advantages of this approach are ease of implementation and low memory usage.

However, the common `switch` implementation does have disadvantages. First, the `switch` implementation is not very object-oriented [Sweeney00]. Adding states involves modifying the `switch` statement. When these modifications are combined with inheritance and function overloading, the end result is often 'spaghetti' code. Also, for large projects with multiple developers, the non-object-oriented design of the `switch` implementation can lead to significant maintenance and debugging problems.

Second, the performance of this implementation is dependent on the size of the FSM. Most `switch` statements are converted into `if-then-else` statements by the compiler and are difficult to optimize. For an FSM having n states, the program will average about *n/2* if-then-else comparisons before finding the appropriate state function call. If the FSM is distributed over a class hierarchy, the search for an appropriate state function might require several virtual function calls up the class hierarchy in addition to the if-then-else comparisons.

A more object-oriented solution to the function-mapping problem is to encapsulate the state function calls within the current state variable. Since the state functions are usually associated with the game object, implementing the state functions directly within a state object is not practical. However, the state functions can effectively be stored within a state object through the use of function pointers.

Function Pointers

Function pointers in C are very straightforward, but the syntax is somewhat cryptic.

```
<return type>(*<pointer>)(<arguments>)
```

In C++, nearly all function calls are made to class member functions. Function pointers to these functions require significantly more syntax because the functions are class-specific. Accordingly, the declaration syntax requires the class name.

```
<return type>(<class>::*<pointer>)(<arguments>)
```

Let's assume IsOdd() is a member function of a class called "CMath." The function pointer declaration to IsOdd() would be:

```
bool (CMath::*pfnFunction)(int)=&CMath::IsOdd;
```

The class-specific nature of function pointers to member functions extends beyond the declaration syntax. Function pointers to member functions cannot point to functions in a derived class unless the function is already declared in the base class [Stroustrup97]. This is a serious limitation because all functions must be declared in the base class, resulting in severe code bloat. On the plus side, function pointers to virtual functions will resolve to the proper function call using the virtual function call mechanism. This allows function pointers to member functions to work properly in derived class hierarchies (assuming the functions are declared in the base class).

Execution of a member function through a function pointer also presents a problem. Member functions use a different calling convention from regular functions as they pass the class instance to the function via a hidden parameter (the this pointer). Thus, execution of a member function through a function pointer requires a class instance. The code below illustrates the execution of the IsOdd() member function through the pfnFunction function pointer.

```
CMath Instance;
bool bResult=(Instance.*pfnFunction)(5);
CMath *pInstance=&Instance;
bool bResult=(pInstance->*pfnFunction)(3);
```

With these limitations, the use of function pointers to store the state functions seems difficult at best. For the moment, let us assume that workarounds exist, so we continue to examine the use of function pointers in an FSM implementation. (For more on function pointers, Lars Haendel's "The Function Pointer Tutorials" [Haendel01] is an excellent reference on function pointers, and it is available online.)

The Function Pointer Implementation

In a function pointer implementation, each state is now represented as an object. Within this object, the state function calls are stored in function pointers, and the function mapping occurs when the state is initialized. The FSM tracks the current state by maintaining a pointer to the current state object, and the state function calls are executed directly from the state object through the function pointers.

The primary advantage of the function pointer implementation over the switch implementation is its object-oriented design. The function mapping is now part of the state object and not the game object. This difference in implementation avoids the necessity of extending the FSM execution code into the game object classes. Instead of overloading the Update() function in the derived class, new states can be added to the FSM by merely including new state objects.

Another advantage of this implementation is that the performance is independent of the number of states within the FSM. Since each state object knows exactly what functions to call, there are no if-then-else comparisons and no traversal of the game object's class hierarchy.

This implementation does have some disadvantages, however. Implementation is more difficult due to the limitations inherent in function pointers to member functions. In addition, this implementation requires significantly more memory, as the state function mapping is now stored as a set of function pointers instead of being compiled into the code.

The Implementation (CFSM)

In order to best satisfy the design requirements, the CFSM implementation will consist of a base class using the function pointer implementation, as previously described. The CFSM implementation has two separate parts: the state objects and the FSM.

The State Objects

In the game object assumptions, we stated that each state in the game object would be represented as a set of functions. In the CFSM implementation, each state is represented by three functions. As an example, let us create a game object class called CEnemy, which implements an idle state.

```
class CEnemy : public CFSM
{
    void BeginStateIdle();
```

```
        void StateIdle();
        void EndStateIdle();
};
```

The `BeginStateIdle()` and `EndStateIdle()` functions are called during state transitions and provide a convenient location for initializing and cleaning up states. The `StateIdle()` function is the main state function and is called every tick from the `Update()` function. Since three functions make up each game object state, the CFSM state object uses three function pointers to store the state functions.

To create state objects, a two-class hierarchy is necessary. The base class, `CState`, provides a generic interface for executing the stored state functions.

```
class CState
{
public:
    virtual ~CState() {}
    virtual void ExecuteBeginState()=0;
    virtual void ExecuteState()=0;
    virtual void ExecuteEndState()=0;
};
```

The second class, `CStateTemplate`, is derived from `CState`. To avoid the problem of class-specific function pointers, `CStateTemplate` is a template class.

```
template <class T>
class CStateTemplate : public CState
{
protected:
    typedef void (T::*PFNSTATE)(void);
    T *m_pInstance;
    PFNSTATE m_pfnBeginState;
    PFNSTATE m_pfnState;
    PFNSTATE m_pfnEndState;
public:
    CStateTemplate() : m_pInstance(0),
            m_pfnBeginState(0),
            m_pfnState(0),m_pfnEndState(0) {}

    void Set(T *pInstance,PFNSTATE pfnBeginState,
            PFNSTATE pfnState,PFNSTATE pfnEndState)
    {
        m_pInstance=pInstance;
        m_pfnBeginState=pfnBeginState;
        m_pfnState=pfnState;
        m_pfnEndState=pfnEndState;
    }

    virtual void ExecuteBeginState()
    {
        (m_pInstance->*m_pfnBeginState)();
    }
    virtual void ExecuteState()
```

```
    {
        (m_pInstance->*m_pfnState)();
    }
    virtual void ExecuteEndState()
    {
        (m_pInstance->*m_pfnEndState)();
    }
};
```

CStateTemplate implements the three state function pointers as well as a pointer
to the class instance. The execution functions from the CState class are overloaded
and implemented in CStateTemplate. Since CState is the base class for CStateTemplate, a game object can create class-specific state objects using CStateTemplate
instances. The FSM implementation, however, can use the state objects generically by
treating them as instances of CState and thus avoids having to know the details of a
game object in order to execute its state functions.

The FSM

With state objects now defined, the CFSM base class can now use them to implement
the FSM.

```
class CFSM
{
protected:
    CState *m_pCurrentState;
    CState *m_pNewState;
    CStateTemplate<CFSM> m_StateInitial;
public:
    CFSM();
    virtual ~CFSM() {}
    virtual void Update();
    bool IsState(CState &State);
    bool GotoState(CState &NewState);
    virtual void BeginStateInitial() {}
    virtual void StateInitial() {}
    virtual void EndStateInitial() {}
};
```

The current state, m_pCurrentState, is a pointer to a CState object. The use of a
CState pointer allows the FSM to completely implement the state function execution
code within the CFSM's Update() function. In addition to the current state pointer, a
CState pointer, m_pNewState, is also declared. This variable is tracked by the FSM and
will cause the FSM to execute a state transition if set.

The CFSM implementation defines an initial state using the CStateTemplate class
and stores it in the state object m_StateInitial. This state is provided so that the
FSM implementation always has a state to execute. The CFSM constructor initializes
the initial state along with the pointers to the state objects.

```
CFSM::CFSM()
{
    m_StateInitial.Set(this,BeginStateInitial,
            StateInitial,
            EndStateInitial);
    m_pCurrentState=static_cast<CState*>(
            &m_StateInitial);
    m_pNewState=0;
}
```

The execution of the state functions occurs in the Update() function.

```
void CFSM::Update()
{
    if (m_pNewState)
    {
        m_pCurrentState->ExecuteEndState();
        m_pCurrentState=m_pNewState;
        m_pNewState=0;
        m_pCurrentState->ExecuteBeginState();
    }
    m_pCurrentState->ExecuteState();
}
```

Upon entering the Update() function, the FSM checks for a state transition using the m_pNewState variable. If one is pending, Update() calls the ExecuteEndState() and ExecuteBeginState() functions, and changes the current state.

The GotoState() and IsState() functions are provided to simplify the handling of state objects. The GotoState() function sets the new state variable and causes a state transition on the next Update() function call.

```
bool CFSM::GotoState(CState &NewState)
{
    m_pNewState=&NewState;
    return true;
}
```

The IsState() function provides a syntax-friendly method of comparing the current state to any given state.

```
bool CFSM::IsState(CState &State)
{
    return (m_pCurrentState==&State);
}
```

Using CFSM

By way of example, we are now going to create a game object that simulates a light-bulb. The game object will use the FSM introduced at the beginning of this gem, and the CFSM class will provide the FSM functionality.

Adding CFSM to a Class

First, we create a class called `CLightBulb` and derive it from the `CFSM` base class. To implement the states, we add two state objects using the `CStateTemplate` class and the corresponding state functions. The two input events are handled through the `SwitchOnEvent()` and `SwitchOffEvent()` functions.

```
class CLightBulb : public CFSM
{
protected:
    CStateTemplate<CLightBulb> m_StateOn;
    CStateTemplate<CLightBulb> m_StateOff;
public:
    CLightBulb();
    virtual void SwitchOnEvent();
    virtual void SwitchOffEvent();
    virtual void StateInitial();
    virtual void BeginStateOn();
    virtual void StateOn() {}
    virtual void EndStateOn() {}
    virtual void BeginStateOff();
    virtual void StateOff() {}
    virtual void EndStateOff() {}
};
```

The constructor initializes the `CFSM` base class and initializes the two state objects.

```
CLightBulb::CLightBulb() : CFSM()
{
    m_StateOn.Set(this,BeginStateOn,StateOn,
        EndStateOn);
    m_StateOff.Set(this,BeginStateOff,StateOff,
        EndStateOff);
}
```

Next, we add the `SwitchOnEvent()` and `SwitchOffEvent()` functions for handling the input events and state transition logic.

```
void CLightBulb::SwitchOnEvent()
{
    if (IsState(m_StateOff))
        GotoState(m_StateOn);
}

void CLightBulb::SwitchOffEvent()
{
    if (IsState(m_StateOn))
        GotoState(m_StateOff);
}
```

Since this is a simple example, the state functions are mostly stub functions. However, the `BeginStateOn()` and `BeginStateOff()` functions contain code for displaying the current state so we can follow the FSM's execution.

```
void CLightBulb::StateBeginOn()
{
    cout << "State: On" << endl;
}

void CLightBulb::StateBeginOff()
{
    cout << "State: Off" << endl;
}
```

Finally, the StateInitial() function is overloaded to 'jump-start' the lightbulb FSM.

```
void CLightBulb::StateInitial()
{
    GotoState(m_StateOff);
}
```

Changing an FSM's Behavior in a Derived Class

Let us create a new class to simulate a flashing light. Since a flashing lightbulb is similar to an ordinary lightbulb, we can use the CLightBulb class and simply extend its behavior. First, we need to derive a new class called CFlashingLightBulb from CLightBulb. We then need to add a new state for handling the flashing and overload the *On* state functions from CLightBulb.

```
class CFlashingLightBulb : public CLightBulb
{
protected:
    CStateTemplate<CFlashingLightBulb> m_StateOnDim;
    unsigned int m_uTimer;
public:
    CFlashingLightBulb();
    virtual void SwitchOffEvent();
    virtual void BeginStateOn();
    virtual void StateOn();
    virtual void BeginStateOnDim();
    virtual void StateOnDim();
    virtual void EndStateOnDim();
};
```

Like the previous example, the new state is initialized in the constructor.

```
CFlashingLightBulb::CFlashLightBulb() : CLightBulb()
{
    m_StateOnDim(this,BeginStateOnDim,StateOnDim,
        EndStateOnDim);
}
```

The flashing behavior will be handled by cycling between the *On* and *On Dim* states, with a timer controlling the flash interval. The *On* state functions from CLightBulb are overloaded to reflect the new behavior.

```
void CFlashingLightBulb::BeginStateOn()
{
    CLightBulb::BeginStateOn();
    m_uTimer=10;
}

void CFlashingLightBulb::StateOn()
{
    --m_uTimer;
    if (m_uTimer==0)
        GotoState(m_StateOnDim);
}
```

Likewise, we implement the *On Dim* state functions.

```
void CFlashingLightBulb::BeginStateOnDim()
{
    cout << "State: On Dim" << endl;
    m_uTimer=10;
}

void CFlashingLightBulb::StateOnDim()
{
    --m_uTimer;
    if (m_uTimer==0)
        GotoState(m_StateOn);
}
```

Finally, we update the SwitchOffEvent() function to take into account the new state.

```
void CLightBulb::SwitchOffEvent()
{
    if (IsState(m_StateOn) || IsState(m_StateOnDim))
        GotoState(m_StateOff);
}
```

During execution, the FSM will cycle between the *On* and *On Dim* states, thus simulating the behavior of a flashing light. This example illustrates both the use of new states and the overloading of existing states to extend the behavior of the FSM.

Conclusion

This gem illustrates an FSM implementation using function pointers that allows developers to quickly add FSM functionality to either new or existing game objects. While applicable for game development in its current form, the FSM implementation presented here is minimal and intended mainly to be used as a starting point for developers wishing to create their own FSM implementations. Accordingly, there are many areas of possible modification, including memory optimizations, more-complicated state-transition logic, customized state objects, and additional error checking.

References

[Calder94] Calder, Brad, Dirk Grundwald, and Benjamin Zorn, "Quantifying Behavioral Differences Between C and C++ Programs," available online at http://www.cs.colorado.edu/department/publications/reports/docs/CU-CS-698-94.ps, January 1994.

[Dysband00] Dysband, Eric, "A Finite-State Machine Class," *Game Programming Gems*, Charles River Media, Inc., 2000: pp. 237–248.

[Haendel01] Haendel, Lars, "The Function Pointer Tutorials," available online at http://www.function-pointer.org, October 2001.

[LaMothe99] LaMothe, Andre, *Tricks of the Windows Game Programming Gurus*, Sams, 1999: pp. 729–734.

[Stroustrup97] Stroustrup, Bjarne, *The C++ Programming Language, Third Edition*, Addison Wesley Longman, Inc., 1997: pp. 418–421.

[Sweeney00] Sweeney, Tim, "Unreal Technology FAQ," available online at http://unreal.epicgames.com/UnrealScript.htm, June 2000.

[Woodcock00] Woodcock, Steve, "Game AI: The State of the Industry," *Game Developer Magazine*, August 2000: pp. 34–43.

[Woodcock01] Woodcock, Steve, "Game AI: The State of the Industry," *Game Developer Magazine*, August 2001: pp. 24–32.

3.4

Terrain Analysis in an RTS— The Hidden Giant

Daniel Higgins,
Stainless Steel Studios, Inc.
dan@stainlesssteelstudios.com

As children (and, well, even as adults), we strive to understand the world around us. By the time we enter school, we can easily recognize and identify many things. We know what a street is, or a building, and can recognize the sky, the ocean, a hill, and a forest. Even if we had silly notions as kids, such as the woods behind our suburban home actually being part of a forest that stretched on for miles, we at least recognized these terrain elements and many of their properties.

Moving into the virtual world, computer games strive to provide a rich environment for players by creating a world that is full of interesting terrain elements. Just as a teenager can decide either to cut through the woods to get to a friend's house or go by way of the street, programmers can use the same type of terrain information to make decisions. Programmers might have a virtual teenager avoid traveling through the forest if it's after sunset, or perhaps take a chance on the forest if they are walking with a group of friends.

Gathering the information about the world environment is called *terrain analysis*. It is a vital element of today's computer games, especially real-time strategy (RTS) games. Unfortunately, this important task can be overlooked or grossly underestimated in terms of development time. Make no mistake—writing a terrain-analysis engine can be a gigantic undertaking, depending on how much information you want to analyze. However, it is one of the most important developmental tasks in an RTS game.

Areas

The first step in terrain analysis is planning. When choosing what terrain elements to analyze, we must consider: "What areas do I need to know about?" Will you want to recognize forests, choke points, or oceans in your game? Brainstorm a list of world areas you will want to recognize.

After brainstorming a list of areas, you might find that these areas need to be divided into two major categories: static and dynamic. Despite conceptual differences, static and dynamic areas can be represented very similarly (if not identically) in code. Since both are very similar, you should consider writing a generic "Area" base class full of virtual methods that will facilitate easier future programming.

Static Areas

Static areas don't change throughout the course of the game. Generally, static areas tend to have the most points (or tiles) and cover the largest areas. In contrast to dynamic areas, static areas must be preprocessed before the game starts. This is an advantage over dynamic areas because dynamic areas might need frequent processing before, during, and after the game.

Reprocessing a very large area during runtime could make the game slow down to a crawl, or it could even freeze the game world. That would be a disaster for a game and obviously should be avoided. Static areas are therefore a necessity in order to reduce processing time during a game.

Some examples of static areas are:

- **Continents**: Continents are one of the most important areas of terrain analysis. Every point on every map should exist on some type of continent, even if the point is a cliff, an ocean, or a waterfall. Continents are used to determine the accessibility properties of different parts of the map. You might have naval units that can only travel in ocean continents, land units that can only traverse land continents, or air units that can fly over all continent types.
- **Hills**: If an RTS engine makes use of true line of sight or gives an advantage to fighting on an elevation, then detecting hills is a good idea. In *Empire Earth,* we defined a hill as a collection of points adjacent to each other that are above a certain elevation level. We found hills to be very useful for adding to the perception that the computer player played intelligently. Archers owned by the computer player might flee to a nearby hill to attack from an elevated point, or perhaps the computer player would choose a hill near a resource site as a good spot for a guard tower.
- **Shore Tiles**: A shore tile is defined as a tile that meets the ocean and the land. This means some shore tiles exist mainly in the ocean and some exist in the shallow water where most land units can walk. A game with shore waves can use shore tiles to determine if they should make a wave, how far out it should start in the ocean, and what its neighboring waves should look like. Shore tiles can also be very useful for determining at what point a transport ship should pick up or drop off a unit.
- **Shore Rings**: Shore rings are defined as tiles that exist within some distance of land. If a tile exists two tiles from land, then it would be stored in 'shore ring 2.' Shore rings work great for RTS games with units that can span multiple tiles. Since collision detection with large units can be a tricky issue, one way to keep gigantic ships like aircraft carriers from traveling too close to the land is to build rings around the coastline. Any number of rings can be used to keep different

sizes of ships from reaching the land. If keeping ships away from coastlines is not an issue, this is probably not an area that needs to be processed.

Dynamic Areas

Dynamic areas, which change with the runtime variations of the world, help keep a game from getting stale and add longevity to a product. Computer players that react to a changing world provide a greater illusion of intelligence to human players and can give players a fresh gaming experience every time they play.

In the code, dynamic areas look much the same as static areas, but dynamic areas carry an inherent danger with them. If an area is very large and needs to be reprocessed often during a game, it can cause the game to run poorly or even freeze. This can be avoided with some creative tricks, but efficiently reprocessing dynamic areas goes beyond the scope of this gem.

Some examples of useful dynamic areas in an RTS are:

- **Forests**: Forests are defined as a collection of trees that all touch each other. Forests need to be dynamic, since if a player chops down a tree, the old location of the tree should no longer report that it belongs in a forest. If we assume people understand and recognize forests, then it's easy to put them to good use. The uses of forests should be intuitive. For example, if the player selects a citizen, then clicks on a tree in the middle of a forest, the player will probably expect that the citizen (or unit) would harvest from a tree in the vicinity of the unreachable one that was clicked on. If we have analyzed the forest, then we have a variety of simple ways to find the perfect tree to chop. One technique is simply to go to the closest tree to the unit. Another technique is to calculate the line from the unit to the selected tree, find the first tree in the forest that the line intersects, and then send the unit to that tree. The AI can also use knowledge about the forest for various tasks, such as planning where to build a wall or where to hide units for an ambush.

- **Towns**: In the everyday world, most people think of a town as a collection of buildings that are within proximity of each other. The concept is much the same in an RTS, with the exception that in the game world, towns should be represented as a convex hull in which a number of buildings live (see Figure 3.4.1).

    Towns are dynamic because they can grow, shrink, or even merge when a building is created or destroyed. Towns also differ from most other areas because the convex hull encompassing all the points is more significant than the points inside (individual buildings). In a sense, if one wants to see if a given point were inside a town, then they would need to get its convex hull and do a point-in-polygon test instead of checking its actual points.

    Towns are created and destroyed when buildings are built or razed. The process of assigning a building to a town starts with the newly constructed building checking its distance to each town's convex hull. The distances are then used to determine if the new building should join a town, merge two or more towns,

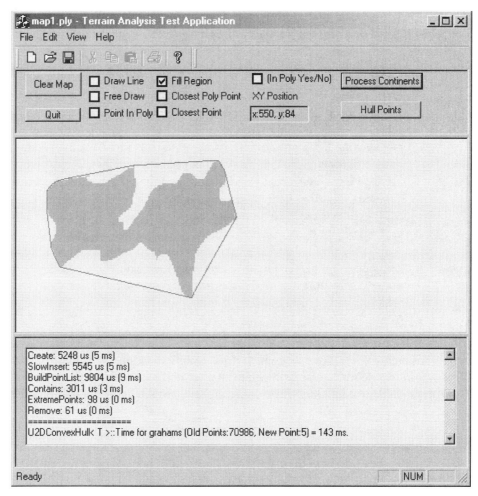

FIGURE 3.4.1   *Highlighted area indicates a town.*

or create a new town of its own. If a building is within the acceptable distance of two towns, the towns merge and become a single, larger town.

An identified town can also serve a greater purpose than just mapping out a cluster of player buildings. Storing information about a town can help the AI units make intelligent decisions about where to attack, with what units, and what strategy is best for approaching a town.

A few of the many pieces of information that can be stored about a town are:

• **IsCoastal:** In many situations it can be quite useful to know if a town is located near an ocean. The most obvious use for this is to let the computer player quickly know if they should bother bringing in sea units to bombard the town.

- **TownCost:** Computing the economic cost of all the buildings in the town can tell the computer player if this is the enemy's biggest town, or if it's really just a small hamlet.

- **Choke Points**: Choke points are defined as a narrow routes, such as between two forests, which provide passage through to other regions. Choke points are useful for RTS computer players in that they can indicate good guard locations, ambush spots, and wall building locations. They can even help a computer player avoid blocking itself in by indicating where *not* to construct buildings. A more detailed choke point description and algorithm can be found later in this gem.

- **Herds**: Herds are packs of similar animal units that share a territory and group dynamics. Tracking herds as areas provides a way to keep the herd acting realistically, such as having territory disputes or moving around the game world as a group.

- **Armies**: Armies are certainly dynamic. They can grow and shrink many times in the course of a game. They are primarily useful for the computer player and its player interaction, but there are other creative game-engine uses for armies as well, including group movement and group behaviors.

Building Generic Areas

Object-oriented programming (OOP) techniques can sometimes have a large up-front development cost; but in general, they make subsequent development faster and easier. Designing a generic area system is an example of how OOP can make life easier in the long run.

An area class needs only a few data members. It needs to know the points inside them, the convex hull of those points (more on that soon), the type of area they are, and lastly, it needs to have a unique ID. In addition to data, areas should have some virtual methods to make using them a snap.

Virtual methods should include:

- Create(): Creates the area.
- GetClosestPoint(): Gets the closest point to a given point.
- GetClosestPointToArea(): This method takes another area and returns the closest point between the two areas.
- GetClosestPointToHull(): This is different than GetClosestPoint() because it relies on checking the hull. You could make your derived classes call GetClosest-PointToHull() in the GetClosestPoint() method. This is most useful for areas like towns, which have few actual points (the buildings); but you want it to seem like every point in a town is actually stored inside this object (instead of just the few that were used to make the hull).
- GetRandomPoint(): This is probably the most useful area-related method. Using this for computer-player guard destinations saves development time and can help create the illusion of intelligence.

Optimization Tip: When you derive a continent area, consider putting lots of other areas inside the continent class. For example, have a vector of choke points on the continent so that programmers can quickly get the choke points that they want. This can also serve as a memory optimization for other areas. Using continents as sort of a hash table can cut down the search time for tasks, like finding which forest's hull a user clicked in. If you return the continent the user clicked on and only search that forest, you've cut down your search time.

Building your area system with a generic base class will make using your areas a lot easier. Your computer player can often make intelligent decisions just by performing some basic actions on areas without having to know much about the area with which they are interacting.

Convex Hulls

One of the more-complex areas of simulating human intelligence deals with the computer's lack of vision. A human can receive an enormous amount of data in a few blinks of an eye, while our computer companions cannot. We can simulate this behavior by using a simple and powerful geometric shape, the *convex hull.*

A convex hull is a shape that does not fold in on itself. If one were to walk clockwise around the edges of a hull, they would turn only to the right and never to the left. Also, If you were to draw a line between those points, the line would never leave the convex hull.

While a convex hull is a shape that can exist in many dimensions, for reasons of efficiency and usefulness to most RTS engines, it's generally safe to focus on the 2D case. Certainly, developing a hull system that works in multiple dimensions has its benefits given the development time or specific need for them.

Why Use Convex Hulls?

Convex hulls take up very little memory, can be very efficient, and provide a fuzzy level of accuracy. On one end of the spectrum, you could have perfect accuracy by just keeping a list of all the points, but this would be costly in terms of memory usage as well as performance. A concave hull could be more accurate, but it would cost more in memory and performance. On the other end of the spectrum, you can use bounding boxes or bounding circles to approximate the areas in question. Both of these use very little memory and can be more efficient (performance-wise), but they suffer from poor accuracy in representation. The convex hull brings all of these together, giving us good accuracy, good performance, and low memory usage.

Convex hulls can be used in almost every area of an RTS game engine. They are ideal for determining if a unit is hidden in the vicinity of a forest or if a unit has crossed the borders of a town. They also make the creation of complicated AI behaviors simple to implement because they provide the programmer with a quick representation of an area. Being a special geometric shape, they are bound to mathematical rules that allow the AI to make optimizations and assumptions based on those rules (see Figure 3.4.2).

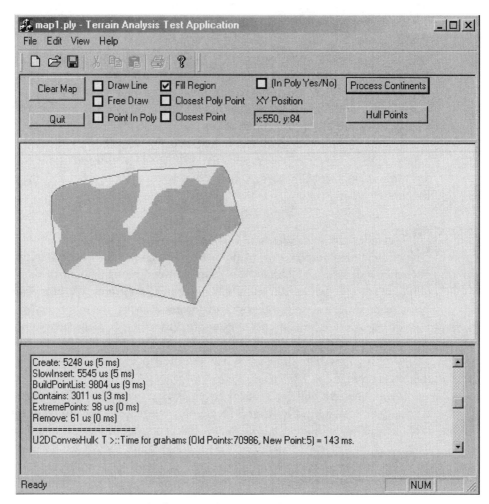

FIGURE 3.4.2   *A convex hull surrounds an area (shown in a test application).*

It's not just the useful tasks alone that make the investment in convex hulls so appealing. The development time for hulls is fairly short, since the math knowledge required for writing 2D convex hulls is small (i.e., implementation shouldn't be difficult for programmers who aren't math gurus).

What's in a Hull?

A convex hull is really a polygon with special rules. It therefore makes sense to begin the construction of a convex hull class by constructing a base polygon class. It is also a good idea to make the polygon/convex hull class a template, since most tasks in an PC-based RTS game can use integer-based hulls for added performance. Otherwise, we use float-based hulls.

Table 3.4.1 Data Members for a Polygon Class

Type	Variable	Description
vector<U2DPoint<T>>	mPoints	All the vertices of the polygon.
U2DRectangle<T>	mBoundingBox	Quick representation of the area of the polygon. Its area covers the extreme points of the hull or polygon. The box has two points, one at top left, and the other at bottom right.
U2DPoint<T>	mCenterPoint	Center of mass point. This is very handy for making quick, fuzzy decisions about distances to a polygon, or as a homing beacon for this shape.
float	mArea	The area inside the polygon.

Note: U2DPoint<T> is a template *xy* point class, and U2DRectangle<T> is a template rectangle class with top, left, right, and bottom coordinates.

Data members for a polygon class might appear like those shown in Table 3.4.1. Since this is a base class, there are quite a few necessary virtual methods that it should provide in addition to the normal Get/Set and construction/destruction methods.

- CalculateArea(): Determines the area of the polygon or hull.
- ClearPolygon(): Clears the polygon's data.
- Contains(): This inline version does a fast point-in-rectangle check before calling the virtual and more-expensive ContainsInPoly() method.

```
inline bool Contains(const U2DPoint<T>& inPoint) const
{ return (this->mBoundingBox.Contains(inPoint)) ?
        this->ContainsInPoly(inPoint) : false; }
```

- ContainsInPoly(): This virtual method does the appropriate point-in-polygon test for the given point.
- Create(): This creates the polygon, and an optional sorted flag is passed as an optimization for shapes like the convex hull.

- CreateCenterPoint(): This virtual method computes the center point using the appropriate algorithm. One way to compute the center point is the center-of-mass method described here.

```
U2DPoint<float> theSums(0.0f,0.0f);
long            theSize = this->mPoints.size();
long            theLoop;
```

```
/* Sum up all the points. */
for(theLoop = theSize - 1; theLoop >= 0; theLoop--)
{
    // cast to floats regardless of template type.
    theSums.SetX(theSums.GetX() +
    ((float)mPoints[theLoop].GetX() /(float)theSize));

    // cast to floats regardless of template type.
    theSums.SetY(theSums.GetY() +
    ((float)mPoints[theLoop].GetY() / float)theSize));
}

// cast it into the right format:(template function)
theSums.CopyTo(this->mCenterPoint); }
```

- Expand(): A handy method for increasing the size of polygons proportionally by expanding outward, a simple expand algorithm would be to draw a line from each vertex to the center point and project that vertex away from the center.
- GetClosestPoint(): One of the most useful methods for a convex hull, GetClosestPoint() returns a potentially fabricated point on the hull. It's a good idea to have two closest-point methods, one for returning the closest vertex and one for returning the closest line-intersection point on the hull or polygon.
- GetClosestPoints(): Use this method to find the closest point given two polygons or convex hulls.
- GetIntersection(): Returns true if the two polygons intersect and can optionally create a polygon representing the intersection.
- SortPoints(): This is a template function used to sort the points.

```
template<class K> // inFO is a function object.
inline void SortPoints(const K& inFO)
{ std::sort(mPoints.begin(), mPoints.end(), inFO); }
```

- TrimToVitalPoints(): This is where the convex hull-creation algorithm should run; however a normal polygon would probably do nothing in this method.

Deriving from U2DPolygon<T>, the convex hull class needs to overload some of the polygon's base class methods, and one of the most important methods is Create().

The Create()method is the entry point for the convex hull-creation algorithm. Picking the right algorithm to construct a hull will make a big difference in hull-creation performance. There are many published convex hull-creation methods and utility functions [O'Rourke98]. One of the favorites among programmers, and the method used in *Empire Earth,* is Graham's algorithm [O'Rourke98].

Optimization Tip: The most expensive part of Graham's algorithm is sorting the points; passing in an 'already sorted' flag for those rare occasions when you already have a list of sorted points will save you some CPU time.

TIP

Convex hulls are very effective elements in terrain analysis as they allow the programmer to create lots of incredible features in relatively little time. Powerful features and low development costs are two things that designers, gamers, and programmers can all smile about.

The Giant in the Matchbox

Having the convex hull of an area is terrific—until you need to get an actual point from the area. If you want a real point (a point that exists on a continent, for example, and not just in its convex hull), then you will need a data structure to contain all of the continent's points.

Egads! You're probably imagining thousands or millions of points floating around in memory. It is true that gigantic maps and even some smaller maps will be serious memory hogs unless we can employ smarter techniques.

What we need is a memory superhero, something to crunch all these evil points into a tiny space without causing a major CPU hit. Answering the call for this crisis is: Major Matchbox—the template-based U2DMatchboxContainer class.

The U2DMatchboxContainer class, known throughout the rest of this gem as the "matchbox container," is a series of linked lists that contain point ranges and simulate actual points. A matchbox container is really just a one-dimensional array in *x*, which can contain linked lists of start and end *y* value nodes.

Consider a square blank map that consists of a single land continent. If the map is 400 × 400, then the continent contains 160,000 points. If we put these points inside a matchbox container, the 160,000 points end up turning into only 400 points, since we only need to store one point for each *x* value. This is because the continent is already convex (it's a square). If we take a more-complicated example and store the points from Figure 3.4.3a in a matchbox container, the end result would look much like Figure 3.4.3b.

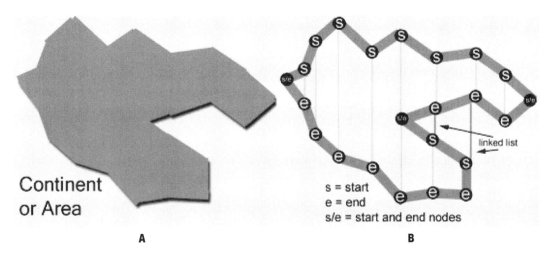

Continent or Area

s = start
e = end
s/e = start and end nodes

linked list

A   B

FIGURE 3.4.3 *(a) A continent or area. (b) How a continent's points would be stored in a matchbox container.*

What's in the Matchbox?

There are three important structures in the matchbox system—the matchbox container node, the matchbox container list header, and the manager of all these: the matchbox container. Inside the matchbox container lives an array of header nodes. The array represents the *x*-axis, although it could just as easily represent the *y*-axis, or even be dynamically based, which would take up less memory.

Data members for the matchbox container are shown in Table 3.4.2. Note that this should be made into a template class; but for simplicity, this is being shown as an integer container.

Table 3.4.2 Data Members for the Matchbox Container

Type	Variable	Description
`vector<MatchboxListHeader*>`	`MPointArray`	*X*-axis representation of points. Each element in the array is a *y* (start-end) point range-linked list.
`long`	`MOffset`	Odds are that *x* won't start at zero; but we want our array to start at zero, so we will shift all incoming *x* coordinates by this amount. This means if our points go from *x,y* (10,50) to (25,99), then our offset would be 10.
`long`	`MSize`	Number of points inside this container.

Some of the methods for the matchbox container are:

- `BuildPointList()`: Fills the incoming vector with all of our points. In a sense, it puts all of our points into an array format. Passing in a step level is important for template versions because, if this container used floating-point numbers instead of integers, the step level would indicate at what rate we increment each value as we generate our list of points.
- `ComputeCenterPoint()`: This handy method uses a center-of-mass computation to determine the center of all these points.
- `Contains()`: Returns true if the passed-in-point exists (real or implied) inside this container.
- `Create()`: Creates our container from the passed-in-points.
- `GetClosestPoint()`: Odds are, you'll eventually want to quickly retrieve the closest point to a passed-in-point or another matchbox container.
- `GetOnlyExtremeEdgePoints()`: This gets only the extreme edges of a polygon. This means if a continent is doughnut shaped, none of the inner-rim doughnut

points would be returned. This is ideal for optimizing the computation of a convex hull. It's a huge optimization to build a hull with 200 points instead of 80,000. It's also possible to write a very fast convex hull-creation method based on previously known extreme points and incorporating the sorting implied in the storage of this structure.

- `GetRandomPoint()`: By passing in a random number generator, you can have a get-random-point method that will be used more than you might expect.
- `Insert()`: Having three insert methods is useful. One method takes a point, another takes a vector of points, and a third method takes a matchbox container.
- `Remove`: Given a point or a vector of points, this method should remove them from the container.
- `Operator[]`: A useful method that simulates an array traversal.

MatchboxListHeader

This class contains a linked list of container nodes and a size. It does most of the work by inserting, removing, and merging nodes.

Matchbox Container Node

The matchbox container node contains a start y and an end y coordinate. All methods in it are based on checks to see if a passed in point or coordinate exists within its start-to-end range.

A `Contains()` method would look like this:

```
inline bool Contains(long inNum) const
{ return (inNum >= this->mStart && inNum <= this->mEnd); }
```

By putting the pieces of the matchbox nodes, header, and container together, you'll have a fast data structure capable of handling many points in a small amount of memory. It's an incredibly useful tool for optimizing terrain analysis and other areas. Most game engines use points, and therefore should have this or a similar structure in their toolbox.

Choke Points

You will recall that choke points are narrow passages that provide access to other regions. That being said, the method of creating choke points is really unique to every game. In the RTS game *Empire Earth,* choke points are created when two or more large areas—such as a forest, cliff, ocean, or edge of the map—are near each other but do not touch (see Figure 3.4.4).

From out of the Blue

Imagine it is a bright sunny day and you want to send a cavalcade of riders and villagers north toward the plains to build a settlement. You seem cheery and optimistic as you set out on your journey. You anticipate a smooth trip, since reports of enemy sightings along the road have been minimal.

While on your journey, you approach a passage that is flanked by a forest on either side. The passage seems harmless enough as your traveling companions bask in the bright morning sun and smile at the sound of singing birds. Midway through the wooded lane, the songs of the birds become drowned out by a volley of curses and the thunder of hooves, which seem to come from all directions. The passage, once a tranquil scene, now seems to be collapsing in around you with a hail of fiery arrows and charging horsemen! Screams fill the air as you beckon your troops to turn back. You wheel and turn, only to have lines of despair crease your forehead. You watch helplessly as the rear of your army collapses under a mass of enemy troops. Your army breaks in a panic, and you stare, too shocked to move, at the helpless villagers that were under your protection. You put your hands to your ears, attempting to block the screams that were once laughing, joking voices. There is no escape, the enemy is everywhere at once, and the only choice is to charge blindly into the rising dust at either the front or the rear of the passage. You know what must be done; and you begin your final assault. You are now one of the screaming horde, sword raised, horse charging, and for the few moments before you are cut down, you try to even the score a bit.

The Plan

How did the computer player plan such an evil encounter? Was it good planning, luck, or perhaps just knowing information about the terrain? As you might imagine, choke points are great for planning ambushes. Let's walk through how the computer was able to plan this attack.

First, the computer must pick a choke point from which to launch its ambush. Maybe it selected a random choke point or found a highly traveled one, or perhaps it even selected one between the enemy (the human player) and the main town. Regardless of how it was chosen, the computer might choose to divide its ambush troops into four divisions and place them all at opposite, extreme points of the choke point, as indicated in Figure 3.4.4.

Notice that the four black Xs are the farthest points of the choke point. This is where the computer player hides its troops and waits for the enemy to pass. It waits and watches until the enemy has reached the center of the choke point (the + sign), then the computer lets out a howl and attacks!

In *Empire Earth,* having the choke point, together with its points and its convex hull, made planning and executing this ambush simple. The computer player did not have to do a lot of intensive CPU planning. Instead, it simply picked a good spot and then waited for its opportunity to attack.

Finding the Choke Point

The algorithm for finding a choke point temporarily costs a large amount of memory and CPU time, all of which fortunately go away once the choke points have been

FIGURE 3.4.4 *Ambush in a choke point.*

computed. Most of the memory requirements involved go into making the algorithm run quickly, so you can trade performance for memory if you wish.

Before we describe the algorithm, keep in mind that you'll need quite a few (mainly integer) arrays that are the size of the world. Don't panic; this is only temporary memory and will be returned after the choke points are computed. If you can't afford the memory even temporarily, consider breaking the world down into continents or some other area division first, and then use the bounding box of the continent or area as the 'map of the world.'

The idea behind this algorithm is that each terrain area is given an influence (called throughout the rest of this gem as an "aura") that can grow. The number of passes this algorithm will perform determines how much this aura will grow. If two or more auras intersect each other, then a choke point is formed.

The main loop of the algorithm is as follows:

```
// copy the original map into choke point map.
CopyOriginalMapIntoChokePointMap(inMap,theOutMap);

// inPasses controls how much area's auras grow.
for(theLoop = inPasses - 1; theLoop > 0; theLoop--)
{
```

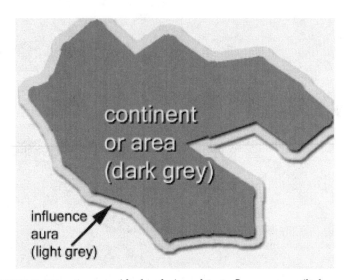

FIGURE 3.4.5   *An area (dark color) and its influence aura (light gray).*

```
// copy the map. (uses cached map from above
// the loop)
CopyOriginalMapIntoChokePointMap(inMap,
    theResultMap);

// apply the algorithm
ApplyChokePointAlgorithmToMap(theOutMap,
    theTempMap, theMaxX, theMaxY));
}
// create the final choke points.
CreateChokePointAreas(inMap);
```

Before the main loop begins, we have to generate and cache a map of obstacles. If a tile has an obstacle on it, then the tile gets a blocked cost (whatever is appropriate for your game), otherwise it gets a zero cost.

Then, for every tile in the world:

```
// cache the XY array position
long theXY = ((theXLoop * theMaxX) + theYLoop);

// if this tile is blocked, fill in the areas id
if(ChokePoint::IsBlockedTile(inMap->GetTile(theXLoop,
    theYLoop), theXLoop, theYLoop, theAreaID))
{
    // store the blocking area's id and set a cost.
    ChokePoint::sTerrainIDMap[theXY] = theAreaID;
    ChokePoint::sCostMap[theXY] = kBlockedCost;
}
else
```

```
{
    ChokePoint::sTerrainIDMap[theXY] = 0;
    ChokePoint::sCostMap[theXY] = 0;
}
```

After caching these values in the static cost/terrain ID map, subsequent calls to `CopyOriginalMapIntoChokePointMap()` will simply do a `memcpy()` of the `sCostMap`.

The real algorithm is in the `ApplyChokePointAlgorithmToMap()` method. This method must loop through every tile in the world ("tile" in this case means the map of open and obstacle tiles). If a tile does not have an obstacle, then for each of this tile's neighbors, we sum up all the costs for all the nonblocking tiles. To add up each neighbor's cost, we simply refer to the 'current cost map,' which means we get all the costs from previous algorithm passes. Using the costs from prior passes is what makes the auras grow.

If we get a tile with a cost when looping through the neighboring tiles, we then cache its area ID. This tells us from which area the aura grew. That's not enough, however, since we have to identify whether this cost came from our aura or a different one.

As the auras grow, they mark tiles as being from their aura. If the auras intersect, they mark tiles with a 'compound-area' ID. If we see that one of our neighbors has either the compound-area ID or an aura ID that is not our own, then we keep this cost. Otherwise, we set our cost to zero if no neighbors have a cost and come from either a different aura or a compound aura. This keeps areas from creating choke points with only themselves.

At the end of our tile loop, each tile takes the sum of its neighbors (zero if they were not a compound aura or a different aura) and divides the sum by the number of qualified neighbors that contributed to our sum. That tends to give the choke points an hourglass shape, but you can fine-tune this to achieve different results.

After executing all the desired passes, you end up with an array of scores that are either zero, blocked, or some other score. The last step is to gather the adjacent scores and create choke points out of them. The perfect tool for this (and all other terrain analysis detection tasks) is the A* machine described in the book *AI Wisdom* [Higgins02a]. If you don't want to create an A* machine, then a flood-fill algorithm can gather these scores and create the choke point areas.

This algorithm sounds expensive, but with the right optimizations, it can be very fast.

Performing Terrain Analysis

When you write a terrain-analysis engine, much of its success is determined by how generic it can be written and how optimized it is. In *Empire Earth*, we used an A* machine, which is a highly optimized and generic tool that can be used for everything from path-finding units to creating forest areas and other terrain-analysis tasks as well.

Conclusion

Certainly, one of the major tasks faced when creating an RTS engine is terrain analysis. Successful games can still ship without complex terrain analysis, but the more tools provided to programmers, the more plentiful and advanced the game features will be. Terrain analysis demands a high-performance, generic engine, and developing such an engine takes a significant amount of time. However, if done well, and if the terrain information is used creatively, it pays for itself many times over.

References

[Higgins02a] Higgins, Daniel F., "Generic Path-finding," *AI Game Programming Wisdom,* Charles River Media, Inc., 2002.

[Higgins02b] Higgins, Daniel F., "How to Achieve Lightning Fast A*," *AI Game Programming Wisdom,* Charles River Media, Inc., 2002.

[O'Rourke98] O'Rourke, Joseph, *Computational Geometry in C,* Second Edition, Cambridge University Press, 1998.

3.5

An Extensible Trigger System for AI Agents, Objects, and Quests

Steve Rabin, Nintendo of America, Inc.

steve@aiwisdom.com

When your players exhaust the single-player version of your game and then search online for more levels or the level editor, you should be prepared to quench their thirst. Extensible levels and quests are the hallmark of a well-designed game, and enable a faithful following to extend your game's normal life span. Whether your game is an RTS, an RPG, or an action game, you should allow the player some way to customize the levels and build new areas to conquer.

Baldur's Gate, *StarCraft*, and *Dungeon Siege* are all great games that allow the player to create new quests, and in certain cases, modify and extend the AI. However, the player is not a programmer, and you shouldn't force them to learn a fictional programming language and debug their creations. Simplicity is the key to allowing the average player to tinker with your game, and it can be achieved by implementing an extensible *trigger system*.

Introducing the Trigger System

A trigger system is a centralized piece of code that does one thing: It evaluates conditions and executes responses. If a set of conditions is met, a set of responses is executed. This simple system is elegant, easy to implement, and easy to data-drive [Rabin00]. It can solve a variety of problems and is especially good at being modified by designers and players. Best of all, it makes it easy to create exciting, new, interactive environments for the players to explore.

Consider a game where you take a brave band of adventurers to explore a dungeon. As you trace through the catacombs, a pillar crumbles and almost crushes your leader. As you reach an impressive stone door, an icy draft snuffs your torches. After lighting your last torch, you decipher the inscription on the door and it reads, "Heavy are the hearts who pass through this doorway." With a little thought, you place the members of your party on the heart-shaped floor tiles, and the door slowly grumbles open.

Each of the previous events can be specified with a trigger system using the simple condition-and-response paradigm. When a party member walked within a meter of a particular pillar object, it responded by falling. When the party walked within two meters of the door, the response was to play a sound effect for wind and extinguish the surrounding torches. When each heart-shaped floor tile was touched by a member of the player's party, the response was to slide open the door and play a stone-grinding sound effect.

A trigger system can be made with just enough hooks that both your designers and your players can spend hours making innovative scenarios and quests. The *Star-Craft* level editor is a fine example of a trigger system that you should examine and play with. Many of the following ideas will expand on that particular functionality.

Object-Owned Trigger Systems

While a master trigger system seems like the natural choice (as demonstrated in [Orkin02]), perhaps a more-powerful architecture is to consider a trigger system class that any agent, object, or quest can own. Not every object requires one, but the ability to own an instance of a trigger system keeps data encapsulated within the objects and makes the system more flexible and object-oriented. It's also natural to think of triggers existing on particular items, so the concept is still easy for players to grasp.

Consider the pillar that falls over when someone stumbles near it. We could define such a pillar in a level editor and attach a trigger definition that encompasses the falling behavior. Then, a designer or player could place dozens of these pillars in the game and they all magically display the same behavior, since the trigger behavior is directly attached to the object. In this way, any agent, object, or quest can own a trigger system that is completely dedicated to that single entity.

Defining a Condition

A condition can be any event or state that you can quantify in your game. Conditions are fixed in the executable, but are highly configurable through arguments or a level editor. Below is a list of possible conditions:

- Player within radius R of spot (x, y, z)
- Player within boxed area position (x, y, z)
- Proximity of an enemy to the player
- Life of the player below X%
- Object X in player's inventory
- Object X equipped by player
- Player was killed
- Player reached X level
- Player talked to character X
- Player killed enemy X
- Player received message X

Conditions Connected with Boolean Logic

In order to make conditions even more flexible, it is advantageous to allow conditions to be linked together with Boolean operators, such as AND, OR, NOT, or XOR. For example, if a door is to open when you are equipped with the ice sword, ice shield, and ice armor, these conditions must be ANDed together. If a door opens if you are holding either the silver key or the skeleton key, then those conditions must be ORed together. Figures 3.5.1 and 3.5.2 demonstrate these conditions with a tree structure.

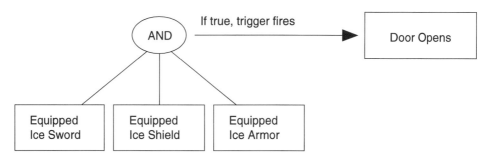

FIGURE 3.5.1   *If all three conditions are "true," then the door will open.*

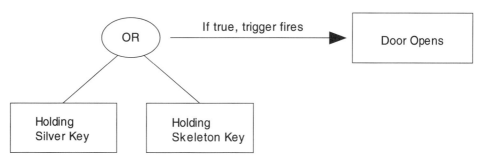

FIGURE 3.5.2   *If either condition is "true," then the door will open.*

The situation gets even more interesting if you require that the player have the ice sword, ice shield, and ice armor equipped, as well as possessing either the silver key or the skeleton key. Figure 3.5.3 shows this configuration.

The visualization from these first three figures is important, since it provides a good way to structure the code. If each element is a class, we can have two types of classes: an Operator class and a Condition class. The Operator class can be configured to behave like any Boolean operator. It also contains a list of pointers to Operator instances or Condition instances, which are the subjects of the single Boolean operator. The Condition class is able to evaluate any testable condition and contains the arguments that customize it.

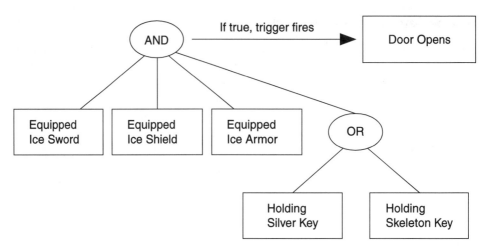

FIGURE 3.5.3   *A more-complicated set of conditions for the door to open.*

Defining a Response

A response can be any state or action in the game that you want to change. Again, these are fixed in the executable, but they can be customized through arguments or a level editor. The following is a list of possible responses:

- Level/Quest complete
- Hurt/Heal player by X points
- Give player X experience
- Open/close/lock/unlock door
- Spawn X creatures of type Y
- Kill X creatures
- Play sound
- Play random sound from list
- X% chance of playing sound
- Move player/enemy X to spot (x,y,z)
- Spawn special effect in spot or on player/enemy
- Set player/enemy X on fire
- Poison player/enemy X
- Stun player/enemy X
- Make player/enemy X invincible
- Make player/enemy X invisible
- Reset trigger
- Send message X to player

If a particular set of conditions is met, the response will be executed. However, the responses can be further expanded to include a list of responses, instead of just one. In this way a single trigger can either affect several things simultaneously when it fires or randomly choose between several possibilities.

Evaluating a Trigger

Once a trigger is defined by its conditions, we need an architecture for evaluating when it should fire. The first consideration is if a particular condition should be event-driven (waiting for an event to be reported to the trigger system), or if it should poll the world (checking for the truthfulness of the condition every couple of game ticks). In practice, you'll want the flexibility to create conditions that are either event-driven or polled; it will be advantageous to build in this dual functionality.

For conditions that are event-driven, we need an interface for events to enter the trigger system. The simplest mechanism is to use event messages. Event messages are simply a notification that some event has occurred, along with any relevant data. For a more in-depth discussion of event messages, refer to [Rabin02].

For conditions that are polled, we can call an update function within the trigger system that allows for each polling condition to do its work. Event-driven conditions would ignore this update.

Whether an event message or a polling update enters the trigger system, we need a way for it to propagate through the conditions. Figure 3.5.4 shows an example of a condition set that requires both event messages and polling. The left condition is waiting for a collision event, while the right condition will poll for the condition when a polling update is received.

When an event message or polling update enters the trigger system, it is routed to the root Operator instance of each trigger. The Operator then passes it through to its children and expects either a "true" or "false" to be returned. Each child in turn passes

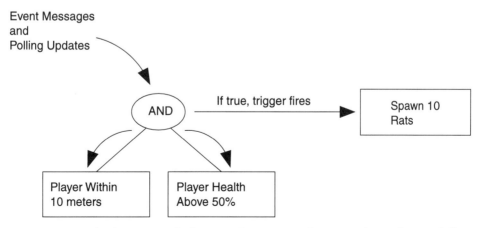

FIGURE 3.5.4   *A trigger example that contains an event-driven condition (bottom left) and a polling-based condition (bottom right).*

it to its own children. When it reaches a condition, the child then returns "true" or "false" based on the new state of the condition. The return values are then evaluated at every Operator instance, and then passed up to its parent.

It is important to note that the Operator class should use lazy evaluation when processing its children. If any condition is not satisfied according to the operators, the trigger testing is abandoned at this time. For the example in Figure 3.5.4, an event message sent to the left condition, which happens to result in "false," should cause the event message to never be sent to the right condition. This will help reduce the amount of processing required.

Another important thing to note when using event-driven conditions is that they must remember events until they are manually reset. With the example in Figure 3.5.4, if the player gets within 10 meters, a collision event should be sent to the trigger. The condition should remember that event and always return "true" upon further event messages or polling updates.

At some point, the conditions for the specific trigger will all return the proper value, causing the trigger to fire. Once a trigger is fired, it will remember and not fire again.

Single Shot and Reload Times

All triggers should have two additional properties that are defined by the designer:

```
bool SingleShot;   // Whether the trigger should only
                   // fire once.
float ReloadTime;  // If it should fire multiple
                   // times, how long before it
                   // resets.
```

These two properties allow triggers to fire more than once. The SingleShot property determines whether the trigger should fire once or be allowed to fire multiple times. If SingleShot is "false," then the ReloadTime determines how long before the trigger resets all of its conditions and accepts events again.

Combining Triggers with Flags and Counters

Triggers can be combined together only if they are able to set intermediary states that every trigger within the system has access to. Thus, every trigger system can be outfitted with a set of flags and counters to keep track of triggers that have fired. To make this as general as possible, we'll let each trigger create arbitrary flags simply by referring to them with a string name. The trigger system will create a flag as it is referenced, or set and keep it around until the system is destroyed.

Consider these new conditions:

- Is flag_name true/false?
- Is flag_name even/odd?
- Is flag_name1 and flag_name2?
- Is flag_name1 and not flag_name2?

- Is `flag_name1` OR `flag_name2`?
- Is `flag_name1` XOR `flag_name2`?
- Is `flag_name1` and `flag_name2` and `flag_name3`?
- Is `flag_name` count equal to X?
- Is `flag_name` count more than X?
- Is `flag_name` count less than X?

Consider these new responses:

- Increment the value represented by `flag_name`.
- Decrement the value represented by `flag_name`.
- Set the value represented by `flag_name` to a value of X.
- Set the value represented by `flag_name2` to the value of `flag_name1`.
- Toggle the boolean value represented by `flag_name`.
- Set the boolean value represented by `flag_name` to TRUE.
- Set the boolean value represented by `flag_name` to FALSE.

With these flags and counters, we can have the trigger system mark or count events, such as counting how many times a player visits a particular area. In addition, the trigger system can now be made to only trigger on particular sequences of events, like stepping on three individual tiles in a specific order. Because these flags and counters hold state information, many more types of triggers are now possible.

The example in Figure 3.5.5 shows how to cause a clue to be dropped if the player can't get through a particular door and is visiting certain areas over and over

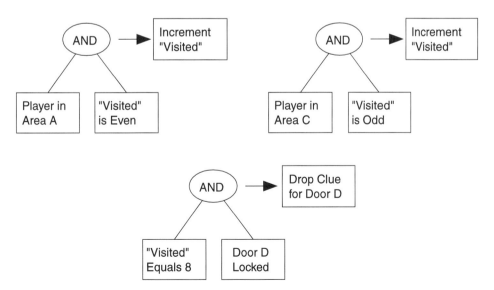

FIGURE 3.5.5   *Three triggers that work together through a counter named "Visited." If the player visits Areas A and C alternatively eight times without unlocking Door D, then a clue is dropped.*

again in desperation. Note that there are three separate triggers that are cooperating through a counter named "Visited."

Note that with the addition of flags and counters, the trigger system becomes strikingly reminiscent of a blackboard architecture [Isla02]. The flags and counters make up the blackboard, and the triggers are the knowledge sources (KSs) that operate on the blackboard data. However, since the triggers mostly act on data coming from outside of the blackboard, the trigger system is not formally a blackboard architecture.

Trigger Systems Versus Scripting Languages

You have probably noticed that the functionality of the trigger system, especially with the addition of state information, is becoming strikingly similar to the functionality of a scripting language. While the functionality does overlap, consider these benefits of using a trigger system instead of a full-featured scripting language:

- *A trigger system can be specified completely within a GUI.* Scripting languages are rarely focused enough to allow this type of simplified and robust authoring. Incorrect syntax isn't a problem, since triggers are structured around conditions and responses.
- *A trigger system is very accessible to users.* The concept is easier to understand, and more people will actually try to use it.
- *A trigger system is constrained.* Since the trigger system is well-constrained, the user is unlikely to crash the game, since they can only perform a small, focused, well-tested set of actions (responses).
- *A trigger system is quick to implement and modify.* A trigger system can be implemented in a fraction of the time of a full scripting language. The time scale is on the order of weeks compared to a scripting language, which can take months or years to implement [Tozour02], [Brockington02].
- *A trigger system is easy to document.* A trigger system is relatively simple to write documentation and examples for—something always needed if you want the user to roll their own after the game is released.

Limitations

The main limitation of the system described is that it doesn't scale well. However, this can be fixed with some extra code to cull irrelevant triggers. Proximity culling has proven to be quite effective.

Another limitation of the system is that the vocabulary for defining conditions and responses is fixed within the executable. Thus, hooks into the code have to be deliberately placed by programmers. This is also a good thing, since it helps to safeguard your game from random or malicious tinkering.

Conclusion

An extensible trigger system might be a luxury for many games with tight development schedules, but it's a worthy feature that will add value and depth to your game. In addition, an extensible trigger system is also an effective way to have level designers construct logic without having to become proficient programmers. While a trigger system at first glance can seem too simple a solution, the goal is to empower designers and players. The easier it is to define content and level-specific logic, the bigger your game can be and the more fun your players will have.

References

[Brockington02] Brockington, Mark, and Mark Darrah, "How Not To Implement a Basic Scripting Language," *AI Game Programming Wisdom*, Charles River Media, Inc., 2002.

[Isla02] Isla, Damian, and Bruce Blumberg, "Blackboard Architectures," *AI Game Programming Wisdom*, Charles River Media, Inc., 2002.

[Orkin02] Orkin, Jeff, "A General-Purpose Trigger System," *AI Game Programming Wisdom*, Charles River Media, Inc., 2002.

[Poiker02] Poiker, Falco, "Creating Scripting Languages for Non-Programmers," *AI Game Programming Wisdom*, Charles River Media, Inc., 2002.

[Rabin00] Rabin, Steve, "The Magic of Data-Driven Design," *Game Programming Gems*, Charles River Media, Inc., 2000.

[Rabin02] Rabin, Steve, "Enhancing a State Machine Language Through Messaging," *AI Game Programming Wisdom*, Charles River Media, Inc., 2002.

[Tozour02] Tozour, Paul, "The Perils of AI Scripting," *AI Game Programming Wisdom*, Charles River Media, Inc., 2002.

3.6

Tactical Path-Finding with A*

William van der Sterren, CGF-AI

william@cgf-ai.com

If all games were just about getting from point A to point B, AI would solely have to provide the shortest paths. A standard A* algorithm could do the job. However, often when trying to reach point B, the AI also needs to avoid being seen or shot at. This is called *tactical path-finding*, a situation where the AI needs to balance short travel times with avoiding hostile observation and fire (see Figure 3.6.1). Whether handling a tank platoon retreating behind a ridgeline or an X-Fighter sneaking through a cloud of meteoroids, the AI needs to consider enemy positions and their lines of fire.

Tactical path-finding not only adds a realistic touch to AI movement, but it also presents a more-rewarding and less-predictable opponent for the player. This gem will help you to extend the standard A* algorithm so it generates tactical paths.

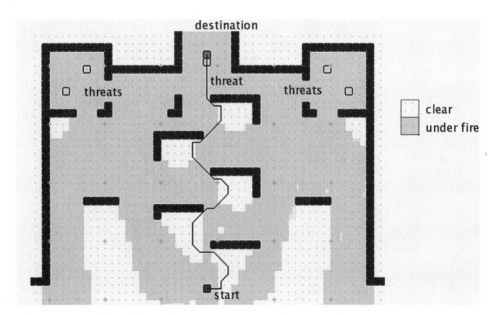

FIGURE 3.6.1 *A path that alternates exposure with cover and concealment.*

First, we will introduce a small change to the 'shortest-path' A* algorithm by increasing the costs for movement through locations subject to enemy observation or fire. As a result, A* will generate paths that attempt to avoid enemy observation and fire. These attempts, however, often look artificial and are not tactically sound.

We will then look at a few of these 'flawed' tactical paths, figure out why these paths are flawed, and how we can correct this in our A* cost function. We will also compare the computing costs of finding tactical paths with those of finding shortest paths. Obviously, finding tactical paths will be more expensive, but we will look into a few techniques and tricks to limit the overhead of the A* search and the line-of-fire evaluations that need to be done during the tactical path computation.

ON THE CD

On the CD-ROM, you will find an extended version of James Matthews' A* Explorer tool [Matthews01]. With this tool, you can experiment with tactical A* (and follow all the examples included in this gem).

A*, But More Risky

A* is a generic search algorithm. To allow it to find paths for our AI, we equip it with a cost function and a heuristic function [Stout00]. For path-finding, the cost function computes the exact cost of moving from one location to another. These movement costs are computed from the distance traveled and the speed allowed by the terrain.

The heuristic function for path-finding typically provides an estimate of the remaining costs to the destination, such as the vector length divided by the maximum speed. Listing 3.6.1 shows an example of a cost function and a heuristic.

Listing 3.6.1   Cost function and heuristic for evaluating shortest paths.

```
float MovementCostNodeToNode(node* aFromNode, node* aToNode) {
    float dist, fromMoveCost, toMoveCost;
    dist = (aFromNode->origin −
        aToNode->origin).Length();

    fromMoveCost = aFromNode->GetLocalMovementCosts();
    toMoveCost   = aToNode->GetLocalMovementCosts();

    // take the average
    return kTravelTimeFactor * dist *
        (fromMoveCost + toMoveCosts) / 2;
}

float HeuristicNodeToDestination(node* aToNode,
        node* aDestination) {
    float dist;
    dist = (aToNode->origin −
        aDestination->origin).Length();

    return kTravelTimeFactor * dist *
        (minimalMoveCostForAnyLocation);
}
```

Using such a cost function and heuristic A* will find and return a path with the lowest costs to the destination. Typically, the AI is interested in the path that gets it to the destination most quickly, so the costs are expressed as time.

If we now introduce additional costs for visiting locations in the enemy's line of sight and line of fire, the resultant generated paths will also attempt to avoid observation and hostile fire. Our revised A* algorithm will automatically balance short travel time versus visiting risky locations, based on the weights for each type of cost [Reece00].

Listing 3.6.2   Cost function for evaluating tactical paths.

```
float TacticalCostNodeToNode1(node* aFromNode,
      node* aToNode) {
   float travelTime, riskFrom, riskTo, riskTotal;
   travelTime = MovementCostNodeToNode(aFromNode,
      aToNode);

   // use duration of move, and average risk of
   // both locations
   riskFrom =
      GetRiskOfEnemyObservationOrFire(aFromNode);
   riskTo   =
      GetRiskOfEnemyObservationOrFire(aToNode);
   riskTotal = (riskFrom + riskTo) / 2 * travelTime;

   // return the weighted combination of travel
   // and risk costs
   return kTravelTimeFactor * travelTime +
      kRiskFactor * riskTotal;
}
```

You'll find an example of a more-tactical A* cost function in Listing 3.6.2. The additional risk costs depend on the risk sampled at each of the nodes and the travel time needed to move from one node to the other. If the nodes are not too far apart, this approximates the total risk of moving from one node to the other. Otherwise, you might need to sample the risk at additional locations between the nodes.

The GetRiskOfEnemyObservationOrFire() function determines the risk of a given node by checking the enemy's ability to observe or fire at that position from all of the known or presumed enemy positions. This typically involves performing a number of ray casts in the game world geometry. Because these ray casts are often expensive, this gem will also discuss how to create small lookup tables of precomputed line-of-fire information.

Listing 3.6.2 explicitly does not provide a tactical version of the heuristic. Because we don't know about the risk in the remaining part of the path, we can only estimate the remaining travel time. The HeuristicNodeToDestination() already does this, so we'll just leave it alone.

Have a look at the results in Figure 3.6.2. In Figure 3.6.2a, you see a 'traditional' shortest path, happily passing through potential hostile fire (gray areas). In Figure

3.6.2b, you see the result of our `TacticalCostNodeToNode1()` cost function. Just by adding costs for the risk of being under fire, we can obtain paths that show a clever and convincing balance between speed and cover.

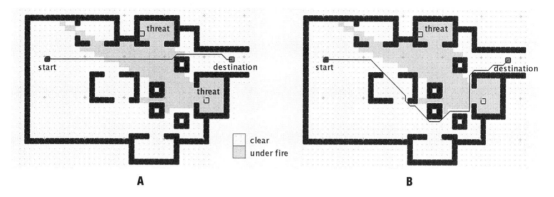

FIGURE 3.6.2   *(a) Shortest path. (b) Path offering protection and concealment.*

We are not done yet! In a large number of situations, this simple tactical A* cost function will provide paths that are tactically flawed and break the illusion of intelligence. Another problem is that the 'tactical' nature of path-finding also comes with a (CPU) cost.

In the remainder of this gem, we will first identify and correct a number of tactical flaws in our cost function. Then, we will investigate the additional costs of tactical path-finding and come up with some ways to limit these costs.

Tactical Improvements to Flawed Paths

It only takes one AI flaw to break the illusion of intelligence. When the player has carefully led wingmen, squads, or his tank platoons to an assault position, there is nothing more annoying than seeing them getting killed due to a lack of tactical understanding. Unfortunately, the tactical cost function defined previously lacks this understanding in a couple of places:

- It does not distinguish between long and short exposures to hostile fire, but simply adds up the total exposure;
- It assumes that threats remain static during the path's duration.

We will look into each of these problems and come up with improvements to the tactical-cost function to try to solve them.

Exposure Time and Enemy Modeling

Imagine a helicopter traversing some terrain defended by surface-to-air missile launchers. Imagine that the helicopter can reach its destination via two paths of identical length. One path exposes the helicopter to the missile launcher only once but for 20 continuous seconds. The other path exposes the helicopter for 20 seconds also, but in four stretches of 5 seconds, each exposure separated by at least 5 seconds of conceal-ment. Both paths are equal to our cost function, TacticalCostNodeToNode1(), which simply adds up the amount of exposure. So, which one should the helicopter really choose?

To the enemy, the duration of the helicopter's exposure is very important. The single 20-second exposure might just be long enough for a missile launcher to detect *and* lock on to the helicopter so it can launch a smart missile. If the helicopter picks the path with four brief exposures, however, this is less likely to happen. Whether it's missile launchers that need to lock on, snipers requiring time to properly aim, or guards turning around in response to some noise—they all prefer their target to have long exposure times with only brief intervals of cover.

To take into account the enemy's 'aiming' ability, therefore, we need to extend our nodes and cost function:

Listing 3.6.3   A* node with one additional field to take into account the enemy's aiming quality.

```
struct node {
    node(): aiming(0) { }; // default ctor: start
                           // with zero aim
    node(float anInitialAim) : aiming(anInitialAim) { };

    float   location[3];
    float   aiming;
};
```

In the cost function, we use and update the aiming information detailed in List-ing 3.6.4.

Listing 3.6.4   Cost function tactical path.

```
float TacticalCostNodeToNode2(node* aFromNode,
        node* aToNode) {
    float travelTime, riskFrom, riskTo,
        riskTotal, aiming;

    // compute travelTime and riskTotal
    ...

    // update aiming quality based on risk,
    // and add it to risk
    aiming  = aFromNode->aiming;
    if ( riskTotal > 0 ) { // spotted,
                                    // so increase aiming
        aiming = min(kMaxAiming, aiming + travelTime);
    } else { // not spotted, so decrease aiming
        aiming *= power(kAimingDamping, travelTime);
```

```
    }
    riskTotal += kAimingFactor * aiming;

    // store aiming quality at destination
    aToNode->aiming = aiming;

    // return the weighted combination of
    // travel and risk costs
    return kTravelTimeFactor * travelTime +
        kRiskFactor * riskTotal;
}
```

Figure 3.6.3 shows a simple test case generated against the helicopter path problem, and the graphs below the image show the exposure and aiming quality for each path.

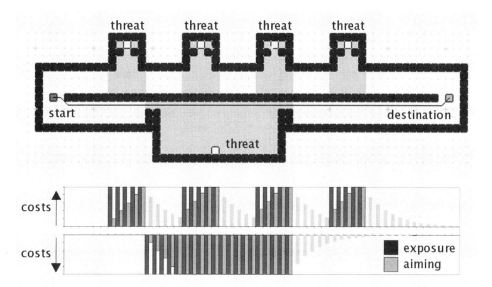

FIGURE 3.6.3 *A flawed tactical path where one long exposure is preferred over four brief ones.*

Both paths feature the same amount of exposure to hostile fire—20 seconds. In the top path, the exposure (dark bars) consists of four intervals separated by an interval of cover of equal length. In the bottom path, the exposure consists of one interval of 20 seconds. For both paths, aiming by the threat (gray bars) starts as soon as the path is exposed. The aiming quality increases with each exposure until a maximum has been reached. As soon as the path is no longer exposed, the aiming decreases (gray bars). The threat might predict the movement on the covered path for a while, but the aiming decreases with time. For the top path, the total amount of 'aiming' when exposed is less (gray bars with borders) than that for the bottom path. The intervals of cover between the exposures decrease the enemy's aiming ability and prevent it from staying at its maximum.

Similarly, when the AI starts a search for a tactical path from a position already exposed to hostile fire, it should start assuming the enemy has a maximum aiming quality. This will result in paths that try to visit nearby cover early on its path.

Thus, by also modeling the enemy's ability to improve its observation and aim in our A* cost function, we get tactically better paths. Our A* now prefers brief exposures separated by long intervals, rather than the alternative of long exposures and short intervals of cover, which definitely looks more intelligent.

Threats Don't Remain Static....

Unfortunately, in most games, threats are not static. They patrol an area or move out upon spotting a unit in their path. Our current tactical A* solution, however, will happily plan a movement lasting perhaps 10 seconds, using the exact threat positions at a single moment. By ignoring the threat's movement, much of the 'tactical quality' of the path is left to chance, and so is the player's perception of the AI.

To obtain better tactical paths, we must anticipate the enemy's movements. This is less complex than it sounds and can be done without using 'chess AI with minmax-trees' to anticipate the most likely enemy movement. Instead, we can just assume that the enemy also occupies each and every position within a few steps of their current position. Have a look at Figure 3.6.4:

Note how much the path in Figure 3.6.4a depends on the initial position of the threat. The path chosen is not robust against threat movement, and it ignores the larger presence of obstacles and the cover on the left side of the map.

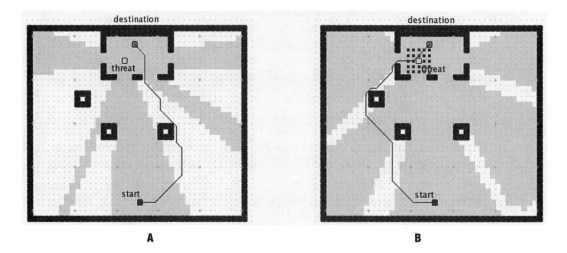

FIGURE 3.6.4   *(a) Tactical path assuming threats remain static. (b) A path assuming threats move two steps.*

When we assume that threats occupy all positions within two steps of their initial position, we indeed pick a more pessimistic scenario. The result, as shown in Figure 3.6.4b, is more robust against threat movement and also favors the higher availability of obstacles on the left side of the terrain. It's hard to fault the AI for picking this path.

Most game AI implementations provide a fast way to obtain all positions within a few steps of the threat. These usually correspond with the outgoing waypoints or neighboring nodes.

More Tactical Improvements

Going from point A to point B, our AI is now able to use cover and concealment in a plausible and effective way. There is more to tactics than just cover and concealment. Here are some more tactical considerations that can easily be taken into account by our tactical A* cost function.

Not all lines-of-fire are equal. If the AI will face only a few enemies, it is wise to count the number of hostile lines-of-fire to a given path position, rather than just distinguishing 'cover' and 'risk' positions. The distance to the threat and the threat's weapon might also have a large influence on the risk of being in the line-of-fire.

Games rewarding stealth and/or locations with shade, foliage, or small objects offer important protection from observation. The path-finding algorithm will prefer these locations if the cost function includes a small penalty for all other locations.

Even in the absence of known threats, there can still be tactical path-finding. Rather than avoiding known and suspected hostile lines-of-fire, it is now important to avoid weak combat positions. For example, a tank should not unnecessarily cross ridgelines because its weaker bottom might be exposed, or it might stand out against the skyline. Similarly, a marine should avoid using ladders because his movement on a ladder is very predictable, and he is unable to return fire while climbing it. Visiting the location of a recently shot squad member probably isn't smart either. Many tactical properties of a location can be analyzed and precomputed, as is explained in [Sterren01]. By introducing additional costs for visiting these locations, the paths generated by our tactical A* path-finding will try to avoid them.

Performance

Obviously the added tactical ability of A* described here comes with some additional CPU and memory costs as compared to a standard A*. Our approach compares even less favorably with the fast, yet predictable precomputed path lookup tables used by some games. As a point of reference, finding a tactical path with A* was about 10 times more expensive than finding a shortest path for squad AI in a *Quake*-based game.

On the other hand, most AI movement does not require a tactical path. Often it suffices to replan a squad's tactical path once every three seconds or so. The individual squad members then move in brief, 'shortest path' hops along this path, and a few line-of-sight checks are used to find cover.

Let's have a look at the origins of some of these additional costs, what they add, and what we can do to limit them. First, we'll consider the line-of-fire tests, which often add the largest costs. Then, we'll look at A* and its tactical cost function, and the larger search space involved.

Efficient Line-of-Sight/Fire Tests

In many games, line-of-sight and line-of-fire (LOF) tests consume considerable CPU time. For tactical path-finding, however, it suffices to use approximations of the actual lines-of-fire (the AI might not have spotted all threats and threats may move or look the other way). Trading CPU time for a lookup table of sampled lines-of-fire might be a good option in this case.

If the terrain is not too large, you might consider using a lookup table with one or more bits per line-of-sight/fire, as described in [Lidén02]. Such a lookup table consumes $O(N^2)$ memory. Alternatively, you can record the incoming lines-of-sight and lines-of-fire per location in terms of sectors, consuming $O(N)$ memory. This approach and the results for our 2D example are illustrated in Figure 3.6.5.

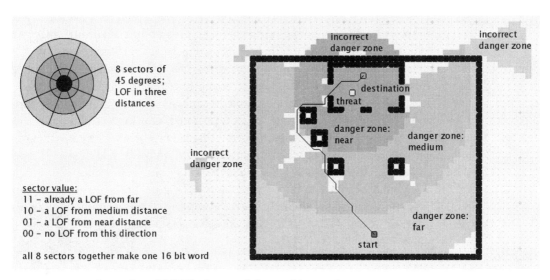

FIGURE 3.6.5   *Sector-based LOF lookup and the resulting path.*

Using one 16-bit word per location, information is precomputed and stored. For each location, every sector describes the worst-case distance from which a potential enemy in that sector can have a line-of-fire to that location. This worst-case distance is represented using four values, from 'no line-of-fire at all in this sector' to a 'line-of-fire at the maximum engagement distance.' Note that the value stored is a pessimistic one: a single position in the sector that has a line-of-fire is sufficient to mark that sector as having a LOF from locations in that direction.

During an A* search, an approximation of the line-of-fire from a given threat position can be efficiently determined using the sector-based lookup table (see Listing 3.6.5). For the threat and position, the corresponding 45° sector and distance are computed. The lookup table then tells us whether it is possible for the location to be fired at from the threat's sector and for the threat-to-fire into the location's sector. If both lines-of-fire are feasible, the threat likely has a line-of-fire.

Obviously, such a small sector-based lookup table does not represent all lines-of-fire correctly. You can easily verify this by comparing the lines-of-fire in Figure 3.6.4 with the danger zones in Figure 3.6.5. In many cases, the (pessimistic) errors correspond to lines-of-sight easily achieved by the threat if the threat were to move. In other cases, such as the danger zones outside the box, the errors are more serious. With a few more bits and smaller sectors, however, you can easily reduce the number of errors.

For 3D environments and for games offering partial cover (which removes the symmetry in lines-of-fire), you might need to store some more bits. Still, this sector-based lookup approach stores lines-of-sight for some 1,000 locations in a few tens of kilobytes and is generally quite efficient.

Listing 3.6.5   Computing an approximate risk using sector-based, precomputed LOF information.

```
float GetApproximateRiskFromThreat(node* threat,
      node* location) {
   int    sector = GetSectorForLine(threat, location);
   int    reverse_sector = (sector + 4) % 8;
   float distance =
      GetDistanceForLine(threat, location);

   if (HasLineOfFireFromSector(location->id,
        sector, distance)
           && CanFireIntoSector(threat->id,
               reverse_sector, distance))
      return distance / kMaxDistance;
   else
      return 0.0;
};

bool HasLineOfFireFromSector(int index, int sector,
      float distance) {
   unsigned int allsectors = sectors[index];
   unsigned int mask  = (0x3 << sector);
   unsigned int value = ((allsectors & mask) >>
      sector);

   return (    (value == 3 && distance < kMaxReach   )
          || (value == 2 && distance < kFarReach    )
          || (value == 1 && distance < kMediumReach));
};

bool CanFireIntoSector(int index, int sector,
```

```
            float distance) {
    // assume firing is symmetric, otherwise
    // an extra table is needed
    return HasLineOfFireFromSector(index,
        sector, distance);
}
```

Extended A* Costs

As mentioned earlier, in its tactical format, A* consumes more CPU and memory, primarily through the tactical cost function and the larger search spaces being explored by A*. One source of additional cost is the floating-point arithmetic in the tactical cost function. You can gain performance by implementing approximate versions of floating-point computations using integer math. You should do this only after having verified and tuned the path-finding with the more 'exact' floating-point cost functions to avoid introducing other problems.

The space being searched by the tactical A* algorithm is typically much larger than one for a standard A* algorithm, as is shown in Figure 3.6.6. The larger search space is a result of the added line-of-fire obstacles that typically are placed between the start and destination position of the path. A* will spend a lot of effort exploring locations to the rear and the sides, since those seem safer. It does not help that the heuristic cannot reflect these added line-of-fire obstacles.

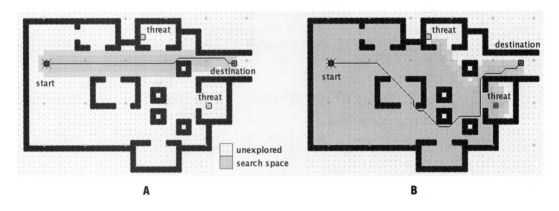

FIGURE 3.6.6   *(a) Search space for shortest path. (b) Search space for tactical path.*

One way to reduce the search space is to introduce even more-costly 'virtual' obstacles. If you want your AI to find a tactical path to a forward destination, why not restrict its attempts to evaluate positions deep in the rear or far to the sides by temporarily marking those nodes 'off-limits'? Nothing says you can't use the algorithm to ignore these areas.

Another way of reducing the search space is to use hierarchical path-finding, executing the path-finding in 'layers.' First, generate a shortest path search at a higher level between areas of the map. Then, select the areas used for that shortest path and their neighboring areas, and run the tactical path-finding to the locations within the selected areas. Both Board/Ducker [BoardDucker02] and White [White02] address area navigation in their gems.

The ASE Program

ON THE CD

As an experiment with tactical path-finding, we invite you to play with the A Star Explorer (ASE) application on the CD-ROM. James Matthews [Matthews01] laid the foundation for this A* tool. The tactical enhancements and line-of-fire approximation described in this gem were added. Note that the A* implementation in this ASE is not representative of a high-performance tactical A*. Instead, the algorithm has been designed for hosting alternative cost functions and visualization.

Conclusion

Finding tactical paths with A* is a bit more complex than treating locations under enemy fire as terrain that is expensive to visit. You also should look at the path from an enemy perspective and deal with enemy aiming and movement in the cost function. These features will ensure paths that intelligently use stretches of cover and concealment to limit the risk of hostile fire, even when the enemies move. Using a similar approach, you can extend A* to pick paths that stay in touch with friendly or hostile elements, if that is important. Hopefully, this gem offers sufficient help to add these features to your game with efficiency.

References

[BoardDucker02] Board, Ben and Mike Ducker, "Area Navigation: Expanding the Path-Finding Paradigm," *Game Programming Gems 3,* Charles River Media, Inc., 2002.

[Lidén02], "Strategic and Tactical Reasoning with Waypoints," *AI Programming Wisdom*, Charles River Media, Inc., 2002.

[Matthews01], A* Explorer, available online at http://www.generation5.org, 2001.

[Patel99] Patel, Amit J., "Amit's Thoughts on Pathfinding", available online at http://www-cs-students.stanford.edu/~amitp/gameprog.html, November 18, 2001.

[Rabin00] Rabin, Steve, "A* Speed Optimizations," *Game Programming Gems*, Charles River Media, Inc., 2000.

[Reece00] Reece, Doug, et al., "Tactical Movement Planning for Individual Combatants," Proceedings of the 9th Conference on Computer Generated Forces and Behavioral Representation, available online at http://www.sisostds.org/cgf-br/9th/, 2000.

[Sterren01] van der Sterren, William, "Terrain Analysis for 3D Action Games," Game Developers Conference 2001 Proceedings, paper and presentation available online at www.cgf-ai.com, 2001.

[Stout00] Stout, Bryan, "The Basics of A* for Path Planning," *Game Programming Gems*, Charles River Media, Inc., 2000.

[White02] White, Stephen, "A Fast Approach to Navigation Meshes," *Game Programming Gems 3*, Charles River Media, Inc., 2002.

3.7

A Fast Approach to Navigation Meshes

Stephen White and Christopher Christensen, Naughty Dog

swhite@naughtydog.com,
cchristensen@naughtydog.com

A common problem in video games is how to navigate around objects in a complex environment. In the case of *Jak and Daxter: The Precursor Legacy*, we wanted creatures to be able to maneuver around highly detailed 3D environments, where each level was composed of millions of polygons and filled with many creatures and obstacles. We wanted the creatures to move intelligently and to exhibit several types of movement behaviors. Due to the density of creatures in our world, we needed a system that was faster than the more-common navigation techniques, such as A*; but it still needed to be flexible, accurate, and give the appearance of intelligent movement. To solve this problem, we developed our own navigation mesh technology, which admirably solved our needs, but also had a few interesting limitations.

Static vs. Dynamic Obstacles

The most fundamental problem of navigation is how to get from point A to point B. The shortest distance between these two points is a straight line. However, a straight line isn't appropriate when there is an obstacle blocking a direct movement between the two points. Obstacles can be broken down into two categories: static and dynamic. Static obstacles are obstacles that don't move, ever. These are our favorite type of obstacles since there are many optimizations that can be made to navigate around them. Examples of static obstacles are cliffs, walls, trees, and pillars. Dynamic obstacles are obstacles that can move or be removed, such as other creatures, the player, moving platforms, and crates. Dynamic obstacles are more difficult to deal with since their ability to move makes it difficult to use precomputed solutions. To make things worse, a dynamic obstacle might move in such a way as to invalidate a previously computed path. Since static and dynamic obstacles have so many different advantages and disadvantages, we chose to approach the problems separately.

Nav Meshes

The most common type of static obstacle encountered in *Jak and Daxter* was the terrain. Natural boundaries, such as walls and cliffs, described an area within which a creature could maneuver. Inside that boundary there could be other static obstacles, such as trees, large rocks, pillars, gaps too large to leap across, and other things that the creature should not be allowed to pass through.

To describe where a creature was allowed to maneuver within an area, the artists modeled a 'nav mesh.' The mesh was a collection of triangles, and each triangle represented a valid area where the creature could maneuver. The mesh was modeled to the extent of the natural boundaries of the desired area, and holes in the mesh were used to represent areas where the creature could not travel within the natural boundaries. Note that our nav meshes were largely two-dimensional in nature and defined a two-dimensional area where a creature could travel. There was, however, a three-dimensional element to our meshes, which will be explained later.

As an example, suppose there is a clearing that we want a creature to be able to navigate within (see Figure 3.7.1). In this clearing, there is a large rock that the creature should not pass through. The artist would model a nav mesh that would both describe the extent to which the creature can travel as well as a hole cut out around the rock (see Figure 3.7.2). Each triangle in the mesh would describe a valid area where the creature is allowed to travel. By restricting the creature's travel to the two-dimensional space described by the mesh triangles, the creature could neither exit the clearing nor pass through the rock.

The beauty of this system was in its simplicity. Both area-boundary and inner-obstacle problems were solved using the same solution. A fairly simple nav mesh could even represent highly detailed and complicated terrain.

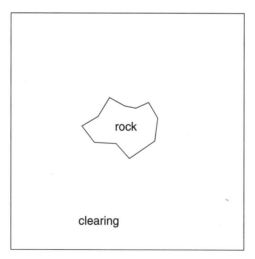

FIGURE 3.7.1   *A clearing with a static obstacle.*

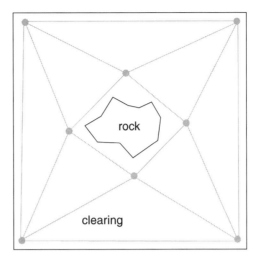

FIGURE 3.7.2 *A clearing with a nav mesh added.*

Portals

The triangles of the nav mesh do more than just establish an area where a creature can walk—they also establish what we refer to as "portals." Portals can be thought of as doorways to other triangles. In the case of our nav meshes, the portals were represented by the edges of the triangles. As a simplification, we established that our meshes could not contain any T-junctions, which simply meant that we only allowed an edge to be shared between no more than two triangles. Since a triangle has three edges, this means that a single triangle could be connected to at most three other triangles; so a single triangle has at most three portals leading to other connected triangles. This limitation did pose some three-dimensional issues, but it did give us some nice data characteristics. For one thing, we could use two bits to specify a portal of a triangle (first portal, second portal, or third portal) and still have one value left over for other uses.

Suppose our problem is moving from point A to point B. If point A represents the creature, point B represents the desired destination of the creature, and both points are within the same triangle, then we know that the creature can move directly toward point B, since we already know that the creature can move anywhere within the triangle. A problem arises when the destination is not contained within the same triangle as the creature. In this case, the creature might need to choose a direction that will both keep the creature on the nav mesh and intelligently move the creature along a path that will reach the desired destination, even if that path temporarily moves the creature in a direction away from the desired destination.

So, if we're on some triangle and our desired destination is on some other triangle, how do we decide which way to go? The solution that we used was to precompute a two-dimensional array that specified the portal to use to get from any triangle to any other triangle on the mesh. Remember that it only took two bits to specify a portal, so the memory cost of our table was roughly equal to squaring the number of triangles in the mesh and dividing by four. This means that the table for a mesh of 256 triangles (the maximum our implementation allowed) cost only 16 KB of memory. In practice, our nav meshes rarely exceeded more than 64 triangles (one kilobyte of memory) and were often smaller. Also, since multiple creatures typically shared the same nav mesh, there were relatively few nav meshes overall, so the memory cost was not significant. Now, consider the advantages of having this two-dimensional table. Figuring out which portal to use is now extremely fast, since it is a simple table lookup. The entry in the table is found by using the index of the source triangle and the index of the destination triangle. If the table was composed of byte values instead of two-bit values, then the C code might look like the following:

```
portalIndex = portalTable[destTriIndex][srcTriIndex];
```

Of course, using a byte table would quadruple the memory cost for little gain, so our bit-packed table code becomes:

```
bitIndex = 2*(destTriIndex*triCount + srcTriIndex);
byteIndex = bitIndex / 8;
byteShift = bitIndex & 7;
portalIndex = (portalTable[byteIndex] >> byteShift)&3;
```

Once we know the portal to use for a given triangle, we can take the desired direction vector from point A to point B and then solve for the point on the portal that most closely matches our desired direction. The creature then moves in the direction of the point on the portal until it reaches the portal, where it transitions to the triangle on the other side of the portal. If point B is within the creature's new triangle, then the creature can move directly to point B. If point B is still not within the creature's new triangle, then another look-up in the table is done to determine which portal to use next. The logic repeats until the creature eventually reaches the triangle that contains point B.

As an example, refer to Figure 3.7.3. Point A starts the creature out located within triangle 0, and point B (its destination) is located within triangle 3. Since point A is not in the same triangle as point B, a look-up in the table is done to determine which portal to use, and the returned value tells us to use the portal connecting triangle 0 to triangle 1. A point is found on that portal that most closely matches the desired direction of point B, and the creature is moved to that point. The creature is then considered to be within triangle 1. This behavior is repeated until the creature enters triangle 3, which is where point B is located; and the creature can then move directly to point B.

Although the above example was fairly simple, the same logic works for far more complicated cases. Consider Figure 3.7.4 (on page **000**), which shows the same simple logic applied to navigating a more complicated mesh.

This logic works for forking and looping paths. When there is more than one portal that can be used to reach a destination, the table entry specifies which portal

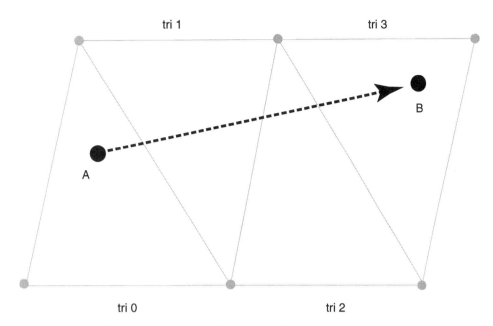

FIGURE 3.7.3   *Navigating from A to B on a simple mesh.*

represents the shortest route to the destination. However, there is actually one complication to consider. A triangle represents an area, and not a single point. This means that the distance between a point on one triangle and a point on another triangle can vary dramatically, depending on where the points are located on their respective triangles. Since the precomputed table tells us how to get from one triangle to another triangle, rather than how to get from an exact position on a triangle to an exact position on another triangle, the precomputed portal might not actually lead to the shortest path to the destination. In practice, however, this was rarely a problem, since if more than one path covered a similar distance, then it really didn't matter that the chosen path wasn't always the shortest.

Building the Table

So, how do you precompute the table? Several methods could be used, but the method that we chose was to compute a point to represent the center of each triangle. Preferably, this was a point that was equidistant to the three corners of the respective triangle. We then used a simple flood-fill algorithm to find the paths connecting the triangles. If more than one path was found between two triangles, then the algorithm would discard the longer path.

An important item to consider when constructing the nav mesh is that it represents a single path to each destination. Each portal should provide a single, clear route between any two areas in order to produce acceptable results. Providing more than

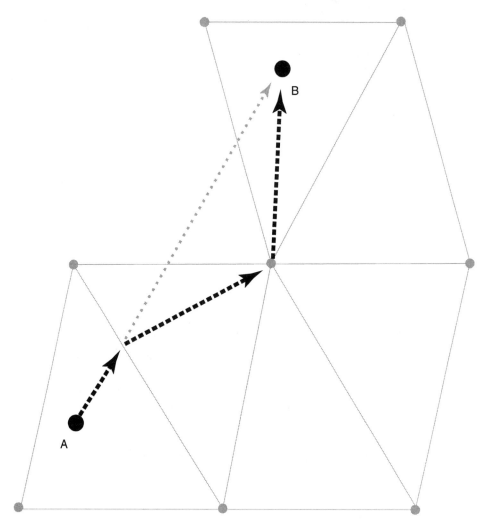

FIGURE 3.7.4   *Navigating around a corner.*

one portal to pursue a single path could result in zigzagging movement. Figure 3.7.5 shows a case where it is unclear at precompute time which portal is the best way to get from point A's triangle to point B's triangle. In this example, only one portal is chosen at precompute time, which would be inappropriate at runtime, since it does not intersect a direct path from point A to point B. Figure 3.7.6 shows the proper way to construct this nav mesh, where the direct path is always taken.

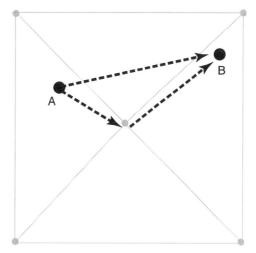

FIGURE 3.7.5   *Poor mesh construction.*

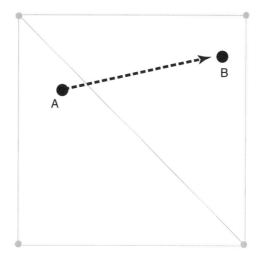

FIGURE 3.7.6   *Good mesh construction.*

Additional Portal Issues

Although the concept of using portals is quite simple, there are a few complications in their implementation. One such complication is that as point A approaches a portal edge, the test for whether the vector from point A to point B intersects the portal edge might become unreliable. For example, floating-point round-off errors might shift point A outside of the current triangle, causing the test to go awry. Also, when the source-to-destination vector is nearly parallel to the portal edge, the intersection test can give unreliable results. To avoid these problems, we checked to see if the source point was closer than some chosen epsilon distance to the portal edge. When it was, we simply looked ahead to find the next portal on our path that wasn't so close to the source point and used that as our portal.

Another item to consider is choosing alternate directions when the desired direction vector does not intersect the portal. It might not be clear which of the two portal endpoints is the best choice to follow. Choosing an endpoint based on which endpoint most closely matches the desired direction might not be sufficient. For example, if the desired direction vector is perpendicular to the portal and moving away from it, then either of the portal's endpoints is equally desirable. Floating-point precision and other minor variations could cause undesirable oscillations. One method that can resolve this ambiguous situation is to look ahead at successive portals until a portal is found that clearly indicates which endpoint of the current portal is closest to our future path. This 'look-ahead' technique also has the added benefit of creating more-direct navigation as the creature travels around winding pathways. Since this technique is rarely needed and usually only requires a few triangles of look-ahead, the extra CPU cost is minimal.

Representing Creatures

Using a nav mesh, we are able to travel intelligently from one point on the mesh to another point on the mesh. Most creatures, however, occupy more space than a single point, and so a question arises about how to account for their thickness. Since efficiency was more important to us than accuracy, we simply used a circle to represent the two-dimensional area of a creature on the nav mesh, where the radius of the circle represented the thickness of the creature. Using circles gave us some problems with creatures that were not very circular in shape. For example, a horse doesn't look very circular when viewed from above. If you made the circle big enough to enclose the entire horse, then other creatures would avoid the sides of the horse, and the horse itself wouldn't be able to squeeze into an area that it visually should fit into. If you made the circle smaller so that creatures could get closer to the horse, then you'd let the ends of the horse poke out of the circle, where they might occasionally overlap something else.

Despite these problems, we felt that the advantages of using circles outweighed the disadvantages. For *Jak and Daxter*, we were always able to find a radius that appeared to be a reasonable compromise between these two adverse effects. Another advantage to using circles was that rotation didn't have to be factored in when checking for collision with the nav mesh or other dynamic obstacles.

Instead of trying to adapt our nice, simple, point-to-point nav mesh logic to a much more computationally expensive circle-to-circle logic, we opted to preshrink our nav meshes to account for the radii of the creatures that may be using it. The concept is simple in that instead of modeling the nav mesh to exactly abut against obstacles, the mesh is modeled to stay at least some radius from all obstacles. Figure 3.7.7 shows how a nav mesh might be modeled for a small creature, and Figure 3.7.8 shows

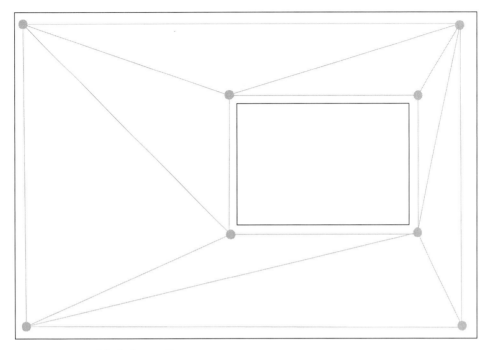

FIGURE 3.7.7   *Mesh for small creatures.*

the same scene with a nav mesh modeled for a larger creature. If we guarantee that the distance from the edges of the nav mesh to all static obstacles is greater than or equal to the radius of the creatures that use the nav mesh, then the creature can be represented by a point instead of a circle.

This is an enormous optimization, since moving a point around the nav mesh is much simpler than moving a circle around the mesh, though it does come with some problems. The biggest problem is that different types of creatures might want to use the same nav mesh, and some creatures might have significantly larger circles than other creatures. If the nav mesh is modeled to work for the larger creatures, then the smaller creatures might not be able to move very close to the static obstacles. In general, this wasn't a problem for us, but occasionally we had situations where the distance of the nav mesh was far enough from static obstacles that the player could stand next to a wall and a smaller creature couldn't get close enough to the wall to attack the player. To fix this undesirable behavior, we would adjust the distance of the nav mesh to any surrounding static obstacles until we found a compromise in which larger creatures would overlap the static obstacles slightly, but smaller creatures would be able to reach the player.

Our second biggest problem was that it was often difficult to judge what distance to use when modeling a nav mesh. The appropriate distance to use was based on the radii of the circles representing the creatures on the mesh, and the types of creatures and radii of their circles were subject to occasional design and programming changes.

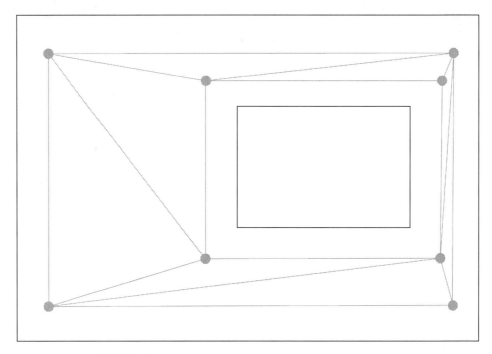

FIGURE 3.7.8   *Mesh for large creatures.*

Dynamic Obstacles

Using circles to represent creatures gave us the advantage that we could treat creatures as points when moving them around the nav mesh. This is also true for moving creatures around dynamic obstacles, such as other creatures. Instead of using computationally expensive logic for moving a circle around other circles, we can simply inflate the circles of surrounding obstacles by the radius of the creature currently being moved. For example, Figure 3.7.9 shows a creature of radius r and two dynamic obstacles with different radii, and Figure 3.7.10 shows how we treat the creature as a point by adding its radius to the obstacles. By inflating surrounding circles before moving a creature, we've unified the representation of a creature to being a single point and reduced our navigation issues to the relatively simple problem of moving a point inside the bounds of a mesh while avoiding surrounding circles.

To navigate the point among the circles, we checked to see if the direction that we wanted to travel would cause us to collide with any nearby circles. If not, then we could go ahead and move in the desired direction. If it was determined that a collision would occur, we computed two new vectors that would steer us clear of the collision (see Figure 3.7.11).

These two vectors could be considered as rotations away from the original vector: a rotated vector to steer to the left of the obstacle, and a rotated vector to steer to the

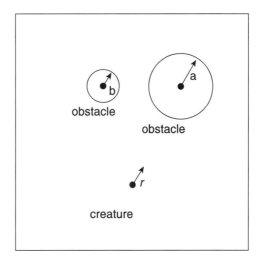

FIGURE 3.7.9   *Creature as circle with two circular dynamic obstacles.*

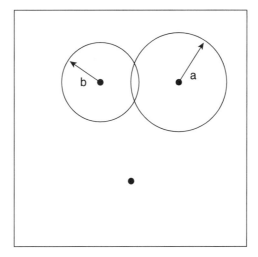

FIGURE 3.7.10   *Creature simplified to a point with obstacles enlarged to compensate.*

right of the obstacle. We would then check these two new vectors to see if either of them would collide with any other obstacles. If so, then we would appropriately rotate the right-most vector to the right or rotate the left-most vector to the left to avoid any additional obstacles. Once all potential obstacles had been accounted for, the two resulting vectors showed two possible ways to move that would avoid the dynamic

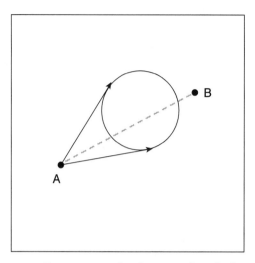

FIGURE 3.7.11   *Getting around a dynamic obstacle that intersects our desired path.*

obstacles' blocking the originally desired direction of movement. To avoid an undesirable cyclic movement behavior and to keep things simple, we usually chose the vector that more closely matched the creature's last direction.

One problem we had with this approach was that the creature could occasionally become stuck inside of other dynamic obstacles. This was commonly caused by floating-point precision issues, but it could also occur due to various other movement behaviors. Instead of trying to solve the thorny problem of not allowing overlaps to occur under any situation, we opted to have an embedded creature attempt to move away from the obstacles that overlapped it. Basically, we identified which circle the creature overlapped the most, and after computing the directions to avoid the other circles, we blended those results toward the direction away from the overlapping circle, proportionate to the amount of the overlap. This technique caused overlap cases to resolve themselves in a reasonable manner.

Another potential problem was that a creature could become completely surrounded by other dynamic obstacles such that the left and right vectors both faced exactly opposite of the originally desired vector. We chose to ignore handling this case, which meant that a creature could potentially move to a position that would cause them to overlap one of the surrounding dynamic obstacles. In practice, however, this wasn't an issue for us, especially since creatures naturally tended to move away from overlaps.

Navigation of Both Static and Dynamic Obstacles

Our final logic for maneuvering creatures turned out to be quite simple and broke down into the following steps. First, we found the best direction to reach our destination using the nav mesh and its portals. We then checked to see if the resulting direction would hit any dynamic obstacles (circles). If so, we modified the direction to avoid them. Finally, we checked to see if this new direction would lead us off of the nav mesh. If so, we clamped the movement to the nav mesh.

The final step of clamping movement to stay on the nav mesh was done for efficiency and required a little bit of finesse. One problem was that a creature might become blocked and be forced to stop. Another issue was that we sometimes allowed a creature's movement vector to be bent against the edge of the nav mesh instead of being simply clamped. The bent vector allowed the creature to continue moving, but we didn't do an additional check to see if the bent vector would cause the creature to overlap nearby circles; so a creature might subsequently become embedded within another creature. Since our circle avoidance logic made creatures naturally want to move away from overlaps, this usually wasn't an issue between two moving creatures. We did, however, encounter issues when a moving creature overlapped a dynamic obstacle that didn't move, such as a crate. To eliminate this problem, we made sure that nonmoving dynamic obstacles, such as crates, were not placed near the boundaries of a nav mesh.

Additional Nav Mesh Thoughts

Our nav meshes predominantly denoted two-dimensional areas where dynamic obstacles were allowed to move. This sufficed in most cases, since most creature setups can be described using two-dimensional boundaries. However, we occasionally had situations that required three-dimensional information. For example, if we wanted to put a creature on a circular staircase that spiraled upward, it would not be sufficient to use just a two-dimensional nav mesh to describe the staircase. For this type of situation, we had a maximum height that the creature could be from the surface of a nav mesh triangle in order to be considered on that triangle. This gave the ability for a nav mesh to have three-dimensionally crisscrossing triangles, as long as the triangles that occupied the same two-dimensional space were at sufficiently different elevations so that it was clear which triangle a creature was using.

Another enhancement that we made to our nav mesh system was the ability for creatures to jump across certain obstacles to reach the desired final destination. For example, a creature might jump across small chasms in pursuit of the player. Modeling triangles across the chasm and marking those triangles as special 'gap triangles' accomplished this ability. When a creature crossed a portal into a gap triangle, a search found the triangle on the far side of the gap, and the creature was sent a message telling it to jump across the gap to that triangle. In order to keep the creature from landing on top of a dynamic obstacle on the other side of the gap, the creature used a temporary circle that reserved a safe landing place.

Conclusion

Our navigation mesh system admirably fit our needs for the development of *Jak and Daxter* (see Plate 3). We were able to create many different types of creatures that exhibited a variety of behaviors while intelligently navigating our complex three-dimensional environments. Although navigational approaches exist that might provide more-robust general solutions to this difficult problem, our system excelled at being both fast and conceptually simple, creating a winning combination for us.

3.8

Choosing a Relationship Between Path-Finding and Collision

Thomas Young, PathEngine

thomas@pathengine.com

For many games, the AI is all about characters moving around within an environment. It's no use having sophisticated decision-making systems if the resulting decision can't be executed when the player moves behind a bunch of crates. On the other hand, if a character correctly understands how to deal with the obstructions in its environment, then even a very simple decision-making structure can result in impressive-looking AI.

We can think of the pathfinder as a system with the responsibility of understanding collision. The relationship between path-finding and the collision system is a key architectural issue when creating characters that understand how to react to the obstructions in their environment. Three different approaches to this architecture and the implications of each approach will be explained in this gem.

Moving Under the Control of Collision

We don't want characters walking through walls, tables, or other obstructions. To prevent this from happening, character movement can be controlled by a collision subsystem. Decisions made by the AI are subject to arbitration by this subsystem before being implemented as character movement.

This creates a strong dependency between code that generates character movement and collision code that arbitrates that movement. Behavior code depends on the results of the collision code in order to work as intended. Imagine the situation where behavior code thinks a character can walk directly toward the player, but in fact that character is snagged on an obstruction. The behavior code must take collision into account.

The Collision Model for Path-Finding

A pathfinder allows certain possibilities for movement and disallows others. This implies a certain understanding about how collision works. We can call this the pathfinder's collision model.

We can often describe this collision model in terms of *path-finding space* and *obstructed space*. In a tile- or cell-based pathfinder, path-finding space is defined by the set of unobstructed tiles or cells. Figure 3.8.1a shows a tile-based path-finding space (white cells) and obstructed space (black cells). In a points-of-visibility- or waypoints-based system, the path-finding space is represented explicitly along with a set of points. Figure 3.8.1b shows what the path-finding space might look like in this case. (Note that this path-finding space must correspond with the set of points used, otherwise the pathfinder will not function correctly.) When generating a path, the pathfinder allows the possibility of movement within the path-finding space, but it does not allow paths to cross through obstructed space.

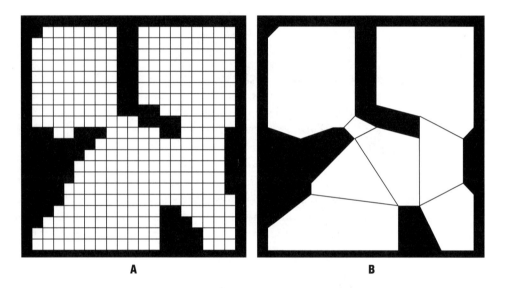

A   **B**

FIGURE 3.8.1   *Path-finding space for (A) a tile-based system and (B) a points-of-visibility system.*

It is the relationship between this collision model for path-finding and the collision actually applied to movement that differentiates the three approaches to be discussed.

Approach #1: Fault-Tolerant AI

A defined relationship between the collision model used by path-finding and collision actually applied means that there is an interdependency, or linkage between these two systems. The implication is that whoever codes the path-finding system will need to be aware of any changes to the collision system (or vice versa) to make sure that the relationship is not broken.

From an architectural point of view, reducing interdependencies is good practice. Human behavior doesn't depend on our knowing the precise physics behind collision with our environment. We have a rough idea of how to move through our environment, get by with feedback mechanisms and so on, and avoid collisions. Can we use a similar approach for our AI and thereby avoid direct linkage with the collision system?

The idea behind the fault-tolerant approach is that the collision model for path-finding need only roughly correspond to the actual, more-detailed collision applied to movement. The pathfinder's representation might perhaps be edited manually to approximate collision, or it could be built automatically from the same world and object representations used by collision without any further assumptions about how that collision works. The pathfinder is used to generate guide paths, and then the AI uses fault-tolerance methods to ensure that characters can actually move along those paths under arbitration by the collision system.

In Figure 3.8.2, collision takes place between a character and the obstacles drawn in black. The pathfinder approximates this with a polygonal path-finding space, drawn in white. The black line shows a guide path returned by the pathfinder. The gray line shows the direction in which the character must move to avoid collision (with the obstructions in black) while continuing in the general direction of the guide path. [Reynolds97] describes how steering behaviors can be combined to achieve this kind of effect.

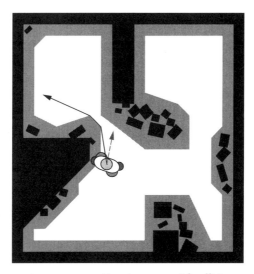

FIGURE 3.8.2 *Steering to avoid collision.*

The fault-tolerant approach is attractive because it produces plausible results from the point of view of modeling real-world behavior. If we have simple collision and a relatively small world to test our behaviors against, then this approach can work well. The more closely path-finding space approximates real collision, the better this approach will work. However, if we have reasonably complex collision, then it will be difficult to approximate this with a pathfinder. If our behaviors will be applied in a large number of different situations, then we can also expect problems with this method.

In some situations, it is difficult to find the correct steering. For the character in Figure 3.8.3, it is necessary to change direction several times in order to get through the gap. The squiggly gray line in Figure 3.8.3 indicates the steering that is required. If the correct steering cannot be found in a situation like this, the result will probably just be a character floundering momentarily against an obstruction. In a more extreme situation, the result could be a character getting stuck in between obstructions.

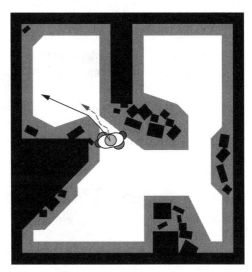

FIGURE 3.8.3   *Steering correctly can be a complex problem.*

To find the correct steering in a difficult situation requires future possibilities for movement to be taken into account. The gray line in Figure 3.8.3 is really a detailed path for planned movement as opposed to a steering vector. A combination of path sections needs to be found to solve for movement through the gap. The first section of this needs to correctly position the character for movement along the second section, and so on. In this case, finding the correct steering really requires planning and some detailed understanding of collision.

Sometimes, it might not actually be possible to move along the guide path. Consider for example a gap slightly narrower than that in Figure 3.8.3. In this case, we would like characters to recognize in advance that a gap cannot be passed and choose another, more appropriate path. Again, this requires planning and detailed understanding of collision.

We can perhaps extend the fault-tolerant approach to address these problems by using planning mechanisms that adapt to feedback from collision. The first time a character arrives at the gap in Figure 3.8.3 and fails to find a way through with reactive behaviors, we could mark that gap as blocked in our path-finding representation. This kind of fault tolerance is difficult to implement and still does not provide any real guarantees about behavior. There is nothing to stop a character from walking into a situation that they cannot steer out of.

Another approach might be to use machine-learning techniques, such as neural network training, to build behavior directly from collision feedback. These kinds of techniques effectively automate the linkage between collision and behavior—but note that a dependency on collision still remains. The results of these kinds of techniques depend very much on the exact nature of the collision, so any change in the collision system introduces the risk of breaking behaviors. Even if the collision system doesn't change, these techniques do not work well in collision situations that are different from those they were trained on.

If we need guarantees about behavior, then we are probably better off accepting linkage between AI and collision. This enables us to design an understanding of collision into our AI.

Approach #2: Path-Finding in a Subset of Unobstructed Space

With this approach, we can define a relationship between collision and path-finding while avoiding the need for interdependencies between these systems. Specifically, we need to guarantee that all points in path-finding space are unobstructed by collision; or in other words, that *valid space* for the pathfinder is a subset of *true unobstructed space*.

True unobstructed space means the set of positions where a character can be placed without being in collision. If the orientation of a character affects whether that character is in collision, then that orientation adds an extra dimension(s) to unobstructed space, and therefore a position in unobstructed space will include orientation as a component. For this approach, path-finding space can be represented in fewer dimensions than true unobstructed space, and the boundary of path-finding space is simplified. What is important is that the movement through positions in path-finding space is guaranteed to be collision-free.

Figure 3.8.4 shows how path-finding space might be constructed for this approach. In this case, the rotational dimension of collision is eliminated by using a bounding box that is large enough to fit the character at any rotation. Sets of obstructions are simplified by taking convex hulls and then expanding the resulting geometry by the shape of our bounding box. (See [Young01] for more detail.) The result is that we can guarantee that our character will not collide at any rotation of that character for any position in path-finding space.

We can use a similar approach for tile-based path-finding. In this case, we can render expanded shapes into the path-finding grid and flag any grid tiles overlapped by these shapes as obstructed.

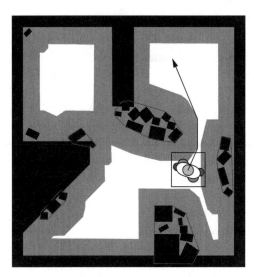

FIGURE 3.8.4   *Path-finding in a subset of unobstructed space.*

The advantage of this approach is that the pathfinder can now tell us how to move without colliding. A path returned by the pathfinder can be followed without the need for a layer of reactive behaviors because we know that the path will be unobstructed. The AI still doesn't know how to get through the narrow gap, but now this is integrated into movement-planning so that our behavior can choose another path or do whatever is appropriate. If we want our character to be able to get into the top-left part of our environment, then we will need to widen the gap; but now we can use the pathfinder to tell us about this kind of problem automatically.

Because path-finding space is only a subset of true unobstructed space, we must deal with the possibility that characters might find themselves outside of valid space. Characters should never get to an invalid position by following paths returned by the pathfinder; but we must consider the possibility that characters might be pushed outside of path-finding space by interactions with other characters, the force of an explosion, or whatever.

The pathfinder cannot tell a character outside path-finding space how to get back into path-finding space without colliding. Once a character is outside of path-finding space, we have the same kind of problems as with the previous approach. We can use reactive methods to get back to a valid position, but if a character is pushed into a narrow gap, then there is still a possibility that the character might get stuck. This situation is a lot less likely because characters will not move into gaps by themselves; hence, the reactive methods can be focused on simply getting characters back to a valid point. They are simpler to code and more functional.

A good, practical solution that enables us to give guarantees about character behavior is to allow characters to cheat collision when moving back into path-finding space. If everything works correctly and problematic configurations of geometry are avoided, then this shouldn't be needed, but designing this into our system can give us a lot more peace of mind during beta testing. (Beware of potential consequences of cheating collision, as discussed below.)

Finding a Valid Position

The simplest way to obtain a valid position for a character that has somehow found itself outside of path-finding space is to keep track of the last known good position. This can give bad results if a character moves a significant distance while outside path-finding space (see Figure 3.8.5a). Additionally there will be times when we need to deal with a position outside path-finding space for which there is no last-known good position.

A more elegant approach is for the pathfinder to provide a query that returns the closest point inside path-finding space to a given point outside that space. This works pretty well and applies more generally; but in certain situations, the resulting point might be on the other side of a wall from a character's current position (Figure 3.8.5b). If this happens, the character will not be able to get back into valid space by moving toward that point unless they are allowed to cheat collision. If they are allowed to cheat collision, then the result is that a character gets through a wall and into another part of the game. This can sometimes have humorous consequences, but is nonetheless a pretty serious bug.

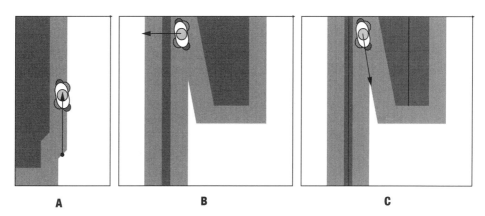

A   **B**   **C**

FIGURE 3.8.5 *(A-C) Finding a valid position.*

Putting Backbones in the World

We can improve the closest valid point method by adding an extra level of hard-collision 'backbones' to the world (Figure 3.8.5c). These backbones can be represented explicitly or can be based on the existing world representation. If the world is already divided into cells, then it could be sufficient to use boundaries between cells as backbones. The closest valid point query is then modified to look for the closest point that does not involve crossing a backbone. This gives us a more appropriate result.

For the case where characters are allowed to cheat collision while returning to path-finding space, the backbones provide a way for us to enforce constraints about connectivity in the game world. Theoretically, this means that path-finding around backbones might now be required in order to maintain our guarantee that characters can always get back to a valid position; but in practice, this will probably not be necessary. If we do implement path-finding around backbones, then this will also be useful for hierarchical path-finding (see [Rabin00]).

Approach #3: Using the Pathfinder Itself for Character Collision

Both of the previous approaches are complicated by the possibility of situations where obstruction by the collision system is not understood by the pathfinder's simpler model. We can avoid this with a third approach, which uses the pathfinder itself to provide character collision. This approach guarantees that characters cannot be pushed out of path-finding space and, therefore, that the pathfinder will always be able to understand a character's current position (and that paths returned by the pathfinder can always be followed). This gives us a simplified architecture and reliable character movement, but at the cost of having to use simplified mechanics for character collision.

There are other advantages to using simplified character collision. The collision will be extremely fast, robust, and predictable. We can use the collision system to implement constraints on game progression or to trigger scripts and be confident that this will all work exactly as intended. On the other hand, we potentially lose a lot of interesting interaction between the character and the world, which a sophisticated collision system would have provided.

Characters might still need to deal with target positions outside path-finding space, and for this, we might still need a query to find the closest valid point. The advantage is that we no longer depend on these methods to extract a character from potentially being stuck in positions.

Layered Collision

In order for the AI to understand the mechanism that controls character movement, we need to simplify this mechanism; but complex collision interaction is necessary if we want to create an interesting and believable environment. The trick to meeting both of these requirements at the same time is to use a layered collision architecture.

If behavior is implemented in terms of movement through path-finding space and the pathfinder understands the system that governs that movement, then we have all the guarantees that we need. Movement through path-finding space will often mean the translational part of the movement of a character's local origin. In our layered architecture, a path-finding collision layer deals with this part of character movement. More-sophisticated interactions can be provided in a world collision layer as long as those interactions do not affect this movement of the character's origin.

PLATE 1 *Natural Selection: The Evolution of Pie Menus: Pie menus in The Sims.*

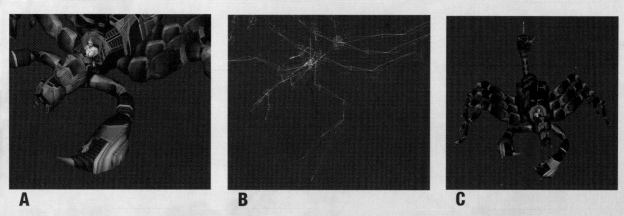

A   B   C

PLATE 2 *Scorpion tank mesh (A) is assigned a constrained bone structure (B) and uses inverse kinematics to reach a purple "effector" point (C). The red, green, and blue arcs in B indicate how the rotation angles are limited about each joint's x-, y-, and z-axes. Courtesy of Jason Weber.*

PLATE 3 *An overhead view of a portion of the game Jak and Daxter: The Precursor Legacy with navigation meshes shown drawn over the background. Creatures use the navigation meshes to intelligently negotiate the terrain and exhibit various complex movement behaviors. Plate courtesy of Jane Mullaney. © 2001 by Sony Computer Entertainment America. Jak and Daxter: The Precursor Legacy is a trademark of Sony Computer Entertainment America, Inc. Reprinted with permission.*

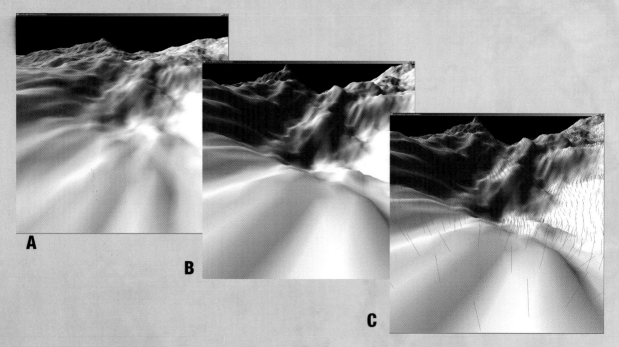

PLATE 4 *(A) A fractal terrain at 1/8th of its full height. The lighting formula uses vertex normals to highlight terrain detail. (B) A fractal terrain rendered at full height. As the heightfield grows, the normals diverge and the lighting effect becomes more pronounced. (C) The same terrain with the normals superimposed at each vertex. Normals are depicted as line segments with green bases and red tips.*

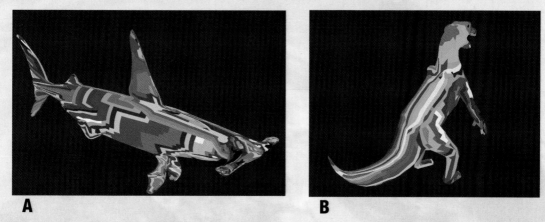

A

B

PLATE 5 *This plate shows the triangle strips from a (A) shark model and (B) dragon. Each color represents a new triangle strip. The shark model contains an average triangle strip length of 20 vertices, and the dragon model contains 243 triangle strips with an average of 27 vertices per tri-strip. Courtesy of Carl S. Marshall.*

PLATE 6 *This real-time hatching demo has a single static light source with precomputed shadow volumes. The outlines are computed within a pixel shader using an edge-detection method. Plate courtesy of Alex Vlachos and Drew Card, ATI Research, Inc. Reprinted with permission.*

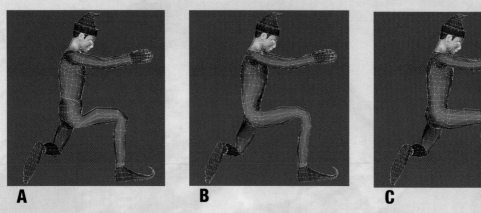

A   **B**   **C**

PLATE 7   *A mesh exported with authored weights (A) is used to automatically generate new weights (B), and is then enhanced with smaller subbones at the joints (C), nearly eliminating the shrinking and stretching that commonly plagues basic skinning algorithms. Courtesy of Jason Weber.*

PLATE 8   *Three methods of generating pseudo-3D images from a 2D image source: Dual image elevation maps (top row), procedural image warping (middle row), and the interlaced texture approach (bottom row). Plate courtesy of Greg Snook. Original 3D model, © Glen Mel 2002. Reprinted with permission.*

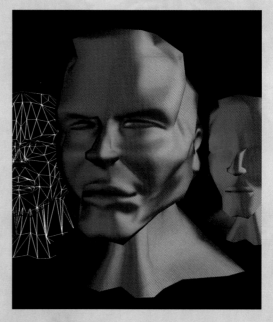

PLATE 9   *High-resolution mesh simulation for a head model using a normal map generated with the Max4 plug-in (see the Gem "Curvature Simulation Using Normal Maps," by Oscar Blasco.) The models have been rendered in real-time with soft phong illumination using a normal map in object space. (Head modeled by Julio Cesar Espada.)*

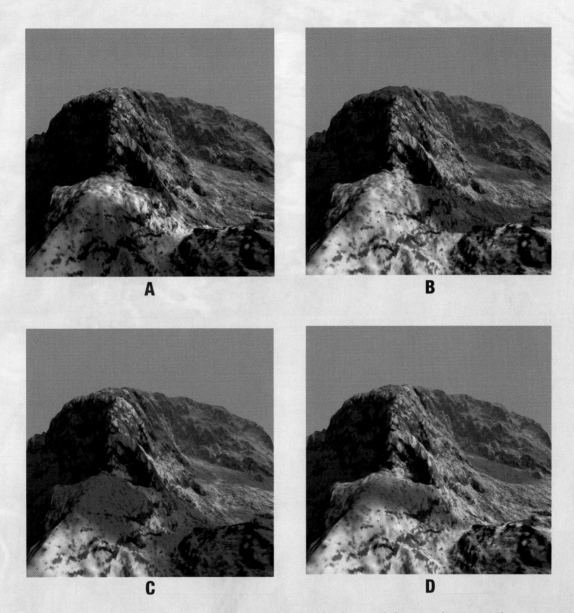

PLATE 10 *(A-D) Photorealistic-quality terrain lighting under changing lighting conditions in real-time. Courtesy of Naty Hoffman and Kenny Mitchell.*

PLATE 11   *Animated clouds with shadows on terrain using one cube map. Courtesy of Kenneth L. Hurley.*

A   **B**

PLATE 12   *Two examples of procedurally generated textures: (A) A 3D noise texture on a teapot. (B) A 3D noise texture with alpha.   Courtesy of Simon Green.*

PLATE 13   *The NVIDIA Wolfman demonstrates real-time volumetric fur, rendered on a fully animated character model. The fur is rendered using the "shells and fins" technique, using eight concentric shells for the body of the fur plus fin geometry to improve the silhouette, for a total of 100,000 polygons per frame. The character is animated via matrix palette skinning in the vertex shader, with 61 bones and 4 bones per vertex. The fur is lit using the pixel shaders with a per-pixel anisotropic lighting model, and every surface is fully self-shadowed using shadow maps. © NVIDIA Corporation 2002. Reprinted with permission.*

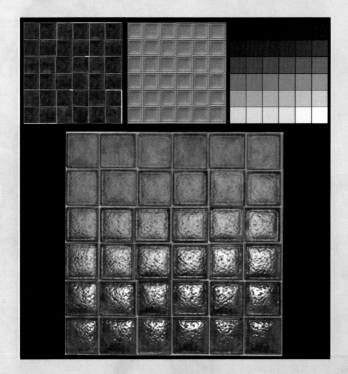

PLATE 14   *The base map (upper left), a bump map (upper middle), and specular exponent map (upper right) are combined to make the bottom image, which has different specularity. Courtesy of Alex Vlachos, John Isidoro, and Chris Oat, ATI Research, Inc.*

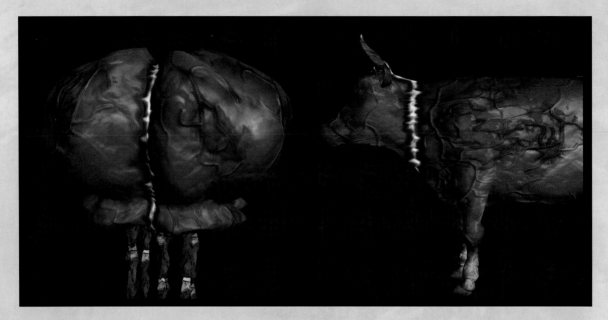

PLATE 15 *An irridescence texture shader on a brain (left) and a cow (right). Courtesy of Alex Vlachos, John Isidoro, and Chris Oat, ATI Research, Inc.*

PLATE 16 *Different normal density functions (NDFs) applied to a piece of cloth. Courtesy of Jan Kautz.*

World collision can take responsibility for extra dimensions of the character's position (such as the vertical coordinate of that position or the orientation of the character) if those dimensions are not relevant to the pathfinder's collision model. Note that if a character needs to turn in a certain direction in order to move, then we have to be careful when applying world collision to character orientation. World collision can also give us 3D interactions between a character's limbs and the environment as long as that character's skeleton remains anchored to the character's origin.

By designating certain events as temporary or exceptional, we can add more-interesting interactions to the system. It makes sense for certain events to interfere with the ability of a character to move along a path; so for these types of events, we can allow world collision to affect movement through path-finding space. Consider for example the blast from an explosion or interaction with a projectile. The only constraint for these types of events is that the character should not be moved outside path-finding space by the interaction, so we know that the character will be able to get up afterward and resume path-finding. Figure 3.8.6 shows how a force resulting from a 3D interaction might be fed back into the path-finding collision layer.

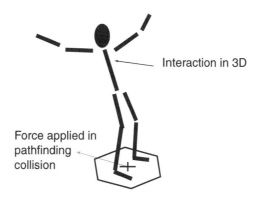

Interaction in 3D

Force applied in pathfinding collision

FIGURE 3.8.6   *Interaction between collision layers.*

Implementing Movement Along a Path

For the second and third approaches, we assume that a character moving along a path will not leave path-finding space. In order to ensure that this is true, we have to be careful exactly how movement along a path is implemented.

It is quite common to implement character control through a turn-and-move interface. A range of angles might be used to detect success in turning toward the next path target before moving forward. However, this will result in characters clipping corners (Figure 3.8.7a). Even if we get the angle exactly right, a character might still end up at an invalid position by overshooting a path target (Figure 3.8.7b). With approach number two, this means the pathfinder must find the closest valid point,

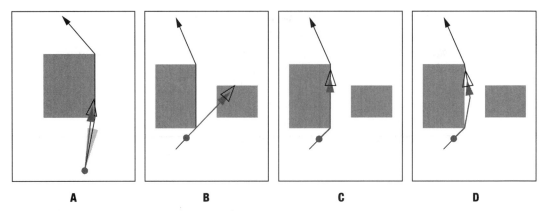

FIGURE 3.8.7   *(A-D) Moving along a path.*

but moving to that point will interfere with smooth movement along the path. For approach number three, these problems can result in a character being blocked by path-finding collision and unable to move along the path. Making the characters slide along the edges of path-finding space will help in many cases, but not all.

The code required to eliminate these kinds of errors in a turn-and-move interface gets quite complex. We can simplify the situation by switching to parametric movement along a path (Figure 3.8.7c). Turn constraints can still be satisfied before starting to move along a path, but for turn constraints during movement along the path, we are better off modifying the path to satisfy the constraints (Figure 3.8.7d).

Even with parametric movement, there are issues about the approximation for points along a path. The most common problem will be when a path follows a diagonal boundary of path-finding space, as shown in Figure 3.8.8a. Approximating a point at a given distance along this path might result in a point that is just outside path-finding space. In this case, we could avoid the problem by choosing the direction of approximation, depending on the direction of the path before and after this section.

However, choosing the direction of approximation will not solve a situation such as that shown in Figure 3.8.8b. Here, even though we've approximated the point in the right direction with respect to the angle of the following corner, we still come up with a point inside an obstacle. A more general solution is to attempt to move to a first approximation, and only if this fails generate another point by approximating in the other direction.

In a situation such as that shown in Figure 3.8.8c, there might be no valid points along a path section. This kind of situation is pretty rare; so for static maps, we can add code to the map-validation routines to check for this possibility and, if it occurs, simply modify the maps to remove the problem. For geometry that changes at runtime, we don't have this option. One solution is to restrict the edges of dynamic geometry to horizontal, vertical, or 45° lines because the problem cannot occur with these kinds of edges.

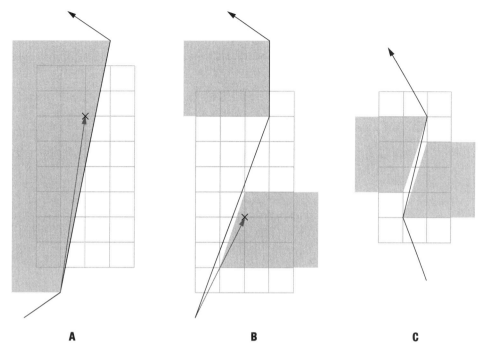

A   B   C

FIGURE 3.8.8   *(A-C) Problems with approximation.*

Conclusion

The relationship between AI, path-finding, and collision is a key issue for movement-based AI. The fault-tolerant approach produces the most plausible results from the point of view of simulating real behaviors and requires minimal constraints on path-finding and collision. However, this approach can add a lot of complexity to the implementation of behavior, which makes it very difficult to build behaviors that will work reliably in all circumstances.

Path-finding in a subset of truly unobstructed space gives reliable behavior most of the time at the cost of requiring some minimal linkage between the path-finding and collision subsystems. Since characters can still get outside path-finding space, we still need to be able to deal with this case. It is possible to guarantee the results of behavior with this approach if we allow characters to cheat collision in certain circumstances.

Using the pathfinder itself to control character collision results in the simplest architecture and the most reliable behavior. If it is essential to guarantee the results of behaviors, then this is the approach to use. More-interesting collision interactions can be provided through a layered collision architecture.

The second and third approaches can perhaps be seen as 'control freak' approaches. To make these approaches work best, we need to extend this attitude to the mechanisms for implementing movement along paths. These approaches do not give the most plausible architecture for behavior simulation, but for games that make difficult demands on the AI, they provide a way to get through beta without too much cost to hair or to sanity.

References

[PathEngine] Path Engine, available online at http://www.pathengine.com, January 2002.

[Rabin00] Rabin, Steve, "A* Aesthetic Optimizations," *Game Programming Gems*, Charles River Media, Inc., 2000.

[Reynolds97] Reynolds, Craig, "Steering Behaviors for Autonomous Characters," available online at http://www.red3d.com/cwr/steer/, September 6, 1997.

[Young01] Young, Thomas, "Expanded Geometry for Points-of-Visibility Path-finding," *Game Programming Gems 2*, Charles River Media, Inc., 2001.

GRAPHICS

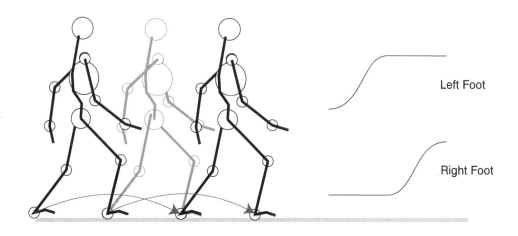

Left Foot

Right Foot

Introduction

Jeff Lander, Darwin 3D, LLC

jeffl@darwin3d.com

This is an incredibly exciting time to work on graphics for games. On game consoles and personal computers, the graphics hardware available to developers for creating the visuals for their games offers staggering capabilities. However, great expectations from game players come along with this power. Players expect each title to be more visually impressive than the previous game, and players demand that developers push the technical limits of the various platforms.

It has only been a few years since a game graphics programmer did not have many tools to work with. All the graphics were created by directly manipulating the pixels on the screen. A programmer's toolkit included things like fast assembly language 'blitters,' which copied chunks of image data to the screen. Any 3D graphics, if used, consisted of simple line-drawing routines, lighting calculations, and flat-shaded or textured triangle rasterization routines. Research consisted of trying to implement known 3D-rendering techniques in a quick way on the system's CPU.

As the systems have improved, developers have extended these techniques to include more-sophisticated 3D-rendering algorithms. Developers have been able to pull techniques from the research done at visual effects companies, educational institutions, and conferences such as SIGGRAPH.

Now, however, developers are at an important crossroads. The capabilities of the game systems have matured beyond the well-defined path of graphics research. The needs of graphics programmers working on games have diverged from the needs of programmers working on other computer graphics applications. Thus, it is time for game developers to devote assets, funds, and energy to help create a new path.

These game-programming gems are steps along this new path. The authors are developers, hardware vendors, and researchers who have contributed their knowledge and expertise to the unique problems facing game graphics programmers. The gems presented here fall into two categories—gems that deal with issues related to game scene geometry, and gems concerned with the rendering of this geometry.

Scene geometry issues include the calculation of elements of the model needed for rendering. We start out with Eric Lengyel's gem, "T-Junction Elimination and Retriangulation," which provides an algorithmic solution for a source of notorious rendering errors.

The computation of vertex normals is incredibly important for lighting the scene. For geometry that deforms, routines that make this computation efficiently are extremely important. Jason Shankel's gem, "Fast Heightfield-Normal Calculations," and Martin Brownlow's "Fast Patch Normals" deal with this topic.

Three gems address data organization and manipulation. The fastest-rendered polygons are the ones you don't draw, as is discussed in "Fast and Simple Occlusion Culling" by Wagner Corrêa, et al. Carl Marshall's gem, "Triangle Strip Creation, Optimization, and Rendering," offers techniques for optimizing the data format. Finally, "Computing Optimized Shadow Volumes for Complex Data Sets" by Alex Vlachos tackles the issue of dynamic shadow creation.

Character animation is an important issue for games; there is a pressing demand for more-realistic characters. "Subdivision Surfaces for Character Animation" by William Leeson presents an alternative to discrete triangular meshes for characters. Jason Weber's "Improved Deformation of Bones" provides a solution to the pinching and folding issues common with skeletal deformation animation systems. When animating characters, mixing and blending animation sets can be difficult (yet manageable), as described in Thomas Young's "A Framework for Realistic Character Locomotion."

With the emergence of programmable graphics hardware, rendering programs, or *shaders,* have become an essential tool in graphics programming. However, these languages are very low-level and API-specific. In "Programmable Vertex Shader Compiler," Adam Lake presents a method for creating a programming language that compiles into platform-specific code.

Several geometry gems begin the crossover into rendering. In "Billboard Beams," Brian Hawkins uses matrix methods to create the illusion of 3D objects using 2D sprites. Another use of 2D art to create the illusion of 3D is presented in "3D Tricks for Isometric Engines" by Greg Snook. Finally, to calculate the normal maps needed for complex, per-pixel rendering of objects, Oscar Blasco uses a dense mesh model in "Curvature Simulation Using Normal Maps."

Geometry processing alone does not create beautiful images. The geometry must be rendered. This section begins with Nathaniel Hoffman's description of realistic and natural outdoor lighting in "Methods for Dynamic, Photorealistic Terrain Lighting." This gem is followed by Kenneth Hurley's "Cube Map Lighting Techniques," which describes the use of hardware-rendering capabilities toward achieving realistic lighting.

Generation of the texture data is a difficult problem for game programmers. As the visuals get more complex, we need more textures. Creating them by hand is expensive from a production standpoint and causes storage and memory issues on game platforms. Textures can actually be created as needed using mathematical models, as described in Mike Milliger's "Procedural Texturing." The next gem, "Unique Textures," by Tom Forsyth, provides a method for dynamically combining textures to provide a more-complex and varied scene.

Many effects in computer graphics are created when complex mathematical operations are computed per pixel. Even programmable graphics hardware is often not flexible enough to perform these operations quickly. However, a great deal of mathematics can be approximated using lookup tables. These tables can be conveniently stored in a texture map. The final gems in this section deal with this idea, and its possibilities are outlined in a gem from the team at ATI, "Textures As Lookup Tables for Per-Pixel Lighting Computations." Jan Kautz then extends his ideas on this technique to include a more artist-driven approach in his gem, "Rendering with Handcrafted Shading Models."

These gems represent a strong step forward along the path toward creating new graphics techniques that are particularly applicable to game production. The authors and I sincerely hope developers will join us in blazing the trail and seek new and challenging horizons in the unexplored gaming frontier.

T-Junction Elimination and Retriangulation

Eric Lengyel, Terathon Software

lengyel@terathon.com

Suppose that a scene contains two polygons that share a common edge as shown in Figure 4.1.1a. When two such polygons belong to the same object, the vertices representing the endpoints of the common edge are usually not duplicated. Instead, both polygons reference the same vertices to save space and bus bandwidth. Graphics hardware is designed so that when adjacent polygons use exactly the same coordinates for the endpoints of shared edges, the rasterizer produces pixels for each polygon that are precise complements of each other. Along the shared edge, there is no overlap between the pixels belonging to one polygon and those belonging to the other; and, more importantly, there are no gaps between the polygons.

A problem arises when adjacent polygons belong to different objects that have their own copy of the endpoint vertices for the shared edge. These vertices might greatly differ in each object's local coordinate space. For instance, when the vertices

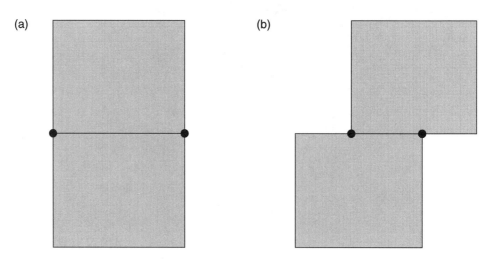

FIGURE 4.1.1 *(A) Adjacent polygons sharing a common edge. (B) Adjacent polygons with edges falling within the same line in space, but not sharing the same endpoints.*

are transformed into world space, floating-point round-off error could produce slightly different vertex positions for each object. Since the vertex coordinates are no longer equal, a seam might appear when the polygons are rasterized.

A greater problem occurs when two polygons have edges that fall within the same line in space, but they do not share the same endpoints, as illustrated in Figure 4.1.1b. In such a situation, a vertex belonging to one polygon lies within the interior of an edge belonging to the other. Due to the shape that the edges form, the location at which this occurs is called a *T-junction*. Because the adjacent edges do not share identical endpoints, T-junctions cause visible seams in any game engine that does not eliminate them.

This gem describes how to detect possible sources of these seams in complex 3D scenes and how to modify static geometry so that visible artifacts are avoided. Since T-junction elimination adds vertices to existing polygons (that are not necessarily convex), we also discuss a method for triangulating arbitrary concave polygons.

T-Junction Elimination

Given an immovable object A in our world, we need to determine whether there exist any other immovable objects possessing a vertex that lies within an edge of object A. We only consider those objects whose bounding volumes intersect the bounding volume of object A. Let object X be an object that lies close enough to object A to possibly have adjacent polygons. We treat both objects as collections of polygons having the greatest possible number of edges. We perform triangulation of these polygons *after* the T-junction elimination process in order to avoid the creation of superfluous triangles.

Before we locate any T-junctions, we first want to find out if any of object A's vertices lie very close to any of object X's vertices. We must transform the vertices belonging to both objects into world space and search for vertices separated by a distance less than some small constant ε. Any vertex $\mathbf{V}_A$ of object A that is this close to a vertex $\mathbf{V}_X$ of object X should be moved so that $\mathbf{V}_A$ and $\mathbf{V}_X$ have the exact same world-space coordinates. This procedure is sometimes called *welding*.

Once existing vertices have been welded, we need to search for vertices of object X that lie within a small distance ε of an edge of object A, but which do not lie within the distance ε of any vertex of object A. This tells us where T-junctions occur. Let $\mathbf{P}_1$ and $\mathbf{P}_2$ be endpoints of an edge of object A, and let $\mathbf{Q}$ be a vertex of object X. The squared distance d^2 between the point $\mathbf{Q}$ and the line passing through $\mathbf{P}_1$ and $\mathbf{P}_2$ is given by

$$d^2 = \left(\mathbf{Q} - \mathbf{P}_1\right)^2 - \frac{\left[\left(\mathbf{Q} - \mathbf{P}_1\right) \cdot \left(\mathbf{P}_2 - \mathbf{P}_1\right)\right]^2}{\left(\mathbf{P}_2 - \mathbf{P}_1\right)^2} \tag{4.1.1}$$

If $d^2 < \varepsilon^2$, then we know that the point $\mathbf{Q}$ lies close enough to the line containing the edge of object A, but we still need to determine whether $\mathbf{Q}$ actually lies between $\mathbf{P}_1$ and $\mathbf{P}_2$. We can make this determination by measuring the projected length t of the line segment connecting $\mathbf{P}_1$ to $\mathbf{Q}$ onto the edge formed by $\mathbf{P}_1$ and $\mathbf{P}_2$. As shown in Figure 4.1.2, this length is given by

$$t = \left\| \mathbf{Q} - \mathbf{P}_1 \right\| \cos \alpha, \tag{4.1.2}$$

where α is the angle between the line segment and the edge. Using a dot product to compute the cosine, we have

$$t = \frac{\left(\mathbf{Q} - \mathbf{P}_1 \right) \cdot \left(\mathbf{P}_2 - \mathbf{P}_1 \right)}{\left\| \mathbf{P}_2 - \mathbf{P}_1 \right\|}. \tag{4.1.3}$$

If $t > \left\| \mathbf{P}_2 - \mathbf{P}_1 \right\| - \varepsilon$, then the point $\mathbf{Q}$ does not lie within the interior of the edge formed by $\mathbf{P}_1$ and $\mathbf{P}_2$. Otherwise, we have found a T-junction, and a new vertex should be added to the polygon of object A between $\mathbf{P}_1$ and $\mathbf{P}_2$, precisely at $\mathbf{Q}$'s location.

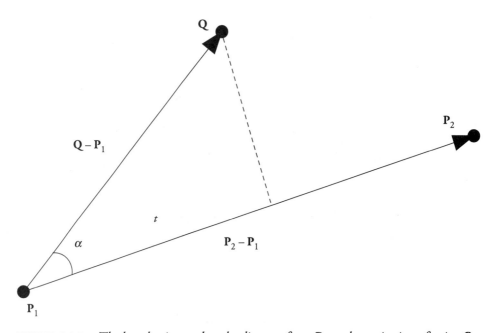

FIGURE 4.1.2 *The length* t *is equal to the distance from* $\mathbf{P}_1$ *to the projection of point* $\mathbf{Q}$, *onto the edge between* $\mathbf{P}_1$ *and* $\mathbf{P}_2$.

Retriangulation

After all the static world geometry has been processed, we must triangulate the resulting polygons so that they can be passed to the graphics hardware. Any vertex added to a polygon to eliminate a T-junction is collinear (or at least nearly collinear) with the endpoints of the edge for which the T-junction occurs. After all T-junctions have been eliminated for a single polygon, its edges might contain several vertices that fall in a straight line. This prevents us from using a simple fanning approach that might ordinarily be used to triangulate a convex polygon. Instead, we are forced to treat the polygon as concave.

The algorithm that we describe takes a list of n vertices wound in a counterclockwise direction as input and produces a list of $n - 2$ triangles. At each iteration, we search for a set of three consecutive vertices for which the corresponding triangle is not degenerate (not wound in the wrong direction) and does not contain any of the polygon's remaining vertices. Once such a set of three vertices is found, the middle vertex is disqualified from successive iterations, and the algorithm repeats until only three vertices remain.

In order to determine whether a set of three vertices is wound in a counterclockwise direction, we must know beforehand the normal direction $\mathbf{N}_0$ of the plane containing the polygon being triangulated. Let $\mathbf{P}_1$, $\mathbf{P}_2$, and $\mathbf{P}_3$ represent the positions of the three vertices. If the cross-product $(\mathbf{P}_2 - \mathbf{P}_1) \times (\mathbf{P}_3 - \mathbf{P}_1)$ points in the same direction as the normal $\mathbf{N}_0$, then the corresponding triangle is wound counterclockwise. If the cross-product is near zero, then the triangle is degenerate. Thus, two of our three requirements for a triangle are satisfied only if

$$\left(\mathbf{P}_2 - \mathbf{P}_1\right) \times \left(\mathbf{P}_3 - \mathbf{P}_1\right) \cdot \mathbf{N}_0 > \varepsilon \tag{4.1.4}$$

for some small value ε (typically, $\varepsilon \approx 0.001$).

Our third requirement is that the triangle contains no other vertices belonging to the polygon. We can construct three inward-facing normals, $\mathbf{N}_1$, $\mathbf{N}_2$, and $\mathbf{N}_3$, corresponding to the three sides of the triangle, as follows.

$$\mathbf{N}_1 = \mathbf{N}_0 \times \left(\mathbf{P}_2 - \mathbf{P}_1\right)$$

$$\mathbf{N}_2 = \mathbf{N}_0 \times \left(\mathbf{P}_3 - \mathbf{P}_2\right)$$

$$\mathbf{N}_3 = \mathbf{N}_0 \times \left(\mathbf{P}_1 - \mathbf{P}_3\right) \tag{4.1.5}$$

As shown in Figure 4.1.3, a point $\mathbf{Q}$ lies inside the triangle formed by $\mathbf{P}_1$, $\mathbf{P}_2$, and $\mathbf{P}_3$ if and only if $\mathbf{N}_i \cdot (\mathbf{Q} - \mathbf{P}_i) > -\varepsilon$ for every $i = 1,2,3$.

Since we have to calculate the normals given by Equation 4.1.5 for each triangle, we can save a little computation by replacing the condition given by Equation 4.1.4 with the equivalent expression

$$\mathbf{N}_1 \cdot \left(\mathbf{P}_3 - \mathbf{P}_1\right) > \varepsilon \tag{4.1.6}$$

This determines whether the point $\mathbf{P}_3$ lies on the positive side of the edge connecting $\mathbf{P}_1$ and $\mathbf{P}_2$.

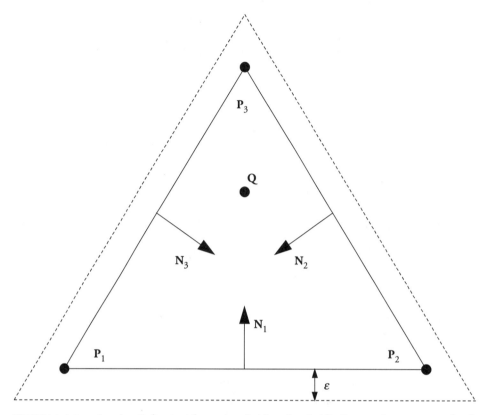

FIGURE 4.1.3   *A point **Q** lies inside a triangle if and only if it lies on the positive side of each of the three edges of the triangle.*

Implementation

ON THE CD

The source code provided on the CD-ROM demonstrates an implementation of the retriangulation algorithm. This particular implementation maintains a working set of *four* consecutive vertices and, at each iteration, determines whether valid triangles can be formed using the first three vertices or the last three vertices. If only one of the sets of three vertices forms a valid triangle, then that triangle is omitted, and the algorithm continues to the next iteration. If both sets of three vertices can produce valid triangles, then the code selects the triangle having the larger smallest angle. In the case that neither set of three vertices provides a valid triangle, the working set of four vertices is advanced until a valid triangle can be constructed.

The method presented by the source code was chosen so that the output of the algorithm would consist of a series of triangle strips and triangle fans. Such triangle structures exhibit excellent vertex cache usage on modern graphics processors. The implementation also includes a safety mechanism. If a degenerate, self-intersecting, or otherwise nontriangulatable polygon is passed to it, then the algorithm terminates prematurely to avoid becoming stuck in an infinite loop. This happens when the code cannot locate a set of three consecutive vertices that form a valid triangle.

Conclusion

Rendering artifacts such as seams between adjacent objects can be avoided by welding nearly-coincident vertices and performing T-junction elimination.

When these operations are performed as a preprocessing step, the resulting set of polygons may contain three or more collinear vertices. Fortunately, these polygons can be triangulated using a simple but robust algorithm that emits a single triangle at a time and recursively triangulates smaller sub-polygons.

4.2

Fast Heightfield Normal Calculation

Jason Shankel, Maxis

shankel@pobox.com

eightfields are two-dimensional arrays of height values, commonly used to store terrain or water surface data, and are also commonly used for calculating bump maps. This gem will describe how we can take advantage of the special characteristics of heightfield meshes to significantly optimize vertex normal calculation.

Normals on an Arbitrary Mesh

Each vertex in a heightfield mesh requires at least one corresponding surface normal if lighting- and/or environment-mapping calculations are needed for the final rendering result. There are two kinds of normals typically associated with a 3D mesh—face normals and vertex normals. Face normals are, as the name implies, normals associated with each face in a mesh. Vertex normals are normals associated with each vertex.

Face Normals

Calculating face normals is relatively straightforward. Pick two edges of the face that share a common vertex and define two vectors (v_1 and v_2) pointing along the edges with their origin at the shared vertex. The face normal (n_f) is a unit vector pointing in the direction of the cross-product, n_f, of v_1 and v_2. Note that any two edges will do for triangles, as shown in Figure 4.2.1.

$$n_f = (v_1 \times v_2)/ \mid v_1 \times v_2 \mid \tag{4.2.1}$$

Vertex Normals

Vertex normals are a little less straightforward. While there is only one correct normal for a given face, a given vertex might have multiple normals, each associated with a particular face or group of faces. However, for meshes that are fairly smooth (which is typical for heightfields), we can find a reasonably unique vertex normal by averaging the normals of each face that touches the vertex. This average should be weighted by the relative angle of each face at the vertex to prevent thin or highly tesselated faces from skewing the result.

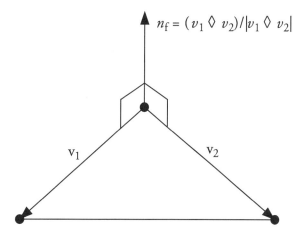

FIGURE 4.2.1   *Calculating a face normal for a triangle.*

Let $\{n_1, n_2, n_3...n_n\}$ be the normals of the faces touching vertex v, and let $\{a_1, a_2, a_3...a_n\}$ be the angles between the edges of faces 1 through n.

The normal at vertex v is given by Equation 4.2.2, as shown in Figure 4.2.2.

$$n_v = \frac{\sum_{i=0}^{n} n_i a_i}{\sum_{i=0}^{n} a_i} \tag{4.2.2}$$

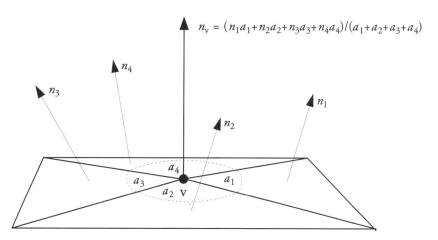

FIGURE 4.2.2   *Calculating a vertex normal using face normals.*

Heightfield Normals

The vertices of a heightfield mesh can be defined as follows by $v_{x,y}$, where

$$v_{x,y} = \left\{ x, y, h(x, y) \right\}. \tag{4.2.3}$$

In Equation 4.2.3, x and y are regularly-spaced indices into the heightfield grid, and $h(x,y)$ is the height at x,y. For a given vertex v in the heightfield, we can arrange the neighboring vertices as shown in Figure 4.2.3. For simplicity, $h_{1...4}$ refer to the values of $h()$ for the four neighbors, and the four vectors which have their origins at v and point to the neighboring vertices are labeled $v_{1...4,}$.

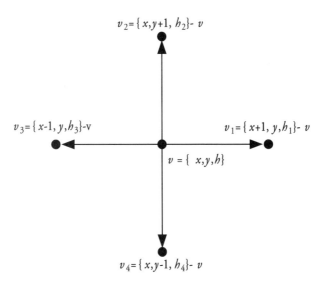

FIGURE 4.2.3   *Heightfield vertex neighbors.*

Simplifying with Assumptions

Given the unique characteristics of heightfield vertices, we can make a number of assumptions that simplify the general vertex normal formula.

First, we can assume that each vertex in the heightfield belongs to exactly four faces. Note that, strictly speaking, this might not be the case. We are assuming that the mesh is composed of quads, when it will most likely be composed of triangles. However, this assumption should not adversely affect the quality of our normals.

Second, we can assume that each of a vertex's faces contributes equally to the vertex normal, thus eliminating the need for performing a weighted average. Again, this assumption is not completely safe. If two neighboring height values greatly diverge, then the angle of their corresponding face will significantly diverge from 90°, thus changing the 'correct' contribution of the face. However, in cases where neighboring height values diverge significantly, the local vertices no longer have unique normals; and any formula, even the 'correct' one, will produce suspect results.

Finally, since the x and y values are regularly spaced, when we set the origin at v, the neighboring vertices will all have x and y values of 1, –1, or 0. These constants will greatly simplify the cross-product formula.

Doing The Math

Let's start with the original formula:

$$n_v = \frac{\sum_{i=0}^{n} n_i a_i}{\sum_{i=0}^{n} a_i} \qquad (4.2.4)$$

Next, since there are only four faces and each contributes equally to the normal, we can simplify the average:

$$n_v = (n_1 + n_2 + n_3 + n_4)/4 \qquad (4.2.5)$$

Now, when we go to calculate $n_{1...4}$, we will find that the cross-products reduce to simple terms:

$$n_1 = v_1 \times v_2 = \left\{ -h_1, -h_2, 1 \right\}$$

$$n_2 = v_2 \times v_3 = \left\{ h_3, -h_2, 1 \right\}$$

$$n_3 = v_3 \times v_4 = \left\{ h_3, h_4, 1 \right\}$$

$$n_4 = v_4 \times v_1 = \left\{ -h_1, h_4, 1 \right\} \qquad (4.2.6)$$

Ideally, we would like $n_{1...4}$ to have equal magnitudes, since variation in their magnitudes will affect the averaging formula. However, since the magnitudes of $n_{1...4}$ only significantly vary in cases where the neighboring height values diverge, we can get away with using $n_{1...4}$ as they are.

Adding up, we get:

$$n_v = (n_1 + n_2 + n_3 + n_4) / 4 = \left\{ 2(h_3 - h_1), 2(h_4 - h_2), 4 \right\} / 4 \qquad (4.2.7)$$

Since the magnitude of n_v is not important at this stage, we can multiply the whole thing by two just to simplify the arithmetic:

$$n_v = \left\{ (h_3 - h_1), (h_4 - h_2), 2 \right\} \qquad (4.2.8)$$

Since $h_{1...4}$ are most likely just memory lookups, it is clear that this formula is significantly faster than averaging four cross-products. It is important to remember that n_v is not a unit vector and might need to be normalized, depending on your application.

Conclusion

Heightfields are often used to store landscapes and other static objects. For these kinds of applications, the speed of vertex normal calculation is probably not an issue, as normals will most likely be calculated offline or only once at data load.

However, for applications that use dynamic heightfields (say, to simulate the surface of a body of water or for procedural bump-map animation), speed is of the essence. This gem has shown how we can significantly improve the performance of the standard vertex normal formula by taking advantage of the special characteristics of heightfield vertices.

Sample Code

ON THE CD

The sample code applies the fast normal formula to a heightfield, which animates between flat and a fractally-generated random landscapes. The sample code uses OpenGL and GLUT. See Color Plate 4 for some screenshots of this application.

References

[Ebert94] Ebert, D., et al., *Texturing and Modeling*, AP Professional, 1994.

[Fernandes00] Fernandes, António Ramires, "Terrain Tutorial," available online at *http://www.lighthouse3d.com/opengl/terrain/*, September, 2000.

4.3

Fast Patch Normals

Martin Brownlow, Shiny Entertainment

mbrownlow@shiny.com

Surface patches are a memory-efficient way of creating smooth surfaces that can be rendered at many levels of detail. However, having a smooth surface is not as useful if you cannot light it properly. For that, you need the normal vector at each vertex. Alas, this needs to be computed afresh for each vertex.

Definitions

Although the method described here works for any basis matrix, for the purposes of this gem, we will limit ourselves to discussion of bicubic Bézier patches (referred to hereafter simply as "patches"). These patches are represented by 16 control points arranged in a 4×4 grid. The control points form a convex hull that the actual surface lies within. Only the four corner control points actually lie on the surface.

A surface normal (hereafter referred to as "normal") is a unit vector that lies perpendicular to the surface at the point it is associated with. This vector has many uses, the most common of which are lighting and collision detection.

A point on a patch is defined uniquely by two parametric coordinates, which are usually referred to as u and v, and have a valid range of [0.0, 1.0]. These are not to be confused with texture coordinates (although they might be used directly as such). If we regard the patch as a 4×4 grid of control points, then the u value represents the horizontal fraction of the way across the grid, and the v value represents the vertical fraction. The actual-world position of a (u, v) point depends entirely on the control points. Indeed, if the control points are not evenly spaced in the world (as is more often the case than not), then a continuous step in the u direction can produce steps of varying lengths in the world.

The efficient tessellation and rendering of patches is beyond the scope of this gem. Many excellent texts exist that detail the different methods for drawing patches (see [Farin96], [Foley96], and [Gallier00]). A description of any single one of them here would be inappropriate, since this method of generating normals is applicable to most, if not all, methods of rendering a patch.

Traditional Approaches

The most obvious approach to generating a patch vertex normal involves examining its neighbors. By considering the previous and next vertex in both the u and v directions of the patch, you can approximate the surface tangents. The normal is then simply the normalized cross-product of these two vectors.

Another method is to use the first derivative of the patch equations to directly generate the two tangent vectors. However, although this does not require any neighbors, it still needs a cross-product and a normalize operation per vertex.

Considerations

In order to efficiently process a patch on current PC graphics hardware, you must use what is called a "vertex shader." This is basically a custom program written in a minimal but powerful instruction set that executes once for each vertex in the vertex stream. To gain the maximum parallelism and throughput, a vertex shader is restricted to operate on only one vertex at a time; it cannot access any vertex other than the one currently being processed. In other words, every vertex in the stream must contain all the information needed to process it. It is also desirable to have the minimum amount of information per vertex to reduce the time spent by the graphics card in actually accessing the data, and to maximize the time spent in processing it. Obviously, our target is to have the vertex stream just contain the patch (u, v) coordinates for each vertex. Since the u and v coordinates have a range of [0.0, 1.0], and it is unlikely that we will need more than about 100 subdivisions, it is possible to encode these into bytes, giving an impressive two bytes per vertex in the vertex stream!

A Simpler Method

These two methods presume that we only know the position at each control point, from which we can generate the curve equations and, ultimately, the normals. What if we also have the normals at each control point to start with?

These are easily generated at each control point using a variety of methods, including the two methods previously described. A control point would then consist of a position and a normal. Any skinning code applied to a control point's position could also be applied to its normal. Given this, all we have to do is interpolate the normal across the patch, just as we do the position. This has the added advantage of being a nonlinear interpolation, which will better approximate the real normal.

This meets all our hardware requirements; it requires only the (u, v) patch coordinates of the current vertex to correctly generate its position, normal, and texture coordinates. It also has the advantages of working for any basis system and using exactly the same code as the position generation, just using control normals instead of control points.

Other Advantages

Another advantage of this method is that by generating the normals in different ways, you can eliminate shading artifacts from curve continuity issues. If we treat the set of control meshes for the whole object as a single continuous mesh, then we can create vertex normals for each control point exactly as we would for a Gouraud-shaded model. Although the normals wouldn't strictly be correct with respect to the curves, it can give the model a much smoother look that would otherwise take the modeler much longer to create. If the normals are generated in this way, we eliminate curve-continuity issues in the model. This method also eliminates any shading issues that are introduced during the skinning process, when the curves lose continuity with each other as they are influenced by different bones.

Most modern graphics architectures use a vector-based processor that operates on four data elements simultaneously. This method uses two vectors, but each contains only three items. We can use this to our advantage and interpolate two extra values across the patch. This could be used for a variety of things, such as arbitrary texture mapping or a varying alpha value for better transparency effects.

Exactly How Accurate Can This Be?

A Bézier curve has the property that the control points form a bounding mesh that the curve never exceeds. This means that the interpolated normal will never be greater than the modulus of the control mesh normals. However, except in the case of a straight curve segment, a Bézier curve never passes through the center two control points. In other words, the modulus of the interpolated normal will always be less than or equal to the modulus of the control normal. The result is an interpolation that is somewhere between linear and the correct arc interpolation. In practice, the normal difference across the patch is not too large, meaning that the interpolation is very close to the correct value.

For other curve basis systems, the problem can be a little more severe, with the normals getting quite large for sudden, sharp turns on the surface. However, with strategic use of most modern graphic cards' ability to automatically normalize normals, this is less of an issue than it would otherwise be.

Conclusion

Patch surfaces are useful for creating smooth, resolution-independent geometry with minimal memory usage. By treating the normal at each control point as a second control mesh, we can quickly approximate the correct surface normal. Although the results are not strictly correct, they can produce superior results by eliminating shading errors due to curve discontinuity introduced during skinning.

References

[Farin96] Farin, Gerald E., *Curves and Surfaces for Computer Aided Geometric Design: A Practical Guide,* Fourth Edition, Academic Press, 1996.

[Foley96] Foley, Van Dam, et al., *Computer Graphics: Principals and Practice, Second Edition in C,* Addison Wesley, 1996.

[Gallier00] Gallier, Jean, *Curves and Surfaces in Geometric Modeling: Theory and Algorithms,* Morgan Kaufmann Publishers, 2000.

4.4

Fast and Simple Occlusion Culling

Wagner T. Corrêa, Princeton University;

James T. Klosowski, IBM Research;

and Cláudio T. Silva,

AT&T Labs-Research

wtcorrea@cs.princeton.edu, jklosow@us.ibm.com,
and csilva@research.att.com

In many graphics applications, such as building walkthroughs and first-person games, the user moves around the interior of a virtual environment and the computer creates an image for each location of the user. For any given position, the user typically sees only a small fraction of the scene. Thus, to speed up the image rendering, an application should avoid drawing the primitives in the environment that the user cannot see. There are several classes of algorithms to determine which primitives should be ignored or culled. *Back-face culling* algorithms determine those primitives that face away from the user. *View frustum culling* determines the primitives that lie outside of the user's field of view. *Occlusion culling* determines the primitives that are occluded by other primitives.

While back-face and view frustum culling algorithms are trivial, occlusion culling algorithms tend to be complex and usually require time-consuming preprocessing steps. This gem describes two occlusion culling algorithms that are practical, effective, and require little preprocessing. The first one is the prioritized-layered projection (PLP) algorithm, which is an approximate algorithm that determines, for a given budget, a set of primitives that is likely to be visible. The second algorithm, cPLP, is a conservative version of PLP that guarantees finding all visible primitives.

The Visibility Problem

Given a scene composed of modeling primitives and a viewing frustum, we need to determine which primitive fragments are visible; that is, which fragments are connected to the eye-point by a line segment that meets the closure of no other primitive [Dobkin97]. Researchers have studied this problem extensively, and many approaches to solve it exist [Cohen-Or01, Durand99]. A recent survey on visibility algorithms, [Cohen-Or01] classifies algorithms according to several criteria. We will now briefly summarize those that are most relevant to our gem.

From-Point Versus From-Region

Some algorithms compute visibility from the eye-point only, while others compute visibility from a region in space. Since the user often stays in a region for some time, the from-region algorithms amortize the cost of visibility computations over a number of frames.

Precomputed Versus Online

Many algorithms require an offline computation, while others work in real-time. For instance, most from-region algorithms require a preprocessing step to divide the model into regions and compute region visibility.

Object Space Versus Image Space

Some algorithms compute visibility in object space using the exact, original 3D primitives. Others operate in image space using only the discrete, rasterized fragments of the primitives.

Conservative Versus Approximate

Few visibility algorithms compute exact visibility. Most algorithms are conservative and over-estimate the set of visible primitives. Other algorithms compute approximate visibility and do not guarantee finding all visible primitives.

The PLP Algorithm

PLP [Klosowski00] is an approximate, from-point, object-space visibility algorithm that requires very little preprocessing. PLP can be understood as a simple modification to the traditional hierarchical view-frustum culling algorithm [Clark76]. The traditional algorithm recursively traverses the model hierarchy from the root node down to the leaf nodes. If a node is outside the view frustum, we ignore the node and its children. If the node is inside or intersects the view frustum, we recursively traverse its children. The traversal eventually visits all leaves within the view frustum.

This PLP algorithm differs from the traditional one in several ways. First, instead of traversing the model hierarchy in a predefined order, PLP keeps the hierarchy of leaf nodes in a priority queue called the *front* and traverses the nodes from highest to lowest priority. When we visit a node (or *project* it, in PLP parlance), we add it to the *visible set*. Then, we remove it from the front and add its *layer* of unvisited neighbors to the front (hence, the algorithm's name, "prioritized-layered projection"). Second, instead of traversing the entire hierarchy, PLP works on a *budget*, stopping the traversal after a certain number of primitives have been added to the visible set. Finally, PLP requires each node to know not only its children, but also all of its neighbors.

An implementation of PLP can be simple or sophisticated, depending on the heuristic to assign priorities to each node. Several heuristics precompute the initial *solidity* of a node and accumulate the solidities along a traversal path. The node's accumulated solidity estimates how likely it is for the node to occlude an object behind it [Klosowski00]. In this gem, we use an extremely simple heuristic to assign priorities to the nodes. The node containing the eye-point receives priority –1, its neighbors receive priority –2, their neighbors receive priority –3, and so on. Using this heuristic, the traversal proceeds in layers of nodes around the eye-point. This is simple to implement, very fast, and quite accurate. We will show accuracy measurements when we present the runtime results. The only precomputation this heuristic requires is the construction of the hierarchy itself.

ON THE CD

We use PLP as a front-end to the hardware's implementation of the z-buffer algorithm [Foley90]. For a given budget, PLP gives us the set of primitives it considers most likely to maximize image quality. We simply pass these primitives to the graphics hardware. The C++ implementation of PLP can be found on the CD-ROM.

The cPLP Algorithm

Although PLP is, in practice, quite accurate for most frames, it does *not* guarantee image quality, so some frames might show objectionable artifacts. To circumvent this potential problem, we use cPLP [Klosowski01], a conservative extension of PLP.

The main idea of cPLP is to use the visible set given by PLP as an initial guess, while adding nodes to the visible set until the front (of the priority queue) is empty. This guarantees that the final visible set is conservative [Klosowski01]. There are many ways to implement cPLP, including exploiting new platform-dependent hardware extensions for visibility computation. The implementation we describe in this gem uses an item-buffer technique that is portable to any system that supports OpenGL.

The cPLP main loop consists of two steps. First, we determine the nodes in the front that are visible. To do this, we draw the bounding box of each node in the front, using flat shading with a color equal to its identification number. We then read back the color buffer and determine the nodes seen. Second, for each front node found to be visible, we project it (adding it to the visible set), remove it from the front, and then add its unvisited neighbors to the front. We iterate the main loop until the front is empty. The bottleneck of the item buffer-based implementation of cPLP is in reading back the color buffer. To avoid reading the entire color buffer at each step, we break the screen into tiles. Tiles that are not modified in one step can be ignored in subsequent steps. The C++ implementation of cPLP can be found on the CD-ROM.

ON THE CD

Discussion

PLP and cPLP are attractive visibility algorithms for several reasons:

- PLP and cPLP are from-point algorithms, and they make no assumption about the model. In contrast, some from-region algorithms assume the model consists of axis-aligned rooms and portals [Teller91, Funkhouser93], which might be a significant restriction.
- PLP and cPLP require little preprocessing. For most heuristics, the precomputation consists of creating the model hierarchy and computing simple summary statistics per node, such as the total number of primitives. This can be done quickly, even for a large model. On the other hand, other techniques [Teller91, Hong97, Zhang97] can require preprocessing times on the order of hours or days, even for relatively small models.
- Although occlusion culling algorithms such as PLP avoid rendering unseen geometry, they might still render small primitives that have little effect on the final image. As shown by [El-Sana01], PLP can be easily integrated with level-of-detail management.
- PLP is suitable for time-critical rendering. Even if we use the lowest levels of detail, the number of visible primitives in a given frame might overwhelm a low-end graphics card. The PLP budget gives the user a convenient way to balance both accuracy and speed. The impact of slightly incorrect images on the user's perception of the walkthrough is often far less than the impact of low frame rates [Funkhouser96].

PLP is most useful when higher frame rates are more important than absolute accuracy—for example, when the user is moving fast to get to a certain point. On the other hand, cPLP is necessary when artifacts are not acceptable, such as when the user has reached his target and is closely examining its details. Ideally, an application should allow the user to switch back and forth between PLP and cPLP on the fly.

Experimental Results

To show what PLP and cPLP can do, we have run tests using the 13 million-triangle UNC power-plant model on a Pentium III, 733-MHz computer with a Nvidia GeForce2 graphics card. We collected statistics for both PLP and cPLP using a 500-frame path. Figure 4.4.1 shows a typical frame of this path using a budget of 140,000 triangles per frame.

For PLP, the average frame rate was 10.1 Hz, with 75% of the tests having a frame rate above 9.3 Hz. For cPLP, the average frame rate was 2.1 Hz, with 75% of the tests having a frame rate above 1.5 Hz. Although the rates for cPLP are lower than the rates for PLP, the image is guaranteed to be 100% correct. We measured the accuracy of PLP by counting the number of incorrect pixels in the images it generated versus the correct images generated. The average accuracy for PLP was 96.3%; and for 75% of the test, the accuracy was above 94.9%.

FIGURE 4.4.1 *Using the prioritized-layered projection algorithm (PLP) to walk through the 13-million triangle UNC power plant model. On a 733-MHz Pentium III computer with Nvidia GeForce2 graphics, PLP achieves an average frame rate of 10.1 Hz and an average accuracy of 96.3%.*

Because of the layered traversal of the model hierarchy, the wrong pixels tend to be at regions far from the eye-point. Sometimes the artifacts are noticeable, but they are usually tolerable and have little impact on the user's experience. Recall that we achieved this level of accuracy with the embarrassingly simple heuristic of traversing the model hierarchy one layer at a time. We believe this accuracy can be even better with more-sophisticated heuristics.

Conclusion

PLP and cPLP are practical solutions to the ubiquitous visibility problem. PLP allows the user to trade off accuracy for speed. With PLP, there is no guarantee of image quality; however, in practice, it is good enough to give the user a sense of smooth navigation. Whenever 100% accuracy is critical, the program could switch to cPLP and still be able to walk through the model at slower frame rates.

There are several ways to improve upon what we have presented in this gem. First, we have presented only one simple heuristic for estimating the visibility of a node. More sophisticated heuristics exist [El-Sana01], and there is still room for improvement. Second, these algorithms could be combined with level-of-detail management [El-Sana01]. Finally, these algorithms could be used to drive caching schemes to handle models that are larger than the available main memory.

References

[Clark76] Clark, James H., "Hierarchical Geometric Models for Visible Surface Algorithms," *Communications of the ACM*, 19(10): 547–554, October 1976.

[Cohen-Or01] Cohen-Or, Daniel, Yiorgos Chrysanthou, Cláudio T. Silva, and Frédo Durand, "A Survey of Visibility for Walkthrough Applications," *IEEE Transactions on Visualization and Computer Graphics*.

[Dobkin97] Dobkin, David and Seth Teller, *Handbook of Discrete and Computational Geometry*, Computer Graphics Chapter, CRC Press, 1997.

[Durand99] Durand, Frédo, "3D Visibility: Analytical Study and Applications," Ph.D. Thesis, Université Joseph Fourier, Grenoble, France, 1999.

[El-Sana01] El-Sana, Jihad, Neta Sokolovsky, and Cláudio T. Silva, "Integrating Occlusion Culling with View-Dependent Rendering," in Proceedings of IEEE Visualization, 2001: 371–378.

[Foley90] Foley, James D., Andries van Dam, Steven K. Feiner, and John F. Hughes, *Computer Graphics: Principles and Practice*, Second Edition, Addison Wesley, 1990.

[Funkhouser93] Funkhouser, Thomas A. and Carlo H. Séquin, "Adaptive Display Algorithm for Interactive Frame Rates during Visualization of Complex Virtual Environments," Computer Graphics Proceedings, SIGGRAPH 1993: pp. 247–254.

[Funkhouser96] Funkhouser, Thomas A., "Database Management for Interactive Display of Large Architectural Models," Proceedings of Graphics Interface '96: pp. 1–8.

[Hong97] Hong, Lichan, et al., "Virtual Voyage: Interactive Navigation in the Human Colon," Computer Graphics Proceedings, SIGGRAPH 1997: pp. 27–34.

[Klosowski00] Klosowski, James T. and Cláudio T. Silva, "The Prioritized-Layered Projection Algorithm for Visible Set Estimation," in *IEEE Transactions on Visualization and Computer Graphics*, April-June 2000, 6(2):108–123.

[Klosowski01] Klosowski, James T. and Cláudio T. Silva, "Efficient Conservative Visibility Culling Using the Prioritized-Layered Projection Algorithm," in *IEEE Transactions on Visualization and Computer Graphics*, October-December 2001, 7(4):365–379.

[Teller91] Teller, Seth and Carlo H. Séquin, "Visibility Preprocessing for Interactive Walkthroughs," Computer Graphics Proceedings, SIGGRAPH 1991: pp. 61–69.

[Walkthru01] The Walkthru Project at UNC Chapel Hill, "Power Plant Model," available online at http://www.cs.unc.edu/~geom/Powerplant/.

[Zhang97] Zhang, Hansong, Dinesh Manocha, Thomas Hudson, and Kenneth E. Hoff III, "Visibility Culling Using Hierarchical Occlusion Maps," Computer Graphics Proceedings, SIGGRAPH 1997: pp. 77–88.

4.5

Triangle Strip Creation, Optimizations, and Rendering

Carl S. Marshall, Intel Labs

Carl.S.Marshall@intel.com

In the current age of high-performance consoles, triangle strips have moved to the forefront of primitive selection when representing and rendering geometry. This gem focuses on how to generate triangle strips from arbitrary 3D polygonal models. We will describe and provide source code for developing long triangle strips. After describing the triangle strip algorithm, we will explain the benefits of triangle strips, the possible pitfalls encountered when creating them, and how to submit them to the graphics API. In addition, several other triangle strip creation algorithms will be reviewed and critiqued.

Triangle Strips

A triangle strip (tri-strip) is a series of connected triangles. The connection of the triangles allows vertex caching so that graphics cards can reuse the shared edges between the triangles. Figure 4.5.1 shows a simple triangle strip with shared edges V_2V_3 and V_3V_4. In order for a triangle to be a part of a triangle strip, the triangle must contain the same smoothing group and material group as the other triangles in the tri-strip. A smoothing group is a group of triangles that all have one normal per vertex, and a material group is a group of triangles that all have the same lighting and texture properties.

Background

The technique of using triangle strips has been around for a long time. Before that, the general format for submitting triangles to the API was to explicitly send each vertex's position, normal, and color. But because fewer vertices need to be sent for triangle strips, this gives them a tremendous advantage over a pure triangle graphics API call. Today, vertex indexing has virtually displaced the earlier process and now is the primary method for submitting polygons to a graphics card. [Marselas00] suggests that by using triangle strips and vertex indexing, it is possible to bring the vertex-to-

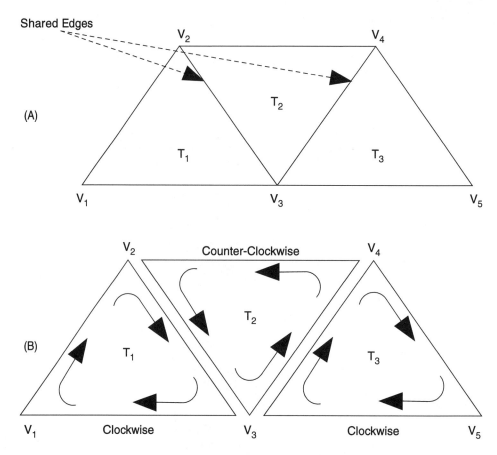

FIGURE 4.5.1   *(A) A simple triangle strip with shared edges V_2V_3 and V_3V_4. (B) The ordering of the triangles in the tri-strip alternate between clockwise and counterclockwise ordering.*

triangle ratio close to 1:1 for certain meshes. This gives tri-strips the advantage of data reduction.

Goals

Triangle strip creation has four goals:

    1. To minimize the number of tri-strips
    2. To minimize the number of repeated vertices
    3. To minimize the number of isolated triangles
    4. To maximize vertex caching

These goals often conflict with one another. For example, it is difficult to generate extremely long tri-strips or cache friendly tri-strips without repeating many vertices. It is also better to have several isolated triangles (tri-strips of three vertices) than a few tri-strips of four vertices because you can batch the isolated triangles into an indexed vertex list.

Benefits

Using triangle strips instead of independent triangles will allow for a reduced submission of vertices or vertex indices. Depending on how the triangle strips are submitted to the graphics hardware, you can receive substantial savings in vertex data, transformation, and lighting. Triangle strips can also give you an advantage with vertex caching on the graphics card.

Triangle Strip Creation

There are several triangle strip creation algorithms in the research space, but each algorithm has its advantages and disadvantages, due to the fact that finding the optimal tri-strips is an NP-complete problem. [Evans96a] uses a quad-based mesh to optimize tri-strips within patches, whereas [Hoppe99] uses a cache-friendly triangle strip approach. The approach we chose is to optimize the length of the triangle strip to overcome the graphics API overhead.

Since it is impossible to have the perfect triangle stripping of a mesh for any situation, we have to create algorithms that will find the most optimal tri-strips for the specific implementation. The algorithm that we use aggressively generates tri-strips from any arbitrary 3D polygonal model. This tri-strip generation algorithm can be placed into any of your favorite 3D authoring tools, or it can be run as a stand-alone tool. The goal is to generate long tri-strips and then write them out into a format that is easily rendered. Color Plate 5 shows a sample image of two models after the triangle strip algorithm has been run on the mesh.

Definitions

Before we go into our creation algorithm, it will help to define a few terms. An *active edge* is the edge of a triangle within the strip onto which new triangles can be added. The active edge is between the second and third vertices of the last triangle to be added to the triangle strip. The bold edge in Figure 4.5.2a shows the active edge, DE, in which the triangle with vertex F can be added. A *swap* is used when the active edge does not align with the neighboring triangle to be added to the strip. Figure 4.5.2b shows a case in which the active edge is DE, but the next triangle to be added is on edge CE. To add the new triangle, vertex C will have to be repeated and then swapped with vertex E. This will keep the proper clockwise, counterclockwise ordering. The last term we will define is called a *flip*, which is when two duplicate vertices have to be added and swapped to add a new vertex, as shown in Figure 4.5.2c.

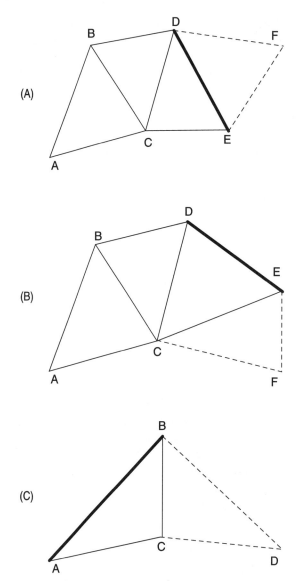

FIGURE 4.5.2   *The various stages in which triangles can be added to a triangle strip. (A) A tri-strip with a vertex index ordering of ABCDE and an active edge DE. Since the active edge borders the new triangle, F can just be added to the end of the tri-strip. The new tri-strip is ABCDEF. (B) Tri-strip ABCDE with active edge DE. To include vertex F, C will have to be duplicated and then swapped with E, since the active edge does not border the new triangle to be added. The new tri-strip is ABCDCEF. (C) A case where reordering the first face of a triangle strip to match the second face is crucial to minimize repeated vertices. If the triangle strip started as CAB, then B and C would have to be repeated to add vertex D. CABBCD is the new triangle strip. If the active edge is facing away from the second triangle, then two vertices have to be repeated.*

Preprocess

The preprocess stage is used to create metrics for generating quality triangle strips.

1. Find a triangle with the smallest area, which we will call the *origin* triangle. To avoid poor triangle stripping, you might want to get the 10 smallest-area triangles in the mesh and select between those triangles for the origin triangle.
2. Select a vertex of the origin triangle or create its centroid, which will be the starting point for the triangle strip algorithm.
3. Create a centroid for each triangle. This can be easily done by averaging the three vertices of each triangle (see Equation 4.5.1). C is the centroid position, and V_1, V_2, and V_3 are the vertex positions of the triangle.
4. For each triangle, calculate and store the Euclidean distance between the starting vertex and the centroid.

$$C = (V_1 + V_2 + V_3) / 3.0 \qquad\qquad (4.5.1)$$

Creation Algorithm

Once we have the preprocess stage complete, we can start generating triangle strips. Each time a triangle of the mesh is added to a tri-strip, mark the triangle invalid.

1. Select a valid triangle. This triangle will be the first triangle of the triangle strip.
2. If the triangle has neighbors, select the triangle with the smallest distance value, and make it the current triangle. Otherwise, end the triangle strip and go to Step 6.
3. Reorient the first triangle so that its active edge matches the second triangle. The edge between the second and third vertices should match the neighboring triangle.
4. Get the neighbor of the current triangle by finding the triangle with the smallest distance value, which was stored in preprocess Step 4. If the triangle does not align with the active edge, then a vertex will have to be repeated with a swap in order to continue creating the triangle strip (see Figure 4.5.2c).
5. Go to Step 2.
6. Check to see if any remaining triangles are not included in a tri-strip. If so, go to Step 1.

The high-level pseudo-code for running the tri-strip algorithm is show in Listing 4.5.1.

LISTING 4.5.1 *High-level pseudo-code for running the tri-strip algorithm.*

```
void main( )
{
    Mesh *pMesh;

    LoadMesh(pMesh); // Load 3D polygonal mesh
    originTriangle = FindSmallestAreaTriangle();
    CalculateCentroidForEachTriangle();

    // Get Euclidean distance from centroid of
    // the origin triangle to the current
    // triangle origin
    CalculateDistanceFromToEachTriangle(
    OriginTriangle);

    // Generate the triangle strips
    TriStripGeneration(pMesh);

    // Run a second pass filter to see if any of
    // the previous triangle strips can be connected
    ConnectTriangleStrips();
    ConvertTriStrips(); //Use custom data structure
}
```

Once the creation algorithm is finished, the output will be *N* triangle strips. Each of these triangle strips will belong in one smoothing group and have the same material ID. Once the tri-strips are stored in memory, you can customize the data into any format that is required by your game I/O.

Connecting Triangle Strips

As a second pass, the triangle strips can be analyzed to see if there are any points at which they can be connected to each other. The analysis starts by finding all of the starting edges and ending edges of each triangle strip along with the face index attached to each edge. Then, the starting and ending edges are compared with those of all of the other triangle strips to see if a match occurs. Once a match is found, the two triangle strips are analyzed to see which stage they fall into (from Figure 4.5.2). Most cases will require some number of vertex repetitions to merge the triangle strips. One of the simpler cases is when an isolated triangle is matched with another triangle strip. In most cases, the isolated triangle's vertices can be reordered to conform to the matching triangle strip.

Optimizations

Since the goal of developing triangle strips is to increase performance, optimizations are a key part of any triangle strip generation algorithm. Optimizations can be placed into several areas of the triangle strip development process: preprocess, generation, and runtime.

Preprocess:

- Create meshes with only a few smoothing groups (more than one normal per vertex).
- Limit the number of material groups per model.
- Optimize the model so that polygonal faces do not swap back and forth between material groups or smoothing groups. This will limit the length of a triangle strip.
- Sort triangle strips via material groups before submitting them to the graphics card.
- Eliminate all *dummy* faces. A dummy face is when two or more of the three vertex locations are equivalent. This can cause the triangle strip to flip inside out and possibly get culled when rendered.

Generation:

- Batch isolated triangles into a single, indexed buffer.
- Try to merge triangle strips that have neighboring beginning or ending triangles, where possible.
- Know the cache size of the hardware, and optimize as appropriate.

Runtime:

- Use an indexed array API call instead of a pure ordered vertex submission call.
- Reduce state swapping and dynamic texture coordinate changes.

Rendering

Most graphics APIs have support for rendering triangle strips. There are usually a couple of formats you can choose from when submitting triangle strips to the graphics card. One format requires sending the vertex data for each vertex in the triangle strip. This is very expensive, since many vertices will be duplicated due to shared edges by multiple triangle strips. Another format requires submitting the triangle strips via an indexed format. An indexed format is one in which you submit a vertex pool, and the triangle strip vertex indices into the vertex pool. One issue with most graphics APIs is that they only allow one triangle strip submission per API call. In some APIs, you can submit dummy vertices to allow the submission of multiple triangle strips. [Neider99] and [Microsoft00] both list the API submission calls for triangle strips. OpenGL uses the primitive type `GL_TRIANGLE_STRIP`, and Microsoft Direct3D uses `D3DPT_TRIANGLESTRIP`.

Cache-Friendly Triangle Strips

Another triangle strip creation algorithm creates triangle strips that are cache friendly by minimizing vertex cache misses [Hoppe99]. [Nvidia00] uses a vertex-caching scheme that will run as a post-process on previously created triangle strips in order to optimize cache usage. The advantage to this approach is that you can optimize triangle strips to a specific graphics card. Of course, the drawback with this routine is that the optimizations can hinder you if the same content is used on another graphics card with a different cache size.

Continuous Level-of-Detail Triangle Strips

Creating triangle strips for a mesh that has a continuous level of detail can be tricky. As soon as a vertex or face is removed from the mesh, it can have a dramatic effect on the triangle strips that were created at the higher resolution by breaking them up and creating invalid faces. There are a couple of ways to solve this problem. The first would be to create a set of triangle strips for every resolution of the model. This is extremely impractical and would balloon your memory usage. The second choice would be to create the triangle strips on the fly and store them in memory until the resolution changes. We chose the second method, only allowing triangles to be added to a triangle strip that neighbored its current active edge or required a swap. If no neighbors existed, then the triangle strip would be ended. The key here is to optimize the data structures for fast neighbor lookup and traversal. The advantage is the ability to use triangle strips with dynamic geometry; however, this will require additional overhead in memory.

Conclusion

This gem described how to create and optimize triangle strips for your game. When you consider rendering primitives for your geometry, triangle strips can help provide a beneficial speed-up compared with submitting simple triangle lists. We encourage you to test your geometry with triangle strips and compare the differences for yourself.

References

[Evans96a] Evans, Francine, Steven Skiena, and Amitabh Varshney, "Optimizing Triangle Strips for Fast Rendering," Visualization '96 Proceedings, IEEE, 1996: pp. 319–326

[Evans96b] Evans, Francine, Steven Skiena, and Amitabh Varshney, "Completing Sequential Triangulations Is Hard," Technical Report, Department of Computer Science, State University of New York at Stony Brook, 1996.

[Hoppe99] Hoppe, Hughes, "Optimization of Mesh Locality for Transparent Vertex Caching," Computer Graphics Proceedings, SIGGRAPH 1999: pp. 269–276.

[Isenburg00] Isenburg, Martin, "Triangle Strip Compression," *Graphics Interface*, pp. 197–204, 2000.

[Marselas00] Marselas, Herb, "Optimizing Vertex Submission for OpenGL," *Game Programming Gems*, Charles River Media, Inc., 2000.

[Microsoft00] *Microsoft DirectX 8.0 Software Development Kit*, available online at http://www.msdn.microsoft.com/downloads, 2000.

[Neider99] Neider, Jackie, et al., *OpenGL Programming Guide, Version 1.2*, Addison Wesley, 1999.

[Nvidia00] Nvidia NvTriStrip v1.1., available online at http://developer.nvidia.com/view.asp?IO=nvtristrip_v1_1, 2000.

4.6

Computing Optimized Shadow Volumes for Complex Data Sets

Alex Vlachos and Drew Card,

ATI Research

Alex@Vlachos.com and DCard@ati.com

As graphics hardware performance increases, shadow volumes become a more relevant topic for the game industry. In this gem, we describe a method for computing the exact front cap geometry visible from a given static light source. This is the exact geometry that is visible from the light's point of view, and it is useful for calculating shadow volumes. Previous work has been done on this topic; however, most methods suffer from either infinite recursion (with complex polygonal models) or fail to solve for cyclically overlapping polygons. The method presented here also works for scenes that have intersecting polygons.

Previous Work

The Weiler-Atherton algorithm [Weiler77] provides an interesting method for computing front cap geometry. The advantage of its method is that it does not require a perfectly sorted list of polygons with respect to the light source. Additionally, the Weiler-Atherton algorithm solves for cyclically overlapping polygons. However, when using even a slightly complex scene, this method lends itself to infinite recursion due to precision errors when using 64-bit, floating-point variables. The method presented in this gem borrows some of the basic methods from the Weiler-Atherton algorithm, but it approaches the problem from a different direction.

The Algorithm

The steps for computing the exact front cap geometry visible from a given static light source are somewhat complex. Starting with all the front-facing polygons that lie in the light frustum, roughly sort them back-to-front. A simple quick-sort based on each polygon's closest vertex will suffice. At this point, you want to assign each polygon a unique ID for later reference. You might also want to store these polygons into bins to enable quicker searching. We call these polygons the "input array." We also need an "output array," which will be initialized as empty.

Now we perform a series of operations on each of the polygons in the input array. First, create a beam (a small frustum) from the light source and the polygon. Three of the four clip planes that make up the beam are simply the planes defined by the light position and each edge of the polygon. The fourth clip plane is the plane of the polygon itself. All of the geometry that we have stored so far in our output array that falls inside the beam's frustum is discarded. The remaining fragments are stored back into the output array (see Figure 4.6.1).

Since it is sometimes impossible to perfectly sort polygons (as with cyclically overlapping polygons), there may be polygons remaining in the output array that obscure the currently selected polygon from the light's viewpoint. To account for this case, we recurse one level deep for each of the obscuring polygons. A temporary array is created with just the current input polygon, and it is clipped using the beams of each obscuring polygon. The remaining polygons (in the temporary array) are copied to the output array. If there are no obscuring polygons, we simply add the input polygon to the output array (see Figure 4.6.2).

After processing each input polygon, we need to run an optimization algorithm on the output polygon array to reduce the amount of polygon splitting. This algorithm is explained in the following section. Note that this step needs to occur at each iteration of the main loop.

After looping through all the input polygons, solve for T-junctions in the final output array to prevent rasterization artifacts. At this point, the clean front caps have been created, and the shadow volume can now be easily generated. Since the front caps do not overlap from the light's point of view, a copy of the final front cap geometry can be projected onto the far plane of a spotlight frustum to generate the back cap. Point lights can be split into eight subregions to facilitate the creation of the volume.

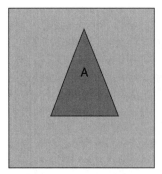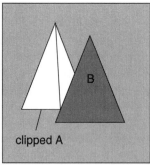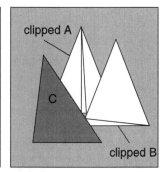

FIGURE 4.6.1 *An illustration of beam construction and output polygon culling. The dark gray polygon is the currently selected one, and the white polygons are in the output array. A beam is created from the light point (in this case the eye-point) and the selected polygon. The output polygons are then clipped against this beam.*

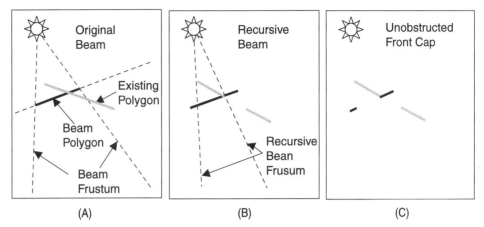

FIGURE 4.6.2 *Dealing with obstructing output polygons. Shown from a top (orthographic) view. (A) The light beam is illustrated by the dotted lines surrounding the (black) beam polygon. (B) The light-gray polygon, which is in the output array, is clipped by the original beam frustum from (A). Since a portion of the clipped polygon obstructs the currently selected (black) polygon, a recursive step is taken to create a beam frustum with the clipped portion, and the original (black) polygon is clipped against it. (C) The result is the exact front cap geometry.*

Optimization Algorithm

As previously mentioned, an optimization algorithm is required in order to avoid numerical inaccuracies and improve performance. In many cases, the repetitive clipping to beam frustums can create excessive numbers of sliver polygons. To help avoid this, all subpolygons created from an original input polygon are collapsed into the smallest number of polygons possible at each pass through the loop.

The input stream should also be optimized before the main loop. This will make it unnecessary to optimize across the original polygon boundaries at every iteration. Optimizing in groups based on the original input polygons does everything that is required.

There are two algorithms that can be utilized to optimize the polygonal mesh. These algorithms, which we will outline here, provide a method for determining which vertex should be removed or which edge collapsed. The remaining n-gon will then need to be retessellated into triangles using a robust tessellation algorithm such as that in [deBerg00].

Vertex Removal

An example of removing a vertex is illustrated in Figure 4.6.3. The first step is to build a mesh from all of the triangles that correspond to an original input triangle (by the triangle ID). Next, build an edge table for all of the edges in this mesh. For each ver-

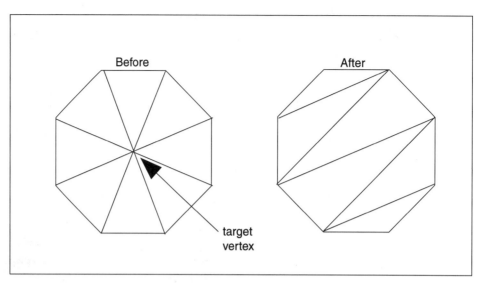

FIGURE 4.6.3   *Removing a vertex.*

tex in the mesh, choose a starting triangle that contains that vertex, and use the edge table to walk clockwise around the vertex to neighboring triangles that also contain that vertex. Continue to walk around the vertex until no more triangles exist in the chain or until the original triangle is reached. If the walk around the vertex is successful (i.e., a full walk back to the original triangle is completed), then the vertex can be removed.

Edge Collapse

An example of collapsing an edge is illustrated in Figure 4.6.4. Similar to the vertex-removal algorithm, the first step is to build a mesh from all of the triangles that correspond to an original input triangle. Now, build an edge table for all of the edges in the mesh. For each vertex in the mesh, choose a starting triangle, which contains the vertex, and use the edge table to walk clockwise around the vertex to neighboring triangles that also contain the vertex. Compare the current triangle's leading edge with the original edge for collinearity, using a cylinder test (or sum up the angles of the triangles and test for equality with 180°). If the two edges are found to be collinear, collapse the edge by combining the two adjacent edges into a single edge and removing the shared vertex.

Note that keeping track of the original edges of the input triangles might also reduce the computation time for the edge collapse. This method allows for the comparison of the edge IDs while also reducing possible error due to floating-point inaccuracies.

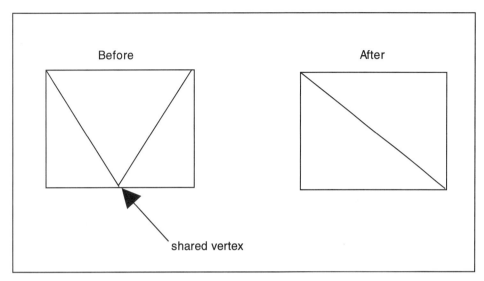

FIGURE 4.6.4   *Collapsing an edge by removing a shared vertex.*

For an example of precomputed shadow volumes combined with other rendering techniques in real-time, see Color Plate 6.

References

[deBerg00] de Berg, van Dreveld and Schwarzkopf Overmars, "Polygon Triangulation," *Computational Geometry Algorithms and Applications,* Second Edition, 2000: pp. 45–61.

[Weiler77] Weiler, K. and P. Atherton, "Hidden Surface Removal Using Polygon Area Sorting," *Computer Graphics,* SIGGRAPH, 1977: Vol. 11, pp. 214–222.

4.7

Subdivision Surfaces for Character Animation

William Leeson, Trinity College, Dublin

wleeson@indigo.ie

Constructing surfaces through subdivision has become popular with high-end rendering packages over the past few years. This is due in no small part to the stunning visuals produced by companies such as Pixar [DeRose98]. These schemes solve many of the problems associated with other curved-surface techniques, such as NURBS surfaces. Since they behave in a way similar to polygonal meshes, there are fewer restrictions. Character skins can be used almost directly with some subdivision schemes. Others require some modification in order to get a good representation of the original mesh.

This gem introduces subdivision surfaces as a means of improving the appearance of game characters. First, we will present the different schemes available, focusing on two implementations of subdivision surfaces. Then, we will explore a number of optimization methods based on culling and preprocessing.

Subdivision Schemes

There are two main types of subdivision surfaces [Kobbelt98], namely approximating and interpolating schemes. The three most important properties of subdivision surfaces, as relates to this gem, are:

- Efficiency
- Affine invariance (i.e., transformation of the control points transforms the surface)
- Continuity (i.e., they can produce smooth surfaces)

Subdivision schemes use a *mask* to define a set of vertices and corresponding weights. There are two types of masks for each scheme: the *odd* mask and the *even* mask. Odd masks are used to produce new vertices, while even masks are used to refine old vertices for the newly produced mesh. These two types can be further divided into edge, crease, and normal masks. Additionally, in order to be able to represent sharp features, special crease masks must be created. For triangular schemes, vertices with a *valency* (number of connected vertices) of six are known as *ordinary* vertices. The others are called *extraordinary*. The masks are applied to each vertex in

FIGURE 4.7.1 *Loop approximating subdivision surface for four iterations.*

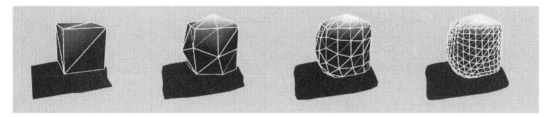

FIGURE 4.7.2 *Butterfly interpolating subdivision surface for four iterations.*

the mesh to produce a new mesh. After successive applications of the mask, the mesh converges to a surface (see Figures 4.7.1 and 4.7.2). The masks can also be applied to the texture coordinates in exactly the same manner. This generates the texture coordinates for each vertex. Generally, approximating schemes are faster because they have fewer constraints imposed on them, as they do not have to interpolate the control points. However, when dealing with edges and noncontinuous surfaces, special masks (which take these circumstances into account) must be applied.

Approximating Schemes—Loop Subdivision

Loop subdivision [Loop87] is perhaps the simplest subdivision scheme. It has a very small support area. The mask for this scheme is given by Equation 4.7.1 (see Figure 4.7.3).

$$v_i = \begin{cases} \dfrac{1}{8}\left(v_1 + v_2\right) + \dfrac{3}{8}\left(v_3 + v_4\right) & even \\[2ex] \displaystyle\sum_{j=1}^{n} \Omega v_j + \left(1 - n\Omega\right)v_i & odd \end{cases} \tag{4.7.1}$$

where

$$\Omega = \frac{1}{n}\left(\frac{5}{8} - \left(\frac{3}{8} + \frac{1}{4}\cos\left(\frac{2\pi}{n}\right)\right)^2\right) \text{ or } \Omega = \begin{cases} \dfrac{3n}{8} & n > 3 \\[2ex] \dfrac{3}{16} & n = 3 \end{cases}$$

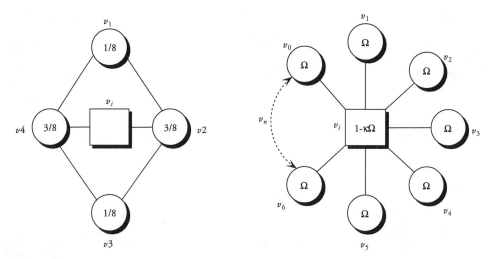

FIGURE 4.7.3　*Loop subdivision mask.*

A convenient feature of the Loop scheme is that the tangent vectors can be computed for each point using

$$t_1 = \sum_{i=0}^{n-1} \cos \frac{2\pi i}{n} v_i$$

$$t_2 = \sum_{i=0}^{n-1} \sin \frac{2\pi i}{n} v_i$$

(4.7.2)

where v_i is one of the n vertices that is connected to the vertex we are trying to find a normal for. Note that different masks are needed for computing the tangents at a boundary edge [DeRose98]. Although sin and cos are expensive to compute, optimizations (which will be described later) can be used to remove them from the computation.

Interpolating Schemes—Modified Butterfly

The butterfly scheme got its name from the distinctive shape of its mask, which resembles that of a butterfly. The original butterfly [Dyn90] method is probably the most common interpolating scheme used, but it does not guarantee a continuous surface for arbitrary meshes. For a small amount of extra work, a modified scheme [Zorin96] can be used. Fortunately, it has the same small support area as the original scheme. Like most interpolating schemes, there is no even mask. The original vertices

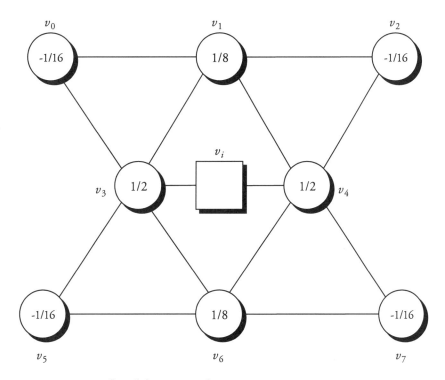

FIGURE 4.7.4 *Butterfly subdivision mask.*

are reused, since the surface must pass through them. An example mask is shown in Figure 4.7.4.

$$
v_i = \begin{cases} v_i & even \\ -\dfrac{1}{16}\left(v_1 + v_3 + v_6 + v_8\right) + \dfrac{1}{8}\left(v_2 + v_7\right) + \dfrac{1}{2}\left(v_4 + v_5\right) & odd \end{cases} \tag{4.7.3}
$$

Unlike the Loop method, computing the tangent vectors can be quite involved. It is probably quicker to compute them from the faces, so that information will not be covered in this gem.

Hierarchical Half-Edge Mesh

One of the most difficult aspects of using a subdivision scheme is creating a suitable data structure [Weiler85] for traversing the nodes so that the subdivision rules can be applied. A half-edge data structure can be created for each level of subdivision. The half-edge data structure uses a vertex, an edge, and a face structure to make up the mesh:

```
struct vertex
{
    edge *p_edge;      /* edge vertex starts */
};

struct edge
{
    edge *p_pair;      /* other half of edge */
    edge *p_next;      /* next edge in face */
    edge *p_prev;      /* previous edge in face */
    face *p_face;      /* face edge is part of */
    vertex *p_vertex;  /* vertex that starts edge */
};

struct face
{
    edge *p_edge;      /* an edge in the face */
};
```

This data structure is similar to a winged-edge data structure. A half edge is an edge that is split between two neighboring faces. Each edge points to its next and previous edges. (Actually, the original half-edge data structure did not have a pointer to a preceeding edge, but it makes some queries easier.) It also references the face it is part of, as well as the vertex starting the edge (see the previous code). Each edge need only point to one vertex. Each vertex points to the edge it starts, and each face points to one of the edges that make up the face (see Figure 4.7.5).

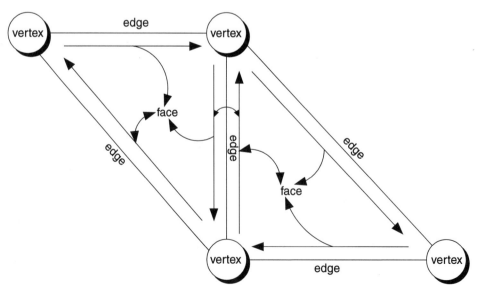

FIGURE 4.7.5   *Half-edge mesh.*

This arrangement allows for easy querying of neighboring faces and connected vertices. For example, to determine all the vertices connected to a given vertex, simply go to the half edge associated with that vertex. Then, move to that half edge's pair edge—this half edge references the first connected vertex. If this is repeated until we return to the initial edge, then all connected vertices will have been found (see Figure 4.7.6).

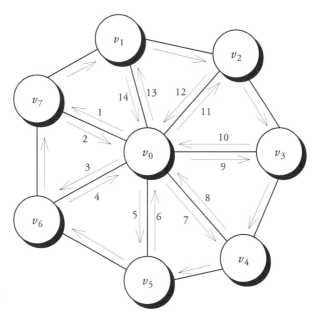

FIGURE 4.7.6   *Connection traversal order for finding connected vertices to v_0.*

Even if the half-edge data structure is not used directly within the subdivision computation, it is a fast and convenient way to determine the relevant indices for the masks. The half-edge data structure is also perfect for examining other properties of the mesh, such as connectivity and error detection (e.g., more than two faces sharing an edge). In order to store the hierarchical information, each face can also store pointers to its siblings. Alternatively, each sibling can be stored at an address in an array $kn + i + 1$, where i is the sibling's number $0...(k-1)$, n is the parent's offset, and k the number of siblings. An important aspect of this structure is that it cannot have an edge shared between more than two faces without undergoing modification. This can cause trouble if there is no checking done when a mesh is loaded (don't say you weren't warned). In any event, the two schemes presented here do not have masks to cater for this situation.

Bone Hierarchy and Vertex-Accumulation Buffer

When animating a character, a bone hierarchy is often needed. Implementing a bone hierarchy is a trivial task, so we won't go into much detail here. The bone hierarchy is a simple transformation hierarchy where a series of transformations are applied to the nodes. As the hierarchy is descended, each node and its vertices are transformed by the current transformation. Fortunately, when using subdivision surfaces for character animation, we only need to transform the control points of the mesh to alter the shape of the skin. This is advantageous, since fewer transformations will be performed.

Weighted Vertex-Accumulation Buffer

Vertex weighting introduces complications to the task of transforming the vertices. To implement skinning, a buffer is used to accumulate the resulting vertices. This is then used as the vertex buffer for the subdivision scheme. As the hierarchy is descended, each node is transformed by the current transformation matrix, multiplied by its weight, and then added to the accumulation buffer. With this method, the initial subdivision mesh is not altered by the skinning procedure. Now the subdivision mesh can be altered at will, preventing the accumulation of floating-point errors. As an added advantage, the subdivision surface and skinning procedures are now separated and will not interfere with each other, making the implementation easier.

Optimizations

When using many subdivision surfaces together, it is important to reduce the overall workload this causes. We will describe four schemes that can be used to reduce the potential workload in two distinct places in the subdivision hierarchy.

Hierarchical Back-Face Culling

The technique of hierarchical back-face culling is based on the clustering idea of hierarchical visibility culling [Kumar96], where faces are grouped together. Since we are using subdivision surfaces, we know that child faces have similar properties to their parents. Therefore, if their parents and neighbors all face away from the view, then so do the children. This technique is very effective, especially when high polygon counts are involved. It is also used to reduce the number of subdivision faces that need to be processed, since we avoid the subdivision of hidden surfaces. A more thorough investigation of this technique was presented in a SIGGRAPH sketch by Carlo Séquin [Séquin01].

View-Frustum Culling

Another optimization method is lazy spatial subdivision, which uses the subdivision hierarchy to skip processing subsurfaces. This method involves using either a k-d

(BSP) tree or an octree to separate faces into visible, hidden, or partially visible status with respect to the view frustum. Thus, if the viewer is looking at the characters' faces, the subdivision is only performed on those faces. This is very important if an optimum frame rate is desired.

Each subdivision mesh is contained in a bounding box. If the whole bounding box is visible, then it is drawn. Otherwise, the box is split into another four boxes, whose visibilities are then determined. This continues until either the maximum depth is reached or the minimum number of faces is reached. Determining these conditions is crucial to optimizing this algorithm and depends on the rendering method or graphics card used. One of the problems with this technique is that some polygons might occupy more than one bounding box. This would cause those polygons to be drawn or tested against the frustum multiple times. To stop this from happening, each face is tagged with the frame number each time its visibility is determined. Then, when processing other nodes, faces that are tagged can be left out, thereby reducing the number of faces that have to be tested against the frustum. By using this test, we can cull out faces where subdivision is unnecessary and only subdivide those that are in the frustum. For small meshes, it is preferable to use the view frustum directly for culling visible faces.

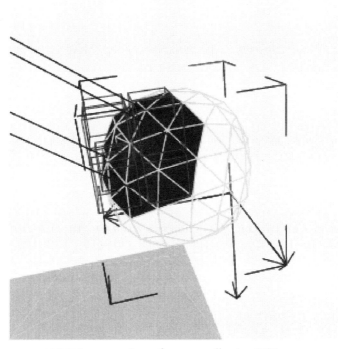

FIGURE 4.7.7 *Lazy frustum cull using BSP tree.*

The two previous approaches are used to mark faces that are deemed either visible or invisible. This data is then used to reduce the number of child faces produced by subdivision or to cull out any faces before they are sent down the rendering pipeline.

The next two optimizations are methods that precompute data in order to reduce the cost of traversing the half-edge data structure. These techniques, unfortunately, can significantly increase the amount of memory required, but they do substantially speed up the display and generation of subdivision surfaces.

Precomputed Face Vertex Indices

Precomputation of the face vertex indices is very useful when it comes time to display a face in the subdivision surface. This is an index array and needs to be done only once for the surface. The idea is to store the indices of the vertices that make up the faces prior to using the subdivision surface. Thus, they do not have to be computed each time the surface is going to be rendered. This is then used as part of a vertex array. The face index array looks like:

$$\left\{ \left(v_{1_1}, v_{12}, v_{13} \right), \ldots, \left(v_{n_1}, v_{n_2}, v_{n_3} \right) \right\} \tag{4.7.4}$$

Precomputed Weights and Vertex Indices

Precomputation of the weights and vertex indices is used for the generation of even vertices and also for the refinement of odd vertices, making traversal of the half-edge mesh unnecessary. Basically, a set of weights (w_i) and indices (v_i) for each vertex (i) in the mask are computed and stored with the destination index (v_d) of the resulting vertex. Thus, a simple for loop is all that is necessary to generate the next set of vertices. This scheme can also be used to compute the tangent vectors for the Loop and butterfly schemes, avoiding the use of sin and cos. The method differs slightly for each subdivision scheme. The butterfly scheme requires less memory, as it has a fixed number of vertices for each mask. Thus, eight vertex indices and weights are stored, as well as the destination index for the resulting vertex. The butterfly weight-and-index array looks like:

$$n \times \left\{ \left(v_0, w_0 \right), \cdots \left(v_8, w_8 \right), v_d \right\} \tag{4.7.5}$$

The Loop scheme is a bit more complicated. The even masks do not have a fixed number of vertices from which the resulting vertices are generated. Thus, to store these, we have to add an extra field that identifies how many vertices are stored. Fortunately, the odd masks have a fixed number and can be stored in a similar manner to the butterfly scheme, but with only four indices and weights. A Loop odd and even weight-and-index array looks like:

$$n \times \left\{ \begin{array}{ll} \left(\left(v_0, w_0 \right), \cdots \left(v_4, w_4 \right), v_d \right) & odd \\ \left(k, \left(v_0, w_0 \right), \cdots \left(v_k, w_k \right), v_d \right) & even \end{array} \right\} \tag{4.7.6}$$

The storage costs can be further reduced. If the vertices are always stored in the same order, then weights are the same for the odd masks. Therefore, they do not need to be stored. To use the arrays, the program simply runs through the sets, multiplying the vertex by its weight and adding that result to the total for the vertex.

Putting It All Together

The implementation of the subdivision schemes is pretty straightforward. In this implementation, a multiple pass approach is adopted, where a new level of the mesh is generated on each pass. This method makes the code fairly simple and enables the optimizations to be performed on each pass, if necessary. For each pass, the vertices are stored in a single array, whose size grows to accommodate the number of vertices needed. On the final pass, the vertices and faces are dumped into a geometry array, which is then sent down the rest of the rendering pipeline.

Storing the Data

Arrays are used to store the data for subdivision surfaces. This is for speed reasons as well as for ease of management. It is also relatively easy to pass the arrays directly to the graphics API in the form of vertex arrays. Arrays are far easier to manage, since only one big allocation is ever needed. Then, if the space is too small, we can reallocate more memory. This way, only the first few frames are slow (until sufficient memory has been allocated). Arrays tend to use less memory because pointers do not need to be stored for simple hierarchical and linear storage schemes. Since the memory is allocated as a single chunk, it caches much better and, therefore, is accessed faster. Another significant advantage of the array-based approach is that when using the accumulation buffer for skinning, the face indices and other reference data need not be regenerated. This is because each vertex generated is stored at the same relative location in the array.

Removing What Is Not Seen

The visibility culling is only performed on the original mesh to save time, since it is an expensive option. While determining the visible faces is relatively easy, deciding which faces are needed to produce child faces is a bit harder. In order to do this, we need to know in advance how many levels of subdivision are required. This is because the support areas required by the subdivision schemes overlap, producing a dependence hierarchy (see Figure 4.7.8). The more levels of subdivision required, the larger the support area must be. An alternative to explicitly determining these regions is to use a lazy evaluation method that generates faces as they are needed. Unfortunately, these methods prove to be slower, as the memory accesses are fragmented.

Luckily, the support areas for the butterfly scheme and Loop scheme are very similar, with the butterfly being marginally smaller (see Figure 4.7.8). This allows us to use the same methods to determine the extra faces needed in addition to those that are

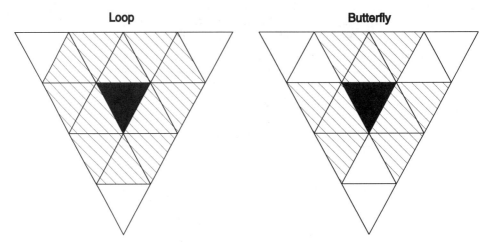

FIGURE 4.7.8   *Support areas required by Loop and butterfly subdivision schemes.*

visible for a given subdivision level. It also highlights the fact that for a mesh with relatively few nodes, such as a cube made with triangles, the child node can be quite dependent on the rest of the mesh.

Rendering the Frame

To render the surfaces, a list of triangles, vertices, normals, and texture coordinates are put into a vertex array and then rendered. A simple API separates the rendering API from the rest of the code. This allows more-complex operations and rearrangement of the scene to facilitate faster rendering by minimizing state changes.

Source Code

ON THE CD

A sample program is available on the CD-ROM.

Conclusion

Subdivision surfaces can be used to create very detailed characters with natural forms. The same formulas can also be applied to the texture parameters to generate proper surface coordinates. In addition, many of today's modeling packages provide support for subdivision schemes. They also furnish a very easy route for increasing the amount of detail. However, these subdivision methods don't provide an easy means to reduce the mesh detail from the initial mesh. This is where progressive meshes [Svarovsky00, Hoppe96] would be more useful. It would be great to combine the two methods—use subdivision to increase detail, and use progressive meshes to reduce it. Subdivision surfaces also reduce the number of transformation operations necessary to perform skinning, as only the initial mesh needs to be modified. Modern accelerators provide T&L support and vertex-weighting extensions, however, using these features with subdivision surfaces is possible. To do this, the view frustum is transformed, rather than the vertices of the mesh. Then, when the culling is done with this modified frustum, the untransformed visible triangles are sent to the graphics card for transformation and display.

References

[DeRose98] DeRose, Tony, et al., "Subdivision Surfaces in Character Animation," Computer Graphics Proceedings (SIGGRAPH 1998): pp. 85–94.

[Dyn90] Dyn, Nira, et al., "A Butterfly Subdivision Scheme for Surface Interpolation with Tension Control," ACM Transactions on Graphics, Vol. 9, No. 2, pp. 160–190, 1990.

[Hoppe96] Hoppe, Hugues, "Progressive Meshes," Computer Graphics Proceedings (SIGGRAPH 1996): pp. 99–108.

[Kobbelt98] Kobbelt, Leif, et al., "Subdivision for Modeling and Animation," Course Notes (SIGGRAPH 1998).

[Kumar96] Manocha, Kumar, et al., "Hierarchical Visibility Culling for Spline Models," *Graphics Interface,* 1996: pp. 142–150.

[Loop87] Loop, Charles, "Smooth Subdivision Surfaces Based on Triangles," Master's Thesis, University of Utah, Department of Mathematics, 1987.

[Séquin01] Séquin, Carlo, et al., available online at http://www.ce.chalmers.se/staff/tomasm/research/subdiv/, December 25, 2001.

[Svarovsky00] Svarovsky, Jan, "View-Independent Progressive Meshing," *Game Programming Gems*, Charles River Media, Inc., 2000.

[Weiler85] Weiler, Kevin, "Edge-Based Data Structures for Solid Modeling in Curved-Surface Environments," IEEE Computer Graphics and Applications, Vol. 15, No. 1, pp. 21–40, 1985.

[Zorin96] Zorin, Denis, et al., "Interpolating Subdivision for Meshes with Arbitrary Topology," Computer Graphics Proceedings (SIGGRAPH 1996): pp. 189–192.

4.8

Improved Deformation of Bones

Jason Weber, Intel Corporation

jason.p.weber@intel.com

Artists can produce beautifully realistic meshes to represent the actors in their games. To bring them to life, these models need to be animated for a wide variety of behaviors. Storing a full set of vertex positions for every frame of animation is not only prohibitively memory-consumptive, it restricts movements to only those actions explicitly created by the artist. So, many applications use a hidden hierarchy of segments that looks and acts very much like a subset of a natural skeleton.

By transforming each vertex of a mesh through multiple matrices instead of just one, and then by doing a carefully weighted average of the results, we are able to smoothly deform these meshes to any position and play back the results at any frame rate. This approach permits a significant reduction in the required animation data and allows the skeleton, and thereby the mesh, to be spontaneously adjusted to any pose, perhaps reacting to unpredictable events in its environment.

However, the popular deformation algorithm has some problems when used in its original form. We will demonstrate how large deflection angles cause joints to shrink, potentially even to a point. Fortunately, this can be overcome by adding a small chain of additional bones at troublesome joints, such as the elbows and knees. By carefully reworking the weighting data to account for these 'links,' we can use the same simple core deformation algorithm and only incur the small additional burden of a few extra bones.

Background

The skeletal structure is a hierarchy of transforms, like a scene graph. At each transform, we define a bone length, which is really a displacement along that transform's local x-axis. By default, the origin of all child bones is positioned at the displaced point on the end of the parent bone. We allow for an arbitrary additional displacement, but in most cases where bones connect end-to-end, it is zero.

A reference pose of the skeleton describes the state of the hierarchy where it aligns with the given undeformed mesh. (Biped, in 3DS Max, calls this the "figure mode.") The motion of the bones away from the reference pose is used to deform the mesh to any arbitrary position. The motion of these bones comes from some driving source, such as motion capture, authored motion, or inverse kinematics [Weber02]. (For a longer description of the background material, refer to the GDC 2000 proceedings [Weber00].)

Simple Methods

The basic skinning algorithm is demonstrated in *Game Programming Gems* by [Woodland00] and is also nicely explained in Jeff Lander's *Game Developer* article [Lander98]. As an example of this technique, consider vertices on an elbow whose position needs to be affected by the current transform of both the upper and lower arm bones. As we pass each vertex in the elbow through each of the two transforms, we get two different resultant vertices. If we then do a weighted average of these transformed vertices, we get a reasonable 'in-between' position. An important guideline here is that these weightings for the vertices should smoothly transition from 100% upper arm to 100% lower arm from the top of the elbow to the bottom. Otherwise, the mesh will stretch abnormally and might appear to tear.

As the deflection angle of the lower arm increases and the difference in the results from each bone increases, serious visual abnormalities could arise. For example, the worst case might be if you twist the child bone 180° about its lengthwise axis. The two transformed resultants are on opposite sides of the elbow, so a 50/50 average is at a point inside the elbow. The overall effect is much like twisting or bending a cardboard paper towel tube. Figures 4.8.1 and 4.8.2 show illustrations of problem cases.

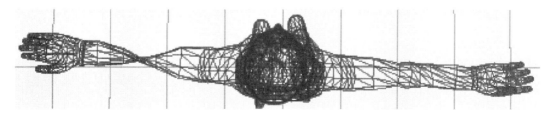

FIGURE 4.8.1   *Twisted elbows: a simple skinning method demonstrated on the left arm contrasted with an enhanced technique on the right arm.*

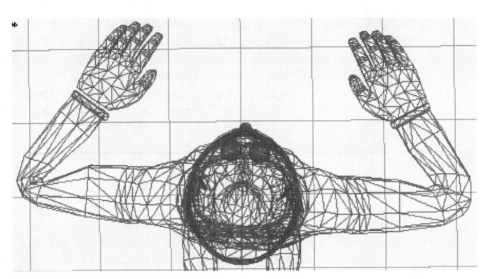

FIGURE 4.8.2   *Corresponding effect with elbows bent. The right arm uses the enhanced technique.*

Adding the Bones

If large angles cause defects, one solution is to limit all deflections to a small angle. We cannot really restrict the motion of the existing bones, but we can distribute these large angles over several smaller bones conveniently placed at the joints. Since a deflection of 60° seems to be a safe limit, using three or so of these 'links' should usually be sufficient. The length of the links can be left to the author of the model. We are often content with a default value derived from the mesh's cross-sectional radius at the joint and the length of the child bone:

```
total_linklength=0.3*child_length+1.5*joint_radius
```

The placement of the bones should look something like a spline. The bones should stay arranged end-to-end, but they may slide together a little as the joint flexes. We don't have to actually shorten the bones, but the overlap will naturally compress the mesh slightly. Our solution is demonstrated in GPGBoneNode::CalcBoneLinks() in GPGBoneNode.cpp on the CD-ROM, and it works as follows.

ON THE CD

To compute the position of the bones, first consider three points, as shown in Figure 4.8.3a—the original joint connection A, the first link center B, and the last link center C. They will form a triangle as the joint flexes. For each link, take two points, one along BC and the other along either BA or AC, depending on whether the link is in the first or second half of the chain. The displacement of these points along these lines is proportional to the ordering of the link along the chain. Once you have these two points, take a weighted average to find the center for the desired link. The weighting goes linearly from 100% of the point on BC at either the first or last link to

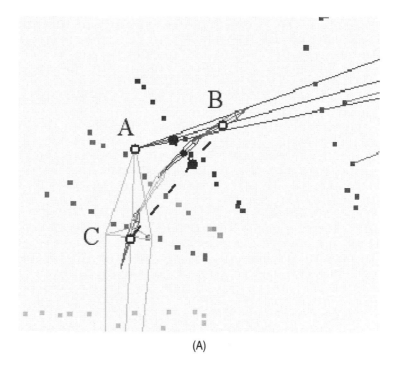

(A)

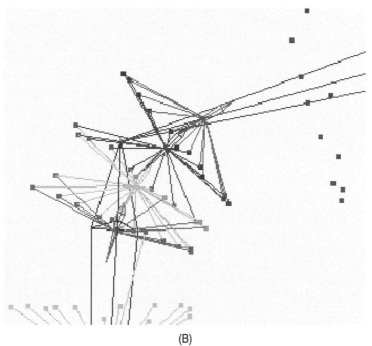

(B)

FIGURE 4.8.3 *(A) A small chain of bones added to the joint. (B) Example of new weighting relationships.*

50/50 for a link in the exact center. Rotations of the links are computed as the linear interpolation of the overall change in angle so that the total deflection is evenly distributed.

The instantiation and weighting of the links only need to occur once. The position and rotation of the links need to be recomputed every time the parent or child moves, potentially every frame.

Changing the Weights

Most of the weights around a bone-linked joint will need to be reassigned. The weights should transition smoothly from the original parent to the first link, then along to each element in the chain, and finally to the original child bone. If there is no fork at this joint and all the original influences were assigned only to this parent and child bone, it is sufficient to use the longitudinal (x) position to find which two bones to attach to (including the new link bones). If we look at the links as an integer number line, with the parent bone as zero and the original child as (`number_of_links+2`), then we use the local x position of the vertex along the chain, scaled to the size of the number line. We find the integer numbers above and below where that vertex falls and use the fractional part to determine the weights. For example, if our local x position scales to 2.3 in 'bone link space,' the new weights will be 70% for the second link bone and 30% for the third link bone.

If there is a fork in the bone hierarchy nearby, more information needs to be considered, even if there is not an explicit sibling to the particular child bone. The hip and shoulder areas are two good examples of this type of situation. The goal for any particular link chain is to only reassign a fair fraction of the parent's influence and leave the remainder of the influence for other bones to consider. For example, a vertex on the chest near the shoulder might be partially influenced by the motion of the upper arm, but it is also well anchored to one or more spinal bones. When adding bones between the clavicle and upper arm, we don't want to reassign the portion that belongs to the spine.

To determine this fair fraction, all the weights are found for the particular vertex that have the same parent as an ancestor to the child in question. These 'competitors' reduce how much influence we can reassign for that child. To make sure the effect is not dependent on the order that the weights are processed, only competitor entries that follow the current weight entry on the weight list are considered. Adding up these competitor weights, we determine the fraction as:

fraction = 1 − *competitor* / (*competitor* + *childweight*)

The weight to be reassigned is then:

fraction * *parentweight* + *childweight*

At this point, we continue as in the unforked case. We adjust the existing stored parent weight in place. For our two new weights, we can first overwrite the previous child entry, which has now been entirely reassigned, and then add a new weight entry for the second influence.

Figure 4.8.4a shows a shoulder joint with reassigned weights. This diagram shows which of the given links the vertices are weighted to. It does not show the magnitude of the weights or any weights to other bones, like the spine. A chain of three links connects the clavicle bone to the upper arm. Lines are drawn from each vertex to the

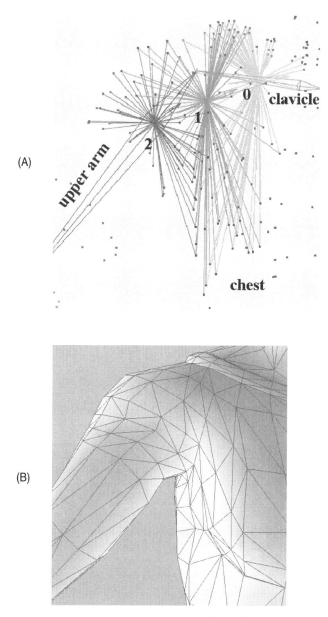

FIGURE 4.8.4 *New weighting with three added links (A) for a shoulder mesh (B).*

center of each bone that the vertex is influenced by. The shade of the line matches the shade of the bone, varied for clarity. Note how the links have influences deep into the chest. These create a gradual stretching of the skin when the arm is moved.

Normal-Derived Influence Fade

There is one side effect we cannot ignore. Since we are reassigning based purely on position, joints with apparent right angles in the mesh can incur excessive bulging. The shoulders tend to display this problem. When the upper arm moves up, the side of the chest will push out sideways, as though it were a very wide region of the arm (see Figure 4.8.5).

We can use the inherent difference in the normal direction to correct for this. We take the dot product of a vertex's normal with respect to the longitudinal bone axis. From this result, we subtract the x displacement of the vertex along the bone, divided by the approximate radius at the joint (the subtracted value and the result both have a floor of zero). This reduction has the effect of isolating the correction toward the parent side of the joint. The secondary result is a fraction from 0.0 to 1.0, which we square for good measure. This fraction is applied to the weight that was previously destined to reassignment. That portion of the weight is not reassigned, but directly added to the parent's weight. In our example code, see GPGSkin::RelinkWeights() in GPGSkin.cpp on the CD-ROM.

ON THE CD

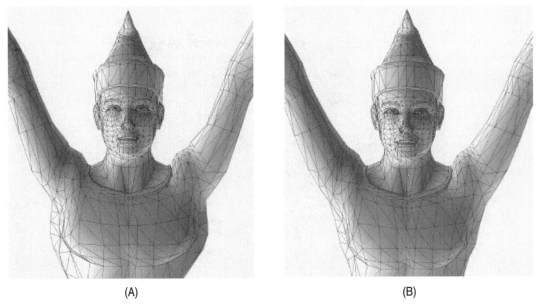

(A)   (B)

FIGURE 4.8.5   *Raised arms (A) without and (B) with normal-derived influence fade.*

Packing It Up and Making It Fast

In order to process the weights and generate the deformed mesh as quickly as possible, it is critical that we lay out our runtime data in a cache-friendly manner. The biggest decision to make is whether to process the weights in a 'bone-major' or 'vertex-major' fashion.

For the bone-major method, you have to first clear all the vertex positions and normals in the mesh. Then for each bone, you process all the vertices that the bone influences, accumulating fractional components to their stored positions and normals. While this will probably keep the current matrix in cache, it reads and writes the mesh in a very scattered manner.

In the vertex-major method, we process the vertices in order, pulling in matrices as necessary. While this may incur some scattered access to the matrix array, the advantages are numerous. First of all, there is no clearing stage. We know when the first write to a vertex occurs, so that access can be a pure *set* instead of an *add*. Since the weights for a vertex are clumped together, we can accumulate the results in a local variable and dump them out with one write per vertex, instead of one read and one write per weight per vertex.

We have tried it both ways, and for all our measurements, the vertex-major approach was *at least* twice as fast, and probably much faster, even with all the optimizations we were able to add later on due to the flexibility of the layout.

Transform Matrices

Every bone in the skeleton has a transform, including the added bone links. Until the actual deformation stage, we use quaternions because of their superior interpolative qualities [Bobick98]. However, for raw vertex transforms, using the matrix form is almost four times faster. So, just before the core deformation loop, we fill in a nicely packed array of 3×4 matrices, one for each bone. Each matrix is assigned the inverse of the bone's reference transform, multiplied by the bone's current transform. In this way, we can transform directly from the original, undeformed mesh without having to store vertex offsets relative to each bone.

ON THE CD

The core deformation loop contains only about 50 lines of code. See GPGSkin::ComputeDeformedVerticesPacked() in GPGSkin.cc on the CD-ROM.

Packweights

Since the vertex weights will usually be a larger data structure than the matrix array or even the mesh, it is important to keep the weight list small in order to reduce the amount of data we need to process each frame. This not only saves space, but it should really optimize our cache usage. However, we also need to be aware that excessive byte conservation might throw off the word alignment, which would be just as detrimental to the process.

The *packweight* structure is a big byte block with alternating sections of one vertex definition and one or more boneweight influences. The vertex definition contains the vertex index, a copy of the undeformed vertex position and normal, and the number of weights to follow. The boneweight block contains just the bone index into the matrix array and the fractional weight. As we read any block, we can prefetch the next one.

Note that storing the vertex position and normal in the weight list means that we can continuously deform to an output mesh without having to retain an undeformed input mesh. If we wanted to allow outside modifications to the input mesh, such as with a morphing modifier, we would not store that data in the weight list, but we would have to take the penalty of rereading vertices from the input mesh every frame. See the file GPGPackWeights.h on the CD-ROM for our example code.

ON THE CD

Normal Renormalization

We can perform a weighted average of multiple normals just like we do with the positions, but the result will have a reduced magnitude. These differences are easy to fix. Since the reduced normals are known to have a range of magnitude from 0 to 1, you can use a modest table to eliminate the sqrt() operation. If you do not renormalize them, they could cause a reduction in lighting intensity. Our observations show very little difference, so you might want to consider leaving them as is or hook the option to a quality toggle.

Conclusion

Bones-based animation can be a key to reducing animation overhead and allowing for spontaneous and unique behaviors. Existing deformation techniques can be made very fast and are easily extended to overcome some inherent limitations.

Additional topics could cover the generation and manipulation of the original vertex weights. Color Plate 7 demonstrates improvements achieved by using a completely automated procedure to generate raw weights, remove anomalies, smooth the distribution, and add bone links.

The improvement in the waist is mostly due to the regenerated weights. The upper leg benefits dramatically from using the links to reduce shrinkage. Even the shoulder and knees improve significantly by eliminating excessive stretching. Also, the chest looks more realistic, since using links in the shoulder permits a wider spread of influences over the surrounding mesh.

References

[Bobick98] Bobick, Nick, "Rotating Objects Using Quaternions," *Game Developer Magazine,* February 1998: pp. 34–42. Also available online at http://www.gdmag.com.

[Lander98] Lander, Jeff, "Skin Them Bones: Game Programming for the Web Generation," *Game Developer Magazine,* May 1998: pp. 11–16.

[Weber00] Weber, Jason, "Run-Time Skin Deformation," Game Developers Conference Proceedings (GDC 2000): pp. 703–721. Also available online at ftp://download.intel.com/ial/3dsoftware/animatedoc.pdf.

[Weber02] Weber, Jason, "Constrained Inverse Kinematics," *Game Programming Gems 3*, Charles River Media, Inc., 2002.

[Woodland00] Woodland, Ryan, "Filling the Gaps—Advanced Animation Using Stitching and Skinning," *Game Programming Gems*, Charles River Media, Inc., 2000: pp. 476–483.

The author will make an effort to maintain a long-term archive and link site for some related resources at http://www.imonk.com/baboon/bones.

4.9

A Framework for Realistic Character Locomotion

Thomas Young, PathEngine

thomas@pathengine.com

With today's hardware, we can render extremely realistic-looking characters. High-fidelity motion-capture systems are widely available for providing animation data. However, in most games, as soon as a character starts to walk, the illusion of reality is destroyed. The character's feet slide against the ground, the character is rotated arbitrarily in mid-animation, or the animation jumps suddenly to a completely different state.

Even a small amount of foot-sliding is noticeable. As soon as we see a foot slide against the floor, we know that breaking friction has been overcome. Without friction between the foot and the floor, there is no mechanism that a character's forward motion can be attributed to, so the movement of the character is strongly perceived as unrealistic.

It is difficult to solve all the constraints for realistic animation at the same time. We can ensure smooth transition between animations with a tweening modifier. This modifier calculates the in-between (or tween) positions in animation poses. We can solve the problem of arbitrary targets for locomotion by modifying the translation resulting from each animation segment. However, a straightforward implementation of these modifiers will result in foot-sliding.

This gem presents a solution to this problem based on adjusting the position of the feet only when they are already in motion. A framework is described for applying this idea to the problem of realistic character animation by using independent modifiers for different parts of a skeleton.

Problem: Locomotion to an Arbitrary Target

Toward the end of the 2D era, we started to see games such as *Prince of Persia* and *Fade to Black*, which featured beautifully sequenced animations. The trick was that the game environment was built from unit-length tiles on a fixed grid. Since the animation was designed around exactly the same unit-length, it was possible to guarantee that the animation ended perfectly, just pixels in front of a wall or a cliff.

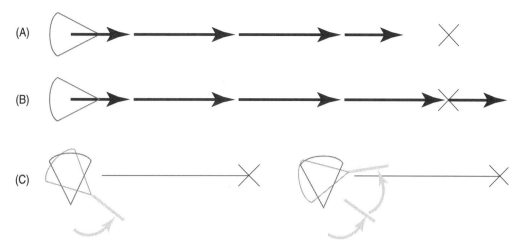

FIGURE 4.9.1 *A character with fixed animations attempting to move to arbitrary points and angles. (A) The character will not reach the point with a start, walk, walk, stop sequence. (B) The character will overshoot the target with a start, walk, walk, walk, stop sequence. (C) The character will not point toward the target with one or two rotation animations.*

As soon as the possibilities for movement include turning in arbitrary angles and moving forward, the situation becomes more complicated because we can no longer constrain this movement to a fixed grid. Now we are stuck with the problem of characters needing to move arbitrary distances and turn in arbitrary angles.

The character in Figure 4.9.1 has an animation for starting to walk, a walk cycle animation, and an animation for stopping. In Figure 4.9.1a, two walk cycles will not take the character far enough, but in Figure 4.9.1b, three will take the character too far. Figure 4.9.1c shows how the same problem applies when turning arbitrary angles. In this case, the character only has one turn animation. Playing the animation once does not turn enough, but playing it twice turns the character too far. We can improve the situation by providing more animations for a character to choose from, but the basic problem remains.

Plan and Modify

We can solve this problem by modifying the translational or rotational offsets for animations as they play. In Figure 4.9.2, the closest set of animations in length is chosen programmatically from the available animations. The offset required to take the end point of the animations to the target is split across the animations and applied as a modification to each animation. The animation sequence now ends exactly at the target point.

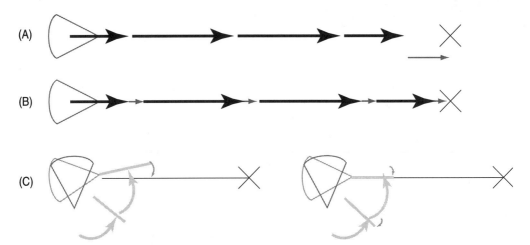

FIGURE 4.9.2 *Plan and modify movement to arbitrary targets. (A) Calculating the necessary adjustment to move to the target. (B) Distributing the adjustment among the fixed animations. (C) The same process with angles.*

In order to modify the translational or rotational result of an animation, we simply apply an offset to the position or orientation of the character origin with a 'ramped' multiplier that goes from 0 to 1 smoothly as the animation is played. However, since this multiplier will change during parts of the animation, such as when a foot is supposed to be stationary, the result is foot-sliding.

Problem: Smooth Transition Between Animations

Motion-captured moves will never start or end in exactly the right stance, no matter how good the actor is. Concentrating on hitting the right stance can also have a negative effect on the quality of motion. It is a shame to discard a capture in which the actor got the movement right, just because the capture ends a bit out of stance. With motion-captured animation, we need to transition smoothly between captures that are out of stance. Even if we are working with hand-animated moves that start and end in perfect stance, we still need to be able to transition early out of a move.

An Approach

The best result will be achieved by transitioning directly between the state of the skeleton at the end of one motion and the state at the start of the next motion, as opposed to transitioning in and out of a predefined stance. Since we do not want to interrupt the flow of movement, a transition should be made while the animation is playing. For the greatest flexibility, we should not project which animation will play next until we must play that animation. Based on these considerations, a good approach to the problem is to modify the start of each animation to be the same as the

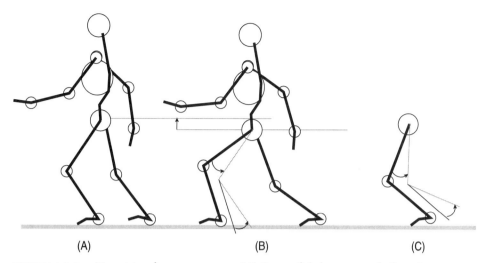

FIGURE 4.9.3 *Transition between stances. (A) State of skeleton at end of previous animation. (B) State of skeleton at start of following animation. (C) Applying the same modification later in an animation causes problems at a foot.*

end of the previous animation, and then ease out this modification as the animation is played.

The character in Figure 4.9.3a shows the state of the skeleton at the end of the previous animation. Figure 4.9.3b shows the skeletal state at the start of the following animation. We need a modification that will transform the skeleton from the state in Figure 4.9.3b to the state in Figure 4.9.3a. We also need to be able to smoothly transition back to the original position as the second animation plays.

A common approach to solving the transition problem is to store the state of a skeleton as a set of hierarchical relative orientations and to interpolate between these orientations. Orientations are often interpolated with the use of spherical linear interpolation of quaternions. (See [Shankel00] for a more detailed description of quaternion interpolation.) If we use this interpolation method, then our modification takes the form of a set of quaternion offsets for each joint. This modification can be eased out by multiplying the offsets by a 'tween ratio' that goes from 1.0 to 0.0, over the duration of the current animation. Figure 4.9.3b shows how a set of rotations at the joints can take the skeleton to the desired position. The origin for the character in Figure 4.9.3 is between the hips. As the height of the origin can vary with animation, our modification should also include an offset to this height.

Problems with this Approach

The first problem with this kind of straightforward interpolation approach is that for any modification that affects the position of the feet, easing out that modification will also affect the feet. If this happens while the foot is supposed to be stationary against the floor, then we get foot-sliding. The amount of sliding will depend on the size of the original discrepancy and the length of time over which our modifier is eased out.

The second problem is that our modifier will give us undesirable results when it is applied to the skeleton later on in the animation. Figure 4.9.3b shows the rotations that will be applied by our modifier to the left leg. We know that these rotations result in a 'correct' position for the skeleton when applied to the first frame of animation because the rotations were chosen to achieve a specific target position when applied at this point. Figure 4.9.3c shows how the application of the same rotations to the leg later on in the animation results in the foot hovering above the floor. The interface between the foot and the floor over a period of animation depends on a combination of translation at the origin and rotation of the leg. Applying a modifier to the rotation of the leg breaks this interface. This will result in feet hovering or interpenetrating the floor, feet being positioned at the wrong angle with respect to the floor, and feet sliding against the floor when they are supposed to be stationary. The problem gets worse as the skeleton gets further from its start position. We can improve the situation by easing out our modification more quickly, but this will affect the smoothness of the transition and make the foot-sliding more pronounced over the ease-out duration. So, once again, while we have an approach for transitioning between two animations, the sliding-feet problem still plagues our result.

A Framework for a Solution: Local Modifiers with Independent Tween Ratios

By modifying an animation slightly as it is played, we can solve some problems in character locomotion. However, if this modification affects the positions of the feet while they are supposed to be stationary against the floor, then there is still a problem.

We can choose when to reduce our tween ratio. If a character jumps in the air halfway through an animation, then we can delay tweening until both feet leave the floor and finish tweening by the time the character lands. This would eliminate problems resulting from changing tween ratio while the feet are on the floor. Unfortunately, most animations will have at least one foot on the floor most of the way through the animation.

Affecting Feet Only When They Are Already Moving

The trick is to use independent modifiers for different parts of a skeleton. This way, we can ease out each modifier over different sections of the animation. Thus, to modify an animation without introducing foot-sliding, we use a separate modifier for each leg. For a walk animation in which the left foot moves first, followed by the right foot, we ease out the left-leg modifier while the left foot is moving forward, then we wait until the right foot starts to move before easing out the right-leg modifier.

We can generalize this to any kind of animation and automate the process of determining when to perform the ease-out for each modifier. Figure 4.9.4 shows a two-step animation with the corresponding movement profile for each foot. We can

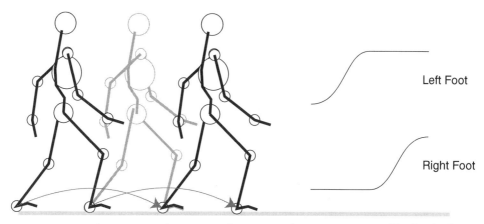

FIGURE 4.9.4 *A two-step animation with corresponding movement profiles for the feet.*

take the tween ratio for each leg directly from this movement profile. The tween ratio at a given point can be set as the movement up to that point divided by total movement over the course of the animation.

If a foot does not move at all during the animation, or if there is insufficient total movement (and so the rate of tweening would be too fast), then we can choose either to allow some foot-sliding for that animation or allow the modifier to remain at the end of the animation without being eased out completely.

Because the feet will move slightly as a result of error accumulation down the skeleton hierarchy and/or because of error in the original motion capture, it helps to set a threshold for foot movement and ignore any movement below that threshold.

Application: Locomotion to an Arbitrary Target

For the problem of locomotion to an arbitrary target, we need the animation to be unmodified at the start, but uniformly offset at the end. By applying an offset at the character origin, we already bring the feet and legs to the correct position by the end of the animation. However, to apply our framework to this problem, we need some way to apply this offset at different times for each foot.

The solution is to keep track of three tween ratios. A straightforward, ramped tween ratio controls a global offset applied to the character origin. Tween ratios, determined from the movement profiles of the feet, keep track of the desired amount of offset at each foot. A modifier is then applied at each leg to correct the difference between the tween ratio already applied by the global modifier and the desired tween ratio for that foot. Figure 4.9.5 shows how this would apply to the two-step animation in Figure 4.9.4. Halfway through the animation, the global tween ratio is 0.5; the left foot has finished its step and therefore should be at 1.0, and the right foot has not moved yet, so it should be at 0.0. To correct the positions of the feet, the left leg needs to be modified by 0.5 and the right leg by –0.5.

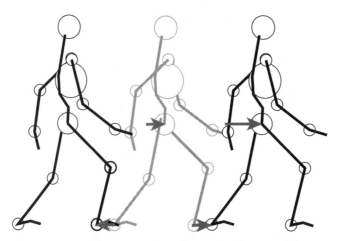

FIGURE 4.9.5   *Correcting a global modifier. The arrows show modifications applied to a skeleton at different points in a two-step animation. The skeleton in gray shows the situation halfway through the animation.*

A rotational or translational modifier will need to be set up as required to create the same effect as the global modifier, when the modifier is applied with a positive value, or to cancel that effect when the modifier is applied with a negative value. If the character origin is at the hips, then a rotational modifier can simply rotate the leg by changing the orientation of the hip joint. A translational modifier will be more involved, and we have some choices about how to implement this.

Translational Modifiers

A translational modifier for a foot needs to apply an offset to the position of that foot and set up the rest of the leg appropriately, without affecting the position of the hips. This is a classic problem for inverse kinematics (IK) (see, for example, [Tolani00]). With an IK approach, a set of constraints is solved for the leg, with the goal of putting the foot in the desired position. We have to take into account the possibility that the IK can fail. In this case, we could put the foot at the closest position that we can achieve within the given constraints. Figure 4.9.6a shows a required offset for the foot. Figure 4.9.6b shows how an IK solution might achieve this offset as a combination of rotations at the joints.

A simpler alternative is to point the ankle in the desired direction by rotating the hip joint and then apply scaling to the leg to bring the ankle to the correct position, as shown in Figure 4.9.6c.

At first glance, the IK solution looks better because it maintains skeletal constraints correctly throughout the animation, but there are some problems with this approach. A straightforward IK solution does not take into account the need for consistency across frames. Small changes in the position of the IK target can lead to big

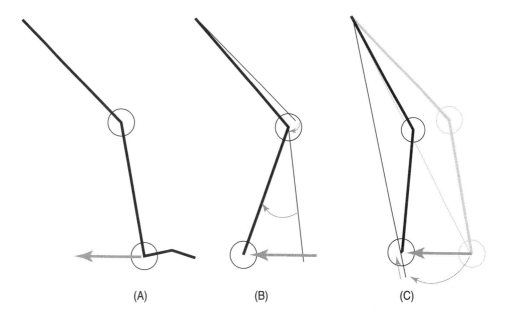

(A)   (B)   (C)

FIGURE 4.9.6   *Transform modifiers. (A) The required offset. (B) Rotations at joints found by inverse kinematics. (C) A simpler approach rotates the whole leg and then scales to fit.*

changes in the position of the leg and inconsistency between frames. These inconsistencies between frames can result in unnatural animation.

The most important constraint for consistent animation is that the modifier should have a very small effect on the leg for a small offset. In order to enforce this constraint in the IK solution, we need to reformulate the problem for IK. We can redefine the problem and find a modification to the angles in the leg in order to achieve an offset to the position of the foot. Unfortunately, there is no guarantee that the position of the leg in the original animation conforms to the constraints of our IK in the first place.

In practice, the simpler approach is recommended (applying a single rotation at the hip and then scaling). This gives us smoother animation and an acceleration at each point in the leg that corresponds better to the original animation. For a small offset, we are guaranteed a small modification. The angle at the knee is also preserved with this method. Because we do not enforce constraints at the hip, however, the skeleton can get into some strange positions; and while using a small amount of scaling on the leg will not be noticeable, any significant amount will look very odd. For these reasons, we should try to avoid using large values for modifiers and also try to avoid leaving modifiers on characters when they are stationary.

Sometimes, even a small amount of scaling can mess up the skinning. One trick we can use as an alternative to a simple scaling is to stretch the leg along the direction of the bones without scaling in the other directions.

Application: Transitions

We can apply the same framework for transitions between animations. By using separate modifiers for each leg, we can eliminate problems resulting from changing the tween ratio while a foot is supposed to be stationary. However, applying a modifier to the angles of the legs while the character origin is moving will still cause problems at the feet.

The solution is to use an 'anchored modifier.' This essentially does the same thing as the translational modifiers previously discussed, but also affects the orientation of the foot. Instead of specifying an offset, we specify a target position for the foot in world space (or in the character's local coordinate system, if that does not change as the animation plays). The target position for the anchored modifier is the position of the foot at the end of the previous animation. Assuming that the foot is correctly placed with respect to the ground at that point, the modifier will ensure that the foot remains correctly placed with respect to the ground until that foot starts moving. As soon as the foot starts moving, the modifier can be eased out.

An anchored modifier will ensure that the position of the feet corresponds to the end of the previous animation, but it does not do anything about the rest of the leg. Even if the hip and the leg do not move across the transition, if the position of the leg in-between those points does not match up across that transition, then the animation can still appear jerky. We can solve this problem by simply applying spherical interpolation to the leg as before, but with the anchored modifier applied to the result of that interpolation.

Further Details

Single-Step Animations

In a two-step animation where both feet move over the course of the animation, we get the chance to ease out modifiers on both legs while the animation is playing. Transition modifiers enable us to generalize the technique also to single-step animations. Any modifiers not eased out by the end of an animation will be dealt with by modifiers at the start of the next animation.

Keeping Characters Moving

In order to make characters look alive, we must keep them moving. We can use a collection of moving-on-the-spot animations to avoid characters standing completely stationary. If these animations include moving the feet slightly, then this gives the animation system a chance to ease out any remaining modifiers.

The player will most likely notice irregularities in a character's posture when that character comes to a stop. Therefore, it is a good idea to ease out any modifiers when a character stops. If there is a pause key, then the same concerns apply for paused action.

Limiting Modifiers

Degenerate captures, which are a long way out of stance, can result in modifiers with large values. Sequences of animations over which a given foot does not move at all can result in the errors at transitions getting built up into large modifiers. It is a good idea to limit the range of values that can be applied through a modifier in order to prevent strange effects in these kinds of situations.

Conclusion

In order to solve problems in character locomotion, we often need to modify animation. Unfortunately, modifying animation can break the interface between the foot and the floor, and can result in unrealistic-looking movement. By using separate modifiers, and therefore independent tween ratios for each leg, we can apply modifications to each leg at a time when the corresponding foot is already moving and avoid problems of foot-sliding.

References

[Shankel00] Shankel, Jason, "Interpolating Quaternions," *Game Programming Gems*, Charles River Media, Inc., 2000.

[Tolani00] Tolani, Deepak, et al., "Real-time inverse kinematics techniques for anthropomorphic limbs," available online at http://hms.upenn.edu/software/ik/ikan_gm.pdf, September 8, 2000.

4.10

A Programmable Vertex Shader Compiler

Adam Lake, Intel Labs

adam.t.lake@intel.com

This gem discusses the implementation of a compiler for programmable vertex shaders. There are many reasons why it is now desirable for graphics programmers to consider compilers for programmable shading hardware. Some examples include increased readability and greater portability of the programs we write for programmable hardware. As the underlying instruction set changes, we do not need to rewrite our shaders. If the shader is written in a high-level language, we need only retarget the front end of our compiler to a new code generator for the new instruction set. This allows shaders written in a high-level language to be compiled to the shader implementation in OpenGL, DirectX, or an in-house software-rendering library. Also, by writing a shader in a high-level, C-like language, it is easier for us to read and write new shaders. This makes it easier to make changes to your shaders library.

ON THE CD

    The CD-ROM includes a full implementation of a simple vertex shader compiler. It also contains documentation on how to create a workspace for building compilers and an example that compiles the OpenGL lighting equation into a DirectX vertex shader! To give a practical foundation to this gem, we are focusing on the vertex shader implementation in DirectX8. Future implementations might vary, but the framework and infrastructure we provide should still be applicable.

Programmable Vertex Shader

A *vertex shader* is a program that takes the standard lighting equation parameters, such as color, position, normal, and texture coordinates (known as the *vertex* stream), as input and computes the final values that are submitted for rasterization. Material and light parameters are sent to the vertex shader through a set of constant registers that do not change while a specific vertex stream is being processed by the vertex shader. A widely used vertex shader implementation, DirectX8, has 96 constant registers, 12 temporary registers, and 16 vertex registers [Microsoft00] (see Figure 4.10.1). The output of this program (the final vertex properties) are loaded into a set of *output* reg-

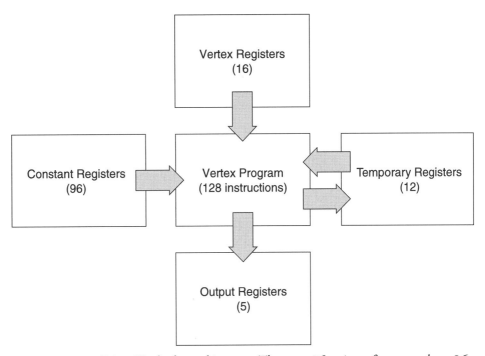

FIGURE 4.10.1   *DirectX8 shader architecture. There are 16 registers for vertex data, 96 for constants, 12 temporary registers, and 5 for output. In DirectX8, there is a limit of 128 instructions per vertex program. Temporary registers are the only registers that are read/write.*

isters that, after transformation and lighting calculations have been performed by the vertex shader, are passed to the pixel shader for final display. All registers are four-component vectors. Individual elements can be referenced in an individual instruction using x, y, z, and w as accessors of the elements. We will not cover pixel shaders in this gem, but more information can be found in the References.

As previously mentioned, the vertex shader program utilizes a set of assembly instructions along with the values in the input registers to compute values to the output registers. Mathematical operations such as add, mult, max, and min are supported, as well as a set of higher-level assembly instructions, such as dp3, dp4, logp, and dst. ([Microsoft00] and [Microsoft01] offer a detailed instruction set.) An example assembly program is given in Listing 4.10.1.

Listing 4.10.1 A cartoon vertex shader in vertex shader assembly [Lake01].

```
;————————————————
; Vertex Transform
;————————————————
; rN is a temporary register
; vN is a vertex register
; cN is a constant register
; oPos and oTo are output registers
;————————————————
; Transform to view space
m4x4 r9, v0, c8;
; Transform to projection space
m4x4 r10, r9, c12;
; Store output position
mov oPos, r10;
;————————————————
; Lighting calculation (N.L dot product)
;————————————————
dp3 oTO.x, c20, v3;
```

The Compiler

The compiler consists of six key components. It will translate the high-level language into a lower-level instruction set. We introduce each here and go into greater detail in later sections (see Figure 4.10.2).

- **Symbol Table**—Contains keywords and variables used in the program. Used to look up and store the register to which a variable has been assigned.
- **Scanner**—Works with the parser to accept or reject a program. Builds *tokens,* or symbols, out of the characters that are passed to the scanner. Passes these tokens to the parser and adds new variables to the symbol table. (*Lex* is short for *lexical* analyzer. In practice we use *flex*, the gnu version of Lex, to create our scanner.)
- **Parser**—Works with the scanner to accept or reject a program. Builds statements from the tokens the scanner passes as input. Uses these statements to create the abstract syntax tree. (*Yacc* stands for *yet another compiler compiler* [Levine92]. In practice we use *bison*, the gnu version of Yacc, to create our parser.)
- **Abstract Syntax Tree (AST)**—Each time the parser accepts a statement, it adds it to the syntax tree. The syntax tree is passed from the parser to the code generator.
- **Code Generator**—Walks the AST and emits code for the vertex shader based on data in the AST.
- **Temporary Register Allocator**—Manages the temporary register set used by the code generator.

The compiler we are generating is simple when compared to the complexity of a standard compiler, which has support for loops, branches, and extensive optimization

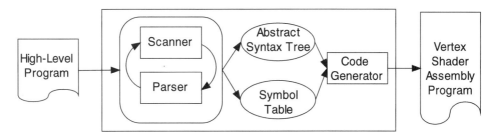

FIGURE 4.10.2 *We start with a high-level program that is passed to our compiler. First, we use our scanner and parser to determine whether we have a valid program. During this process, we also build a syntax tree and a symbol table. Next, we pass these to the code generator. The code generator walks the syntax tree and emits a valid vertex shader assembly program.*

ON THE CD

routines. We could add many enhancements. This is definitely an opportunity for future work, and you are encouraged to experiment, optimize, and augment the example source code provided on the CD-ROM.

Compiler Components

The compiler is broken up into seven components: the language, scanner, parser, abstract syntax tree, symbol table, temporary register set, and code generation.

The Language

The first task is to define the language we are going to compile. Since we are interested in creating a language that is familiar, we based it on a C-like procedural language model. Eventually, we want to support things like parameter-passing, function calls, and loops; but for the first version, we do not handle these constructs. We would also like to migrate many of the features and keywords into a Renderman-like language in the future. While this is too complicated for the vertex shaders, a real-time Renderman language is inevitable in the future of fully programmable graphics pipelines.

Since vertex shaders do not currently support looping or branching, we do not need to support the syntax for these elements. However, we do have a large set of values that we would like to utilize in our vertex shader. These are listed in Table 4.10.1. Each of these values are considered *constant*, or nonvarying across a particular mesh during its rendering. We assign each of the values into a specific *register* in the constant register set. There is an agreement between the application and the shader that the value will be stored in that particular register, and both the application and the compiler agree on which register this value resides in. For example, in our compiler, we store the light direction for the first light, LightDir0, in constant register 26. The application must put the light direction into this register for the shader, or the shader

Table 4.10.1 Keywords Used in Vertex Shading Language

Property Keywords

Vertex	Light	Material	Output
Pos	LightDir0..4	MatAmb	oPos
Normal	LightAmb0..4	MatDif	oColor
TexCoord0..4	LightDif0..4	MatSpec	oFog
	LightSpec0..4	MatShininess	oTexture
	LightPos0..4		

Note: In the example, we do not use the second color channel or the second texture layers that are part of the output register set in DirectX8.

will read bogus data contained in the register. The compiler knows where this value is stored by looking up LightDir0 in the symbol table and returning the register index where it was assigned. In our example, this is the method GetRegNumFromName(char *name) in the class CTempRegSet. Table 4.10.2 lists the math keywords that are used in our vertex shader.

Scanner

The scanner is also known as the "lexical analyzer." The lexical analyzer works with the parser to determine whether your program can be accepted as input. Again, our scanner is simple. We recognize the list of tokens in the symbol table, as well as variables (strings that are not keywords), punctuation, floating-point numbers, math operations, and comments using regular expressions defined in our token list.

ON THE CD

The CD-ROM contains an example in the directory for this gem, (see scanner.l). Lex is used to build the actual C program that is *then* compiled to build the scanner. Details of this process are beyond the scope of this gem, but it's always interesting to take a look at the C file generated, lex.yy.c.

Table 4.10.2 Math Keywords

Math Keywords

dot3	cos	clampTo1	floor	normalize	negate
dot4	sin	sqrt	ceiling	maxWith0	

Note: The math keywords are in addition to the +,−,*,/,^, (, and) operators. Notice there is only support for unary operators. Binary operators would be an obvious addition. For example, max(x,y).

The scanner has three sections. The first section, denoted by the {% and %} operators, includes the C definitions that will be necessary for your scanner. The second section, denoted by the %% at the beginning and end of the segment, includes the actual rules that the scanner recognizes, from highest to lowest precedence. The final section, after the last %%, is used to insert any C/C++ code that is needed by the rules. Typically, these are functions to look up symbols, functions to handle error control, or functions that handle error reporting.

To create a lexical analyzer, or *scanner*, from the file scanner.l, we use the GNU tool *flex*, which is available at [Streett02]. These are not shipped on the CD-ROM and need to be downloaded to compile the example compiler.

Parser

The parser works in conjunction with the scanner to accept or reject a program. While the scanner recognizes tokens, or symbols, the parser accepts or rejects *sets* of symbols, or *statements*. For example, the expression AmbientLight = AmbientMaterial * LightAmb0 is one statement. It is made of six tokens—the variables, the arithmetic symbols, and the semicolon at the end of the statement. As the scanner scans the symbols, it first recognizes the string AmbientLight as a new variable, adds it to the symbol table, and passes it to the parser. The parser can find no statement that consists of just a variable name, but it has several that start with the variable name, so it goes ahead and stores it on a stack of symbols. For this example, assume the stack starts empty, and we are only trying to recognize this statement. Next, = is considered. Again, this symbol is placed on the stack. Eventually, the entire expression is recognized as a set of symbols because it *matches* one of the statements in the language. In this case, it matches the statement Expr T_PLUS Expr. All of these elements are popped off of the stack, and the process begins again with the next statement. If the program is complete, and we are not left with only the start symbol on the stack, then we know that the program has a syntax problem. Similarly, if we are processing a symbol combined with a stack that has no opportunity to match any of the rules of the grammar, then the program has a syntax problem, and parsing stops. The start symbol is assumed to be the first symbol in the grammar description of the parser. In our example grammar file, yaccer.c, the start symbol is Program.

The parser has three sections that are structured similar to the scanner. First, the section between {% and %} contains C-related data structures that are needed in the action section of the grammar. Second, between the pair of %% symbols, is the *grammar*. The grammar is the set of statements the parser will recognize. Each statement in the grammar has an *action* section. An action section is C code that describes what to do if the statement is matched. In other words, if the set of symbols on the stack with the most-recently recognized symbol (or token) matches this statement, then take the following actions. In our parser, the action is to simply add this statement to the abstract syntax tree, as follows:

```
Expr: Expr T_PLUS Expr
    {
        $$ = new CastNode("Expr");
        ((CastNode *)$$)->addChildNode(0,(CastNode *)$1);
        CastNode *pNewNode = new CastNode("T_PLUS");
        ((CastNode *)$$)->addChildNode(1,(CastNode *)pNewNode);
        ((CastNode *)$$)->addChildNode(2,(CastNode *)$3);
    }
```

In this example, the first line contains the rule. It says that if two expressions are found with a plus sign in between, then we are to *pop* these elements off of the stack and *reduce* the stack to the single token, Expr. In addition to this reduction, there are a set of *actions* we are to take between the { and } that consist of C code. The $$ refers to the left-hand-side token Expr. Each of the subsequent $1, $2, and so forth, refer to the right-hand-side (RHS) tokens from left to right, respectively. Here, we are creating a new node in our AST and adding children to that node that correspond to the tokens on the RHS. The (CastNode *) type cast is necessary because we have declared each of these tokens as type void. (For more information, see [Levine92].)

The preceding description of the scanner and parser are only meant to provide you with enough information for a basic understanding of how these tools are used in the context of the vertex shader compiler. If you are interested in adding symbols, changing their names, or changing their assigned registers, the information presented here should be sufficient. However, any reader interested in doing their own nontrivial modifications to the compiler (adding functionality like type-checking or a more sophisticated symbol table) is encouraged to read the how-to manual on Lex and Yacc [Streett02]. Another excellent reference is the classic by John Levine [Levine92]. All three should be consulted if you are building your own compiler.

Abstract Syntax Tree

The abstract syntax tree is the data structure produced by the parser as it validates the statements during parsing. As each statement is determined to be valid, it is added to the AST. When the parsing is complete, the AST is passed to the code generator, which walks the tree and emits code for each statement in the parse tree. It is considered an *abstract* syntax tree because it does not contain all of the syntax elements of the grammar [Aho86]. For example, the semicolons are not stored in the tree because they are not needed to emit the code. In contrast, a *concrete* syntax tree would keep every token that is parsed.

Symbol Table

The symbol table stores symbols that are used in the compiler. At startup, it is initialized with all of the keywords and symbols used in the language. As the compiler parses the program, new variables are added to the symbol table. If the symbol already exists, then a reference to that symbol is recorded in the symbol table (see Table 4.10.3).

Table 4.10.3 A Symbol Table Entry

Name	Type	Scope	Token	Register Type	Register Number	Register Component (x,y,z,w)	Pointer to next Entry
"LightDir1"	"Keyword"	0	T_STRING	eRegTypeConst	37	eRegCompAll	NULL

Note: An entry consists of the name of the symbol, the symbol type, its scope, and the token that represents the symbol in the scanner. It also contains the register number, type of register, and the specific component of the four-component register once the symbol has been assigned to a register. Finally, we place a pointer to the next symbol in the table. An example symbol table is contained in the file CSymbolTable.cpp on the CD-ROM.

Temporary Register Set

Figure 4.10.1 showed that there is a set of temporary registers that we use as our working set when creating our assembly instructions. We have created a CRegister class that simply marks a register as empty or full. From this class, we construct a CTempRegisterSet class that manages the temporary registers. The types of things we can do to a register are: mark it as full or empty, MarkAsFilled() and MarkAsEmpty(); request a specific register, RequestSpecificReg(); or get the next available register, GetNextAvailableTempReg(). This class is used in the code generator.

Code Generation

The code generator contains the heart of the compiler. The code generator takes in an AST that was produced from a correct grammar. It then walks this AST and emits code for each statement it finds. Two alternatives for optimization exist at this point. The first and most obvious is to run different algorithms over the tree; each algorithm does a different type of optimization. Another would be to output an intermediate-level language description and run your algorithms on that intermediate language. Several of these techniques are discussed in [Muchnick97]. The point of this gem is to get you started with a working compiler that you can then extend by adding enhancements and optimizations appropriate to your target platform—this is where that customization can begin!

Conclusion

To see the results, compile the example vertex shader compiler with the shader on the CD-ROM as input. Now, imagine that you are working on a new shader. Would you rather debug the high-level code or the assembly that is generated? There will always be a need to get close to the hardware for certain applications, but having a compiler handy to do the dirty work is probably a better solution in many cases. This compiler has been used to generate shaders successfully for applications using DirectX8. As with all projects, there are plenty of opportunities for improvement, and we welcome any contributions that readers would like to make.

Acknowledgments

None of this work would have been possible without the support of the management of the Intel Labs Graphics and 3D Technologies team (G3D). I'm especially grateful to Carl Marshall and Stephen Junkins for continuing to push me that little bit further to complete the task and rise to the next challenge. Thanks also to Jeff Lander and Mike Macpherson for reading early drafts and providing feedback.

References

[Aho86] Aho, Alfred, Ravi Sethi, and Jeffrey D. Ullman, *Compilers: Principles, Techniques, and Tools,* Addison Wesley, 1986.

[Lake01] Lake, Adam, "Cartoon Rendering Using Texture Mapping and Programmable Vertex Shaders," *Game Programming Gems 2,* Charles River Media, Inc., 2001.

[Levine92] Levine, John, Tony Mason, and Doug Brown, *Lex and Yacc,* O'Reilly and Associates, 1992.

[Möller 02] Möller, Tomas and Eric Haines, *Real-Time Rendering,* Second Edition, A.K. Peters, Ltd., 2002.

[Microsoft00] *Microsoft DirectX 8.0 Software Development Kit,* available online at http://www.msdn.microsoft.com/downloads, 20000.

[Microsoft01] *Microsoft DirectX 8.1 Software Development Kit,* available online at http://www.msdn.microsoft.com/downloads, 2001.

[Muchnick97] Muchnick, Steven S., *Advanced Compiler Design and Implementation,* Morgan Kaufmann, 1997.

[Olano00] Olano, Marc "Interactive Shading Language, Language Description," Course Notes on Approaches for Procedural Shading on Graphics Hardware (SIGGRAPH 2000).

[Proudfoot01] Proudfoot, Kekoa, William R. Mark, Svetoslav Tzvetkov, and Pat Hanrahan, "A Real-Time Procedural Shading System for Programmable Graphics Hardware," Conference Proceedings (SIGGRAPH 2001).

[Streett02] http://www.monmouth.com/~wstreett/lex-yacc/lex-yacc.html. Flex and bison ports to Win32, including source and documentation.

[Upstill89] Upstill, Steve, *The Renderman Companion: A Programmer's Guide to Realistic Computer Graphics,* Addison Wesley, 1989.

[Woo99] Woo, Mason, et al., *OpenGL Programming Guide,* Third Edition, Version 1.2, Addison Wesley, 1999.

4.11

Billboard Beams

Brian Hawkins, Seven Studios
winterdark@sprynet.com

Dazzling special effects are a key component to the graphical flair of many games, and an effect that appears again and again is the laser light beam. Beams are used for everything from spacecraft weaponry to magic spells, and solid beams can also be used to create structural elements in buildings.

Several methods are available for creating a beam effect, each of which has its own disadvantages. The simplest technique uses multiple spherical billboard sprites along the line of the beam. This can require a large number of sprites to create a small number of beams, and the visual illusion can break down under numerous conditions, such as during the production of larger beams. A much more economical technique uses only a single rectangle rotated around the axis of the beam to face the camera as completely as possible. This efficiently produces a convincing beam from the side view, but the polygonal nature of the beam becomes apparent as the view approaches a straight-on perspective.

These two methods can be combined to create a better method that is both efficient and maintains visual integrity under most conditions. Two triangles are oriented toward the camera to form the endpoints, and two more triangles form the main beam section. The rest of this gem describes in detail the positioning and texture mapping of the triangles to create the illusion of a three-dimensional beam.

Matrices

A billboard matrix is determined for each endpoint, given the camera-to-world matrix, and the two endpoints of the beam. An ordinary billboard matrix for a camera-oriented sprite uses the same orientation as the camera-to-world matrix with a different position. However, for a beam, the billboard matrices should be oriented along the beam's screen direction. Therefore, the front vector remains the same as the camera-to-world matrix, but the up and right vectors must be modified. First, a directional vector for the beam is obtained from the two endpoints:

$$B = B_1 - B_2$$

Next, a directional vector, termed the "eye vector," from the camera position to one of the beam endpoints is calculated:

$$\mathbf{E} = \begin{bmatrix} M_{03} & M_{13} & M_{23} \end{bmatrix}^{\mathrm{T}} - \mathbf{B}_1 w$$

Then, the cross-product of the eye vector and the beam vector produces a vector that is oriented perpendicular to the beam vector in screen space:

$$\mathbf{P} = \mathbf{B} \times \mathbf{E}$$

Finally, the normalized cross product of the perpendicular vector and the camera-to-world front vector provides the up vector for the billboard matrices:

$$\mathbf{F} = \begin{bmatrix} M_{00} & M_{10} & M_{20} \end{bmatrix}^{\mathrm{T}}$$

$$\mathbf{U} = \frac{\mathbf{F} \times \mathbf{P}}{\left\| \mathbf{F} \times \mathbf{P} \right\|}$$

From this, the right vector is easy to calculate:

$$\mathbf{R} = \mathbf{F} \times \mathbf{U}$$

Now, the billboard matrices for each endpoint are generated from the orientation vectors and the endpoint positions:

$$\mathbf{M}_1 = \begin{bmatrix} F_x & U_x & R_x & B_{1x} \\ F_y & U_y & R_y & B_{1y} \\ F_z & U_z & R_z & B_{1z} \\ 0 & 0 & 0 & 1 \end{bmatrix} \text{ and } \mathbf{M}_2 = \begin{bmatrix} F_x & U_x & R_x & B_{2x} \\ F_y & U_y & R_y & B_{2y} \\ F_z & U_z & R_z & B_{2z} \\ 0 & 0 & 0 & 1 \end{bmatrix}$$

Vertices

Figure 4.11.1 shows the two triangles that will form the end caps of the beam, whose radius is specified by $\mathbf{S}$, once transformed by the appropriate billboard matrix. Vertices $\mathbf{V}_1$, $\mathbf{V}_2$, and $\mathbf{V}_3$ are transformed by $\mathbf{M}_1$, and $\mathbf{V}_4$, $\mathbf{V}_5$, and $\mathbf{V}_6$ by $\mathbf{M}_2$. Vertices $\mathbf{V}_2$, $\mathbf{V}_3$, $\mathbf{V}_4$, and $\mathbf{V}_5$ can then be used to form the other two triangles that make the beam. The two end triangles will then be camera-oriented, which in turn will cause the other two triangles to be camera-oriented as well.

A further optimization can be achieved on most modern architectures by passing the triangles as a triangle strip, thus reducing the number of vertices sent per beam from 12 to 6. For this to work, the vertices are sent in order from $\mathbf{V}_1$ to $\mathbf{V}_6$, and shared vertices must share the same properties. This second requirement is of particular importance when considering texture mapping.

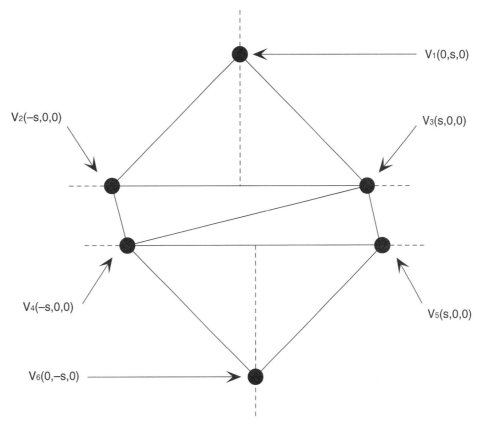

FIGURE 4.11.1   *Vertex coordinates before transformation.*

UV Mapping

Figure 4.11.2 shows the two main texture mapping alternatives that allow for triangle strip creation. Vertices V_1 to V_6 are matched up with the corresponding texture coordinates T_1 to T_6. When choosing which layout to use, consider the tradeoffs between the two options. The first method, shown in Figure 4.11.2a, matches the actual shape of the beam better and therefore suffers fewer graphical artifacts. However, the texture space left is broken into two triangles that might be hard to use for other textures. The second method, presented in Figure 4.11.2b, is more efficient in its use of texture space, but it achieves this by stretching the texture in such a way that visual artifacts could be introduced in the final image. This problem is not seen in most beams, making the second method the preferred choice unless a noticeable visual problem is encountered.

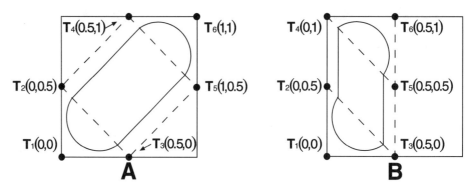

FIGURE 4.11.2 *Example texture layout with texture coordinates.*

Conclusion

The algorithm presented here provides a generic method of efficiently rendering beams. The performance could be enhanced by tailoring the algorithm to take advantage of particular architectural features of the platform that is used, while still maintaining the visual effect desired. Let the fireworks begin.

4.12

3D Tricks for
Isometric Engines

Greg Snook, Bungie Studios

gregsn@microsoft.com

Isometric engines are one of the last bastions of two-dimensional graphics left in the game industry. While this gem proposes some 3D methods to enhance what is essentially a sprite-based display system, it tries to preserve the essence of sprite-based graphics. While you could simply represent a majority of the game objects with 3D models to get the same visual effect, the ideas presented here maintain the use of sprites by adding a few tricks to make them appear as flexible as 3D models. The concepts may also be useful in other 3D engines as a replacement for flat billboard sprites or as a means to represent distant objects at a lower level of detail.

Consider an isometric game engine where each game object is created in some 3D modeling package. The game world itself is divided into rectangular volumes, which we will call "cells." Each cell is represented in the game by a single 2D image. These images are orthographic projections of the cell contents onto a plane placed at the front of the cell (see the projected texture created in Figure 4.12.1). Since we view the game through an orthogonal camera, rendering the game world is a matter of figuring out which cells are onscreen, and then drawing the image of each cell's contents at the appropriate screen coordinates. There is no scaling or perspective correction needed to display the cells, so our 2D cell projections have completely replaced the original 3D models.

To move into a 3D, perspective-correct environment, we need to add what our 2D projections are lacking—depth information. This converts our 2D images into something approaching a voxel representation. We will look at a few methods to render these depth-enabled images in a 3D setting.

Moving into the Third Dimension

The first step in moving into 3D is to change our rendering method. The most common way to draw 2D images within a 3D system is through the use of billboards. These are flat pieces of geometry onto which the individual cell images are texture-mapped. If one billboard is used for each of the game cell images, and the scene is rendered through an orthogonal camera, then the display will look nearly identical to the original 2D version. The billboards have become a replacement to the traditional

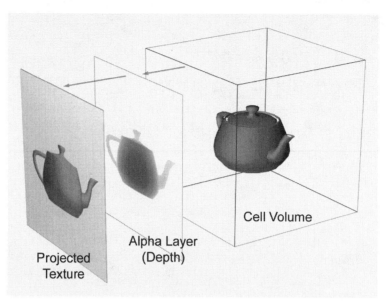

FIGURE 4.12.1 *An orthogonal projection of the original cell contents creates both the texture image and per-pixel depth information, stored as shades of gray in the alpha channel.*

drawing method, yielding the same result. Using a nonorthogonal camera will handle all the distance-related scaling and parallax effects, but will immediately show the billboard's lack of depth.

To create the illusion of depth in the billboards, some volumetric data for each texture must be recorded. Remember that each image placed on the billboard cards is intended to represent the objects within a certain volume of space. This is essentially a projection of the cell's contents onto a plane. Per-pixel depth information can be recorded, representing the distance from the projection plane to the point of intersection with the cell's contents (see Figure 4.12.1). This per-pixel depth information is the catalyst for each of the three methods presented here for creating a volumetric representation from the billboard image. It also proves useful when calculating per-pixel bump-mapping information for the texture—a technique that can be used in tandem with any of the methods described here.

Method 1: The More Billboards the Better

The elevation map method, first described by Sim Dietrich [Dietrich00], is a technique that uses multiple billboards to represent a volume of space. Each billboard is textured with a slice of the cell volume, so that together they approximate the original geometry when stacked facing the camera. Dietrich also showed that all the billboards in a cell group can be mapped with a single texture containing depth information for the cell within the alpha channel of the texture. Using hardware-enabled alpha test-

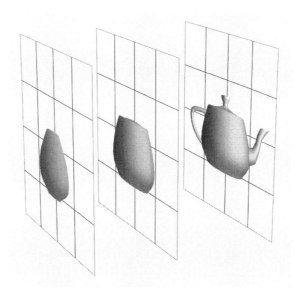

FIGURE 4.12.2 *An exploded view of multiple-depth slices, texture-mapped on stacked billboards to emulate a solid object.*

ing, individual depth layers of the cell texture can be drawn on each billboard. This allows for the creation of a pseudo-volumetric solid with a few polygons and a single texture (see Figure 4.12.2).

The desired depth value is placed in the alpha component of each vertex's diffuse color. Using a subtraction operation within the texture stage, this value is subtracted from the alpha channel of the texture sample. The hardware is set up to perform an alpha test to reject pixels that are less than zero after the subtraction operation. This ensures that only those portions of the texture that have a depth value higher than the value set into the vertex color are drawn.

In DirectX8, the setup is just a few simple render and texture states:

```
SetRenderState(D3DRS_ALPHATESTENABLE, TRUE);
SetRenderState(D3DRS_ALPHAREF, 0);
SetRenderState(D3DRS_ALPHAFUNC, D3DCMP_GREATER);

SetRenderState(D3DRS_ALPHABLENDENABLE, TRUE);
SetRenderState(D3DRS_SRCBLEND , D3DBLEND_ONE);
SetRenderState(D3DRS_DESTBLEND , D3DBLEND_ZERO);

SetTextureStageState(0, D3DTSS_COLORARG1, D3DTA_TEXTURE);
SetTextureStageState(0, D3DTSS_COLORARG2, D3DTA_DIFFUSE);
SetTextureStageState(0, D3DTSS_COLOROP, D3DTOP_SELECTARG1);

SetTextureStageState(0, D3DTSS_ALPHAARG1, D3DTA_TEXTURE);
SetTextureStageState(0, D3DTSS_ALPHAARG2, D3DTA_DIFFUSE);
SetTextureStageState(0, D3DTSS_ALPHAOP, D3DTOP_SUBTRACT);
```

Depending on the camera type used to view the scene, it might be necessary to draw the cell from some wide angles. The elevation map holds up quite well in these situations, but might begin to show silhouette artifacts as the viewing direction approaches a parallel angle to the billboards. To account for this, additional angled billboards can be added to handle the wider viewing angles. Because the desired depth value for each billboard is encoded into the diffuse color of its vertices, Gouraud shading between the vertex colors allows for the slice to occur on just about any angle needed.

Another drawback of the elevation map technique is that it deals with depth as a height map. Only one height value is used per pixel to define the image volume, giving the resulting object an extruded appearance when viewed from an angle. To help alleviate this problem, a second depth map can be used to define the rear of the object, giving us two values per pixel: one to define the depth value at the front of the object and one to define the back.

This is created in the same manner as our current depth texture using a camera placed on the opposite side of the cell volume. During rendering, a pixel shader can be used to perform a second subtraction operation, this time using the depth information in the second texture. If both subtraction operations provide a positive result, the point in question is between the front and back depth buffer values, and is output to the screen. If either subtraction operation is negative, the point is either in front or in back of our object volume and is rejected. The sample application included on the CD-ROM shows this technique in action.

ON THE CD

Method 2: Warping Textures

While not the fastest method for representing a cell's contents on a billboard, procedurally warped relief textures do provide the benefit of no additional geometry. What they suffer from is a preprocessing step to warp the billboard texture each time the viewing angle changes. Because this can be somewhat costly in terms of performance and requires a discrete texture for each cell, it is only useful for unique objects in the game. However, single-instance objects, such as the player's character or boss monsters, can get a strong sense of depth from relief textures.

The notion of relief textures is borrowed from Manuel Oliveira and Gary Bishop, who developed the technique at the University of North Carolina at Chapel Hill [Olivera99]. The idea is based on the fact that the texture contains per-pixel depth information for the cell, which can be reprojected onto the billboard plane to emulate another viewing angle. Given a camera position, each pixel in the texture can be offset to a new position on the texture, given its original texture position and depth value. The resulting texture, created after all pixels have been offset, describes the cell contents as seen from the position of the viewer (see Figure 4.12.3).

The trouble is that this is a two-pass operation. Pixels must first be offset along the u axis of the texture, then again along the v axis to locate their final resting place. In the interest of speed, the v-offset operation can often be skipped and still produce

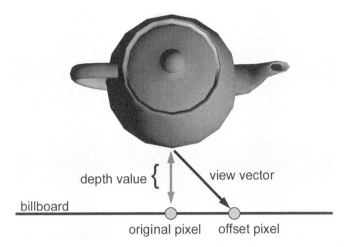

FIGURE 4.12.3 *Viewed from above, this diagram shows the reprojection of a pixel onto the billboard plane. The offset location is calculated from the original pixels (x, y) location on the billboard and the depth information encoded into the texture's alpha channel.*

a believable result. The nature of most isometric game objects (usually tall, thin entities such as bipeds) and the screen's aspect ratio help to hide the effects of this cheat. In the sample code provided, only the *u* offset is performed during the texture warp.

When performing the *u*-offset operation, there is the possibility of holes being created in the image (locations to which no pixels have been offset), and occlusion problems (locations where more than one pixel offset to the same position) might occur. To handle occlusion, the texture must be processed in the direction of the pixel offset. This ensures that pixels closer to the camera overwrite those further away. For example, if the billboard is located on the camera's left side, the pixels will be offset to the right. In this case, the texture must be processed from left to right to ensure that pixels closer to the camera (toward the right of the image) overwrite those further away. If the billboard is to the right of the camera, the opposite is true, and the texture must be processed in right-to-left order. In the worst case, where the billboard straddles the camera's view vector, the texture must be processed in both directions, occluding toward the center.

Holes are created when two adjacent pixels in the original texture map to two nonadjacent positions after the warp is performed. In these cases, the desired view of the object is from an angle not accounted for in the original orthographic projection of the depth values. A suitable result can still be obtained by performing a blend between the two separated pixels to fill the gap.

The final result yields a texture that is properly warped for the given viewing angle. This texture can then be mapped directly on the billboard for display. The sample program provided on the CD-ROM shows this technique in action.

ON THE CD

Method 3: Vertically Interlaced Textures

The final method presented here builds off of the relief textures used earlier. Using the programmable pixel shaders in Direct X8 (or greater) on suitable hardware, a blend between prewarped versions of our texture can be performed during rendering. This will emulate various viewing angles.

Think of the texture mapped across the billboard as a sheet of paper riddled with pinholes, through which the cell contents can be seen. Each texel is a pinhole, and the color placed there is what is seen though the hole. What the relief textures do, in a sense, is compute what would be seen through the pinholes at various angles.

In this final method, a texture is created that contains four views of the cell contents interlaced as vertical strips. Using a pixel shader and a second utility texture, the interlaced strips are blended on the GPU. This provides nearly the same quality as the relief texture method, without the need for a procedural texture warp. The downside is that some texture resolution is lost along the *x*-axis of the texture in order to pack in the various image samples. For every pixel in the original image, there must instead be a horizontal sample set of four pixels, one for each viewing angle. This method can also extend into the *v*-axis of the texture, but at the cost of more texture resolution (see Figure 4.12.4).

The pixel shader is built around the bump environment map instruction (texbem). It works in two basic steps. First, it converts the incoming (u, v) coordinates, pointing them to the start of the desired sample set. Second, it offsets the new *u* coordinate to the desired viewing angle within that set, using the texbem instruction. The result is a per-pixel blend between two of our four viewing angles, packed into the texture.

The first step of the shader uses the utility texture mentioned earlier. This texture contains a lookup table that converts our incoming *uv* coordinate pair to the start of

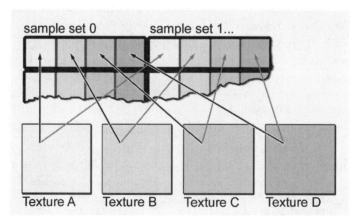

FIGURE 4.12.4   *The interlaced texture is created by sampling identical pixel locations in the source textures and organizing them into sample sets of four pixels each.*

the sample set in the second texture. This texture should be the same width as the interlaced texture and is filled with the value ($u*4$) for every pixel on the *u*-axis. If the billboard is given texture coordinates along *u* from 0.00 through 0.25, then the utility texture will convert the incoming value to the range [0.0, 1.0] in steps that are equivalent to a four-pixel span within the interlaced texture. This forces each incoming texture coordinate to point to the start of our four-pixel sample set.

The second step is to offset this value to select the desired pixel within the sample set. This offset value is in the range [0.0, four_pixel_span], which can be calculated in a vertex shader and written into a second set of *uv* coordinates for each vertex. The four_pixel_span value is the width, in texture space, of four pixels. This can be calculated as 4 divided by the width of the image in pixels.

ON THE CD

Finally, the texbem instruction performs the offset from the start of the sample set to the desired sample within, resulting in a per-pixel blend of the two closest camera views. Source code on the CD-ROM shows the implementation details of both the vertex and pixel shader. Also, Color Plate 8 shows three methods of generating psuedo-3D images from a 2D image source.

Conclusion

While no billboard method can fully replace a complex 3D model, these techniques demonstrate that prerendered images can still be used in a 3D environment with great effect. With some careful content creation, it is certainly possible to create an object that is nearly indistinguishable from the original model. Whether you wish to update an isometric sprite engine or need an easy way to bring more objects into your 3D world, we hope these ideas will prove useful.

References

[Dietrich00] Dietrich, Sim, "Elevation Maps," available online at Nvidia's developer-support Web site: http://developer.nvidia.com/docs/IO/1334/ATT/Elevation-Maps2.doc, January 2000.

[Olivera99] Olivera, Manuel M. and Gary Bishop, "Relief Textures," available online at UNC's Image-Based Rendering Web page: http://www.cs.unc.edu/~ibr/projects/RT/RT.html, April 1999.

4.13

Curvature Simulation Using Normal Maps

Oscar Blasco, Aside Software

oscar@asidesoft.com

Today's in-game models are still far from being realistic. Prelit textures are the common way to simulate curvature using low-detail models. Nevertheless, current hardware is now capable of calculating per-pixel lighting equations (both the common and not-so-common). This gem explains how to perturb the normals on a surface to simulate the curvature of a denser model by using bump mapping. We will enhance the visual quality without losing speed or having to abandon more-traditional ways of adding detail (e.g., handmade bumps; see Figure 4.13.1 and Color Plate 9).

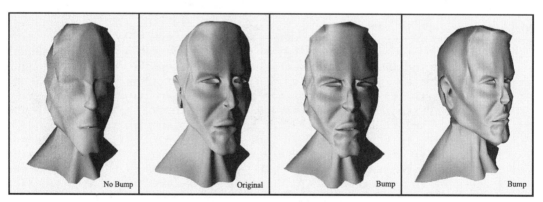

FIGURE 4.13.1 *Result of the bump-mapping process. Left to right: The low-resolution model, the original model, and two examples of the final result using bump mapping.*

Normal Maps

Bump mapping is a per-pixel process that disturbs the intensity of the light at the current point. This means that we can lighten or darken the pixel that is being rendered. In other words, we can compute the lighting equation on a per-pixel basis rather than on a per-vertex basis. Equation 4.13.1 shows a simple and common lighting equation with a specular component:

$$color = \left(n \cdot l\right) \cdot Surface\_Color + \left(n \cdot h\right)^8 \qquad (4.13.1)$$

In our case, n is stored as a texel in a texture (the coordinates of the vector codified as an RGB color), which is called a *normal map*. The hardware is responsible for calculating the dot product between n and l (the same for n dot h), and then uses the result as a modulation factor for the surface color. Note that l is transformed to local space, and the dot product is done in *texture space* (more on this later).

Overview of the Process

The curvature simulation algorithm presents a general scheme for obtaining the detail of a dense model so that it can be used on a lower-resolution model for real-time rendering. By modulating the lighting across the low-resolution model surface, we will simulate the captured detail.

The first model is a dense mesh, which is modeled as if it were going to be used for nonreal-time rendering. A second, similar model has a more reasonable number of triangles to be used for rendering at interactive rates. It also has *uv coordinates* for texturing. The low-resolution model does not need to be a simplified version of the dense one, which is why this technique is a viable solution. It allows the modeler to modify the low-resolution mesh to fix problems or to simply use another mesh with no direct relationship.

As we said, our objective is to store the detail that is not present in the low-resolution mesh into a normal map. This is done by capturing the curvature of the original model while taking into account that our low-resolution mesh has a curvature of its own. This curvature is defined by the normals on the dense model, so we need to capture those normals and store them into a map.

At runtime, the generated texture will perturb the normal for each point on the low-resolution mesh. This changes the dot products in the lighting equation (Equation 4.13.1) and produces the simulation of curvature. Each texel is perturbed to make the surface seem like the original object at that point (note that our normal map must have a finite size). The algorithm can be outlined as follows:

- Preprocessing
- Computing the map
- Post-processing

Computing the map requires:

- *Rasterizing* each polygon into the map (using the *uv* coordinates of each vertex).
  - Calculating the perturbed normal at each texel.

Preparing Our Data

We will need some data before starting:
For the high-resolution model:

- Normals at each vertex, which are smooth across the model.

For the low-resolution model:

- A tangent-space basis at each vertex (smooth tangent, binormal, and normal)
- The *uv* texture coordinates of vertices

The tangent-space bases are needed to transform the computed normals into texture space.

It is easy to see why the object has to be *uv* mapped; otherwise we would not know how to map the low-resolution mesh map to the texture. (See "Known Issues" to explore the common problems related to *uv* coordinates.)

Casting Rays

Now let's discuss how to calculate the perturbed normal at each texel. Since the two meshes do not share vertices, we have to shoot rays from the low-resolution mesh surface and check where they intersect with the dense model.

Sander, et al. [Sander] discuss about two ways to choose the direction of the rays. The first and easiest way is to use the normal of the current face (closest-point). A second way requires interpolation of the normals along the surface to use as the directions (normal-shooting).

As you can see in Figure 4.13.2, normal-shooting parameterization leads to better results, while closest-point produces more discontinuities.

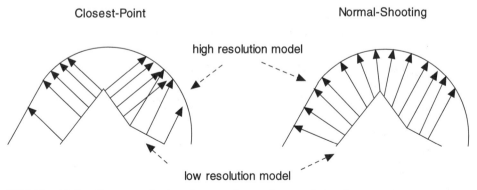

FIGURE 4.13.2 *Rays traced using closest-point and normal-shooting.*

For each ray, once we have shot the ray and obtained the point of intersection with the dense model, the normal at that point is computed using the barycentric coordinates within the triangle.

Barycentric coordinates are an easy way to define a point inside a triangle. Let P be our intersection point defined in object space, and v_0, v_1, and v_2 will be the vertices of the triangle. We can calculate them as follows:

$$u = \frac{\left\|\left(v_2 - v_1\right) \wedge \left(P - v_1\right)\right\|}{\left\|\left(v_1 - v_0\right) \wedge \left(v_2 - v_0\right)\right\|} \tag{4.13.2}$$

$$v = \frac{\left\|\left(v_0 - v_2\right) \wedge \left(P - v_2\right)\right\|}{\left\|\left(v_1 - v_0\right) \wedge \left(v_2 - v_0\right)\right\|} \tag{4.13.3}$$

$$w = 1 - \left(u + v\right) \tag{4.13.4}$$

The barycentric coordinates are relative to the areas of the subtriangles defined by the intersection point and the triangle vertices (Figure 4.13.3).

They are useful for collision checking because any property defined per-vertex can be interpolated using u, v, and w. For example, the intersection point is defined as:

$$\vec{P} = u \cdot v_0 + v \cdot v_1 + w \cdot v_2 \tag{4.13.5}$$

The steps that we have covered in this section are: First, for each point on the lower-resolution mesh, shoot a ray along the interpolated normal and obtain the intersection point in a triangle of the high-resolution model. Second, compute its barycentric coordinates so we can interpolate the normal of the high-resolution mesh at that point. As you can see, we now have what we are looking for—a normal vector. Now we must store it into the normal map.

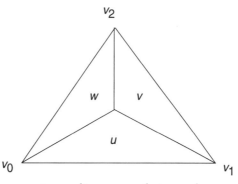

FIGURE 4.13.3 *Barycentric coordinates are relative to the area of each subtriangle.*

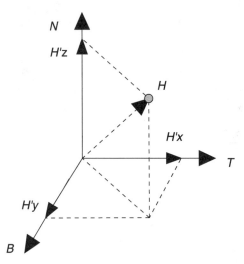

FIGURE 4.13.4   *The captured normal (H) is converted to texture space (H').*

Getting the Detail

Since we chose to evaluate the lighting in texture space, a transformation of space is needed to use the captured normal (see Figure 4.13.4).

The tangent, binormal, and normal at any point on the surface form a matrix (Equation 4.13.6), which is a transformation from model space into texture space. (Equation 4.13.7 is the transformed normal.) *T*, *B*, and *N* are also called the *tangent space basis* [Lengyel01].

$$\mathbf{M} = \begin{bmatrix} T \\ B \\ N \end{bmatrix} = \begin{bmatrix} Tx & Ty & Tz \\ Bx & By & Bz \\ Nx & Ny & Nz \end{bmatrix} \tag{4.13.6}$$

$$\bar{H}' = \begin{bmatrix} x \\ y \\ z \end{bmatrix} = \begin{bmatrix} Tx & Ty & Tz \\ Bx & By & Bz \\ Nx & Ny & Nz \end{bmatrix} \bullet \begin{bmatrix} Hx \\ Hy \\ Hz \end{bmatrix} \tag{4.13.7}$$

Post-Processing

After computing the normal map, it will still have many empty regions. During rasterization, texture filtering will alter the normals we use, due to these gaps in the normal map. We solve this by filling the normal map with a light blue color—RGB (127, 127, 255) or vector (0.0, 0.0, 1.0).

The blue color is often sufficient, but we can do something else to achieve better results. With an edge-expansion filter, we can expand the colors of the polygon edges in the texture. This will fix any hardware filtering issues.

Save your texture using an image format that does not alter the texels. For example, JPEG is not a good idea, since it uses a lossy compression algorithm that denormalizes the normals.

Known Issues

There are two reasons for problems that we might encounter when using the ray-tracing scheme presented here. One is the *uv* coordinates, and the other one relates to missed rays or incorrect intersections.

If the models have significant differences (e.g., a ray intersects the surface of the dense mesh twice), we will get wrong normals. It is important to instruct the modelers to avoid such situations (see Figure 4.13.5).

As for *uv* coordinates, there are two major problems that need to be addressed:

• *Discontinuities in the tangent space bases.* This problem is common to any bump mapping that computes the lighting in texture space. Doing the lighting in texture space allows us to change the geometry and still use the same normal map. The problem is that due to the *uv* mapping, the tangent space bases are not smooth along the model surface, which produces discontinuities in the light vector. Doing the lighting in model space completely avoids the problem; although

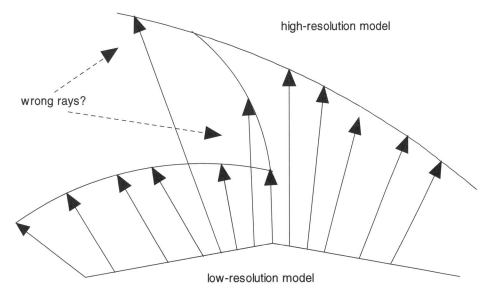

FIGURE 4.13.5   *The ray-casting algorithm does not know which intersections are incorrect.*

it has a counterpart: If the normals were defined in model space, we would need to change them each time the geometry is deformed. However, you can transform the light into the new space defined by the deformed geometry to solve the problem. In any event, this all depends on the engine design and quality desired.

- *Incorrect mapping.* The algorithm has a huge dependency on *uv* coordinates. The object needs to be well mapped in order to avoid strange results.

Another Approach

It is interesting to talk about other approaches for computing the normal map, particularly when the models have spatial similarities. We will consider that the low-resolution mesh was obtained directly from the dense one using some simplification algorithm, and that this algorithm only used the vertices from the original model. Moreover, the original model was already *uv* mapped, or it was added using some scheme. With those conditions, we can easily make a direct relationship between the models for each texel, since they have common vertices (the same *u* coordinate and *v* coordinate).

This scheme can be simplified if we do not transform the normals into texture space. Since this is exactly the same as drawing the normals of the dense model directly to the normal map, we can implement this scheme using 3D hardware rasterization. This is very useful if we are able to *uv* map the model.

Conclusion

This gem strives to make the algorithm presented as general as possible, though generalization also implies less accuracy and less speed. By 'general,' we mean it does not depend on any relationship between the models. The exact goal was to make an approach, which allows the artist to modify the vertices of the low-resolution mesh. Other algorithms used to extract the original curvature depend on the fact that the models share vertices (and their properties, like *uv* coordinates). A simplification algorithm that uses edge collapses is often used to obtain the low-resolution mesh from the dense model. The disadvantages of this are obvious: Simplification tends to create faces with no uniform size, and the mesh is hard to unwrap (map with *uv* coordinates). Also, if the original objects were already *uv* mapped, the mapping usually gets corrupted. Nevertheless, there are cases in which you might want to use this.

After generating the normal map, we can still add hand-made bumps for small details; in fact, it is actually desirable to do so. Modeling such details in a dense mesh is hard and completely inefficient. The ray tracing will not be able to get the same precision as if we were to add it with hand-made bumps. They can be added to the generated normal map with simple normal-map combiner code; only a perturbation of the normal stored in the texture is needed.

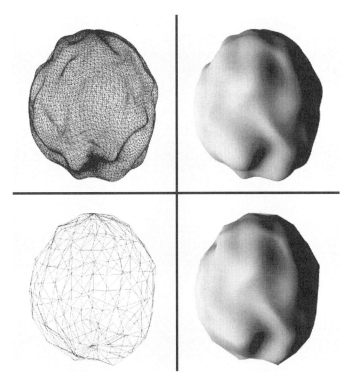

FIGURE 4.13.6 *Example of a perturbed sphere. The top two images are the original object, the bottom two are the final result using the algorithm.*

Acknowledgments

I would like to thank Julio Cesar Espada for all the models he created (especially for the head in Figure 4.13.1) and for his feedback in using and testing this technique. I would also like to thank Ignacio Castaño for his comments and support.

References

[Ebert] Ebert, David S., et al., "Texturing and Modeling: A Procedural Approach," (SIGGRAPH).

[Kilgard] Kilgard, Mark J., "A Practical and Robust Bump-Mapping Technique for Today's GPUs," paper available online at nVIDIA site: http://developer.nvidia .com/docs/IO/1329/ATT/bumpmap.pdf.

[Lengyel01] Lengyel, Eric, *Mathematics for 3D Game Programming & Computer Graphics*, Charles River Media, 2001.

[Sander] Sander, Pedro V., et al., "Silhouette Clipping," SIGGRAPH 2000 Proceedings: pp. 327–334. Available online at http://research.microsoft.com/~hoppe/.

[Watt92] Watt, Alan H. and Mark Watt, *Advanced Animation and Rendering Techniques,* Addison Wesley, 1992.

[Wynn] Wynn, Chris, "Implementing Bump-Mapping Using Register Combiners," available online at nVIDIA site: http://developer.nvidia.com/docs/IO/1273/ATT/BumpMappingWithRegisterCombiners.pdf.

4.14

Methods for Dynamic, Photorealistic Terrain Lighting

Naty Hoffman and Kenny Mitchell,

Westwood Studios,

naty@westwood.com,
kmitchell@westwood.com

Current rendering technologies enable us to include expansive and detailed outdoor scenes in our games, using large numbers of triangles. However, an important part of the visual complexity and appeal of an outdoor scene is due to its lighting, not just its geometry. If the lighting is static, it is simple enough to precompute a high-quality lighting solution—but what should we do when the lighting changes dynamically? This gem will present several methods for producing high-quality, physically based lighting solutions for terrain under dynamic lighting conditions.

Background

The first step is to quantify light correctly. Light is electromagnetic radiation in the visible portion of the spectrum (about 400–700 nm). The most common metric for light is *radiance*, or light flux along a ray. To understand how radiance is defined, visualize a small square (area A) centered on the light ray and perpendicular to it (see Figure 4.14.1a).

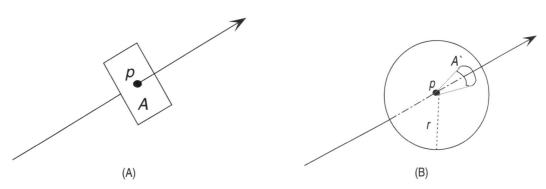

(A) (B)

FIGURE 4.14.1 *(A-B) Radiance area* A *along a light ray and patch* A' *on the radiance sphere.*

Light energy continuously passes through this square in all directions and frequencies. In RGB space, this energy (and any quantity derived from it) is specified as three numbers. This can roughly be thought of as dividing it into three 'buckets,' based on frequency. At a given point in time, we measure the rate of energy over time (light power or *radiant flux* Φ). The amount of flux going through the square depends on the size of the square, and doesn't really indicate the amount of light along the ray. We can measure the flux per area at the intersection point p ($M = d\Phi / dA$, or power per area, measured in watts per square meter). However, M includes light going in all directions, not just along the ray—we need to take direction into account. In Figure 4.14.1b, we see a sphere (radius R) centered on p, and a small patch (area A') on this sphere surrounding the ray. A part of M (which we will call M') goes through this patch—M' does not depend on the radius of the sphere, but only on the part of the sphere's area covered by the patch. This represents a range of directions and is called a *solid angle* ($\omega = A' / R$, measured in steradians). The quantity of light along the ray is the radiance ($L = dM' / d\omega$, measured in watts per meter squared per steradian). Radiance is power per *projected area* per solid angle—the projected area being measured perpendicularly to the ray. If we use an area that is at an angle to the ray (e.g., when looking at light reflected from a surface), then a correction factor equal to the dot product between the surface normal and the ray is needed.

In outdoor scenes, radiance can vary by six orders of magnitude [Debevec98], but most hardware limits us to a small range of light values. In this gem, we will compress all light values into the [0, 1] range. A related issue is the nonlinear relationship between pixel values and display radiance. The human visual response to light introduces other issues. We have chosen to ignore these problems and deal only with linear radiance values.

Another important quantity used in measuring light is the *irradiance, E*. This is similar to the flux per area, M above (with the same units), except that instead of measuring the total of all the outgoing light at a point, it measures the total incident (incoming) light. Since this is measured at a surface, the incoming radiance at a point p is integrated over a hemisphere $H(p)$ that is centered on the surface normal $\mathbf{N}(p)$:

$$E(p) = \int_{\mathbf{V} \in H(p)} L_i(p, -\mathbf{V}) \, \mathbf{N}(p) \cdot \mathbf{V} \, d\Omega \tag{4.14.1}$$

Here, $\mathbf{V}$ is an outgoing unit vector in the hemisphere $H(p)$, $L_i(p, -\mathbf{V})$ is the incident radiance at p from $-\mathbf{V}$, and $d\Omega$ is the differential solid angle used for integration. The dot product is the projected area correction factor.

In this gem, we deal only with Lambertian (diffuse) terrain surfaces. For such surfaces, the outgoing radiance L_o is the same in all directions and is equal to the irradiance multiplied by the color $C(p)$ divided by π:

$$L_o(p) = \frac{C(p)}{\pi} E(p) \tag{4.14.2}$$

The color is an RGB triple, in which each value is between 0 and 1. A color of 0 reflects none of the incoming energy in the relevant band of frequencies, and 1 reflects all of it.

The problem we are trying to solve here is the calculation of $L_o(p)$ for all the points on a heightfield terrain (at a finite resolution) under changing lighting conditions. Since the terrain is Lambertian, and we assume that $C(p)$ is known, this is equivalent to calculating $E(p)$. For this, we need to know the incoming radiances from all directions in $H(p)$. These directions are divided into three groups: those from which the sun is visible, those from which the sky is visible, and those from which other terrain points are visible. We assume that certain data is available at each moment in time: the sun's position, angular size, and radiance. We might also want information about cloud positions, and other data. Note also that the sky's radiance might vary over different parts of the sky.

Now, the directions in which other terrain points are visible pose a difficult problem. In order to know the incoming radiance for these directions, we need to first know the outgoing radiance for other terrain points. If the radiance and positions of the sun and sky were static, we could use an iterative algorithm such as radiosity to precalculate a solution, but this is not practical in the dynamic case.

A Taxonomy of Solutions

We will present a range of techniques to solve the radiance calculations. These techniques will differ in the amount of precalculation and storage needed for the results, their limitations and assumptions, and how well the outcomes approximate the correct results. Most of them require too much precalculation to be usable with deformable terrain (we will note the exceptions). Since there are two sources of light—sun and sky—we can split the problem into a 'sunlight-only' subproblem and a 'skylight-only' subproblem. Most of these techniques solve only one of these subproblems, in which case two techniques must be used and the resulting radiances summed.

Some of these solutions involve calculating light values on the CPU and uploading light maps to the graphics card. In this case, care must be taken so that the CPU and bandwidth consumptions are not too high. Since lighting values usually change slowly, we can amortize the update over multiple frames. We experimented with multithreading for a while; however, we ended up with a single-threaded, double-buffering scheme that calculated and uploaded chunks of an active texture while using the previous texture for rendering. When the active texture was complete, we swapped the active and rendering texture and started again.

Sunlight: Horizon Angles,
Shadow Ellipses, and PTMs

The solutions in this section solve the 'sunlight-only' subproblem. Most of the solutions to this subproblem ignore light reflected from other terrain points. Our experience has shown that as long as inter-reflections are taken into account in the skylight subproblem, the results are acceptable. That said, it is preferable to take sunlight inter-reflections into account if possible, and we will show one technique that does so. Without inter-reflections, the sun's contribution to the irradiance at p is

$$E_{sun}(p) = \int_{V \in S \cap H(p)} L_{sun} \, N(p) \cdot V \, d\Omega \qquad (4.14.3)$$

where S is the set of directions that point at the sun. Since the sun's solid angle, ω_{sun}, is small, then we can assume that the result of the dot product is constant, and we get

$$E_{sun}(p) = O_{sun}(p)\omega_{sun}L_{sun}N(p) \cdot V_{sun} \qquad (4.14.4)$$

where V_{sun} is the direction to the sun's center and $O_{sun}(p)$ the percentage of the sun that is outside $H(p)$ or otherwise occluded at p. The two quantities, which vary between terrain points, are the dot product and the occlusion factor. To reduce the cost of calculating the dot product, we quantized the normals of all the terrain points into a 256-entry normal table in a preprocessing stage. Then, for each frame, we calculated the dot product between each entry in the table and the current sun vector. This reduced the dot product calculation for each point to a simple table lookup. Another possibility is to use a normal map and dot3 texture blending in hardware.

There are several methods for calculating the occlusion factor. One of these methods uses *horizon mapping*, which was introduced by Max in [Max88]. This idea is based on storing the horizon angles for each point in a given set of directions (see Figure 4.14.2a). If the sun motion is restricted to an arc that passes through the zenith, then two horizon angles suffice. Given this information, determining whether a point is in shadow or not is simply a matter of comparing the angle of the sun to the horizon angle in that direction. If the sun angle θ is below the horizon angle φ, the point is in shadow ($O_{sun}(p) = 0$). Otherwise, it is not ($O_{sun}(p) = 1$). Soft shadows can be supported by tracking two angles for the sun (θ_{top} and θ_{bottom}, the angles to the sun's top and bottom) and comparing both to the horizon angle. If $\varphi \geq \theta_{top}$, then $O_{sun}(p) = 0$. If $\varphi \leq \theta_{bottom}$, then $O_{sun}(p) = 1$. If $\theta_{top} > \varphi > \theta_{bottom}$, then $O_{sun}(p) = (\theta_{top} - \varphi) / \alpha$, where α is the angular diameter of the sun. We have had good results with storing the horizon angles as 16-bit fixed-point numbers and doing the calculations on the CPU, as well as storing them in 8-bit texture channels and performing the calculations in a pixel shader. For efficiency, the direction along which the horizon angles are defined should correspond to rows in the heightfield array. This will help when calculating horizon angles. You should scan along the heightfield to a fair distance on each side, since hills can cast quite long shadows when the sun is at oblique angles. Note that horizon angles must always be clamped to $H(p)$, or errors will result (see Figure 4.14.2b.).

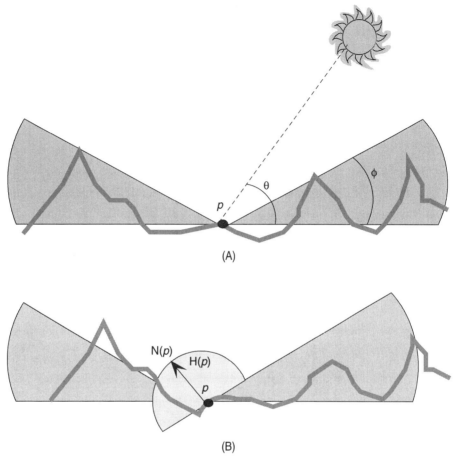

FIGURE 4.14.2   *(A) Terrain profile showing sun angle* θ *and horizon angle* φ. *(B) Horizon angles must be clamped to H(p).*

Of all the sunlight methods, horizon mapping requires the least amount of pre-processing. It would be possible to handle occasional local changes to the heightfield (such as small craters) by recalculating the horizon maps in the affected area and to some distance on both sides.

Occlusion can also be calculated using *shadow ellipses*, introduced in [Heidrich00]. Here an ellipse is fitted to the set of visible angles from each point. This ellipse is parameterized using six numbers, which can be stored in two RGB texture maps. Software, register combiners, or pixel shaders can then be used to evaluate sun occlusion for each point. This method cannot do soft shadows easily. Its main advantage over horizon angles is that it can handle arbitrary sun positions. (See [Heidrich00] for details and [Kautz00] for implementation details using hardware under OpenGL.)

Polynomial texture maps (PTMs), introduced in [Malzbender01], can also be used for evaluating sunlight. This is one of the few techniques that can handle terrain inter-reflections for sunlight. To create a terrain PTM, first render a series of N images of the terrain using a radiosity package, with the sun at several different positions. The sun does not need to move in an arc through the zenith as it does in horizon mapping, but it does need to be restricted to a one-dimensional arc. Use a sun color of RGB(1,1,1). Then process the resulting N images into a single PTM. The first step is to separate the color and luminance values for each image. Then, fit a quadratic uni-variate polynomial $(a_0x^2 + a_1x + a_2)$ to the N luminance values for each pixel, with the sun's position along its arc as the variable. Finally, generate two RGB textures: One stores one color value per pixel (by averaging across all images), and the other stores the three coefficients of the per-pixel luminance polynomials. At runtime, the poly-nomials are evaluated with the current sun position, either in software or in a pixel shader. The result is combined with the color value and modulated with the current sun color. (More details on PTMs are in [Malzbender01], and tools for implementing them are available in the download section of the associated Web site. Note that the paper deals mostly with bivariate polynomials requiring six coefficients, which is more complex and expensive than is needed for the purposes of this gem.)

If lighting conditions depend only on a single variable (like the time of day), it is possible to use PTMs to get the full lighting solution. In this case, a separate polyno-mial will probably need to be stored for each R, G, and B channel to capture the color variations, requiring nine values per pixel instead of six (three + an RGB color).

Skylight: Radiosity Approximations and Patches

The solutions in this section solve the 'skylight-only' subproblem. First, we will han-dle the case where the entire sky is assumed to have the same radiance. This approxi-mation is not as bad as it would seem. We have used it with good results. In this case, all we need to do is calculate the lighting for our terrain with a sky radiance equal to RGB(1,1,1), and then store the result in a RGB texture. At runtime, we multiply this texture with the current RGB sky radiance to get the desired result. The color in the texture will be relatively subtle, since it will result from inter-reflections with the col-ored terrain. If space is at a premium, the texture could be converted to 8 bit-per-pixel grayscale with a small loss in quality.

If precalculation time and space are not a problem, then the best way to generate the skylight texture is to use a radiosity package, with the terrain and a hemispherical distributed light source as input. If this is not practical (for time or space reasons, or because the terrain might change), then there is a useful approximation that can gen-erate a very similar result in far less time. Stewart and Langer found in [Stewart97] that in a scene lit by a diffuse hemispherical illuminator, a point p tends to 'see' other points in the scene that have a similar radiance value. So, we can assume that for all $\mathbf{V}$ in $H(p)$, where another terrain point is visible, $L_i(p, -V) = L_o(p)$. Stewart and Langer showed that the error introduced by this approximation is small. The significance of this is that it breaks the interdependence between different terrain points, enabling us to derive a closed-form expression for $E(p)$. Stewart and Langer have derived a closed form using horizon angles to determine which directions are covered by terrain. Their formulation uses any number of horizon angles. We have had good results with eight (which is a convenient number for computation, since it corresponds to the rows, columns, and diagonals of the heightfield array). Assuming there are eight horizon angles (measured from the vertical, and not from the horizontal, as with sunlight) φ_0, φ_1, φ_2, φ_3, φ_4, φ_5, φ_6, and φ_7, the sky's contribution to the irradiance, including inter-reflections, at p is:

$$E_{\text{sky}}(p) = \frac{L_{\text{sky}} I(p)}{1 - C(p)\left(1 - \dfrac{1}{\pi} I(p)\right)} \tag{4.14.5}$$

$$I(p) = \frac{1}{2} N(p) \cdot \sum_{i=0}^{7} \left(\left(\varphi_i - \frac{\sin 2\varphi_i}{2}\right)\Delta \sin_i \quad \left(\varphi_i - \frac{\sin 2\varphi_i}{2}\right)\Delta \cos_i \quad \frac{\pi}{4} \sin^2 \varphi_i\right) \tag{4.14.6}$$

$$\Delta \sin_i = \sin\left(\frac{\pi}{4}(i+1)\right) - \sin\left(\frac{\pi}{4}i\right) \tag{4.14.7}$$

$$\Delta \cos_i = \cos\left(\frac{\pi}{4}i\right) - \cos\left(\frac{\pi}{4}(i+1)\right) \tag{4.14.8}$$

(For details on the derivation of Equations 4.14.5–8, see either the original paper [Stewart97] or the summary in [Hoffman01].) The horizon angles used here can be scanned to a relatively short distance, unlike those used for sun shadows. Of course, if you are already calculating horizon angles for sunlight shadows, there is no reason not to use those for two out of the eight angles. Since this technique uses relatively little preprocessing, it can also handle occasional minor edits to the heightfield (e.g., small craters) by recalculating the skylight texture in the affected area and a small distance around it.

If assuming a single radiance value for the sky does not produce acceptable results, the sky subproblem can be further broken up into sub-subproblems. For example, the sky could be divided into N patches, and N skylight textures could be calculated, each one based on the terrain being illuminated only by the relevant patch. At runtime, each of the skylight textures is modulated by the radiance of the relevant patch, and the results are summed together. Each of these skylight textures is essentially a basis function for calculating the final skylight solution. These basis functions can be calculated either via radiosity or by Stewart and Langer's method ([Stewart98] derives the necessary math). Another possibility is to use the method in [Sloan 02], which can handle very complex skylight distributions.

Animated Cloud Shadows

Clouds are seldom absent from an outdoor scene, and the shadows cast by clouds are equally important to overall realism. Clouds' shadows are cast onto terrain through the occlusion of light from the sun. With increasing cloud density, sunlight is obscured more, resulting in darker areas on the ground. Therefore, it follows that a simple model of such shadows can be incorporated into a scene by multiplying the inverted cloud density with sunlight and adding the result to the sky's light contribution

$$E(p) = E_{sky}(p) + \left[1 - D(p)\right] E_{sun}(p) \qquad (4.14.9)$$

where $D(p)$ is the cloud density as projected onto the point p. Strictly speaking, the mapping of a cloud to its shadow on the ground is a perspective projection from the sun onto the earth's curved terrain at an angle. However, as the sun's distance is very far relative to the area cast in shadow, it is common to assume a planar projection. A less accurate assumption frequently made in the calculation of texture-mapping coordinates for cloud shadows is that the sun is located vertically above the terrain. This assumption permits optimization by directly applying the ground-plane world-space location (G_{pos}) of terrain vertices to texture coordinates using only scale and bias factors:

$$uv = G_{pos}\ Scale + Offset \qquad (4.14.10)$$

Without this assumption, a more complex texture projection matrix is required, resulting in more cycles per vertex. This per-vertex cost is particularly important with terrain meshes, which involve large numbers of vertices. However, when modeling the change in time of day, the sun's angle should be taken into account in the texture-projection calculation.

With the exception of events like storm clouds and twisters, clouds generally travel in a linear direction. So, animating the movement of clouds is reduced to updating texture offsets in the direction of cloud movement. However, care must be taken in the projection to avoid generating out-of-range texture coordinates.

ON THE CD

On the CD-ROM, a DirectX8 PC cloud-mapping sample demonstrates the use of vertex- and pixel-shading hardware for the method just described. First, the vertex program transforms the world-space vertex position to the screen. Doing this as early as possible is important in order to permit the graphics hardware to determine whether to reject the vertex through clipping.

```
dp4 oPos.x, VPOSITION, c[CV_VIEW_PROJECTION_0]
dp4 oPos.y, VPOSITION, c[CV_VIEW_PROJECTION_1]
dp4 oPos.z, VPOSITION, c[CV_VIEW_PROJECTION_2]
dp4 oPos.w, VPOSITION, c[CV_VIEW_PROJECTION_3]
```

The terrain's color texture is mapped as a planar projection and is performed using the world-space vertex position in the ground plane. This is then scaled and biased using the single multiply add (mad) instruction.

```
mad oT0.xy, VPOSITION.xz, [CV_BASE_TEX_PROJ].xy,
    c[CV_BASE_TEX_PROJ].zw
```

The sunlight texture is mapped in the same way, but the projection is redone, as it is more efficient to recalculate here than to store the result and copy to the output texture register.

```
mad oT1.xy, VPOSITION.xz, c[CV_BASE_TEX_PROJ].xy,
  c[CV_BASE_TEX_PROJ].zw
```

Next, the cloud layer is mapped. Again, this is simply a case of scale and bias operations, with the addition of the animation of the texture offset.

```
mad o T2.xy, VPOSITION.xz, c[CV_CLOUD_TEX_PROJ].xy,
  c[CV_CLOUD_TEX_PROJ].zw
```

The second cloud layer projection is applied to a fourth set of output texture coordinates in the same way, with alternative scale and bias parameters. Note that the only input stream to the vertex program is the world-space location of the vertex. Everything else is generated procedurally from that. This benefits us by reducing the bandwidth to the vertex processor (again this is an important concern with high-density meshes, such as terrains).

In the pixel shader, each texture is combined according to Equation 4.14.9 to yield the final rendered result. After the texture declarations, the average density of the two cloud layers is calculated.

```
add_d2 AVG_CLOUD_DENSITY, TEX_CLOUD_LAYER_0,
  TEX_CLOUD_LAYER_1
```

This is then inverted and multiplied by the contribution from the sunlight texture.

```
mul CLOUD_SHADOW_LUM, TEX_SUNLIGHT,
  1-AVG_CLOUD_DENSITY
```

Next, a constant skylight color factor is multiplied by the terrain texture color.

```
mul SKYLIGHT, TEX_TERRAIN_COLOR, CP_SKYLIGHT
```

Finally, the skylight contribution is added to the shadowed sunlight factor, times the terrain color.

```
mad OUTPUT_REG, CLOUD_SHADOW_LUM, TEX_TERRAIN_COLOR,
  SKYLIGHT
```

For this example, the constant sky radiance factor and sun radiance textures were statically pregenerated using Terragen [Terragen01]. They were extracted from Terragen images using the following methods:

- For the color texture, place the sun vertically above the terrain and disable terrain shadows.
- For the skylight factor, render terrain with a gray surface with sun at an angle, and sample the darkest point in the image.
- For the sunlight texture, subtract the skylight factor from the above image.

The cloud density texture was generated by hand. This texture could also be used to render the clouds themselves.

Video-Based Solution

A brute-force method for generating dynamic terrain lighting is to render canned sequences using an advanced offline rendering tool, then play back the sequence onto a video texture. Any view-independent lighting effects could be represented entirely in the video texture. Certain view-dependent effects, such as fog, might be applied to the video texture with traditional techniques. Furthermore, a novel, detailed bump-map effect can be achieved by applying a lit video texture to the terrain at a smaller scale.

With no time constraints imposed, unlimited complexity could be applied to this solution. However, a serious caveat is the high offline cost of generating video sequences. This time-consuming process must be appropriately budgeted during the developmental process. With that in mind, the remaining challenge of this technique is the efficient playback of video textures in the 3D scene.

PC and console hardwares are moving toward accelerated support for video textures in 3D, albeit at a slower pace than vertex and pixel processing. For example, the image-processing unit (IPU) on the PlayStation2 accelerates decompression of mpeg frames. However, the path that video data must take via the IPU before reaching video memory is somewhat convoluted [Hoffman01]. On the PC, such support is presently orthogonal to textured geometry support in 3D, although advanced video-decompression hardware has existed for some time.

An attractive potential hardware solution would be to decompress a video texture format from video memory prior to the pixel shader stage. This would have the benefits of greatly reduced bandwidth and accelerated decompression.

Nonterrain Objects

A large task to consider when rendering outdoor environments with dynamic lighting is the effect of objects, such as buildings and vehicles, on the terrain. Many methods exist for rendering general shadows in real-time [Haines01], which can be applied to terrain shadows in various situations.

In one technique, *decal shadow texture projection*, the texture is pregenerated (or generated by rendering the shadow to a texture surface) and mapped onto the terrain. A slight z-bias is required to avoid z-buffer conflicts when the projected decal mesh does not match the underlying terrain mesh [McNally99]. This method produces detailed soft shadows, can quickly shadow large numbers of static objects (such as trees), and can easily be integrated with a shadow level-of-detail scheme.

For dynamic objects, techniques range from drop shadows to stencil- and shadow-buffer methods. The choice depends on hardware performance and constraints. However, the need for fast projection onto an arbitrary terrain mesh is common among these methods. This can be optimized by assuming an axis-aligned sun position and, in the case of a heightfield, an axis-aligned mesh.

Conclusion

We have presented various methods for achieving photorealistic, quality terrain lighting under changing lighting conditions in real-time. For an example of photorealistic terrain lighting in real-time, see Plate 10. The methods have differing tradeoffs and characteristics in order to fit different types of games, platforms, and development pipelines. If you are developing a game with outdoor environments, we hope at least one of these methods will prove useful.

References

[Debevec98] Debevec, Paul, "Rendering Synthetic Objects into Real Scenes: Bridging Traditional and Image-Based Graphics with Global Illumination and High Dynamic Range Photography," Computer Graphics Proceedings (SIGGRAPH 1998), pp. 189–198.

[Haines01] Haines, Eric, et al., "Real-time Shadows," GDC 2001 Conference Proceedings, also available online at http://www.gdconf.com/archives/proceedings/2001/haines.pdf.

[Heidrich00] Heidrich, Wolfgang, et al., "Illuminating Micro Geometry Based on Precomputed Visibility," Computer Graphics Proceedings (SIGGRAPH 2000): pp. 455–464. Also available online at http://www.cs.ubc.ca/~heidrich/Papers/.

[Hoffman01] Hoffman, Naty, et al., "Photorealistic Terrain Lighting in Real-Time," *Game Developer Magazine* (July 2001): pp. 32–41.

[Kautz00] Kautz, Jan, et al., "Bump Map Shadows for OpenGL Rendering," available online at http://www.mpi-sb.mpg.de/~jnkautz/projects/shadowbumpmaps/.

[Malzbender01] Malzbender, Tom, et al., "Polynomial Texture Maps," Computer Graphics Proceedings (SIGGRAPH 2001): pp. 519–528. Also available online at http://www.hpl.hp.com/ptm/.

[Max88] Max, Nelson, "Horizon Mapping: Shadows for Bump-Mapped Surfaces," *The Visual Computer* (July 1988): pp. 109–177.

[McNally99] McNally, Seamus, "Treadmarks Engine." Phone conversation available online at http://www.vterrain.org/.

[Sloan02] Sloan, Peter-Pike, et al., "Pre computed Radiance Transfer for Real-Time Rendering in dynamic, Low-Frequency Lighting Environments," to appear, Proceedings of SIGGRAPH2002. Available online at http://research.microsoft.com/~ppsloan/.

[Stewart97] Stewart, James, et al., "Towards accurate recovery of shape from shading under diffuse lighting," *IEEE Transactions on Pattern Analysis and Machine Intelligence* (September 1997): pp. 1020–1025. Also available online at http://www.cs.queensu.ca/home/jstewart/papers/.

[Stewart98] Stewart, James, "Fast horizon computation at all points of a terrain with visibility and shading applications," *IEEE Transactions on Visualization and Computer Graphics* (March 1998): pp. 82–93. Also available online at http://www.cs.queensu.ca/home/jstewart/papers/.

[Terragen01] Fairclough, Matt, "Terragen." Software available online at http://www.planetside.co.uk/terragen.

4.15

Cube Map Lighting Techniques

Kenneth L. Hurley, NVIDIA Corporation

khurley@nvidia.com

Cube maps were introduced to game developers in DirectX7. In 1999, NVIDIA introduced the Geforce 256 and brought cube maps to the mass PC gamer market. Until now, they had been mainly used to render shiny objects. However, the cube map can be used in more-interesting ways. This gem will describe some ways to encode different lighting conditions as well as other properties within cube maps. It will give a brief overview of the properties of cube maps and how to index into them. Some references for fallback methods will also be given. This gem is DirectX-centric, but the same principles can be applied to OpenGL.

Physical Properties of Cube Maps

Cube maps are represented as six textures in hardware. Each texture represents a side of a cube. Normally, code is written so that a reflection vector is used to index into the cube map. A three-component vector is then passed into the hardware, which gives the hardware the information needed to pick the correct face and select the *uv* coordinates for that face (Figure 4.15.1). The hardware uses the longest component of the three components to select the face. For instance, if the vectors (0.4f, 0.5f, 0.7f) were passed into the hardware, it would select the positive *z* face of the cube map, since 0.7 is the largest component. The hardware would then use the other two components (0.4f, 0.5f) to select the *uv* coordinates. One difference between cube maps and regular texture addressing is that the *uv* coordinates are signed values, and the texture is addressed such that the center of the cube face is *uv* coordinate (0, 0). Normal texture mapping uses the upper-left corner as the (0, 0) *uv* coordinate.

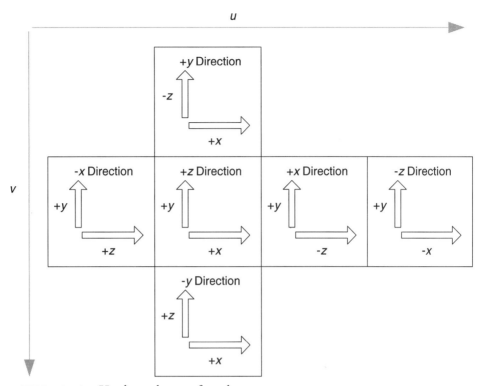

FIGURE 4.15.1 *Hardware layout of a cube map.*

How To Get Data to/from a Cube Map

Loading cube maps in DirectX8 can be accomplished in several ways. The easiest way to create a .dds cube map file is to use Microsoft's DirectX Texture Tool, which is included with DirectX8. The following code demonstrates loading a cube map from a .dds file.

```
LPDIRECT3DCUBETEXTURE8 m_pCloudTexture;

D3DXCreateCubeTextureFromFile(m_pD3DDev, "cloudtex.dds",
    &m_pCloudTexture));
```

Make sure to use D3DXCreateCubeTextureFromFile and not D3DXCreateTexture-FromFile with a LPDIRECT3DTEXTURE8 pointer, as DirectX8 will accept the call, but strange results will occur upon rendering. To render the selected texture, simply set the texture in one of the texture stages. The following code is a sample of how to do this.

```
m_pD3DDev->SetTexture(0,(LPDIRECT3DBASETEXTURE8)m_pCloudTexture);
```

Another way to load the texture is from six individual bitmap files. This requires a call to D3DXCreateCubeTexture to create the cube map texture and then a call to

GetCubeMapSurface for each face of the cube map. Alternatively, the texture maps can be loaded with one of the D3DXLoadSurface* functions.

Rendering with the Cube Map

Setting up the 3D texture coordinates for a cube map can be done in one of several ways. Prior to DirectX8, a programmer would use code similar to the following to set up rendering of cube maps:

```
for( LONG i = 0; i < cV; i++ )
{
    // eye vector (doesn't need to be normalized)
    FLOAT fENX = m_vEyePt.x - pVIn->v.x;
    FLOAT fENY = m_vEyePt.y - pVIn->v.y;
    FLOAT fENZ = m_vEyePt.z - pVIn->v.z;

    FLOAT fNDotE = pVIn->v.nx*fENX + pVIn->v.ny*fENY +
                   pVIn->v.nz*fENZ;
    FLOAT fNDotN = pVIn->v.nx*pVIn->v.nx + pVIn->v.ny*pVIn->v.ny +
                   pVIn->v.nz*pVIn->v.nz;
    fNDotE *= 2.0;

    // reflected vector
    pVIn->v.tu = pVIn->v.nx*fNDotE - fENX*fNDotN;
    pVIn->v.tv = pVIn->v.ny*fNDotE - fENY*fNDotN;
    pVIn->nz = pVIn->v.nz*fNDotE - fENZ*fNDotN;

    pVIn++;
}
```

This code calculates the reflection vector on a per-vertex basis and places the vector into the 3D texture coordinates that are to be passed to the hardware.

DirectX8 introduced a new method for dealing with cube maps. Vertex buffers can now be set up to use either the fixed function pipeline or vertex and pixel shaders. The fixed function pipeline of DirectX8 is very similar to that of DirectX7. It can be set up by specifying texture stage states and render states, with the cube map-specific render states for the fixed function pipeline being D3DRS_LOCALVIEWER and D3DRS_NORMALIZENORMALS. The texture stage state that needs to be considered is D3DTSS_TEXCOORDINDEX. For this gem, the D3DTSS_TCI_PASSTHRU texture stage state value is the focus. This instructs the hardware to use the texture coordinates directly without transforming them in any way.

In DirectX8 and above, vertex shaders can be used to change the normal based on a rotation. The vertex shader then puts the normal into the output texture coordinate that corresponds to the texture stage where the cube map was selected. The following code snippet demonstrates how to do this.

```
;transform normal, put into texture coordinate output
dp3 oT0.x, srcNormal, c[CV_ROTATION_X]
dp3 oT0.y, srcNormal, c[CV_ROTATION_Y]
dp3 oT0.z, srcNormal, c[CV_ROTATION_Z]
```

Encoding Cloud Cover

Encoding cloud cover into a cube map is not as straightforward as it might at first appear. Fractional Brownian motion (fBm) and Perlin noise [Perlin85] are used extensively to create 2D cloud textures. This technique works quite well and allows the regular textures to tile seamlessly; however, these images cannot be loaded into cube maps without apparent seams. The reason for these seams is that the edges of the 2D image only match with parallel edges. The top and bottom edges will only match with each other, but not with the side edges, since they do not tile with the top or bottom edges. This poses a problem for cube maps, since all the edges must match in order to prevent seams. The solution is to use a 3D fBm or Perlin noise function to encode the clouds into a cube map. The following code will do this.

```
D3DXVECTOR3 tVec;

// now loop through each pixel of the cube map, gathering the fBm
for (i=0; i<CUBEMAP_TOTAL_DIR; i++)
{
    dest = m_CubeFacesData[i];
    for (pos.y=0; pos.y < m_CubeSize.cy; pos.y++)
    {
        for (pos.x = 0; pos.x < m_CubeSize.cx; pos.x++)
        {
            GetCubeVector(i, &pos, &m_CubeSize, &tVec);
            *dest++ = fBm(tVec);
        }
    }
}


//========================================================================
// Function:    GetCubeVector
// Description: returns a 3 vector given a from an x,y, face of a cube
//                       map
// Parameters:  face = face of cube map to calculate vector from
//              tInfo = x,y, width and height of cube map face texture
//              vecOut = 3 vector pointer for output
// Returns:     pointer to vecOut
//========================================================================
D3DXVECTOR3 *CCubeMapDoc::GetCubeVector(DWORD face, const CPoint *pos,
                            const CSize *size, D3DXVECTOR3 *vecOut)
{
    float s, t, sc, tc;

    // move pixels to center
    s = ((float) pos->x + 0.5f) / (float) size->cx;
    t = ((float) pos->y + 0.5f) / (float) size->cy;
    sc = s*2.0f - 1.0f;
    tc = t*2.0f - 1.0f;

    switch (face)
    {
    case CUBEMAP_POS_X:
        vecOut->x = 1.0f;
```

```
            vecOut->y = -tc;
            vecOut->z = -sc;
            break;
        case CUBEMAP_NEG_X:
            vecOut->x = -1.0f;
            vecOut->y = -tc;
            vecOut->z = sc;
            break;
        case CUBEMAP_POS_Y:
            vecOut->x = sc;
            vecOut->y = 1.0f;
            vecOut->z = tc;
            break;
        case CUBEMAP_NEG_Y:
            vecOut->x = sc;
            vecOut->y = -1.0f;
            vecOut->z = -tc;
            break;
        case CUBEMAP_POS_Z:
            vecOut->x = sc;
            vecOut->y = -tc;
            vecOut->z = 1.0f;
            break;
        case CUBEMAP_NEG_Z:
            vecOut->x = -sc;
            vecOut->y = -tc;
            vecOut->z = -1.0f;
            break;
    }

    D3DXVec3Normalize(vecOut, vecOut);
    return vecOut;
}
```

To use this cube map for a sky sphere, create a sphere that is representative of the world's atmosphere and use the coordinates as lookups into the cube map. There is no need to normalize the coordinates, since the lookup into the cube map does not require a normalized vector. Here is a code snippet for a vertex shader that demonstrates this technique.

```
vs.1.1

;transform position
    dp4 oPos.x, srcPosition, c[CV_WORLDVIEWPROJ_0]
    dp4 oPos.y, srcPosition, c[CV_WORLDVIEWPROJ_1]
    dp4 oPos.z, srcPosition, c[CV_WORLDVIEWPROJ_2]
    dp4 oPos.w, srcPosition, c[CV_WORLDVIEWPROJ_3]

; Output texture coordinates
    mov destTexCoord, srcPosition
```

Animating the clouds is fairly straightforward. Using DirectX8, rotate the sky sphere using a rotation matrix passed into the vertex shader.

A side benefit of encoding the clouds in a cube map is that shadows from the clouds can be drawn onto the terrain. The alpha can be encoded with the inverse grayscale image of the clouds, minus the sky color. The color can also be obtained in a pixel shader by taking one minus the color from the original cloud cube map. The positions for the terrain are used as indices into the cube map, and the alpha component is used to darken the terrain. This has the added benefit of creating soft shadows from your preblended clouds with semitransparent edges. The lighting calculations for the terrain, with regards to the sun, could also be altered by using this value. For instance, the light calculation can be blended with half of the alpha channel values, giving the effect of semitransparent clouds.

Encoding Lights in a Cube Map

Static and dynamic lights can be encoded in a cube map in a number of ways. Infinite static lights, like the sun, can be prerendered into the cube map using the techniques described to index into the cube map. The normal of the vertex is used to index into the cube map and retrieve the light that is rendered into the cube map. This works well for infinite static lights, but not for dynamic lights. Dynamic lighting usually requires multiple texture passes. The idea is to render the moving lights into the cube map by using a 90° field of view and pointing the camera at each side of the cube. The camera position to render from would be the position of the object that is being lit. This technique would work well for rendering a scene that had, for example, a disco ball where there could be 100 lights or so in the scene. Rendering the disco room and objects in the room could be accomplished using this technique. The cube maps do not have to be very big for this technique to work convincingly, so keep this in mind when calculating the rendering time.

Encoding Diffuse Lighting in a Cube Map

Diffuse maps can also be incorporated into scenes with many lights by using the above code that traversed through a cube map to build the cloud texture. For each uv coordinate on a face of a cube map, a vector n (normal) is calculated. For vector n, another vector l (light) is calculated from each uv coordinate of each cube face. These two vectors are used in a dot product operation to determine the cosine of the angle between the two vectors. This is the same calculation used in standard vertex lighting. If the result of the dot product is negative, it is safe to assume that vector l is not contributing to vector n. Otherwise, the result of the dot product is the weighting factor that is used to blend the pixels of the cube map together. The pixels chosen for the blending operation are from the uv coordinates that were used to calculate the two vectors n and l. This, in essence, samples a hemisphere of pixels centered about vector n. The cube map in Figure 4.15.2 is the result of this sampling. To use this cube map for lighting, the sample should be gamma corrected, as some range is lost in the conversion into low dynamic range.

FIGURE 4.15.2   *Encoded diffuse cube map.*

Encoding of a specular map can be accomplished in much the same way as the diffuse map by following the same guidelines for traversing the cube map and sampling each direction as before. Instead of taking a dot product for the weighting of the two vectors, take the nth root of the dot product, where n is specified as the specular exponent. Some user interaction will have to occur for this phase, as the specular exponent varies on a material-by-material basis.

Encoding a Day/Night Cycle into the Cube Map

Day/night cycles can also be used with the cloud cube map by using the technique described to create a cloud cube map and only encoding the grayscale portions of the clouds. When lighting the sky sphere, clamp the dot product with a value that represents the lowest point on the horizon that changes color. The sky color is passed to the pixel shader as part of the lighting calculation, and, as the sun rotates, the color of the sky sphere can be changed by writing the color to vertex memory. As the sun approaches the horizon, the sky color can be ramped from blue to orange. After the sun passes the horizon, simply ramp the colors, based on time, from orange to black. The nice thing about clamping the dot product is that any color can be picked based on the clamp value.

Conclusion

Cube maps can be used for a wide variety of effects besides rendering shiny reflective objects. This gem describes some more-interesting uses for cube maps. Note that hardware that doesn't support cube maps can still take advantage of these techniques by using sphere maps or dual-paraboloid maps [Heidrich99]. In this case, the calculations will have to be done using texture coordinate generation or using the CPU to calculate the *uv* coordinates.

The source code for a few demonstrations of the described techniques can be found on the CD-ROM. An animated cloud cube map over terrain and the diffuse lighting (envlight.nvp) code snippet are included. Also, see Color Plate 11.

References

[Debevec97] Debevec, Paul E. and Jitendra Malik, "Recovering High Dynamic Range Radiance Maps from Photographs," (SIGGRAPH 1997): pp. 369–378.

[Elias02] Elias, Hugo, "Perlin Noise," available online at http://freespace.virgin.net/ hugo.elias/models/m_perlin.htm, January 5, 2002.

[Heidrich99] Heidrich, Wolfgang and Hans-Peter Seidel, "Realistic, Hardware-Accelerated Shading and Lighting," Computer Graphics Proceedings (SIGGRAPH 1999): pp. 171–178.

[Perlin85] Perlin, Ken, "An Image Synthesizer," *Computer Graphics Proceedings* (SIGGRAPH 1985): pp. 287–296.

4.16

Procedural Texturing

Mike Milliger, 2015, Inc.

mikem@2015.com

Procedural texturing is an area of research that includes topics ranging from Fourier synthesis to stochastic models to creating textures based on chemical gradients. Darwyn Peachy, in *Texturing & Modeling*, defines procedural as a way "to distinguish entities that are described by program code rather than by data structures [Ebert98]." In the context of games and this gem, we are mainly concerned with the ability to map a texture image onto a surface through mathematical functions.

Whenever discussing procedural texture mapping with artists, almost invariably their first response is, "So, you are trying to put me out of a job?" All the content creators can put their sharp objects down; in the end, hand-painted textures will always look better than pure texture synthesis done through the use of programs. Using a procedural system exclusively for a title would not only be inefficient task-wise for a balanced development team, but the system would also be inadequate from an aesthetic point of view. A combination of procedural and traditional methods will strengthen the artwork of a game and make the game environment look more natural. Not only can we generate unique, new textures with procedures, we can manipulate the various properties (color, location, aspect ratio, etc.) of pregenerated images. The goal of this gem is to introduce basic concepts for using procedures to manipulate and synthesize images for games and to give simple guidelines for implementation.

Parameters and Procedures

The creation of a procedural texture requires two elements—a procedure that will be used to generate the texture and the parameters that control this procedure.

Parameters

Parameters passed into generating procedures guide the outcome of the texture. Manipulating variables in mathematical functions generally creates the variations in procedural textures. Much as an audio engineer mixes sound signals by using a variety of electronic processing gear, the visual-effects artist manipulates a variety of signal generators and processing functions to create a unique texture. Often, we use the same terminology. Signals (or base textures) are generated at various wavelengths and are filtered and blended through a variety of controls. Common parameters for procedural algorithms include terms like "frequency," "amplitude," and "bias." However, instead of manipulating sound, these functions are used to manipulate texture properties, such as color values and translucency.

Procedures

The majority of procedural effects used in games have been based on Ken Perlin's family of procedural algorithms, known as "noise." A pseudo-random number generator (PRNG) is at the heart of most noise procedures, and this randomness helps generate natural-looking effects. Noise is the workhorse of procedural textures and the most-applicable and widely used type of procedure for games. There are many derivations of noise—value noise, gradient noise, value-gradient noise, lattice convolution, and sparse convolution. All of these procedures are variations on the idea of turning pseudo-random numbers into sources of textures for graphic images [Macri00]. The PRNG generates a lattice. A lattice refers to an n-dimensional, smoothed grid of uniformly distributed points in texture space, each containing a random number (float). The spacing of these points determines the frequency. Several sources of noise of different frequency can be combined together. Each of these noise sources (or octaves) can be added together to form a final image using various mathematical methods. These methods are then fine-tuned to create specific effects. For example, Kim Pallister's gem in *Game Programming Gems 2* [Pallister01] explains how to use noise to generate dynamic, procedural clouds by summing octaves into turbulent noise.

Noise algorithms are a direct method for the creation of a procedural texture source. Another method for texture generation takes a texture source and evolves it over time using an algorithmic procedure. One such procedure is cellular automaton [Macri00]. When used to generate procedural textures, an initial texture is divided into a number of discrete samples called "cells" or "texels." The color at every texel in the image defines the current state of the cellular automaton system. At every iteration of the procedure, each texel in the texture is modified according to a set of rules. These rules generally involve setting each texel to be the weighted average of a specified set of the neighboring texels. Using these simple systems, a great variety of effects can be achieved. For example, setting each cell's value to be the averaged value of the neighbor cells beneath it can simulate a fire effect. At each iteration of the system, the virtual flames in the texture spread upward [Macri00].

Iterative procedures, such as cellular automaton, complement direct methods, like the noise functions. For example, a pseudo-random noise procedure can generate a group of randomly scattered points that can then be used as the initial system state for the iterative algorithm.

Focusing on Games

Procedural texturing techniques have been used in a variety of computer graphics applications, such as scientific visualization and visual effects. This gem is focused on the use of these techniques in game applications.

Uses of Procedural Textures

Procedural texturing is still in the early stages as far as prime-time game development is concerned. Most of the effects in past games have been simple water or fire effects. However, procedural texturing excels at representations of natural phenomena and can be used to generate textures for wood, marble, snow, grass, stars, or volumetric effects, such as clouds [Pallister01]. These are exactly the type of surfaces that are commonly needed in game projects.

A generated texture can be used in a static manner much like any other form of texture. By using the texture-transformation capabilities of modern graphics hardware, the texture can be moved over the image's surface. A series of textures can be generated and then played back as an animated texture. This is a common practice in many games. However, a predictable pattern can often be seen on the surface, and the effect is easily spotted when the animation repeats. To some extent, this takes the viewer out of the immersion of the game. The real power of procedural textures is achieved when the textures are generated in real-time within the game project. Because the procedures are mathematical and with endless variation, repetitive cycles are eliminated.

In addition to their use as color source material, procedural textures can be used as bump, diffuse, specular, or dynamic environment maps in multitexture systems. A procedural texture could be used to show cracks or dents in a surface by perturbing the texture space normals using a function. Diffuse mapping with noise can break up large areas of solid color and show unevenness (large areas of solid color tend to stand out and look fake). Fractal terrain is often a noise image used as a heightfield (displacement map) on a dense mesh. Many outdoor engines use this technique to generate the geometry for unique terrain instead of storing all the data. Since the noise image is made by a seeded PRNG, the terrain can be generated again into the same shape if the player returns to the same area.

Advantages of Procedural Textures

There are many advantages to using procedural textures in your game. The decision to use them often boils down to a classic problem in computer science: the trade-off between computation time and memory size. Even though it takes processor time to build the texture, there is virtually no memory footprint. Also, procedural textures are not limited by bandwidth constraints. There is no need to continually load and reference texture memory for pixel colors. Since the texture is regenerated every frame, there is no reduction in the fidelity of the image. This is especially beneficial in first-person games where the view can move extremely close to a surface. A bark texture on a tree could be regenerated each frame as a player moves toward the tree, increasing in detail as the view moves closer.

While most procedures are written in highly optimized assembly code, rendering scenes with a lot of different procedural textures will lower the frame rate. We can have a large number of surfaces that utilize procedures in a single level, as long as most of them are not visible at the same time. It is simple to cull textures that do not appear on the screen and to skip the calculations. Procedural textures lend themselves to reuse, and we can use the same texture for multiple objects, like a fire procedure for all the torches in a hallway. Although procedures are hard to debug, given their lack of control and randomness, this can also be the source of pleasant surprises (serendipity) [Ebert98]. Even so, procedures can be controlled to some extent by parameters that change the outcome texture rather than being limited to a fixed image.

Procedural textures can be one-, two-, or three-dimensional. Three-dimensional textures serve as new tools for artists and programmers to create effects. A procedurally generated, three-dimensional texture will allow a plane, intersecting at any angle with the volume (color space), to be textured appropriately and in relation to the rest of the color space. This technique is also known as "solid texturing." The color space incorporates the use of a 3D array of color values for texturing, and the textured object is placed within this color space. Destructible environments are becoming more common in games, and solid texturing will amplify the reality of objects in the scene. Imagine a pillar mapped with procedurally generated marble getting caught on the wrong end of a rocket launcher and blown into large chunks. Not only will the inside of the remaining pillar be mapped with the continuous veins of marble, the chunks blown off of the pillar will be mapped as well, as long as they are in the color space. Believable caustics and clouds can also be achieved with this technique. Procedural textures have no fixed area and can cover arbitrary-size areas without repetitions and seams. To add detail for large areas, increase the number of octaves in the procedure.

Getting Procedural Textures in the Game

There are two basic types of procedural textures that can be used in your game: real-time and pregenerated. Pregenerated procedural textures can be made in content applications such as Lightwave or Photoshop, or in a professional procedural texture package such as DarkTree, and then mapped in the traditional method (losing some benefits of calculating them in real-time). DarkTree allows users to modify parameters visually by piping functions into each other, generating different effects. Results are displayed in real-time, giving the user instant feedback about the effect. Animated textures can also be saved out on a frame-by-frame basis.

If you want to implement a real-time procedural system in your game engine, then there are some general heuristics that will be helpful. The first step is to create a solid workflow that is fairly simple. A top priority should be to make it simple for noncoder types. An authoring tool with sliders and an instant previewing window is more than worth the effort of writing it. The key is to allow content creators to continue doing what they do best, making art instead of typing arcane parameters in a text editor. The authoring tool should save out the parameters and procedure name for the surface to a shader file; and when the level or area loads, the parameters generated by the tool are passed into the procedure when drawing the surface. Assign reasonable defaults to surfaces that can be overridden if values exist for the surface description.

In the future, games can look forward to a more Renderman-like environment for texturing and shading. Most game engines already have, or are moving toward, shader systems. A standardized, shading language for games would allow a clean method for defining parameters and applying functions to materials.

Other Uses for Procedural Functions

While this gem mainly focuses on image synthesis, most procedural techniques can be extended to other aspects of game development. We have already discussed using noise to make terrain. When it comes to animation, a user could apply noise to IK-based death animation so that several bad guys that die in the same room do not end up in the same death pose. When using morph targets, add a noise weight to the vertices in order to get different results, such as random blinking or variable tail flips on dolphins. Perlin has demonstrated the use of noise for generating facial expressions [Ebert98]. Procedural modeling is an increasing area of interest for game designers, especially for memory-challenged architectures. Trees and their branches could be procedurally spawned, resulting in a variety of vegetation without the need to store massive amounts of geometry.

Hardware Acceleration

Calculating the texture during runtime on a per-pixel basis takes a lot of computational time. Having the majority of per-pixel work done by the graphics hardware instead of the main processor is one way to offset the computational cost of procedural calculations. Now, with the latest consumer graphics hardware, we can have real-time procedural textures in games without a large performance hit on the main processor. If you don't have the graphics chipset that can handle per-pixel operations and coloring effects, then the calculations will take place on the main processor.

The main issue for real-time generation of procedural textures is the ability of the graphics hardware to render directly to a surface. This can be done with capable hardware using either Direct 3D or OpenGL. As an example, a pseudo-random function can be used to create several source noise textures of various frequencies. These source noise textures can then be combined by rendering them to a surface using the available hardware blending and filtering modes. On graphics hardware that supports multitexture rendering, several textures can be combined in a single pass. The results of these operations can then be used as a texture that is applied to an object in the game scene.

Beyond this kind of direct, procedural texture creation, it is even possible to create iterative cellular automaton system directly in hardware. Using hardware that supports blending four simultaneous textures, and feeding the results back into the system, effects such as animated fire and water can be generated [James01].

Conclusion

Procedural texturing is a powerful and flexible way to generate new textures and modify existing textures. The techniques have not found their way into a lot of games, even though procedures would strengthen the artwork of a game. This is mainly due to the time necessary to perform the per-pixel operations needed to generate the texture. With consumer-level hardware now able to perform pixel operations on the graphics chipset, which frees up the main processor, we should see more procedurally generated effects in future games. There is no doubt that the most popular families of procedures, noise and cellular systems, will be leading the way.

The included sample demonstration code from Simon Green (NVIDIA) shows the use of graphics hardware to create dynamic procedural 3D textures. It uses a single precomputed 3D noise texture, which is accessed multiple times using the texture matrix to control the frequency and the register combiners to weight and sum each layer and produce the final color.

The 3D texture is 64×64×64 texels in size and uses the single-channel 'luminance' format, and therefore consumes only 256 KB of memory. It is interesting to note that although the period of this texture is relatively small, it is surprisingly difficult to see any repeating patterns once the octaves have been combined together. The novel part of this technique is that the noise texture is prefiltered using a cubic filter. This helps avoid some of the artifacts that would occur if we just used a texture with random texels and let the hardware linearly interpolate between them. It also allows us to precompute the absolute function that is needed for the Perlin 'turbulence' function.

To produce the final fractal noise pattern, we use four or more 3D texture lookups for the noise texture. Each layer is known as an octave, since the frequency typically doubles each time, just as in a musical scale. We use the texture matrix to scale each set of texture coordinates and thereby increase the spatial frequency for each octave, but this could also be done easily using a vertex program. Interesting animated effects can also be created by translating or rotating the texture coordinates of each layer at different rates. This is much cheaper than actual four-dimensional noise would be. The best results seem to be achieved when the speed of animation for each octave is proportional to the spatial frequency.

Finally, the register combiners are used to weight the value from each octave by the correct amplitude and sum the contributions of all the octaves together. Once we have the final (scalar) summed noise value, there are various ways to produce a color from this. For simple coloring effects, the register combiners can be used to interpolate between two or more colors based on the noise value, but for more nonlinear patterns (such as veined marble), we can use a color table. One way to achieve this involves rendering the scene to a texture, and then in a second pass, drawing a screen-aligned quad using the `dependent_gb` texture shader and a one-dimensional texture that maps the noise values to colors. The alpha test function of the graphics hardware can also be used to discard pixels that are above or below a certain threshold, creating interesting 'corroded' looks. Future programmable hardware will be able to do this (and more) in a single pass and provide much more flexible procedural texturing possibilities.

Acknowledgments

Thanks to Simon Green and NVIDIA for providing the demonstration code and Color Plates 12 and 13.

References

[Ebert98] Ebert, David, et al., *Texturing & Modeling*, Second Edition, AP Professional, 1998.

[James01] James, Greg, "Operations for Hardware-Accelerated Procedural Texture Animation," *Game Programming Gems 2*, Charles River Media, Inc., 2001. Demos available online at http://developer.nvidia.com.

[Macri00] Macri, Dean, and Kim Pallister, "Procedural 3D Content Generation," available online at http://cedar.intel.com/, February 8, 2001.

[Pallister01] Pallister, Kim, "Generating Procedural Clouds Using 3D Hardware," *Game Programming Gems 2*, Charles River Media, Inc., 2001.

4.17

Unique Textures

Tom Forsyth, Mucky Foot

tomf@muckyfoot.com

In the real world, no two surfaces are the same. They have a myriad of tiny differences—wood grain, surface texture, dirt marks, scuffs, faded paint, footprints, graffiti, and so forth. Nevertheless, computer games reuse the same textures over and over again. In the past, this was done for practical reasons. Video memory was in short supply, and using a different texture for each surface in a scene would have caused excessive paging in and out of textures, even for static views.

Now, video memory is relatively cheap and plentiful, but there are new problems. We demand higher-resolution textures, which chew memory at a prodigious rate. Also, we are creating such mammoth worlds to play in that no single team of artists could possibly create unique data for every surface, even if there was the disk space to store them all.

Many of these problems can be solved by generating textures in a more procedural way, rather than relying on the hand of the artist to generate every single texel. The core idea that we will explore in this gem is how to use a relatively small number of artist-generated source textures and combine them at runtime using a variety of blends, fractal methods, and random numbers to create the textures required for the scene.

Procedural Textures

As described in Mike Milliger's gem in this section [Milliger02], the use of procedural textures allows artists to do less actual pixel-pushing, and start generating *descriptions* of classes of surfaces. These descriptions can then be applied to large areas of levels and multiple objects in that level. Because the descriptions use pseudo-random numbers for some of their values, each instance will be slightly different in exact appearance, just as they are in real life. The important thing is to allow the artists to take back full control at any stage of the process—for certain important items, they will want to lock down a finished article and not have it change in any way. However, for almost all the terrain and scenery in a game world, this rigid control is not necessary.

Because each surface's texture is uniquely generated, each one can adapt to the geometry of the object it is mapped onto. The most obvious benefit is that texture seams vanish—continuous textures, such as rock or wood, can flow smoothly and continuously around any geometry. Artists frequently struggle with conventional methods, and it is hard to hide seams while avoiding excessive texel distortion. Also, exposed corners can be scuffed, concealed corners can gather dirt, and surfaces exposed to the sun will be bleached.

Smart Texture Caching

At the heart of a typical graphics system is a texture cache. The graphics system can then composite the various source textures together in cunning ways to create the final result. In some cases, this composition might be complex and slow, so it is important to avoid cache thrashing in order to be compatible with 'dumb but fast' caches (e.g., the Direct3D texture cache).

If you expect or find the texture cache to be relatively slow, some simple refinements can be made to improve performance. For example, you can work out the highest-resolution mipmap level that will be required for a given texture on an object. This is usually as simple as dividing a constant (calculated offline) by the object's distance and taking the base-2 logarithm. This gives a conservative estimate and assumes that the texture will be viewed perpendicular to the viewer's line of sight. More-aggressive estimates that take viewer/surface orientation into account can be made, but they are more expensive (for example, on a curved surface, it is likely that some part of the texture will always be roughly perpendicular to the viewer).

Composition Model

The simplest method is the Photoshop 'stack' method—a series of RGBA layers, each with a source texture, composited on top of the last result with a type of blend. However, any useful blending controlled by random numbers requires a more-complex system based on a tree of blends, not just a single stack. In addition, you are often required to composite together many alpha channels and then do a color blend using the resulting alpha channel. Since these alpha channel-only blends are common, there needs to be an explicit way of labeling layers and blends as alpha-only to ensure that full 32-bit RGBA textures are not used all the time—thus, ensuring more-efficient memory access.

The tree model is only required for a tenth of the blends in most cases. We will refer to layers and blends between them, rather than tree nodes and leaves, regardless of the internal representation.

Layer Mapping and Transforms

The most fundamental aspect of a layer is its mapping onto the geometry. This is usually determined by the 3D package: either by explicit *uv* mapping, or by some sort of planar or spherical projection. This includes the layers representing source textures, the intermediate layers, and, most importantly, the target layer—the texture that will be generated by the composition and actually passed to the graphics chip to texture the image.

The mapping of the source and target layers do not need to have any relationship to each other. Frequently, a single source will be mapped over a join between two or more target textures, ensuring a smooth transition between the two. Typically, data on source layers and for mapping will be determined per-vertex rather than per-triangle, which allows textures to be combined to flow continuously over any surface shape. In many cases, at a particular vertex, some layers will be discontinuous (such as paint schemes on walls or vehicles), while others will be continuous (such as dirt or scratch marks). When designing the data structures, it is important to remember that in most cases, an object cannot simply be partitioned into different materials with one texture per material. Once the composition is done and the target textures are generated, this is precisely what happens to the data that is passed to the low-level mesh rendering system, but this model does not work at a higher level.

In addition to raw layer *uv* mapping data, additional data can be held at each vertex. This data can control aspects of the blends performed and will usually be linearly interpolated between the vertices. For example, the random numbers that control a blend might be biased and scaled by values held at each vertex; this way the artist can label some vertices as more dirty or less dirty, rougher or smoother, and so on. Getting these values into the 3D model is a problem that some 3D packages do not handle very well (vertex coloring is poorly supported, and multiple channels can be even trickier). In some cases, these values might need to be encoded into another texture layer instead and possibly converted to per-vertex values later by a preprocessing stage.

Layers can also have their *uv* mappings perturbed or determined by various other methods. For example, rotations, scales, skews, and so on are all possible (usually controlled by random numbers), as are hard-coded complex methods—for example, a brick wall might be generated by compositing many individual source bricks, each brick taken randomly from a selection of 20 or so. In this case, the source of the brick is a random number, quantized to 20 positions, and the destination is the staggered-brick pattern of the wall. This would normally be done with two transforms, one to shift the chosen source brick to the upper-left corner and one to shift it into the correct position on the target texture. At runtime, the two would be combined in an overall *uv* transformation before any texels were actually read.

Layer Sources and Filters

The layers can be derived from a variety of methods. For example, the artist can supply a bitmap, or procedural data, such as Perlin noise [Perlin], or cellular automata (CA) to generate moss or wood grain [Ebert94]. All the parameters for these various methods can be derived from per-pixel or per-vertex factors supplied by the artists or from pseudo-random numbers derived from the supplied information.

The sources can also be filtered. The most usual filter is a simple scale and bias on the RGB or alpha values, especially when applied to noise functions or other similar remappings, such as sigmoid curves or step functions. Interpolating splines of 1° to 4° can be useful and give the artist gamma, contrast, and brightness controls with a single graph. Most of these methods simply generate a 256-entry lookup table (or sometimes three different RGB tables), and this is then applied to the image. Other common filters are blurs and edge-finding methods, and similar 2D convolution-kernel-based techniques. These are implemented as single-source blends.

Compositing Methods

Most of the standard Photoshop blends should be supported, such as the standard alpha blend, multiplicative, additive, subtractive, and so on. Table 4.17.1 shows some simple Photoshop blending methods with their equivalent mathematics and alpha-blend settings. Note that these blends will frequently be applied using alpha blends, not using multitexture. Although in many cases using multitexture methods is theoretically more efficient than multiple alpha-blending passes, in practice it is sometimes a struggle to conform to the restrictions of multitexture.

In some cases, triadic blends—blends with three sources—can be required, for example, in a blend between two alpha channels with the blend factor determined by a third alpha channel. Sometimes this requirement can be worked around using multiple two-argument blends, but this will be slower and less flexible, so it is worth keeping the blend architecture open enough to allow blends that take any number of

Table 4.17.1 Photoshop Blending Methods and the Equivalent Multipass Alpha Blend Settings

Photoshop Blend	Mathematical Operation	Alpha Blend (source, combine, destination)
Normal	Arg1*alpha + Arg2*(1-alpha)	SRCALPHA, ADD, INVSRCALPHA
Multiply	Arg1 * Arg2	DESTCOLOR, ADD, ZERO
Additive	Arg1 + Arg2	ONE, ADD, ONE
Subtractive	Arg1 − Arg2	ONE, SUBTRACT, ONE
Screen	Arg1+Arg2-Arg1*Arg2	INVDSTCOLOR, ADD, ONE
Lighten	Max (Arg1, Arg2)	ONE, MAX, ONE
Darken	Min (Arg1, Arg2)	ONE, MIN, ONE

inputs. Triadic blends should be implemented using multitexture hardware if possible, as this avoids additional temporary textures.

Number Controls

As a result of using unique texturing systems, artists require increasingly sophisticated ways to generate numbers as blend factors or mapping transforms. At first they need obvious things in the system—a slider they can move, a pseudo-random number generator with fixed scale and bias, and so on. Then they might want to make a hundred of the objects and only use one slider to control the parameters of all the objects.

You might find the need for variables and mathematical operations on them, in which case you could employ a full programming language (Python, LUA, LISP, etc.—take your pick). However, artists prefer more-visual programming techniques— boxes that hold variables, arithmetic operations, and so on. So, you might want to consider a graphical representation. In practice, we found that a tree structure presented in a similar style to file-selector trees was best for calculating values. We added draggable rubber-band lines between them for showing where the results were used in the blends or other calculations.

Dynamic Textures

Another powerful technique changes the layers according to gameplay. The most obvious examples are footprints, blood splatters, bullet holes, and explosion scorch marks. These are typically simple layers that have their *uv* mappings determined in real-time. The advantages of these over conventional geometry decals is clear: There are no *z*-fighting issues, no extra geometry required to draw each frame, a much wider variety of effects and texture variations are possible without losing batching efficiency, and much 'smarter' blends are possible.

One example when dynamic texture blends might be useful is on bump maps. Simply alpha-blending multiple Dot3 bump maps together does not work very well. They overlap (e.g., multiple footprints in sand), and typically the interaction between them does not make sense—one footprint simply obscures part of the another completely. However, we can composite the individual heightfields of the footprints using a *max* blend that takes the maximum of the two height values (or indentations). Once they are composited, the result is added to the original surface's heightfield. Only then is the complete heightfield turned into a Dot3 normal-map texture with a filter. With standard decals that simply alpha-blend into the frame buffer, this sort of compositing is impossible.

Another use of this method is to composite multiple shadow maps together in a scene. For example, in a forest, the shadow maps of trees do not actually need to precisely match the shape of the trees—using just three or four different maps can easily provide enough variation to fool the eye. This method would increase texture-cache performance. As an additional bonus, the shadow map can be recomposited if, for example, any trees are destroyed during gameplay. Alternatively, as the sun moves, the shadow maps can be recomputed with the new light-source direction in mind.

Scalability

Scalability and portability are important on PC systems as well as consoles. It is important to spend the available cycles and memory where the player can see it.

Unique texture systems already have scalability built in. Using a simple distance-based estimation of the maximum size of mipmap level, the compositing is done only on the texels that are likely to be visible. This optimizes CPU time and enables video memory to be used more efficiently to generate higher-resolution textures only on the objects that are visible.

Using a scalable system also allows for more realism when it's most needed. For example, in a hectic firefight, players care about frame rate, not the quality of the textures. When the firefight is over, the player can admire their gruesome handiwork. With less movement, fewer textures are being brought into the cache every second, and frame rate is not so crucial, so the composition system can spend more time on the textures.

Things that can be done to enable this scalability are:

- Reduce the size of source textures, using smaller mipmaps. This increases memory cache efficiency and reduces disk accesses on a demand-loaded or virtual-memory system.
- Reduce the size of target textures. This means fewer texels to composite and reduces swapping of textures in and out of video memory.
- Simplify sampling filters. Instead of Gaussian or trilinear filters, use bilinear filters or even-point filters.
- Simplify image filters. Light blurs or edge-enhancements can be omitted altogether, and filters that use large convolution kernels can be replaced by lower-quality versions using smaller kernels.
- Reduce the number of blends by marking certain blends with a level-of-detail factor. For example, detail textures and decals can be removed or reduced without too much quality loss. They can always be added back in when the scene's level of detail increases again.

Some of these items can also be applied selectively to distant textures.

Something to be careful *not* to do is recompositing all textures when the scene-wide level of detail changes. This will lead to two problems: First will be a large frame-rate stall as every texture in the scene is recomposited. Second, all the textures will visibly change, giving a nasty, popping effect. A far better method is to only recomposite textures when they are offscreen. If a texture does need to be recomposited while onscreen for whatever reason, at least spend the time to alpha-blend between the two versions in order to eliminate the visible pop.

CPU or Graphics Chip Compositing?

Ideally, all compositing would be performed by the graphics chip. That is what the graphics chip is designed to do—take several textures, apply *uv* transformations to them, apply some pixel effects to them, and then blend them with an existing image. It is designed to do all this in parallel, achieving amazing throughput. Unfortunately, some of the filters and blends that are required are fairly complex, and hard or impossible to do on the majority of graphics chips. Additionally, there are often problems or speed penalties when swapping source and target textures in and out of video memory, and performing the compositions on the graphics chip can become counterproductive. There will always be a blend that an artist vitally requires near the end of a project that just cannot be done by the graphics chip. For this reason, it is a good idea to always have a method of composition that is entirely CPU-based, even if a lot of the operations can then be moved to the graphics chip for speed.

PC

The PC's CPU is good at compositing. The MMX (SIMD small-integer) instructions are powerful and fast, and most simple blends and filters will be limited by memory bandwidth rather than CPU speed. Memory is plentiful and backed by a 'huge' virtual memory store that is itself a form of cache.

Using the graphics chip to perform composition is trickier for PC games than for console games. The wide diversity of PC graphics cards makes life particularly difficult here. Render-to-texture capabilities vary widely (even on recent cards) from no support to full support. Additionally, the range of blends and filters available again varies widely, and many require multiple passes to emulate, reducing speed.

XBox

The XBox shares some similarities with the PC. The CPU is the same, and it has very fast MMX instructions for image composition, so that part of the pipeline can be shared. However, the graphics chip is smart and can do 90% of the filters and blends that are required without CPU assistance. Best of all, the graphics chip and CPU share the same memory, which means that at each stage of the composition, the faster of the two can be used for that stage. Since graphics data is all stored in system memory, there is no need to worry about copying the data back and forth. Unfortunately, this does create some bandwidth and fill-rate issues.

The Demo

ON THE CD

The demo provided on the CD-ROM shows a very simple procedural landscape. There is only one source texture used, which has been colored differently according to the terrain type at each vertex. The texture is also shifted randomly at each vertex before being applied. When compositing a particular texture, the terrain types for each of the 25 vertices on that texture are blended together. Then, any decals (here a simple-colored 'splat') are alpha-blended over the top. The data for the decals hangs off the nearest landscape vertex, so retrieving the relevant list of decals for a particular texture is very quick.

Holding down the shift key shows a false-color picture of the different mipmap levels used—all the mipmap calculations are done as if the camera were placed in the middle of the landscape. The central mipmaps are 256×256 texels, reducing by a factor of two each time with distance.

This demo illustrates several things. Seamless texturing using a small number of source textures (just one in this case) is simple and effective. A large number of decals can be applied to a surface with relatively minor speed penalties, unlike traditional frame-buffer composition. A smart texture cache and simple distance-based mipmapping substantially reduces the amount of compositing and texture memory required. Finally, even a software implementation of composition can be quick and effective—this demo uses no graphics hardware capabilities for its compositing.

Conclusion

Unique texturing encompasses a whole range of interesting features. The main aim is to make every texture in the world unique and to remove the cookie-cutter look from games. The same technology can be used for cunning effects.

Immersion is improved by having surfaces change depending on their positions in the game world. Extra details normally produced with detail textures, light maps, and decals can be added more efficiently, cheaper, and with more flexibility. Artists' time is reduced by freeing them from large amounts of tedious pixel-pushing, even on huge and diverse worlds, while allowing them more time to fine-tune the really important bits of a scene.

Finally, using a scripting language to drive the texture-composition engine gives artists and designers awesome flexibility and opportunity to create worlds with a look not commonly seen in today's computer games.

References

[Ebert94] Ebert, et al., *Texturing and Modeling: A Procedural Approach*, AP Professional, 1994.

[Milliger02] Milliger, Mike, "Procedural Texturing," *Game Programming Gems 3*, Charles River Media, Inc., 2002.

[Perlin] Ken Perlin's page about noise: http://mrl.nyu.edu/~perlin/doc/oscar.html.

4.18

Textures as Lookup Tables for Per-Pixel Lighting Computations

Alex Vlachos, John Isidoro, and Chris Oat; ATI Research

Alex@Vlachos.com, jisidoro@atil.com, coat@ati.com

The latest generation of graphics hardware has brought forth a new level of per-pixel programmability for real-time applications [Microsoft02]. However, they are limited by both the size and the types of instructions that can be performed. Because of this limitation, programmers need to utilize a new set of tricks to perform more-advanced graphics algorithms on a per-pixel basis. In this gem, we show ways to use texture maps as a means to solve functions through a lookup table, focusing on lighting computations. This technique saves precious pixel shader instructions, and in many cases, it is the only way to make certain per-pixel effects possible on the current generation of hardware.

Specular Per-Pixel Lighting Without Using a Cube Map for Normalizing *h* (*n.h/h.h* Mapping)

A common problem with performing specular lighting calculations in a pixel shader is that the halfway vector, *h*, can become denormalized when it is linearly interpolated across a polygon. One standard solution is to use a normalization cube map to renormalize the halfway vector [Baker01]. Normalization cube maps have the disadvantages of requiring an additional texture fetch as well as consuming a lot of texture memory. An alternative to using normalization cube maps followed by a 1D specular texture fetch is to use an *n.h/h.h* map as a lookup table in your shader. This optimization reduces the number of texel fetches required per pixel from two to one. However, the normalization cube map is still used to normalize tangent space light vector, *l*.

- Fetch *n* (per-pixel normal) from the normal map (bump map).
- Halfway vector (H) is stored as a 3D texture coordinate and interpolated across the polygon causing it to be denormalized at each pixel.

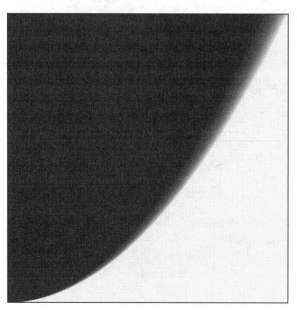

FIGURE 4.18.1   n.h/h.h *Map (k = 32). An example of a procedurally created* n.h/h.h *map that allows for per-pixel specular lighting with a specular exponent of 32.*

- Store *n.h* in the first component of the texture coordinate.
- Store *h.h* in the second component of the texture coordinate.
- Using this 2D texture coordinate, fetch into the *n.h/h.h* map. The resulting texel fetched is the specular lighting term raised to some constant power *k*.

Creating the *n.h/h.h* map is relatively simple (see Figure 4.18.1). The map is a monochrome image that potentially uses 1/18th of the texture memory required by a normalization cube map (six RGB color faces of a cube). The *n.h/h.h* map is essentially a lookup table for the following function:

$$f(s,t) = \left((s.t) \, / \left((t.t)^{0.5} \right) \right)^{k} \tag{4.18.1}$$

which can also written as

$$\left((n.h) \, / \, \|h\| \right)^{k} \tag{4.18.2}$$

The following is a DirectX8.1 pixel shader (Version 1.4) that performs the *n.h/h.h* mapping:

```
;(0.0, 0.5, 1.0, 1.0)
SetPixelShaderConstant 0 psCommonConst
SetPixelShaderConstant 1 ambient
SetPixelShaderConstant 2 diffuse
```

```
SetPixelShaderConstant 3 specular
StartPixelShader
    ps.1.4
    texld r0, t0 ;normal map n
    ;tangent space H (not necessarily normalized)
    texcrd r2.rgb, t2
    ;tangent space L (normalizer cube map lookup)
    texld r4, t1
        dp3_sat r4, r0_bx2, r4_bx2 ;(n.l)
        dp3_sat r3.r, r0_bx2, r2 ;(n.h)
        dp3_sat r3.g, r2, r2 ;(h.h)
    phase
    ;Base map
    texld r1, t0
    ;(n.h)/(h.h)^k map lookup
    texld r2, r3
        ;light = n.l * diffuse + ambient
        mad r5.rgb, r4, c2, c1
        ;basemap * light
        mul r5.rgb, r1, r5
        ;(specular * color) + (basemap * light)
        mad_sat r0.rgb, r2, c3, r5
        +mov_sat r0.a, c0.b
EndPixelShader
```

Per-Pixel Specular Exponent Using an $(n.h)^k$ Map

Using a method similar to the one previously described, it is possible to specify a unique specular exponent on a per-pixel basis. This requires some additional math in the pixel shader. A specular exponent (shininess) map, as well as the creation of an $(n.h)^k$ texture, is also required. The grayscale specular exponent map is often stored in the alpha channel of the base texture. This is what an artist paints to define the specular exponent k at each pixel.

- Fetch n (per-pixel normal) from the normal map (bump map).
- Fetch k from the exponent (shininess) map.
- Halfway vector (H) is stored as a 3D texture coordinate and interpolated across the polygon causing it to be denormalized at each pixel.
- Store $(n.h)^2$ in the first component of the texture coordinate.
- Store $(k*h.h)$ in the second component of the texture coordinate.
- Store $(h.h)$ in the third component of the texture coordinate.
- A projective, dependant texture fetch is required into the $(n.h)^k$ map. The projection causes the first two coordinates to be divided by the third, resulting in $((n.h)^2/(h.h), k)$. The texel fetched with these coordinates is the specular lighting term raised to the per-pixel power k.

Just like the $n.h/h.h$ map, the $n.h^k$ map is used to reduce the amount of math you would otherwise have to do explicitly in the pixel shader (such as normalizing h and raising $n.h$ to a power of k). In this case, $k = [0.0, 1.0]$, where 0.0 corresponds to the minimum k value used during $(n.h)^k$ texture creation, and 1.0 corresponds to the maximum k value in the $n.h^k$ texture. When doing the dependent texture fetch, use the projective divide (_dz in D3D) to divide the first two coordinates by the third. This projective divide causes the resulting texture lookup coordinates to be:

$$s = \left(\left(n.h\right) * \left(n.h\right)\right) / \left(h.h\right) = \left(n.h\right)^2 \|h\|^2 \qquad (4.18.3)$$

$$t = k$$

For $n.h^k$ mapping, the texture lookup table computes the following function:

$$f(s,t) = s^{0.5*t} \qquad (4.18.4)$$

By performing the texel fetch from this map, using the above coordinates, the equation becomes:

$$\left(\left(n.h\right) / \|h\|\right)^k \qquad (4.18.5)$$

This results in the standard Phong specular lighting component raised to the exponent k. The beauty of this technique is that the projective texel fetch both normalizes the h vector and performs the exponentiation. The tiled quad at the bottom of Color Plate 14 was rendered using an $(n.h)^k$ map to achieve varying degrees of specular lighting on a per-pixel basis. The specular exponent varies per-pixel as defined by the exponent map shown in Figure 4.18.4. Figure 4.18.3 is an example of a procedurally generated $(n.h)^k$ map that allows for per-pixel specular lighting with a per-pixel exponential range of [0, 64].

FIGURE 4.18.2   *An RGB texture of a tiled surface without any lighting.*

FIGURE 4.18.3   *A procedurally generated $(n.h)^k$ $(k=[0,64])$ map that allows for per-pixel specular lighting with a unique specular exponent specified at each pixel.*

FIGURE 4.18.4   *Grayscale specular exponent map that is used in combination with the texture from figure 4.18.3 to obtain artist-editable per-pixel specular exponents.*

```
;(0.0, 0.5, 1.0, 1.0)
SetPixelShaderConstant 0 psCommonConst
SetPixelShaderConstant 1 ambient
SetPixelShaderConstant 2 diffuse
SetPixelShaderConstant 3 specular
StartPixelShader
    ps.1.4
    ;dot 3 map (specular exponent stored in alpha)
    texld r0, t0
    texcrd r2.rgb, t2 ;tan H
    ;tangent space L (normalizer cube map lookup)
    texld r4, t1
        dp3_sat r4, r0_bx2, r4_bx2 ;(n.l)
        dp3_sat r3.b, r2, r2 ;(h.h)
        dp3_sat r3.r, r0_bx2, r2 ;(n.h)
        mul  r3.g, r3.b, r0.a ;k*((h.h))
        mul  r3.r, r3.r, r3.r ;(n.h)^2
    phase
    ;Base map
    texld r1, t0
    ;Attenuated (n.h)^k map
    texld r2, r3_dz
        ;n.l * diffuse + ambient
        mad r5, r4.r, c2, c1
        ;diffamb = basemap * (n.l * diffuse + ambient)
        mul r5.rgb, r1, r5
        ;diffamb + (specular * specular color)
        mad_sat r0.rgb, r2, c3, r5
        +mov_sat r0.a, c0.b

EndPixelShader
```

Color-Shift Iridescence

Another rendering effect using texture lookup tables is color-shift iridescence. This type of iridescence can be seen on insects' wings, certain finishes on glasswork, and pearl-like objects. The effect this algorithm simulates is based on the empirical observation that the color at a particular point on an object tends to change in hue depending on the angle between the view vector and the surface normal. This is usually caused by a thin layer of semitransparent film on an object that diffracts different frequencies of incident light in different directions. The base algorithm performs standard Phong lighting and then multiplies the specular highlight color by a texel fetched from a 1D, hue-based gradient texture addressed by $(n.v)$, where n is the per-pixel normal, and v is the tangent space view vector. See Color Plate 15 for images of hue-based gradient and objects rendered using color-shift iridescence. The following pixel shader performs the color-shift iridescence. Note that this example uses the $(n.h)^k$ technique of the previous subsection.

```
;(0.0, 0.5, 1.0, 1.0)
SetPixelShaderConstant 0 psCommonConst
SetPixelShaderConstant 1 ambient
```

```
SetPixelShaderConstant 2 diffuse
SetPixelShaderConstant 3 specular
StartPixelShader
    ps.1.4
    ;dot 3 map (specular exponent stored in alpha)
    texld r0, t0
    ;tan H
    texcrd r2.rgb, t2
    ;tangent space L (normalizer cube map lookup)
    texld r4, t1
    ;tangent space V (normalizer cube map lookup)
    texld r5, t3
        dp3_sat r4.gb, r0_bx2, r4_bx2 ;(n.l)
        dp3_sat r4.r, r0_bx2, r5_bx2 ;(n.v)
        dp3_sat r3.b, r2, r2 ;(h.h)
        dp3_sat r3.r, r0_bx2, r2 ;(n.h)
        mul  r3.g, r3.b, r0.a ;k*((h.h))
        mul  r3.r, r3.r, r3.r ;(n.h)^2
    phase
    ;Base map
    texld r1, t0
    ;Attenuated (n.h)^k map
    texld r2, r3_dz
    ;Iridescent map 1D tex map lookup
    texld r3, r4
        ;Iridescent * Specular
        mul_sat r0.rgb, r2, r3
        ;n.l * diffuse + ambient
        mad r5, r4.g, c2, c1
        ;diffamb = basemap * (n.l * diffuse + ambient)
        mul r5.rgb, r1, r5
        ;diffamb + specular * specularcolor
        mad_sat r0.rgb, r0, c3, r5
        +mov_sat r0.a, c0.b
EndPixelShader
```

Per-Pixel Point Lights with Correct Per-Pixel Falloff

Another useful application for texture lookup functions is correct per-pixel light attenuation. Computing distance falloff for point lights is traditionally sampled at the vertices and the distance is then linearly interpolated for per-pixel effects. The problem with this approach occurs when a light is near the surface of a large polygon, and there is no vertex to catch the light near the light source.

The approach for this algorithm is to calculate the distance from each pixel to the light source instead of each vertex. This results in the exact falloff value, based on a given light source, thus avoiding the common problems with the vertex-based approach.

The vertex shader computes the vertex position in *normalized light space* (NLS) instead of directly using the distance from the vertex position. The NLS transform is a translation by (–lightPos), then a uniform scaling by (1 / lightFalloff). This

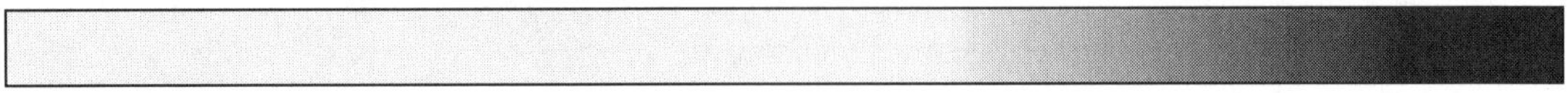

FIGURE 4.18.5   *1D point light texture that renders light color and intensity change as a function of distance from the point light source.*

gives us each vertex's position in NLS. The pixel shader then computes the distance squared on a per-pixel basis by simply taking the dot product of this interpolated vertex position with itself. Then, a 1D texture is sampled using the NLS distance squared as the texture coordinate. This allows you to vary the intensity and color of the light using distance in any way possible. The per-pixel nature of the algorithm solves any vertex-sampling issues. Since NLS position is linear by definition, this approach works perfectly without artifacts. This method hides a per-pixel square-root function in a texel fetch (see Figure 4.18.5).

Per-Pixel Spotlights and Directional Lights with Correct Per-Pixel Falloff

A natural extension of the per-pixel point light attenuation is to model spotlights and directional lights. This technique is similar to the point light shader above, but it requires slightly different vertex and pixel-shader operations. Instead of creating a 1D texture for the light, a 2D texture is required. The *u* axis of the texture is indexed with distance squared in the same way as a point light. However, the *v* axis of the texture encodes falloff based on the spot angle (the angle between the NLS vertex position vector and the spotlight direction).

To use this 2D texture, we extend the notion of normalized light space to represent a rotation, as well as extending a scale factor and a translation. This rotation matrix is composed of the light's orthonormal basis with the light direction as the *z*-axis.

In the vertex shader, similar to point lights, the vertex position is transformed into normalized light space. In the pixel shader, we can load this new position into a register as a set of texture coordinates and perform a dot product with itself to get the NLS distance squared (exactly like point lights, above). This NLS position is also loaded into a separate register with a projection modifier, causing the first two components to be divided by the first. This will compute the projected position. This projection performs a divide by *z* in NLS, which gives the spotlight its cone-like shape. Then, by doing a dot product with itself, we get a squared, scaled distance from the NLS *z*-axis, which acts like an 'angle' in the range 0-1. If the dot product is done without a modifier, this value represents an angle of 0°-90°.

These two dot product values are then used as a lookup into a 2D texture, which is a visually convincing approximation to the usual spotlight distance multiplied by the angle equation, assuming squared values as input.

Table 4.18.1 Available Scale Factors and Resulting Frustum Angles

Scale Factor	_d8	_d4	_d2	None	_x2	_x4	_x8
Frustum Angle (°)	165.7	151.9	126.8	90.0	53.1	28.1	14.3

If we simply do a dp3 as written below, the 2D texture map represents values within a 0°-90° light frustum. This means that the texture created for the spotlight must encode the full 0°-90° frustum. For lights with larger or smaller cones, texels can be better utilized by selecting an appropriate range. Using scale factor instruction modifiers, the 2D texture can represent other frustum angles. The formula for frustum angle is 2*arctan(1/scale factor). Table 4.18.1 shows the available scale factors and the resulting frustum angle:

By using the scale factors for the frustum angle, the y resolution of the texture lookup table can be decreased for smaller frustum angles because much less space is being represented. If the desired frustum angle is not listed in the table, just choose the closest table entry that is larger than the frustum to be represented, and make up the difference by scaling down the lookup table in the y direction.

```
;(0.0, 0.5, 1.0, 1.0)
SetPixelShaderConstant 0 psCommonConst
StartPixelShader
    ps.1.4
    ;NLS pos
    texcrd r1.xyz, t1.xyz
    ;NLS pos in xy plane scaled by 1/z
    texcrd r2.xy, t1_dz.xyz
        ;distance squared from light
        dp3 r1, r1, r1
        ;Set z = 0
        mov r2.b, c0.r
        ;(dist in xy plane scaled by 1/z)^2
        dp3 r1.g, r2, r2
    phase
    ;Base
    texld r0, t0
    ;Light attenuation
    texld r1, r1
        ;Base*light
        mul r0, r0, r1_x2
        ;  "  * N.L
        mul r0, r0, v0
EndPixelShader
```

Removing the _dw from the second texcrd instruction provides a cylindrical directional light frustum. This removes the scaling by 1/z of the distance in the xy-plane and gives the light's domain a cylindrical shape (see Figure 4.18.6). Note that this light still has a position and a falloff from that position. If positional distance falloff is not desired, just remove the first dot product and use the second dot product to index into a 1D texture.

FIGURE 4.18.6   *2D spot/directional light texture that renders how, along one axis, light color and intensity changes as a function of distance from the light source. The other axis renders how the light changes as a function of angle from the light vector. This example assumes a 90° frustum and is a perfect candidate for using the 53.1° frustum to save texture usage.*

Conclusion

We have shown a variety of effects using textures as function lookups. Using this idea, many graphics algorithms that have been per-vertex-only techniques can now be performed per-pixel. Of course, these are just a few useful examples of the many effects that can be achieved with this technique.

References

[Baker01] Baker, D. and C. Boyd, "DirectX 8.0 Shader Applications (Per Pixel Lighting)," DirectX Developer Day, 2001, available online at http://www.microsoft.com/corpevents/gdc2001/developer_day.asp.

[Microsoft02] MSDN.Microsoft.com, "DirectX 8.1 Pixel Shader Reference," available online at http://msdn.microsoft.com/library/default.asp?url=/library/en-us/dx8_c/directx_cpp/Graphics/Reference/Shader/Pixel/Instructions/Instructions.asp, February 2002.

4.19

Rendering with Handcrafted Shading Models

Jan Kautz,

Max-Planck-Institut für Informatik

kautz@mpi-sb.mpg.de

Quite a few techniques have been proposed on how to implement more-complex and more-realistic shading models for graphics hardware [Heidrich99, Kautz99], making them useful for games. Still, these techniques are rarely used, probably due to two reasons: complex implementation issues and unintuitive parameters for the shading models used. We propose to use a simple technique called *normal distribution function (NDF) shading*. It allows an artist to handcraft shading models, with the shape and color of highlights simply stored in bitmaps. The technique uses per-pixel shading, and can also be used in conjunction with bump mapping. Anisotropic shading models can also be created.

Shading Models

A shading model determines how much light reflects off a surface, depending on the direction to the light source, *l*, the direction toward the viewer, *v*, and the surface normal, *n*.

So far, most-interactive rendering systems use the Blinn-Phong [Blinn77] model, due to its simplicity:

$$L_o = k_d \left(n \cdot l \right) + k_s \left(h \cdot n \right)^N \tag{4.19.1}$$

The parameter k_d is the diffuse coefficient, usually stored in a color texture map; k_s is the specular coefficient, often chosen globally, but sometimes stored in a gloss map; and the parameter N is the specular exponent, which changes the shininess of the material. The vector h is the normalized halfway vector between the view and light directions.

As you can see, this model mainly uses simple operations, except for the one exponentiation. On today's graphics hardware it can be implemented with a pixel shader [Kilgard00, Mitchell01], since dot products and dependent texture reads are available.

Nonetheless, the lit objects often look like shiny plastic. It is nearly impossible to make a piece of cloth look like cloth. For anisotropic shading, which is used to render materials like brushed aluminum, Blinn-Phong cannot be used at all, since it is only isotropic (i.e., orientation independent).

Previous Methods for Incorporating Better Shading Models

A few methods have been proposed that can incorporate better shading models [Heidrich99, Kautz99], but these usually have limitations, such as unintuitive parameters, or require measured data that is not widely available.

Microfacet-Based Shading Models

Shading models that are based on microfacets (see [Cook81]) assume that the surface consists of tiny specular facets pointing in different directions (Figure 4.19.1). These microfacets are so small that they cannot be discerned, but the overall distribution of their orientations governs the shape of the specular highlight. Hence, all the microfacet-based shading models use the distribution of the microfacet normals n_m. We denote the NDF with $p(n_m)$. What does this distribution tell us? If we look up a value with $p(h)$, it gives the percentage of the surface's microfacets that face toward direction h.

As previously mentioned, microfacet models assume that all the microfacets are small, perfect mirrors. If the halfway vector between the view and light directions is the same as the normal of a perfect mirror, we see the reflection of the light source.

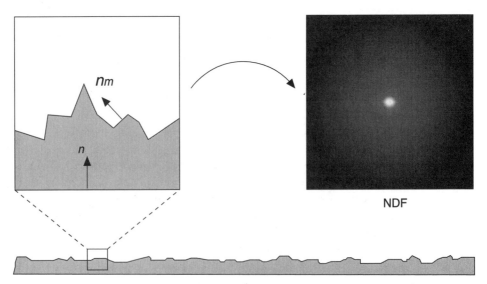

FIGURE 4.19.1   *A surface consisting of tiny microfacets and its normal distribution function.*

This is almost true for a surface consisting of tiny microfacets. If there are microfacets with a normal n_m that is equal to the halfway vector h between the light and view directions, we see light reflected from the light source, but at the microfacet scale. The distribution function $p(h)$ tells us what percentage of the incoming light is reflected, since not all microfacets are oriented in the same direction.

The specular part of the Blinn-Phong model can be seen as a simple microfacet-based shading model. It assumes that the orientations of the microfacets have a cosine to the power of N distribution.

NDF Shading

The shading model that we want to use is just a slight modification of the original Blinn-Phong model:

$$L_o = k_d\left(n \cdot l\right) + k_s p\left(h_{local}\right), \quad h_{local} = \left(h \cdot t, h \cdot b, h \cdot n\right) \tag{4.19.2}$$

As you can see, the only difference is that instead of the fixed $\cos^N$ distribution, we use an arbitrary normal distribution function. The surface tangent t, binormal b, and the normal n define the local surface coordinate frame, which is also needed for bump mapping. If the normal distribution function happens to be $p(n_m) = (n_{m,z})^N$, we get the original Blinn-Phong model. However, since the normal distribution now depends on the full local halfway vector, instead of only its z coordinate (simply $h \cdot n$), we can also create anisotropic highlights.

How To Store the NDF

How can we store the normal distribution function so that it can be used with graphics hardware? We store it in a 2D texture map. Assuming the microstructure of the surface is a heightfield, the orientations of the microfacets can only vary within the upper hemisphere; in other words, the z coordinates of the microfacets' normals n_m are always positive. Therefore, it is sufficient to use the following two coordinates to index into our 2D $p(n_m)$ texture:

$$u_x = \frac{n_{m,x} + 1}{2}, \quad u_y = \frac{n_{m,y} + 1}{2} \tag{4.19.3}$$

Figure 4.19.1 illustrates an example of a normal distribution function that was stored in such a way. Imagine a hemisphere where all the values of the normal distribution function lie. Now, we project this hemisphere onto a square plane. This is exactly what is shown in Figure 4.19.1 and what the mapping detailed here does.

Rendering/Pseudo-Code

So, how do we render an object with this new shading model? Well, it is not much more complicated than the standard Blinn-Phong model. If we have already created a texture by storing a normal distribution function, then we need to do the following to render the specular highlight:

Given:
a light source at position $\mathbf{p}_{light}$

- a viewer at position $\mathbf{p}_{viewer}$

Bind NDF texture
For every vertex $\mathbf{v}_i$ of a polygon:

- Compute the normalized vector $\mathbf{l}$ from $\mathbf{v}_i$ to $\mathbf{p}_{light}$
- Compute the normalized vector $\mathbf{v}$ from $\mathbf{v}_i$ to $\mathbf{p}_{viewer}$
- Compute the halfway vector $\mathbf{h} = \mathbf{v}+\mathbf{l}$

Normalize $\mathbf{h}$
Retrieve the tangent $\mathbf{t}_i$ and the binormal $\mathbf{b}_i$

- Compute $u_x = (\mathbf{h}^*\mathbf{t}_i+1)/2$
- Compute $u_y = (\mathbf{h}^*\mathbf{b}_i+1)/2$
- Set texture coordinates (u_x, u_y)

Render polygon

The diffuse term can be added either later or in the same stage if multitexturing is supported. An additional gloss map can also be applied, if desired.

Generating the NDF Texture

So how do we create such an NDF texture? We use a paint program to model our normal distribution, which is equivalent to drawing the highlight itself! Figure 4.19.2 shows a few highlights and how they look on objects.

Usage

We now will suggest how to use the diffuse term and the new specular NDF term to generate interesting shading models. If a standard highlight (as in the original Blinn-Phong model) is desired, then the NDF texture should probably be grayscale, so that you can change its color according to the light source. The texture should not contain a directional diffuse term. In Figure 4.19.2, two different NDFs are applied to some geometry; a standard diffuse term was added as well.

More-interesting shading effects can be achieved by including a (colored) *directional* diffuse term. In contrast to the normal diffuse term, the directional diffuse term depends on $h \cdot n$. Therefore, we can include it in the NDF. This directional diffuse term can, of course, have some color, which makes it possible to achieve interesting effects.

In Color Plate 16, on the left, you can see a piece of cloth rendered with a bluish directional diffuse NDF plus a red diffuse term. The cloth looks mostly purple, but at

FIGURE 4.19.2 *NDFs applied to a piece of cloth and a teapot.*

grazing angles, the red diffuse term has more influence than the blue directional term, making the cloth more reddish. In the middle, you can see an NDF that varies from dark red to bright red at grazing angles of the halfway vector, which is the opposite way an NDF usually looks like. Applying this NDF to the piece of cloth gives it a velvet-like look. On the right side, we created an anisotropic NDF, which goes from red to blue. Now, the cloth looks like anisotropic satin.

Bump Mapping with NDFs

NDF shading can be easily incorporated with bump mapping, as long as you have dependent texture reads. It is almost equivalent to bump mapping with the Blinn-Phong model, only you have to compute the texture coordinates, u_x and u_y, with the tangent and the binormal for the lookup. This makes it necessary to store them in texture maps as well. Here is a pixel shader (DirectX8.1 notation) that will do this computation:

```
ps.1.4
texld r1, t0  ; Normal (tex1)
texcrd r2.rgb, t1 ; Tangent Space l vector
texcrd r3.rgb, t2 ; Tangent Space Halfangle vector
texld r4, t0  ; Binormal (tex4)
texld r5, t0  ; Tangent (tex5)

dp3_sat r1.xyz, r1_bx2, r2 ; r1 = max(n*l,0)

dp3 r2.x, r4_bx2, r3 ; r2.x = b*h
dp3 r2.y, r5_bx2, r3 ; r2.y = t*h
add_d2 r2.xy, r2, one ; r2 = (r2+1)/2
```

```
phase
texld r0, t5   ; tex0.rgb = k_d and tex0.a = k_s
texld r2, r2   ; NDF is in texture unit 2

mul r0.rgb, r0, r1  ; k_d * (Nn*l)
mul r1.rgb, r0.a, r2 ; k_s * NDF()
add r0.rgb, r0, r1  ; k_d * (Nn*lL) + k_s * NDF()
```

Extensions

The shading model could be extended with a Fresnel term and a (so-called) self-shadowing term, which refers to the self-shadowing of microfacets. This is commonly used in more-accurate microfacet models [Cook81]. Although these two terms do change the resulting shading, in many cases they do not significantly add to the shading model, especially if point light sources are used for illumination.

One other extension is to include the area foreshorting of incident light for the specular term as well:

$$L_o = k_d(n \cdot l) + k_s p(h_{local})(n \cdot l) \qquad (4.19.4)$$

This makes a big difference in the shading, especially if a directional diffuse term is encoded in the NDF texture. In the end, however, the use of this additional term depends on the effect/material you wish to create.

Conclusion

We have presented a shading technique that is easy to implement and easy to use. A wide variety of materials can be simulated. An artist can modify the appearance of an object in an intuitive way by just painting a highlight and/or a directional diffuse term into a texture! See Color Plate 19 for an example of NDF shading applied to the Standford Buddha model combined with a diffuse color. Although there is some physical explanation behind this shading technique, it does not accurately model any real world surfaces. Nonetheless, the visual richness that can be achieved with this shading model is fascinating.

References

[Blinn77] Blinn, J., "Models of Light Reflection for Computer Synthesized Pictures," Computer Graphics Proceedings (SIGGRAPH 1977), pp. 192–198.

[Cook81] Cook, R. and K. Torrance, "A Reflectance Model for Computer Graphics," Computer Graphics Proceedings (SIGGRAPH 1981): pp. 307–316.

[Heidrich99] Heidrich, W. and H. P. Seidel, "Realistic, Hardware-Accelerated Shading and Lighting," Computer Graphics Proceedings (SIGGRAPH 1999): pp. 171–178.

[Kautz99] Kautz, J. and M. McCool, "Interactive Rendering with Arbitrary BRDFs Using Separable Approximations," Tenth Eurographics Workshop on Rendering, pp. 281–292, June 1999.

[Kautz01] Kautz, Heidrich W. and H. P. Seidel, "Real-Time Bump Map Synthesis," Eurographics/ SIGGRAPH Workshop on Graphics Hardware, August 2001, pp. 109–114.

[Kilgard00] Kilgard, M., "A Practical and Robust Bump-Mapping Technique for Today's GPUs," available online at http://developers.nvidia.com, July 2000.

[Mitchell01] Mitchell, J., "Advanced Vertex and Pixel Shader Techniques," available online at http://www.ati.com/developer, September 2001.

NETWORK AND MULTIPLAYER

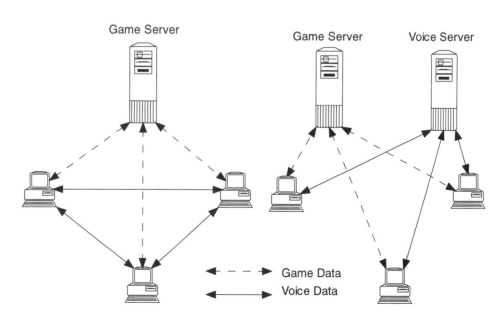

Game Server

Game Server   Voice Server

Game Data

Voice Data

Introduction

Andrew Kirmse, LucasArts
Entertainment Company
ark@alum.mit.edu

The inclusion of a networking section in this book is evidence that online gaming is coming of age. Many of the top PC games are multiplayer or online-only, and network gaming is beginning to spread to consoles and mobile platforms. The gems in this section cover networking—from the small (David Fox's "Wireless Gaming Using the Java Micro Edition") to the very large (Justin Randall's "Scaling Multiplayer Servers" and Thor Alexander's "A Flexible Simulation Architecture for Massively Multiplayer Games").

Real-time strategy (RTS) games have a special place in the history of networking as the genre that brought online gaming to the masses. Jim Greer and Zachary Simpson present their event-locking strategy for RTS games in "Minimizing Latency in Real-Time Strategy Games," and Jan Svarovsky gives practical implementation advice in his "Real-Time Strategy Network Protocol." Both articles draw on actual experience with building commercial games.

Online gaming is a young discipline—there are still many choices to make in a game's low-level networking architecture. In many client/server games, security is a paramount consideration. Pete Isensee's "Secure Sockets" describes elements of IPsec, the secure protocol used by Microsoft's Xbox console. A different option for PC games is Microsoft's DirectPlay, which has recently been rewritten. Gabriel Rohweder outlines its features, including voice communication, in "Creating Multiplayer Games with DirectPlay 8.1." At a higher level of abstraction, Jason Beardsley presents a method for automatically communicating C++ objects in "Template-Based Object Serialization." My gem, "A Network Monitoring and Simulation Tool," can be used to simulate poor network connections on a LAN to test any of these low-level methods.

These gems record our first steps in the implementation of real-time distributed systems. As we gain more experience building online games, we should try to turn these early efforts into portable and reusable components. When networking becomes a commodity, we can focus our efforts on higher-level systems, and ultimately build better games faster.

5.1

Minimizing Latency in Real-Time Strategy Games

Jim Greer, EA.com, and
Zachary Booth Simpson, Mine Control

jamesfgreer2@yahoo.com,
oink54321@yahoo.com

Multiplayer real-time strategy games have different networking requirements than twitchy action games. Rather than transmitting the millisecond-by-millisecond movements of the player, they must manage hundreds of semi-autonomous units. This allows their network protocol to be optimized in ways that action games cannot. In this gem, we will describe *event-locking*, a time-synchronized method well-suited to the coordination of real-time strategy games. The technique could also be applied to simulation games and other nontwitch games.

Frame-Locking Versus Event-Locking

Early networked games, often written for local area network (LAN) play, used a technique called *frame-locking*. Under this method, the clients send out an update every frame; at a minimum, this includes all the user input that occurred during the frame. This update might be sent to all other clients (in a peer-to-peer arrangement) or to a central server that processes it and echoes the results to all clients. In practice, some such frame-locked games render more than one frame before sending an update; but the updates typically happen at some fixed interval. While this method is suitable for LAN play, it does not extend well to Internet play, even under low to moderate latency (150–300 ms).

Consider a network architecture with a central server. As long as all clients are sending in their updates at the same pace, everything is fine. However, if one client's update is not received due to network latency or other reasons, then the server and all other clients must freeze, awaiting the arrival of the update. If they were to proceed without waiting for the delayed client's input, the game would immediately be out of synchronization—the player would see the results of their actions, but no one else would.

Figure 5.1.1 shows an example of this arrangement as an event timeline. For the first update at time 0, Clients A and B send their updates to the server. The server

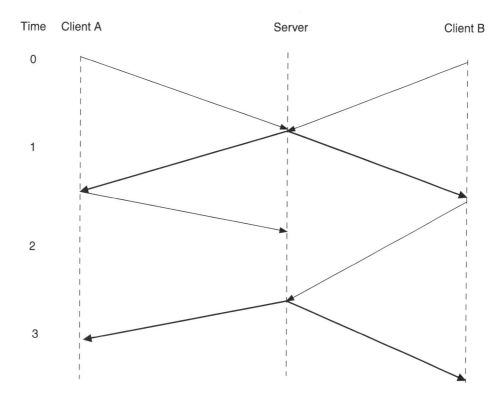

FIGURE 5.1.1   *Freezing under frame-locking: Server and Client A are held up by Client B.*

receives both updates at nearly the same instant and sends the results immediately. However, for the second update, Client B's update takes longer in transit due to network latency. The server waits, and so does Client A.

This behavior makes pure frame-locking suitable only for LAN games, but with modifications, it can handle longer latencies. For example, *Age of Empires* [Bettner01] used a peer-to-peer architecture with adaptive communication turn lengths. Pauses would occur when communications weren't received from one machine, but then the turn length would be increased to compensate. Instead of more pauses, players would experience slightly diminished responsiveness overall. Unfortunately, the performance of the game was still limited by the slowest network connection among the players.

Event-Locking

What is needed is a method that, in contrast to frame-locking, avoids slowing down all clients to the speed of the slowest one. We propose event-locking as an efficient method. Under this method, each client sends requests for events, which are evaluated by the server and, if approved, broadcast to all clients simultaneously.

For example, imagine a typical real-time strategy game in which one player decides that they want to move a tank. The player issues the movement command on their client, which performs preliminary legality checking. If legal, the client sends a `RequestMoveTank` packet to the server. The server then performs its own authoritative legality check, and upon determining that the movement is legal, sends a `MoveTank` packet to all clients, including the one that originally made the request. (For more discussion about selecting what actions to use as events, see [Dickinson01].)

Note that not all clients will receive the event packets at the same time. Therefore, events must be structured so that clients can begin execution at the appropriate time. For example, a movement event such as the `MoveTank` packet described above might contain a series of waypoints, each encoded with an arrival time. A client that receives the packet later can either warp the tank to the appropriate current position or, if the difference is small, simply animate its movement slightly faster.

It might appear that this arrangement would introduce unacceptable delays for players. If it takes 300 ms or more for their tank to start moving, won't they be frustrated? The answer is to give the player immediate 'request feedback.' In the simplest case, this feedback might be a client-side animation or sound effect. Or, for movement requests, it could be safe to start 'unofficial' movement on the client if server denial is unlikely. For example, in the `MoveTank` example, the tank driver can say "Yes, sir!" and start moving immediately, assuming that the server will confirm the movement the vast majority of the time. Figure 5.1.2 illustrates this example.

There will be cases when the server rejects a client's request or sends a path different than the one the client generated. For example, perhaps just prior to Client A issuing a `RequestMoveTank`, Client B requested the construction of a building near the tank. Client A might create a path that rolls the tank to the north and begins the movement in anticipation of the server's authorization. However, because the server knows that a building now exists in the tank's northerly path, it reroutes it to the west. When Client A receives the correct path, it must warp the tank from the unofficial path to the correct one, and this might be extremely disconcerting to the player. However, unless latency is very high, significant warping will be rare; furthermore, for many games, uncommon but dramatic warping is preferable to the alternative of common, but less-dramatic freezing. Furthermore, the warping will only be experienced by the player with the poorer connection.

The fact that some units might be in unofficial positions on a given client means that all important decisions must be handled by the server. In games that don't have a single final authority, out-of-sync bugs can be a big problem [Bettner01]. In many real-time strategy games, one of the client machines is also the server. Typically, unit creation, destruction, path-finding, and targeting decisions are server-controlled and broadcast. However, movement and attacks are animated independently on each client, generating no network traffic.

The following code illustrates how path-finding packets might be exchanged between the client and server.

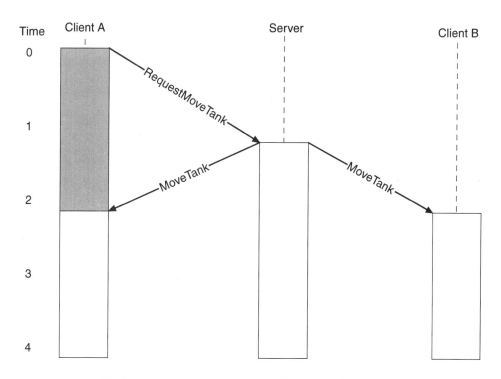

FIGURE 5.1.2 *Tank movement example—the tank moves in boxed areas (gray is unofficial movement). All players see the tank arrive at the same time.*

```
void MoveableUnit::moveRequest( Coord destination ) {
    // GENERATE a temporary path and
    // begin traversing it. This will
    // probably be the same as the path the
    // server finds but not guaranteed:
    setActivePath(generatePath(destination));

    // SEND a RequestMovement the server,
    // even if this client also happens
    // to be the server:
    sendRequestMovement( destination );
}

void handleRequestMovement(
    MoveableUnit &unit,
    Coordinate destination
) {
    // This is the handler for the destination
    // request packet. Note that all clients send
    // requests, even the client who also happens
```

```
    // to be the server

    // This can only run on the client who
    // is also the server
    assert( thisClientIsAlsoTheServer );

      // ENCODE which unit is to move and compress
      // the path into a compact form:
    Path path = unit.generatePath( destination );
    MovementPacket p = makeMovementPacket(unit, path);

    // SEND the packet to every client
    // including the original sender
    // even if that sender is also the server:
    broadcast( p );
}


void handleMovement(MoveableUnit &unit, Path &path) {
    // This function is called in response to
    // a MovementPacket.

    // Note: setting the path may induce warping if the new
    // path is not the same as the temporary path on
    // the requesting client
    unit.setPath( path );
}
```

Transport Layer for Event-locking—TCP

Assumed in the implementation of event-locking is a reliable delivery protocol, such as TCP [Postel80-2]. In other game protocols—for example, those that might be used in a flight simulator, where units generate traffic as they move—dropped packets are noncatastrophic because newer data will soon arrive to correct the loss. However, in event-locking implementations, the server sends each critical event only once; and therefore, the transport layer must ensure delivery. We have used and were pleased with TCP for this. Some game developers have written their own reliable protocols on top of UDP [Postel80-1], working under the theory that they can reduce latency by 'improving' upon the TCP algorithms. *We strongly advise against this approach.* Not only is the complexity of the task often underestimated, but so also are the ramifications. Smooth operation of the Internet depends upon the well-defined and well-tested flow-control mechanisms of TCP. Attempting to override this flow-control with a custom algorithm can induce catastrophic router feedback and possibly even temporary denial of service. (In the case that the game developer deploys their own centralized servers, this denial-of-service would most likely occur on their own routers). One final point against UDP is that it is often firewalled on corporate networks because it is more difficult to secure. This implies that game developers will need to consider a TCP connection as a protocol-of-last-resort, even in the case that they implement a custom UDP-based system.

Time Synchronization

Performance of event-locking is significantly improved by time-synchronizing the clients. For example, imagine that when a unit moves, the server broadcasts a message like: "Move unit X such that it will arrive at position P at time T in the future." Without clock synchronization, time T on one client could differ from another client's by as much as the current packet latency (which might be much higher than the average latency). In such a case, a player with lower latency will have an advantage because they will see the world closer to the way the server sees it and are thus less likely to have requests denied.

Existing Clock Synchronization Protocols

Clock synchronization is a topic of major importance, and several well-developed protocols already exist. The simplest technique is incorporated in the Simple Network Time Protocol (SNTP) [Mills96]. In this protocol, the client machine to be synchronized sends a datagram (UDP) packet to the server, which then immediately replies to the receiver with the time as it is known to the server. Although simple, the SNTP algorithm is not useful when accuracy is critical and latency is variable, because it does not attempt to measure or compensate for latency.

Unlike SNTP, the Network Time Protocol (NTP) [Mills92] does attempt to compensate for latency by sophisticated statistical methods. Unfortunately, NTP is very complicated and, more importantly, slow to converge on the accurate time delta. This makes NTP less than ideal for network game play where players expect games to start immediately and are unwilling to allow for dedicated synchronization time.

Further complicating matters, NTP and SNTP both use UDP in place of TCP to avoid the anomalous latency measurements induced by hidden retransmits that TCP might generate. As noted above, UDP is often firewalled by many Internet service providers, especially by corporate WANs, and is therefore undesirable.

A Simple Alternative: High Mode Elimination

An alternative to SNTP and NTP is required for games. Ideally, the protocol should be reasonably accurate (150 ms or better), quick to converge, simple to implement, and able to run on stream-based protocols, such as TCP.

We propose the following algorithm, which we call "stream-based time synchronization with elimination of higher order modes":

1. The client stamps the current local time on a 'time request' packet and sends it to the server.
2. Upon receipt by the server, the server stamps its time and returns the packet.
3. Upon receipt by the client, a time delta is calculated by *delta* = (*currentTime − sentTime*) / 2.

   (Note that so far this algorithm is very similar to SNTP)

4. The first received result is immediately used to update the clock, since it will get the local clock at least into the right time zone.

5. The client repeats Steps 1 through 3, five or more times, pausing a few seconds each time. Other traffic might be allowed in the interim, but should be minimized for best results.

6. The time deltas of each packet are accumulated and sorted in lowest-latency to highest-latency order. The median is determined by picking the midpoint sample from this ordered list.

7. All samples above that are approximately 1.5 times the median are discarded, and the remaining samples are averaged using an arithmetic mean.

The only subtlety of this algorithm is the discarding of samples with a time delta more than 1.5 times the median. The purpose of this is to eliminate packets that were retransmitted by TCP. To visualize this, imagine that a sample of 10 packets was sent over TCP, and there happened to be no retransmission. In this case, the latency histogram will have a single mode (cluster) centered on the median latency. Now, imagine that in another trial, a single packet of the 10 is retransmitted. The retransmission will cause this one sample to fall far to the right on the latency histogram, typically more than twice as far away as the median of the primary mode. By simply cutting out all samples that fall far from the median, these stray modes are easily eliminated, assuming that they do not comprise the bulk of the statistics, which is likely that they do not.

One very important consideration in time synchronization is that while the synchronization is running, *time might go backward!* It is extremely critical that any time-dependent checks used during time synchronization (e.g., animations during the startup phase or startup timeouts) do not slave themselves to the clock being synchronized. Failure to heed this warning could result in odd 'lock-up' bugs that will not manifest themselves until play-testing with players who span more than one time zone and are therefore likely to be mysteriously unreproducible within the developer's workplace.

This basic algorithm was tested in *NetStorm: Islands At War*, a real-time, Internet strategy game co-implemented by the authors at Titanic Entertainment (1997). The results were satisfactory and usually resulted in synchronizations of less than 100 ms. Anecdotal evidence in large-scale trials suggested that bad synchronizations due to retransmission were infrequent, and when they did occur, were often symptomatic of an unusually bad Internet connection that would eventually cause more-catastrophic errors (such as dropped connections), rendering the failure due to time-sync moot.

The following code sample demonstrates the statistical technique:

```
// GLOBAL variables holding time samples:
//————————————————————————————
typedef double Time; // or appropriate type for platform
Time timeSamples[MAX_TIME_SAMPLES];
int numTimeSamples;  // Num valid samples in the timeSamples
```

```
// CODE that calculate the time correction:
//——————————————————
assert( numTimeSamples > 2 );

// FIND the median:
sort( timeSamples, numTimeSamples );
Time median = timeSamples[ numTimeSamples/2 ];

// FIND mean of samples less than 1.5 times the median:
sum = (Time)0.0;
int count = 0;
for( int i=0; i<numTimeSamples; i++ ) {
    if( timeSamples[i] - median < (Time)1.5 * median ) {
        sum += timeSamples[i];
        count++;
    }
}
Time correctedDelta = sum / (Time)count;
```

Conclusion

We had great success using the event-locking method. Our first multiplayer RTS, *NetStorm: Islands at War*, was released by Activision in 1997, and despite having heavy action with hundreds of units animating at once over eight clients, it required only a 9600-baud modem on the server machine and even less on the clients. *Next Generation* magazine described the network play as "smooth as silk" even on terrible connections. We hope you'll have similar results.

References

[Bettner01] Bettner, Paul and Mark Terrano, "GDC 2001: 1500 Archers on a 28.8: Network Programming in Age of Empires and Beyond," Game Developer Conference, 2001, available online at http://www.gamasutra.com/features/20010322/terrano_01.htm.

[Dickinson01] Dickinson, Patrick, "Instant Replay: Building a Game Engine with Reproducible Behavior," Gamasutra.com, July 2001, available online at http://www.gamasutra.com/features/20010713/dickinson_01.htm.

[Mills92] Mills, David, "Network Time Protocol (Version 3) Specification, Implementation and Analysis," University of Delaware, March 1992, RFC-1305, available online at http://www.eecis.udel.edu/~mills/ntp.htm.

[Mills96] Mills, David, "Simple Network Time Protocol (Version 4)," University of Delaware, October 1996, RFC-2030, available online at http://www.eecis.udel.edu/~mills/ntp.htm.

[Postel80-1] Postel, J., "User Datagram Protocol, STD 6," USC/Information Sciences Institute, August 1980, RFC-768.

[Postel80-2] Postel, J., "Transmission Control Protocol, STD 6," USC/Information Sciences Institute, August 1980, RFC-761.

5.2

Real-Time Strategy Network Protocol

Jan Svarovsky

jan@svarovsky.com

This gem aims to explain a simple and practical system for connecting up to 10 computers over the Internet to play dynamic strategy, management, or combat games. *StarTopia* [StarTopia01] is a real-time strategy (RTS) game that supports four-player multiplay over the Internet. Player interaction involves placing and maintaining facilities, interacting with individual characters, and ordering troops around the battlefield. This gem is based on the simple network protocol we used for this game. Although this gem is primarily a description of the general principles, it includes our experiences, both good and bad, in an actual commercial implementation.

First, we will briefly discuss common protocols that we have come across, then cover the basic principles. Following that will be some refinements to the protocol, a description of modules we found useful, and some of the pitfalls we encountered. We will also include a simplified example game. Part of the system found in *StarTopia* is on the CD-ROM.

ON THE CD

Other Protocols

The systems that concern us here are for games involving up to 10 players, rather than those for massively multiplayer online games.

Client/Server: First-Person Shooter

The most common protocol for first-person action games is that each player is sitting in front of a 'client' program, which could almost be considered as a dumb terminal. A server runs the game, effectively remote from any client, even if in practice it resides on the same machine as one of the clients. The server tells each client what it can see. Each client tells the server what it wants to happen, based on player controls. There are refinements to smooth out the game, based on the client's prediction of server response.

This protocol benefits from its simplicity and its ability to avoid cheating (since the server can veto some illegal acts). Clients can drop in and out, but the game on the server lives on. However, it does require that the client's visible game state is small enough that it can be repeatedly transmitted. This limitation eliminates this protocol as an option for real-time strategy games where a tremendous amount of game state is involved.

Peer-to-Peer

With the peer-to-peer protocol, no computer in the game is more important than any other. Each computer 'owns' a part of the game state and has a final say on what happens to that part (typically, the game-player entity and a few AI agents).

The benefit of this protocol is that the game state owned by the computer is instantly updated. In an ideal world, your computer owns the AI agents that are closest to you, since they are not as important to other players that are farther away. The downside is that any interaction between two characters or objects in the game must have a corresponding network packet so that different computers can establish a consistent outcome. Of course, as the size of the game state increases, the number of packets sent around the network communicating state increases quadratically.

Lockstep

As the name implies, a game using this protocol runs in lockstep with all computers involved. They start with the same game state, and game time is split into turns. With each turn, each computer models the game world to advance the action by one step. At the end of the turn, each machine tells every other machine what actions the user has performed. Since all of the computers know what all users are doing, they can collectively model the next game turn and stay synchronized.

This is an easy protocol to implement and has a relatively low bandwidth, since user input (which might be idle for many frames) is all that needs to be transmitted. The bandwidth is also unrelated to the size of the game state, which is a big advantage for real-time strategy games.

A problem with this protocol is that the number of game turns per second is limited by the round-trip network delay; at the end of each game turn, the machines must receive at least an acknowledgement from all the other machines before modeling the next turn. Keeping the machines synchronized is also fairly difficult. You have to ensure that no user actions directly affect the game, but rather indirectly affect the game via the network code. This ensures that all machines are acting on the same information, and this discipline must be followed. Similarly, you have to keep their random-number generators synchronized.

In a similar way to the client/server system, some cheats are difficult because any illegal changes enacted on the game state will cause that machine to fall out of sync with the other machines. On the other hand, because the entire game state is available on each machine, other cheats become possible—for example, changing the game to be able to see more of the map than usual.

Our Protocol

We based our protocol on the lockstep system, with several changes to limit its short-comings. One machine is declared the server in order to keep the network traffic linearly proportional to the number of players. Otherwise, the network traffic is proportional to the square of the number of players. Each client only sends one packet per event (to the server), rather than one to each of the other clients. This method enables the server to be in charge of negotiating the game state when a machine drops its connection.

With lockstep, the clients collect input from the others between each game turn. However, we can remove this round-trip network delay between turns. The server simply broadcasts 'advance the turn' packets on a regular basis, and user input from each client is broadcast to all machines upon being received by the server. This means that each user-input event must make the trip to the server and back before it can be processed, but the game turns continue to occur at a steady pace in the meantime (see Figure 5.2.1).

The main features of this system are as follows:

- At the start of play, the state of the game on all machines is identical.
- The server then sends an identical stream of packets to the clients. This is a steady stream of 'advance the turn' packets, interspersed with user input.
- The game progresses forward based solely on information received from the server, which is identical for all machines. Therefore, the game stays synchronized across the network.
- For this reason, it is vital to decouple local user input from the local game state. User input gets transmitted to the server, which in turn broadcasts them to the other machines so that parallel action can take place.
- Game turns don't necessarily happen absolutely simultaneously on all computers, but game events occur in the same order.
- There is at least one round-trip delay between a user input and its effect on-screen. (This will be discussed in the next section.)
- All network packets must have guaranteed delivery. You want all user actions to get processed, so packets to the server must arrive. Also, packets from the server must arrive in order, so that all clients receive identical event streams.

Number of Game Turns per Second

Several factors must be considered when deciding how many game turn updates should be issued per second. As will be discussed in the next section, the graphics engine does not draw the game state as it is, but rather as an interpolated version. This means that the number of turns per second is not directly visible to the player, so we must look elsewhere for this design decision.

There is a balance, of course. Lowering the game-turn rate has the following advantages:

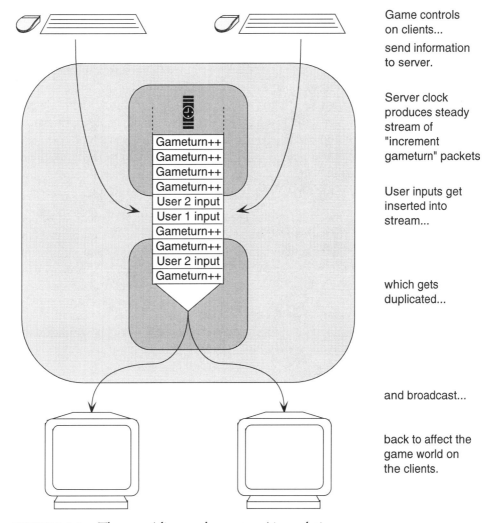

Game controls
on clients...

send information
to server.

Server clock
produces steady
stream of
"increment
gameturn" packets

User inputs get
inserted into
stream...

which gets
duplicated...

and broadcast...

back to affect the
game world on
the clients.

FIGURE 5.2.1   *The server/client and game turn/time relations.*

- Most of the time, the only network activity that occurs is the server issuing game-turn update packets, so a lower number of turns lowers this expected bandwidth.
- Most game-turn processing is at a constant cost per turn, no matter how many turns per second there are. The simplest example is the movement of objects with a constant velocity. Lowering the game-turn rate reduces the CPU cost of modeling the game.

On the other hand, there are advantages to higher turn rates:

- Some game processing has a constant cost per second, rather than cost per game turn. For example, if your robots are meant to scan the surrounding area once per second, then halving the number of turns per second will double the amount of scanning that has to be done per turn. In the extreme, the processing of the world will be visible as a pause in the smooth rendering. In *StarTopia*, it was possible to create this effect by running a very low-spec computer with a higher-spec video card and then filling the game area with lots of activity. The frame rate is high, but the computer struggles with processing the game.
- When user input arrives, its effect is only realized in the game the next time it is modeled. This means that, on average, the response time of the game is lagged by half of a game turn. If game turns happen more often, this effect is reduced.

In *StarTopia*, we eventually settled on six turns per second. The *Dungeon Keeper* team [Keeper01] used four turns per second. In both cases, different numbers were experimented with, and in fact varied frequently during game development. A similar number of turns per second should work for most real-time strategy games.

Refinements

Once the basic protocol has been implemented, there are some improvements that will make the whole game much more playable.

Interpolating Between Game Turns

First, the clients anticipate when game turns will arrive from the server and try to interpolate the scene smoothly between turns. In reality, all that is arriving is permission from the server to model the next turn, possibly with some new user input.

Though the world is modeled at a steady number of updates per second, what is shown on-screen can be updated as frequently as each client computer can handle. Players with faster machines get a much smoother view, but the game is the same for all players.

It is impossible to correctly anticipate the precise arrival of the next turn, of course, so any prediction system that comes close is acceptable. We found that basing the prediction on the weighted average of the previous few arrival times was adequate.

This improvement needs no prediction of future game state. You just interpolate between the last two game turns you modeled. This interpolation can be linear for most things, such as object position, even when there are as few as four turns per second. Ideally, the system will correctly anticipate the moment the next game turn occurs, so you can continue with the interpolation. This adds up to one extra game-turn lag, which can be a significant time, but it allows for better gameplay.

Hiding the Lag

The main issue that remains is the very noticeable delay between player actions and their effects on the game world. User input only affects the game after the event has made the trip to the server and back, adding a game-turn delay plus an extra turn for the interpolation.

You can effectively conceal this lag in a management-style game by separating the game into the interface, the network code, and the game state. The game state is the only thing that must stay synchronized. The 'interface' is expanded to include as much of the response of the game to the user as possible.

Examples of game state that we (re)classify as interface are:

- In a game where the player creates rooms or buildings, partially designed room layouts are all done locally, and only the final room design is broadcast.
- The AI's response to commands is delayed, but the user interface response to commands, such as flashing circles around targets, gets immediately processed locally. The fact that your tank actually turns to fight its target a quarter of a second later is unnoticeable to the player.
- Camera movement doesn't usually need to be transmitted if where you're looking doesn't affect the game.
- Finishing touches to the GUI should happen only on the local machine. For example, our characters' heads track the mouse pointer around the screen when they are being talked to directly.

It is, in fact, possible to use this protocol in a game that involves more-direct interaction with the world, such as a first-person shooter, but it is awkward. One example is player character movement. The 'move left' packet would change to 'I want to have moved left on game turn x.' The image displayed to the local user would update as if the move had been allowed. Every client, on receipt of the event packet from the server, would decide whether or not the move was possible. However, the decisions would be identical on all machines, leaving the local machine with the task of covering up any denied actions.

Host Migration

Since one machine is dedicated as the server, a problem arises when that machine leaves the game. This is quite likely to happen, since players are unlikely to be willing to leave their machines connected for the sake of the others.

To handle this situation, you must first make sure that there is as little state as possible on the server. The system described above is ideal because the server is merely a clock that counts game turns and acts as a short-term holding bay for user input packets.

The remaining clients must decide which machine will host the new server. Different clients might have received different amounts of the event stream from the server. The most up-to-date version must be used because the client that has received the most-recent events will not be able to roll back.

For a more seamless transition, clients should check if they had sent any packets to the server that did not make it into the new broadcast stream. These should then be resent. Storing perhaps five seconds of network packets is not particularly expensive, due to the small nature of the packets.

In *StarTopia*, we supported server dropout to a lesser extent than this. Most games were just one-on-one, so server dropout happened less often than expected. We had a frequent autosave system (every minute or so). If, for some reason, the server left, the remaining machines could just restart from their latest autosave with very little effect on the game.

Handling a Slow Computer

The server will keep generating game turns at a steady rate, which might be too fast for one of the clients, even if only for a short while. If game turn update requests are arriving four times a second, but the client takes half a second to model a game turn, it will never catch up and will freeze, unable to advance the game fast enough.

We simply added an occasional extra packet that clients would send to the server, which would not be rebroadcast. This would tell the server what percentage of CPU time was taken by modeling the game. The server could then slow down gameplay and allow the slower client to catch up by ensuring that the CPU modeling cost had dropped sufficiently for all the clients.

Useful Modules

Next, we will describe four other techniques that we found useful.

Simulating Lag in Single Player

Even in the single-player game, there should be a simulated network lag. This worked wonders for us, because the majority of game development and testing was done in the single-player mode. When we started testing the network game, the testers were very worried about the effect the network lag would have on playability. At this point, we could smugly point out that they'd been playing with lag all along. The game was programmed and tested against network lag by incorporating it from the start.

Pointer-to-Unique-ID

Although the game state might be completely synchronized, pointers won't necessarily be equal across machines, so any object (in C++) that must be referred to by network packets, such as 'I'm clicking on this unit' needs a unique ID. This is relatively effortless; simply derive all referenced objects from a base class that contains a unique numerical ID (and a pointer-to-number conversion function), and include a lookup table for number-to-pointer conversion.

There are some subtle pitfalls to watch out for. For instance, when objects are destroyed and new objects are assigned the same number, some network packets might exist that refer to the old object. This is fixed by attaching a small extra number to each ID, which is incremented when the object dies and the ID is used for another object. An alternative is to simply use a much larger number of object IDs and never reuse IDs, or reuse them in least-recently used order. This will increase the size of the lookup table for ID-to-pointer conversion, or it can be turned into a hash table. In *StarTopia,* a surprisingly large number of objects were created and destroyed in a typical session.

Debugging Out-of-Syncs

The major part of network game debugging was tracking down reasons why clients went out of sync with each other. Detecting that the game was out of sync was done by a simple checksum system. The checksum included the number and position of objects, and little else.

Once the game is out of sync, looking at the differences in the game state tells you very little. So, the best strategy is to litter the code with `printf`s, especially around decision points in the code. You then compare the output from the two machines to find where they went out of sync.

Of course, `printf`s are expensive. Hence, since most of what we printed were numbers and constant strings, we kept a large queue of little structures, which could contain either pointers to strings or numbers. The `printf` operation simply wrote onto the end of this queue. The pointers were then dereferenced to produce the 'sync dump' only when the game went of sync. For simplicity, the output was written out to a shared network drive with a machine-specific filename.

Packet Loss

As previously mentioned, all network messages in our system must be guaranteed to arrive in the right order. We found it worthwhile to roll our own guaranteed messaging system, which was effectively a layer under the protocol described here. There is a stream of messages from each client to the server, consisting of user input and some housekeeping packets. There is also one stream from the server to each client, containing game-turn increments and user events. Though each client receives the same information, the streams were handled independently.

Pitfalls in *StarTopia*

We will describe the most common problems we had when implementing this system. Of course, this section is specific to *StarTopia,* but the lessons we learned will hopefully help you with your project.

Out-of-Sync

As mentioned above, this was by far our biggest problem, but it was not insuperable. Although there was a huge amount of detail in the game, we reduced the out-of-syncs to the point that we were unable to find them during testing. At this point, we #defined out the 'syncdebug' module and put in a message suggesting that people try restarting the game from the latest autosave. This message was never found (unless we cheated to trigger it).

Our main cause of out-of-sync bugs was that, out of necessity, we had written a large portion of the game before the network protocol was incorporated. So, legacy code that was left in by accident would break the rules of the protocol. The most common out-of-sync bugs due to this were [Ireland01]:

- Changing game state directly rather than making the change via a network packet that would be broadcast around to all clients.
- Game code referring to the player that is local to the player's machine.
- Game code referring to the camera.
- Game code referring to the system clock for timing, rather than the game turn.

These problems can be avoided by keeping the interface and game state as far apart as possible. For example, no code that controls game state should know which player is sitting in front of the machine or where the player is looking. Once you have complied with this principle, the remaining common reasons for out-of-sync scenarios are:

- Uninitialized data.
- Different versions of data files. Once the game is shipped, this is less of a problem. But during development, when people can be running many different versions, it is almost worth having a checksum of all data loaded into the game.
- Different executables. Again, the simplest solution is to make the game insist that all players use identical executables, though this can get in the way of some testing.

Event Packets Becoming Irrelevant

The typical instance of this pitfall or bug is that an event packet refers to some object that is destroyed during the time the packet makes the trip to the server and back. Alternatively, a packet describes a change for an object, but the object is no longer in an appropriate state to receive this event. (For a while, we could hire and fire characters in our game, even if they died in the meantime!)

Of course, the tests for this are simple—the unique-ID system described above catches object deaths. In addition, you should always check if your object is in a fit state to respond to an event. What makes this a pitfall is that it happens most often when players are sending many packets or if they are simultaneously referring to the same object. These situations happen more frequently toward the end of game development, when the game is near enough to completion for big showdowns to be played. Hence, these bugs can go unnoticed for an inconveniently long time.

Example Game

ON THE CD

Sync debug has been included on the CD-ROM. We encourage you to look at the code and comments. More-complete modules, such as `syncdebug`, have been included, so they are a good basis for a practical implementation. We encourage you to look at the code and comments.

Conclusion

This protocol was easy to implement and worked well for our game. It gave us great freedom to write a game full of many concurrent events, without worrying about their effect on network bandwidth. We hope this gem will help you, should you wish to try our protocol.

I would like to thank the other members of the team who built *StarTopia*, especially Tom Ireland, who gave me helpful comments as I wrote this gem.

References

[Ireland01] Ireland, Tom, list compiled during game development, July 2001.
[Keeper01] Bullfrog, *Dungeon Keeper II*, PC game, information available online at http://www.dungeonkeeper.com, June 1999.
[StarTopia01] Mucky Foot, *StarTopia*, PC game, information available online at http://www.muckyfoot.com, July 2001.

5.3

A Flexible Simulation Architecture for Massively Multiplayer Games

Thor Alexander, Hard Coded Games

thor@hardcodedgames.com

Massively multiplayer (MMP) games offer fun and addictive gameplay to hundreds of thousands of players who meet online and battle each other or join forces to fight common foes. Constructing such large and persistent Internet-based playgrounds is one of the most challenging aspects of game development and possibly software development in general. An MMP consists of many components, including networking, rendering, database access, and game simulation. This gem focuses on game simulation, and it presents a solution that provides for a flexible simulation architecture that can be reused to create many different styles of online games.

A commercial MMP game is much more of a service than a product. A successful online game service will have a lifetime of at least five years. Over this time, the code base must be maintained and modified in a timely fashion into a production or *live* environment with hordes of pesky players critiquing every change. To survive in such an environment, a code base needs to be built on a solid engineering foundation. To achieve this, we will leverage techniques from both the Design Patterns tools and UML.

Design Patterns are very useful and proven software engineering tools that have gained favor in recent years. A pattern is a recurring solution to a standard problem. For more information on patterns, see [Gamma94]. The Unified Modeling Language (UML) is a design process for visualizing and specifying a software system. This gem presents UML class and sequence diagrams. For an in-depth discussion of UML, see [Booch98].

Architecture Overview

First, let us overview the architecture we wish to achieve for MMPs.

Client/Server Components

At its core, an MMP is a client/server system. It provides a network layer that relays message packets across the Internet between the client and server processes.

These message packets are received and interpreted by the game-simulation layer. This layer is responsible for maintaining the consistency of the game state-space on the client and the server. Detailed simulation of the physical representations of the objects that occupy this state-space is handled by the physics layer. Since the client rendering layer presents only what the player can perceive, the number of objects simulated at any given time on the client need only be a subset of those on the server. This allows the client to perform the physics simulation at a much higher level of detail than the server physics layer. See Figure 5.3.1 for an overview of this architecture.

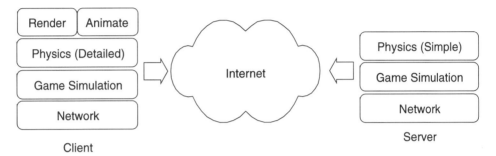

FIGURE 5.3.1   *Client/Server game architecture.*

Simulation by Proxy

The game-simulation layer on the server holds the one true representation of the state-space. It must serve as the arbitrator if any clients that it serves fall out of synch. The server broadcasts changes to the actors and objects in the state-space as simulation events to the client. The client uses these events to update the proxy objects that make up its local copy of the state-space. The user interacts with the server simulation by sending action requests that the server simulation layer must validate before the action takes place. Figure 5.3.2 depicts the request/event flow. For security reasons, an

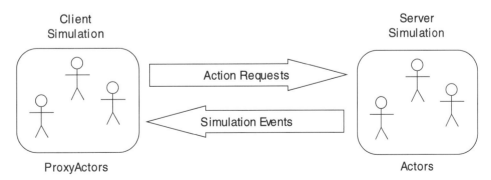

FIGURE 5.3.2   *Client/Server simulation via Actors and Proxies.*

MMP design must never trust the client's representation of state-space. For a detailed discussion on issues surrounding simulation by proxy, refer to the Virtual Simultaneity section of [Perlin96].

Support Classes

Before we jump into the core classes of our architecture, we need to define a few support classes that we will layer to construct the core classes of the system.

Dictionary/Hash Tables

A dictionary is an abstract data type that stores items associated with values. Basic operations are AddEntry, LookupEntry, and RemoveEntry. A good dictionary implementation method is the hash table, which is an associative array in which keys are mapped to array positions by a hash function. Figure 5.3.3 shows the class diagram for such a dictionary. This dictionary will prove to be the workhorse data structure of this architecture.

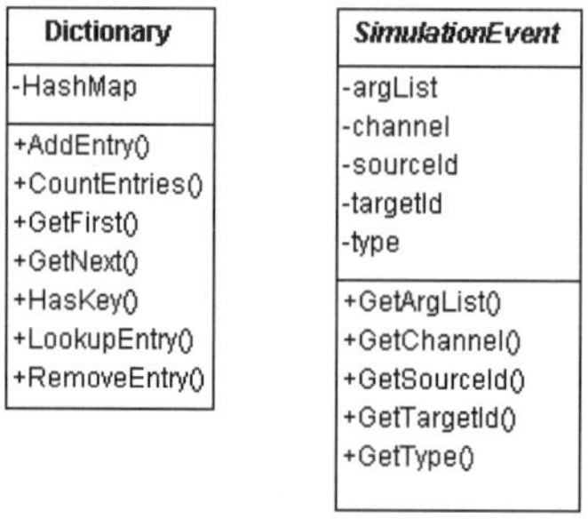

Dictionary
-HashMap
+AddEntry()
+CountEntries()
+GetFirst()
+GetNext()
+HasKey()
+LookupEntry()
+RemoveEntry()

SimulationEvent
-argList
-channel
-sourceId
-targetId
-type
+GetArgList()
+GetChannel()
+GetSourceId()
+GetTargetId()
+GetType()

FIGURE 5.3.3 *Support class diagrams.*

Simulation Events

Simulation events are the transactional objects of this system. When an actor interacts with the environment by performing actions, the results of these actions are broadcast to other actors that can perceive them as events. An event object contains the event type, source-actor ID, and target-actor ID, as well as a list of arguments specific to the event type. Additionally, it has a channel attribute that is used by the receiver of the event to filter out the categories of events that it is interested in.

SimulationState

SimulationState is our implementation of the *state pattern*. For the sake of clarity, we present a simplified version of the pattern that does not include a state machine or state manager. (For a detailed and more-robust implementation, see [Boer00] and

[Dybsand00].) SimulationState serves as the base class for all states in our architecture. Basic operations are CanTransition and Transition. The base CanTransition is a pretest method that validates if the specified context object can make a valid transition to this state. Derived state classes can implement additional checks to meet their individual needs. The Transition method is where all of the real work takes place. Each child class will need to implement this method and provide any specific behaviors that occur when this state is entered.

ActionState

ActionStates are the typical game-simulation operations, such as slapping an opponent or opening a door. Each ActionState has its own durationTime attribute that details how long this action takes to execute. Typically, this attribute is used to synchronize the server simulation with the animation play-back time on the client. The Action-State also maintains the startTime attribute. This is useful for calculating the time index into an animation when a spectator enters the view of the actor sometime after that actor has already transitioned into an ActionState (see Figure 5.3.4).

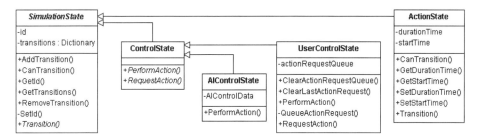

FIGURE 5.3.4 *Simulation state class diagrams.*

ControlState

A *ControlState* defines from where the associated actor can accept commands. This allows the actor to be under player control, AI control, or in some additional mode, such as a scripted state for use with in-game cut-scenes. The ControlState can be swapped on the fly to transition the actor between these states. Another use for ControlStates is for training by observation. When in such a training state, the players control the actor as they would in the user-controlled state, with the computer eavesdropping in on the actor and learning from their actions. (For more details on training by observation, refer to [Alexander02a].)

UserControlState

The *UserControlState* maintains a queue of pending action requests that have been received on the server from the user on the client. This control state's PerformAction method will pull requests from this queue when it is called.

AIControlState

The *AIControlState* is responsible for determining the appropriate action to perform when an actor in this state calls its PerformAction method. This decision process should be implemented with an AI technique that best suits a given simulation's game mechanics, such as finite state machines, neural nets, or fuzzy logic. For one example of such a decision subsystem, refer to [Alexander02b].

Core Classes

Now, let us discuss the core classes for this architecture.

SimulationObject

A *SimulationObject* (SOB) forms the base for all of the core classes that the simulation deals with, including actors, areas, items, and obstacles. Figure 5.3.5 shows the core-class hierarchy. An SOB is assigned its own ID that designates it as a unique object. SimulationObjects communicate with each other by sending simulation events. They can subscribe to the events that they care about with other simulation objects. Each SOB maintains a *subscribers* dictionary that it uses to publish events that it generates.

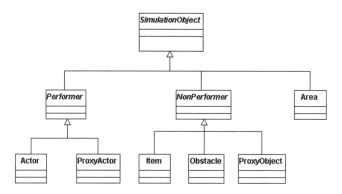

FIGURE 5.3.5   *Core class hierarchy.*

An SOB might contain other SimulationObjects. Each SOB maintains a *contents* dictionary of the objects that it contains, as well as an *ownerId* that refers to the SOB that contains it. SimulationObject containment serves as an abstract concept that can facilitate many features for the child classes. Actor subclasses can use it to implement inventory-item management systems. Items can become in-game containers, like chests and bags, which contain other items. Areas, which are abstract spatial representations, make use of containment to track other SimulationObjects that enter and exit their boundaries.

Similar to containment, SimulationObjects also maintain a dictionary of links to each other. Links provide an aggregation, or 'whole/part' relationship, between

SOBs. This provides for a simple, yet powerful way to enable objects to receive events from component parts on a transitory basis. Links can be used to implement portals or doorways between areas that can be opened and closed. Compound items can be constructed from parts by linking items together.

SimulationObjects also provide a *property* dictionary for storing game system-specific attributes per-object in a data-driven fashion. Each `simulationObject` subclass can add its own properties to the dictionary as needed. The contents of this dictionary can be replicated down to the associated proxy object on the client in an intelligent, just-in-time fashion that minimizes the network-traffic overhead. Examples of properties include attributes like the object's location in the world space, movement speed, hit points, mana, and so forth.

Finally, SimulationObjects provide a persistence mechanism that allows the simulation layer to interface with storage systems in a generic fashion. Each `simulationObject` maintains a *dirty* flag that is set when persistent properties and data are changed. The simulation layer can call the `Store` method on the SOB when needed. `Store` tests the dirty flag and archives the object if it is set. The `Restore` method performs the converse operation and loads the object into the simulation. These methods can be implemented in the target application to save the objects to flat-file formats, such as XML or relational databases such as Oracle or MS-SQL (see Figure 5.3.6).

FIGURE 5.3.6 *SimulationObject class diagram.*

Performer

The abstract *Performer* core class provides for the shared client/server functionality and common interface of the *Actor* and *ActorProxy* simulation object classes. The Performer class maintains a `schedulePriority` attribute that is used by the simulation for scheduling. A performer also maintains the object's `currentActionState`, which represents the action that the object is currently performing. This attribute is determined and set by the `PerformAction` method. More-advanced simulations can be implemented by expanding the object to contain several parallel action states for mutually exclusive activity layers, such as movement states, posture states, conversation states, and so forth (see Figure 5.3.7).

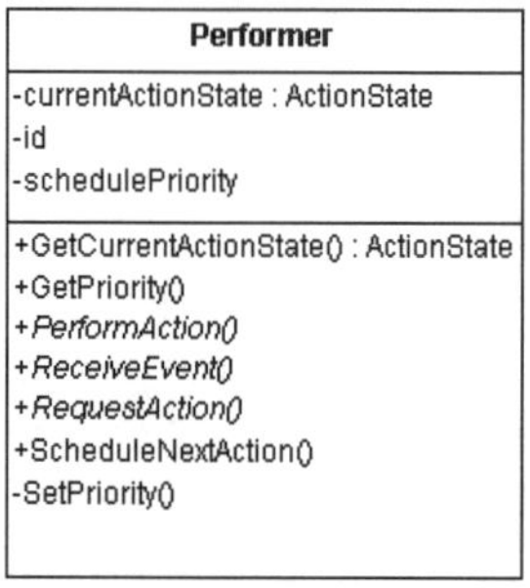

Performer
-currentActionState : ActionState
-id
-schedulePriority
+GetCurrentActionState() : ActionState
+GetPriority()
+*PerformAction()*
+*ReceiveEvent()*
+*RequestAction()*
+ScheduleNextAction()
-SetPriority()

FIGURE 5.3.7   *Performer class diagram.*

Actor

An *Actor* is defined to be a server-side simulation object that is capable of interacting with the simulation environment. Actors have a *ControlState* that allows them to be controlled by a number of different agents, including players, AI, and scripted cutscenes. The `PerformAction` and `RequestAction` methods are delegated down to the current control state, where the controlling agent is responsible for providing the appropriate implementation. The Actor class also maintains an *eventQueue* that is populated by the `ReceiveEvent` method (see Figure 5.3.8). This queuing of events allows the Actor to batch them up and defer handling them until its next scheduled `PeformAction` method.

This passive, just-in-time event-handling scheme allows the system to avoid having to decide what it needs to do every time an Actor receives an event. In a high-

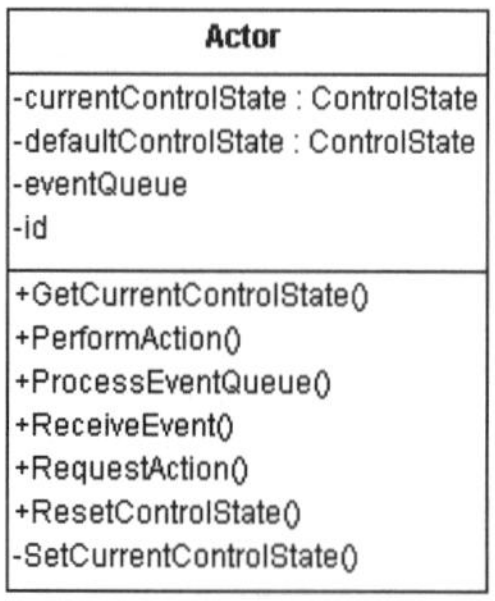

Actor
-currentControlState : ControlState
-defaultControlState : ControlState
-eventQueue
-id
+GetCurrentControlState()
+PerformAction()
+ProcessEventQueue()
+ReceiveEvent()
+RequestAction()
+ResetControlState()
-SetCurrentControlState()

FIGURE 5.3.8   *Actor class diagram.*

event simulation, like MMP games where the actors need to be aware of everything going on around them, this is a critical improvement. The ReceiveEvent method can also filter out event types that require immediate attention and bypass the queue to perform the required handling when the event is received.

ActorProxy

An *ActorProxy* is the client-side counterpart of an Actor. It shares the same SimulationObject ID as its Actor and replicates the actor's relevant data. The client-side simulation will route all incoming events to the appropriate actor proxy, where it will be handled by the ReceiveEvent method. The proxy also provides a RequestAction method that routes outbound action requests to the associated actor on the server. Finally, there is a PerformAction method available to process any client-side-only behavior that does not need to be replicated by the server simulation, such as dynamic soundtrack selection or triggering of UI elements (see Figure 5.3.9).

FIGURE 5.3.9 *ActorProxy class diagram.*

Nonperformers

Much simpler than performers are the other core classes that do not directly interact with the simulation environment. These objects do not perform actions and do not receive any scheduled processing time from the simulation. All events must be handled actively as these objects receive them. These objects include:

- *Items*—Small game objects that can be picked up, moved, and dropped by actors.
- *Obstacles*—Nonmoveable objects in the game that cannot be picked up.
- *ProxyObject*—Client-side counterpart of the Item and Obstacle classes.
- *Area*—Abstract spatial representations used to partition the simulation space down into manageable sections, Areas define the local potential visible set that is used to filter who can and cannot see (or if needed, hear) simulation events.

Managers and Factories

Managers and factories are implemented as singletons [Gamma94]. A singleton comes in handy when a single global object needs to be accessed by several different classes and objects. They are created when the simulation layer is initialized, and they remain in service until the layer is shut down. Parallel managers are maintained independent of each other on both the client and server.

SOBFactory

The *SOBFactory* is responsible for creating simulation objects and guaranteeing that they have a unique ID number. To achieve this, the SOBFactory is the sole keeper of the `nextSobId`. The factory provides a `Create` method that takes an SOB-type argument that specifies what subclass of `simulationObject` (Actor, Area, Item, etc.) it creates. If the client-side simulation needs to create local simulation objects, it can maintain its own SOBFactory, which will need to implement a scheme to ensure that client-side SOB IDs do not conflict with those generated on the server (see Figure 5.3.10).

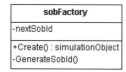

FIGURE 5.3.10   *SOBFactory class diagram.*

SOBManager

An *SOBManager* is responsible for maintaining a dictionary of simulation objects. The main function of this manager is to resolve SOB IDs into object references via the `LookUpById` method. This manager also provides methods to `Store` and `Restore` all of the objects under its supervision. These two methods delegate the actual object-persistence implementation down to the specific simulation objects. This allows for a single call to be made transparently from the simulation layer to save or load all of the objects within it (see Figure 5.3.11).

FIGURE 5.3.11   *SOBManager class diagram.*

ScheduleManager

The *ScheduleManager* is responsible for scheduling a `PerformAction` method callback for all of the Performer simulation objects that are active in the simulation (see Figure 5.3.12). It also provides the `ProcessTasks` method that takes a time slice argument and calls all of the pending scheduled callbacks that it can process within that time, sorted by the Performer's `schedulePriority`. Although an effective schedule can be implemented with a directory, as shown here, a more optimized solution is the priority queue. (For an excellent article, on implementing priority queues refer to [Nelson96].)

FIGURE 5.3.12   *Class diagram for ScheduleManager.*

LookupManager

The *LookupManager* provides a fast and effective mechanism for accessing static game data at runtime (see Figure 5.3.13). Typically, this data is stored in relational or object databases and loaded on simulation startup. The data is mapped into a nested dictionary with a primary *Table* key and secondary *Entry* keys. Some examples of static game data include initial ActionState data, SimulationEvent types, and SimulationObject properties.

FIGURE 5.3.13   *Class diagram for LookupManager.*

Putting It All Together

Now that we have defined the support, core, and manager classes, we need to wrap them all up in a nice top-level interface for managing the client/server simulation layers. The *BaseSimulation* class provides such a common interface. It contains all of the object references to our manager singletons, as well as a reference to the root simulation object. This object represents the entire simulation universe and provides a pointer to anchor all top-level Area simulation objects to. The simulation maintains two instances of the SOBManager, an *areaManager* and an *actorManager*. This separation of simulation objects is useful for debugging, maintenance, and archival purposes (see Figure 5.3.14).

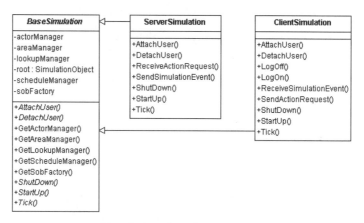

FIGURE 5.3.14   *Simulation class diagrams.*

Attaching Users to Actors

The *ServerSimulation* and *ClientSimulation* classes each implement `AttachUser` and `DetachUser` methods, providing a mechanism to request that the calling user be mapped to a specific Actor instance on the server, as well as its associated ActorProxy on the client. Attaching a user to an Actor allows that user to send action requests and receive simulation events. It is up to the current control state of the target actor to arbitrate whether or not the actor will accept or decline the attach request. Such an attachment mechanism has the added benefit of supporting advanced features, such as allowing multiple users to attach to the same Actor. A few uses for this feature in an MMP are to allow customer-support personnel to take over control of a troublesome player's character, or to be able to see the game from the exact perspective of a newbie player who is having trouble and requesting help.

Action Requests

Once attached to a user on the server, the client's primary outbound communication comes in the form of action requests. The `SendActionRequest` method on the ClientSimulation takes an `ActionStateId` and an argument list representing the user's desired action, and passes them to the server simulation layer. The server, in turn, delegates these requests down a chain of responsibility from the attached Actor to its currentControlState, where it is processed or rejected. Figure 5.3.15 illustrates the action-request sequence.

Action Scheduling

The *ServerSimulation* provides a single `Tick` method that can be called from outside the simulation layer to trigger all processing of pending actions. This method is responsible for calculating the available time slice for simulation processing and hand-

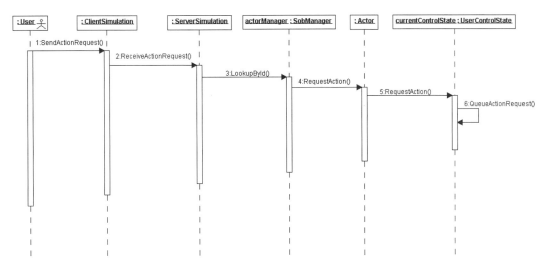

FIGURE 5.3.15   *Action request sequence diagram.*

ing it over to the schedule manager via the ProcessTasks method. Since the server physics layer typically requires processing at a higher frequency than the simulation layer, the Tick method serves as a good callback method to be registered with the physics layer that maintains the main game loop (see Figure 5.3.16).

Optimized Event Broadcasting and Handling

The PerformAction method on the ControlState determines the desiredActionState for the calling Actor to attempt to transition. If this actionState passes its CanTransition

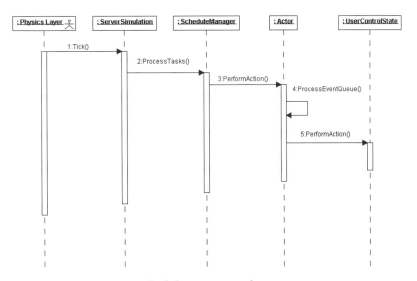

FIGURE 5.3.16   *Action-scheduling sequence diagram.*

pretest, then its Transition method is called to do the heavy lifting. Each actionState needs to provide its own specific implementation. Typically, this implementation will need to inform other simulation objects of the state transition. This is accomplished through simulation events. The acting simulationObject maintains the subscribers dictionary of other objects that have registered an interest in its actions. These subscribers are notified by calling their ReceiveEvent method. The receiver can determine if it needs to give the event immediate or passive attention. In the former case, it is handled as it is received; in the latter case, it is queued and is processed on the receiver's next PerformAction tick. Figure 5.3.17 shows this sequence diagram.

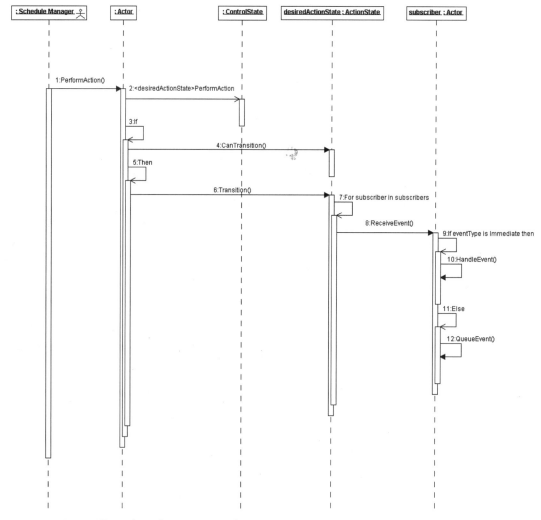

FIGURE 5.3.17   *Event-broadcast sequence diagram.*

Conclusion

Developing an MMP is a vast undertaking and presents many challenges that are unique. Starting with a solid and well-engineered foundation, like the one presented here, will carry you far and allow you to spend more time and effort on innovative game mechanics, rather than bug fixes and workarounds.

References

[Alexander02a] Alexander, Thor, "GoCap: Game Observation Capture," *AI Game Programming Wisdom*, Charles River Media, Inc., 2002.

[Alexander02b] Alexander, Thor, "An Optimized Fuzzy Logic Architecture for Decision-Making," *AI Programming Wisdom*, Charles River Media, Inc., 2002.

[Boer00] Boer, James, "Object-Oriented Programming and Design Techniques," *Game Programming Gems*, Charles River Media, Inc., 2000.

[Booch98] Booch, Grady, "The Unified Modeling Language User Guide," Addison Wesley, 1998.

[Dybsand00] Dybsand, Eric, "A Finite-State Machine Class," *Game Programming Gems*, Charles River Media, Inc., 2000.

[Gamma94] Gamma, et al., "Design Patterns," Addison Wesley Longman, Inc., 1994.

[Nelson96] Nelson, Mark, "Priority Queues and the STL," *Dr. Dobb's Journal.* Also available online at http://www.dogma.net/markn/articles/pq_stl/priority.htm, January 1996.

[Perlin96] Perlin, K. and A. Goldberg, "Improv: A System for Scripting Interactive Actors in Virtual Worlds," Computer Graphics Proceedings (SIGGRAPH 1996), ACM, 1996.

5.4

Scaling Multiplayer Servers

Justin Randall,
Sony Online Entertainment
logic@jrlogic.dyndns.org

Years ago, multi-user dungeons (MUDs) would often see 50 to 100 players interacting simultaneously. Even during these humble, early stages of multiplayer gaming, players suffered from lag and server resource starvation. Server administrators, implementers, and wizards fought constant battles against bugs, cheaters, grief players, and 'bots' running on player machines. Yesterday's problems live on today, but with added complications of scale. The complexity of game systems and designs leave servers open to more exploits. The amount of throughput required to simulate an interactive 3D world for thousands of players exacerbates lag. As the technology advances, so do the tools used to decipher, automate, peek, cheat, crash, or otherwise ruin a gameplay experience. We are fighting the same battles, but they are bigger and require some different tactics to win.

This gem will describe strategies to improve fair gameplay, as well as methods of clustering server processes and optimizing systems to reduce throughput requirements while improving process performance.

Strategies to Improve Fair Play

Never trust the client to send good information back to the game server. Assume every packet is malformed. Players will send false packets to move faster in a game, to inflict more damage, or to crash servers. They might do it to exploit data duplication bugs, or they might do it just to inflict grief on server administrators and other players. For whatever reason, they will send garbage—and the server must be prepared to throw out the trash.

Exploits in a multiplayer game fall into two general areas:

- Data that is sent from the client—the client lies to the server about what it is doing or assaults another client on the network.
- Data that is on the client—the player sneaks a peak at the data to gain unfair advantage.

It is impossible to exploit information that is not available. Game clients usually use information that is relevant to maintain the world simulation. It is helpful to have as much information on the client as possible to prevent objects from 'popping' into existence or to prevent lagging while waiting for simulation data to arrive. This 'potentially relevant' information can be exploited to give a player an advantage beyond the scope of normal gameplay. The client only *presents* portions of information, while the player extracts the rest through some other means (e.g., third-party software).

Strategy 1: Don't Send the Data

Data sent to the client should be on a 'need-to-know.' basis. Less data on the client equates to fewer opportunities for exploitation, lower bandwidth costs, and better perceived performance.

For example, the health point value of a foe might be useful during combat to improve client-side simulation, but sending health points for all potential foes in the world will let the player pick and choose their prey without interacting directly with the game. Programs like ShowEQ [ShowEq01] and proxy bots in first-person shooters are examples of how black-hat users exploit extraneous information sent to the client. If the data is not available, these kinds of exploits are impossible.

Strategy 2: Temporarily Lock the Data

Of course, the realities of gameplay in the context of limited bandwidth require that some precaching data be sent to improve the simulated experience on the client. All is not lost! Another strategy is to encrypt precache data with *a randomly generated key that is not sent to the client*.

The data is in ciphertext when it reaches the client. The client, not having a key to decrypt the data, can only resort to an attack on the cipher itself. The time required to make a brute-force assault on a cryptographically strong cipher like Twofish [Schnier98] far exceeds the relevance of the precache before it becomes interactive. After all, precaching information is sent because the client will likely be interacting with it in the near future (probably within the next 60 seconds).

When the decryption key (16 bytes is usually large enough) is sent, the data magically 'appears' on the client. The time required to send tens or hundreds of kilobytes is amortized, and the data becomes relevant in the time it takes to send those few bytes to decipher precaching information.

Some information, such as how to draw an object, could be in the clear as a precache message to request a background load of assets; while game information like experience values, health points, object name, and so forth are ciphertext. This strikes a balance between network-send latencies, blocking disk reads, CPU-lag loading assets, and fair play.

Strategy 3: Clients Send Commands, Not States

If the client is not authoritative for position, health points, combat results, or whatever, then it is not possible for the player to say, "I have 65536 health," or "Joe is dead." Instead, the client should only be allowed to send commands like "walk," "run," or "attack Joe."

Strategy 4: Server Validates Client Output

The player might not be allowed to send the message "Attack Joe," or might send a packet of garbage that is not valid. If the server receives an invalid command, it should be ready to either discard the data or discard the client altogether by disconnecting it.

Strategy 5: Never, Ever Tell a Client the Network Address of Another Client

If a player knows the network address of another player, any number of attacks could be launched against the remote client. For example: The player is engaged in combat with Joe, and Strategy 3 has already been implemented, meaning only commands may be sent. However, the player might employ a denial of service (on the game network port) against Joe during combat. Joe is effectively incapacitated and cannot issue any commands. He is summarily executed in a duel, the denial of service disconnects Joe's computer, and the black-hat player wins the battle.

The game design might require high-bandwidth services, such as voice communications. In this case, peer-to-peer communications are attractive solutions to problems of throughput and the cost of ownership. There will be a tradeoff, however, between lower operational expenses and customer experiences. Permitting players to activate peer communications selectively, explaining the risks to them when they do it, and allowing them to choose who they peer with are some compromises that might be acceptable.

Designing Scalable Servers

It is important to prepare the server code for the consequences of a high-throughput application. Data delivery should be efficient. Using the network system in game code should be simple and safe. Efficiency, simplicity, and safety are common-sense goals, but these goals can often be lost in the details of implementing massively multiplayer servers.

Efficiency—Use Modern System Interfaces

Everyone would like code to be portable. By writing a `select`, `connect`, `accept`, `listen`, `send`, and `recv`, wrapped with a few `#ifdef`'s to handle nuances of Winsock versus BSD sockets, a network subsystem can be authored with very little code in a couple of hours, and it can be reasonably portable.

This is fine for low-volume network services handling a few dozen connections, but it does not scale well when writing services handling hundreds or thousands of active sessions. Most modern operating systems provide extended APIs that are more efficient than basic BSD socket services.

poll() and POSIX2 AIO

POSIX2 defines an asynchronous I/O system (AIO) that is better suited to high-throughput applications. Unfortunately, it is not very well-supported on all platforms. As of 2001, glibc provides fallbacks for AIO, and Linux supports AIO only for files that allow lseek(). At some point, however, AIO will be the preferred approach to high-volume networking.

But for today, game code has to work on real-world platforms that are tested and stable. An alternative to POSIX2 AIO for UN*X is the poll() system call. poll() is closely related to select(). File descriptors (specifically, poll file descriptors) are passed to the call, and it returns the number of descriptors that have some events pending.

It does not, however, tell the application *which* descriptors are ready. The application must iterate through the descriptor list to see which of them have events.

poll() is better suited than select(), because the events are posted in the descriptor list directly. The network system does not have to leave user space to find descriptors with pending events. Finding pending sockets in a set of hundreds, or even thousands, now only takes a few milliseconds, without the pains associated with making system calls querying for events on each socket.

This code is an example of using the poll call:

```
int result = poll(fds, count, 0);
int c = 0;
for(i = 0; i < count, c <= result; ++i)
{
    if(fds[I].revents == POLLIN)
    {
        c++;
        // .. receive data
    }
}
```

Win32 I/O Completion Ports and Overlapped I/O

Microsoft introduced IOCP with Winsock2. IOCP is an asynchronous I/O API that efficiently presents I/O events to an application. Rather than using select()or other asynchronous methods, a socket is associated with a *completion port,* and normal Winsock operations commence. When an event occurs, however, the completion port is queued by the operating system. The application can then query the kernel for completion ports. Microsoft indicates that this is the best way to implement high-volume network server applications [MSDN00]. This code roughly demonstrates IOCP usage:

```
void foo()
{
    SOCKET s = socket(AF_INET, SOCK_STREAM, 16);
    HANDLE iocp = CreateIoCompletionPort(
        s, g_iocpGroup,
        0, 0);
}

void updateNetwork()
{
    bool success = true;
    while(success)
    {
        int ok = GetQueuedCompletionStatus(
        iocp, // completion port of interest
        &bytesTransferred, // number of bytes sent or
                           // received
        &completionKey,
        &overlapped,
        0 // timeout immediately if there are no
        // completions
        );

        if(ok)
        {
            success = true;
            // handle event
        }
        else
        {
            success = false;
        }
    }
}
```

Safety—Message Serialization

A server written in a strongly typed language can catch message-type errors at compile time, before mistakes are introduced to a running application. Enforcing type safety over a network is no more difficult than ensuring type safety when storing objects on disk. In fact, the same design and strategies used for file-based persistence should be used for network-based data synchronization, with a few exceptions.

When persisting data to disk, programs might often assume that the data will be reread by the same program on the same host that wrote the data. When writing data to the network, this is not necessarily the case. Simply throwing a raw chunk of memory containing some structs or classes to the network will definitely break, even if two hosts are of the same endian architecture. The local and remote systems might both be x86 systems, but running applications compiled with different word-alignment options (Dev Studio aligns at 8 bytes by default and gcc at 4 bytes). The client might be a little-endian x86, and the server might be a big-endian 64-bit alpha (with little-endian emulation disabled). Perhaps they are of the same architecture today, but servers could be upgraded next year. There are no guarantees about byte alignment or endianness when dealing with the network.

Opt for serialization that is common to network messaging, file I/O, and database persistence (if a database is in use). Unified serialization might be used to apply deltas to object data as well as to construct whole objects. For example, a database process might receive a position update network message, interpret it as SQL, and write only the object position to the back-end database. The database could then be treated like any other server receiving updates. The interface is common; the implementation is what differs.

Enforcing type safety saves time in the long run, provides a more-stable application, and permits better reuse of code as development progresses. One of the most effective uses of a typed message system is in dispatching data to server systems.

Simplicity—Message Dispatch

Typically, a protocol will identify messages with a short one- to four-byte header. As the message is received, the header is read, and more data is extracted from a packet until the whole message has been processed. This often happens in a single function with a large switch statement that forwards a network buffer to other functions for further processing.

This is a method that gets the job done, does it efficiently, and is easy to understand. It is also somewhat painful to add new messages. When enough message types are introduced to the system, the switch statement can grow to a ten thousand-line behemoth that is unreadable. With each new addition to the messaging system, the switch implementation induces increasingly large build times. Most importantly, the dispatch code is tightly coupled with each new message. New message code cannot leverage old code to implement new behavior. The old code must be updated to understand the new message data. Unused data paths might remain in the code base undetected.

The typed-message system mentioned earlier might be used to avoid some of this pain. It would be beneficial if an application could say to the dispatching system. "when connection X sends message Y, invoke my member function Z to handle it."

With this kind of dispatching system, there should be no prior knowledge of what types of objects are requesting a message or what types of messages are handled. Once the dispatch system is written, it need not be touched again, and it will be far less than ten thousand lines of code!

ON THE CD

How it works (see the code provided on the CD-ROM for full implementation details):

- A connection object has a dispatch object.
- Another object in the system registers itself with the dispatch object.

  - It provides a 'connect' method that accepts a reference to a dispatch object that it listens to—a 'this' from the object invoking 'connect' and a pointer to a member function that is executed when the requested message is emitted.

- The connection object adds the requestor's dispatch object and callback function to a container of recipients by type.
- When the dispatch system receives a network message, it constructs the message and 'emits' the message, which was already resolved to the proper dispatch method at compile time.
- Requestor objects have their member functions invoked with the message as an argument.

This requires some meta-programming magic with templates if C++ is used. It provides type-safe message dispatch and compile-time errors when message types (or requestor methods) are unresolved.

In the context of a network messaging system, a connection receives a network buffer, constructs a new message of a specific type, and dispatches it:

```cpp
void Client::Client(Connection * connection) :
myCallbackObject()
{
    myCallbackObject.connect(
        connection->getEmitter(),
        this,
        &Client::onDisconnect);
}

void Client::onDisconnect(DisconnectMessage & d)
{
    cleanup();
}

void Connection::onReceive(const Archive::Stream & data)
{
    Archive::Stream::ReadIterator r = data.begin();
    Message & m = MessageFactory::create(r);
    emitMessage(m);
}
```

This can be used for far more than network messaging. Consider a monster object on the server process. When the monster dies, it should be removed from all clients that see the monster.

```cpp
void Client::onCreateMonsterOnRemote(Monster * m)
{
    myCallbackObject.connect(
        m->getEmitter(),
        this,
        &Client::onKilledMonster);
}

void Client::onKilledMonster(KillMessage & k)
{
    RemoveObjectMessage r(k.getMonster()->getId());
```

```
        send(r);
    }

    void Monster::onKilled(Character * destroyer)
    {
        KillMessage k(this, destroyer);
        emitMessage(k);
    }
```

Later in development, designers might decide that the character object has to know if it kills a monster. In this case, the character only wants to know about monsters that are killed when it is in combat. Perhaps all characters involved in combat with the monster gain experience points. Using the dispatch system, the single kill message that was emitted by the monster in the old code can trigger new code in a new character object.

```
    void Character::onEnterCombat(Monster * m)
    {
        myCallbackObject.connect(
            m->getEmitter(),
            this,
            &Client::onKilledMonster);
    }

    void Character::onKilledMonster(KillMessage & k)
    {
        experiencePoints +=
            k.getMonster()->getExperienceValue();
    }
```

As an additional bonus to using this particular (C++) implementation of a dispatch system, function pointers that are passed as callbacks can be protected members, thus hiding interface details, yet exposing them selectively to individual objects when they need to handle particular messages. No one may invoke the protected members directly, unless they are exposed explicitly within implementation code of the object that defines them.

Distributing the Load

Ensuring that server systems can scale to arbitrarily large connection counts often entails clustering host systems and running multiple processes. Game services spanning several processes introduce technical design challenges. How does a client find the right service? How do services cooperate to present a unified world simulation? Where does the world persist game data between process startup and shutdown? How are processes spawned? What happens when clients need to interact with objects on multiple servers? These are just a few of the problems nearly every distributed-game server will have to address.

Once solutions are implemented, meeting the demands of the game ceases to be as much of a technical problem as an economic problem. Ideally, throwing more hardware at the server cluster would increase capacity.

Consider Using a Front-End Process To Interact with Clients

Separating client traffic from the rest of the servers is a good first step to solving problems of location (How does a client find the right service?) and presenting a unified world simulation. When a client connects to a game server, it is really interacting with a front-end process (FEP). Several front-end processes might cooperate to increase the total connection count that a server cluster handles.

How Does a Client Find the Right Service?

A common design employs a well-known login service that will validate a client, then present the client with several 'servers' with which it may interact. Each server is one of several front-end processes that separate the client from back-end game processes. Once the client connects to an FEP, that process will communicate with other back-end processes to insert a player's character into the world simulation so that it may begin gameplay (see Figure 5.4.1). How the world is presented to the client and which back-end process interacts with the client depends on the design of the game. If there is a process for each city in a role-playing game, then the city that the player was last in might be the target process for the new client.

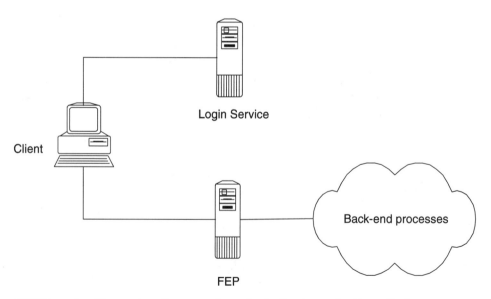

FIGURE 5.4.1   *Connection diagram using a Login Service and a Front-End Process (FEP).*

The back-end will likely consist of other location services. Which objects are on which servers? Which players are on which servers? This relationship is abstracted from the client. It will only interact with the FEP. There is no need for a client to connect directly to a locator service or any other back-end process. Back-end locators need a single connection with each FEP, which in turn can successfully redirect client communications to a world-simulation service somewhere in the back-end.

How Do Services Cooperate To Present a Unified World Simulation?

FEPs facilitate the presentation of a unified world simulation. A unified simulation is one in which the game world appears as a single server covering a contiguous simulation through a single connection. If a client has to move from one back-end game-server process to another, there is no reconnection process necessary on the client. This might all be handled with interactions between the FEP and the game-server processes involved.

The FEP introduces a single process to filter packets. A FEP might handle compression and encryption for client connections, dumping raw, uncompressed clear text to back-end processes in order to save precious CPU resources for other activities (like AI or physics). Because the FEP is the single point of entry for client data, packets might also be validated on the FEP, without requiring protocol upgrades (e.g., if a client attempts to send a malformed packet to crash game servers).

Front-end processes safeguard clients from game-service failures on the back-end. If there is a recovery scenario implemented, clients need never know that the server died a horrible death. The connection between the FEP and the client can remain active while the back-end starts a new game service and redirects the clients to the new process. Meanwhile, the developer can browse the core files, while players happily continue abusing their servers.

Of course, every design has its flaws. Introducing a FEP will induce latency as data is read from the network, dispatched to the appropriate connection on the back-end, committed to the wire, and read on a back-end process. It is another process to manage when maintaining or diagnosing server clusters.

Distributing server processes does not necessitate the use of FEPs. Some game designs that involve autonomous game servers (i.e., there is no requirement for a unified world simulation) requiring near-real-time latencies are probably not candidates for using front-end processes.

Interprocess Interaction

The majority of technical exploits arise when players interact across process boundaries. A player trading items for gold with an NPC or player on another process is a great example of a duplication exploit. If Joe (on Server A) is accepting plate mail armor offered by Jane (on Server B), and Joe (or anyone else) manages to crash Server B, he might be able to duplicate the plate mail armor. This happens if Joe's server commits the transaction while Server B is crashing and has not committed the transaction. Jane still has plate mail armor; so does Joe. There are two plate mail armors in the world where before there was only one. Next time they trade 2 armors, then 4, 8, 16, and so on, until they have an obscene amount of armor to loot.

The liberal use of UML [Larman01] sequence diagrams is indispensable when identifying interprocess exploits. As diagrams are built, assume one or both servers will crash at some point during an interprocess interaction. Identify what will happen to the state of the game if this happens.

When building sequence diagrams, take time to consider interactions with overloaded servers and how these affect gameplay. It would be unfair to keep a player locked in a trade screen while it waits for a server that might never return. Messages sent between processes might not be processed right away. Assume that one or more processes will have a 100% CPU load and might never have an opportunity to process an interaction. Thinking asynchronously will help to design a system that the player perceives as better-performing. It will be more tolerant to unfair demands on some processes and can help to build load-balancing systems to even out the CPU load on a server cluster.

Optimization

Three-dimensional clients limit the number of polygons sent to a rendering pipeline to what is potentially visible in the scene. This is done to save the amount of processing necessary to draw a scene. Large-scale, distributed servers are under a much heavier load, interacting with more objects than a client scene has polygons. N^2 operations between one million objects that are scattered over 20 or more processes will quickly demonstrate a requirement to cull objects on the server as well!

On a client, culling happens relative to a single camera in a single scene. On a server, the problem balloons out of proportion. Each object has its own perspective on the world! The strategies that worked so well on a single game client are not an exact fit for the complications presented by the server—it cannot afford to spend most of its CPU in sorting and culling algorithms, leaving only a few cycles for AI, messaging, physics, persistence, and the plethora of other tasks it must complete.

It is desirable, even necessary, to limit what each object can interact with to some very small subset of other objects in the world. A system that could rapidly sort and update objects, independent of any perspective presented by a single object, and use less than 10% of the CPU would be ideal.

Those systems do exist, and which one is right for a server really depends on the simulation. This gem will focus on a particular subdivision system proposed in a previous article by John Ratcliff in *Game Programming Gems 2*—the Sphere Tree [Ratcliff]. It will also present a perspective strategy for objects that fit well with a distance-based culling system.

The Sphere Tree

Distance-based culling is best suited to large worlds that cover a lot of area and have clusters of populations scattered throughout world space. Interactions aggregate around objects close to one another and cull objects that are far off in the distance. The sphere tree is an ideal distance-based spatial sorting algorithm.

Sphere trees make speedy distance queries, quickly returning a solution set of objects that are within an arbitrary sphere. They also have the property of extremely rapid resorting of objects in motion. These characteristics can be employed to maintain a perspective-independent sorting and subdivision system to facilitate limited interaction between objects in the world simulation.

A sphere tree organizes objects in a hierarchy of spheres. There is a root node containing all child spheres (see Figure 5.4.2). Children are subdivided into progressively smaller spheres until suitable-size bounding spheres populate the tree. As an object moves within a sphere, it checks its parent's boundaries. If it exceeds the boundary, the parent either resizes itself to accommodate the new position, or, if some maximum size has been reached, the object is sorted into the parent's parent sphere, and a new child sphere is created.

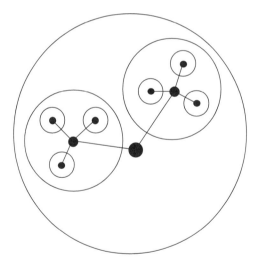

FIGURE 5.4.2 *A three-level sphere tree depicting a root node, two super spheres, and six child spheres.*

Sphere-to-sphere testing is a reasonably efficient process and compares vector distances. This process can be further optimized by comparing square distances to avoid a slow sqrt() call. Because objects in a sphere tree are sorted based on bounding spheres, when a range-based query is made to the tree, it tests the top-most nodes in the tree. Those spheres that satisfy an intersection are further queried. Their child spheres are tested against the query. This process repeats recursively through the tree until a set of objects that satisfy the range query are identified.

Performance of the query depends on the size of the range requested. The smaller the query, the fewer top-most nodes will be included for recursion. This is the second useful property of sphere trees with distance-based culling.

Each object has a bounding sphere so that it properly sorts into the tree. Additionally, it has an 'interest' sphere, in which it has its own perspective on the world, based on some distance. As the object moves, so does the interest sphere. That sphere is used to query the sphere tree. When the query returns a new object to interact with, then it is 'in view,' relative to the object moving. The new object is placed in a set of potentially interactive objects.

When the server checks for interactions between objects, it need only query the potentially interactive set. This is a much smaller subset (depending on the interest radius) than the total number of objects in the world.

As the new object is added, the server might also check to see if it is a player character moving about in the world. If it is, then when the object is added to the potentially interactive list, and baseline information for the new object might be sent to the client. As the object moves or changes, the client can receive updates about that object. The server will only have to send updates about objects that are potentially interactive with the client. Likewise, when objects are removed from the potentially interactive set, they might be unloaded from clients.

It is tempting to place an interest radius on a client's character object. This provides a single interactive set that the client can query for new information. It is more efficient, however, to have interactive sets relative to other objects. A building might have a long range of interaction (it might be visible for hundreds of meters in game-world space), while a shrubbery next to the building might have a visible range of only a few meters.

By storing the interactive set on the viewed objects rather than the viewer, updates can be 'pushed' to viewers by the observed object. This will prevent excessive polling, incurring CPU usage only as events take place.

For the most part, objects are not in motion, and so they do not query the sphere tree to update their interactive sets. Objects that are in motion will need to collide with the interaction spheres of stationary objects. The building will want to know when a character is close enough to see it when the character walks toward the city.

Interaction spheres might be bounding spheres placed into a sphere tree as well. Collision tests with spheres in the tree are efficient. When a collision occurs, the target might receive notification and add the source (mover) to its interactive set. Using this method, stationary objects such as buildings or idle nonplayer characters can be added to a client's world-view and update the client if their state changes.

This same approach can be used to cull server-to-server interactions. Reducing server-to-server traffic is at least as important as server-to-client traffic. Servers will need to perform some processing on remote objects if they interact. Forcing all server processes to spend CPU on all objects in the world will quickly bring a server cluster to its knees.

Sphere trees are not the only solution to problems of spatial sorting and culling interactions, but they are a reasonable solution for large worlds where distance matters. Quadtrees and octrees are just as reasonable for large worlds, but these have their own drawbacks. Some worlds consisting of interconnected spaces are better suited to a portal-based system to cull interaction. Portals, quadtrees, octrees, sphere trees, and many other algorithms are at the disposal of the developer. The hard part is not in implementing the right solution; the hard part is to find the right solution to implement.

Conclusion

This gem has described several techniques that are useful in the design of scalable multiplayer servers. Be sure to take advantage of the server platform's most efficient network API, even at the expense of portability, so that servers can handle the greatest possible number of connections. Architectural features like front-end processes and sphere trees for culling provide high server performance and isolate back-end servers from direct contact with client machines. Spending extra time early in the development process to build simple, safe, and reusable APIs, like message dispatching and message factories, will ensure more-rapid implementation of gameplay features as the project nears completion.

References

[Larman01] Larman, Craig, *Applying UML and Patterns: An Introduction to Object-Oriented Analysis and Design and the Unified Process*, Prentice Hall, 2001.

[MSDN00] Microsoft Corporation, "Windows Sockets 2.0: Write Scalable Winsock Apps Using Completion Ports," available online at http://msdn.microsoft.com/msdnmag/issues/1000/Winsock/Winsock.asp, MSDN, October 2000.

[Ratcliff] Ratcliff, John W., "Sphere Trees for Fast Visibility Culling, Ray Tracing, and Range Searching," *Game Programming Gems 2*, Charles River Media, Inc., 2001.

[ShowEq01] HackersQuest. "HackersQuest" is available online at http://www.hackersquest.org/, March 2002.

[Schnier98] Schnier, Bruce Twofish, "A 128-bit Block Cipher," available online at http://www.counterpane.com/twofish-paper.html, Counterpane Labs, 1998.

Template-Based Object Serialization

Jason Beardsley, NCsoft Austin

jbeardsley@ncaustin.com

For a networked game, either client/server or peer-to-peer, it is important to have an efficient method of converting objects to and from a network-friendly representation, most typically a stream of raw bytes. This process is known as serialization.

Even for non-networked games, serialization is useful for dealing with the file system (e.g., when loading resources from disk or saving game state). However, file-based schemes often trade space efficiency for capabilities that are not usually required in a network environment, such as random access, in-place modification, a hierarchical directory structure, or versioning. This makes them unsuitable for network communication.

This gem presents a serialization method designed for network usage. It achieves a high degree of flexibility and uniformity in handling all types of objects—built-in types, STL containers, and user-defined classes.

Existing Solutions

Serialization itself is nothing new. One commonly employed method is to define a structure containing the data to be serialized, fill it in, and simply use memcpy() to convert it into a format suitable for network transmission. This approach is very fast and satisfactory for many applications, but it has some inherent limitations:

- It only works when the bit-level representation of data is exactly what should be sent over the network. This is not generally true for C++ classes—in particular, those that use dynamic storage or have embedded pointers, or any class with virtual methods.
- Care must be taken when in laying out the structure in order to minimize padding by the compiler. In a cross-platform environment, any padding must be applied equally by all compilers.
- Any byte order conversions must be done explicitly before copying.
- Handling variable-length data, such as strings or arrays, is clumsy at best.

In summary, the 'struct/memcpy()' serialization method is only applicable when dealing with fixed-size structures containing plain data types. Another standard practice involves the use of an object that has methods to store and retrieve each desired type. This class might look something like the following:

```
class Serializer
{
public:
    // plain ol' data
    bool Put(int val);
    bool Get(int& valOut);
    bool Put(float val);
    bool Get(float& valOut);
    // standard classes
    bool Put(const std::string& val);
    bool Get(std::string& valOut);
    // STL containers
    template <typename T>
        bool Put(const std::set<T>& val);
    template <typename T> bool
        Get(std::set<T>& valOut);
    // et cetera
};
```

Note that Put() and Get() are overloaded instead of being named for the type they handle (e.g., PutInt() or GetString()). This is essential for STL container support. If the methods were not overloaded, then the code for handling an STL collection could not be written in a generic fashion (i.e., by calling Put() and Get() on its respective elements).

When it comes to user-defined classes, we face a dilemma—should Serializer be extended to directly support every class, or should the class have its own serialization methods? The answer to the first question is a resounding "**NO**," for a variety of reasons. First, Serializer must have access to the internals of any nontrivial class (requiring friendship). Second, every time support for a new type is added, there might be a large amount of unnecessary recompilation. In addition, Serializer's interface could easily grow out of control. In short, this is a maintainability nightmare, not to mention very inelegant.

Therefore, serialization support should be incorporated into each class directly. Typically, this involves defining an abstract interface class with pure virtual methods to support serialization:

```
class Serializable
{
public:
    virtual bool PutInto(Serializer& s) const = 0;
    virtual bool GetFrom(Serializer& s) = 0;
}
```

Then, extend `Serializer` to support serializable objects:

```
bool Serializer::Put(const Serializable& obj)
    { return obj.PutInto(*this); }

bool Serializer::Get(Serializable& obj)
    { return obj.GetFrom(*this); }
```

There is nothing wrong with this idea, but it has some drawbacks. It requires modification of the class to be serialized, which is fine, if possible. However, what if the class is provided by a third-party library and cannot be changed? There are performance implications, forcing what might otherwise be a very simple, standalone class into an inheritance hierarchy. For a game, where speed is of the utmost importance, introducing virtual methods into a simple class might be an unacceptable price to pay.

Aside from the requirement that user classes be derived from `Serializable`, and accepting some other minor performance problems (e.g., the header declaring `Serializer` must include all STL container headers, increasing compilation times), this satisfies the goal of a consistent, extensible serialization system. The question is, can it be refined further to eliminate (or reduce in scope) these last few problems? The answer is "Yes," but before we can present the final method in detail, some background material is in order.

Portability

Networked games, especially those of the client/server variety, are often multiplatform applications. The client might run on Windows, Macintosh, or PlayStation2, whereas the servers might be a mixture of Linux, Solaris, and Windows, running on different processor architectures. Any serialization library must therefore be highly portable, which means it must be ported to (and *tested on*) each target platform.

One of the first lessons learned when writing multiplatform code is that the C++ language does not dictate the exact size (in bits) of built-in types, such as `int` and `float`. For serialization, this poses a problem, because the exact size of an object must be known. Otherwise, a value could be written using 32 bits, but read out using 64 bits, leading to undefined results. The most recent C standard addresses this by providing the `<inttypes.h>` header, but it could be some time before all compiler vendors implement this. The next best thing is to define (via `typedef`) a group of fixed-size primitive types (`int8`, `int16`, `int32`, `int64`, `uint8`, ..., `uint64`, `float32`, `float64`), and use only these when serializing data. Care must be taken when dealing with data that might be implicitly converted to more than one of the supported types—enumerated types and manifest constants should be explicitly cast to an appropriate numeric type before being stored or retrieved.

The next complication with cross-platform code is that of byte order. Different chip architectures store multibyte values (both integers and floating-point numbers) in memory using either 'big-endian' or 'little-endian' order [Kernighan99]. Thus, the serialization system must be able to convert to and from a standard byte order in order for the low-level data format to be truly portable. Which specific byte order (big or little) is chosen is not extremely important, so long as it is consistent. A good rule of thumb is to go with the native format on the server side, since clients presumably have more CPU cycles to burn. Regardless, byte swapping should never be a noticeable performance problem. Since we are using our own primitive types, we must implement our own set of conversion functions instead of using the standard `htonl()` and friends.

Speaking of primitive types, floating-point numbers might prove to be a significant barrier to portable code, depending on the target platform. Fortunately, almost every processor manufactured today uses the standard IEEE formats, so bit-level copying of floating-point data is actually portable. Keep in mind that floats also have a byte order, which is almost certainly the same as the integer order, so they might need to be swapped. It is not difficult to write a program to test a particular architecture for IEEE compliance, though what to do on a nonconforming platform is left as an exercise for the unlucky reader.

The Serializer Class

The goals for the serialization system are as follows:

- Present a consistent interface for storing and retrieving all types of data.
- Support primitive types, STL containers, and user-defined classes, with minimal code changes to the latter.
- Be as efficient as possible, while still remaining portable.

As the title of this gem suggests, the key to meeting these goals is the use of templates—specifically, the use of member function templates.

Suppose we declare `Put()` and `Get()` inside `Serializer` as follows:

```
class Serializer
{
public:
    template <typename T> bool Put(const T& obj);
    template <typename T> bool Get(T& obj);
};
```

All that is necessary now to support any type `T` is simply to define specialized versions of each function. For example, the standard C++ string class:

```
template <>
bool Serializer::Put(const std::string& obj)
    { /* implementation */ }

template <>
bool Serializer::Get(std::string& obj)
    { /* implementation */ }
```

Regrettably, it is at this point when another lesson in cross-platform programming is learned—not all compilers are created equal. While the above code is standard C++, it is not accepted by all compilers. Microsoft Visual C++ 6.0, for example, does not support member template functions defined outside the enclosing class declaration. Working around compiler differences is standard operating procedure for the network coder, and as is the case with many programming problems, the answer lies in introducing another layer of indirection.

If there were auxiliary functions that handled the low-level details of storing (PutInto()) and retrieving (GetFrom()) the bits for any given type T, safely tucked inside the SerializeHelper namespace to avoid any conflicts, then we could trivially implement Put() and Get() in the following manner:

```
template <typename T> bool Put(const T& obj)
{
    return SerializeHelper::PutInto(*this, obj);
}

template <typename T> bool Get(T& obj)
{
    return SerializeHelper::GetFrom(*this, obj);
}
```

The task then becomes defining PutInto() and GetFrom() for all of the requisite types: integers, floats, strings, STL containers, and so forth. Since the namespace can be extended arbitrarily and in separate compilation units, user-defined types are easily and efficiently supported.

Input and Output Storage

Serializer makes use of a 'byte-buffer' utility class that handles the mundane details of reading and writing to memory, including automatically resizing itself when being written to. The partial interface for this class is as follows:

```
class Buffer
{
public:
    bool Write(const void* data, int len);
    bool Read(void* dataOut, int len);
    const void* GetData() const;
    int GetLength() const;
};
```

Handling Simple Fixed-Length Types

Integers, floats, and bool can be dealt with in two ways—using functions inside the SerializeHelper namespace or directly inside Serializer itself (i.e., by overloading Put() and Get()). Since these types are so fundamental, we will employ the latter method, as it might also speed up compile times.

The code for each type is similar. Convert the value to network byte order (if necessary), and copy the bits. For `bool`, first convert to a `uint8` (true = 1, false = 0), since the underlying representation might be a larger integral type.

Handling Simple Variable-Length Types

Two types fall into the simple variable-length types category: C-style strings and untyped byte arrays. Since strings are null-terminated, it is possible to store the character array with its null terminator, without a Pascal-style lengthfield. Nonetheless, explicitly storing the length (and omitting the terminator) is safer overall, even if it is marginally less space-efficient. Both `string` objects and `char*` can be passed to `Put()`. However, there is no `Get(char*)` function, because the size of the output cannot be determined.

Wide character strings are a portability issue, because the size of `wchar_t` is not strictly defined by the language. Even on a single platform, the exact size can vary, depending on compiler options. Therefore, there is no built-in support for wide strings. One workaround is to define an application-specific wide-string class (perhaps based on the `basic_string` template), and make it serializable.

Raw byte arrays also pose something of a problem. The interface to `Put()` takes in a single argument, but it is necessary to know the number of items to write (as well as the maximum number of items that can be read). Fortunately, we have introduced a class that can act like a byte array (`Buffer`), and it is easily made serializable. There will be times, however, when using `Buffer` is not possible, or when doing so might involve extra copying. Two additional methods, `PutRaw()` and `GetRaw()`, provide low-level access to the serialized stream. These take a length parameter that indicates the number of bytes to be written or read, respectively.

Handling STL Containers

Storing the contents of an STL container is straightforward. First, write out the number of elements, and then walk from the container's `begin()` to `end()`, writing out each individual item (calling `Put()` again). The code to implement this is virtually identical for all containers, so naturally it would be nice to only have to write it once.

Programmers familiar with the STL know that the key to working with STL containers (and the true power of the STL) is effectively using iterators [Meyers01]. The many algorithms that come with the STL (e.g., `find_if()`) use iterators almost exclusively. Serialization is no different, and although `Put()` and `Get()` do operate on containers explicitly, underneath the hood are a pair of functions that only manipulate iterators—`PutRange()` and `GetRange()`. These are in the `SerializeHelper` namespace and only rely on the public interface of `Serializer`.

Here is the implementation of `PutRange()`. Note that it could compute the number of items by using the `distance()` algorithm, but it is generally more efficient for the caller to compute it (using `size()`), and pass it in as a parameter.

```
template <typename Iterator>
bool SerializeHelper::PutRange(Serializer& s,
                                   const Iterator& begin,
                                   const Iterator& end,
                                   uint32 size)
{
    if (!s.Put(size)) return false; // store size
    for (Iterator it = begin; it != end; ++it)
        if (!s.Put(*it)) return false; // store item
    return true; // success
}
```

Retrieving the elements of a container is slightly more complicated. This process has two extra wrinkles—first, the type of objects contained must be determined (e.g., for set<T>, figure out what T is); and second, once an element has been unserialized, it must be inserted back into the container. Given this, it is a matter of reading the number of elements and then reading each element out one-by-one, adding to the container. Fortunately, the designers of the STL have provided the necessary functionality in the iterator_traits class and the concept of insert iterators [Josuttis99], [Austern98].

```
template <typename Inserter>
bool SerializeHelper::GetRange(Serializer& s,
                                   Inserter it)
{
    uint32 size;
    if (!s.Get(size)) return false;
    for (uint32 i = 0; i < size; ++i)
    {
        iterator_traits<Inserter>::value_type obj;
        if (!s.Get(obj)) return false;
        *it = obj; // inserts into container
    }
    return true; // success
}
```

Once again, compiler differences (or more accurately, STL differences) arise and make this piece of code nonportable. The culprit here is iterator_traits, which is not fully functional on all platforms. The workaround is something of a hack. What is needed is a way to determine the type of the contained objects. The caller of GetRange() certainly knows this, and thus can pass in a null pointer of that type T, which becomes another template argument. The result (differences in bold) is:

```
template <typename T, typename Inserter>
bool SerializeHelper::GetRange(Serializer& s,
                                   Inserter it,
                                   T* /* unref */)
{
    uint32 size;
    if (!s.Get(size)) return false;
    for (uint32 i = 0; i < size; ++i)
```

```
        {
            T obj;
            if (!s.Get(obj)) return false;
            *it = obj; // inserts into container
        }
        return true; // success
}
```

Given `PutRange()` and `GetRange()`, writing the other helper routines for an STL container is straightforward. For `list`, this is the code:

```
template <typename T>
bool SerializeHelper::PutInto(Serializer& s,
                              const list<T>& l)
{
    return PutRange(s, l.begin(), l.end(), l.size());
}

template <typename T>
bool SerializeHelper::GetFrom(Serializer& s,
                             list<T>& l)
{
    l.clear(); // destroy any existing contents
    return GetRange(s, back_inserter(l), (T*)0);
}
```

The rest of the STL containers are handled similarly, with the only difference being in the number of template arguments (e.g., `map` requires two types—key and value) and the creation of the insert iterator in the call to `GetRange()`. Sequence-based containers use the `back_inserter` adapter (which calls `push_back()`), while the others use a plain `inserter` (which calls `insert()`).

In order to completely support associative containers (`map`, `hash_map`, etc.), we must also define serialization functions for the utility template class `pair`. Note that STL containers of any serializable class are supported (including nested containers), so long as the class has a default constructor.

Handling User-Defined Classes

The final piece to the system is dealing with user classes (i.e., any arbitrary class that you want to serialize). Classes (or structures) whose public interface can be used to read and write an object's complete state, and which are not part of an inheritance hierarchy, are simple: define `PutInto()` and `GetFrom()`, and that's it. No changes to the class are necessary!

When a class has private data, the `SerializeHelper` functions will have to be made friends. If these are viewed as external member functions, then this does not really break encapsulation. In fact, it is similar to adding `iostream` support to a class.

A class hierarchy makes life interesting. For example, say we have an abstract base, `Message` class, and concrete subclasses, `MoveMessage` and `ChatMessage`. The base class has members that need serialization, as do the subclasses. Since more message classes will probably be added in the future, the network layer (where messages are serialized before going out on the wire) only knows about Message objects. How can this layer properly serialize an arbitrary Message, and how can it create an arbitrary Message out of a bunch of received bytes?

For serialization, the answer is to reintroduce the serializable concept. Make the base class Message directly serializable (i.e., define PutInto() and GetFrom()). Have these functions call into pure virtual methods that Message subclasses must define in order to handle class-specific data. On the receiving end, use the factory pattern [Gamma95] to create the right type of Message before unserializing. In order for the receiver to know which kind of Message was sent, and therefore which kind to manufacture, a header with type information (e.g., a 'message-class id') is also required.

Pointers and Arrays

Dealing with pointers is pretty easy—simply dereference them and call the existing methods. Defining Put() and Get() that take pointer arguments does not work, because it gives the compiler a choice of which template to instantiate (Put<T>(T*) or Put<T*>(T*)), and this is an ambiguity error. Compilers do not like choices. As a result, this means that STL containers of pointers cannot be automatically serialized.

The interface must change to properly support arrays, because we need to know how many elements are to be written in Put() and the maximum number that can be read in Get(). Since one of the overriding goals is a consistent interface, this is undesirable. However, working with plain arrays is of obvious importance for efficiency, so templatized PutArray() and GetArray() functions (taking a length parameter) are included—but in general, using the STL vector class is every bit as fast as arrays. Just like pointers, an STL container of arrays is not going to work out-of-the-box, although this hardly sounds like a limitation.

Extensions and Optimizations

A Variable-Length Count

Strings, buffers, and STL containers store their sizes in serialized outputs. The question is: What kind of integer should be used for this lengthfield? To minimize output size, it should be as small as possible. Requiring the length to fit inside (say) a uint16 limits the ability to serialize large collections, which might impact user code. Using a uint32 certainly provides enough space, but will waste bytes in most cases.

An idea that minimizes the output size yet allows for large lengthfields, is to encode the length in a variable number of bytes. Each byte contains seven data bits, and one 'stop' bit. To encode a count with N significant bits, a total of $(\lfloor N - 1 \rfloor / 7 \rfloor + 1)$ bytes are required. This format will end up using 5 bytes to encode a value with 29 or more significant bits, but if there are that many elements being stored, the extra byte will hardly be noticeable.

You might be tempted to use this process for all multibyte integers. However, this is a bad idea if the values being stored fall into an even distribution across the type's entire range, because the average encoded length will actually be larger than the fixed length. Encoding is beneficial only because most of the values being serialized are small.

Keyed Serializer

Scripting languages often have a built-in 'generic' hash table, capable of storing a mapping from just about any object to any other—Perl's associative array and Python's dictionary types are two examples. Using serialization, this same concept can be implemented in C++. The goal is to create a class that maintains a mapping from some known type T to any arbitrary type of object—like an STL map with no restrictions on the value type. As might be expected, this class is a template (with member template functions), and has the following interface:

```
template <typename KEY>
class KeyedSerializer
{
public:
    template <typename T>
        bool Put(const KEY& key, const T& value);
    template <typename T>
        bool Get(const KEY& key, T& value);
};
```

The implementation is actually pretty simple. It has an internal map from KEY to the Buffer class defined earlier. Put() first serializes value into a Buffer, and then adds to the map. Get() does the reverse (leaving the map unchanged—so it can be called multiple times with the same key). One interesting characteristic of KeyedSerializer is that it, unlike Serializer, allows random access to its stored objects. If an object is never retrieved, its (potentially complicated) deserialization code is never invoked. Finally, KeyedSerializer can itself be made serializable, and this is where it becomes truly useful in a network context.

Partial Serialization

Network programmers know that bandwidth is money. Just about anything a network game can do to minimize the size of messages being sent between client and server (or client peers) is worth trying. In light of that, the KeyedSerializer class can be quite useful for sending partial updates over the network.

For example, suppose a 'game object' has the following basic properties: position, orientation, velocity, scale, color, and type. If an object update message contained every one of these values, and updates were sent on a regular basis, it is pretty clear that bandwidth would be wasted—an object's scale, color, and type are not likely to change very frequently, if ever. Obviously, individual message types could be used for each property, but as the number of properties grows, the number of potential messages (including combinations of related properties) can grow quite large. However, if an object update contained a KeyedSerializer (perhaps using uint8 as the key type), a single message can handle any combination of properties, use a single code path, and with minimal overhead.

Object Tagging

There is a potentially serious problem with Serializer. This is type safety—or, the lack thereof. If two objects serialize into the same number of bytes (e.g., float32 and uint32), then it is possible to store one type and read the other. Of course, this is a bug in the application and not in the serialization library, but the fact remains that it can happen without any indication of error (except for whatever odd side-effects result).

The solution is to introduce a measure of safety by preceding each object with a tag. When reading, the tag is checked against what is expected. If the tags do not match, then an error is returned. To compute the tag for a given type, another function inside the SerializeHelper namespace is used (and therefore must be defined for all supported types). Using a one-byte tag, this is the resulting code (changes in bold):

```
template <typename T> bool Put(const T& obj)
{
    uint8 tag = SerializeHelper::ComputeTag(obj);
    return WriteTag(tag) &&
            SerializeHelper::PutInto(*this, obj);
}

template <typename T> bool Get(T& obj)
{
    uint8 expected = SerializeHelper::ComputeTag(obj);
    return ReadAndCheckTag(expected) &&
            SerializeHelper::GetFrom(*this, obj);
}
```

It goes without saying that this will increase the size of the serialized output. However, this additional overhead can be eliminated by making the tag processing optional (e.g., only in debug builds or as a runtime toggle). The auxiliary functions WriteTag() and ReadAndCheckTag() hide all of the details, so that is where conditional processing of tags takes place. If tags are turned off, these simply do nothing and return true.

Future Work

There are a number of ways by which Serializer and its related classes can be extended further. Here are a few ideas:

- Generalize the storage mechanism (instead of always using Buffer) to use an abstract interface and implement serialization to/from files, both binary and human-readable text (useful for debugging).
- Integrate support for a favorite scripting language.

- Write adapters that allow the stream operators (<< and >>) to be used for some syntactic sugar (be careful to consider proper error-handling).
- Build a code generator that automates the creation of serializable classes, based on a specification with types and field names.
- Add encryption and/or compression at the serialization layer.
- Port the code to a new compiler or platform.

Conclusion

This gem has presented a system for object serialization that is efficient, extensible, and minimally intrusive. Using the power and expressiveness of templates, it provides a great deal of functionality in a relatively small amount of code.

References

[Austern98] Austern, Matthew H., *Generic Programming and the STL*, Addison Wesley, 1998.
[Gamma95] Gamma, Erich, et al., *Design Patterns*, Addison Wesley, 1995.
[Josuttis99] Josuttis, Nicolai M., *The C++ Standard Library: A Tutorial and Reference*, Addison Wesley, 1999.
[Kernighan99] Kernighan, Brian W. and Rob Pike, *The Practice of Programming*, Addison Wesley, 1999.
[Meyers01] Meyers, Scott, *Effective STL*, Addison Wesley, 2001.

5.6

Secure Sockets

Pete Isensee, Microsoft Corporation

pkisensee@msn.com

Cheating and hacking in multiplayer games is a common problem that can destroy a gaming experience. One way to prevent cheating is by using cryptography, encrypting and authenticating network traffic. This gem explores the Internet Protocol Security (IPSec) standard and shows how games can leverage portions of the standard to protect network packets and prevent spoofing, sniffing, and replay attacks.

IPSec

IPSec is an Internet standard developed by the Internet Engineering Task Force based on academic and government research. It is published in [RFC2401] through [RFC2411], as well as [IPSec2]. IPSec provides services for authentication, integrity, and confidentiality, and is widely used to implement virtual private networks (VPNs). IPSec is designed to be implemented at the network layer (network stack) and is typically hidden from applications. Unfortunately, native IPSec is not a viable option on most gaming platforms. Even when IPSec is available in a given OS (e.g., Windows 2000), it's neither on by default nor required that applications support it. Nevertheless, game programmers can learn a lot from IPSec, and many of the features of IPSec can be implemented within the context of game network code.

Authentication means verifying who sent a message; integrity means ensuring that a message was not modified. IPSec implements authentication and integrity using keyed cryptographic hashes like MD5 [RFC1321] and SHA-1 [RFC3174]. "Confidentiality" is the term used to describe obscuring data, which implies encryption. IPSec uses symmetric encryption algorithms like DES [RFC2405] and AES [AESDraft]. For game traffic, it usually makes sense to choose a high-performance algorithm. Data requiring a higher level of encryption (e.g., player damage packets, tournament scores, etc.) can use stronger, slower algorithms. (For a good summary of algorithm performance, see [WeiDai01].)

Cryptography alone cannot prevent replay attacks. An authentic, encrypted message that is intercepted and resent by an attacker will authenticate and decrypt just fine. Therefore, IPSec also includes a mechanism for preventing replay attacks by using a combination of sequence numbers and a sliding replay window.

Caveats

One of the most critical steps in establishing a secure system is key management. This gem does not cover key-exchange techniques or the proper ways to generate, expire, and update keys. The assumption here is that both ends of a secure connection have the same keys and that the keys were established and exchanged in a secure fashion. Another process essential to secure systems is the proper generation of truly random bits for keys, shared secrets, and initialization vectors [Isensee01]. This gem assumes that keys use cryptographically random values.

The IPSec standard requires the implementer to embed a copy of the IP header into the payload of the packet, which is in turn both encrypted and authenticated. This allows the receiver to verify that the actual IP header wasn't altered. Implementing this level of authentication is both complicated and usually unnecessary, since the authentication of the payload proves that the packet came from someone who knows the proper authentication key. This gem does not cover IP authentication.

IPSec implementations are closely tied to the fragmentation system of the IP protocol. To avoid this issue altogether, this gem assumes that all packets are sent using unfragmented UDP packets and not via TCP, avoiding fragmentation. Most games use UDP packets anyway, so this assumption is not unreasonable. This gem also assumes that all messages are less than the maximum transmission unit (MTU). Applications must implement their own sequence mechanism for messages larger than the MTU.

Security Associations

A security association (SA) is a logical 'connection' created for security purposes. The SA defines how traffic is secured from one node to another. An SA includes cipher and authentication keys, modes, algorithms, and other data that define the packet format. The `SecurityAssociation` class included with this gem contains the information shown in Table 5.6.1.

SAs almost always occur in pairs, with an SA on the sender exactly matching an SA on the receiver. In a client-server game, the server might have a list of one SA per client, and each client would have a single SA that matched an SA on the server. In a peer-to-peer game, each peer would have a list of SAs. The list of security associations maintained by a host is called the "security association database" (SAD). For games, this 'database' typically resides in the memory of the game or game server.

Prior to sending or receiving secure data, the communicating pair must establish a security association. This gem does not cover the means by which the SA data is exchanged by the sender and receiver. Some of the data, like the algorithms, could be baked into the code. Other data, like the keys, should change on a regular basis for maximum security, and should be exchanged using secure protocols like EKE, Kerberos, or Diffie-Hellman [Schneier96]. Be sure to use different keys for authentication and encryption in order to maximize security.

Table 5.6.1 Security Association Data

Data	Description
Authentication Algorithm	The cryptographic hashing algorithm used for authentication (e.g., MD5, SHA-1)
Authentication Key	The symmetric key data used for authentication
Encryption Algorithm	The symmetric encryption algorithm used when encrypting and decrypting packets (e.g., DES, AES)
Encryption Key	The symmetric key data used by the encryption algorithm
Sequence Number	The next sequence number to be used by a packet sent on this SA
Last Sequence Number	The highest sequence number received on this SA
Replay Window	A bitmask used as the sliding window for rejecting replay attacks
IV Size	The size of the encryption initialization vector (2-8 bytes)
ICV Size	The size of the integrity check value (8-12 bytes)
Max Padding Blocks	The maximum number of additional random padding blocks (0-4 blocks). The block size is based on the encryption algorithm.

Packet Format

Implementing secure sockets is a matter of encrypting and stamping a hash on data before sending it, and authenticating and decrypting the data when receiving it. Table 5.6.2 shows the format of a secure packet, detailing which portions of the packet are authenticated and encrypted.

Table 5.6.2 Secure Packet Format

Data	Size (bytes)	Default Size (bytes)	Authenticated	Encrypted
Security Parameters Index (SPI)	1-4	2	Yes	No
Sequence Number	4	4	Yes	No
Initialization Vector (IV)	2-8	4	Yes	No
Payload	Variable	Variable	Yes	Yes
Padding	0-255	0-255	Yes	Yes
Pad length	1	1	Yes	Yes
Integrity Check Value (ICV)	8-12	10	No	No

Security Parameters Index

The security parameters index (SPI) is a handle that uniquely identifies a security association in a security association database. An SPI is transmitted in every secure packet so the receiver can select the SA under which the packet will be processed. The size of the SPI is game-specific, and depends on the maximum number of SAs that

ON THE CD

will be active at any one time. The example implementation included on the CD-ROM generates random, unique two-byte SPIs. The SPI is not, and cannot be encrypted, because it is used to identify the SA that defines the algorithms and keys. If an attacker modifies the SPI, the packet validation will fail, since the SPI is always authenticated.

Sequence Number

The 'sequence number' is a monotonically increasing counter value. The first packet sent using a given security association will have a sequence number of one, the next packet will be number two, and so on. The receiver uses the sequence number to ensure that duplicate packets and 'old' packets are ignored. The sender must ensure that if there's a possibility of the sequence number rolling over to zero, the two endpoints of the connection generate a new pair of security associations and expire the old SAs prior to rollover. The sequence number is not encrypted so that replay attacks can be detected without having to decrypt the packet. This can also reduce the effect of a denial-of-service attack. If an attacker modifies the sequence number, the packet validation will fail, since the sequence number is always authenticated.

Initialization Vector

An initialization vector (IV) is a binary blob of random data used to initialize a symmetric encryption algorithm. The IV ensures that even if the same plaintext data is sent multiple times, it will encrypt to different ciphertext. The IV is initialized by the sender with random data and is fed to the encryption algorithm. The receiver initializes its decryption routine using the same IV. Each encryption algorithm defines a standard IV length, with most symmetric algorithms using an IV of eight bytes. To minimize bandwidth at the expense of less security, an implementation can transmit smaller IVs. The example implementation uses four-byte IVs as the default. The remainder of the IV is set to the sequence number when it is used during the encryption or decryption phase.

Payload

Payload refers to the original plaintext data. This data is encrypted in the packet that is sent over the wire.

Padding

Padding is appended to the payload before encryption. Padding is used for two reasons. First, the encryption algorithm might require a certain block size. For instance, many symmetric encryption algorithms use eight-byte blocks. Second, it might be desirable to add a random amount of padding to hide the true size of the payload. Padding bytes are initialized with a series of integer values (starting at one) that can be verified by the receiver, providing an additional level of security.

Pad Length

The pad length is a one-byte field that stores the number of padding bytes in the packet.

Integrity Check Value

ON THE CD

The integrity check value (ICV) is a truncated, hash-based message authentication code (HMAC). An HMAC is a keyed hashing algorithm that uses a combination of a standard cryptographic hash algorithm and a secret symmetric key [RFC2104]. Like a thumbprint uniquely identifies a human being, an HMAC uniquely identifies a secure packet. Truncating the HMAC is a well-known security practice. The example implementation on the CD-ROM truncates the hash to eight bytes by default.

The sender calculates the ICV by hashing the encrypted packet data using the authentication key of the SA. The receiver performs the same calculation and compares the ICV it computed with the ICV that was sent. If they match, the packet is valid—it was sent by someone with a matching SA (authentic) and it was not modified in transit (integrity intact). If not, the packet is bogus and is thrown away.

Sending Data

Sending data is a matter of encrypting the payload and generating a cryptographic hash of the data to be sent. The following sections describe the details used by the example implementation.

Establishing a Security Association

Prior to sending secure data, the sender establishes a security association with the receiver. Once the SAs and SPIs have been set up, each end of the communication link has the data it needs to encrypt, decrypt, and authenticate traffic sent between the two endpoints.

Building the Header

The header includes the SPI, the sequence number, and the encryption IV. The SPI corresponds to the SA used to encode and authenticate the payload. The current sequence number is also found in the SA. Once a sequence number has been used, it is incremented in the SA. The encryption IV is generated randomly. If the SA encryption algorithm requires a larger IV than what is sent in the packet, the remaining bytes are set to the sequence number.

Generating Padding

Padding is generated based on the size of the plaintext payload and the SA encryption algorithm. Additional random padding might be added to hide the true size of the payload. The amount of random padding is configurable. The padding bytes are initialized with a series of integer values, starting at one.

Encrypting the Payload

The encrypted portion of the packet includes the original payload, the padding, and the pad-length byte. The symmetric encryption is initialized with the IV generated above, and the encrypted payload is generated using the SA symmetric encryption key and SA symmetric encryption algorithm. The resulting ciphertext is appended to the header.

Generating the Authentication Code

The last step before sending the data is to generate the ICV. The HMAC algorithm is initialized with the SA cryptographic hash algorithm and authentication key. The hash algorithm is then applied to the packet header and encrypted payload/padding. The resulting hash value is appended to the ciphertext. The hash value is not encrypted.

Sending the Secure Packet

The secure buffer is now ready to be sent using whatever UDP socket mechanism the game uses, typically send().

Receiving Data

On the receiving end, the order of operations is critical for security and performance. The receiver must validate the packet SPI, ICV, and sequence number. The receiver may then decrypt the packet and validate padding. Only after all validation checks are complete can the receiver process the packet payload. If any validation check fails, the packet must be thrown away. If the receiver is a game server, the server might also want to audit the failure event as a way of detecting and tracking cheaters.

Receiving the Secure Packet

The secure packet is received using whatever UDP socket mechanism the game uses, typically recv().

Validating the Packet

The simplest check that can be made on the packet is validating the SPI. If the SPI does not match a security association in the receiver's security association database, the packet is deemed invalid. Assuming an SA match, a quick check is made on the size of the block, based on the minimal amount of data that must be included in the secure packet.

The next step is to validate the packet against the ICV. The HMAC algorithm is initialized with the SA cryptographic hash algorithm and key. The hash algorithm is then applied to the packet header and encrypted payload. The resulting hash value is truncated and compared with the ICV received. If it matches, we have an authentic packet.

The last step prior to decrypting the packet is to check the sequence number. If the packet is a replay or too 'old,' there's no reason to decrypt it. The example implementation uses a 64-bit sliding window to reject replay attacks and yet still allow out-of-order packets, which can occur with UDP. The 'right' edge of the window represents the highest validated sequence number received on the SA. Packets that contain sequence numbers lower than the 'left' edge of the window are rejected (they're too old). Packets falling within the window are checked against the list of received packets. If a packet with a matching sequence number is received, it is a replay and is ignored. New packets set the corresponding bit in the window. Packets with a sequence number larger than the right edge cause the window to shift.

Decrypting the Payload

The first step of decryption is to extract the IV. The IV is extended with the sequence number if necessary and then used to initialize the decryption algorithm. The payload and padding bytes are deciphered using the SA symmetric decryption key. The resulting plaintext includes the original payload, padding bytes, and padding size.

Validating Padding

The padding size is validated to ensure that it's reasonable. The padding bytes are then validated to ensure that they contain a series of integer values. Finally, all padding information is stripped from the plaintext, leaving the original payload.

Example Implementation

ON THE CD

The sample code on the CD-ROM, which is included with this gem, includes C++ classes that wrap cryptographic functions, security associations, and secure buffers. Table 5.6.3 shows the list of classes provided.

The essential implementation details are contained in `SecurityAssociation` and `SecureBuffer`. The next section shows how the classes are used in a game for sending and receiving secure data.

Table 5.6.3 Secure Socket Classes

Class name	Description
`CryptContext`	Win32 CryptoAPI cryptographic service providers
`Key`	Cryptographic keys and algorithms
`Cipher`	Encryption and decryption functions
`Hash`	Hashing algorithms
`Buffer`	`std::string<unsigned char>`
`SecurityAssociation`	Security association data
`SADatabase`	`std::map<SpiType, SecurityAssociation>`
`SecureBuffer`	Functions for encrypting, decrypting, and authenticating payloads

Creating a Security Association

Create a security association and add it to the security association database (SAD):

```
// One-time association of SAD to SecureBuffers
SADatabase sad;
SecureBuffer::SetSADatabase( &sad );

// Generate random keys. This example uses the
// DES cipher for encryption and MD5 for hashing
Key keyAuth( CALG_DES );
Key keyCrypt( CALG_DES );

// Create a new SA using the specified keys
// and algorithms; other values get defaults
SecurityAssociation sa( keyAuth, keyCrypt, CALG_MD5 );

// Generate a new SPI and add the pair to the db
SpiType nSPI = sad.GenNewSPI();
sad.Insert( nSPI, sa );

// Securely exchange nSPI and keys with other end
// of connection . . .
```

Sending a Secure Packet

Generate and send a secure packet:

```
// Associate SecureBuffer with SA via SPI
SecureBuffer sb( nSPI );

// Generate the encrypted and authenticated buffer.
// Encryption and hashing happens here.
sb.Create( "payload", 7 );

// Send the secure packet
send( sock, sb.GetDataPtr(), sb.GetSize(), 0 );
```

Receiving a Secure Packet

Receive and process a secure packet:

```
// Receive the secure packet
char pData[ 1024 ];
int n = recv( sock, pData, 1024, 0 );
if( n == 0 || n == SOCKET_ERROR )
   return false;

// Validate the packet
SecureBuffer sb( pData, n );
if( !sb.IsAuthentic() )
   return false;

// Extract the original payload
if( !sb.GetPayload( pData, &n ) )
```

```
    return false;

// Adjust the replay window
sb.SetAccepted();
return true;
```

CryptoAPI

The cryptographic algorithms and key management use the Windows CryptoAPI. All of the crypto code is modularized into crypto.cpp so that you can replace the low-level crypto with other implementations (e.g., Crypto++) [WeiDai01]. One of the frustrating features of the CryptoAPI is that it doesn't provide direct access to key data. There are no APIs that allow you to directly set or get a key. However, Microsoft KnowledgeBase article Q228786 [KB228786] discusses a method for directly accessing key data, and that method is used by the Key class.

Because of the way the CryptoAPI is designed—using cryptographic service providers—not all potential algorithms or key lengths are available on all versions of Windows. Be sure to check the return codes for failure cases.

Performance

There are two major performance issues involved with using secure sockets. The first is additional bandwidth requirements. Using the default settings and an encryption algorithm with eight-byte block requirement (e.g., DES), minimum packet overhead with the sample implementation is:

2 (SPI) + 4 (SeqNum) + 4 (IV) + 0–15 (Padding) + 1 (PadLen) + 10 (ICV) = 21–36 bytes

Those 21–36 bytes are in addition to the standard UDP packet overhead. You can tweak the SA parameters to reduce the overhead, but only at the expense of security. To reduce the effects of the overhead, consider changing from small, frequent payloads to larger payloads sent less frequently. To avoid unnecessary padding, send payloads whose size+1 is evenly divisible by the block size of the SA cipher. (The +1 accounts for the pad length byte.)

The second performance issue is encryption/decryption and authentication. Table 5.6.4 shows the costs of creating, authenticating, and decrypting one kilobyte of payload data, which indicates that performance is not unreasonable. The most important factors at work here are the speed of the algorithms and the size of individual packets. Choose algorithms and key lengths that provide solid security at a reasonable performance cost.

These values were generated on a Pentium III, 866 MHz, running Windows 2000, and using the default SA settings with DES encryption (64-bit keys) and MD5 hashing. The "Create" column is the time in milliseconds required to repeatedly call SecureBuffer::Create on total payload data using the given payload size. The

Table 5.6.4 Performance

| | Time to process one kilobyte of payload data | | |
Payload Size (bytes)	Create (ms)	Authenticate (ms)	Decrypt (ms)
64	2.07	0.90	1.07
128	1.06	0.45	0.57
256	0.59	0.24	0.34
512	0.35	0.14	0.23
1024	0.23	0.09	0.16

"Authenticate" column shows the time spent in `SecureBuffer::IsAuthentic`, and the "Decrypt" column shows the time in `SecureBuffer::GetPayload`. Performance increases as the payload size increases, since relative packet overhead decreases for larger packets.

Security

The intent of this gem is to present an implementation that strikes a balance between extremely robust security with huge packet overhead and reasonable security with minimal packet overhead. The quality of security provided is primarily dependent on the strength of the algorithms used. Don't use XOR as an encryption or authentication algorithm and expect to have packets that are never cracked. Choose well-known, standard algorithms with solid implementations, like DES, Triple-DES, Blowfish, and AES for encryption, MD5 and SHA-1 for hashing. Understand the security levels and performance trade-offs between the algorithms. Use large keys (128-bits) when they're supported by the algorithm. Change keys regularly. Don't reduce the IV size to less than four bytes or the ICV size to less than eight bytes, or security will be substantially diminished.

Although it's technically possible to turn off encryption and only use authentication, be aware that an authenticated packet without encryption exposes your game to sniffing attacks, which can result in cheating that's just as bad as spoofing attacks (and harder to detect).

Conclusion

As more games support features like tournaments and prize competitions, secure communication not only reduces cheating, but also becomes an essential requirement of the game. The IPSec specification includes security elements that can directly benefit networked games. Although the packet overhead is not insignificant, performance is good, and the benefits of secure traffic are considerable.

References

[AESDraft] "The AES Cipher Algorithm and Its Use With IPSec," draft available online at http://www.ietf.org/10.html, November 2001.

[Howard02] Howard, Michael and David LeBlanc, *Writing Secure Code*, Microsoft Press, 2002.

[IPSec2] "IP Encapsulating Security Payload (ESP)," updated draft available online at http://www.ietf.org/ID.html, November 2001.

[Isensee01] Isensee, Pete, "Genuine Random Number Generation," *Game Programming Gems 2*, Charles River Media, Inc., 2001.

[KB228786] "How to Export/Import Plain Text Session Key Using CryptoAPI," available online at http://support.microsoft.com; q228786, July 2001.

[RFC1321] "The MD5 Message-Digest Algorithm," available online at http://www.ietf.org/rfc/rfc1321.txt, April 1992.

[RFC2104] "HMAC: Keyed-Hashing for Message Authentication," available online at http://www.ietf.org/rfc/rfc2104.txt, February 1997.

[RFC2401] "Security Architecture for the Internet Protocol," available online at http://www.ietf.org/rfc/rfc2401.txt, November 1998.

[RFC2403] "The Use of HMAC-MD5-96 within ESP and AH," available online at http://www.ietf.org/rfc/rfc2403.txt, November 1998.

[RFC2404] "The Use of HMAC-SHA-1-96 within ESP and AH," available online at http://www.ietf.org/rfc/rfc2404.txt, November 1998.

[RFC2405] "The ESP DES-CBC Cipher Algorithm with Explicit IV," available online at http://www.ietf.org/rfc/rfc2405.txt, November 1998.

[RFC2406] "IP Encapsulating Security Payload (ESP)," available online at http://www.ietf.org/rfc/rfc2406.txt, November 1998.

[RFC3174] "US Secure Hash Algorithm (SHA1)," available online at http://www.ietf.org/rfc/rfc3174.txt, September 2001.

[Schneier96] Schneier, Bruce, *Applied Cryptography*, Second Edition, John Wiley & Sons, 1996.

[Schneier99] Ferguson, Neils and Bruce Schneier, "A Cryptographic Evaluation of IPSec," available online at http://www.counterpane.com/ipsec.html, February 1999.

[WeiDai01] Dai, Wei, "Crypto++ Cryptographic Class Library," available online at http://www.eskimo.com/~weidai/cryptlib.html, November 2001.

5.7

A Network Monitoring and Simulation Tool

Andrew Kirmse, LucasArts Entertainment Company

ark@alum.mit.edu

ON THE CD

Most online games are developed under ideal conditions on a high-bandwidth, local network with extremely low latency. In contrast, online games are typically played in low-bandwidth, high-latency environments with unpredictable network behavior between machines. This gem describes a Windows-based simulation tool called "NetTool" that you can use to make a LAN behave more like the Internet. Complete source code and Win32 binaries are on the CD-ROM.

Interface

Figure 5.7.1 shows a picture of the NetTool interface. The top section defines a set of *filters*. Each filter describes the behavior of the network between two (IP address, port) pairs. TCP filters, being connection-oriented, allow communication in both directions, so only one filter is required between any two hosts. UDP filters are one-way—the 'Add reverse' button will take the currently selected filter and create a new one with the endpoints reversed. This is useful in the common case where the hosts use the same port to send and receive data.

NetTool simulates network latency on a per-packet basis according to a Gaussian distribution. The interface allows you to set the mean and variance of each filter's latency distribution.

There are several other controls available on each filter. Incoming packets are only forwarded when the Enabled box is checked, allowing you to selectively restrict traffic from individual hosts. Checking the Listed box causes incoming packets to be displayed in the large list box on the lower right of the screen. The UDP Options settings apply only to UDP filters, and are described later.

The title bar displays all of the IP addresses assigned to the machine running Net-Tool.

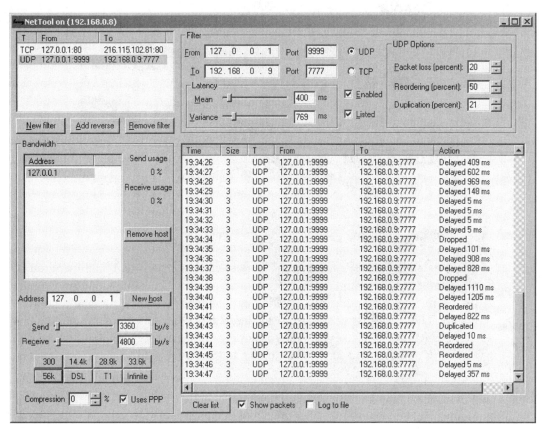

FIGURE 5.7.1   *The NetTool interface.*

Network Monitoring

As packets arrive, NetTool dispatches them according to the settings of the filters that they match. If the Show packets box is checked, a summary of each packet is displayed in the list box in the lower right on the interface. This shows the packet's arrival time, payload size, incoming and outgoing addresses, and the action that was taken by NetTool. The action will be one of the following:

- Sent immediately: No extra latency is required for this packet, so it's sent right away.
- Delayed *X* ms: The network simulation requires that the packet be delayed before being forwarded. The amount of delay is a combination of the filter's latency settings and the host bandwidth simulation (to be addressed later in this section).
- Dropped: The packet was not forwarded. This occurs only for UDP packets when the filter's Packet loss setting is nonzero.

- Reordered: The packet was sent before another packet that arrived previously. This can only occur for UDP packets when the Reordering setting is nonzero.
- Duplicated: The packet was sent twice. This occurs only for UDP packets when the filter's Duplication setting is nonzero.
- Wait for connect: For a TCP filter, data arrived before the remote connection completed. It will be sent as soon as the connection succeeds.

If the Log to file box is checked, the same summary information will be logged to the file log.txt.

TCP Simulation

TCP is a reliable, stream-based protocol: Data arrives in the order it was sent, in arbitrary-size chunks. NetTool appends all incoming data on a filter to a single queue. It then polls the queue, forwarding as much data as the sender's and receiver's bandwidth simulations will allow.

Several subtleties arise in NetTool because of TCP's connection-oriented nature. For example, data can arrive from the sender before the connection to the receiver has completed, or the sender can shut down the connection before previously sent data has been forwarded. These cases are accounted for and should be transparent to applications.

UDP Simulation

UDP is message-oriented, meaning that data arrives in the same chunks in which it was sent. UDP is also unreliable, meaning that individual messages might be lost in transit, arrive out of the order in which they were sent, or even arrive multiple times. On a local network, UDP packets are almost never lost; but on the Internet, packet loss is common.

NetTool drops packets with a probability given by the Packet loss box. These packets are simply thrown away, much like a router on the Internet might do under a heavy load.

If a packet is not dropped, it might be duplicated (sent twice) with a probability equal to that shown in the Duplication box. The latency model is applied to the two duplicate packets independently. If reordering is enabled, it's possible that the duplicated packets will not arrive one after the other.

Packet reordering will only occur under certain circumstances. Suppose two UDP packets, *A* and *B*, arrive on the same port. The latency simulation is applied to each packet independently, causing *A* and *B* to be scheduled for transmission. If, as a result, *A* is scheduled before *B*, no reordering will occur. However, if *B* is scheduled before *A*, NetTool will preserve this ordering with the probability given in the Reordering setting. In order to force reordering to occur for testing purposes, it's useful to introduce latency with a high variance to make this second scenario more probable.

Host Bandwidth Simulation

In addition to latency arising from network delays, latency is also induced at the endpoints of a connection by the available bandwidth. For example, on a 300-bps modem connection, it takes an entire second just to send 30 bytes (assuming 8 bits per byte, plus a start bit and a stop bit). In the lower-left section of the interface, you can set the bandwidth available at each host. The send and receive bandwidth can be set separately, as this is actually a common case with 56k modems (which can only upload at 33.6k), and with asymmetric DSL connections. Several predefined bandwidth settings are available on buttons below the bandwidth sliders; these values are only approximate.

The NetTool bandwidth calculations take into account the size of the header attached to each packet. For UDP, this is 28 bytes (20 bytes IP header plus 8 bytes UDP header), though this can be reduced to a simulated 7 bytes if Uses PPP is checked, as PPP compresses the IP header. For TCP, the header would normally be 40 bytes, but most slow consumer connections use VJ header compression, which reduces the size to about 8 bytes. In addition, many modems have optional compression, which can be simulated by setting a compression percentage in the lower-left corner. This bandwidth simulation is somewhat simplistic, but it is sufficient to produce the approximate behavior of a client connection.

Conclusion

NetTool is a convenient way to simulate consumer Internet connections on a LAN. It is particularly useful for stress-testing under poor network conditions; an ideal use would be testing an implementation of reliable communication on UDP. Please forward any improvements you make to the author so that they can be shared with others.

5.8

Creating Multiplayer Games with DirectPlay 8.1

Gabriel Rohweder,
Microsoft Corporation

grohwed@hotmail.com

Adding multiplayer functionality to a game can be a daunting task. Often, developers will write their networking engines specifically to meet the needs of one title. Porting this code over to another title can be more of a headache than starting a new one from scratch. DirectPlay helps provide solutions to these problems with a generic, extensible network-gaming API that is both easy to use and easy to maintain. This gem is meant to explain some of the more-intricate details of using DirectPlay, as well as offer tips for avoiding common pitfalls. If you don't have any experience with Direct-Play, review the sample code in the DirectX SDK before reading this gem. DirectPlay supports two types of networking architectures—client/server and peer-to-peer. Although there are many successful games on the market today that use the peer-to-peer architecture, this gem will focus mainly on the client/server architecture.

Inside DirectPlay

To reap the greatest rewards from DirectPlay, you should be familiar with how the API is constructed. DirectPlay consists of three separate layers: core layer, protocol layer, and service provider layer.

Your application will interact directly with the core layer, as seen in Figure 5.8.1. The core layer is responsible for various tasks, such as initialization and maintaining the player list. DirectPlay 8.1 utilizes a push model of information exchange. This means that your application will need to register a reentrant callback function with the core layer, which will be called by the core layer when relevant messages are received from the protocol layer.

The protocol layer is responsible for the construction and interpretation of packets. DirectPlay adds 4 bytes to each packet—this is called the "packet header." Direct-Play is built on the UDP protocol, so these 4 bytes are in addition to the 28 bytes required for the UDP and IP headers. The header contains information that the receiving side needs to know in order to process the packet correctly. This protocol is

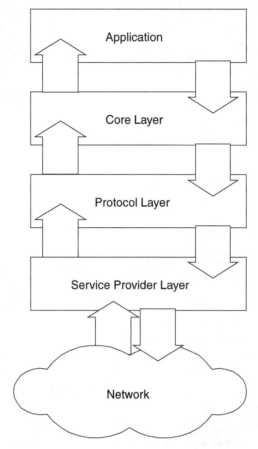

FIGURE 5.8.1   *The DirectPlay message flow.*

also responsible for throttling data (which will be explained later) and verifying that incoming packets are formed correctly.

The service provider layer provides the transport for your session. It allows you to support many different methods of networking, such as TCP/IP, serial, and IPX.

Another element of DirectPlay that is worth mentioning here is DPNSVR. DPNSVR is an optional service that maintains a list of all the current hosts on your machine. Doing this helps to ensure that your application doesn't try to host a session on a conflicting port and allows your client applications to enumerate all of the available sessions hosted on a particular machine by querying port 6073. DPNSVR supports only the IPX and IP service providers at this time.

Transmitting Data

It was mentioned earlier that DirectPlay is a generic API. By 'generic,' it is meant that DirectPlay was not designed around a specific game genre. One of the most popular types of games on the shelves today is the first-person shooter (FPS). The FPS generally requires very frequent transmission of small amounts of data. The fast action associated with the FPS dictates the use of nonguaranteed messaging for most of your game data. If a packet is lost on the wire, it could be irrelevant by the time it was successfully resent by the client. For this reason, most FPS network layers are built on UDP. UDP offers fast transmissions of data, with no guarantee that the packets will arrive in the correct order or even arrive at all. There are times, however, when you will want to make sure a packet gets to its intended recipient, and in the order sent. Player deaths and level changes are examples of when you would want to do this. DirectPlay will handle all of these scenarios for you, because it allows the programmer to specify if an individual packet is to be sent guaranteed, nonguaranteed, sequentially, or nonsequentially. A typical client-side send in DirectPlay is implemented as follows:

```
MYMSG_OBJECT          msgShoot;
DPN_BUFFER_DESC       buffDesc;
DPNHANDLE             hAsync;

msgShoot.dwType       = MYMSGTYPE_SHOOT;
buffDesc.dwBufferSize = sizeof(MYMSG_OBJECT);
buffDesc.pBufferData  = (BYTE*)&msgShoot;
pClient->Send(&buffDesc,1,0, NULL,&hAsync,0);
```

By default, DirectPlay sends messages nonguaranteed and sequential. The last parameter in the call to Send() is the dwFlags parameter. This parameter is used to specify your send characteristics. For example, if you wanted to send your data guaranteed and nonsequential, you would use the following call:

```
DWORD dwFlags = DPNSEND_GUARANTEED |
                DPNSEND_NONSEQUENTIAL;
pClient->Send(&buffDesc,1,0,NULL,&hAsync,dwFlags);
```

After a call to Send() or SendTo(), your message is placed into the DirectPlay internal send queue for that player. The reason for this is that DirectPlay throttles data, a process whereby the protocol layer will increase or decrease the frequency of sends, depending on link conditions and how quickly the recipient can process them. There is an associated send queue with every connection in a session. This ensures that one slow connection will not affect the performance of all players in that session. In order to increase performance in your application, it is important to process network traffic as efficiently as possible. (See Reentrant Callbacks for tips on how to process data more effectively in your callback function.) You can check the status of your send queue by calling GetSendQueueInfo(), as shown in the following code. The server interface takes an additional parameter, specifying which player's send queue information to return.

```
DWORD dwNumMsgs; //number of msgs in the send queue
DWORD dwNumBytes; //number of bytes in the send queue
pClient->GetSendQueueInfo(&dwNumMsgs, &dwNumBytes, 0);
```

A message will remain in the send queue until it is either sent or a timeout occurs. A timeout value can be associated with each message, dictating the maximum amount of time that the message should be allowed to remain queued. If the message will become invalid after a certain amount of time, as was discussed earlier, it would be wise to specify a timeout value for that message. The following code specifies a time-out value of 30 ms:

```
DWORD dwTimeOut = 30; //time in milliseconds
pClient->Send(&buffDesc,1,dwTimeOut,NULL,&hAsync,0);
```

If you notice that your send queue is growing too large, there are two possibilities to consider. One possibility is that you are blocking the receive threads on the receiver, prohibiting DirectPlay from processing incoming messages. The other possibility is that you are sending data more quickly than the receiver can process it, causing dropped packets. If your message queue is growing too large, but the number of bytes queued is relatively small, try coalescing your data. Coalescence means combining two or more messages into one larger message. DirectPlay will not do this for you because it is a generic API, and as such has no idea how to logically group your data. One thing to be wary of when grouping your data is mixing message types. For instance, you probably wouldn't want to combine a message telling the server that a player is now invisible, with a message saying that the player has fired a railgun. If you send the message nonguaranteed, then you run the risk of losing the invisibility message, because the packet might be dropped and not resent. On the other hand, if you send the message guaranteed, the player might start sporadically firing their railgun at an inopportune moment.

Once a message is received, the recipient sends back an ACK to the sender. An ACK is a special message telling the sender that the recipient received the message. If no ACK is received by the sender for a particular packet, then it is considered unde-livered. The difference between a guaranteed send and a nonguaranteed send is how the sender will handle an undelivered packet. With a *nonguaranteed* message, the sender will simply continue sending data from the message queue, ignoring the dropped packet. With a *guaranteed* message, the sender will retry sending the dropped packet until it is received, or until a timeout occurs. It is important to note here that this timeout value is different from the one mentioned earlier. When a guaranteed message times out in this manner, DirectPlay determines that the connection has been lost, and issues `DPN_MSGID_TERMINATE_SESSION` and `DPN_MSGID_DESTROY_PLAYER` messages as appropriate. In DirectPlay, an ACK rides piggyback on a normal data packet to maximize throughput. In the event that there are no data packets to piggy-back, DirectPlay will create a special ACK packet and attempt to deliver it to the sender. Although it is optimized for bidirectional traffic, the frequency at which DirectPlay will create these special ACK packets is high enough (around 100 ms) to avoid causing throttling issues on the sender in the event that your data stream is uni-directional.

One other popular type of game today is the massively multiplayer, online role-playing game (MMORPG). While this genre of game shares some similarities with the FPS networking model, there are many differences. An MMORPG tends to cater to thousands of players, simultaneously interacting in an expansive virtual environment. Current implementations of this model tend not to send network traffic for every key press a player makes; instead, it sends state information across the wire. If you've ever played an MMORPG, you will probably have noticed that while engaged in combat, the results are not governed by your keyboard or mouse dexterity as they are in an FPS, but rather by your character's attributes and abilities. You send a message to the server that you are entering combat mode and what your current target is—the server handles the rest. State information can also be used to communicate other data to the server, such as movement. When sending this kind of information across the wire, you want your messages to be guaranteed. If the player's client is telling them that they are in combat mode and fighting a mountain troll, but the server is recognizing them as standing idle while being beaten to a pulp by a mountain troll, you will have some angry players. Managing thousands of simultaneous connections is another big issue with the MMORPG. DirectPlay scales well when properly implemented and offers the programmer some handy tricks to help things go smoothly. One such trick is grouping.

Grouping

Grouping allows the application developer to perform fewer sends, because they can transmit to a group of players, rather than transmitting the same data to all of them separately. In the MMORPG, the landscape is usually broken into zones or sectors. This is an excellent way to group players. You can create a group of all the players in a certain sector and send out your data to that one group. There is an overhead to adding and deleting players from groups, so you must be careful how you partition them. In an FPS, it probably would not be beneficial to group players geographically. Due to the size of the average FPS map, a player could be switching from one sector to another every few seconds. Instead, you could use teams or some similar method to group players. The following code shows how to create a group in DirectPlay:

```
DPN_GROUP_INFO dpnGrpInfo;
DPNHANDLE hAsync;
ZeroMemory(&dpnGrpInfo, sizeof(DPN_GROUP_INFO));
dpnGrpInfo.dwSize        = sizeof(DPN_GROUP_INFO);
dpnGrpInfo.dwInfoFlags   = DPNINFO_NAME;
wcscpy(dpnGrpInfo.pwszName,"ThievesGuild");
pServer->CreateGroup(&dpnGrpInfo,NULL,NULL&hAsync,0);
```

Once this code has been executed, your server interface's callback function will be invoked with a message of type DPN_MSGID_CREATE_GROUP, containing a DPNID. A DPNID is a unique identifier assigned to each player or group in a session. Once the DPN_MSGID_CREATE_GROUP message is received, it is safe to start adding players to the group. To send a message to the group, you would need to supply the returned DPNID to the SendTo() method of the server interface. You can also send a message to all players in your session by setting the DPNID_ALL_PLAYERS_GROUP constant in place of the DPNID.

When you send a message, DirectPlay creates an internal copy of that message. This copying process carries an overhead. To optimize performance, there is a DPNSEND_NOCOPY flag that you can specify in your call to Send() or SendTo() that will prevent DirectPlay from making that internal copy. The down side to this is that the buffer being sent must remain valid until the send completes. If you allocate your message on the local stack, you should not use asynchronous Send() operations because the memory containing your message will go out of scope when your function returns. Instead, allocate the buffer from the heap, and free it when the asynchronous send completes. For best results, you should use a pool of buffers to avoid the cost of allocating and freeing each message. Sending a message synchronously will not encounter this condition, since the Send() call will not return until the message has been sent.

Reentrant Callbacks

One of the hardest issues to tackle in any application is multithreading. This is not only because it can be tricky to program, but because it can be tricky to debug as well. Likewise, multithreading issues tend to be one of the biggest problems faced by developers because DirectPlay relies heavily on reentrant callback functions. You must be careful when writing your code, as an unexpected context switch could crash your application. When designing your data structures, such as linked lists, keep in mind that they could be accessed by two separate threads. Add reference counters to them to avoid resource conflicts. Use critical sections whenever accessing a global variable or other shared resource in your callback function. Besides the obvious need to avoid deadlocks, be aware that waiting for locks or performing other lengthy operations in your callback function prevents DirectPlay from using that thread to process other data. This might cause the sender to throttle back, artificially limiting your throughput.

One way to avoid holding DirectPlay threads is to queue up your incoming messages, and have a separate thread process them, thus freeing up the DirectPlay threads to do more work. Returning DPNSUCCESS_PENDING from the DPN_MSGID_RECEIVE message event will allow you to avoid the overhead of copying the buffer to your queue because DirectPlay will temporarily hand ownership of this buffer over to your application. If you choose to do this, you must call ReturnBuffer() when you are finished processing the message so that DirectPlay can free those resources.

```
case DPN_MSGID_RECEIVE:
{
    PDPNMSG_RECEIVE pRcvMsg;
    pRcvMsg = (PDPNMSG_RECEIVE)pMessage;
```

```
                //lock the queue to avoid race condition
                LockMyQueue();
                //pass the hBufferHandle to the queue because
                //you will need that in your
                //call to ReturnBuffer()
                AddToMyQueue(pRcvMsg->pReceiveData,
                             pRcvMsg->hBufferHandle );
                UnlockMyQueue();
                return DPNSUCCESS_PENDING;
        }
```

Once the queue has processed the message, make the call to `ReturnBuffer()`:

```
    pClient->ReturnBuffer(hBufferHandle,0);
```

If your application needs to scale to a larger number of connections, a single queue could hamper your performance. In this case, you might wish to devise a more sophisticated way of offloading message processing from your callback function.

As a side note, it is not always a bad thing to hold DirectPlay receive threads. It is possible that the network is able to handle more data than a CPU-bound receiver can process. If the receiver continues to queue these messages, the queue will grow without bounds. One solution is to queue received data until a limit is reached, and then begin blocking new `DPN_MSGID_RECEIVE` callbacks. If and when all threads are blocked, the senders will be forced to 'back off.'

DirectPlay lets you specify the size of your thread pool by calling `SetSPCaps()`. By default, DirectPlay spins up $2n + 2$ threads, where n is the number of processors in your system. If your CPU is not being utilized to its fullest and message queues are starting to back up, you could consider increasing your threadpool size. Most likely, many of your threads are busy waiting for disk I/O or critical sections. Therefore, you won't cause the CPU to thrash if you spin up more threads to handle DirectPlay messages. On the other hand, if your application seems to be CPU bound, then you might want to decrease the number of threads DirectPlay can use. When setting the number of threads in your DirectPlay application, remember that the threadpool can only be increased, not decreased, once a call to `Host()`, `Connect()`, or `EnumHosts()` is made. Prior to these function calls, the threadpool can be set to whatever size you deem appropriate. The threadpool is shared among all interfaces in a process. You can retrieve the thread count available by DirectPlay to process incoming messages by calling `GetSPCaps()`.

```
    DPN_SP_CAPS dpnCaps;
    pClient->GetSPCaps(&CLSID_DP8SP_TCPIP,&dpnCaps,0);
    dpnCaps.dwSize = sizeof(DPN_SP_CAPS);
    if(dpnCaps.dwNumThreads < 16)
    {
        dpnCaps.dwNumThreads = 16;
    }
    pClient->SetSPCaps(&CLSID_DP8SP_TCPIP,&dpnCaps,0);
```

Refer back to Figure 5.8.1. When a message arrives, the service provider directly invokes the protocol layer, the protocol layer invokes the core, and the core invokes your callback function, all in the same thread from the service provider. This reduces the amount of context-switching between the time a message is received on the wire and when it is passed to your application.

DirectPlay gives you a few tools to help you with multithreading and performance issues in your callback function, one of them being the context value. A *user context* is a value that you pass to DirectPlay, and DirectPlay will pass that value back to you in related calls to your callback function. Why is this helpful? Imagine that you have an application with two client interfaces, one for data and one for voice (as you'll see later in this gem, a DirectPlay voice connection requires a DirectPlay client or peer interface). Although you have two client interfaces, you might only want to code one callback function for them both. When the core layer calls into your callback function, you have no idea which interface the new message belongs to. Specifying a user context value in the call to Initialize() allows you to determine for which client object the newly arrived message is relevant. A context value can also be associated with every player in the session. This player context value can play a large part in optimizing the time you spend inside of your callback function. When a client connects to a session, you can associate its context value during the DPNMSG_INDICATE_CONNECT or DPNMSG_CREATE_PLAYER messages. All subsequent messages arriving from that client will contain a pointer to the relevant player. Notice in the following code that once a player joins the session, its context value is set. Later, when a message is received from that same player implying that it now has a damage modifier, the server can use the player context as an index into the player list. This quickly adds up to a lot of saved processing time.

```
HRESULT WINAPI DPClientMsgProc(PVOID pvUserContext,
                               DWORD dwMessageType,
                               PVOID pMessage)
{
    HRESULT hr = S_OK;
    switch(dwMessageType)
    {
        case DPN_MSGID_CREATE_PLAYER:
        {
            //add player to your list and
            //set their user context value
            PDPNMSG_CREATE_PLAYER pMsg;
            pMsg = (PDPNMSG_CREATE_PLAYER)pMessage;
            MYPLAYER mpPlayer;
            mpPlayer.dpnid = pMsg->dpnidPlayer;
            LockMyPlayerList();
            pAddress = AddPlayerToList(&mpPlayer);
            UnlockMyPlayerList();
            pMsg->pVUserContext = pAddress;
            break;
        }
        case DPN_MSGID_RECEIVE:
```

```
        {
            PDPNMSG_RECEIVE pRcvMsg;
            pRcvMsg = (PDPNMSG_RECEIVE)pMessage;
            MYPLAYER * pPlayer = NULL;
            LockMyPlayerList();
            pPlayer = GetPlayerFromList(
                pRcvMsg->pvPlayerContext);
            if(pPlayer == NULL)
            {
                hr = DPNERR_GENERIC;
                UnlockMyPlayerList();
                break;
            }
            MYMSGTYPE * pMsg = NULL;
            pMsg = (MYMSGTYPE*)
            pRcvMsg-> pReceiveData;
            switch( pMsg->dwType )
            {
                case MYMSG_QUADDAMAGE:
                {
                    pPlayer->DamageFactor *= 4;
                    break;
                }
            }
            UnlockMyPlayerList();
            break;
        }
    }
    return hr;
}
```

Another benefit that DirectPlay provides you is the serialization of callbacks. Serialization means that you are guaranteed that any two messages involving a particular player will not be handled on separate threads at the same time. A good example here would be a server receiving a message from a client to join a session. Immediately after joining the session, however, the client decides to disconnect. If a DPN_MSGID_ DESTROY_PLAYER message were to arrive before the server has had time to complete its player initialization code, the server could be left trying to access an invalid object in its player list. The DirectPlay callback serialization guarantees us that this will never happen.

Sending Voice with DirectPlay

Whether it is to discuss tactics, taunt your enemies, or just chat with a friend, communication is an important part of any multiplayer game. Unfortunately, text-based chat interfaces can be distracting when you are trying to play a game, and canned audio can become monotonous after you've heard the same words repeated for the hundredth time. Luckily, there is another option. If you're using DirectPlay for your networking layer, you can easily add voice communications to your game, and it only takes a little extra work.

The DirectPlayVoice interface allows you to send voice data over your network connection, using a DirectPlayClient or DirectPlayPeer connection as a transport. You will need to register a callback function in your call to Initialize(), just as you did for your client interface. Assuming that you already have your client/server DirectPlay session setup for your voice data to use as a transport session, getting DirectPlayVoice up and running is simple. The following code is all you need to get a voice server to host a session:

```
//pServer is your IDirectPlay8Server interface pointer
//and must be currently hosting a session
pVoiceSrvr->Initialize(pServer,SrvrProc,NULL,NULL,0);

DVSESSIONDESC dvSesDesc;
ZeroMemory(&dvSesDesc, sizeof(DVSESSIONDESC));
dvSesDesc.dwSize        = sizeof(DVSESSIONDESC);
dvSesDesc.dwFlags       = DVSESSION_NOHOSTMIGRATION;
if(fMixingServer == TRUE)
{
    dvSesDesc.dwSessionType     =
        DVSESSIONTYPE_MIXING;
}
else //Forwarding server
{
    dvSesDesc.dwSessionType     =
        DVSESSIONTYPE_FORWARDING;
}
//this value must be retrieved by a call to
// GetCompressionTypes()
dvSesDesc.guidCT = MyCodecGuid;
dvSesDesc.dwBufferQuality  =
    DVBUFFERQUALITY_DEFAULT;
dvSesDesc.dwBufferAggressiveness =
    DVBUFFERAGGRESSIVENESS_DEFAULT;
pVoiceSrvr ->StartSession(&dvSesDesc, 0);
```

Initializing and connecting a voice client to a hosting session is similarly easy. The following code will initialize, connect, and set transmit targets for your voice client:

```
//pClient is your IDirectPlay8Client interface pointer
//and must currently be joined to a session
pVoiceClient->Initialize(pClient,VoiceProc,NULL,0,0);
DVCLIENTCONFIG dvClientConfig;
ZeroMemory(&dvClientConfig, sizeof(DVCLIENTCONFIG ));
dvClientConfig.dwSize  = sizeof(DVCLIENTCONFIG );
dvClientConfig.dwFlags              =
    DVCLIENTCONFIG_AUTOVOICEACTIVATED |
    DVCLIENTCONFIG_AUTORECORDVOLUME;
dvClientConfig.lPlaybackVolume      =
    DVPLAYBACKVOLUME_DEFAULT;
dvClientConfig.dwBufferQuality      =
    DVBUFFERQUALITY_DEFAULT;
```

```
dvClientConfig.dwBufferAggressiveness =
    DVBUFFERAGGRESSIVENESS_DEFAULT;
dvClientConfig.dwThreshold      = DVTHRESHOLD_UNUSED;
dvClientConfig.lRecordVolume    = DVRECORDVOLUME_LAST;
DVSOUNDDEVICECONFIG dvSDConfig;
ZeroMemory(&dvSDConfig, sizeof(DVSOUNDDEVICECONFIG));
dvSDConfig.dwSize = sizeof(DVSOUNDDEVICECONFIG);
dvSDConfig.guidPlaybackDevice   =
    DSDEVID_DefaultVoicePlayback;
dvSDConfig.guidCaptureDevice    =
    DSDEVID_DefaultVoiceCapture;
dvSDConfig.hwndAppWindow        = hDlg;
pVoiceClient->Connect(&dvSDConfig,&dvClientConfig,0);
DVID dvid = DVID_ALLPLAYERS;
pVoiceClient->SetTransmitTargets(&dvid, 1, 0);
```

DirectPlayVoice manipulates audio using DirectSound, allowing the developer to do effects processing, such as voice warping or lip synching, on the receiving end of an audio stream. DirectPlayVoice also supports 3D positional audio, which can greatly enhance the realism of voice transmissions in 3D games.

DirectPlayVoice can be set up in one of three different configurations:

- A *peer-to-peer* configuration allows all players to send their voice data directly to their intended target. The advantage to this is that a dedicated server is not needed to process the voice data. This method is great for games with a limited amount of players, but it does not scale well at all.
- A *forwarding* configuration sends the voice data to a central server, where it is forwarded to the receiving players. With this configuration, a client only needs to send one voice message out with a list of intended recipients, cutting down bandwidth requirements. Bandwidth requirements on the server, however, are much higher, as it must send out several voice messages to different players.
- The third configuration is the *mixing* server. This is the best choice if you have a dedicated piece of hardware available to perform mixing operations on incoming voice data. A mixing server, like the forwarding server, allows clients to send one voice stream out with a list of intended recipients; but where they differ is that a mixing server will combine all of the audio destined for one target together and send it out as a single audio stream. This reduces the bandwidth requirements on the client and server, but it requires more processing power.

If you want to use a peer-to-peer configuration with your voice data, you must have a peer-to-peer DirectPlay session hosted. However, it is not required that it be the same session that you are using to transport game data. Thus, Figure 5.8.2 shows two valid networking models for a client/server game with voice: one with a peer-to-peer voice configuration and the other with a separate voice-forwarding or voice-mixing configuration.

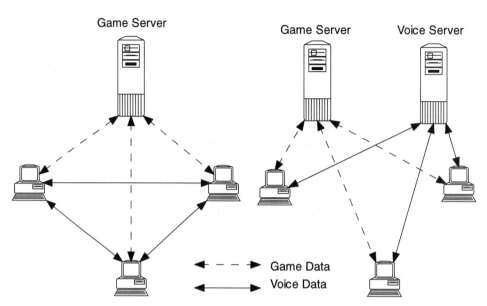

FIGURE 5.8.2   *Left: Peer-to-peer voice configuration. Right: Client/Server voice configuration.*

Resources

If you are having trouble with some aspect of DirectPlay, there's a likely chance that someone else has, too. There are many resources on the Internet that can provide help with your DirectPlay networking layer, most notably the Web networking newsgroups at microsoft.public.directx.networking and microsoft.public.win32.programmer.directx.networking. These newsgroups are frequently monitored by members of the DirectPlay team and experienced users of the API, and can be an invaluable resource during the development of your game.

5.9

Wireless Gaming Using the Java Micro Edition

David Fox, Next Game

davidfox@ureach.com

In an era of supercharged consoles, photo-realistic monsters, and rich 3D universes, writing games for a wireless device can feel lackluster. The screen is miniscule—less than 100×100 on most mobile phones. You have little dynamic memory to play around with—only a 32-KB heap on many phones. And there's limited network connectivity; most second-generation wireless networks send data at 9.6 kbps (kilobits per second). The processors on wireless devices are also hundreds of times slower than an average desktop computer.

On the plus side, it's becoming harder to find people who don't carry network-enabled devices with them. At the end of 2001, there were more than 600 million mobile phone users worldwide. If a compelling wireless game caught fire, it would find a massive audience.

While it might seem silly to try to achieve a rich, meaningful immersion on a tiny screen, there's one thing mobile phone games offer that even the best consoles can't provide: They're always with you and can be played anywhere you go. Furthermore, many wireless networks implement some form of mobile positioning. As this feature becomes more accessible, a game can track exactly where a player is in the real world. Wireless games are not only portable and convenient to play, but with some clever design, wholly new types of experiences can seamlessly meld virtual space with reality.

Another burgeoning field is in creating wireless extensions to existing games. For example, a mobile interface can tap into a persistent multiplayer game world that is usually played in full visual splendor on a console. A mobile gamer could be instantly notified of attacks and surreptitiously logon during meetings to tweak settings or make important decisions.

The difficulty lies in achieving meaningful network interaction given extreme limitations.

Network Characteristics

Latency is the time it takes for a packet of data to travel from one point to another, and is usually based on distance and number of hops between the two points.

Bandwidth is the amount of data that can be sent per second, and is usually based on the physical hardware being used to transfer data.

Multiplayer game programmers struggle with the Internet's high latency and the average home user's low bandwidth. Second-generation (2G) wireless networks, however, make the Internet seem downright speedy.

European mobile phones primarily operate on the Global System for Mobile Communication (GSM), which sends data at 9.6 kbps. Most networks in North and South America, Russia, Israel, Eastern Asia, and Central Africa transfer data based on a standard called Code Division Multiple Access (CDMA), which runs at a peppier 14.4 kbps. Some networks use Time Division Multiple Access (TDMA), which is similar to GSM and has the same 9.6-kbps limit.

Providers in Japan, Hong Kong, South Korea, and Singapore use what can be thought of as a 2.5-generation (2.5G) network. This is achieved using a variant of CDMA (IS-95B), which achieves a 64-kbps data transfer rate. In the United States, CDMA 2000 has been deployed in select markets, eventually hoping to offer speeds of up to 144 kbps. Furthermore, most GSM networks are being upgraded to use General Packet Radio Services (GPRS), which can theoretically reach speeds of 170 kbps.

Third-generation (3G) networks are slowly being rolled out. Most 3G standards are built on top of Internet Protocol (IP) services, allowing for high-speed mobile access. The plan is for networks to scale up gradually, starting with 2.5G technologies and ramping up to speeds of around 300 kbps, and finally reaching 2400 kbps (2.4 Mbps), which is even faster than today's home DSL connections. Deployment of 3G, however, is extremely expensive and fraught with all sorts of challenges. We should not expect to see widespread 3G networks anytime soon.

Wide area wireless networks are also high latency because of the inherent interference and noise of radio wave communications. Most wireless networks force data packets to hop over many high-latency routers. Satellite-based wireless networks generally add even more latency. It is not rare to experience network delays of one or even two seconds.

For the time being, then, wireless game designers should assume that they are working with a thoroughly high-latency, low-bandwidth connection.

Java Micro Edition

Java (Sun Microsystems) is emerging as a standard language for wireless devices. Java runs in a virtual machine, which means that as long as developers follow the right procedures, the same Java byte code can run on any supporting platform. Java is also extremely easy to use. It is object-oriented with no pointers, no complicated memory operations, and automatic garbage collection. Most importantly, Java applets cannot access functions or memory outside of their secure 'sandbox,' which means that it is virtually impossible to write malicious code or viruses.

Java 2 Micro Edition (J2ME) [J2ME01] is an attempt to take the best aspects of standard Java and pare them down for smaller devices, such as mobile phones, pagers, and handheld organizers. Most major mobile phone manufacturers have joined with Sun to create the CLDC (Connected, Limited Device Configuration) [CLDC01], along with the MIDP (Mobile Information Device Profile) [MIDP01]. A Java applet written for a mobile phone, therefore, is called a "MIDlet."

Various device manufacturers have released extension APIs for J2ME. For example, Siemens has an extensive game API that sits atop MIDP. NTT DoCoMo does not use MIDP, but has a separate Java profile known as "I-Appli."

Qualcomm has created a virtual machine and language called the Binary Runtime Environment for Wireless (BREW), which is based on C++. Qualcomm has embedded BREW right onto the chipset for CDMA phones. While BREW is a J2ME competitor in some sense, a Java Virtual Machine can be written in BREW.

Mobile phone manufacturers have embraced Java in a way that not even PC manufacturers have. Java is emerging as the platform of choice for mobile devices.

J2ME Networking Nutshell

In the world of Java Standard Edition, the large and intricate `java.io.*` and `java.net.*` packages are used to great effect. These packages contain most any type of networking class you want, such as `Socket`, `DatagramSocket` or `ServerSocket`. Each class has different methods and different ways of being used.

In the world of J2ME, however, we don't have the luxury of being so complete. For starters, we have no idea what type of network transport protocol a phone is using. Devices that work over circuit-switched networks can use streaming always-on connections, such as the Transport Control Protocol (TCP). However, packet-switched networks might only be able to handle its network data in discrete, nonguaranteed packets using protocol such as the User Datagram Protocol (UDP).

The CLDC's `Connection` interface was created to be as general as possible. The `Connection` class is a catch-all that can, in theory, handle any kind of network connection. A special class known as the "`Connector`" can tap into any CLDC class that extends from the `Connection` interface.

Every `Connector`'s open method accepts a string with the familiar syntax: "`protocol:address:parameters`". For example, to open a typical HTTP connection:

```
Connector.open("http://java.sun.com/developer");
```

To open a socket:

```
Connector.open("socket://123.123.111.000:9000");
```

And to open a datagram connection:

```
Connector.open("datagram://www.myserver.com:9000");
```

You can then create a datagram and send it as follows:

```
Datagram dgram = dc.newDatagram(message, msglength,
```

```
        "datagram://www.myserver.com:9000");
dc.send(dgram);
dc.close();
```

The remote 'server' could, of course, be another mobile device. Most wireless devices can easily communicate in a peer-to-peer fashion with each other. Peer-to-peer latencies are lower—there's no need to use a middleman. However, in peer-to-peer games, one of the peers generally acts as a server, and the other acts as a client. The size of this extra server code could make such a scheme infeasible. To have a MIDlet deal with incoming traffic, just create an endless loop that listens to a port and waits for some data:

```
DatagramConnection dc = (DatagramConnection)Connector.open
    ("datagram://:"+receiveport);
while (true)
{
    dgram = dc.newDatagram(dc.getMaximumLength());
    dc.receive(dgram);
    reply = new String(dgram.getData(), 0,
     dgram.getLength());
    }
```

Since the Datagram protocol is standard, we could write an extremely simple server component in Java Standard Edition (or any other language), running on any PC. For instance:

```
DatagramSocket receiveSocket = null;
DatagramPacket receivePacket = new DatagramPacket(bytesReceived,
  bytesReceived.length);
receiveSocket.receive(receivePacket);
```

As you can see, the MIDP specification makes it extremely easy to pass data back and forth. Unfortunately, many wireless devices do not support datagrams. A `Connec-tionNotFoundException` will be returned if the device you are using does not support the protocol you requested.

The only protocol that MIDP devices *must* support is HTTP. As such, it is recommended that you design wireless games for the lowest common denominator—using HTTP.

HTTP Limitations

HTTP is a widely supported protocol. It is exceptionally easy to design Java servlets or other Web technologies to be able to deal with HTTP [Fox01]. Additionally, HTTP rides atop TCP, so there will be no out-of-order or missing packets. You will not need to bulk up your MIDlet with extra networking code.

However, HTTP's simplicity is also its downfall. HTTP is a request-response protocol designed to deliver static content. A TCP connection is made, a browser asks for a document (request), a Web server delivers it (response), and the connection is closed. HTTP Version 1.1 is a little more advanced, allowing for arbitrary amounts of chunked data and for connections that stay alive. But HTTP is still very much a half-duplex protocol—you cannot transmit in two directions at the same time.

If your game is a simple turn-based game, you might not need full-duplex connections at all. Latency and bandwidth will not be much of a problem, either. Only one player may make a move at a time. A player moves, the new game state is sent down to all players, and then the next player can make a move.

However, if your game is more advanced and has unpredictable data packets coming in constantly, you're in trouble. And what if you want to tap into a complicated, full-featured game server that uses UDP?

Use Multiple Connections

One way to achieve full-duplex communication is by having your MIDlet client create multiple connections—one that sends data to the server and one that stays alive, retrieving server data. The first connection should use chunked transfer encoding. The server creates an open connection and assigns it some sort of unique ID. This ID is then sent down to the client.

The client can now create one client-to-server connection with an incredibly large *"Content-length"* heading, passing in the proper ID. The server can then handle request data as it flows in from the client and channel an appropriate response to the open server-to-client connection.

Some servers and proxies might not be able to handle a request with a long content length, and might buffer the request and wait for it to be completed. In this case, the client can break each message into a chunk and send it as an individual request. The client should send the ID along with each request, either as a custom header element or as part of the payload. The server can then parse this ID number and send the appropriate response back to the client.

Proxy Power

Another way of creating robust wireless communications is to write your game server using any protocol you wish. You can then tap into the game server via an HTTP proxy. This is a simple enough system—the MIDlet communicates with a proxy instead of a game server. It will, of course, add extra latency. However, it will also allow you to create a better experience for devices that support better network protocols. For example, devices that support datagrams can try communicating directly with your game server. If a `ConnectionNotFoundException` is thrown, the game can revert to using HTTP via a proxy instead.

Optimizing Packets

So how do we create meaningful game traffic using HTTP over a high-latency, low-bandwidth network? In effect, the challenge of creating a wireless game is similar to that of any other multiplayer game: Packets must be as small as possible, and designing the game around network limitations is tantamount.

There are many network programming subtleties and rules of thumb to deal with the design of TCP/IP. For better or worse, a lot of these subtleties do not have to be dealt with in wireless games—latency and bandwidth are too limited to warrant being bothered.

Better Latency

The following game scenario illustrates a basic problem involving latency. Rat A and Rat B spot a piece of cheese at the same time, and both make a mad dash for it. Because it takes a second or more for each player to be notified of the other's location, both rats see themselves as the first one to grab the snack.

There are many techniques for dealing with this. Dead reckoning [Aronson01] is a method to extrapolate and predict a game character's movement. Latency can also be dealt with by locking the game frames in step [Bettner01]. Both of these techniques, however, involve every client keeping a detailed simulation of every entity in the game. This might require more memory than a wireless device offers.

It might also be wise to have your game server measure the latency of packets it receives and deal accordingly. A typical multiplayer shooter-game server sends data at a rate of 10 frames per second (fps). This will most likely be unfeasible for a wireless game. Since animation rates for wireless devices are slower (often only 10 fps), network rates of 2 fps to 3 fps are acceptable, given the general slowness.

Better Bandwidth

Bandwidth is usually not as much of an issue as latency, since game packets can often be made quite small. The most important rule of thumb is that, like never before, every bit adds up.

Rather than send the game state every frame, you should delta-compress your information, only transmitting the data that has changed. Additionally, MIDP does not support floating-point operations. Most games that involve graphics will simulate floating-point math using a long integer. Try to reduce and simplify such values to 8 bits or 16 bits whenever possible. The simplest form of data compression is byte-packing—don't waste a whole byte to send a boolean value. Instead, tweak individual bits to send eight flags at once.

There are more-advanced forms of data compression that can take large packets and reduce their size by 30% or more. These include gzip. The downside to compressed packets, however, is that already-high latency will become even higher because of the time it takes to compress and decompress. The code to handle compressing might also take up too much room in the MIDlet. In most cases, simply packing your data into bytes will be sufficient.

The game server should prioritize messages. Some messages are necessary for the game to function properly. Others, such as a chat message or score update, are not as essential. If a message is not immediately relevant to a game scene, you should avoid sending it altogether.

Try to tokenize messages as much as humanly possible. In other words, try not to send the phrase "Your tank was hit!" Instead, send a single byte macro that is mapped on the client to a hard-coded list of phrases.

Retrieving Images from the Server

Version 1 MIDlets can only display graphics using the PNG file format. Unfortunately, there is no method to directly grab an image from the network. Rather, the createImage method accepts only two types of parameters: a string (for filenames) or a byte array:

```
createImage(byte[] imageData, int imageOffset, int imageLength);
```

The way to retrieve images using MIDP is to download the binary contents of an image, and then feed that array directly into the createImage method:

```
public Image grabImge(String url)
{
    InputStream is = null;
    HttpConnection hc = null;
    Image img = null;
    try {
    hc = (HttpConnection)Connector.open(url);
    // If we've got a connection...
    if (hc.getResponseCode() ==
        HttpConnection.HTTP_OK) {
        // Open the stream
        is = hc.openInputStream();
        // How big is the file?
        int len = (int)hc.getLength();
        // Create a byte array that size
        byte[] data = new byte[len];
        // Read in the file
        int actual = is.read(data);
        // Create an image from the raw data
        img = Image.createImage(data, 0, len);
        }
    } catch (Exception e) {
        System.out.println("IO Exception+"+e);
    } finally {
        if (is != null) {
        try {
            is.close();
        }
        catch (Exception e) { }
        }
        if (c != null)
        {
        try {
            c.close();
```

```
        }
        catch (Exception e) { }
        }
    }
    return img;
}
```

If you want images to look as good as possible on various mobile devices, it is recommended that you create an image server. That way, your game can send the device's screen size, color abilities, and other parameters. The image server can then take large, colorful images and convert them on-the-fly into tiny, grayscale PNGs. The Java Advanced Imaging API [JavaImage01] and other such packages can do most of this work for you.

Conclusion

The biggest challenge in wireless networking, other than the limitations of the network itself, is to balance limited device space, speed, and memory with advanced networking techniques. While using dead reckoning, frame locking, compressed packets, and other tricks might be effective in theory, many mobile devices only allow 10 KB to 50 KB of space for your byte code. Fitting both the game code and the networking code into this box is often a harrowing experience.

Designing games cleverly in order to make the most of limitations is always the best bet. For example, you might opt to use tanks instead of soldiers in a war game. Tanks move slowly, can only fire a round occasionally, and take a long time to change their direction. Of course, there's only so far this approach can take you. Ultimately, some types of games will simply not be possible until better wireless networks and devices are rolled out.

But if these challenges are faced, the results can be worth it. Wireless devices offer always-on networking and in-pocket interactivity. Given the pervasiveness of handheld devices and the potential for reaching a wider audience than ever before, a truly original wireless game concept can revolutionize the face of entertainment.

References

[Aronson01] Aronson, Jesse, "Dead Reckoning: Latency Hiding for Networked Games," *Gamasutra*. Available online at http://www.gamasutra.com/features/19970919/aronson_01.htm, September 19, 1997.

[Bettner01] Bettner, Paul and Mark Terrano, "1500 Archers on a 28.8: Network Programming in Age of Empires and Beyond," Game Developer's Conference Proceedings, 2001. Available online at http://www.gdconference.com/archives/proceedings/2001/terrano_1500arch.doc.

[CLDC01] Sun.com, "CLDC Information Page," available online at http://java.sun.com/products/cldc/.

[Fox01] Fox, David, "Creating Games Using J2ME," *Gamasutra*. Available online at http://www.gamasutra.com/resource_guide/20010917/fox_01.htm, September 17, 2001.

[J2ME01] Sun.com, "J2ME Information Page," available online at http://java.sun
     .com/j2me/.

[JavaImage01] Sun.com, "Java Advanced Imaging API," available online at http://
     java.sun.com/products/java-media/jai/.

[MIDP01] Sun.com, "MIDP Information Page," available online at http://
     java.sun.com/products/midp/.

AUDIO

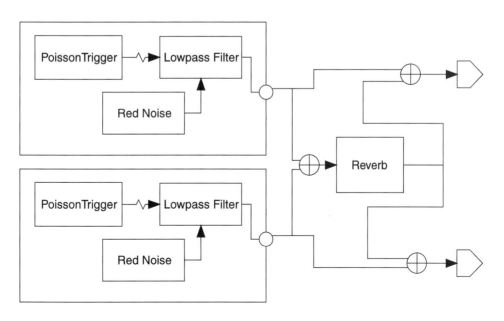

Introduction

Scott Patterson, Next Generation Entertainment

scottp@tonebyte.com

Programming audio for games has much in common with game programming in general. For example, the game design and target platform dominate development decisions. It is also typical for audio programmers to program the basic functionality and then move on to enhancements. Game design is the basis for determining which audio enhancements are the most valuable, and the target platform is the basis for determining which enhancements are the most practical. Today, the computer processing power available for game-audio programmers makes many new enhancements practical. Recommending some of the ideas and implementations for these enhancements is the song of this section.

Getting more audio content in games through compression techniques is very common, yet free access to high-quality audio compression algorithms has been very uncommon—until now. Jack Moffitt introduces psychoacoustic compression in his article "Audio Compression with Ogg Vorbis." While Ogg Vorbis could easily be the name of a science-fiction character, it is actually the name of an open source, patent-clear, and general-purpose audio codec. Jack describes typical scenarios of audio compression in games and demonstrates how to use the Ogg Vorbis API.

Many game platforms now include 3D audio capabilities. Garin Heibert gives us practical tips on programming 3D audio in his article "Creating a Compelling 3D Environment." He presents details of OpenAL and DirectSound3D API programming. In "Obstruction Using Axis-Aligned Bounding Boxes," Carlo Vogelsang explains an efficient technique for calculating how much an obstruction diverts the 'path' of sound between source and listener.

Greater variety of sound playback in games can be achieved with real-time digital audio-processing techniques. Phil Burk introduces a useful and multipurpose filter in his gem, "Using the Biquad Resonant Filter." He also demonstrates important filter-implementation techniques, such as permuting an algorithm and denormalizing floating-point values. In "Linear Predictive Coding for Voice Compression and Effects," Eddie Edwards explains how it is possible to change the character of a voice with an effect called the vocoder, and also achieve remarkable compression at the same time.

Real-time control and intricate audio response is possible with procedural generation techniques. Phil Burk shows how stochastic synthesis techniques can procedurally generate interactive sounds in his gem, "Stochastic Synthesis of Complex Sounds." A configurable system for procedural generation and processing of audio is discussed in Frank Luchs' "Real-time Modular Audio Processing for Games." Using systems like this, a passionate future of game audio will include the flexible routing of audio generation and processing modules to produce involving and immersive sounds.

So with techniques in your arsenal, you can add experimentation, enhancement, and excitement to game audio. You can pack more sample content into the same sized box. Your creatures can emit spacially dynamic sounds that seem to creep around corners. Your robots can talk with vocal cords made from industrial machinery. Your engines can clank, whine, and roar with greater complexity and response. Even the wind can howl in new evolving ways. If you breathe new life into game audio, you breathe new life into games.

6.1

Audio Compression with Ogg Vorbis

Jack Moffitt, Xiph.org Foundation

jack@xiph.org

Ever since computers could produce sound, audio has been a part of games in some form or another. Originally, beeps and bloops were all that were possible. MIDI was later used, as it contained a lot of information about the sound in a small amount of space. Then, as sound cards became prevalent, MOD-type files became more popular, offering a combination of sampled sounds with sequencing and limited effects. Once the CD-ROM became the standard media on which games shipped, Redbook audio (normal CD audio) started to become popular, and finally games used high-quality music.

Unfortunately, as the music became better, music files also became larger. While CDs can easily hold an hour's worth of great-quality audio, not much else will share the same disc. ADPCM is one compression standard that has been used in commercial games to try and alleviate the size of music files while retaining the quality, but its size savings are not fantastic. High-quality music is now a must for any game, and since game developers are going to continue to push the envelope with respect to audio and music in games, music files will have to get smaller.

Enter psychoacoustic compression.

Psychoacoustic Compression

Psychoacoustic compression works by eliminating all the parts of the sound that the ear can't hear or considers unimportant. Unlike some other forms of compression, psychoacoustic compressors are lossy. The original signal is irreversibly modified, even though to most ears the sound remains the same.

The compression ratios for psychoacoustic compressors are generally between 10:1 and 20:1. This is far better than the ratios offered by the other sound compression alternatives.

How It Works

There are a few basic principles behind psychoacoustics. First, there is the absolute threshold of hearing. This is represented by the graph in Figure 6.1.1.

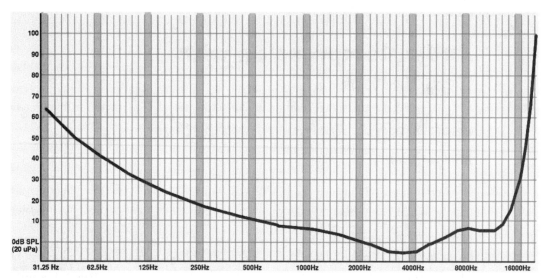

FIGURE 6.1.1   *The absolute threshold of hearing. The x-axis represents frequency, the y-axis represents loudness.*

The absolute threshold of hearing represents how loud a sound has to be at a certain frequency range in order for the human ear to perceive it. Any sounds that are below the curve can't be heard. If you take away all the sounds that fall under the curve from the original sound, the resulting sound should be perceived identically.

Another basic concept of psychoacoustics is masking. Just as bright background light sources will mask foreground objects, loud sounds will mask quieter ones. A strong tone will mask weaker tones at higher and lower frequencies. Even after a strong tone is gone, it will still mask some sounds, due to temporal masking. Since a fair amount of the sound is masked, psychoacoustic encoders won't include them, and the human ear is none the wiser.

How Do Sound-Compression Techniques Compare?

Now that we have a basic understanding of how psychoacoustic compression works, let's take a look at how it compares to the other forms of audio compression that might be more familiar. Audio is normally transmitted as raw PCM samples. These are uncompressed, so each stereo 16-bit sample takes 4 bytes. For CD-quality audio, there are 44,100 of these every second, or around 10 MB of audio a minute.

Typical ways of reducing the bulk of audio data include downmixing and resampling. Downmixing reduces the stereo channels into one channel, cutting the total size by half. Resampling uses fewer samples per second to represent the sound. Usual resampling rates are 22,050 Hz and 11,025 Hz. Both of these methods result in greatly reduced file sizes, but they come at the cost of quality and the loss of stereo.

ADPCM is a 4:1 compression format that encodes the differences between successive samples. It is sometimes used in games to shrink audio without the unacceptable loss of quality that downmixing or resampling creates. ADPCM is also lossy, though, and does degrade audio quality. It also only compresses audio to one quarter of the size, meaning that an hour's worth of audio can still be almost 200 MB.

There are several lossless methods available as well. While these do not sacrifice any quality, their compression ratios are not very good. Typical lossless compressors get between 1.5:1 and 2:1 in the general case. Many of them can be quite slow, but their compression ratios alone make them unusable for most situations.

Why Ogg Vorbis

Psychoacoustic compression seems to be the clear choice for music compression. High compression ratios and almost no discernable quality loss makes it appealing, but the question still remains—which codec to use of the ones that are widely available?

Ogg Vorbis [OggVorbis02] stands above the rest as the perfect fit for games and other applications. Its royalty-free licensing makes it a much cheaper alternative than the rest of the codecs. Its open-source implementation gives developers the freedom to customize and tweak it if necessary. Also, its broad platform support ensures that the same code will work on Windows, Macintosh (Classic and OS X), Linux, BeOS, and even console platforms.

In addition to these advantages, Ogg also has several unique features that make it specifically appealing to game developers. It supports multiplexing the audio data with other kinds of information. There are already implementations that intertwine MIDI with CD-quality audio for synchronized device control. It also supports multiple channels, meaning that you can encode and play back in surround sound or even something more ambitious.

For example, using Ogg, a game developer could add synchronized mouth movements to compressed vocals, to give a much more-realistic sense of talking or singing. With other formats, this is more difficult and not directly supported.

If game developers want to keep advancing the current state of the art, the audio and sound will not only have to be compact, but also quite flexible. This is where a lot of the other codec options fall short, and this is where Ogg Vorbis shines.

Compression Scenarios

Using Ogg Vorbis as the implementation choice, we can now cover how best to fit compressed music into a game, considering several possibilities about speed requirements and the type of audio being used. Although Ogg Vorbis will be specifically discussed, most of the ideas presented here should work with other codecs.

There are several things to consider when using a codec with a game. Most games have tight speed requirements, so the amount of processor time necessary to decode audio is an important factor. Desktop computers can generally decode psychoacoustically compressed audio in about 2% to 5% of the total processor time on Pentium III-class machines.

Also, the type of sound being decoded is important as well. For instance, background music generally only consists of one stereo track and switches between different tracks. More-complex music might layer tracks together, requiring the decoding of several files at once. Sound effects are generally short sounds and are keyed to events. The latency between the time the event happens and the sound is played is very important. Many sound effects might be playing simultaneously.

With these situations in mind, let's outline some ways that compressed audio can be effectively integrated into games.

Scenario 1: Decoding On-the-Fly

The most common method of using Ogg in a game would be to decode audio on-the-fly. This uses a little CPU time, but it allows the files to remain on a mass storage device, such as a hard drive.

In this scenario, an audio stream has been completely encoded in Ogg format and is decoded and played in real-time while the game is running. There is no need to make the user wait for entire files to be decompressed before playback, and there's no large, uncompressed audio files sitting around on the player's hard drive. In addition, allowing the player to add his or her own music to a game is simple with this method of integration.

Scenario 2: Decoding to Cache

In some situations, decoding to cache is a better fit. If there are many pieces of audio to be played at once, decoding all of them in real-time might not be possible or might use up too much of the processor time. In this case, decoding the files to a cache on level changes or on startup might be the right solution. This allows a game implementation to keep all audio data compressed that is not needed to be immediately available by gameplay.

This is also a nice way to produce sound effects. The game could decode them on-the-fly the first time they were used, and play the already decoded audio on subsequent requests. If latency is a problem with decoding, the sound effects could be decoded on level changes or at startup, as previously described, and then played back with no decoding latency at all.

Scenario 3: Compressed Transport

In cases where none of the previous scenarios make sense, compression can still be used for end-to-end transport. The game distribution CD-ROM and/or downloadable packages can use Ogg to make the download smaller and leave more room for graphics and code. When the game or demo is installed, all of the music can be decompressed to the hard drive. This scenario would also apply well to game patches or additional packages to go along with the game.

Code Examples Using Ogg

A few code examples will illustrate how easy it is to use Ogg Vorbis. To use the *vorbisfile* library, the code will need to include the API headers:

```
#include <vorbis/vorbisfile.h>
```

ON THE CD

and link against the vorbisfile, *vorbis*, and *ogg* libraries. Under Windows, these can be statically linked or dynamically linked, depending on personal preference (see the SDK files and API reference on the CD-ROM for details).

Uncompressing Files to Memory

Uncompressing files to memory is easy with the vorbisfile API. First, we declare the OggVorbis_File variable:

```
OggVorbis_File vf;
```

Then, we must open the Ogg Vorbis file with an already open FILE*. Note that you must open a file in binary mode for vorbisfile. On some platforms, binary files are default for calls like fopen(), but on Windows, this is not the case, and you must specify binary mode explicitly.

```
int err;
err = ov_open(fp, &vf, NULL, 0);
```

The fp is our FILE* to an already open file. The vf is the OggVorbis_File struct, and the other two parameters are typically set to NULL and zero, as in our example. (If you're curious as to what these mean and when you should use them, please consult the API reference.)

The ov_open will return zero on success or less than zero on failure. On failure, the return value will map to one of the standard error codes of the API (which you can find explained in the API reference).

Now that the Ogg file has been opened by the vorbisfile library, the library owns the file. It will close the file when it's done, and you should no longer use that file pointer in external file operations. Once the file is opened, the file info must be read:

```
vorbis_info *vi;
vi = ov_info(&vf, -1);
```

The vorbis_info struct will contain information about the opened Ogg file, such as its sampling rate, the nominal bit rate, and its number of channels. The second parameter specifies which logical bitstream to return information for (–1 means the current logical bitstream). Optionally, you can read the comments from the file with the ov_comment() function.

Before we can decompress the Ogg to memory, we must first allocate some space for it. To find out the total space required, we must call ov_pcm_total() to find the total number of PCM samples, and multiply this by the number of channels and the number of bytes per sample (usually 2 bytes for 16-bit audio).

```
int size;
char *buffer;

size = vi->channels * 2 * ov_pcm_total(&vf, -1);
buffer = (char *)malloc(size);
```

Now that we have a buffer allocated for the entire decoded output, ov_read() is called in a loop to retrieve PCM samples into the buffer.

```
int eof = 0;
char *buf = buffer;
int current_section;

while (!eof) {
    long ret = ov_read(&vf, buf, 1024, 0, 2, 1,
                &current_section);

    if (ret == 0) {
        /* 0 return value means end of file */
        eof = 1;
    } else if (ret < 0) {
        /* < 0 return value indicates an error */
    } else {
        /* advance the buffer pointer on success */
        buf += ret;
    }
}
```

The code is fairly simple. It doesn't do any error checking (although when working with Ogg, most errors are normally benign and can be ignored) or overflow checking, but all the hard work is done for you in the vorbisfile library.

Once a file is finished, you must cleanup with ov_clear():

```
ov_clear(&vf);
```

Decoding in Real-Time

Decoding in real-time is very similar to the previous situation of decoding to a memory buffer, except that instead of decoding all at once, real-time decoding takes place a piece at a time. After reading each block from ov_read(), the code then sends it to the next stage of the pipeline. In the most common case, this is an audio output device.

For the sake of simplicity, system specifics of audio output won't be covered here. Instead, the code assumes that there is an audio_output() function that takes a buffer of samples and a size, and does the right thing.

Using the previous example as a base, the only thing that needs to be modified is the decode loop. At the top of the loop, there is still the call to ov_read():

```
char pcmout[4096];

while (!eof) {
    long ret = ov_read(&vf, pcmout, sizeof(pcmout),
                       0, 2, 1, &current_section);
    /* ... */
}
```

Notice that the buffer is now a fixed size, since the code only processes output in small blocks.

In the `success` clause of the previous example's `if` blocks, we advanced a buffer pointer. Since we only process a block at a time for real-time decode, we just need to send the current block to the `audio_out`:

```
audio_out(pcmout, ret);
```

On `success`, `ret` will be the number of bytes placed into the buffer.

Encoding

The last part to a fairly comprehensive understanding of using psychoacoustic compression in your game is encoding and production. There are several knobs to tweak when making compressed Ogg files, and understanding these will lead to better-sounding music and sound effects in your game.

Quality and size are integrally related in Ogg, and both are controlled by a single knob. In most codecs, you adjust the 'size' knob, which implicitly changes the quality. In Ogg, you adjust the 'quality' knob, which implicitly changes the size. In general, the bigger you're willing to make the file, the better it will sound; and conversely, the less quality you need, the smaller the file can be. There are some practical limits to this relationship, though.

The size of compressed audio is measured by bit rate: the amount of bits used to store one second of audio. The average gamer is not going to be able to hear subtle quality loss, so pushing the bit rate past a certain point will have diminishing returns. Ogg files should sound quite good at 64 kbps (kilobits per second) and should hardly be discernable from the original, which is around 128 kbps.

Since, with most games, the music is not the primary focus of the gamer's attention; lower-bit-rate Ogg files should be more than enough to give gamers an excellent-quality experience.

Two other knobs are the number of channels and the sample rate of the audio. While these affect quality (e.g., mono sound is not as good as stereo), the rate of quality change to size change is not linear. If you halve the size by going from stereo sound to mono sound, the quality is only slightly diminished in most cases. Similarly, if you halve the sample rate, the audio sounds worse, but possibly not much worse. If space is at a premium, you can downmix and resample before compressing with Ogg. This leads to smaller files with an acceptable loss of audio quality.

Conclusion

As game audio grows in importance, it seems obvious that better forms of compression must be utilized to reduce audio's bulk. Since many games are developed on a tight financial budget, an open and royalty-free solution is the natural choice. So, on your next project, consider psychoacoustic compression with Ogg Vorbis.

References

[OggVorbis02] Ogg Vorbis, available online at http://www.vorbis.com, June 2001.
[XiphHome02] Xiphophorus, http://www.xiph.org, June 2001.
[XiphName02] Xiphophorus names and logos, available online at http://www.xiph
.org/xiphname.html, June 2001.

6.2

Creating a Compelling 3D Audio Environment

Garin Hiebert, Creative Labs, Inc.

garinh@hibyte.com

This gem will provide you with techniques for creating compelling 3D audio in your games by applying a few simple rules to your audio engine design and the samples used. We will introduce some basic concepts of 3D audio rendering, provide tips on how to maximize the effectiveness of your audio engine, and offer examples of how to apply these tips. DirectSound 3D and OpenAL are used as examples of prominent 3D audio APIs, but the concepts should be transferable if you are using another API. Complete sample code is included on the CD-ROM.

3D Audio Core Concepts

Many modern games are designed to take place in a 3D world, even in genres that in the past would have used two-dimensional representations of their world. The fundamental idea of a 3D audio engine is to provide a way to use the same three-dimensional world representation for all aspects of the game, with the same data being used for audio and video components. The following subjects are fundamental to 3D positional audio rendering and are critical to your audio engine design.

Single Listener

There is a single 'listener' object representing where the sound is heard in the 3D environment. The listener has a position and orientation in the game-world space, which is used to calculate the appropriate speaker output.

Multiple Sources

Each sound-producing object in the environment is represented by a source. All the sources are mixed and represented at the listener's position, and each corresponds to a voice on the sound card.

Multiple Buffers

A buffer object contains the actual audio data. In DirectSound 3D, a buffer and a source are combined into one object. In OpenAL, the audio data is separated from the sources, in which case there are commonly more buffers allocated than there are sources.

Voice Management

There must be a scheme implemented to allocate the audio data (in buffers) among the available voices on the sound card. The game often needs to play more sounds concurrently than the system can play. Voice management solves this problem by invoking a method, based on distance and/or priority, to decide which sounds will be played at any given time. In DirectSound 3D, a buffer and a source are the same thing, and a voice-management scheme is used internally to determine which buffers are audible using the current hardware. In OpenAL, a source object directly corresponds with a voice on the audio hardware, and there can be a much larger number of buffers that can be played on the limited number of sources. Voice allocation in this case is done by any scheme the programmer decides to use.

Determination of Speaker Output

The end user might have any of a variety of speaker output configurations, any of which should convincingly portray the 3D audio world. To do this, the audio-rendering system (e.g., DirectSound, OpenAL) must minimally figure out what the panning and attenuation characteristics are for each source at the listener's position. The relative positions and orientations of the listener, and each source can be used to figure out the panning of the speakers. The distance between each source and the listener determines the attenuation of each source, and the resulting audio is then mixed and played. For an even more compelling audio experience, reverberation and filtering can also be applied (either globally or on a per-source basis) before the final mix.

Using Your Audio Engine Effectively

The following tips (in order of their application to the audio-processing chain) will help you maximize the quality of a 3D audio engine.

Tip #1: Use Normalized Samples

Before importing a sample into your engine, make sure it is taking full advantage of the amplitude range of your sample bit depth by normalizing it. Otherwise, you might find that a particular sample is always too soft, and then you might have to adjust the levels of everything else. This hassle is avoided by normalizing the sample to begin with.

Tip #2: Use 'Dry' Samples

If you intend to apply effects to your audio, make sure there are no effects applied to the original sample. (Samples without effects are called "dry.") Applying reverberation or filtering at an early stage makes it impossible to recover from the effect during run-time processing.

Tip #3: Decide on Your Units

Make sure you know what units are used in the design of the game world. It is critical to provide the correct information to the low-level API so that it can render the audio properly. This means that the audio API needs to understand the physical parameters of the game world. If the audio world units are in meters, but the game world is in feet, then certain audio effects (e.g., Doppler effects or air absorption) might not work as intended, forcing you to recalibrate the effects for another set of units. Using consistent units throughout the engine will allow the API to work the way it was designed.

Tip #4: Understand and Use the Capabilities of the Low-Level API

Decide on a low-level API and plan to take advantage of its features. In addition to 3D position, the low-level API (e.g., DirectSound 3D, OpenAL) will have global and per-source properties, such as roll-off factor or per-source gain. Plan on providing this data to the low-level API. For example, if you followed Tip #1 and normalized your audio, then you will need to set per-source reference distance appropriately. Both OpenAL and DirectSound 3D have a notion of directional audio as well—an under-utilized feature of both APIs.

Tables 6.2.1 and 6.2.2 show a few of the global and per-source properties that can be applied using OpenAL or DirectSound 3D.

Table 6.2.1 Examples of Global Properties in OpenAL and DirectSound 3D

Description	OpenAL Property	DirectSound 3D Property
Master gain	AL_GAIN	Master Volume, set using mixer API
Speed of sound	AL_DOPPLER_VELOCITY	DistanceFactor, applied to listener
Doppler effect	AL_DOPPLER_FACTOR	DopplerFactor, applied to listener

Table 6.2.2 Examples of Per-Source Properties in OpenAL and DirectSound 3D

Description	OpenAL Property	DirectSound 3D Property
Pitch multiplier	AL_PITCH	Frequency
Gain	AL_GAIN	Volume
Position	AL_POSITION	Position
Velocity	AL_VELOCITY	Velocity
Direction	AL_DIRECTION	ConeOrientation
Head relative/Absolute modes	AL_SOURCE_RELATIVE	Mode
Reference distance	AL_REFERENCE_DISTANCE	MinDistance

Tip #5: Add Effects

Process the audio to accommodate the game environment. Using an API such as EAX, occlusion, obstruction, reverberation panning, and other effects can be added to enhance the player's experience. A fallback scheme for lack of hardware-accelerated effects does not need to be limited to dry audio, either—filtering and additional attenuation can be applied. For example, in a first-person shooter, intervening walls should muffle sounds. Applying occlusion via EAX or using a low-pass filter function with additional attenuation can make this situation sound much more realistic and at the same time provide the player with information about the environment.

Implementation

ON THE CD

A demo program is provided on the CD-ROM with an audio engine incorporating the above tips. The demo program is simple in many regards, but it still illustrates typical audio engine flow with four high-level events:

1) Loading Audio Data

All the audio data is loaded once when the program starts. In most games, the audio data is loaded for each level as part of the loading of that level's other data (e.g., geometry, textures, etc.). But in general, the loading of audio data is an infrequent event. Tips #1 and #2 apply to this event. The audio data should be normalized and dry.

2) Apply Global Parameters

The global parameters are all applied only once, and after the audio data is loaded. A game might not be able to get away with only a single setting of the global parameters, but this will normally be a very infrequent event compared to other audio events. For example, the physical parameters of the game world, such as the Doppler factor and master volume, shouldn't require constant adjusting.

Tips #3 and #4 apply to this event. The setting of any parameter should use the correct units, and the selection of parameters should make use of the API's capabilities.

3) Adjust Per-Source Parameters

Per-source parameters are set once for every frame of graphics displayed, which is similar to how most games will operate. Some games set the audio parameters less frequently than the video updates occur, but this event is still part of the main loop of the program.

Tips #3 and #4 apply to this event. The setting of any parameter should use the correct units, and the selection of parameters should make use of the API's capabilities.

4) Adjust Effects Parameters

Both global and per-source effects are being used in the demo program. If EAX capability is detected, the global EAX preset can be changed while the demo runs. In addition, the demo program is also constantly looking for the opportunity to apply per-source EAX effects. Any game will need to apply both global and per-source effects, depending on the effects available. This event is part of the main loop of the program and takes place concurrently with the per-source parameter changes.

Tips #3 and #5 apply to this event. Some effects rely on the physical properties of the game world being set correctly, and an appropriate level of effects should be used when available.

Conclusion

Creating a compelling 3D audio environment for your game is a difficult job with many subtleties. Using the five tips in this gem, the job will be less stressful, take less time, and provide your players more compelling audio.

Resources

[Creative02] Creative Technology, Ltd., "Creative Labs—Developer Central," available online at http://developer.creative.com, March 2002. The "Games" section has information on EAX as well as OpenAL, including documentation and SDKs.

[Loki01] Loki Entertainment Software, "OpenAL | Open Source Audio Library," available online at http://www.openal.org, March 2002. The OpenAL source code and a mailing list are hosted.

6.3

Obstruction Using Axis-Aligned Bounding Boxes

Carlo Vogelsang, Creative Labs Inc.

cvogelsang@creativelabs.com

This gem will describe how axis-aligned bounding boxes can be used to simplify the calculations for proper sound obstruction caused by arbitrary objects in your game. It will demonstrate actual techniques used by EAGLE™ and EAX-Manager, developed by Keith Charley at Creative Labs. The result is a good audio experience with low calculation cost and enough flexibility for general usability.

The Problem

When sound is heard indirectly, this means that the sound waves cannot travel directly from source to listener. We call this *obstruction* [Jot99] since the direct path is being obstructed. Figure 6.3.1 shows the unobstructed and obstructed sound source.

We want to obtain a value that represents the amount of this obstruction. It turns out that sounds waves with a bigger wavelength (or lower frequency) diffract around solid objects better than sound waves with a smaller wavelength (or higher frequency). So once we have obtained a value that represents the amount of obstruction, we can use that value to determine the gain of a low-pass filter applied to our sound source [I3DL2]. This filter is used to simulate the attenuation of higher frequency sounds diffracting around solid objects.

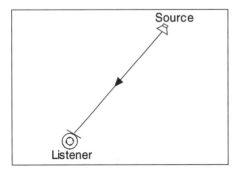
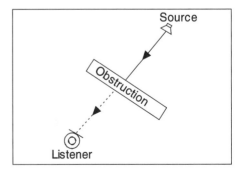

FIGURE 6.3.1 *An unobstructed (left) versus obstructed (right) sound source.*

In the following section, an algorithm is explained that determines a value from 0 (silent, the sound is completely obstructed) to 1 (full level, the sound is completely unobstructed).

The Solution

The solution proposed in this gem involves finding an approximation for the path that sound must take to 'bend' around the corner of an obstruction. The corner we choose to evaluate is the edge closest to the sound source. To calculate this bend, we build an angle, α, from the vectors that go from source to corner to listener. When this angle is at a maximum (180°), there is no obstruction. The smaller the angle calculated, the more the sound is being obstructed [Kutt00]. You can see in Figure 6.3.2 that this results in a vector that intersects the obstruction object. An accurate path around the obstruction would not intersect, but we are trading accuracy for speed.

To speed up the process even further, we can use axis-aligned bounding boxes (AABB). A small error is still introduced, but the computational time is drastically reduced. You can see the error introduced by comparing Figure 6.3.2 and Figure 6.3.3. Any object that is not cubical and axis-aligned will accrue some error in α. Figure 6.3.3 shows the resulting α when using AABBs.

To calculate this angle given our source position, listener position, and obstruction bounding box, we start by computing two bit vectors, one for the source and one

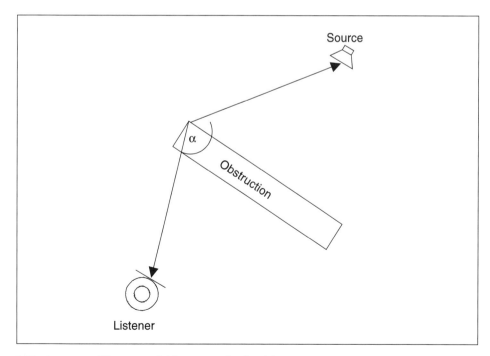

FIGURE 6.3.2   *Biggest angle/shortest path algorithm.*

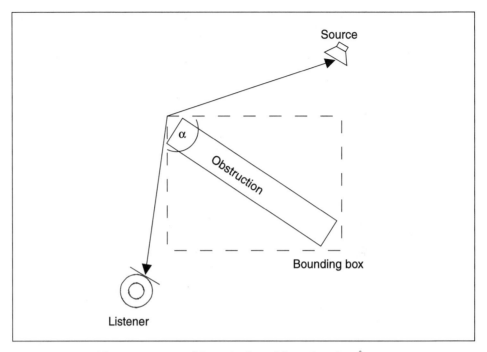

FIGURE 6.3.3   *Obstruction covered by axis-aligned bounding box.*

for the listener. Six bits are used to represent each of the six planes of the 3D bounding box. A set bit indicates that the source or listener is *in front* of that plane; this code example computes the listener bits corresponding to the front and back (*xy-*) plane:

```
if (ListenerPosition.Z < BoundingBox.vMin.Z)
    lListenerFlags |= 0x02;
else if (ListenerPosition.Z > BoundingBox.vMax.Z)
    lListenerFlags |= 0x01;
```

Using these two bit vectors, we can quickly determine if an obstruction is possible. If both bit fields share any true bits, then there cannot be an obstruction, because the source and the listener are in front of the same plane. The check can be performed by:

```
if (lListenerFlags & lSourceFlags)
    continue;
```

If we have determined that an obstruction is possible, we create a list of the bounding-box planes closest to the source. This is accomplished by using the bit vector to determine the zone that the source is in (26 possible zones *outside* of the bounding box and 38 zones *inside* of the bounding box, adding up to a total of $2^6 = 64$ zones). One of the valid 26 outside cases is shown in the switch statement code presented here. The 38 inside cases are invalid and are handled by the `default` case statement.

```
switch (lSourceFlags & 0x3f)
{
case 0x01:// Behind bounding box
    vPlanePoint[0] = BoundingBox.vMax
    vPlaneNormal[0] = {0, 0, 1};
    lPlaneType = BACK;
    lNumPlanes = 1;
    break;
    ..
default:    // Invalid combination (inside)
    lNumPlanes = 0;
    break;
}
```

After this switch statement, we may have up to three bounding box planes specified. For each plane, we check to see if it intersects the source/listener vector. If an intersection is found, we compute the intersection point:

```
for (i = 0; i < lNumPlanes; i++)
{
    SVector svIntersection;
    FindPlaneIntersectionPoint(..,&svIntersection);

    if (PointInPlane(svIntersection,..))
    {
    ...
    }
}
```

Now that we know there is an intersection somewhere on the bounding box's hull, we need to find and move the intersection point to the closest edge. The following code block performs this.

```
switch (lPlaneType)
{
    case FRONT:
    case BACK:
    if (Listener->fY < Box.vMin->fY &&
    Listener->fY > Box.vMax->fY)
    {
        fMidPoint = Box.vMin->fX - Box.vMax->fX;
        fMidPoint /= 2;
        fMidPoint += Box.vMax->fX;
        if (svIntersection.fX < fMidPoint )
            svIntersection.fX = Box.vMax->fX;
        else
            svIntersection.fX = Box.vMin->fX;
    }
    else
    {
```

```
            fMidPoint = Box.vMin->fY - Box.vMax->fY;
            fMidPoint /= 2;
            fMidPoint += Box.vMax->fY;
            if (svIntersection.fY < fMidPoint )
                svIntersection.fY = Box.vMax->fY;
            else
                svIntersection.fY = Box.vMin->fY;
        }
        break;
    default:
        break;
    }
```

With the intersection point now on an edge of the bounding box, we can compute the angle, α, between the intersection point-to-source vector and the intersection point-to-listener vector.

```
long lLevel = MAX_OBSTRUCTION;

CVector cvListener(*psvListener);
cvListener -= svIntersection;

CVector cvSource(*psvSource);
cvSource -= svIntersection;

cvSource.Normalize();
cvListener.Normalize();

float fAngle = cvListener.DotProduct(cvSource);
if ( fAngle >= 0 )
    return lLevel;

fAngle += 1;

float fMaxAngle = (float)m_lDifAngle;
fMaxAngle /= 90.0f;

if ( fAngle >= fMaxAngle )
    return lLevel;

lLevel = (long)(((float)lLevel * fAngle) / fMaxAngle);
```

Now that we know α and, thus, the amount of obstruction imposed by the edge, we will take the biggest value (meaning the *least* amount of obstruction) found. Note that this algorithm will only consider the closest edge to the source; if the bounding box is fairly thin (e.g., walls, crates, etc.), this will work fine. For larger bounding boxes, the influence of the edge closest to the listener can cause greater inaccuracies.

Implementation

ON THE CD

A sample implementation that handles all the calculations needed for a single bounding box is on the CD-ROM. This is actual code from EAXMan, by Keith Charley at Creative Labs, Inc.

Conclusion

In this gem, we have shown how to simplify the obstruction calculations by using axis-aligned bounding boxes. This dramatically reduces the amount of computations required, yet the overall result is very convincing and adds an important audio cue to give players a definite advantage.

References

[I3DL2] IASIG, "Interactive 3D Audio Rendering Guidelines Level 2.0," available online at http://www.iasig.org, Los Angles, CA, 1999.

[Jot99] Jot, J. M., "EAX 4.0 Specification," Creative Labs, Inc., Milpitas, CA, 2001.

[Kutt00] Kuttruff, H., *Room Acoustics*, Fourth Edition, Spon Press, London, U.K. 2000.

6.4

Using the Biquad Resonant Filter

Phil Burk, SoftSynth.com

philburk@softsynth.com

This gem will discuss the biquad infinite impulse response (IIR) filter, which is a multipurpose resonant filter. By changing the filter coefficients, it can perform various filter-pass operations, such as low pass, band pass, high pass, band stop, and others. We will describe how digital filters work, how to implement an efficient biquad filter, and how to calculate coefficients for various functions. Several examples of the sound-filtering techniques and synthesis tricks will be provided.

You can use a filter to change the character of a sound. Sounds can be thought of as being composed of sine waves at various frequencies. Filters change the amplitude of those sine waves, depending on their frequency. You can emphasize the high frequencies or the low frequencies to make something sound brighter or have more boom.

This is particularly handy when playing samples because they tend to always sound the same. However, if you pass a sample through a filter while changing parameters, you can vary the sound every time the sample is played. You can dynamically change these filter parameters to track the state of the game. Changing a sound to appropriately match the current game state will make your game more realistic. (Examples of using a biquad filter to create complex sound effects are also given in Gem 6.6, *The Stochastic Synthesis of Complex Sounds,* by Phil Burk.)

How Digital Filters Work

When you add sine waves of the same frequency together, they can cancel each other out or reinforce each other, depending on their relative phase. Delaying a complex signal by a fixed amount, say one sample period, will change the phase of all its frequency components by differing amounts. A one-sample period delay might cause a very small phase change for a low frequency because it has a long period, while a higher frequency sound will have a greater phase change because the time delay is a larger fraction of the waveform's period. This gives us a mechanism by which we can affect different frequencies in different ways.

A typical digital filter contains a delay line made up of successive, one-sample delays, or *taps*. The original input signal is called x_n. So the taps are labeled x_{n-1}, x_{n-2}, and so on. The taps are scaled and added or subtracted to cause cancellation or reinforcement of various frequencies.

An *averaging* filter, for example, produces an output, y_n, that is an average of the current input sample and the previous input sample. The equation for a simple low-pass filter is:

$$y_n = 0.5 * (x_n + x_{n-1}). \tag{6.4.1}$$

Because low frequencies are not phase-shifted very much by this one-sample delay, they remain relatively unaffected by this filter. However, high frequencies are shifted significantly in phase and can undergo cancellation. In fact, the higher the frequency, the greater the cancellation. Because this filter passes low frequencies more than high frequencies, we call this simple averaging filter a *low-pass* filter.

A high-pass filter can be constructed by changing the plus (+) sign in the equation for the low-pass filter to a minus (–) sign. Then, low frequencies that are not shifted very much in phase cancel themselves out. The simple high-pass filter equation is:

$$y_n = 0.5 * (x_n - x_{n-1}). \tag{6.4.2}$$

IIR Versus FIR Filters

Finite impulse response (FIR) filters only process the incoming sound. So, when the input goes to zero, the output goes to zero within a few samples, depending on how many taps there are.

Infinite impulse response (IIR) filters use delayed versions of both the incoming sound, and the resulting output. This feedback allows the filter to wiggle forever, even when the input goes to zero. The characteristic ringing filters of electronic music are IIR filters.

The Biquad Filter Implementation

The biquad filter has three taps on the input side and two on the output side [Dodge97, p. 214]. The equation for this filter is:

$$y_n = a_0 * x_n + a_1 * x_{n-1} + a_2 * x_{n-2} - b_1 * y_{n-1} - b_2 * y_{n-2}. \tag{6.4.3}$$

By changing the coefficients, a_0, a_1, a_2, b_1 and b_2, you can make the filter behave as a low-pass, high-pass, band-pass, band stop, peaking EQ, or other type of filter.

There are several things we can do to optimize the filter. The most optimal place for the filter operation is in a loop. Most compilers will load the values into the registers once and then perform the loop calculations without having to reload them. The following listing is an implementation of the biquad excerpted from the file Unit_BiquadFilter.cpp available on the CD-ROM.

```
for( i=0; i<GGSYNTH_FRAMES_PER_BLOCK; i++)
{
// Generate outputs by filtering inputs.
    xn = inputs[i];
    yn = (a0 * xn) + (a1 * xn1) + (a2 * xn2)
        - (b1 * yn1) - (b2 * yn2);
    outputs[i] = yn;

// Delay input and output values.
    xn2 = xn1;
    xn1 = xn;
    yn2 = yn1;
    yn1 = yn;
}
```

Permuting the Variables

Another optimization to the biquad filter is to reduce the data movement associated with the delay lines by *permuting* the algorithm. First, we modify the loop so that we perform two filters per loop. Instead of moving data, we can just leave the data in place and change the equation to use the right values. The following code is a permuted version of the previous code. To make this clearer, look at the second IIR equation in the following code, where we multiply (a2 * xn1). We would normally have set xn2=xn1 to implement the delay line, and then done (a2 * xn2). However, we can take a shortcut and just multiply (a2 * xn1), and get the same result. Some optimizing compilers will do this trick by themselves, but it doesn't hurt to give the compiler a hint.

```
for( i=0; i<GGSYNTH_FRAMES_PER_BLOCK; i+=2)
{
// Generate outputs by filtering inputs.
        xn = inputs[i];
        yn2 = (a0 * xn) + (a1 * xn1) + (a2 * xn2)
            - (b1 * yn1) - (b2 * yn2);
        outputs[i] = yn2;

// Permute filter operations to reduce data movement.
// Just substitute variables instead of xn1=xn, etc.
        xn2 = inputs[i+1];
        yn1 = (a0 * xn2) + (a1 * xn) + (a2 * xn1)
            - (b1 * yn2) - (b2 * yn1);
        outputs[i+1] = yn1;

// Only move a little data.
        xn1 = xn2;
        xn2 = xn;
}
```

Also, many of the filter types have coefficients that are the same or zero; so, you could eliminate one of the multiplications. If, for example, a0 equals a2, then the term (a0 * xn2) + (a1 * xn) + (a2 * xn1) becomes (a0 * xn2) + (a1 * xn) + (a0 * xn1), which can be shortened to (a0 * (xn2 + xn1)) + (a1 * xn).

Avoiding Denormalization

Recursive algorithms that operate on their previous output are subject to a vexing problem. Imagine performing this calculation many times:

```
x = 0.99 * x;
```

The value x will continue to get smaller and smaller, and will eventually become too small to represent as a valid floating-point number. This can happen in a game if you leave it paused for a long time. When this happens, some FPUs will interrupt the CPU and ask for a fix, which could render a computer sluggish.

Luckily, there is a simple solution. Just inject a little bit of energy into the filter to prevent it from decaying to such a small value. You can pulse it with a number so small that you will never hear the effect, but it is enough to prevent the interrupts. After you calculate a block of samples using the aforementioned loop, just add a very small number to one of the delayed values. The tiny spike will prevent the filter from decaying too close to zero. The following is an example solution.

```
yn1 += 1.0E-26; /* prevent denormalization */
```

Controlling the Filter

There are two parameters that control the behavior of the filter: the cutoff frequency and the resonance (Q). For a low-pass filter, frequencies above the cutoff frequency will gradually fall off. For a high-pass filter, frequencies below the cutoff frequency will gradually fall off. The resonance value (Q) can be used to increase the amount of feedback in the filter. This can cause frequencies near the cutoff to be emphasized. The filter can even be made to oscillate at a sufficiently high value of Q. A Q value of 1.0 is considered normal resonance.

Calculating Coefficients for the Filter

The coefficients that we are using for the various filter types are based on a cookbook published by Robert Bristow-Johnston on the music-dsp mailing list [RBJ]. Note that the A and B coefficient names are reversed relative to his document in order to be consistent with many textbooks. Calculation of coefficients involves trigonometric calculations, which are expensive and should only be performed when the input parameters change.

Digital filters simply operate on a stream of numbers or samples. For a given set of coefficients and input samples, the output samples will be the same regardless of the actual sample rate. So before calculating the filter, we convert the cutoff frequency (in hertz) to a radial velocity, *omega*, that is proportional to the sample rate. The sine and cosine of omega are used several times in the calculations, so we only calculate them once (`sin_omega` and `cos_omega`).

```
omega = (2.0 * PI * frequency) / sampleRate;
sin_omega = sin( omega );
cos_omega = cos( omega );
```

All of the coefficients are scaled by a common factor. We fold that factor into the coefficients instead of doing an extra multiply.

```
alpha = sin_omega / (2.0 * Q);
scalar = 1.0 / (1.0 + alpha);
```

Low-Pass Filters

Low-pass filters reduce the high frequency content of a sound and pass the low-frequency content.

```
/* Coefficients for LowPass Filters */
A0 = 0.5 * (1.0 − cos_omega) * scalar;
A1 =   (1.0 − cos_omega) * scalar;
A2 = A0;
B1 = -2.0 * cos_omega * scalar;
B2 = (1.0 - alpha) * scalar;
```

Low-pass filters, when combined with reverberation, can make a sound seem more distant. They can be used to make a sound seem muffled when it is behind a wall or inside a box or tunnel. Ringing low-pass filters can be use to create unusual alien vocal chirps or synthetic-sounding weapon noises. A whistling wind sound can be produced by passing white noise through a filter and slowly, randomly varying the cutoff frequency and Q.

High-Pass Filters

High-pass filters reduce the low frequency content of a sound and pass the high-frequency content.

```
/* Coefficients for HighPass Filters */
A0 = 0.5 * (1.0 + cos_omega) * scalar;
A1 =   -(1.0 + cos_omega) * scalar;
A2 = A0;
B1 = -2.0 * cos_omega * scalar;
B2 = (1.0 - alpha) * scalar;
```

High-pass filters can be used to make a voice sound tinny, like it is on a telephone or radio. It can also be used to brighten a sound.

Band-Pass Filters

Band-pass filters reduce the frequencies on either side of a center frequency. We call it a center frequency instead of a cutoff frequency because if you look at the frequency response curve of a band-pass filter, this frequency will be at the center of the peak.

```
/* Coefficients for BandPass Filters */
A0 = alpha * scalar;
A1 = 0.0;
A2 = -A0;
B1 = -2.0 * cos_omega * scalar;
B2 = (1.0 - alpha) * scalar;
```

Combining Filters in Series

You can combine low-pass and high-pass filters in series by passing the output of one filter to the input of another. Each filter will subtract from the previous filter. You can also combine low-pass and high-pass filters to create custom band-pass filters with a broad pass band.

Combining Filters in Parallel

Several filters can be placed in parallel by mixing or adding their outputs together. This collection of filters is called a *filter bank*. An example is the set of band-pass filters in a graphical EQ that you might have on your stereo.

Combining three or more band-pass filters can create formats that create vocal sounds. These may be useful for creating alien creature sounds.

Software

ON THE CD

A keyboard-driven C++ program is provided on the CD-ROM that enables you experiment with all three of the filter types described in this gem. You can pass white noise or an impulse train through the filters to hear how they sound. You can also change the resonance of the filter. The filter frequency is slowly swept up and down using a sine wave. Updates to this software will be posted on the Web at: http://www.softsynth.com/gamegems/.

The example program uses PortAudio, which is a simple, cross-platform audio API. The program should be able to run on Win32, Macintosh, Unix with OSS, SGI, and other platforms. To check for updates to PortAudio for your platform, visit them on the Web at: http://www.portaudio.com/.

Conclusion

A biquad filter gives us a simple way to modify the character of a sound without using a large amount of memory. It allows us to get more use out of a smaller number of samples, or to generate interesting sounds without the use of any samples. This gem shows us how to implement a filter efficiently, and the example software shows us how to filter sounds and play the result.

References

[Dodge97] Dodge, Jerse, *Computer Music Synthesis, Composition and Performance*, Simon & Schuster, 1997.

[Moore90] Moore, F. Richard, *Elements of Computer Music*, Prentice Hall, 1990.

[RBJ] Bristow-Johnson, Robert, "Cookbook Formulae for Audio EQ Biquad Filter Coefficients," available online at http:// http://www.musicdsp.org/.

6.5

Linear Predictive Coding for Voice Compression and Effects

Eddie Edwards

eddie@tinyted.net

A vocoder is a device for altering speech, now made famous by that Cher song, *Believe* [Cher98]. Vocoders are best known for the robot voices they produce, from daleks in the *Dr. Who* series [Nation63] to the battle droids in *Star Wars* [Lucas99], but they can also produce bizarre alien voices, as well as "singing" guitars and similar effects. In addition, vocoders are used as the basis for several voice-compression methods, including the GSM digital mobile phone standard [ETSI00].

Although voice effects and voice compression seem like different problems, the same approach can apply to both. The program on the CD-ROM demonstrates voice effects, but a side effect of the approach is that only 500 bytes of data are required per second—this is 350 times less data than CD audio, which would allow us to store almost three *weeks* of speech on one CD-ROM! The full GSM algorithm is available in the public domain [Degener00] and achieves about 200:1 compression over CD audio.

This sort of magic can happen because of the way a vocoder works. There are several different types of vocoders, but they all work on the same basic principle: Split the sound up into constituent parts (analysis), manipulate the parts, and then put them back together again (resynthesis). We can then either play around with the data in the middle to create effects, or we can compress it. Clearly, we can also store and retrieve it, so the analysis and synthesis parts do not have to happen together—or even on the same machine. A vocoder is like any codec in this respect, with logically distinct encoding and decoding phases (see Figure 6.5.1).

Consider comparing this arrangement with the familiar set up of JPEG compression. There, each block of pixels is transformed into the frequency domain (analysis), where it can be more easily compressed. The pixels are transformed back again (resynthesis) when the JPEG is decompressed.

A vocoder is ultimately defined by which algorithm it uses for analysis and resynthesis. When that algorithm is the Fast Fourier Transform (FFT), we get a *phase*

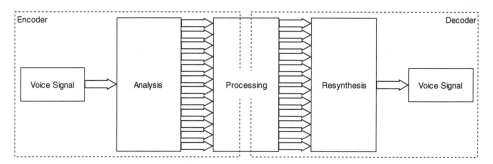

FIGURE 6.5.1   *A vocoder.*

vocoder. The algorithm we present here is called *linear predictive coding* (LPC) and gives us an *LPC vocoder.*

Modeling the Voice

LPC attempts to model the way speech is produced in the human body, but in such a general way that it can also model sound production under different circumstances. The basic model has only two parts, which are usually termed the *oscillator* and the *resonator* (see Figure 6.5.2).

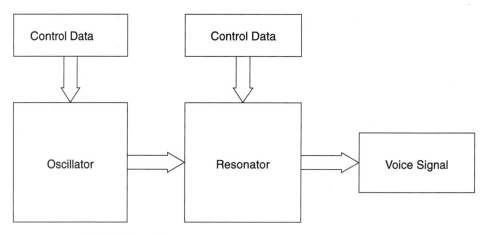

Figure 6.5.2   *The LPC model.*

You can't produce a sound without an oscillator—this is the physical object that vibrates, producing sound waves. Anything that makes a sound contains some kind of oscillator, from a played violin (the strings) to a pencil dropped on a desk (the pencil vibrates). The human voice is no exception; the person's vocal chords is the oscillator.

Oscillators are well understood, and simulating them on a computer provides little challenge.

Many systems make a sound of one form or another, but some are *designed* to do so (either by evolution or ingenuity). These systems are distinguished by the presence of a *resonator*. A resonator acts as a natural amplifier for the sound produced by the oscillator. All musical instruments have them—for instance, an acoustic guitar has a hollow body that amplifies the strings (an electric guitar has a solid body, and its strings are virtually inaudible until you plug the guitar into an amplifier). However, the resonator isn't a simple amplifier, by any means. It amplifies different frequencies by different amounts, depending on the characteristics of the resonator. In violins, the resonance helps to actually *reduce* inharmonic sounds from the strings. It is the quality of the resonator in a violin that distinguishes a Stradivarius from a Yamaha. In brass instruments, the only way to produce different notes is to *change* the configuration of the resonator, since the oscillator (mouthpiece) is incapable of changing pitch. By pressing a key, the player opens an air vent in the side of the resonator, changing its characteristics and producing a new note.

The resonator in the human voice is formed by the human head—specifically, the interior cavities of the head, through which the sound from the vocal chords travels before it reaches the mouth. This resonator is certainly not fixed, and by moving the tongue, jaw, and lips, the speaker can change the resonator's characteristics quite quickly. If you hum with your vocal chords and make your mouth larger and smaller you can hear the effect—clearly, most word sounds come from this mechanism and not the vocal chords. (There are other mechanisms at work too, which we discuss later.)

Since the resonator can change its characteristics over time, we break the modeling process up into *frames* of around 20 ms each. The resonator is assumed to have fixed characteristics over a single frame. The size of each frame is a parameter to the LPC algorithm.

A Software Simulation

Simulating this model in software is actually fairly straightforward. The oscillator can be simulated with a sample player, and the resonator is modeled with a digital filter. The oscillator feeds samples to the filter, and speech is produced.

The digital filter is quite simple in principle. It takes a sequence of input samples and produces a sequence of filtered output samples. The filter works by calculating each output sample as a weighted sum of the previous N input samples. The weights determine the filter's characteristics. This is usually implemented as a function that takes a single parameter (the most recent sample) and remembers the last N samples in an internal state vector.

In LPC, we use a slightly different formulation, which is more physical than mathematical in nature. We model the resonator as a long pipe made up of segments of different widths. When a sound wave travels between two segments, some is

reflected. The amount that is reflected at each point is given by a *reflection coefficient*.
A set of these coefficients describes the whole tube, and the number of coefficients is
a parameter of the LPC algorithm. The filter keeps a state vector corresponding to the
pressure in each segment. This allows reflected waves to actually travel back down
the simulated tube. The function given below does the work.

```
// s = input sample
// FFS[] = forward filter state
// rc[] = reflection coefficients

for (int ii = order; ii--;)
{
    // s -= FFS[ii] * rc[ii]
    // FFS'[ii + 1] = FFS[ii] + s * rc[ii]
    s -= FFS[ii] * rc[ii];
    FFS[ii + 1] = FFS[ii] + s * rc[ii];
}
return s;
```

An interesting note is that this function is invertible, and this is the key to LPC
(see Figure 6.5.3). If we invert that filter and run the *speech* through it, we will get the
oscillator output signal. (When we run the filter this way, the oscillator signal is called
the *residual*.) The inverse of this function is listed here.

```
// s = input sample
// IFS[] = inverse filter state
// rc[] = reflection coefficients

float ifsp = s;

for (int ii = 0; ii < order; ii++)
{
    // IFS'[ii + 1] = IFS[ii] + s * rc[ii]
    // s += IFS[ii] * rc[ii]
    float tmp = IFS[ii] + s * rc[ii];

    s += IFS[ii] * rc[ii];
    IFS[ii] = ifsp;
    ifsp = tmp;
}
return s;
```

This is exactly what we need. In our analysis phase, we have the speech signal, but
not the oscillator signal. Now we can extract the oscillator signal (residual) to be used
for resynthesis. All we need are the reflection coefficients. The problem is that *any* set
of coefficients will do. Each will produce *some* kind of "oscillator signal" when run
through the code above. We need to choose the set of coefficients that gives us the
"best" oscillator signal in some sense.

LPC defines the best residual to be the one that has the least energy in it. This is
reasonable, since it means that the inverse filter has removed the highest-energy parts

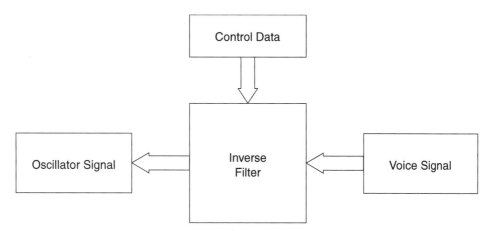

FIGURE 6.5.3 *Reversing the filter.*

of the signal—that is, the most important ones. The forward filter will then re-emphasize those parts of the signal.

Solving this then becomes a matter of constructing a large, simultaneous linear equation and finding the least-squares solution to it. Describing this in detail is beyond the scope of this gem, but the basics might be found in a suitable linear algebra text. The code on the CD-ROM uses Schur's algorithm [Degener94], which is highly optimized for this specific case. This is reproduced as follows:

```
// G[], H[] = working arrays
// AC[] = autocorrelation vector for input signal
// rc[] = (output) reflection coefficients

for (ii = 0; ii < order; ii++)
{
    G[ii] = H[ii] = AC[ii + 1];
}

// one iteration per coefficient
for (ii = 0; ii < order; ii++)
{
    // calculate rc and update error
    float r = -H[0] / error;

    rc[ii] = r;
    error += H[0] * r;

    // update G & H
    for (int m = 0; m < order - ii; m++)
    {
        H[m] = H[m + 1] + r * G[m];
        G[m] = H[m + 1] * r + G[m];
    }
}
```

The code in linearpredictor.cpp performs all these tasks and provides a black-box solution for LPC coding. We are left with a two-step process—analysis plus synthesis—which (barring rounding errors) reproduces the original speech sample precisely. The only parameters are frame time (in samples) and filter complexity (number of reflection coefficients). The test code uses frames of 20 ms (160 samples at 8 kHz) and eight reflection coefficients.

Replacing the Vocal Chords

Once the LPC encoder has done its magic, we will want to play around a little to create our robot or alien voices. The easiest thing to do is to replace the oscillator signal with a synthesized sound. This synthesized sound is then filtered, and the end result is as if the synthesizer were in the speaker's throat instead of his own!

The important thing to remember here is that the synthesized sound is merely being filtered, so any frequencies that are not in the sound to begin with will not be in it afterwards. If we use a simple sine wave, it only contains a single frequency and will not generate interesting sounds. It would be like illuminating a multicolored mural with monochromatic laser light—only the single color is reflected back. So we must try to use a sound that is rich in frequency content.

The best choices are a pulse waveform or a sawtooth waveform, since these contain all the harmonics. A square waveform contains all odd-numbered harmonics. These choices all give relatively intelligible "robotic" speech, and they are all very quick to generate in code.

Alternatively, a bass-heavy waveform will give a bass-heavy voice; and one with only certain frequencies will remain tuned to those frequencies, which will be modulated. These choices give more alien-sounding voices, with weirder input waveforms giving weirder speech sounds—although you can no longer hear *what* is being said! Slightly more complex waveforms can be obtained through FM synthesis.

A sample can simply be played back as well. If that sample is the residual, we get excellent-quality results (perfect, allowing for rounding errors). If it is something else, like a guitar riff, we get a bizarre, "speaking-guitar" effect: an "all your base are belong to us" pedal instead of just a "wah" pedal!

Another interesting choice is simple white noise. When we whisper, we do not activate our vocal chords at all, and the oscillator signal is just a hiss. We also seem to tone down our intonation. Using noise with a line spoken loudly produces a strange kind of hybrid "whisper" that sounds quite evil.

Controlling the Resynthesizer

The only difficult part of generating the new oscillator signal is getting the pitch and volume right. These can be extracted (with some difficulty) from the residual.

The volume is the most important factor, since you need silence in the right places. It is also the easiest to calculate, by performing a root-mean-square calculation over the residual for each frame of the sound. In output, it is a good idea to interpolate this volume so the sound doesn't click or pop.

Pitch is more difficult. The method used on the CD-ROM works as follows. First, assume the pitch is less than 1 kHz, and filter the residual using a low-pass filter to remove any frequencies higher than this. Then, normalize the waveform and center-clip it. This distorts the waveform so that it looks like a series of spikes. Next, compare this waveform with a set of pulse waveforms of different frequencies, and choose the best match (by a least-squares comparison). Finally, for each frame, choose the *median* pitch calculated for the last three frames (this helps smooth the results out). The method is by no means perfect—it is just as much of a hack as it sounds! Nevertheless, it gives reasonable results—the oscillator seems to follow the lilt of the input speech quite well, and some amount of unrealism is actually desirable!

The production of each frame now progresses according to the diagram shown in Figure 6.5.4. The pitch and volume for each frame control the synthesizer, which is creating a waveform according to the parameters chosen for a specific *speaker*. This waveform then passes through the filter to give the resultant resynthesized speech. Note that another possibility is not shown on the diagram—the frame size on *output* can be different to the frame size on the *input*. By doing this, the speech can be sped up or slowed down relative to the input speech.

Note that the parameters of the *speech* (pitch, volume, and reflection coefficients) are separate from the parameters of the *speaker* (they control the synthesizer parame-

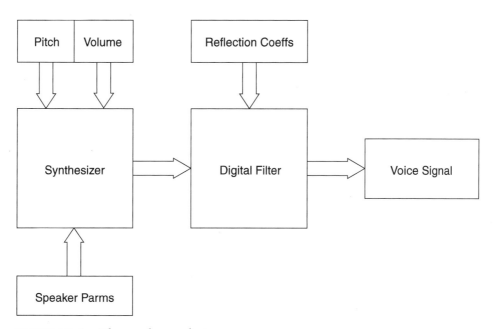

FIGURE 6.5.4 *The speech resynthesizer.*

ters and the speed). So, the same speech data can in principle be used with a variety of speakers. For instance, every robot might have a different pitch so that the player can tell them apart, or some robots might speak more slowly than others. Damage might even affect this, so a broken robot might speak very fast!

Increasing the Depth of the Speaker

Since our reflection coefficients reflect a physical model of a resonator, we can change the resonator by changing the coefficients. The easiest thing to do is to make it longer, and hence deeper. If we begin with 8 reflection coefficients, we could generate 16 coefficients by inserting zeroes between the numbers. The result is a deeper resonance (one octave lower), which sounds more evil.

Alternatively, by cropping reflection coefficients off, the filter becomes more 'shallow'—the speech becomes indistinct and sounds as if the speaker has just been to the dentist. Processing the reflection coefficients is much less intuitive than processing the residual, but many effects are possible in theory.

Encoding the Data

Given the pitch, volume, and eight reflection coefficients, we now have 10 numbers per frame describing everything we need to generate a robotic or alien voice. If we quantize each number into a single byte, that translates to only 500 bytes per second, or 30 KB per minute, as quoted earlier.

For some games, this is as far as we need to go. Other games might require higher-quality speech, or more natural, human-like speech. Perhaps we could try to generate a variety of male voices from a single source sample. It is the encoding that must be addressed in these cases.

The residual signal is quite hard to encode, because it does contain a lot of "missed" information. For instance, most speech sounds use the vocal chords, but some are *unvoiced*, which means the vocal chords are relaxed, and just a hiss of air is released into the vocal cavity. The letter "s" is a good example. In these cases, the residual is like white noise. We could improve the encoding by trying to detect white noise in this case.

Other sounds, like a "p", are made by a different process altogether—in this case, the air "explodes" through the lips making the p-sound. These sounds are called *plosives*. The plosive is not well modeled by the vocal-chord-plus-filter model, so most of the information ends up in the residual. We might be able to model these sounds too, if we spent enough time on it.

To capture all these nuances simply, we should encode the entire residual. Then, the recreated speech will be as near as possible to the real thing. There are many ways we might do this—vector quantization, peak detection, or ADPCM coding for instance. We might even happily store the entire residual as a PCM waveform. We won't have saved space (quite the opposite), but the cost might be worth it if we can perform special effects very cheaply. [Degener94] describes how GSM [ETSI00] encodes the residual into about 1.5 kbps (kilobits per second).

Speed

Not only does the algorithm bless us with low data rates, it also performs admirably (even on consoles from two generations ago). While encoding is difficult to get into real-time, decoding is very fast indeed.

The core of the replay algorithm is the filter. This performs two loads, two adds and two multiplies per coefficient per sample. Assuming eight reflection coefficients, this is about 50 cycles per sample, or 400,000 cycles per second at eight kilohertz. An unoptimized version would, of course, be slower; while a vectorized version could be a lot faster (if the hardware supports it).

In an optimized implementation, the waveform generator would be combined with the filter in the inner loop, alongside the envelope generator, using only a few cycles per sample. The creation of speech therefore takes around 500,000 cycles per second—only 3% of a 16-MHz processor.

Encoding is less critical for game purposes, unless you want to use LPC to transmit speech across the Internet. In this case, some work would have to be done on the encoding end, but a current-generation machine should be able to handle this fairly easily.

Experiments

ON THE CD

The program on the CD-ROM demonstrates almost everything this gem has described, so please play with it for a while. You can load speech samples into the program (an example is supplied), which converts them using the LPC algorithm. These can be played back using either the residual or a voice defined in the program. Several example voices are supplied. The program includes full source code (Microsoft Visual C++), and full instructions are provided in the ReadMe.txt file.

References

[Cher98] Cher, *Believe,* WEA/Warner Bros., 1998.

[Degener94] Degener, Jutta, "Digital Speech Compression," *Dr. Dobbs Journal* (December 1994), available online at http://www.ddj.com/documents/s=1012/ddj9412b/.

[Degener00] Degener, Jutta, "GSM 06.10 Lossy Speech Compression," available online at http://kbs.cs.tu-berlin.de/~jutta/toast.html, July 2000.

[ETSI00] "Digital Cellular Telecommunications System (Phase 2+); Full Rate Speech; Transcoding," (GSM 06.10 version 5.2.1 Release 1996), Third Edition, European Telecommunications Standards Institute, 2000. Available online (free registration required) at http://webapp.etsi.org/pda/.

[Lucas99] Lucas, George, *The Phantom Menace,* 20th Century Fox, 1999.

[Nation63] Nation, Terry, *Dr. Who: The Dead Planet,* British Broadcasting Corporation, 1963.

6.6

The Stochastic Synthesis of Complex Sounds

Phil Burk, SoftSynth.com

philburk@softsynth.com

Stochastic synthesis is a type of audio synthesis that uses random numbers. You can use random numbers at a low level to generate noise. This noise can be used as a sound source or a modulation source. You can also use random numbers at a higher level to control sounds or to trigger sounds. These randomly controlled and triggered sounds can then be used to create soundscapes.

Most games use digital audio samples to create sounds. One advantage of using samples is that they accurately reproduce the original sound. However, a disadvantage of using samples is that they can be repetitive. You can change the sample's playback rate and its amplitude, but that doesn't eliminate the repetitiveness. Real-world sounds do not sound the same every time. Take, for example, a dog's barking. Each bark is a little different. A dog that barked exactly the same every time would be suspect.

Samples are sometimes used to create continuous sounds, such as wind. However, this method eventually requires samples to loop, and the repetition can be audible. A solution to this problem is to synthesize the sounds directly. An advantage of using synthesis is that the sound designer has control over many more parameters. You can change the character of the synthesized wind by making it whistle, or you can make it fluctuate more rapidly. You are not limited to just amplitude and pitch changes.

We will provide examples including wind, sonar pings, rain, rocket engines, and helicopter rotors. The examples will be constructed out of simple, atomic units called *unit generators*. These will include filters, noise generators, oscillators or tone generators, and effects processors, such as reverbs.

Linear Congruential Algorithm

You cannot generate truly random numbers using software. This is because computers generate reproducible, deterministic results. Like most game programmers, however, we are not above cheating. We can generate sequences of numbers, which will sound random, even if they aren't really random.

The most common and cheapest pseudo-random number generator is the linear congruential algorithm (LCA). It is based on doing multiplications and additions, and producing a numerical result that is so large that it overflows the word size of the computer. By carefully selecting the coefficients of the equation, we can generate a sequence of 2^{32} numbers before repeating the sequence [Chamberlin80]. If we generate a stream of samples at 44,100 Hz, then it would only repeat after 27 hours.

To use the LCA function described here, pass a starting value to the function, then feed the result back into the function to generate a sequence of random numbers.

```
/* Calculate pseudo-random 32 bit number using
 * the linear congruential method. */
static unsigned long GenerateRandomNumber(
    unsigned long previous )
{
    return ((previous * 196314165) + 907633515);
}
```

The most significant bits of this function are more random than the lower bits. So, if you want to generate 16-bit random numbers, shift right and use the top 16 bits instead of masking off the lower 16 bits.

Types of Noise

The direct result of the Linear Congruential Algorithm is *white noise*, which sounds like static ("shshshsh"). White noise contains equal energy across the entire frequency spectrum. By modifying the algorithm, you can generate noise with different spectra.

You can generate *red noise* by calculating a new random number every few samples and interpolating between them for the intervening samples. This method, which is demonstrated by the following code and Figure 6.6.1, gives you some very simple control over the frequency content.

```
// phase ranges from 0.0 to 1.0
phase += phaseInc;
if( phase >= 1.0 )
{
// grab a new random target whenever the phase wraps
    source = target;
    target = randomFloat();
    delta = target - source;
    phase -= 1.0f;
}
// linear interpolation between random values
outputs[0] = source + (phase * delta);
```

You can also generate noisy signals using fractal mathematics (feedback on non-linear functions). An example is a simple sine wave with feedback [Roads96]. Iterate over the following code to generate samples or a control signal.

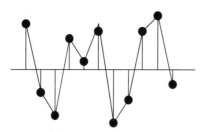 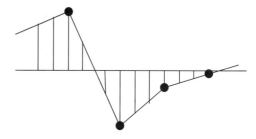

FIGURE 6.6.1 *(Left) White noise with new random values for every sample. (Right) Red noise with samples interpolated between random values.*

```
phase += phaseIncrement + (feedback * x );
if( phase > 1.0 ) phase -= 2.0;
else if( phase < -1.0 ) phase += 2.0;
x = sin( PI * phase );
```

In this example, phase ranges from –1.0 to 1.0. As you raise the feedback coefficient, you will start to get a noisy, chaotic signal.

Software Examples

ON THE CD

The following sections describe actual examples using the techniques described. The source code to the various components described is on the CD-ROM.

Generating a Wind Sound

A wind sound can be generated using a white noise generator (WhiteNoise) as the sound source. The noise signal passes through a low-pass filter (LowPassFilter) with a frequency of 1000 Hz. By increasing the Q of the filter to around 16, you can make a good whistling wind sound.

See Figure 6.6.2 for an overview of the wind example. A red noise generator (Red-Noise) controls the cutoff frequency of the filter and mimics the random rising and falling of the wind. The modRate parameter controls how rapidly the wind fluctuates. The modDepth controls the size of the fluctuation. You then multiply the RedNoise output by the modDepth and add the result to the frequency value to generate the actual cutoff frequency value for the filter. Mixing (or adding) together several of these generators will create a more realistic sound. Try setting modRate to 0.6, and modDepth to 350.

Generating a Sonar Ping

A sonar ping sound consists of a short sine wave burst that echoes off various objects underwater. The sound slowly fades away over time. We can generate the sine burst by hitting a resonant LowPass filter with an impulse spike, similar to hitting a bell

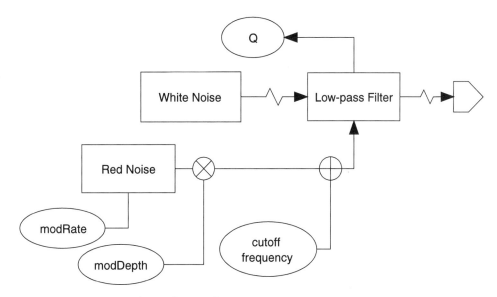

FIGURE 6.6.2   *A wind sound example.*

with a hammer. To implement this, you want to set the filter cutoff frequency to about 700 Hz. To make the filter ring for a longer time, set the Q to larger values, like 1000. To increase the sound of the 'ping' try setting the Impulse amplitude to seven.

The sound we have so far is just a pure sound wave. To make it sound like it is reflecting off of submerged objects, we need to roughen it up a bit. We could add large amounts of reverb, but there is a cheaper trick, which should appeal to game developers. We can modulate the LowPassFilter cutoff frequency by using a RedNoise generator. Set the RedNoise frequency to about 180 Hz and its amplitude to about 80 for the desired result.

The circuit is identical to the wind sound example shown in Figure 6.6.1, except that an ImpulseOscillator replaces the WhiteNoise generator.

Generating the Sound of Rain

The sound of rain is composed of the sounds produced by millions of raindrops hitting cars, trees, windows, dogs, etc. We cannot generate the sound of each individual raindrop, but we can come close. When each raindrop hits, it generates a little 'plop' sound. We could assign an oscillator to each plop sound, but we would need too many oscillators. So, instead we use the familiar ringing filter to generate the plop. An advantage to using a ringing filter is that we can hit one filter with lots of little impulses and get the same result as if we had a filter per impulse. We set the filter frequency to 250 and the Q to 2.

The ringing filter will always generate the same pitch every time we hit it unless we modulate the frequency. We can frequency modulate the filter using a fast Red-

Noise generator, as we have in the previous examples. We set the modRate to 10 and the modDepth to 90 to achieve the desired result.

The next trick is to generate lots of randomly distributed impulses to feed the filter. We can use a comparator to look at a random signal. Whenever the signal exceeds the threshold, we can output a random value, as in the code shown here. Otherwise, we output zero. This will give us occasional random pulses that we can use to excite, or ping the filter (see Figure 6.6.3).

```
threshold = 1.0 - rate;
excitation = (nextRandom() > threshold) ?
    nextRandom () : 0.0;
```

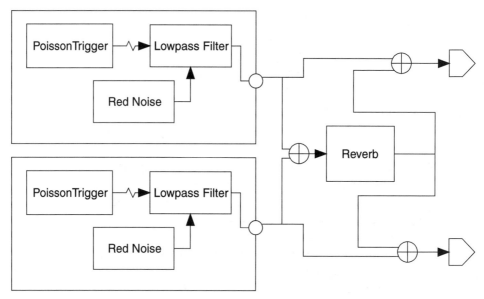

FIGURE 6.6.3   *A rain example. Two raindrop generators share a reverb.*

We can use the rate value above to adjust how hard it is raining.

The ringing filter will give us the sound of individual raindrops that are near to us. Now, we need to generate the millions of drops in the surrounding area that make up the dull roar of rain. We can use a reverb effects processor to echo the sound of a few raindrops and create the sound of many raindrops. The reverb is constructed from six comb filters and an all-pass filter. [Moore90]. The comb filters include a low-pass filter that muffles the sound of the other raindrops and makes them seem farther away. The reverb also uses a much longer delay than normal, between 200 ms and 350 ms, so that the echo effect is less noticeable. We then mix the close raindrop sound with the reverberated sound to get a complete rain sound, as shown above in Figure 6.6.3.

You could add different resonators to this patch to simulate the sound of rain hitting a tin roof or a glass skylight. Just replace the low-pass filter with a more-complex formant filter bank or cross-coupled modal filters.

Generating a Rocket Engine Sound

A decent rocket engine sound can be generated using just two `RedNoise` generators. A single `RedNoise` generator has a discernable pitch and doesn't have the crackle of a good rocket sound. So we can use one `RedNoise` generator to modulate the frequency of another. You want to set the center frequency of the carrier, the `RedNoise` that you hear, to 1300 Hz, and set the modulator's frequency to a value around 731 Hz. Avoid having the modulator frequencies be a simple ratio of the carrier, and set the modulator amplitude to about 600 Hz.

We also need a way to quickly ramp the sound's amplitude up and down as we turn the rocket on and off. Imagine a thruster firing under a pilot's control. We can do this with a slew rate limiter. The limiter tracks its input but won't move faster than a given rate, as shown in the code that follows. This allows us to suddenly set the amplitude to zero, but the actual level will drop more slowly.

```
if( input > value )
{
    value += increment;
    if( value > input ) value = input;
}
else if( input < value )
{
    value -= increment;
    if( value < input ) value = input;
}
```

We then control the output amplitude of the circuit by multiplying the `RedNoise` signal by the `SlewRateLimiter` value. Figure 6.6.4 illustrates the rocket engine sound logic.

Generating a Helicopter Rotor Sound

The noise from a helicopter has two main components, the engine noise and the rotor noise. The rotors cut through the air, causing a whooshing sound. Because the rotors are spinning, they are sometimes going away from us and sometimes coming toward us. This causes a Doppler shift that raises and lowers the pitch of the whoosh. Imagine a car driving past you on a road. It sounds higher pitched when it is approaching you and lower pitched as it goes away. This is because the sound waves are compressed as the car moves toward you, and shorter wavelengths have a higher frequency.

This sound uses filtered white noise as the source sound as in the wind example. It then passes the sound through two variable delays. The two delays are swept back and forth using a sine wave modulator. Set the sine waves 180° out of phase to model

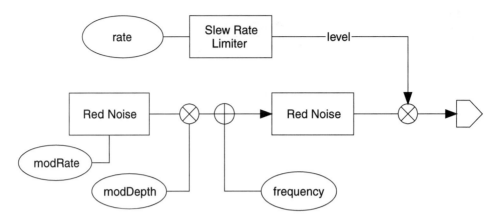

FIGURE 6.6.4   *Rocket engine sound using red noise pair and an envelope generated by a slew rate limiter.*

two blades opposite each other. So, as one delay is increasing, the other is decreasing. This is illustrated in Figure 6.6.5.

Next, we can tune the delay times to match the diameter of the rotor blades. The minimum delay time is when the blade is closest to us, and vice versa.

```
delayRange = rotorDiameter / speedOfSound;
modDepth = delayRange / 2.0;
```

A UH-1 Huey helicopter has a rotor diameter of 48 feet. The speed of sound is approximately 1100 feet per second, so the modDepth for the Doppler shift is about 0.022 seconds. The previous code example generates the proper modDepth.

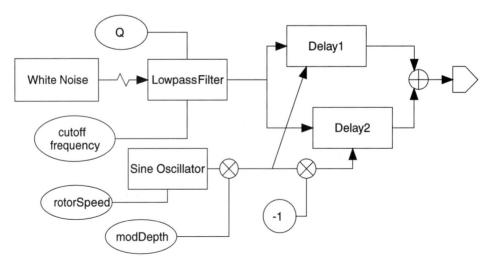

FIGURE 6.6.5   *Helicopter rotor sound created using Doppler shifts 180° out of phase.*

Software

ON THE CD

A keyboard-driven C++ program is provided on the CD-ROM that enables you to experiment with these sounds. You can turn sounds on and off, and change parameters interactively. Look in the index.html file for more information on the software design. To check for updates to this software, visit [Softsynth02].

The example program uses PortAudio, which is a simple, cross-platform audio API. So, the program should be able to run on Win32, Macintosh, Unix with OSS, SGI, and other platforms. To check for updates to PortAudio or to get source code for your platform, visit [PortAudio01].

Conclusion

Using just a few simple unit generators, you can synthesize a wide variety of sounds without the use of samples. This gives you more control over the sound parameters and helps you avoid the artifacts associated with sample loops. Stochastic functions are particularly useful because they can add a lot of complexity without adding a significant computational load. The technique of modulating a single filter with Red-Noise is particularly handy and can be used to replace multiple unmodulated filters. Stochastic processes are also useful at a higher level to trigger short sound events, such as raindrops. Reverberation can be used to make it sound like there are many more sound generators than are actually present in the circuit. Hopefully, these techniques can be used to add some sonic spice in your next game.

References

[Chamberlin80] Chamberlin, Hal, *Musical Applications of Microprocessors*, Hayden, 1980.

[Dodge97] Dodge, Jerse, *Computer Music Synthesis, Composition and Performance*, Simon & Schuster, 1997.

[Moore90] Moore, F. Richard, *Elements of Computer Music*, Prentice Hall, 1990.

[PortAudio01] Bencina, Ross, "PortAudio—an Open-Source Cross-Platform Audio API," available online at http://www.portaudio.com/, 2001.

[Roads96] Roads, Curtis, *The Computer Music Tutorial*, MIT Press, 1996.

[Softsynth02] Burk, Phil, "Biquad Filters and Stochastic Synthesis," available online at http://www.softsynth.com/gamegems/, 2002.

6.7

Real-Time Modular Audio Processing for Games

Frank Luchs, Visiomedia Software Corporation

gemsaudio@visiomedia.com

This gem will describe how to incorporate modular audio processing into your game to procedurally generate sounds in real-time. Often games use one-shot or looped samples to play game sounds. While this can frequently be effective, these static one-shot or looped samples are limited in how they can change in response to user actions. Procedural sound generation with modular audio processing provides many more controls and variations that offer greater realism of sound interaction through a greater interaction between gameplay and audio.

Sound can shape the picture as much as the picture can shape the sound. Real-time procedural audio should become part of a continuum, changing dynamically over time—sometimes subliminal and sometimes impressive. It should resonate with the game's environment and flow with the player's interaction.

Modular Audio Processing

Modular audio processing systems can be created in software using virtual modules and cables that are quite similar to those of vintage modular synthesizer systems. Both systems have no fixed signal path. You create a sound by connecting units like oscillators, filters, and envelope generators—building an audio chain. Using units makes it possible to synthesize various sounds with maximum flexibility, without the need for hard-coding all the countless possible connections.

The data flow of audio processing is determined by the connections that are chosen between the units. The units are encapsulated entities that perform specific operations on the data stream.

Forty years ago, synthesizers were so large that they filled up an entire room, and the only way to save a patch with all its connections was by shooting a Polaroid. Today pure-software systems allow you to create and save millions of patches on your hard disk. Patches are created by appending DSP units to a processing chain. Complex components can be built on top of simpler patches, using units that represent familiar mathematical operations.

As with the vintage hardware monsters, a deep knowledge of digital signal processing is not required, since you can learn by ear while experimenting with connections between modules.

Procedural Sound Generation

There is a great variety of procedural sound-generation methods, and many have a long history in electronic synthesis. Here, we mention some of the common techniques used by many synthesizers that are both effective and practical for current real-time software synthesis.

Classical synthesizers are based on the idea of subtractive synthesis. The typical subtractive synthesizer has an oscillator that generates the basic audio tone, mostly a harmonically rich waveform. This sound goes through a low-pass filter, truncating the upper harmonics, and finally through an amplifier. Each stage can have its own modulators; so over time, the sound changes dynamically in pitch, timbre, and loudness.

Two types of modulators are common. One is the low-frequency oscillator (LFO), which is an oscillator running in the subaudio range (below 20 Hz). It produces cyclic modulations. Connected to an audio oscillator, you will get vibrato. Connected to a filter, you get a kind of "wah-wah." Connected to the amplifier, the result is a tremolo effect. The other modulator is the envelope generator (EG) for one-shot modulations, often triggered by the keyboard. The EG gives the sound a shape.

Another important synthesis method is FM modulation, a frequency (or phase) modulation in audio range. This is perfect for creating a rich spectrum from of a few oscillators. Of course, oscillators can also provide simple linear-interpolated wavetable playback. (For additional information on historical applications of synthesis, see [Smith91].)

The Sphinx MMOS System

ON THE CD

In the following sections, we introduce a system called "Sphinx MMOS," which can be used to generate procedural sounds in your games. Source code and executables for this system can be found on the CD-ROM.

Sphinx MMOS builds on the ideas of PD [PDRef], MAX [MAXRef], and Generator [GENRef], with an extensible object-oriented model that allows users to create instruments at different levels. It simplifies development of audio applications using the well-known patch model.

Different terms are used for the individual elements of such a system. Table 6.7.1 compares the terminology used in Sphinx MMOS with other common terms.

Sphinx MMOS is a data flow-oriented system. In such a system, you build a data-processing network by connecting primitive units together. Each unit (here called a "processor") has input pins that accept data from processors connected upstream and one or more output pins that send processed results to the following downstream processor. For efficiency, all the data is processed blockwise, and the blocksize in

Table 6.7.1 Terminology Used in Sphinx MMOS

Name in Sphinx MMOS	Other Names
Processor	Unit, Filter, Block, Node, (DSP) Module
Pin	Input/Output, Inlet/Outlet, Slot, Port
Signal	Data, Media, Stream, Samples, Payload, Information
Patch	Graph, Chain, Network

Sphinx MMOS defaults to 256 samples. Having a sample rate of 44,100 Hz makes a buffer duration of ~6 ms, which corresponds to a frame rate of ~172 Hz.

Processors

There are many kinds of processors available in Sphinx MMOS. The most common types are oscillators, noise generators, envelopes, filters, and mixers. In order to control triggering of sounds, there are processors for impulse generation, sequencing, and selection. Each processor defines the particular connections that are available.

Table 6.7.2 shows a list of some of the processors in the Sphinx MMOS system. We will discuss how to connect these processors together in the next section.

Table 6.7.2 Some of the Processors in Sphinx MMOS

Oscillators
CGASineOscillator
CGATriangleOscillator
CGASquareOscillator
CGASawtoothOscillator
CGASinCosOscillator
CGASineXOscillator
CGASawtoothOscDSF
CGASawtoothOscBlit
CGAWaveTableOscillator

Envelopes
CGATriangleEnvelope
CGAHalfCosineEnvelope
CGAGaussEnvelope
CGARampEnvelope

Filters
CGAButterworthLPF
CGAResonator

Noise Generators
CGARandomGenerator
CGANoiseGenerator

Miscellaneous
CGAAverager
CGAGlide
CGAInterleaver
CGAThreshold

Trigger & Selection
CGAImpulseGenerator
CGASequencer16
CGASelector

Mixers
CGAMixer2,3,4,6
CGABalance

Patch File Introduction

Sphinx patch files are simple text files that you can edit with any text file editor. Let's look at a simple patch. It's an oscillator with a base frequency of 200 Hz, modulated by an LFO at 3.5 Hz. FMAttenuation is set to 0.1, which limits the modulation depth to +/– one octave. All processors of the audio chain are listed inside the patch. Also, all parameters are contained inside the object's brackets.

```
CGAPatch "Sine Oscillator with LFO Modulation"
{
    CGASineOscillator LFO
    {
        Frequency = 3.5;
    }

    CGASawtoothOscillator OSC
    {
        Frequency = 200;
        FMAttenuation = 0.1;
    }

    Connection = LFO, OSC, SampleOut, FM;
}
```

The last line of the patch connects the sample output of the LFO with the (bipolar) frequency modulation input of the VCO. This is what it looks like to hardcode that patch right into your game:

```
void SamplePatch()
{
    IGAPatch* pPatch = CreatePatch(
        "Sine Oscillator with LFO Modulation");

    // 0 modulator
    IGASineOscillator* pLFO =
        PCREATE(pPatch,SineOscillator);
        pLFO ->SetFrequency(3.5f);

    // 1 oscillator
    IGASawtoothOscillator* pSaw2 =
    PCREATE(pPatch,SawtoothOscillator);
    pSaw2->SetFrequency(200.0f);
    pSaw2->SetFMAttenuation(0.1f);

    // connections
    pPatch->Connect(0,1, SampleOut, FM);
}
```

The first line creates a new patch and appends it to the application's patch list. With the two PCREATE lines, we create the two processors. PCREATE is a convenient macro that casts to the type of processor specified by the CID, creates the object, and appends it to the list of processors in our patch. The order of creation is important, because it defines the order of processing in the chain. The last line connects the two processors. The arguments are the processor indices in the chain and their pins. Here we connect the pin SampleOut of oscillator zero with the input pin FM of oscillator one.

Shown next are the steps needed to initialize Sphinx MMOS, create and play the patch, and clean up.

```
g_pGASystem->Initialize()

SamplePatch();

g_pGASystem->Start();

// run application loop here and handle
// start/stop and parameter setting somewhere
// in your event handling
RunLoop();

g_pGASystem->Terminate()
```

The g_pGASystem is a global that represents the singleton audio object in our application. If not specified otherwise, all rendering is done to the default stream. For audio rendering, the current version of Sphinx MMOS uses its own set of wrapper classes that encapsulate the excellent PortAudio system [Burk01].

Patch File Applications

Now that we have described the basic patch-definition language, we have the power to create complex sounds. Because any signal path can be formed by describing processors and their connections, an infinite variety of patches are possible. Also, these patches can be controlled by games because we can choose game variables to take the place of certain processors in a given patch, thus giving us organic control over digital sound generation and signal processing. We even can connect any dynamic value from our game data or user interface to a CGAController to modify the audio stream at the sample rate.

To show how we can apply this patch system to games, we will now describe how patch configurations can be designed to simulate engine sounds. Rather than covering all of the specific details of the patches, we will highlight some of the important features. We will also show how the complexity of patches can be incrementally increased to improve the quality of engine simulation.

ON THE CD

The patches described in the following subsections can be found in the patches provided on the CD-ROM.

Motor Vehicles

A vehicle sound is a complex signal produced by several sources. Many deterministic and stochastic components occur simultaneously. The deterministic components are correlated to the revolutions per minute (RPM) of the engine. The stochastic components are primarily due to turbulent airflow from the air intake and exhaust systems. At low speed, the sound signature is dominated by these deterministic components, while at high speed, the signature is dominated by the stochastic components.

The basic idea behind an engine patch is to simulate the alternating phases of a sound. In order to generate sophisticated and less-predictable sounds, we combine looped and simple one-shot samples with synthesized sounds. We will use a sequencer to control the timing of the sounds. An impulse generator triggers a selector switch. Each impulse at the input of the selector selects the next sound source input, and it also resets the sample start. This is somewhat like programming a drumbox. The difference lies in speed. We accelerate the cycle up into the audio range. While a drum sequence might groove at 120 beats per minute, our engine will climb to 4000-RPM cruising speed and higher.

- The **PowerStroke** patch simulates the generic, four-cylinder, four-stroke engine. These four repeating strokes are referred to as *Intake, Compression, Power,* and *Exhaust.* We can simulate three of the engine phases with samples. At the beginning of the patch file, we load the samples into the CGASignal objects and give them appropriate names (Intake, Impulse, Exhaust). These names (not the filenames) are used as a reference value for the WaveTable parameter of a CGAWavetableOscillator.

  The wavetable oscillator can play loops or one-shots. We want to trigger the waves from a CGAImpulseGenerator, so we set the Repeat parameter to one. The speed of the impulse generator, the RPM, is controlled by a low-frequency oscillator. Each impulse selects the next input at the CGASelector. To activate four inputs, we set the Selection parameter to 15 (1 + 2 + 4 + 8). We have no input for the compression phase, which means this phase will be silent and the selector will just fill in zeros.

- The **PowerStroke with Muffler** patch has two additional filters of type CGAResonator to simulate the muffler resonances. The original signal and the signals of the resonators are mixed in a CGAMixer3 object. In order to get a roaring sound at higher speed, we set the input gain of the resonances high, but control the AM by the speed controller.

- The **PowerStroke 2 Cylinders with Muffler** patch adds cross-fading between sounds over the range of RPMs. Across the RPM range, the sound components should vary slightly to produce a convincing timbre change.

Helicopters

- The **Turbine** patch plays a turbine sample loop. The sample contains both pitched and noisy components. In contrast to the common sample editing philosophy, the loop points here are chosen to not suppress the cyclic character.

  The CGAWavetableOscillator is frequency modulated by a smoothed LFO source. In order to get a complex and bright sound with varying overtones, we now add a bit of audio FM to the CGAWavetableOscillator. We need a CGAMixer here to combine the modulation signals from the LFO and the VCO. The result is the Turbine AudioFM1 patch. We can change the character in a more interesting way if we add some FM modulation to the VCO that modulates the sample. In lower ranges, this results in amplitude modulations, which enhance the slow rotating effect (Turbine AudioFM2).

- The **Rotor—Enveloped Sample** patch demonstrates a looping sample that is amplitude modulated by a CGAGaussEnvelope to give soft attack and release. The sample m_propeller01.wav consists of a strong noise component and a low-frequency distorted sine wave. The envelope is triggered by a CGAImpulseGenerator. The trigger points are independent of the loop start point, which results in little sound variations.
- **Turbine + Rotor** is a combination of the AudioFM2 Turbine and the enveloped rotor. The turbine's frequency and the trigger speed of the envelope are controlled by the same LFO.
- The **Helicopter with Turbine, Rotor and Flap Fx** patch uses sequenced wavetables and feedback FM techniques to simulate engine and air chop. Exactly as with the car engine, we use the balance parameter of the CGAMixer to cross-fade between its inputs. Components of this patch are the Jet/Turbine Engine with its Intake and Exhaust sounds, the basic main and tail rotor sounds with the blade parameters, an additional generator to intensify air noise at greater speeds, and the flanging impulse for the characteristic flap effect.

  Far away, the helicopter sound has strong amplitude fluctuations and an indirect muffling effect caused by air turbulence. For short bursts, the sound sometimes disappears completely or is just a single but strong impulse. In our patch, we simulate this characteristic interference effect by adding a four-millisecond delayed version to the original flap sample. The delay time is slowly modulated by an LFO. This results in moving notches in the audio spectrum and gives a nice flanging effect.

- **Turbine Controlled by Keypad** is an interaction demo that shows how to control the turbine sample by the keypad. The frequency of the loop is controlled by a value assigned to a key of the numpad. Play with the numbers one to nine in order to glide to different turbine speeds. For the gliding effect, we connect a CGAGlide between the CGANumPadController and the CGAWavetableOscillator.

Submarines

The tonal components of a submarine are machinery and equipment noise, hull resonances, and propeller-radiated noise. The broadband components are flow noise, cavitation, and the background of the ocean's natural noises. In order to generate the sound signature of a submarine, we use two special oscillators to generate pink noise-modulated sine waves. These simulate the combination of irregular and stochastic processes of turbulent noisy bubbles and the tonal noise that contains the discrete resonance frequencies of the ship's hull. The continuous part of the spectrum is characterized by a maximum in the area of 50 Hz to 100 Hz, but convincing frequency values might have a range of up to 1000 Hz.

The propeller sound is simulated by a looped sample containing higher frequencies. When the propeller's excitation frequency corresponds to the hull's natural frequency, we get strong tonals from the hull. Also, singing can occur when the vortex-shedding frequency matches the blade's natural frequency. This is a speed-dependent feedback effect in a narrow speed range and can happen at different speeds.

As the boat passes through the water, turbulent flow noise is generated along the hull. This hydrodynamic noise increases significantly as the speed rises. Cavitation and flow noise extend well beyond 10 kHz.

- **The Sonar—Noise Modulated Sine Patch** is a sine wave of 2000 Hz, with amplitude modulated by a descending ramp and frequency modulated by noise. The noise modulation is shaped by an envelope to get a fade-in effect, thus the tone is clear at the beginning, but gets more and more distorted.
- **The Submarine—Engine Only** is just an amplitude-modulated sample with an engine loop. A CGASinCosOscillator is used for fading. The next turbulence patches introduce two special oscillators for tonal noise generation, the CGANoiseMSineOsc with default settings and the CGASineXOscillator with a frequency setting of 860 Hz for turbulences in a higher range.
- **Submarine—Engine, Turbulences** is a mix between the engine sample, the lower noise generated by the CGANoiseMSineOsc, and the higher noise generated by the CGASineXOscillator. We use a three-channel mixer, the CGAMixer3, and set the gain of the higher part very low to get a convincing, filtered, underwater effect. No additional filter is used for this patch.
- In the patch **Submarine—Engine, Turbulences, Sonar,** we include the elements of the above sonar patch and add frequency modulation on the engine sample to simulate a Doppler effect. In conjunction with a low-pass filter at 400 Hz, this makes the flow-by effect more convincing.

Source Code

On the CD-ROM, you will find the Sphinx MMOS system source code, executables, patch files, and samples. Some patch files demonstrate the various processors, and some contain the engine simulations discussed in the previous section. Updates are available at the Visiomedia Web site [Visiomedia].

There are three methods for incorporating this audio system into your application:

1. Write new C++ classes to handle audio processing and management, and build your own version of the library with customized source code.

2. Write a plug-in containing C++ classes using the Sphinx base interface, IGAProcessor, and load your plug-in along with the original Sphinx MMOS plug-in.

3. Use the system as is, and only create new patch files.

Conclusion

This gem has provided insight into how to combine modular audio processing and procedural generation of sounds to procedurally generate various vehicle sounds for games. The main difference between real-time procedural audio and conventional playback systems is the complexity management and the responsiveness of the processed sounds to the game context. The combination of samples sequenced at audio rate in conjunction with traditional synthesis techniques lets you build spectacular sound transformations for your interactive applications.

References

[Ackermann94] Ackermann, Philipp, "Design and Implementation of an Object-oriented Media Composition Framework," available online at http://citeseer.nj. nec.com/ackermann94design.html, 1994.

[Burk01] Burk, Phil and Ross Bencina, "PortAudio - An Open-Source Cross-Platform Audio API," available online at http://www.portaudio.com, 2001.

[GENRef] Generator by Native Instruments, available online at http://www.native-instruments.net/.

[MAXRef] MAX / MSP by Cycling 74, available online at http://www.cycling74.com/index.html.

[PDRef] Puckette, Miller, "Pure Data Dot Org," available online at http://www.pure-data.org/.

[Rabin00] Rabin, Steve, "Classic Super Mario 64 Third-Person Control and Animation," *Game Programming Gems 2*, Charles River Media, Inc., 2001.

[Sim-Schmitz99] Sim, Ben and Fredric Schmitz, "Acoustic Phasing and Amplification Effects of Single-Rotor Helicopter Blade-Vortex," Proceedings of the 55th Annual National Forum American Helicopter Society, 1999.

[Smith91] Smith, Julius O., "Viewpoints on the History of Digital Synthesis," *Proceedings of the International Computer Music Conference*, October 1991: pp. 1–10.

[Visiomedia] Updates to the Sphinx MMOS system, available online at http://www.visiomedia.com/rooms/labor/src/sphinxmmos/index.htm.

[Wang99] Wang, Geng, "Prediction of Rotorcraft Noise with a Low-Dispersion Finite Volume Scheme," available online at http://www.ae.gatech.edu/~lsankar/CERT/ 1999.

APPENDIX

About the CD-ROM

The CD-ROM that accompanies this book contains a wide variety of useful information designed to make your life easier as a game developer. Here are some of the things that are included:

- Source code listed in the book
- Demos of many techniques described in the book
- The DirectX 8.1 SDK
- The OpenGL Utility Toolkit (GLUT).
- The glSetup Monolithic version
- High-resolution versions of the color plates

Complete installation and usage instructions are included on the CD-ROM in the AboutThisCD.htm file; please read it first.

These gems contain information on the CD-ROM:

- 1.1 Scheduling Game Events
- 1.2 An Object-Composition Game Framework
- 1.3 Finding Redeeming Value in C-Style Macros
- 1.5 Handle-Based Smart Pointers
- 1.6 Custom STL Allocators
- 1.7 Save Me Now!
- 1.8 Autolists Design Pattern
- 1.11 Using Lex and Yacc to Parse Custom Data Files
- 1.13 Real-Time Input and UI in 3D Games
- 1.15 Lightweight, Policy-Based Logging
- 1.16 Journaling Services
- 1.17 Real-Time Hierarchical Profiling
- 2.1 Fast Base-2 Functions for Logarithms and Random Number Generation
- 2.5 Constrained Inverse Kinematics
- 2.7 Coping with Friction in Dynamic Simulations
- 3.2 Area Navigation: Expanding the Path-Finding Paradigm
- 3.3 Function Pointer-Based, Embedded Finite-State Machines
- 3.6 Tactical Path-Finding Using A*
- 4.1 T-Junction Elimination and Retriangulation
- 4.2 Fast Heightfield Normal Calculation
- 4.4 Fast and Simple Occlusion Culling
- 4.5 Triangle Strip Creation, Optimizations, and Rendering

- 4.7 Subdivision Surfaces for Character Animation
- 4.8 Improved Deformation of Bones
- 4.10 A Programmable Vertex Shader Compiler
- 4.11 Billboard Beams
- 4.12 3D Tricks for Isometric Engines
- 4.13 Curvature Simulation Using Normal Maps
- 4.14 Methods for Dynamic, Photorealistic Terrain Lighting
- 4.15 Cube Map Lighting Techniques
- 4.16 Procedural Texturing
- 4.17 Unique Textures
- 5.2 Real-Time Strategy Network Protocol
- 5.4 Scaling Multiplayer Servers
- 5.5 Template-Based Object Serialization
- 5.6 Secure Sockets
- 5.7 A Network Monitoring and Simulation Tool
- 6.1 Audio Compression with Ogg Vorbis
- 6.2 Creating a Compelling 3D Audio Environment
- 6.3 Obstruction Using Axis-Aligned Bounding Boxes
- 6.4 Using the Biquad Resonant Filter
- 6.5 Linear Predictive Coding for Voice Compression and Effects
- 6.6 The Stochastic Synthesis of Complex Sounds
- 6.7 Real-Time Modular Audio Processing for Games

Also, be sure to visit the Web site http://www.GameProgrammingGems.com for more information about the series and about game programming!

INDEX

A

A* algorithm
  costs, 295–296, 298–300, 304–305
  performance, 301–302
  A Star Explorer program, A* tool, 305
  tactical pathfinding, 294–305
Abstract syntax trees (AST), for programmable vertex shader compiler, 410
ActionState class
  GoCap, 231–232, 233–234
  for MMPs, 509
Actor class
  GoCap, 232
  for MMPs, 512–513
ActorProxy class for massively multiplayer games, 513
ADPCM audio compression format, 589, 620–621
AI. *See* Artificial Intelligence (AI)
AIControlStates, for massively multiplayer games (MMPs), 509–510
Aiming, tactical pathfinding and, 298
Air, cellular automata to model currents and pressure, 200, 206
Alexander, Thor, *xxiii*
  articles by, 231–239, 506–519
Alien voices, 613–621
Allocators
  allocation function, 51–52
  allocation strategies, 56
  on CD-ROM, 58
  comparing, 54
  construction, 51–53, 52–53
  copying of, 51
  custom allocators, creating, 55–57
  deallocation, 52
  default allocator object described, 54–55

  destruction, 52–53
  per-object data and, 57
  rebind, 53–54
  temporary register allocation, 406, 411
  typedefs and, 50–51
  utility functions, 51
Anchored modifiers, 402
Animation
  cloud shadows, 436–438, 440–442, 447–448
  foot-sliding, 396–399
  inverse kinematics and, 192–198
  movement to arbitrary targets, 394–396, 399–400
  noise to add randomness, 456
  realistic locomotion, 394–413
  smooth transitions between motion captures, 396, 402
  subdivision surfaces for, 372–383
  translational / rotational offsets, modification of, 395–396
  see also Bones
Approximating functions, Taylor series, 179–180
Area navigation, AI path finding, 240–255
  algorithm summarized, 245–246
  path transversal, 249–253
  regularizing the world for, 247–249
Armies, 272
Arrays
  macro to determine number of elements in, 30
  serialization and, 542
Artificial Intelligence (AI)
  AIControlStates, for MMPs, 509–510
  area navigation, 240–255
  choke points and, 279–283

Artificial Intelligence (*cont.*)
cluster maps for floating-point valued rules, 237–238
ControlState, 233
convex hulls and, 273–277
function-based pointer FSMs, 256–266
game industry and, 229–230
GoCap for machine learning, 231–239
movement-based AI, 321–331
navigation meshes, 307–320
path-finding, 240–255, 307–320
rules definition, 234–236
simulation and schedulers, 13
swapping control to AI, 238–239
tactical pathfinding, 294–305
training with GoCap, 233–236, 236–237
trigger systems, 285–293
ASE program, 305
Asserts
compile-time assert macro, 30
descriptive comments, macro to add, 29
AST (abstract syntax trees) for programmable vertex shader compiler, 410
A Star Explorer program, 305
Asynchronous I / O, 523–524
Attenuation, per-pixel light sources, 473–476
Audience
demographic trends, *xvii–xviii*
world markets, developing games for, 92–108
Audio
ADPCM compression format, 589, 620–621
axis-aligning bounding boxes for obstruction, 600–605
band-pass filters, 610
biquad resonant filter, 606–612
caching decoded sound, 590
compression methods, 585, 588–589, 620–621
decoding speed, 589–590
demo on CD-ROM, 598–599

digital filters described, 606–607
DirectSound 3D, 571, 595–599
downmixing, 588–589
filters, 585
FIR *vs.* IIR filters, 607
helicopter sounds, 627–628, 635–636
high-pass filters, 610
interactive sound, 586, 630–638
low-pass filters, 610
modular audio processing, real-time, 630–638
noise generators, 622–629
obstruction of sound, 600–605
OpenAL, 595–599
patch files, 633–637
positional audio rendering, 595–596
procedural sound generation, 631
resampling, 588–589
resonators described, 615
rocket engine sounds, 627
sampling tips, 596–598
sonar pings, 624–625, 637
Sphinx MMOS systems, 631–638
stochastic synthesis of complex sounds, 622–629
synthesizers, 630–631
3D audio environments, 595–599
vocoders, 613–621
voice communications with DirectPlay, 569–571
voice compression and effects, 613–621
wind sounds, 624
Authentication
described, 546
hash-based message authentication code (HMAC), 550–551
performance and, 555
recommended algorithms for, 555
Autolists, 64–68
cost of, 66
defined, 68
inheritance issues, 66, 67–68

nested iterations, 66
storage of classes, 67
without constructors and destructors, 66
Axis-aligning bounding boxes for audio
obstruction, 600–605

B

Bandwidth
NetTool bandwidth simulator, 560
packet compression and latency, 578
secure sockets requirements for, 554
wireless devices and, 574, 578–579
Barycentric coordinates, 427
Base-2 logarithms of integers, 157–159
Beams, special effects, 413–416
Beardsley, Jason, *xxiii*
article by, 534–545
Bézier patches, 349–351
Big integers, 168
Billboards
illusion of depth and, 417–423
matrix for beam effects, 413–416
Binary representations, macro, 28–29
Biquad resonant filters
coefficient calculation for, 609–610
control parameters, 609
denormalization and, 609
implementation of, 607–608
optimizations of, 608–609
Bison parser, 91, 406
programmable vertex shader compilers,
409–410
Bitmask() function, 158–159
Blasco, Oscar, *xxiii–xxiv*
article by, 424–432
Blinn-Phong shading, normal distribution
function (NDF) variation, 477,
479–482
Board, Ben, *xxiv*
articles by, 64–68, 240–255
Bones
applying motion constraints to, 195–198

constrained inverse kinematics and,
192–198
cyclic coordinate descent (CCD),
193–194
deformation of, 384–393
hierarchy of, 192–193, 378
joint flexion and shrinkage, 384–388,
384–393
reference pose of, 384–385
skinning and, 385–386
vertex-accumulation buffer, 378
web address for archives, links, and
resources, 393
weighting of at joints, 388–392
Boolean operators, linking conditions with,
287–288
Bottlenecks
custom allocators and, 56
profiling and, 146
schedulers and, 12
Bounding boxes, view-frustum culling and,
379–380
Broadband distribution, *xviii*
Brownlow, Martin, *xxiv*
articles by, 59–63, 349–352
Buffers
allocation in multi-language games, 106
buffer policy for logging, 132–133
Bugs. *See* Debugging
Bump maps
curvature simulation using, 424–432
hand-made, 430
NDF shading and, 481–482
Burk, Phil, *xxiv–xxv*
articles by, 606–612, 622–629
Burning materials, modeling with cellular
automata, 210–211
Byrd, John, *xxv*

C

Caches, smart texture caches, 460
Callbacks, DirectPlay 8.1, 566–569

Calls, function, function-binding code generator, 38–42
Card, Drew, *xxv*
  article by, 367–371
CCD (cyclic coordinate descent), 193–194
CD-ROM contents, 639–640
Cellular automata
  active scenery, 203–204
  air, modeling air pressure, 200, 206
  converting polygons to cells, 203
  core processing model, 204–205
  defined and described, 201–203
  dynamic update rates, 212–213
  effects to be created with, 200–201
  fire models, 210–212
  flow models, 207–208
  fluid simulation, code listings, 205
  heat models, 209–212
  neighbor cells, 201
  octrees for storage, 204
  passive scenery, 203
  physical size of cells, 202
  physics routines for, 204
  procedural textures and hardware-based creation of, 456
  totally destructible worlds and, 203
  walls, modeling thin walls, 202–203
  water models, 206–207
Cellular phones as game platforms, 573–581
CFD (computational fluid dynamics). *See* Cellular automata
Cheating, preventing in multiplayer games, 520–522
  Internet Protocol Security (IPSec) standard, 546–555
Chinese. *See* Multiple-language games
Choke points, 272, 279–283
Christensen, Christopher, *xxv*
Classes, declaration of, 33–36
Client / server systems for online gaming, 496–497, 501–502
  for MMPs, 506–507

scalable servers for, 522–533
security associations in, 547
server optimizations, 530–533
voice servers and clients with DirectPlay, 569–571
Clocks, 8
  synchronization for online gaming, 493–495
Clouds
  animated cloud shadows, 436–438, 440–442, 447–449
  cube maps and cloud cover, 447–449
Cluster maps, 237–238
Codecs, Ogg Vorbis, 589–593
Code generators, programmable vertex shader compilers, 411
Collaborative work, UML game engine, 73–82
Collision detection
  barycentric coordinates, 427
  character movement and, 321
  path-finding and, 321–332
  probes or sensory for, 235
  sphere trees for, 532
Collision model path-finding
  described, 321–322
  fault-tolerant AI for, 322–325
  implementing movement along the path, 329–331
  layered collisions, 328–329
  unobstructed space, 325–328
Comments, macro to add to asserts, 29
Compatibility issues
  cross-platform compatibility, 69
  portable serialization for online games, 536–545
Compilers
  floating-point exceptions and, 70
  programmable vertex shader compiler, 406–411
  tokenizers for, 40
Compile-time asserts, macro for, 30

Compile-time constants, macro for, 28–29

Component technologies, pie menus, 119–124

Compression
audio compression, 585, 587–594, 613–621
latency and, 578
of quaternions, 187–191
voice compression with vocoder, 613–621

Computational fluid dynamics (CFD). *See* Cellular automata

Concept stage of game development, 16

Conditions
Boolean operators as connectors, 287–288
defined and described, 286

Conduction, modeling with cellular automata, 209–210

Continents, 269

Contributors, bio and contact information for, *xxiii–xl*

ControlState class, 232
for MMPs, 509, 512

Convection, modeling with cellular automata, 209–210, 211

Conversion stage of game development, 16–17

Convex hulls, 273–277
defined and described, 273
Graham's algorithm, 276

Conway's Game of Life, 201

Corrêa, Wagner, *xxv*
article by, 353–358

Cosine approximation techniques. *See* Trigonometric functions, approximation

Coulomb friction, 215–219

Counters, in trigger systems, 290–292

CPLP algorithm, 355–358

CProfileIterator class, 152

CProfileManager class, 150–151

CProfileNode class, 151–152

CProfileSample class, 150

Crashes, causing deliberate, 69–70

Cube maps
cloud cover, encoding, 447–449
data movement, 445–446
day / night effects, 450
defined and described, 444
rendering, 446
as sky spheres, 448
vertex buffers and, 446

Culling
hierarchical back-face culling, 378
in multi-player games, 530–533
occlusion culling methods, 353–358
sphere trees for distance-based culling, 531–533
subdivision surfaces, 381–382
view-frustum culling, 379–380

Cursors
cursor movement testing, 107
mouse and cursor response, 114

Curvature
algorithm to simulate, 425–426
friction and, 225

Custom data files, parsers for, 83–91

Cyclic coordinate descent (CCD), 193–194

Cygwin, 38–39

D

Damage, cellular automata to model, 200

Day / night cycles, 450

Deallocation function, 52

Debug flags, 129–132
configurable flags, 131
flag policy, 131–132
initializing with configuration files, 131

Debugging
debug flags, 129–132
floating-point exceptions, 71
journaling services for, 136–145
logging systems as an alternative debugger, 129
macros, 31–32

Debugging (*cont.*)
  multiplayer games, 503
  time zone "lock up," 494
Declaration of classes, 33–36
Decryption. *See* Encryption
DeLoura, Mark, *xxvi*
  web address, *xvii*
Demachy, Thomas, *xxvi*
Denormal Exceptions, 70–71
Dereferencing operators, 47
Design of games, UML game engine and
  collaboration, 73–82
Design patterns, autolists, 64–68
Destruct function, 53
Development stages, game frameworks and,
  15–16
Dictionaries, for massively multiplayer games
  (MMPs), 508
DirectPlay 8.1
  architecture described, 561–562
  context values (user contexts), 568–569
  data transmission, 562–566
  DPNSVR host monitor, 562
  for First Person Shooters, 563–564
  message flow and messaging in, 562–566
  for MMPs, 565
  multithreading, 566–569
  troubleshooting resources, 571–572
  voice communications, 569–571
DirectSound 3D, 595–599
Dispatch systems for messages, 525–527
Division by Zero Exceptions, 70
Document type definition (DTD), 111–112
Doors, cellular automata and scenery, 203
Downmixing, audio compression, 588–589
DTD (document type definition), 111–112
Ducker, Mike, *xxvi*
  article by, 240–255
Dust, cellular automata to model, 200
Dynamic areas, terrain analysis of, 270–272
Dynamic HTML, implementing pie menus
  with, 119–122

E
Edge collapse, 370–371
Edge-of-the-world problems, vector fraction
  for exact geometry, 160–169
Edwards, Eddie, *xxvi–xxvii*
  article by, 613–621
Effectors, 193–194
  dividing influence of multiple effectors,
  196
Elevation mapping, depth-enabled 2D
  images and, 418–420
Encryption
  CryptoAPI, 554
  initialization vector, 549
  integrity check value (ICV), 550
  key management, 547, 554
  for multiplayer games, 521–522,
  549–552, 554–555
  padding, 549–550, 552
  payload, 549, 551
  performance and, 554–555
  recommended algorithms for, 555
Enemies, aiming ability and tactical path-
  finding, 298
Enums, macro to transform to strings,
  27–28
Errors
  maximal errors, 175–176
  measuring importance of, 170–171
Euler angles, 195
Euler's method, friction formulation,
  220–221
Even masks, 372
Event-locking
  vs. frame-locking, 488–490
  path-finding packet exchanges, 490–492
  TCP and, 492
  time synchronization and, 493–495
Event managers, 6, 9
Event messages, trigger systems and, 289
Events
  event-locking in online gaming, 489–495

frame events, 8
    input events and real-time, 113–114
    scheduling, 5–13, 11
    time events, 8
    types of, 8
    see also Trigger systems
Exceptions and exception handling
    floating-point exceptions, 69–72
    types of floating-point exceptions, 70
Explosions, cellular automata to model, 200
Exporting, parsing text data exported, 87
Eye vectors, calculating, 414

F

Face normals, 344
Face vertex indices, precomputing, 380
Farris, Charles, *xxvii*
    article by, 256–267
FEA (finite element analysis). *See* Cellular
    automata
Feet, sliding during animation, 396–399
Filters
    to approximate trigonometric functions,
        171–172
    audio filters, 585
    band-pass audio filters, 610–611
    biquad resonant audio filter, 606–612
    combining audio filters, 611
    FIR *vs.* IIR filters for sound, 607
    high-pass audio filters, 610–611
    low-pass audio filters, 610
    NetTool network simulator filters,
        557–558
    textures and, 462, 464
Finite element analysis (FEA). *See* Cellular
    automata
Finite impulse response (FIR) filters, 607
Finite-State Machines (FSMs)
    CFSM, 260–263, 263–266
    defined, 256–258
    derived classes and behavior changes,
        265–266

function pointer-based FSEs, 256–266
    implementation of, 258–260
    inherited FSMs, 258
    rationales for use, 257–258
    switch implementation of, 258–259
Fire
    cellular automata to model, 200
    procedural textures for, 456
FIR (Finite impulse response) filters, 607
Flags
    debug flags, 129–132
    dirty flags and persistent properties, 511
    in trigger systems, 290–292
Flex parser (lexical analyzer), 91, 406,
        408–409
Floating-point exceptions, 69–72
    code to enable, 71
    compilers and, 70
    types of, 70
Floating-point optimizations, 182–184
Floating-point representations, *vs.* vector
        fractions, 163–164
Fluid simulation, code listings, 205
Fonts
    characters for multiple-language games,
        93–94
    double and multi-byte character sets, 97
    single-byte character sets, 96–97
Foot-sliding, 396–399
Foreign languages
    fonts and, 93
    spaces in, 93–94
    see also Multiple-language games
Forests, 270
Forsyth, Tom, *xxvii*
    article by, 459–466
Fox, David, *xxvii*
    article by, 573–581
Fractional errors, vector fractions for exact
        geometry, 160–161
Frame-based operation, *vs.* function-based
        operation, 18

Frame events, 8, 11
Frame-locking, 488–489
Frameworks
   game-independent *vs.* -dependent, 17
   implementation, 20–23
   object-composition game framework,
     15–24
   platform-independent *vs.* -dependent, 17
Friction
   Coulomb friction, 215–219
   curvature and, 225
   deceleration and, 216
   dry friction forces, 215–216
   dynamic (kinetic) friction, 215–218, 219
   Euler's method to simulate, 220–221
   geometric issues and, 225–226
   gravity and, 217
   nonsmoothness and, 222–223
   numerical methods for simulation of,
     219–224
   reformulation method to simulate, 221
   regularizing friction, 221
   smoothness and geometric issues, 225
   static friction (stiction), 215, 218–219
   surfaces in contact, 217
   Taylor method (Taylor series), 222–223
   three-dimensional formulation, 224–225
   transitioning between static and dynamic,
     223–224
   viscous damping and, 221
Front-end processing for multiplayer games,
   528–530
FSMs. *See* Finite-State Machines (FSMs)
Function-based operation, *vs.* frame-based
   operation, 18
Function binding, 38–42
   networking and, 42
   scripting and, 42
Function pointers
   CStateTemplate class to avoid class-speci-
     ficity, 261–262
   defined and described, 259–260

Finite State Machine implementation,
   260

G

Game engines, Universal Modeling Lan-
   guage engines, 73–82
Garrabrant, Byon, *xxvii*
   article by, 146–152
Gimbal lock, 155, 195
GoCap
   ActionState class, 231–232, 233–234
   Actor class, 232
   AIControlState, 233
   architecture of, 231–233
   ControlState class, 232
   TrainingControlState, 233
   UserControlState class, 232–233
Goertzel's Algorithm, sine and cosine calcu-
   lation, 172–174
Gomez, Miguel, *xxviii*
Graham's algorithm, 276
Grammars, Yacc parsers, 40–41
Graphics, industry history and trends,
   335–337
Green, Robin, *xxviii*
   article by, 170–186
Greer, Jim, *xxviii*
   article by, 488–495
Grouping in DirectPlay 8.1, 565–566

H

Hacking, preventing in multiplayer games,
   520–522, 546–555
Half-edge data structures, subdivision surfaces, 375–378
Handheld devices. *See* Wireless devices
Handles, 45–46
   see also Smart pointers, handle-based
Hannibal, Søren, *xxviii*
   article by, 69–82
Hardware
   procedural textures and acceleration, 456

world market and configuration of, 106–107

Harvey, Michael, *xxix*
    article by, 5–14

Hash maps, for AI training, 237–239

Hash tables, for massively multiplayer games (MMPs), 508

Hawkins, Brian, *xxix*
    articles by, 44–48, 129–135, 413–416

Heat, modeling with cellular automata, 200, 209–212

Heightfields
    dynamic, fast calculation methods for, 344–348
    fast heightfield normal calculation, 344–348
    lighting heightfield terrains, 433–444

Helicopters, sound effects, 627–628, 635–636

Herds, 272

Hiebert, Garin, *xxix*
    article by, 595–599

Hierarchy
    of bones, 192–193, 378
    object hierarchy, 78
    real-time profiling systems, 146–152

Higgins, Dan, *xxix*
    article by, 268–284

High-level languages, 3

Hills, 269

Hjelstom, Greg, *xxx*
    article by, 146–152

Hoffman, Naty, *xxx*
    article by, 433–443

Hopkins, Don, *xxx*
    article by, 117–128

Horizon angles and horizon mapping, 436–437

HTTP, 575–577

Hulls, convex, 273–277
    Graham's algorithm, 276

Hurley, Kenneth, *xxx–xxx*i

article by, 444–451

I

ICV (integrity check values), 550

Identifiers, for pointers, 46

IIR (Infinite impulse response) filters, 606–612

Industry trends, *xvii–xix,* 487
    see also World markets, designing for

Inexact Result Exceptions, 70

Infinite impulse response (IIR) filters, 606–612

Infinite loops, macro to prevent, 31–32

Inheritance
    downward casting and autolists, 66
    multiple inheritance and autolists, 67
    vs. object composition, 18
    ownership issues, 19

Initialization vector, 549

Input
    asynchronous I / O, 523–524
    buffered data mode, 113–114
    Input Method Editors (IMEs), 94–95
    keyboard input, 113
    lag times, 115, 488–495
    mouse and joystick input, 114
    onscreen virtual keyboards, 94–95
    real-time input, 109–116
    touchscreens, 124
    world market design considerations, 99–100
    see also User interfaces (UI)

Integrity check value (ICV), 550

Interfaces
    debug flags, 129–130
    macro to simplify class interfaces, 33–36
    systems_t class and, 20–21
    TaskSys_t class, 21
    user interface testing, 107–108
    world market design considerations, 99–101, 107–108
    see also User interfaces (UI)

Internet Protocol Security (IPSec) standard, 546–555

Intersections, vector fractions and, 160–169

Invalid Exceptions, 70

Inverse kinematics
applying to bones, 195–198
constraint of, 192–198
cyclic coordinate descent, 193–194
rotational constraints, 195

I / O, asynchronous, 523–524

IOCP asynchronous I / O, 523

IPSec (Internet Protocol Security) standard, 546–555

Iridescence, creating, 472–473

Irradiance, terrain lighting and, 434

Isensee, Pete, *xxxi*
articles by, 49–58, 546–556

Isidoro, John
article by, 467–476

Isometric engines, 3D tricks for, 417–423

J

Japanese. *See* Multiple-language games

Java 2 Micro Edition (J2ME)
described, 574–575
HTTP and, 575–577
image retrieval, 579–580
MIDlets, 575, 579
multiple connections, 577
networking on, 575–576
optimizing packets, 577–579
proxies, 577

Joints, flexion and shrinkage problems, 384–388

Journaling services
architecture of, 137–140
information reports, 143
interactive reports, 145
interface for, 141–142
tracing information, 143–144

Joysticks, 114

K

Kautz, Jan, *xxxi*
article by, 477–483

Kelly, Paul, *xxxi*
article by, 83–91

Keyboards
input in multiple-language games, 99–100
onscreen virtual, 94–95
real-time input, 113

Kirmse, Andrew, *xxxii*
articles by, 487, 557–560

Klowsowski, James, *xxxii*
article by, 353–358

Knuth, Donald, quoted, 4

L

Lag times. *See* Latency

Lake, Adam, *xxxii*
article by, 404–412

Lander, Jeff, *xxxii–xxxiii*
article by, 335–337

Languages, macro for specialized languages, 32–33

Laser beams, billboard beam effects, 413–416

Latency
defined, 573
front end processing and, 529
input, 115
NetTool, network latency simulator, 557–560
in online games, 488–495, 500–501, 502
packet compression and, 578
simulating network lag time, 557–560
wireless devices and, 573–574, 578

Layers, FramePlayer_t to manage, 21–23

LCA (linear congruential algorithm), 623–624

Leeson, William, *xxxiii*
article by, 372–383

Lengyel, Eric, *xxxiii*
article by, 338–344

Lerp (linear interpolation)
  optimizing calculations, 175
  substitutes for, 179–185
Level-of-detail, triangle strips and continuous LOD, 366
Lexers, 84–85
Lexical analysis
  flex, 91, 406, 408–409
  lex, 83–91
Lex (lexer), 83–91
  code listing for custom data file, 88–89
  Yacc parser generator used with, 85–86
Lifetimes, dynamic *vs.* static, 19
Lights and lighting
  attenuation of per-pixel light sources, 473–476
  beam effects, 413–416
  cube maps, encoding lights in, 449–450
  curvature simulation and, 424–432
  day / night effects, 450
  diffuse lighting, 449
  disco ball effects, 449
  dynamic, realistic, 433–443
  irradiance, 434
  per-pixel lighting computation, 467–476
  radiance, 433–434
  shadow volumes and visibility, 367–371
  static lights, 449
  sunlight, calculation of radiance, 436–438
  sunset / rise effects, 450
  of terrain, 433–443
  vertex normal calculation, 344–348, 349–352
  video-based, 442
Linear congruential algorithm (LCA), 623–624
Linear interpolation (lerp)
  optimizing calculations, 175
  substitutes for, 179–185
Linear predictive coding (LPC), voice compression and effects, 613–621
Line breaks, foreign languages and, 93–94

Line-of-sight / fire tests, 302–304
Lip synching, 589
Lists, autolists, 64–68
List::splice, 57
Loading, load manager on CD-ROM, 63
Localization
  process for world-market games, 101–103
  testing, 107
  user interfaces and, 112
Lockstep protocols, 496–505
  event-locking, 489–495
  frame-locking, 488–489
  game-turn rates, updates, 498–500
  interpolating between turns, 498–500
  pointer-to-unique-ID, 502–503, 504
  single-player gaming, 502
  updates, game turn rates, 498–500
Locomotion
  anchored modifiers, 402
  to arbitrary targets, 394–396
  pauses in, 402
  single-step animations, 402
  smooth transitions between animations, 396–398
  translational / rotational offsets, modification of, 395–396
  tween ratios, 398–399
LOF (line-of-fire) tests, 302–304
Logarithms, base-2 logarithms of integers, 157–159
Logging, lightweight, policy-based logging system, 129–135
LookupManager for massively multiplayer games, 515
LPC algorithm, voice compression and effects, 613–621
LPC (linear predictive coding), voice compression and effects, 613–621
LPC vocoder, 613–621
Luchs, Frank, *xxxiii*
  article by, 630–638

M

Machine learning, GoCap, 231–239
Macros
  class interface simplification, 33–36
  compile-time constants from binary representations, 28–29
  debugging, 31–32
  descriptive comments, 29
  enum to string transformation, 27–28
  for infinite loop prevention, 31–32
  journaling service macros, 143–145
  LINE to string conversion, 31–32
  number of elements in array, 30
  profiling systems, 147–149
  save tables created with, 61–62
  state machine languages, 32–33
  utility of, 26
Maps and mapping
  bump maps, 424–432, 481–482
  cube maps, 444–451
  curvature simulation with, 424–432
  elevation mapping for depth, 418–420
  horizon mapping, 436–437
  layer mapping for textures, 461
  n.h. / h.h. maps, 467–469
  $(n.h)^k$ maps, 469
  normal maps, 425, 429, 430
  PTMs (polynomial texture maps), 438
  specular maps, 450, 469–472
  triangle strip mapping alternatives, 415–416
  UV mapping of triangle strips, 415–416
Marshall, Carl S., *xxxiii*
  articles by, 5–14, 359–366
Masks, subdivision surfaces and, 372–376
Massively multiplayer games (MMPs)
  action requests, 516
  action scheduling, 516–517
  ActionStates class, 509
  ActorProxy class, 513
  Actors and Actor class, 512–513
  AIControlStates class, 509–510
  architecture overview, 506–508
  BaseSimulation class, 515
  ControlStates class, 509
  core classes for, 510–513
  dictionaries for, 508
  DirectPlay 8.1 for, 565
  event broadcasting and handling, 517–518
  grouping players, 565–566
  hash tables for, 508
  LookupManager, 515
  managers and factories, 513–515
  Nonperformer class, 513
  Performer class, 511–512
  properties of SimulationObjects, 511
  proxies, simulation by, 507–508
  simulation events for, 508
  SimulationObject (SOB) class, 509–510, 510–511
  SimulationState class, 508–509
  SOBFactory, 514
  SOBManager, 514
  support classes for, 508–510
  top-level interface for, 515–518
  UserControlStates class, 509–510
Matchbox containers, Major Matchbox, 277–283
  data members for, 278
  methods in, 278–279
Mathematics
  rationales for using, 155–156
  trigonometric functions, approximations to, 170–185
McNeill, James, *xxxiv*
  article by, 157–159
Mechanical engine sounds, 627, 634–635
Mechanical systems, friction and modeling of, 215
Memory allocation
  character sets and, 97–98
  custom STL allocators, 49–58
Menus, pie menus, 117–128

Meshes
  arbitrary meshes, 344–345
  heightfield meshes, 344–348
  subdivision surfaces and, 372–383
  see also Navigation meshes
Messages and messaging
  message dispatch systems, 525–527
  serialization of messages, 524–525
  trigger systems and event messages, 289
Microfacets, shading models and, 478–479,
    482
MIDlets, 575, 579
Milliger, Mike, *xxxiv*
  article by, 452–458
Minimax polynomials, 180–182
MMORPG. *See* Massively multiplayer
    games (MMPs)
MMPs (Massively multiplayer games). *See*
    Massively multiplayer games (MMPs)
Moffit, Jack, *xxxiv*
  article by, 587–594
Monitoring, online games, 558–559
Motion
  cloud shadows, 436–438, 440–442,
    447–449
  realistic, 394–403
Motion captures, smooth transitions
    between, 396–398
Motor vehicles, sound effects, 627, 634–635
Mouse, input with, 114
Movement
  to arbitrary targets, 394–396, 399–400
  collision model path-finding and,
    329–331
  movement-based AI, 321–331
Multiplatform portability, serialization and,
    536–545
Multiplayer games
  data encryption methods, 521–522,
    549–552, 554–555
  data security and cheating, 520–522,
    546–555

  DirectPlay 8.1 to create, 561–572
  MMPs, 506–519
  scaling multiplayer servers, 520–533
  wireless extensions for, 573
Multiple-language games
  character sets, 96–98
  developing games for world markets,
    92–108
  Input Method Editors (IMEs), 94
  line breaks and sorting, 93–94
  localization and user interface for, 112
  memory allocation and character sets for,
    97–98
Multithreading, 13
  DirectPlay 8.1, 566–569
Music. *See* Audio

N

N-ary trees, 147
Navigation meshes
  creatures, representing on, 314–316
  described, 308–309
  dynamic obstacles, 316–319
  portals and, 309–311, 313–314
  precomputing tables for, 311–313
  static obstacles, 318–319
  static *vs.* dynamic obstacles and, 307
NetTool, online game monitor and network
    simulator, 557–560
Network gaming. *See* Online gaming
Network Time Protocol (NTP), online gam-
    ing and, 493
N.h. / h.h. maps as lookup tables,
    467–469
Nicholls, Aaron, *xxxiv*
  article by, 92–108
NLS (normalized light space), 473–474
Nodes, allocation of, 53–54
Nodes, in matchbox containers, 278–279
Noise
  Perlin noise, 453
  stochastic synthesis of, 622–629

Nonperformer class for massively multiplayer games, 513
Normal distribution function (NDF) shading, 477, 479–482
rendering, 479–480
storing as texture maps, 479
Normalized light space (NLS), 473–474
Normal maps
saving, 429
UV mapping and, 430
Normals
on arbitrary meshes, 344–345
face normals, 344
heightfield normals, 346–348
surface normals, fast patches, 349–351
vertex normals, 344–345
NTP (Network Time Protocol), online gaming and, 493

O

Oat, Chris, *xxxv*
article by, 467–476
Object-composition game framework, 15–24
Object-oriented programming (OOP), 73
Objects
composition *vs.* inheritance, 18
serialization of, 534–545
tagging for type safety, 544
Obstacles, pathfinding and, 307, 316–320
Obstruction of sound, 600–605
Occlusion
cPLP algorithm, 355–358
culling methods, 353–358
horizon mapping, 436–437
PLP algorithm, 354–355, 356–358
shadow ellipses, 437
Octrees
cellular automata and, 204
loose octrees, 204
Odd masks, 372
Ogg Vorbis, audio compression

code example using, 591–592
decoding, real-time, 592–593
encoding, 593
psychoacoustic compression described, 587–589
Oil, cellular automata to model, 200
Online gaming
client / server protocols, 496–497, 501–502
client / server systems for, 496–497, 501–502, 506–507, 522–533
event-locking, 489–495
frame-locking, 488–489, 488–490
freezing and frame-locking, 488–489
function binding and ?, 42
game-turn rates, updates, 498–500
high mode elimination for synchronization, 493–495
industry trends, 487
lockstep protocols, 488–495
monitoring network activity, 557–560
out-of-synchs, debugging, 503–504
packet loss, 503
path-finding packet exchanges, 490–492
peer-to-peer protocols, 496–497
serialization methods for, 534–545
slow computers and, 502
synchronization, 493–495, 500–501, 503–504
TCP-based systems, 492
time synchronization, 493–495
time zone "lock up" bugs, 494
UDP-based systems, 492, 493
voice communications in, 569–571
see also Latency
Onscreen virtual keyboards, 94–95
OpenAL audio, 595–599
Operations, dynamic *vs.* static operation order, 19
Optimizations
crashes to analyze performance, 69
floating-point optimizations, 182–184

high-speed trigonometric approximations, 170–185

profiling strategies, 146–156

StackAlloc for memory allocation, 50

template-based object serialization, 542–544

triangle-strips, 364–365

vector fraction implementation, 168–169

Out-of-synchs, online gaming, 503–504

Overflow Exceptions, 70

P

Packweights, 392

Padding, 549–550, 552

Pallister, Kim, *xxxv*

article by, 3–4

Parsers and parsing

bison, 91, 406, 409–410

of custom data files, 83–91

for programmable vertex shader compiler, 406, 409–410

syntax trees and, 406

XML, 112

Yacc parser generator, 40–41, 83–91, 85–86, 89–90

Patches, surface, fast patch normals, 349–351

Path-finding

with A* algorithm, 294–305

area navigation method, 243–246

attraction and repulsion, 249–251

cost function and heuristic for evaluating shortest paths, code listing, 295–296

cost function for evaluating tactical paths, code listing, 296

costs, 295–296, 298–300, 304–305

dynamic landscapes and, 251–253

looping and forking paths, 310–311

navigation meshes and, 307–320

obstacles and, 307, 316–319

path transversal, 249–253

shortest paths, 295–296

3-D environments, 253–254

traditional methods, inefficiency of, 241–243

valid (unobstructed) space, 325–328

vector fractions for exact geometry, 160, 162–163

see also Collision model path-finding

Patterson, Scott, *xxxv*

articles by, 15–25, 585–586

Payload, 549, 551

Peer-to-peer systems, 522

DirectPlayVoice configuration, 571

security associations in, 547

Performance

logging and, 133–134

monitoring, 12

optimizing, 69

profiling strategies, 146–152

Performance monitors, 12

Performer class for massively multiplayer games, 511–512

Phones, mobile phones as game platforms, 573–581

Phong shading, 477–478

$(n.h)^k$ maps and, 469–472

Photoshop, unique textures created with, 460, 462–463

Pie menus, 117–128

effectiveness of, 118–119

Feng GUI design considerations, 117–118

implementing, 119–124

JavaScript pie menus, 119–122

learning curve for, 118–119

in *Sim* games, 124–127

touch screens and motion detectors used with, 124

PIMPL design pattern, debugging flags, 131

Pitch and yaw, 188, 190

Euler angles and, 195

Placement new operator, 52–53

Platforms
  cellular phones as game platforms, 573–581
  cross-platform compatibility, 69
  frameworks, platform-independent *vs.* -dependent, 17
  serialization and multiplatform portability, 536–545
Platforms, cross-platform compatibility, 69
Playability stage of game development, 16
Pointers
  dumb pointers, 45
  handle-based smart pointers, 44–48
  in multiplayer games, 502–503, 542
  serialization and, 542
  unique identifiers for, 46
Policies, defined and described, 129
Poll(), 523
Polygons, adjacent polygons and common edges, 338–339
Polynomial approximations, 179–185
  accuracy and degree of, 184–185
Polynomial texture maps (PTMs), to calculate sunlight, 438
Portals, navigation meshes and, 309–311, 313–314
PortAudio, 611
POSIX2 asynchronous I/O system, 523
Pouratian, Allen, *xxxv*
  article by, 38–43
PowerStroke patches, audio files, 634–635
Primitives, culling, 353
Procedural modeling, 456
Procedural textures
  advantages of use, 454
  natural phenomena represented by, 454
  noise algorithms and, 453
  optimization and, 454–456
  parameters and, 452–453
  real-time *vs.* regenerated, 455–456
  sample code explicated, 457–458
  solid texturing, 455

Production stage of game development, 16
Profile trees, 147
Profiling systems
  browsing profile data, 149–150
  implementation of, 150–152
  real-time hierarchical profiling, 146–152
  usage example, 147–150
Prototype stage of game development, 16
Proxies
  ActorProxy class, 513
  Java Micro Edition HTTP proxies, 577
  MMPs and, 507–508, 513
Pseudo-random number generators
  linear congruential algorithm (LCA), 623–624
  noise and, 453
Psychoacoustic sound compression, 587–589
PTMs (polynomial texture maps), to calculate sunlight, 438

Q

Quaternions
  compression of, 187–191
  described, 187
  polar compression methods, 188, 189–190
  smallest three compression method, 187–188, 189

R

Rabin, Steve, *xxxv–xxxvi*
  articles by, 26–37, 285–293
Radiance, terrain lighting and, 433–434
Radiation, modeling with cellular automata, 209–210, 211–212
Radiosity, skylight, 438=439
Rafie, Bob, about cover art, *xxi*
Rain sounds, 625–627
Randall, Justin, *xxxvi*
  article by, 520–533
Randomness
  Perlin noise algorithms, 453

procedural textures and, 456

Random number generation, bit masks and, 158–159

Range reduction, 176–179

Rasterization artifacts, T-Junctions and, 338–343

Ray tracing, curvature simulation and, 426–428, 429–430

Real time
input and user interfaces, 109–116
journaling services for real-time debugging, 136–145
schedulers, 6–8

Real-time strategy games (RTSs)
game-turn rates, updates, 498–500
industry trends, 487
interpolating between turns, 500
minimizing latency in, 488–495
network protocols for, 496–505
slow computers and, 502

Rebind, 53–54

Red noise, 623

Reflection, inter-reflection of sunlight on terrain, 438

Registers, for programmable vertex shader compilers, 411

Regularization, area navigation, 247–249

Release stage of game development, 16–17

Relief textures, 420–423

Remez Exchange Algorithm, 180–181

Rendering
T-Junction elimination to avoid errors, 338–343
triangle strips, 365

Replay attacks, preventing, 546–555

Resampling audio, 588–589

Resonant filter, sine and cosine calculation, 171–172

Resonators, 615

Responses, defined and described, 288–289

Retriangulation algorithm, 340–343

Robert, Eric, *xxxvi*

article by, 136–145

Robot voices, 613–621

Rocket engine sounds, 627

Rohweder, Gabriel, *xxxvi*
article by, 561–572

Rotational offsets, modification of, 395–396, 400

Round-off errors, vector fractions for exact geometry, 160–161

RTSs. *See* Real-time strategy games (RTSs)

Rules, AI training, 234–239

S

Saving
code for saving classes, 62–63
macros to create save tables, 61–62
overriding defaults, 62
save/load manager on CD-ROM, 63
SAVEMGR class, 60
SAVEOBJ class, 60–61
saving game at arbitrary positions, 59–63

Scalability, textures, 464

Scan codes, characters, 99–100

Scanners (lexical analyzers), 408–409

Scheduling and schedulers
clocks and, 8
design for simple scheduler, 9–11
event managers, 6
multithreading, 13
real-time schedulers, 6–8
scalability of, 11–13
simulation systems and, 13
task managers, 6, 9
uses for, 5
virtual time schedulers, 6–8

Schur's algorithm, 617

Scripts and scripting
function binding and, 42
trigger systems *vs.* scripting languages, 292
Universal Modeling Language (UML) and, 81

Seams, visible, elimination of, 338–343
Secure sockets
    authentication, 546, 551, 555
    bandwidth requirements, 554
    classes on CD-ROM, 552
    CryptoAPI, 554
    IPSec, 546–547
    packet format for, 548–550
    performance issues, 554–555
    receiving data, 551–552, 553–554
    security parameters index (SPI), 548–549,
        550, 551
    sending and receiving secure packets, code
        listings for, 553–554
    sequence numbers, 549, 550, 551–552
Security
    authentication, 546, 551, 555
    confidentiality, 546
    hacking, prevention of, 520–522,
        546–555
    integrity, 546
    Java applications and, 574
    message dispatching systems, 525–527
    security associations and SecureAssocia-
        tion class, 547–548
    type safety of servers, 524–525
    see also Encryption; Secure sockets
Security associations and SecureAssociation
        class
    code listing for, 553
    described, 547–548
    establishing, 550
Security parameters index (SPI), 548–549,
        550, 551
Seegert, Greg, *xxxvi*
    article by, 109–116
Sequence numbers, secure sockets, 549, 550,
        551–552
Sequencing, event managers and, 9
Serialization
    of callbacks in DirectPlay 8.1, 569
    keyed serialization, 543

object tagging for type safety, 544
partial serialization, 543–544
pointers and arrays, 542
portability, 536–537
STL containers, 539–541
struct / memcopy() for, 534–535
template-based object serialization,
    534–545, 537–542
type-based storage and retrieval, 535–536
of user-defined classes, 541–542
variable-length types, 539
Servers
    distributed server processes, 528–530
    front-end processes, 528–529
    load distribution, 527–530
    type safety, 524–525
Shaders. *See* Vertex shaders
Shading
    Blinn-Phong shading, 477–478
    colored highlights, 480–481
    microfacet-based shading models,
        478–479, 482
    normal distribution function (NDF)
        shading, 477–483, 479–482
    patching and shading artifacts, 351
    Phong shading, 469–472, 477–478
Shadows
    cloud shadows, animated, 440–442,
        447–449
    composited shadow maps, 463
    decal shadow texture projections,
        442–443
    shadow ellipses, 437
Shadow volumes, optimizations for,
        367–371
Shankel, Jason, *xxxvii*
    article by, 344–348
Shore rings, 269–270
Shore tiles, 269
SIGGRAPH, 335
Silhouette regions, pathfinding and,
        162–163

Silva, Cláudio, *xxxvii*
    article by, 353–358
Simple Network Time Protocol (SNTP),
        online gaming and, 493
Simpson, Zack Booth, *xxxvii*
    article by, 488–495
Simulation, schedulers, 13
Simulation events, for massively multiplayer
        games (MMPs), 508
SimulationObject (SOB), for massively mul-
        tiplayer games, 509–510, 510–511
SimulationState, for massively multiplayer
        games (MMPs), 508–509
Simulation time, 7
Sine approximation techniques. *See* Trigono-
        metric functions, approximation
Skeletal motion
    inverse kinematics and, 192–198
    rotational constraints, 195
Skeletons. *See* Bones
Skies, color changes, 450
Skylight, radiosity approximations and
        patches, 438–439
Smart pointers, handle-based, 44–49
    construction and destruction of, 46–47
    dereferencing, 47
    equality and inequality testing, 47
    validation of, 47
Smoke, cellular automata to model, 200
Smoothness, friction and, 225
Sniffing, preventing, 546–555
Snook, Greg, *xxxvii*
    article by, 417–423
SNTP (Simple Network Time Protocol),
        online gaming and, 493
SOBFactory for massively multiplayer
        games, 514
SOBManager for massively multiplayer
        games, 514
Sockets, secure. *See* Secure sockets
Sonar pings, 624–625, 637
Sound. *See* Audio

Sound effects
    DirectSound for, 571
    helicopters, 627–628, 635–636
    motor vehicles, 627, 634–635
    rocket engine sounds, 627
    sonar pings, 624–625, 637
    submarines, 637
    voices, robot or alien voice synthesis,
        613–621
    white noise, 622–629
    wind sounds, 624
South Korea, as game market, 92–93
Specular maps, cube mapping and, 450
Speech, linear predictive coding and speech
        modeling, 614–621
Sphere trees, described, 531
Sphere trees, multiplayer game optimization,
        530–533
Sphinx MMOS system, audio processor,
        631–638
    patch files, 633–638
    source code, 637–638
Splice function, 57
Spoofing, preventing, 546–555
Spotlights, per-pixel, 474–476
StackAlloc, 50, 55–56
Stack traces, 143–144
Standard Template Library (STL), allocation
        and deallocation methods, 49–50
State machines
    macro languages, 32–33
    see also Finite-State Machines (FSMs)
Static areas, terrain analysis of, 268–270
Stiction (static friction), 215, 218–219,
        223–224
STL containers, template-based object serial-
        ization and, 539–541
Stochastic synthesis of sound, 622–629
Strings
    concatenating and world markets, 103
    macro to transform enums to, 27–28
Subdivision, sphere trees, 531–533

Subdivision surfaces, 372–383
  arrays for data storage, 381
  bones and, 378
  butterfly subdivision schemes, 374–375, 380, 382
  data structures for, 375–378
  hierarchical half-edge meshes, 375–378
  interpolating schemes, 374–375
  loop subdivision scheme, 373–374, 380–381, 382
  masks and, 372–376
  optimizations for, 378–381
  rendering, 382
  vertex-accumulation buffers and, 378
Submarines, sound effects, 624–625, 636–637
Sunlight, calculation of radiance, 436–438
Suns, static lights, 449
Surfaces. *See* Subdivision surfaces
Svarovsky, Jan, *xxxviii*
  article by, 496–505
Symbol tables, for programmable vertex shader compilers, 410–411
Synchronization, 493–495, 500–501
  out-of-synchs, debugging, 503–504

T

Tactical path-finding, 294–305
  dynamic threats and, 300–301
  enemy modeling and exposure time, 297–298
  line-of-sight / fire tests, 302–304
Task managers, 6, 9
Tasks
  horizontal *vs.* vertical integration of, 19
  interface with task system, 21
  managers, 6, 9
  time budgets and scheduling, 12
Taylor series, 179–180
  friction simulation and, 222–223
TCP
  Java 2 Micro Edition networking, 575

  simulation with NetTool, 559
  TCP-based game systems, 492
Technology, trends in development, *xviii–xix*
Terrain analysis
  armies, 272
  choke points, 272, 279–283
  continents, 269
  convex hulls, 273–277
  dynamic areas, 270–272
  forests, 270
  generic areas, 272–273
  herds, 272
  hills, 269
  Major Matchbox (U2DMatchboxContainer class), 277–283
  shore rings, 269–270
  shore tiles, 269
  static areas, 268–270
  towns, 270–272
Terrains
  generic areas, creating, 272–273
  lighting of, dynamic and realistic, 433–443
  terrain analysis, 268–284
Testing
  danger characters, 105–106
  multiple language games, 104–106
  NetTool network simulator for, 560
  stage of game development, 16
Textures
  blending with stacked layers, 460
  caching textures, 460
  compositing and, 462–463, 465
  creating unique textures, 459–466
  cube maps and, 445–446
  dynamic textures, 463–464
  filters and, 462, 464
  iridescent color-shifting, 472–473
  layer mapping and transforms, 461
  layer sources, 462
  lookup tables for per-pixel lighting, 467–476

mipmaps, 464, 465

normal distribution function (NDF) shading, 477–483

number controls for texturing systems, 463

optimization, 454–456, 456

procedural textures, 452–458, 459–460

scalability, 464

solid texturing, 455

triadic blends, 462–463

vertically interlaced textures, 422–423

warping (relief textures), 420–421

Texture space, 425, 428

Threading, DirectPlay 8.1 and multithreading, 566–569

Time

event scheduling, 5

simulation time, 6–8

virtual time, 6–8

Time events, 8

T-Junctions

defined and described, 338–339

elimination of, 339–340

retriangulation, 340–342

Tokens, tokenizers, 40

Totally destructible worlds, 203

Towns, 270–272

TrainingControlState, 233

Translational offsets, modification of, 395–396, 400–401

Treglia, Dante, *xxxviii*

Trends in game industry, *xvii–xix*

Triangle strips (tri-strips)

beam effects and, 414

cache-friendly triangle strips, 365–366

connecting, 364

creation of, 361–364

defined and described, 359–361

level-of-detail, 366

mapping alternatives and, 415–416

rendering, 365

tri-strip algorithm, pseudo-code for, 364

Triggers. *See* Trigger systems

Trigger systems

conditions, defining, 286

conditions and responses, 286–289

defined and described, 285–286

evaluating triggers, 289–290

event messages and, 289

extensible trigger system for AI agents, objects and quests, 285–293

flags and counters, 290–292

object-owned trigger systems, 286

vs. scripting languages, 292

single shot and reload times, properties of triggers, 290

Trigonometric functions, approximation

Goertzel's Algorithm, 172–174

polynomial approximations, 179–185

range reduction, 176–179

resonant filter, 171–172

table-based, 175–177

Tri-strip algorithm, pseudo-code for, 364

Tri-strips. *See* Triangle strips (tri-strips)

2D images, depth-enabled, 417–423

Typedefs, allocators and, 50–51

Type safety, 524–525

serialization and, 544

U

UDP

DirectPlay 8.1 and, 563–564

Java 2 Micro Edition networking, 575

simulation with NetTool, 559

UI. *See* User interfaces (UI)

UML. *See* Universal Modeling Language (UML)

Underflow Exceptions, 70

Unicode, 98

Universal Modeling Language (UML)

class diagrams for, 76–78

game engines and, 73–82

implementation issues, 80–82

iterative modeling, 78–80

Universal Modeling Language (*cont.*)
  sequence diagrams and interprocess
    exploits, 530
  tools, 82
Updates
  cellular automata, update rates, 212–213
  polling updates as triggers, 289–290
Use cases, 75–76
UserControlState class, 232–233
  for MMPs, 509–510
User interfaces (UI)
  Feng GUI of, 117–118
  localization considerations, 112
  pie menus, 117–128
  real-time input and, 109–116
  specifying elements in, 110–112

V

Valid space, in path-finding, 325–328
Van der Sterren, William, *xxxviii*
  article by, 294–306
Vector fractions, 160–169
  big integers and, 168
  vs. floating-point representations,
    160–161, 163–164
  number ranges, 167–168
  operations using, 165–166
  optimizations, 168–169
  order of intersection, 166
  pathfinding and, 162–163
  rationale for use, 161–163
  3D line and plane intersections, 165
  transversals and, 162–163, 166, 168
  2D line intersections, 164–165
Vectors, yaw and pitch, 188, 190, 195
Vertex-accumulation buffers, 378
Vertex buffers, cube maps and, 446
Vertex indices, precomputing, 380–381
Vertex normals
  described, 344–345
  fast heightfield normal calculation,
    344–348

Vertex shader, programmable compiler
  abstract syntax trees for, 410
  code generator for, 411
  key components described, 406
  language for, 407–408
  parsers for, 406, 409–410
  scanner (flex lexical analyzer), 406,
    408–409
  symbol tables for, 410–411
  temporary registers, 406, 411
Vertex shaders, 350
  attenuation of per-pixel point lights,
    473–476
  cartoon vertex shader, code listing, 406
  defined and described, 404–405
  programmable vertex shader compilers,
    404–412
Vertices
  ordinary *vs.* extraordinary, 372
  T-Junction elimination and retriangula-
    tion, 338–343
  vertex removal and shadow volumes,
    369–370
Video, lighting with video sequences,
  436–438
Virtual time schedulers, 6–8
Visibility
  conservative *vs.* approximate, 354
  cPLP algorithm, 355–358
  from-point *vs.* from-region, 354
  front cap geometry, 367–369
  object space *vs.* image space, 354
  occlusion culling methods, 353–358
  PLP algorithm, 354–355, 356–358
  precomputed *vs.* online, 354
Visual systems, dynamic switching of, 21
Vlachos, Alex, *xxxviii–xxxix*
  articles by, 367–371, 467–476
Vocoders, 613–621
  described, 613–614
  filters in, 615–616
  modeling speech production, 614–621

Vogelsang, Carlo, *xxxix*
    article by, 600–605
Voice communications, DirectPlay 8.1 for, 569–571
Voice compression and effects, linear predictive coding for, 613–621

W
Walls, cellular automata and modeling thin walls, 202
Warping textures, 420–421
Water
    cellular automata to model, 200, 206–207
    procedural textures for, 456
Web addresses
    bones (archives, links, and resources), 393
    contributors, *xxiii–xl*
    Game Programming Gems, 640
    PortAudio updates, 611
Weber, Jason, *xxxix*
    articles by, 192–199, 384–393
Weights
    precomputing, 380–381
    weighting of bones at joints, 388–392
Weiler-Atherton algorithm, 367
Welding, 339
White, Stephen, *xxxix*
    article by, 307–320
White noise, stochastic synthesis, 622–629
Wind sounds, 624
Wireless devices
    CLDC, 575
    game development for, 573–581
    image retrieval, 579–580
Woodcock, Steven, *xxxix–xl*
    article by, 229
World markets, designing for

audio / video and string concatenation, 103
buffer allocation, 106
culture-neutrality, 101
cursor-movement testing, 107
design and planning considerations, 103–104
hardware configuration, 106–107
input, 107
interface and design considerations for, 98–101
keyboard input, 99–100
localization, 101–103, 107
modifying existing games, 104
political sensitivity and, 101
system configuration, 107
video output, 99
see also Multiple-language games
Wrapping stage of game development, 16

X
XBox, 465, 546–547
XML
    pie menus, 119–122
    user interfaces and, 110–112

Y
Yacc (parser generator), 40–41, 83–91
    code listing for custom data file, 89–90
    Lex used with, 85–86
Yaw and pitch, 188, 190
    Euler angles and, 195
Young, Thomas, *xl*
    articles by, 160–169, 321–332, 394–403

Z
Zarb-Adami, Mark, *xxiii*
    article by, 187–191